# The Economics of Aging

A National Bureau
of Economic Research
Project Report

# The Economics of Aging

Edited by **David A. Wise**

The University of Chicago Press

*Chicago and London*

DAVID A. WISE is the John F. Stambaugh Professor of Political
Economy at the John F. Kennedy School of Government, Harvard
University.

The University of Chicago Press, Chicago 60637
The University of Chicago Press, Ltd., London

∞ The paper used in this publication meets the minimum
requirements of the American National Standards Institute for
Information Sciences—Permanence of Paper for Printed Library
Materials, ANSI Z39.48-1984.

**Library of Congress Cataloging-in-Publication Data**

The Economics of aging / edited by David A. Wise.
     p.  cm. — (A National Bureau of Economic Research
project report)
   "Papers presented at a conference held at the Bourbon
Orleans Hotel, New Orleans, Louisiana, 19–21 March 1987"—
Acknowledgments.
  Includes bibliographies and indexes.
  ISBN 0-226-90295-1
   1. Aged—United States—Economic conditions—
Congresses.  2. Old age—Economic aspects—United States—
Congresses.  3. Aged—Housing—United States—
Congresses.  4. Retirement—Economic aspects—United
States—Congresses.  I. Wise, David A.  II. National Bureau
of Economic Research.  III. Series.
HQ1064.U5E26  1988
305.2'6'0973—dc19
                                      88-25159
                                         CIP

### Relation of the Directors to the
### Work and Publications of the
### National Bureau of Economic Research

1. The object of the National Bureau of Economic Research is to ascertain and to present to the public important economic facts and their interpretation in a scientific and impartial manner. The Board of Directors is charged with the responsibility of ensuring that the work of the National Bureau is carried on in strict conformity with this object.

2. The President of the National Bureau shall submit to the Board of Directors, or to its Executive Committee, for their formal adoption all specific proposals for research to be instituted.

3. No research report shall be published by the National Bureau until the President has sent each member of the Board a notice that a manuscript is recommended for publication and that in the President's opinion it is suitable for publication in accordance with the principles of the National Bureau. Such notification will include an abstract or summary of the manuscript's content and a response form for use by those Directors who desire a copy of the manuscript for review. Each manuscript shall contain a summary drawing attention to the nature and treatment of the problem studied, the character of the data and their utilization in the report, and the main conclusions reached.

4. For each manuscript so submitted, a special committee of the Directors (including Directors Emeriti) shall be appointed by majority agreement of the President and Vice Presidents (or by the Executive Committee in case of inability to decide on the part of the President and Vice Presidents), consisting of three Directors selected as nearly as may be one from each general division of the Board. The names of the special manuscript committee shall be stated to each Director when notice of the proposed publication is submitted to him. It shall be the duty of each member of the special manuscript committee to read the manuscript. If each member of the manuscript committee signifies his approval within thirty days of the transmittal of the manuscript, the report may be published. If at the end of that period any member of the manuscript committee withholds his approval, the President shall then notify each member of the Board, requesting approval or disapproval of publication, and thirty days additional shall be granted for this purpose. The manuscript shall then not be published unless at least a majority of the entire Board who shall have voted on the proposal within the time fixed for the receipt of votes shall have approved.

5. No manuscript may be published, though approved by each member of the special manuscript committee, until forty-five days have elapsed from the transmittal of the report in manuscript form. The interval is allowed for the receipt of any memorandum of dissent or reservation, together with a brief statement of his reasons, that any member may wish to express; and such memorandum of dissent or reservation shall be published with the manuscript if he so desires. Publication does not, however, imply that each member of the Board has read the manuscript, or that either members of the Board in general or the special committee have passed on its validity in every detail.

6. Publications of the National Bureau issued for informational purposes concerning the work of the Bureau and its staff, or issued to inform the public of activities of Bureau staff, and volumes issued as a result of various conferences involving the National Bureau shall contain a specific disclaimer noting that such publication has not passed through the normal review procedures required in this resolution. The Executive Committee of the Board is charged with review of all such publications from time to time to ensure that they do not take on the character of formal research reports of the National Bureau, requiring formal Board approval.

7. Unless otherwise determined by the Board or exempted by the terms of paragraph 6, a copy of this resolution shall be printed in each National Bureau publication.

*(Resolution adopted October 25, 1926, as revised through September 30, 1974)*

# Contents

# Acknowledgments

This volume consists of papers presented at a conference held at the Bourbon Orleans Hotel, New Orleans, Louisiana, 19–21 March 1987. It is part of the National Bureau of Economic Research ongoing project on the economics of aging. The majority of the work reported here was sponsored by the United States Department of Health and Human Services, National Institute on Aging Grant Number AG05842. Additional support was provided by The Commonwealth Fund, The W.E. Upjohn Institute for Employment Research, and the National Science Foundation.

Any opinions expressed in this volume are those of the respective authors and do not necessarily reflect the views of the National Bureau of Economic Research or any of the sponsoring organizations.

*David A. Wise*

# Overview

David A. Wise

Increasing longevity is changing every aspect of American life. An older population and longer individual life spans present the most important public policy issues that our society must address. In particular, an aging population raises important concerns about the future well-being of the elderly. The issues highlight the important interactions between demography, health, and economics. How many years Americans work, where and how they live, how well they live, and the kind and amount of health care they receive are all critical questions.

A possibly unforeseen drawback of living longer is that the proportion of one's life that is spent working may decline. If so, each year's earnings while in the labor force must support more years of health care and other needs while out of the labor force. The fact that Americans are living longer, and possibly healthier lives, but leaving the labor force at younger ages has far-reaching implications for the elderly. Not only will there be fewer young persons to support a larger number of elderly, but if current trends continue, a smaller fraction of one's lifetime will be spent working, further limiting the ability of the young to support the old. If policies are adopted to encourage later retirement, which of them would make a difference? What factors affect the age of retirement?

A fundamental determinant of the well-being of the elderly is financial status. Labor market behavior, housing choices, health—all contribute to financial status. Yet some of the critical determinants of the financial status of the elderly are not well understood. Nor are the determinants of the effects of financial status on health status, housing choices, and labor force participation.

This volume contains papers presented at an NBER conference on The Economics of Aging, held in New Orleans in March 1987. The

1

conference was part of NBER's Project on the Economics of Aging. The goal of the project is to further our understanding of both the determinants of the economic well-being and the health status of the elderly, and the consequences for the elderly and for the population-at-large of an increasingly older population with longer individual life spans. The papers in this volume may be grouped into four areas: (1) housing, living arrangements, and family support; (2) labor force participation and retirement; (3) the economics of health and health care; and (4) financial status. Each of the papers is summarized briefly here.

## Housing, Living Arrangements, and Family Support

The savings of a large proportion of the elderly are primarily in the form of housing. The life-cycle theory of consumption would suggest, therefore, that many older persons would reduce housing wealth as they age in order to maintain consumption levels. It is also hypothesized that many elderly are in need of free funds and would like to divest themselves of housing wealth to increase consumption in other forms, were it not for the large transaction costs, both economic and psychic, of moving from one dwelling to another. Both hypotheses are brought into question in papers by Daniel McFadden and Jonathan Feinstein on "The Dynamics of Housing Demand by the Elderly: Wealth, Cash Flow, and Demographic Effects" and by Steven Venti and David Wise on "Aging, Moving, and Housing Wealth." Although the papers were written independently, they use similar methods and reach similar conclusions. The goal of both papers is to study the impact of diverse social and economic variables on the housing decisions of the elderly and, thereby, to isolate the primary facts with which policy must contend. Both papers focus on two aspects of the housing choices of the elderly: (1) the decision to move; and (2) having chosen to move, whether to increase or decrease housing equity and/or annual housing expenses, like mortgage payments and heating. Feinstein and McFadden find that higher satisfaction with current housing is associated with lower mobility and with less downsizing. They conclude that this finding and others call into question the life-cycle model as traditionally formulated. In addition, they find only weak evidence that liquidity constraints affect the housing conditions of the elderly, a result which they conclude is consistent with the apparent lack of enthusiasm among elderly homeowners for reverse annuity mortgages. Their analysis also reveals a strong relationship between retirement and changes in family composition on the one hand and housing mobility on the other.

Venti and Wise confirm that families with high incomes typically also have high housing wealth and that families with low incomes typically have low housing wealth. Thus, they conclude that the potential for a reverse mortgage scheme to increase the consumption of the low-income elderly is limited. They find that families who have high incomes but little housing equity are somewhat more likely to move than families who have low incomes but substantial housing equity—those who are most likely to be liquidity constrained. Their analysis also reveals that the elderly who move are as likely to increase as to decrease housing equity. They also find that the typical mover is not liquidity constrained, and that the economic and psychic costs of moving are apparently not major reasons that the elderly fail to reduce housing equity as they age. They conclude that the absence of a well-developed market for reverse mortgages can apparently be explained by a lack of demand for these financial instruments. Finally, like Feldstein and McFadden, Venti and Wise also find a substantial relationship between retirement and changes in family composition on the one hand and housing mobility on the other.

Similar questions are also addressed by Konrad Stahl in "Housing Patterns and Mobility of the Aged: The United States and West Germany." The age distribution of the West German population today is very similar to the distribution predicted for the United States in the year 2000. His analysis is based on the U.S. Annual Housing Survey for 1978 and the West German 1 Percent Housing Sample for 1978. Stahl finds that in both West Germany and the United States moving is associated with substantial increases in housing-cost–to–income ratios. This is consistent with the findings of Feinstein and McFadden and of Venti and Wise. On the other hand, he finds that consumption of housing services, measured by rooms per family member, declines when the elderly move. This is true in both Germany and in the United States. He also concludes that the potential for adjustment in housing consumption by moving is much greater in the United States than in Germany, since elderly Americans are approximately four times as likely to move as their German counterparts. Finally, Stahl concludes that a strong impediment to mobility in Germany is the apparent rent advantage given to sitting tenants. They typically must pay substantially more for rental housing if they move. Venti and Wise report a similar finding for the United States.

In "Household Dissolution and the Choice of Alternative Living Arrangements among Elderly Americans," Axel Börsch-Supan studies the economic and demographic determinants of the decision to live independently or in a shared accommodation. An important aspect of his work is the decomposition of households into separate family nuclei. He finds that approximately one-third of elderly family nuclei share housing. While this proportion has increased among the general population in the early 1980s, it has decreased among elderly Americans.

More than 70 percent of elderly nuclei who share housing live with their adult children. In most of these cases, the parents head the common household. Among these two-generation households, between 1974 and 1983 an increasing percentage were headed by the parent generation rather than the adult children. He speculates that this development can be attributed to the increasing difficulty of finding affordable housing for first-time home buyers. Children who "take in" their parents have about twice the income level of the average second-generation (children) nuclei family. Finally, he concludes that the choice of living arrangements is determined primarily by demographic variables, not economic factors like income or prices.

Laurence Kotlikoff and John Morris are undertaking a study of the extended family through a special survey sponsored by the NBER and the Hebrew Rehabilitation Center for the Aged. The survey will collect information on children of the elderly residing in Massachusetts. Ultimately, the survey will provide a unique source of information about the behavior of the extended family. Preliminary findings from the survey are reported in the paper, "How Much Care Do the Aged Receive from Their Children? A Bimodal Picture of Contact and Assistance." They indicate that a significant minority of the elderly, many of whom need assistance with activities of daily living, have little or no contact with children, either because they have no living children or because there is little contact with children who are living. Contact between children and "vulnerable" elderly appears to be less than that between children and the nonvulnerable elderly, and the amount of contact between children and the institutionalized elderly appears the least of all. In addition, although many of the parents in the sample are poor, financial support from children to parents, other than in the form of shared housing, is uncommon. The initial impression conveyed by the data is that many of the elderly are well cared for by their children, while a significant minority either have no children or have no children who provide significant time or care.

## Labor Force Participation and Retirement

In "Employee Retirement and a Firm's Pension Plan," Laurence Kotlikoff and David Wise are continuing their work on the incentive effects of private pension plans. They analyze the relationship between pension wealth accrual and retirement, based on the experience of a Fortune 500 firm. For completeness, salary earnings and the accrual of Social Security benefits are analyzed together with pension benefit accrual. The analysis makes it clear that departure rates from the firm are very strongly related to the incentive effects inherent in pension wealth accrual. Because of the strong incentive effects, especially the advantageous early retirement provisions, only about 10 percent of the employees in the firm at age 50 are still working in the firm at age 65; fewer than 50 percent are still working in the firm at age 60. Kotlikoff and Wise note that while a great deal of effort has been directed to estimating the effects of Social Security provisions on labor force participation, much less attention has been given to the effects of private pension plans. They postulate that their data suggest that pension plan provisions have had a much greater effect on retirement than the recent changes in Social Security benefits. They will continue their work with a more formal analysis of data from the same firm.

Douglas Bernheim is working on a series of studies on the relationship between expectations of the elderly about future income, age of retirement, and other variables and their actual realizations. In an earlier paper (Bernheim 1987), he analyzed evidence on individual predictions about future Social Security benefits versus benefits actually received. He showed that estimates of future benefits would be greatly improved if individuals had information on what benefits would be if they were to retire at the current age, say 60; advance calculations would add greatly to individual knowledge. In a companion paper in this volume, "The Timing of Retirement: A Comparison of Expectations and Realizations," he studies the accuracy of expectations concerning the timing of retirement. He finds that expectations about age of retirement are quite accurate. More than 60 percent of the elderly expecting to retire within four years actually retired within one year of the expected date. Both papers are based on data from the Retirement History Survey. An underlying theme of the work is to test explicitly assumptions that are commonly made when modeling retirement decisions and when considering other life-cycle behavior.

John Rust, in a very ambitious effort, has developed "A Dynamic Programming Model of Retirement Behavior." His model accounts for the possibility that retirement plans change over time, and for the role of expectations about uncertain future variables such as the worker's life span, health status, marital and family status, earnings from employment, assets, Social Security, and other variables. The primary work to date has been directed to the development of a computationally tractable algorithm to estimate such a model from observed data. The goal of Rust's work is to demonstrate that rather complex and realistic formulations of the retirement decision can be estimated using his algorithm. He hopes that his procedure will be useful for others in the analysis of similar problems.

**Financial Status**

About 80 percent of the elderly poor are single; 60 percent are widows. Two project papers are aimed at analyzing the reasons for the greater poverty of widows and for their less-favorable future prospects.

In "The Wealth and Poverty of Widows: Assets before and after the Husband's Death," Michael Hurd and David Wise, by tracing backward to the financial status of the couple before the death of the husband, attempt to explain how widows become poor. Their analysis is based on the Retirement History Survey. They find that, based on standard definitions of poverty, the death of a husband very often induces the poverty of a surviving widow. A large fraction of the wealth of the couple is lost when the husband dies; the loss is especially large when the surviving widow is already poor. If the widow had been poor, then almost all the private pension wealth of the prior couple was lost at the husband's death. In addition, the prior households of poor widows, on average, saved less than the households of nonpoor widows. The typical couple had very little life insurance before the husband's death and, therefore, no way to make up the loss in wealth when he died.

In a companion paper on "The Poverty of Widows: Future Prospects," Michael Hurd estimates the future economic status of widows. He begins by estimating the future financial status of the Retirement History Survey population as it ages. The analysis rests on a model of consumption as single persons age. He then considers changes in the initial conditions of the Retirement History Survey population, such as increased pension coverage and increased Social Security benefits, and the implications of such changes for the financial status of widows in the future. By the year 2000, up to 60 percent of the surviving cohort of 1979 widows will be below the poverty level, based on his consumption measure of poverty. His simulations show that increases in private pension coverage and survivorship rules will not do a great deal to reduce the poverty of widows. Only increases in Social Security benefits have a substantial effect on the proportion of widows in poverty. Increase in life expectancy also will have only a small effect on the poverty status of widows. The work highlights the need to understand why some families accumulate wealth while others do not. In general, poverty among widows will only be reduced if couples accumulate more wealth before the husband's death.

## Health

Alan Garber has begun a series of studies on the economics of health care, focusing on long-term care and the worth of medical interventions for the elderly. His study on "Long-Term Care, Wealth, and Health of the Disabled Elderly Living in the Community" is an analysis of the relationship between financial status and the use of hospital, nursing home, and home health care by a sample of noninstitutionalized disabled elderly. It is based on data from the 1982 National Long-Term Care Survey. Among the findings of this initial work is that disabled elderly who live alone make much more use of paid home health care services than those who do not live alone. His preliminary results suggest that most of the disabled elderly who live in the community have significant resources and that home equity and income do not decrease with the number of functional impairments. The results confirm the view that the elderly who live alone use some long-term care services heavily, and that informal supports such as children appear to be an important source of care.

John Shoven, Jeffrey Sundberg, and John Bunker analyze "The Social Security Cost of Smoking." Among the costs of smoking in the United States is a reduction in the expected Social Security benefits resulting from a smoking-induced decrease in life expectancy. The paper estimates the magnitude of this loss for single and married men and women. The analysis rests on separate life tables for smokers and nonsmokers. They find that the expected loss of net benefits accompanying smoking to be very large relative to the estimates of medical costs and lost wages resulting from smoking. The results for single nonsmoking men show that they can expect to receive a net transfer from Social Security of $3,436, while the expected benefits received by smokers fall $17,782 short of their expected contributions. The Social Security costs of smoking for single men thus exceed $21,000 in expectation at age 20. Couples who both smoke have an expected net present value of participation in Social Security about $30,000 below that of nonsmoking couples.

# Reference

Bernheim, Douglas. 1987. Social Security benefits: An empirical study of expectations and realizations. NBER Working Paper no. 2257. Cambridge, Mass.: National Bureau of Economic Research.

# 1    Aging, Moving, and Housing Wealth

Steven F. Venti and David A. Wise

It is often claimed that the elderly live in inappropriate housing. Indeed the claim is that many would like to live elsewhere and would, were it not for the large transaction costs associated with moving. These costs are understood to include not only direct monetary costs, but also the psychic costs inherent in changing neighborhoods, losing contact with longtime friends, and the like. This has been the rationale for the belief that reverse mortgage schemes would be of benefit to the elderly were the market for them easily accessible. This paper is the first stage of research directed ultimately to the analysis of the transaction costs associated with moving for the elderly. It concentrates on the empirical description of the relationship between moving and housing expenditures of the elderly.

There are three themes in the paper. The first is directly motivated by the hypothesis that a significant number of the elderly would like to use housing equity to finance current consumption were that possible without having to incur the large transaction costs of moving. The

Steven F. Venti is Associate Professor of Economics at Dartmouth College and Faculty Research Fellow of the National Bureau of Economic Research. David A. Wise is John F. Stambaugh Professor of Political Economy at the John F. Kennedy School of Government, Harvard University, and a Research Associate of the National Bureau of Economic Research.

The research reported here was supported by the National Institute on Aging, grant no. 3 PO1 AG05842-01 and by a Martin Segal Memorial Fellowship at Dartmouth College. We are grateful to Brian Palmer for developing the data used in the analysis and for many useful suggestions as the work progressed. We have also benefited from discussions with Jim Poterba, the discussant for the paper whose initial comments are in part reflected in this version of the paper, and with Al Gustman and Joyce Manchester. The research is part of the NBER's research project on the economics of aging. Any opinions expressed are those of the authors and not those of the National Bureau of Economic Research or the sponsoring organization.

proposition is not that the elderly live in housing that is inappropriate for them and that they ought to move. It is not, for example, that an elderly couple living in a large house that they want to leave to their children have made an inappropriate housing choice. Rather the question is whether the couple would like to use the housing resources for other purposes. If this were the case, one might expect that when moves occur wealth would be taken out of housing and used to finance current consumption.

A second theme is the extent to which the elderly more generally decrease housing equity as they age. It is well known that a very large proportion of savings is in the form of housing and that many of the elderly have essentially no other assets. Venti and Wise (1986) report that the median level of financial assets among respondents to the 1983 Survey of Consumer Finances was about $1,300. The median level of all assets (excluding Social Security and firm pension plans) was $22,900, the vast majority of which was in housing. Evidence on the assets of the elderly is reported in Hurd and Shoven (1983), Diamond and Hausman (1984), and in Hurd and Wise (ch. 6, in this volume). Diamond and Hausman, for example, report that 20 percent of those aged 45 to 59 had essentially no nonpension personal wealth in 1966. Nearly 50 percent had nonhousing assets of less than $1,000. Given that such a large proportion of personal savings is in the form of housing, one is led to ask whether it is used, as the life-cycle theory would predict, to finance consumption in old age.

The third theme presented here is a descriptive analysis that will serve as the first stage of a more detailed analysis of moving transaction costs among the elderly. It sets forth the empirical regularities with which more formal modeling and analysis must be consistent.

The analysis in this paper is based on the Retirement History Survey (RHS). This ten-year survey follows families headed by persons who were between 58 and 63 years old in 1969. They were reinterviewed every two years until 1979. Data were collected on a wide variety of socioeconomic measures, including income, wealth by detailed asset category, retirement, health status, and many others. Merrill (1984) used data from the 1969 and 1977 RHS interviews to study the home equity of the elderly. The focus of her work is similar to ours, although the details of the two analyses are quite different. In particular, we use each of the six RHS interviews to analyze the moving and housing choices of the elderly. By considering changes in each two-year interval, we are able for the most part to associate changes in housing equity with individual moves. By considering changes over short time intervals, we also minimize the potential effects of attrition from the sample. While our methods differ from hers, her basic conclusions are supported by our findings.

Section 1.1 of this paper describes the frequency of moving by type of housing and by the wealth and income of respondents. Section 1.2 considers the correlates of moving. Who moves? In particular, retirement and death of a spouse are emphasized. In addition, we consider the relationship between income and housing equity, on the one hand, and moving, on the other. The desire to sell a house to finance current consumption might be expected to be concentrated among persons with low current income and relatively higher housing equity. We consider whether there is in fact a concentration of moving among persons in this income-housing-wealth group. Section 1.3 compares changes in housing value, housing equity, and user cost over time for movers compared to nonmovers (stayers). Nonhousing bequeathable wealth is also traced. If wealth is withdrawn from housing at the time of a move, it should show up as an increase in nonhousing bequeathable wealth after the move.

The conclusions of the paper may summarized briefly:

- The elderly typically do not use saving in the form of housing equity to finance current consumption as they age, contrary to the usual life-cycle theory. Indeed, as Bernheim (1984) and Merrill (1984) have reported, housing equity increased with age over the period of the RHS.

- When the elderly move, they are as likely to increase as to decrease housing equity. This suggests that the reason for the virtual absence of a reverse mortgage market may be the lack of demand for such financial arrangements. Even if the transaction costs associated with moving deter many elderly from changing housing, these costs are apparently not what is causing the absence of consumption of housing equity by the elderly. Those who do move do not, on average, withdraw wealth from housing. Thus the typical mover is apparently not liquidity constrained.

- Many of the elderly with little current income also have little housing equity, so that little could be gained by converting it to an annuity, even at an actuarially fair rate. This is consistent with the findings of Manchester (1987) based on data from the Panel Survey of Income Dynamics. That annuity rates are much less than actuarially fair, as shown by Friedman and Warshawsky (1985), may be a further deterrent.

- The attachment to past living arrangements and the maintenance of housing equity may be motivated by a bequest motive, although this explanation is brought into question by the absence of a significant relationship between change in housing equity and whether the family has children, consistent with the findings of Hurd (1986) for nonhousing bequeathable wealth.

- The elderly with high income and low housing equity are the most
  likely to move; those with low income and high housing equity are
  less likely to move than the former group but more likely than other
  elderly families. One may conclude that moving by the elderly is
  just as likely to be motivated by the desire to reallocate more
  income to housing as to use housing wealth to finance current
  consumption. However, among homeowners who move, those with
  low income and high housing equity reduce housing equity the
  most; those with high income and low housing equity increase
  housing wealth the most.
- Moving is strongly related to retirement and to precipitating shocks
  such as change in marital status, in particular the death of a spouse.

## 1.1  Background

### 1.1.1  The Frequency and Nature of Moves

Much of the data that will be presented pertains to changes in housing
between two survey periods. Where the changes do not vary greatly
over the five possible comparisons—1969 to 1971, 1971 to 1973, etc.—
we typically present data for the 1973 to 1975 interval.

The likelihood that a family moves during a two-year interval depends
on housing type, for example:

| 1973 Housing | % of Sample | % Move |
|---|---|---|
| Own | 71.4 | 9.1 |
| Rent | 21.0 | 25.8 |
| Other | 7.6 | 26.5 |

Those who rent are almost three times as likely to move as those who
own. The "other" category includes persons living with relatives, living
in homes owned by others, or paying no cash rent. Most moves are
between the same housing type. This is shown by the following transition matrix for those who moved between 1973 and 1975:

|  | Own | Rent | Other |
|---|---|---|---|
| Own | 78.2 | 15.4 | 6.4 |
| Rent | 17.0 | 69.9 | 13.1 |
| Other | 22.6 | 41.2 | 36.2 |

Almost 80 percent of homeowners who move move to another house.
Change in housing tenure occurs mostly among the elderly who live in
other situations. Thus, when we consider changes in housing type from
one period to the next, we find that the vast majority of people are in
the same type of housing, except the small proportion of the elderly

who are in the "other housing" category at the beginning of the period, as shown below in a transition matrix for all families:

|       | Own  | Rent | Other |
|-------|------|------|-------|
| Own   | 96.7 | 1.8  | 1.5   |
| Rent  | 6.5  | 86.2 | 7.3   |
| Other | 15.1 | 20.1 | 64.8  |

Finally, some people who do not move do in fact change housing tenure. Some rent the housing they used to own or vice versa. Others may transfer ownership to children or to other relatives. In still other cases someone else may assume the rent obligation. Change in tenure without moving is especially common among those in the "other" category.[1] This can be seen in the following transition matrix for stayers (nonmovers):

|       | Own  | Rent | Other |
|-------|------|------|-------|
| Own   | 98.5 | 0.5  | 1.0   |
| Rent  | 2.8  | 91.9 | 5.3   |
| Other | 12.4 | 12.4 | 75.2  |

The transition matrices for the other years look similar to those for the 1973–75 period. The transition probabilities for movers vary with age, however. The RHS respondents were 62 to 67 years old in 1973. In the 1973–75 interval, renters were more likely to change to owning than owners were to change to renting. Transition probabilities for movers by age can be calculated from the RHS by combining data from all of the survey years. Only for the ages 60 through 65 (but not 63) is the transition probability from renting to owning greater than the probability from owning to renting; for all other ages from 58 to 71 the reverse is true. In this respect the RHS data appear to be consistent with evidence from the Annual Housing Survey (AHS).[2]

An indication of the cumulative effect of these transition probabilities over the ten-year period of the RHS is provided by the likelihood of moving between 1969 and 1979 for those who responded in both years. The percentage of respondents who moved at least once during this period is:

| Housing in 1969 | % Move by 1979 |
|-----------------|----------------|
| Own             | 27.0           |
| Rent            | 63.6           |
| Other           | 53.4           |

Many movers, especially renters, moved more than once. Of the original owners who moved and were in the sample in 1979, 73 percent moved once, 18 percent twice, and 9 percent more than twice. Of the original renters who moved, 50 percent moved once, 24 percent twice, and 26 percent more than twice. The following transition matrix for all respondents describes the net result of these moves over the ten-year period:

|  | Own | Rent | Other |
|---|---|---|---|
| Own | 90.3 | 6.6 | 3.1 |
| Rent | 23.0 | 68.3 | 8.7 |
| Other | 26.6 | 31.8 | 41.6 |

There is considerably more movement from renting to owning than from owning to renting. Most of the original owners still own; 7 percent rent. But 23 percent of original renters own at the end of the period. The reason is that renters are much more likely than owners to move, not that when renters move they are more likely than owners to switch tenures, as explained above. Some of the initial respondents died, and others dropped out of the sample for other reasons. This attrition may have some effect on the recorded transition probabilities. Renters, for example, are more likely than owners to drop out of the sample. We do not believe, however, that attrition seriously confounds the interpretation of the data.

Persons who buy often move out of state; renters are much less likely to leave the state. The RHS provides limited information on the distance of moves in the 1973–75 period. For initial owners and renters, distance of moves is indicated in table 1.1. Half of all moves are within the same city, and three-fourths are within the same state.[3] Almost 90 percent of moves from one rental unit to another are within the same state.

### 1.1.2 Income and Wealth

Income and wealth by tenure are shown for 1969 and 1979 in tables 1.2A and 1.2B. Since a large proportion of personal wealth is in housing, it is not surprising that homeowners have much more wealth than renters. Owners also have much higher incomes, much more non-housing bequeathable wealth, and more Social Security wealth, the latter reflecting higher lifetime earnings.

The extent to which housing equity could be used to increase current consumption depends of course on how much housing equity there is. The extent to which individuals might wish to do that may depend on

| Table 1.1 | Percent Distribution of the Distance of Moves, 1973–75 | | | | |
|---|---|---|---|---|---|
| Type of Move | Same City | Same State | Out of State | Other | All |
| Own to own | 35.8 | 29.2 | 22.6 | 12.3 | 43.2 |
| Rent to rent | 69.9 | 17.9 | 8.8 | 3.4 | 36.6 |
| Own to rent | 44.7 | 32.9 | 14.1 | 8.2 | 10.5 |
| Rent to own | 33.3 | 34.6 | 21.8 | 10.3 | 9.7 |
| All | 49.0 | 26.0 | 16.6 | 8.4 | 100.0 |

**Table 1.2A**    **Income by Tenure, 1969 and 1979[a]**

| | Tenure | | | | | |
|---|---|---|---|---|---|---|
| | Owners | | Renters | | Other | |
| Category | Mean | Median | Mean | Median | Mean | Median |
| | 1969 | | | | | |
| Capital income | $ 1,008 | $ 59 | $ 558 | $ 0 | $ 467 | $ 0 |
| Social Security | 432 | 0 | 418 | 0 | 475 | 0 |
| Pension | 653 | 0 | 444 | 0 | 422 | 0 |
| Wages | 14,951 | 13,210 | 10,203 | 8,448 | 5,269 | 2,166 |
| Other | 986 | 119 | 632 | 67 | 541 | 55 |
| Total | 18,030 | 14,810 | 12,254 | 9,484 | 7,173 | 4,049 |
| N | 6,616 | | 2,426 | | 792 | |
| | 1979 | | | | | |
| Capital income | 1,741 | 223 | 895 | 0 | 426 | 0 |
| Social Security | 3,829 | 3,700 | 3,064 | 3,011 | 2,543 | 2,436 |
| Pension | 1,980 | 0 | 1,375 | 0 | 640 | 0 |
| Wages | 2,389 | 0 | 1,232 | 0 | 973 | 0 |
| Other | 954 | 120 | 572 | 45 | 487 | 36 |
| Total | 10,892 | 8,140 | 7,138 | 5,014 | 5,070 | 3,507 |
| N | 5,228 | | 1,526 | | 569 | |

[a]All figures are in 1979 dollars.

housing equity compared to current income. For example, persons with low income but large housing equity stand to gain the most by converting housing equity into current consumption. An indication of the potential for such transfers is provided by the distribution of housing equity by income[4] as shown in table 1.3. Over 40 percent of those in the lowest income quartile also are in the lowest housing equity quartile.

Thus a reverse mortgage may not expand by much the opportunity for this group to increase current consumption. For example, consider a family with housing wealth of $16,334, the maximum in the lowest housing equity quartile (1979 dollars). Assume approximate average male life expectancy at 65 of 15 years. Suppose that the household obtains a loan for the value of the house and uses the proceeds from the loan to buy an annuity. If both the mortgage rate and the annuity "yield" are 10 percent, the annual income from the reverse annuity mortgage would be only $548. In fact, this is an overestimate. The annuity yield is typically much lower than the mortgage rate. In 1979, the average mortgage rate was 10.8 percent and the average annuity yield was 4.8 percent (Friedman and Warshawsky 1985). With these rates, the income from the reverse annuity mortage would be *negative,* −$212 per annum.

**Table 1.2B**        **Wealth by Tenure, 1969 and 1979** [a]

| | Tenure | | | | | |
| | Owners | | Renters | | Other | |
| Category | Mean | Median | Mean | Median | Mean | Median |
| | 1969 | | | | | |
| Nonhousing | | | | | | |
| bequeathable | $ 69,008 | $ 25,912 | $32,265 | $ 8,690 | $16,238 | $ 4,221 |
| Housing | 31,026 | 25,739 | 0 | 0 | 0 | 0 |
| Social | 39,274 | 44,535 | 30,087 | 29,705 | 21,130 | 19,499 |
| Security | 16,222 | 0 | 16,776 | 0 | 14,949 | 0 |
| Pension | 6,274 | 0 | 3,118 | 0 | 5,520 | 0 |
| Other | 161,806 | 110,454 | 82,248 | 52,762 | 57,837 | 37,732 |
| Total | | | | | | |
| N | 6,616 | | 2,426 | | 792 | |
| | 1979 | | | | | |
| Nonhousing | | | | | | |
| bequeathable | 46,262 | 17,476 | 21,480 | 4,710 | 13,919 | 3,116 |
| Housing | 41,735 | 33,000 | 0 | 0 | 0 | 0 |
| Social | 45,078 | 44,528 | 31,319 | 29,556 | 24,779 | 23,464 |
| Security | 7,220 | 0 | 5,564 | 0 | 2,629 | 0 |
| Pension | 12,468 | 0 | 4,518 | 0 | 5,774 | 0 |
| Other | 152,763 | 115,365 | 62,881 | 43,309 | 47,102 | 33,365 |
| Total | | | | | | |
| N | 5,228 | | 1,526 | | 569 | |

[a]All figures are in 1979 dollars.

**Table 1.3**        **Distribution of Housing Equity by Income, 1973**

| | Housing Equity | | | |
| Income | low | 2nd | 3rd | 4th |
| low | 41.0 | 26.0 | 18.3 | 14.8 |
| 2nd | 26.5 | 27.0 | 26.7 | 19.8 |
| 3rd | 18.6 | 27.3 | 31.0 | 23.1 |
| 4th | 8.9 | 19.7 | 28.4 | 43.0 |

Housing equity together with other wealth is possibly a better measure of consumption possibilities. Their joint distribution is shown in table 1.4. Again, those with little nonhousing wealth tend to have little housing equity as well. Close to half of those in the lowest nonhousing wealth quartile are also in the lowest housing equity quartile, and almost three-quarters are in the lowest half. Data for other years look very similar to those for 1973.

**Table 1.4**          **Distribution of Housing Equity by Other Wealth, 1973**

| | Housing Equity | | | |
|---|---|---|---|---|
| Other Wealth | low | 2nd | 3rd | 4th |
| low | 45.6 | 27.6 | 18.1 | 8.8 |
| 2nd | 28.4 | 30.2 | 26.3 | 15.2 |
| 3rd | 14.7 | 26.0 | 33.2 | 26.2 |
| 4th | 6.4 | 16.2 | 26.8 | 50.2 |

## 1.2  Who Moves?

### 1.2.1  Descriptive Data

The likelihood of moving is highest for those with an apparent imbalance in income versus housing equity. The percentage that moved during the 1973–75 period by income and housing equity quartiles is shown for homeowners in table 1.5. The most striking feature of these data is that persons who have relatively high nonhousing wealth but low housing equity are the most likely to move. Persons in the highest nonhousing wealth quartile are more than twice as likely to move if they have low rather than high housing equity. Families with low nonhousing wealth but high housing equity are not unusually likely to move, contrary to what would be expected if moving typically were

**Table 1.5**          **Percentage of Homeowners Who Moved**

A. By Income and Housing Equity, 1973–75

| | Housing Equity | | | | |
|---|---|---|---|---|---|
| Income | low | 2nd | 3rd | 4th | All |
| low | 12 | 7 | 10 | 16 | 11 |
| 2nd | 8 | 7 | 10 | 8 | 8 |
| 3rd | 10 | 7 | 7 | 8 | 8 |
| 4th | 16 | 8 | 8 | 10 | 10 |
| All | 11 | 7 | 9 | 10 | 9 |

B. By Other Wealth and Housing Equity, 1973–75

| | Housing Equity | | | | |
|---|---|---|---|---|---|
| Other Wealth | low | 2nd | 3rd | 4th | All |
| low | 10 | 6 | 10 | 9 | 9 |
| 2nd | 9 | 7 | 8 | 11 | 8 |
| 3rd | 11 | 8 | 9 | 9 | 9 |
| 4th | 20 | 9 | 8 | 10 | 10 |
| All | 11 | 7 | 9 | 10 | 9 |

used to withdraw wealth from housing and reallocate it to current consumption.

According to table 1.5A, however, families with high housing equity but low income are about as likely to move as families with high income but low housing equity. Persons with high incomes but devoting relatively little of it to housing may move to reallocate more of their income to housing. This may simply reflect optimal adjustment to desired housing expenditure, given current circumstances. But it may also be a response in part to government policies. Medicaid rules, for example, often require virtual exhaustion of nonhousing wealth, but not housing equity, before nursing home expenses are paid. Families with low income but high housing equity may move to withdraw wealth from housing because they are liquidity constrained. The evidence in the section 1.3 supports these presumptions.

In principle, homeowners could withdraw wealth from housing by increasing the mortgage on the house. Presumably those with the most housing wealth would be in the best position to do this. And indeed housing equity could be increased by paying off a mortgage. But change in the amount of home mortgages has been rare in the absence of a move. Thus, in practice it would appear that moving is typically the mechanism by which housing wealth has been increased or decreased. Recent tax legislation that eliminates the tax deductibility of interest on consumer borrowing other than mortgages may change the frequency of home equity loans, however.

The probability of a renter moving shows little relationship to income, wealth, or rent. In particular, it does not appear that families with high rent and low income, or with high income and low rent, are more likely than others to move. The percentage of renters who move is shown by income and total wealth quartile and by income and rent quartile in table 1.6.

Moving is often associated with job change. Among the elderly, it is more likely to be associated with retirement. It is also strongly associated with precipitating shocks, particularly the death of a spouse. The relationship of moving to retirement is shown in table 1.7 and to the death of a spouse in table 1.8.[5] Homeowners are slightly less than twice as likely to move if the respondent retires during the two-year interval than if retirement does not occur.[6] The difference is also substantial, although somewhat less, for renters. The death of the respondent almost doubles the likelihood that homeowners and renters move during many of the two-year intervals. (The effect of change in family size is shown in appendix table 1.A. The numbers are close to those pertaining to death of a spouse in table 1.8, although change in family size could occur for many reasons besides death of the respondent.)

Possibly the most informative description of the relationship between age and moving is the empirical hazard rate, the percentage of families

**Table 1.6**          **Percentage of Renters Who Moved**

A. By Income and Total Wealth, 1973–75

|  | Total Wealth | | | | |
|---|---|---|---|---|---|
| Income | low | 2nd | 3rd | 4th | All |
| low | 26 | 25 | 35 | 15 | 26 |
| 2nd | 35 | 25 | 26 | 10 | 27 |
| 3rd | 30 | 30 | 23 | 31 | 27 |
| 4th | 29 | 19 | 18 | 26 | 23 |
| All | 29 | 26 | 24 | 25 | 26 |

B. By Income and Rent, 1973–75

|  | Rent | | | | |
|---|---|---|---|---|---|
| Income | low | 2nd | 3rd | 4th | All |
| low | 24 | 28 | 29 | 24 | 26 |
| 2nd | 27 | 25 | 27 | 30 | 27 |
| 3rd | 32 | 22 | 24 | 33 | 27 |
| 4th | 24 | 15 | 23 | 26 | 23 |
| All | 26 | 24 | 25 | 28 | 26 |

who move in the next two-year interval, given that they have not moved before that. These calculations are shown in table 1.9, by survey year and by age. For example, 7.2 percent of the homeowners who were 58 in 1969 moved in the next two years, by 1971. Looking down the last column, there appears to be a slight increase in the probability of moving at the peak retirement years, 60 to 65, and possibly some decline with age, although both effects are slight. There appear to be no important cohort effects, judging by the similarity of the percentages for

**Table 1.7**          **Percent That Moves, by Retirement, Tenure, and Year**

|  | All | Owners[a] | Renters[a] |
|---|---|---|---|
| Retired: 1969–71 | 21.5 | 12.9 | 38.5 |
| Did not retire: 1969–71 | 12.7 | 6.7 | 26.5 |
| Retired: 1971–73 | 18.4 | 12.6 | 35.1 |
| Did not retire: 1971–73 | 14.5 | 8.8 | 28.5 |
| Retired: 1973–75 | 18.3 | 12.4 | 33.8 |
| Did not retire: 1973–75 | 13.0 | 8.3 | 24.1 |
| Retired: 1975–77 | 16.1 | 9.2 | 33.8 |
| Did not retire: 1975–77 | 12.2 | 7.6 | 25.0 |
| Retired: 1977–79 | 14.7 | 11.1 | 26.3 |
| Did not retire: 1977–79 | 10.9 | 7.2 | 20.5 |

[a]In base year.

Table 1.8    Percent That Move, by Death of Spouse, Tenure, and Year

|  | All | Owners[a] | Renters[a] |
|---|---|---|---|
| Death of original respondent: 1969–71 | 22.5 | 16.4 | 42.0 |
| No death: 1969–71 | 14.3 | 7.7 | 28.8 |
| Death of original respondent: 1971–73 | 23.0 | 17.4 | 43.5 |
| No death: 1971–73 | 15.1 | 9.5 | 29.6 |
| Death of original respondent: 1973–75 | 20.8 | 12.2 | 50.0 |
| No death: 1973–75 | 13.7 | 9.0 | 25.2 |
| Death of original respondent: 1975–77 | 18.5 | 11.9 | 50.0 |
| No death: 1975–77 | 12.5 | 7.6 | 25.5 |
| Death of original respondent: 1977–79 | 15.8 | 13.2 | 29.3 |
| No death: 1977–79 | 11.0 | 7.3 | 20.7 |

[a]In base year.

Table 1.9    Hazard Rates for Homeowners

| | Year at the Beginning of the Interval | | | | | |
|---|---|---|---|---|---|---|
| Age | 1969 | 1971 | 1973 | 1975 | 1977 | All |
| 58 | 7.2 | | | | | 7.2 |
| 59 | 7.4 | | | | | 7.4 |
| 60 | 9.3 | 7.9 | | | | 8.6 |
| 61 | 7.7 | 9.7 | | | | 8.6 |
| 62 | 7.9 | 7.9 | 7.8 | | | 7.9 |
| 63 | 8.1 | 9.0 | 7.4 | | | 8.2 |
| 64 | | 8.8 | 8.9 | 7.5 | | 8.4 |
| 65 | | 9.9 | 8.2 | 6.1 | | 8.3 |
| 66 | | | 7.0 | 6.4 | 7.6 | 7.0 |
| 67 | | | 6.5 | 6.5 | 4.7 | 6.0 |
| 68 | | | | 6.2 | 5.7 | 6.0 |
| 69 | | | | 6.3 | 4.5 | 5.4 |
| 70 | | | | | 7.0 | 7.0 |
| 71 | | | | | 6.3 | 6.3 |
| All | 7.9 | 8.8 | 7.7 | 6.6 | 6.0 | 7.6 |

people of the same age in different years. One might expect that not moving for several years would tend to identify stayers versus movers. If this selection effect exists, it should be revealed by declining moving probabilities along the diagonals that pertain to the same cohort as it ages. Those who enter each successive calculation have not moved for longer and longer periods of time. For all cohorts this effect is summarized in the bottom row. Any such effect does not show up strongly in this tabulation, although it is possibly indicated by the decline from around 8 percent in 1971 to about 6 percent in 1977. Whatever this effect is, it may be indistinguishable from the effect of age. Calculations in section 1.2.2 will help to make the distinction clearer, however.

Comparable data for renters are shown in table 1.10. The data suggest a rather strong selection of stayers in the sample after successive periods without moving. There is on average a substantial decline in the probability of moving as the number of years without moving increases, summarized in the bottom row.[7] On the other hand, there seems to be little effect of age, judged by looking down the columns.

## 1.2.2 Parameterization of Hazard Rates

Finally, these hazard rates are parameterized as simple functions of age, retirement, family status, health status, and income–housing equity quartiles. Given that a person has not yet moved at the time of a survey, the probability of moving by the next survey is estimated as a function of these variables, using a probit functional form. Those who move in a given interval are deleted from the calculations for subsequent intervals. The use of the probit form for the interval probability of moving is consistent with a Brownian motion formulation of a continuous time hazard model.[8]

The Brownian motion version of a hazard model may be described briefly. Suppose that at age $t$ there is a gain $G(t)$ that could be obtained by moving. It may be thought of as $G(t) = M(t) - S(t)$, where $M(t)$ is the utility associated with moving to the best available alternative housing, and $S(t)$ is the utility associated with staying in the present location. The probability of moving is given by $\Pr[G(t) = M(t) - S(t) > 0]$.

**Table 1.10**    **Hazard Rates for Renters**

| Age | Year at the Beginning of the Interval | | | | | |
| | 1969 | 1971 | 1973 | 1975 | 1977 | All |
|---|---|---|---|---|---|---|
| 58 | 24.1 | | | | | 24.1 |
| 59 | 29.1 | | | | | 29.1 |
| 60 | 31.5 | 24.8 | | | | 28.5 |
| 61 | 28.8 | 26.0 | | | | 27.7 |
| 62 | 29.8 | 23.0 | 14.1 | | | 24.7 |
| 63 | 32.0 | 24.9 | 15.6 | | | 26.1 |
| 64 | | 19.0 | 24.6 | 20.9 | | 20.9 |
| 65 | | 26.0 | 23.8 | 12.5 | | 21.8 |
| 66 | | | 19.3 | 18.5 | 17.8 | 18.7 |
| 67 | | | 20.6 | 14.7 | 15.8 | 17.3 |
| 68 | | | | 22.0 | 11.6 | 19.8 |
| 69 | | | | 14.4 | 13.9 | 19.1 |
| 70 | | | | | 16.5 | 16.5 |
| 71 | | | | | 25.4 | 25.4 |
| All | 29.1 | 23.8 | 19.4 | 17.5 | 16.7 | 23.7 |

That $G(t)$ follows a Brownian motion (Weiner) process with drift $u$ means that:

- Every increment $G(t + d) - G(t)$ is normally distributed with mean $ud$ and variance $c^2d$; and
- The increments for every pair of disjointed time intervals are independent.

Because the increments are assumed to be independent, given $G(t)$, $G(t + d)$ is a function only of $G(t)$ and the drift $u$.

If moving is not an absorbing state, meaning that a person could move and then move back again—not a realistic possibility in our case—the probability that a person who has not moved by age $t$ will move by age $t + d$ is given by

(1)     $\Pr[G(t + d) > 0 \mid G(t) = g(t)] = F\{[g(t) + ud]/cd^{1/2}\}$

where $F$ is a cumulative normal distribution function. This is an interval hazard rate with a simple probit functional form.

If moving is an absorbing state, a family could not be in the same house at the beginning and at the end of the period but have moved during the interval. In this case, the interval hazard[9] becomes:

(2)     $\Pr[G(t + d) > 0 \mid G(t) = g(t)] = F\{[g(t) + ud]/cd^{1/2}\}$
        $+ \exp[2ug(t)/c^2] \cdot F\{[g(t) - ud]/cd^{1/2}\}.$

In our case, $d$ is two years, and the starting point $g(t)$ must be estimated. We parameterize $u$ as a function of age; of housing equity and current income; and of changes in retirement, family, and health status. If the interval $d$ is defined to be 1 and $c$ is set to 1, equation (1) is in the form of a standard probit specification. (The variance $c$ is not identified if there is no variation in $d$.) The results for the absorbing-state version of the hazard tell the same story as those using the simple model and are not presented.

An advantage of estimating the interval hazards period by period is that the effect of each variable is allowed to vary freely as persons age. The results for the simple probit are reported in tables 1.11A and 1.11B. Table 1.11A is based on all intervals combined, while table 1.11B presents estimates for selected intervals separately. The last column of the tables shows the change in the probability of moving due to each of the attributes. The change is evaluated at the mean of all the other attributes. For example, if the sixteen variables describing home equity and income in table 1.11A are set to zero—identifying a family with high income and high housing equity—and all of the others are set at their means, the probability of moving is 0.084. If instead of high housing and high income, the family had low housing equity and high income, the probability of moving would be 0.084 + 0.047 = 0.131, or 0.047 higher.

**Table 1.11A**    **Probit Estimates of Interval Hazards for Homeowners, All Intervals Combined[a]**

| Variable | Coefficient | Asymptotic Standard Error | Δ Probability |
|---|---|---|---|
| *Age at Beginning of Period* | | | |
| 58 | 0.0 | — | 0.075[b] |
| 59 | 0.018 | 0.085 | 0.003 |
| 60 | 0.015 | 0.074 | 0.002 |
| 61 | 0.016 | 0.075 | 0.002 |
| 62 | −0.035 | 0.074 | −0.005 |
| 63 | −0.069 | 0.074 | −0.009 |
| 64 | −0.030 | 0.083 | −0.004 |
| 65 | −0.030 | 0.084 | −0.004 |
| 66 | −0.050 | 0.093 | −0.007 |
| 67 | −0.129 | 0.095 | −0.017 |
| 68 | −0.095 | 0.107 | −0.013 |
| 69 | −0.154 | 0.110 | −0.020 |
| 70 | 0.017 | 0.131 | 0.002 |
| 71 | −0.040 | 0.135 | −0.005 |
| *Year at Beginning of Period* | | | |
| 1969 | 0.0 | — | 0.078[b] |
| 1971 | 0.008 | 0.041 | 0.001 |
| 1973 | −0.069 | 0.051 | −0.010 |
| 1975 | −0.141 | 0.065 | −0.019 |
| 1977 | −0.187 | 0.080 | −0.024 |
| *Home Equity–Income Quartile* | | | |
| low–low | −0.124 | 0.056 | −0.018 |
| low–2nd | −0.049 | 0.059 | −0.007 |
| low–3rd | −0.034 | 0.067 | −0.005 |
| low–4th | 0.255 | 0.081 | 0.047 |
| 2nd–low | −0.242 | 0.066 | −0.031 |
| 2nd–2nd | −0.142 | 0.062 | −0.020 |
| 2nd–3rd | −0.222 | 0.064 | −0.029 |
| 2nd–4th | −0.090 | 0.071 | −0.013 |
| 3rd–low | −0.128 | 0.070 | −0.018 |
| 3rd–2nd | −0.183 | 0.064 | −0.025 |
| 3rd–3rd | −0.219 | 0.060 | −0.029 |
| 3rd–4th | −0.049 | 0.059 | −0.007 |
| 4th–low | 0.079 | 0.073 | 0.013 |
| 4th–2nd | −0.103 | 0.068 | −0.015 |
| 4th–3rd | −0.081 | 0.061 | −0.012 |
| 4th–4th | 0.0 | — | 0.084[b] |
| *Retirement Status* | | | |
| no → no | 0.0 | — | 0.046[b] |
| yes → no | 0.341 | 0.074 | 0.044 |
| no → yes | 0.409 | 0.036 | 0.055 |
| yes → yes | 0.285 | 0.036 | 0.035 |

*(continued)*

**Table 1.11A**    (continued)

| Variable | Coefficient | Asymptotic Standard Error | Δ Probability |
|---|---|---|---|
| *Family Status* | | | |
| single → single[c] | 0.0 | — | 0.066[b] |
| married → married | −0.004 | 0.033 | −0.000 |
| married → widowed | 0.322 | 0.056 | 0.052 |
| other change | 1.319 | 0.089 | 0.360 |
| *Health Status* | | | |
| same | 0.0 | — | 0.067[b] |
| better | 0.133 | 0.037 | 0.019 |
| worse | 0.006 | 0.030 | 0.001 |
| Intercept | −1.522 | 0.074 | 0.076[b] |
| Number of observations = 22,914 | | | |
| Log-likelihood = −5864.32 | | | |

[a]The standard errors have not been adjusted for repeated observations for the same person.

[b]The probability of moving in the base case. It is calculated by evaluating all variables within the category (age, home equity and income, retirement status, family status, or health status) at zero and all other variables at their means. The Δ probability for other attributes is the increase or decrease relative to this base. For example, the probability that a move occurs if a person retires is 0.046 + 0.055. The probability associated with the intercept is the probability of moving when all variables are set to their sample means.

[c]Includes single to single, divorced to divorced, and widowed to widowed.

**Table 1.11B**    **Probit Estimates of Interval Hazards for Homeowners, by Interval: 1969–71, 1973–75, 1977–79[a]**

| Variable | Coefficient | Asymptotic Standard Error | Δ Probability |
|---|---|---|---|
| | | 1969–71 | |
| *Age in 1969* | | | |
| 58 | 0.0 | — | 0.071[b] |
| 59 | 0.017 | 0.086 | 0.002 |
| 60 | 0.068 | 0.084 | 0.010 |
| 61 | −0.047 | 0.085 | −0.006 |
| 62 | −0.026 | 0.087 | −0.003 |
| 63 | −0.080 | 0.088 | −0.010 |
| *Home Equity–Income Quartile* | | | |
| low–low | −0.082 | 0.108 | −0.012 |
| low–2nd | −0.001 | 0.111 | −0.000 |
| low–3rd | 0.184 | 0.117 | 0.032 |
| low–4th | 0.306 | 0.148 | 0.058 |
| 2nd–low | −0.257 | 0.125 | −0.033 |
| 2nd–2nd | −0.173 | 0.127 | −0.024 |

**Table 1.11B**     (continued)

| Variable | Coefficient | Asymptotic Standard Error | Δ Probability |
|---|---|---|---|
| 2nd–3rd | −0.296 | 0.128 | −0.037 |
| 2nd–4th | 0.102 | 0.132 | 0.017 |
| 3rd–low | −0.162 | 0.141 | −0.022 |
| 3rd–2nd | −0.368 | 0.141 | −0.044 |
| 3rd–3rd | −0.242 | 0.125 | −0.032 |
| 3rd–4th | −0.200 | 0.125 | −0.027 |
| 4th–low | 0.145 | 0.135 | 0.025 |
| 4th–2nd | −0.342 | 0.152 | −0.042 |
| 4th–3rd | 0.003 | 0.116 | 0.001 |
| 4th–4th | 0.0 | — | 0.085[b] |
| *Retirement Status* | | | |
| no → no | 0.0 | — | 0.054[b] |
| yes → no | 0.280 | 0.168 | 0.038 |
| no → yes | 0.426 | 0.061 | 0.065 |
| yes → yes | 0.283 | 0.074 | 0.039 |
| *Family Status* | | | |
| single → singe[c] | 0.0 | — | 0.062[b] |
| married → married | 0.029 | 0.068 | 0.004 |
| married → widowed | 0.505 | 0.118 | 0.089 |
| other change | 1.434 | 0.164 | 0.397 |
| *Health Status* | | | |
| same | 0.0 | — | 0.064[b] |
| better | 0.179 | 0.072 | 0.026 |
| worse | 0.078 | 0.058 | 0.010 |
| Intercept | −1.592 | 0.109 | 0.079[b] |

Number of observations = 6,121

Log-likelihood = −1581.52

| | | 1973–75 | |
|---|---|---|---|
| *Age in 1969* | | | |
| 58 | 0.0 | — | 0.079[b] |
| 59 | −0.058 | 0.101 | −0.008 |
| 60 | −0.020 | 0.098 | −0.003 |
| 61 | −0.066 | 0.100 | −0.009 |
| 62 | −0.131 | 0.102 | −0.017 |
| 63 | −0.177 | 0.107 | −0.023 |
| *Home Equity–Income Quartile* | | | |
| low–low | −0.181 | 0.121 | −0.028 |
| low–2nd | −0.269 | 0.141 | −0.039 |
| low–3rd | −0.309 | 0.160 | −0.044 |
| low–4th | 0.103 | 0.193 | 0.019 |

*(continued)*

**Table 1.11B**    (continued)

| Variable | Coefficient | Asymptotic Standard Error | Δ Probability |
|---|---|---|---|
| 2nd–low | −0.360 | 0.147 | −0.049 |
| 2nd–2nd | −0.165 | 0.133 | −0.026 |
| 2nd–3rd | −0.426 | 0.145 | −0.055 |
| 2nd–4th | −0.335 | 0.162 | −0.046 |
| 3rd–low | −0.049 | 0.160 | −0.008 |
| 3rd–2nd | −0.245 | 0.155 | −0.036 |
| 3rd–3rd | −0.364 | 0.160 | −0.049 |
| 3rd–4th | −0.046 | 0.146 | −0.008 |
| 4th–low | −0.100 | 0.159 | −0.016 |
| 4th–2nd | −0.221 | 0.140 | −0.033 |
| 4th–3rd | −0.104 | 0.126 | −0.017 |
| 4th–4th | 0.0 | — | 0.099[b] |
| *Retirement Status* | | | |
| no → no | 0.0 | — | 0.036[b] |
| yes → no | 0.538 | 0.162 | 0.068 |
| no → yes | 0.465 | 0.092 | 0.055 |
| yes → yes | 0.413 | 0.079 | 0.047 |
| *Family Status* | | | |
| single→single[c] | 0.0 | — | 0.077[b] |
| married→married | −0.109 | 0.072 | −0.015 |
| married→widowed | −0.138 | 0.146 | −0.018 |
| other change | 1.457 | 0.207 | 0.436 |
| *Health Status* | | | |
| same | 0.0 | — | 0.069[b] |
| better | 0.034 | 0.088 | 0.005 |
| worse | −0.028 | 0.069 | −0.004 |
| Intercept | −1.462 | 0.127 | 0.077[b] |

Number of observations = 4,461

Log-likelihood = −1141.51

| | 1977–79 | | |
|---|---|---|---|
| *Age in 1969* | | | |
| 58 | 0.0 | — | 0.064[b] |
| 59 | −0.227 | 0.131 | −0.024 |
| 60 | −0.120 | 0.127 | −0.014 |
| 61 | −0.245 | 0.134 | −0.025 |
| 62 | −0.020 | 0.122 | −0.002 |
| 63 | −0.060 | 0.130 | −0.007 |
| *Home Equity–Income Quartile* | | | |
| low–low | −0.456 | 0.183 | −0.050 |
| low–2nd | −0.191 | 0.179 | −0.025 |
| low–3rd | −0.638 | 0.279 | −0.061 |
| low–4th | −0.129 | 0.290 | −0.018 |

**Table 1.11B**    (continued)

| Variable | Coefficient | Asymptotic Standard Error | Δ Probability |
|---|---|---|---|
| 2nd–low | −0.474 | 0.215 | −0.051 |
| 2nd–2nd | −0.281 | 0.183 | −0.035 |
| 2nd–3rd | −0.074 | 0.180 | −0.011 |
| 2nd–4th | −0.135 | 0.199 | −0.019 |
| 3rd–low | −0.482 | 0.224 | −0.052 |
| 3rd–2nd | −0.092 | 0.162 | −0.013 |
| 3rd–3rd | −0.278 | 0.155 | −0.035 |
| 3rd–4th | −0.086 | 0.158 | −0.012 |
| 4th–low | −0.310 | 0.253 | −0.038 |
| 4th–2nd | −0.036 | 0.192 | −0.005 |
| 4th–3rd | −0.442 | 0.201 | −0.049 |
| 4th–4th | 0.0 | — | 0.083[b] |
| *Retirement Status* | | | |
| no → no | 0.0 | — | 0.022[b] |
| yes → no | 0.467 | 0.212 | 0.039 |
| no → yes | 0.730 | 0.171 | 0.077 |
| yes → yes | 0.412 | 0.146 | 0.032 |
| *Family Status* | | | |
| single → single[c] | 0.0 | — | 0.054[b] |
| married → married | 0.098 | 0.099 | 0.010 |
| married → widowed | 0.394 | 0.145 | 0.058 |
| other change | 1.468 | 0.314 | 0.390 |
| *Health Status* | | | |
| same | 0.0 | — | 0.049[b] |
| better | 0.212 | 0.111 | 0.026 |
| worse | −0.025 | 0.093 | −0.003 |
| Intercept | −1.656 | 0.194 | 0.060[b] |

Number of observations = 3,266

Log-likelihood = 695.06

[a]The standard errors have not been adjusted for repeated observations for the same person.

[b]The probability of moving the the base case. It is calculated by evaluating all variables within the category (age, home equity and income, retirement status, family status, or health status) at zero and all other variables at their means. The Δ probability for other attributes is the increase or decrease relative to this base. For example, the probability that a move occurs if a person retires in the 1977–79 interval is 0.022 + 0.077. The probability associated with the intercept is the probability of moving when all variables are set to their sample means.

[c]Includes single to single, divorced to divorced, and widowed to widowed.

The estimates support several conclusions. First, as indicated in tables 1.7 and 1.8, moving is often related to retirement and is often precipitated by the death of a spouse or by other changes in family status. For example, based on the estimates for all intervals combined, in table 1.11A the probability that a homeowner moves increases from 0.046 to 0.101 (0.046 + 0.055) if the head retires. The probability that the typical married couple moves is 0.066. If the husband dies during the interval, the probability is 0.118. Other changes in family status, like divorce or marriage, are much more likely to be associated with a move. In these cases, the probability of a move is 0.426 (0.066 + 0.360).[10]

The estimated coefficients on the income–housing equity indicators in table 1.11A show that the probability of moving is greatest for families with the greatest apparent imbalance in income versus housing equity. The estimated hazard rates for the four home equity and income levels distinguished in the probit specification, assuming other attributes at their sample means are shown in table 1.12. The average hazard rate is 7.6 percent. Holding other attributes constant, the hazard rate for families with high income and low housing equity is 13.1 percent. Those with low income and high housing equity are somewhat less likely to move, although they are more likely than the average. These estimates provide no evidence that homeowners typically use housing wealth to increase current consumption. The results in this section together with those below suggest that persons with high incomes and low housing equity are likely to move to increase housing expenditure, while those with low income and high housing equity tend to reduce housing equity when they move. However, the data in section 1.3 show that movers in general do not reduce housing equity.

Change in health status has little effect on the probability of moving, according to our measures (see table 1.11A). An improvement in health is associated with a 0.019 increase in the probability of moving, from 0.067 to 0.086. A worsening of health status is associated with a 0.001 decline in the probability of moving.

**Table 1.12**    **Estimated Hazard Rates for Homeowners, by Income and Home Equity**

| Income | Housing Equity | | | |
|--------|-----|-----|-----|-----|
|        | low | 2nd | 3rd | 4th |
| low    | 6.6  | 5.2 | 6.6 | 9.7 |
| 2nd    | 7.7  | 6.4 | 5.9 | 6.9 |
| 3rd    | 7.9  | 5.5 | 5.5 | 7.2 |
| 4th    | 13.1 | 7.1 | 7.7 | 8.4 |

The parameter estimates show no effect of age on moving. That is, age at the beginning of a two-year period is unrelated to the probability of moving. Note that these variables indicate ages that are two years greater with each successive interval, beginning with 58 at the beginning of the 1969–71 interval. The year effects, indicated by the first year of each of the two-year intervals, are small but declining consistently. They reflect the increasing selection of stayers as the number of years without a move increases. The estimates indicate that those who have not moved before 1977 are 0.024 less likely to move in the subsequent two-year interval than the typical person in the sample in 1969 is likely to move by 1971.

Estimates of the effect of individual attributes on the hazard rates of renters are shown in table 1.13 for all survey intervals combined. As with homeowners, retirement and changes in family status have substantial effects on the probability of moving. There is no age effect. Unlike homeowners, however, there are substantial year effects on the probability that renters move, indicating substantial and increasing selection of stayers as the number of years without a move increases.

**Table 1.13**    **Probit Estimates of Interval Hazards for Renters, All Intervals Combined[a]**

| Variable | Coefficient | Asymptotic Standard Error | Δ Probability |
|---|---|---|---|
| *Age of Beginning of Period* | | | |
| 58 | 0.0 | — | 0.195[b] |
| 59 | 0.135 | 0.101 | 0.040 |
| 60 | 0.196 | 0.095 | 0.058 |
| 61 | 0.118 | 0.094 | 0.034 |
| 62 | 0.075 | 0.092 | 0.021 |
| 63 | 0.091 | 0.093 | 0.026 |
| 64 | 0.098 | 0.115 | 0.028 |
| 65 | 0.129 | 0.117 | 0.037 |
| 66 | 0.149 | 0.135 | 0.044 |
| 67 | 0.117 | 0.142 | 0.034 |
| 68 | 0.207 | 0.164 | 0.062 |
| 69 | 0.035 | 0.176 | 0.010 |
| 70 | 0.219 | 0.225 | 0.066 |
| 71 | 0.398 | 0.235 | 0.127 |
| *Year at Beginning of Period* | | | |
| 1969 | 0.0 | — | 0.294[b] |
| 1971 | −0.197 | 0.056 | −0.064 |
| 1973 | −0.345 | 0.080 | −0.106 |
| 1975 | −0.426 | 0.106 | −0.127 |
| 1977 | −0.492 | 0.132 | −0.143 |

(*continued*)

**Table 1.13**    (continued)

| Variable | Coefficient | Asymptotic Standard Error | Δ Probability |
|---|---|---|---|
| *Home Equity–Income Quartile* | | | |
| low–low | 0.131 | 0.077 | 0.040 |
| low–2nd | 0.157 | 0.080 | 0.048 |
| low–3rd | −0.009 | 0.111 | −0.003 |
| low–4th | −0.006 | 0.164 | −0.002 |
| 2nd–low | 0.209 | 0.090 | 0.066 |
| 2nd–2nd | 0.044 | 0.085 | 0.013 |
| 2nd–3rd | −0.006 | 0.089 | −0.002 |
| 2nd–4th | −0.236 | 0.122 | −0.062 |
| 3rd–low | 0.107 | 0.103 | 0.032 |
| 3rd–2nd | 0.049 | 0.096 | 0.015 |
| 3rd–3rd | 0.027 | 0.082 | 0.008 |
| 3rd–4th | 0.099 | 0.084 | 0.030 |
| 4th–low | 0.139 | 0.130 | 0.043 |
| 4th–2nd | 0.069 | 0.110 | 0.021 |
| 4th–3rd | 0.111 | 0.087 | 0.034 |
| 4th–4th | 0.0 | — | 0.212[b] |
| *Retirement Status* | | | |
| no → no | 0.0 | — | 0.189[b] |
| yes → no | 0.179 | 0.129 | 0.052 |
| no → yes | 0.378 | 0.051 | 0.118 |
| yes → yes | 0.160 | 0.053 | 0.046 |
| *Family Status* | | | |
| single → single[c] | 0.0 | — | 0.209[b] |
| married → married | 0.090 | 0.042 | 0.027 |
| married → widowed | 0.414 | 0.096 | 0.137 |
| other change | 1.187 | 0.138 | 0.438 |
| *Health Status* | | | |
| same | 0.0 | — | 0.212[b] |
| better | 0.200 | 0.056 | 0.062 |
| worse | 0.108 | 0.044 | 0.033 |
| Intercept | −0.982 | 0.087 | 0.237 |

Number of observations = 5,637

Log-likelihood = −2954.0

[a]The standard errors have not been adjusted for repeated observations for the same person.

[b]The probability of moving in the base case. It is calculated by evaluating all variables within the category (age, home equity and income, retirement status, family status, or health status) at zero and all other variables at their means. The Δ probability for other attributes is the increase or decrease relative to this base. For example, the probability that a move occurs if a person retires is 0.189 + 0.118. The probability associated with the intercept is the probability of moving when all variables are set to their sample means.

[c]Includes single to single, divorced to divorced, and widowed to widowed.

The hazard rate declines from 0.294 in the 1969–71 interval to 0.151 in the 1977–79 interval. As shown in table 1.14, low-income families are somewhat more likely to move, but there is no relationship between rent and the likelihood of moving.

## 1.3   Moving, Housing Value, and User Cost

It has been shown that only about 8 or 9 percent of homeowners move in any two-year period, and that only about 25 percent moved over the entire ten-year period. Renters are much more likely to move; about a quarter move in any two-year period, and almost 65 percent of initial renters had moved at least once by 1979. Retirement and death of a spouse are strong precipitating factors associated with moving.

In this section we consider how housing equity and user cost change with moving. In particular, we analyze the extent to which wealth is withdrawn from housing at the time of moving. The market value of housing and housing equity are the principle measures that are analyzed for homeowners.

In addition, we consider the change in nonhousing bequeathable wealth. If wealth is withdrawn from housing at the time of a move, it should show up as an increase in nonhousing bequeathable wealth. This provides a check on the housing equity data. For example, persons may undervalue their houses, especially during a period of increasing housing prices. When the person moves and a new house is bought, its actual market value is revealed. The difference between this value and the estimated value of the previous house could exaggerate the increase in housing value at the time of a move. The change in non-housing bequeathable wealth would not be subject to this potential bias however.[11] If the elderly typically have more wealth in housing than they would like, we would expect to see a fall in housing equity and an increase in nonhousing bequeathable wealth among those who move.

Change in rent is determined for renters. In addition, we follow the change in the user cost of housing for both homeowners and renters. This provides a measure that is comparable for both groups. It also is

**Table 1.14**      **Estimated Hazard Rates by Income and Rent Quartile, for Renters**

| Income | Rent | | | |
|---|---|---|---|---|
| | low | 2nd | 3rd | 4th |
| low | 25.2 | 27.8 | 24.5 | 25.5 |
| 2nd | 26.1 | 22.5 | 22.7 | 23.3 |
| 3rd | 21.0 | 21.1 | 22.0 | 24.6 |
| 4th | 21.1 | 15.1 | 24.2 | 21.2 |

a direct indicator of the extent to which the elderly move to reduce such expenditures. We find that the typical move is just as likely to be associated with an increase as a decrease in housing equity and that user cost is also just as likely to increase as to decrease.

### 1.3.1    Housing Value, Equity, and Nonhousing Bequeathable Wealth

Two types of analysis are discussed. The first is based on changes between adjacent survey years. In this case, the sample includes all homeowners in the sample in each of the two survey periods. The second is based only on respondents who remained in the sample over the entire period of the RHS. This has the advantage of providing data on families both before and after a move. On the other hand, effects of attrition may have a more substantial effect on the calculations when only those who remain in the survey for ten years are included in the analysis. Attrition is unlikely to have an important effect on the calculations based on two-year intervals.[12]

Table 1.15 shows the change in the market value of housing, housing equity, and nonhousing bequeathable wealth for movers and stayers over each two-year interval of the RHS. The comparison with stayers provides a control for economy-wide changes during each interval. In two of the six intervals, the change in housing value for movers is greater than for stayers. In four of the five intervals, more than half of the changes for movers were positive. The equity value of housing was also as likely to increase as to decrease when a move occurred. The median change in equity value was usually somewhat less for movers than for stayers, however, on the order of $1,500 or $2,000. In four of the five periods, the *fall* in nonhousing bequeathable wealth was greater for movers than for stayers. This may be the clearest evidence that wealth is not typically withdrawn from housing at the time of a move. The percentage with a fall in nonhousing bequeathable wealth was typically almost the same for movers as for stayers.

An alternative description of these measures is presented in appendix table 1.B. It shows housing value, housing equity, and nonhousing bequeathable wealth for those who were homeowners during the entire period of the RHS. The data distinguish families by whether they moved or stayed during a particular two-year interval and show the values in each of the other years of the survey as well. Illustrative findings are graphed in figures 1.1a, 1.1b, and 1.1c. The first of each pair of graphs distinguishes those who moved between 1969 and 1971 from those who did not move. Persons in either of these mover or stayer groups may have moved *or* stayed in subsequent years. The second of each pair distinguishes movers and stayers in the 1975–77 interval. Median home value increased over the RHS period for both movers and stayers (fig. 1.1a). Movers typically had greater housing value than stayers. The

**Table 1.15**  **Median Housing Value, Equity, and (Nonhousing) Bequeathable Wealth, by Stay versus Move and by Year, for Homeowners[a]**

| Year and Measure | Housing Value | | Housing Equity | | Bequeathable Wealth | |
|---|---|---|---|---|---|---|
| | Stay | Move | Stay | Move | Stay | Move |
| Median, 1969 | $29,699 | $33,659 | $25,740 | $25,740 | $25,864 | $33,826 |
| Median, 1971 | 28,804 | 32,261 | 26,884 | 26,884 | 25,011 | 34,039 |
| Median Change | − 503 | 363 | 378 | 558 | − 544 | − 1,376 |
| % Change > 0 | 0.46 | 0.53 | 0.54 | 0.54 | 0.45 | 0.45 |
| Median, 1971 | 30,468 | 31,364 | 26,884 | 26,884 | 23,772 | 25,085 |
| Median, 1973 | 32,667 | 32,667 | 29,401 | 24,500 | 21,604 | 22,620 |
| Median Change | 839 | 526 | 1,405 | − 139 | − 632 | − 739 |
| % Change > 0 | 0.61 | 0.55 | 0.63 | 0.50 | 0.31 | 0.28 |
| Median, 1973 | 32,667 | 32,667 | 28,584 | 29,401 | 22,254 | 26,210 |
| Median, 1975 | 31,693 | 33,716 | 26,973 | 25,900 | 19,964 | 25,995 |
| Median Change | − 712 | − 1,758 | − 217 | − 2,323 | − 1,135 | − 1,240 |
| % Change > 0 | 0.43 | 0.43 | 0.48 | 0.42 | 0.42 | 0.42 |
| Median, 1975 | 29,670 | 33,716 | 26,973 | 31,019 | 20,230 | 28,052 |
| Median, 1977 | 33,538 | 35,934 | 29,945 | 29,945 | 19,644 | 28,452 |
| Median Change | 1,569 | 787 | 2,078 | 585 | − 391 | − 2,695 |
| % Change > 0 | 0.62 | 0.51 | 0.64 | 0.51 | 0.45 | 0.40 |
| Median, 1977 | 31,143 | 35,934 | 29,945 | 35,934 | 19,173 | 31,657 |
| Median, 1979 | 35,000 | 39,000 | 33,900 | 32,000 | 17,191 | 34,012 |
| Median Change | 1,044 | 1,464 | 1,615 | − 528 | − 386 | 1,322 |
| % Change > 0 | 0.63 | 0.55 | 0.65 | 0.49 | 0.45 | 0.56 |

[a]All figures are in 1979 dollars. Sample: All homeowners in the sample in adjacent years.

median home value of movers always increased at the time of the move. The median home equity always declines somewhat at the time of the move, but increases thereafter (fig. 1.1b). Movers have more housing equity than stayers, based on these data for those who remained in the survey for its duration.[13] And the difference is typically about as large at the end of the RHS period as at the beginning.

Median nonhousing bequeathable wealth declines continuously for both movers and stayers, and at approximately the same rate (fig. 1.1c). At the time of the move it is as likely to decrease as to increase. (It decreases in both of the graphs shown.) Again, the typical elderly mover appears to withdraw little if any housing equity at the time of the move.[14]

Finally, in table 1.16 we have estimated by linear regression the relationship between family attributes and the change in home equity when the family moves (to another owner-occupied dwelling). The variables are the same as those used to estimate the interval hazard rates in tables 1.11 and 1.13 above. We emphasize the relationship

## Med. Home Value, Movers and Stayers

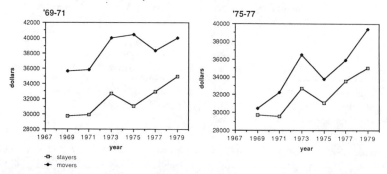

**Fig. 1.1a**

## Med. Home Equity, Movers and Stayers

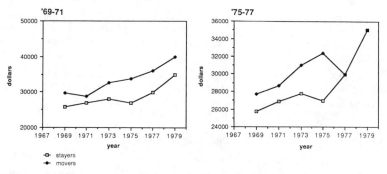

**Fig. 1.1b**

## Med. Beq. Wealth, Movers and Stayers

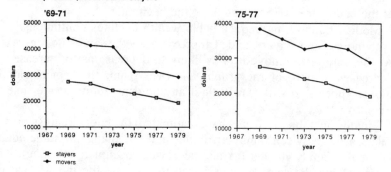

**Fig. 1.1c**

**Table 1.16**    **OLS Estimates of Change in Housing Equity for Homeowners, All Intervals Combined[a]**

| Variable | All Homeowners | | Addition for Movers | |
|---|---|---|---|---|
| | Coefficient | Standard Error | Coefficient | Standard Error |
| *Age at Beginning of Period* | | | | |
| 58 | — | — | — | — |
| 59 | −491 | 833 | 187 | 3,669 |
| 60 | 261 | 612 | 1773 | 2,565 |
| 61 | −1 | 629 | −2,772 | 2,550 |
| 62 | −33 | 511 | 1,123 | 2,095 |
| 63 | −600 | 527 | 5,841 | 2,236 |
| 64 | 329 | 514 | 554 | 2,088 |
| 65 | −601 | 533 | 161 | 2,237 |
| 66 | −289 | 1,093 | 4,182 | 4,912 |
| 67 | 1,147 | 841 | −5,060 | 4,110 |
| 68 | 567 | 734 | −2,509 | 3,521 |
| 69 | 635 | 752 | 4,954 | 3,783 |
| 70 | 673 | 1,065 | −1,189 | 5,240 |
| 71 | −1,675 | 1,092 | −2,076 | 5,467 |
| *Year at Beginning of Period* | | | | |
| 1969 | — | — | — | — |
| 1971 | 446 | 384 | 1,698 | 1,590 |
| 1973 | −1,651 | 341 | −3,534 | 1,437 |
| 1975 | 1,222 | 410 | 274 | 1,838 |
| 1977 | 1,365 | 552 | −440 | 2,609 |
| *Home Equity–Income Quartile* | | | | |
| low–low | 966 | 491 | 4,683 | 2,299 |
| low–2nd | 1,750 | 557 | 5,219 | 2,473 |
| low–3rd | 3,593 | 692 | 5,393 | 2,872 |
| low–4th | 6,182 | 1,033 | 8,396 | 3,211 |
| 2nd–low | 5 | 598 | 3,007 | 2,781 |
| 2nd–2nd | 145 | 571 | 2,683 | 2,526 |
| 2nd–3rd | 1,560 | 579 | 1,381 | 2,783 |
| 2nd–4th | 1,384 | 718 | 9,375 | 2,821 |
| 3rd–low | −1,087 | 671 | 2,114 | 3,154 |
| 3rd–2nd | −870 | 561 | 1,916 | 2,566 |
| 3rd–3rd | −396 | 516 | −4,236 | 2,360 |
| 3rd–4th | 1,374 | 565 | 4,218 | 2,376 |
| 4th–low | −6,005 | 813 | −16,377 | 2,885 |
| 4th–2nd | −3,616 | 667 | −13,790 | 3,160 |
| 4th–3rd | −2,742 | 604 | −949 | 2,324 |
| 4th–4th | — | — | — | — |
| *Retirement Status* | | | | |
| no → no | — | — | — | — |
| yes → no | 278 | 665 | −2,535 | 2,487 |

(*continued*)

**Table 1.16**    (continued)

| Variable | All Homeowners | | Addition for Movers | |
|---|---|---|---|---|
| | Coefficient | Standard Error | Coefficient | Standard Error |
| no → yes | −257 | 370 | −425 | 1,353 |
| yes → yes | −189 | 312 | 2,084 | 1,206 |
| *Family Status* | | | | |
| single → single[b] | — | — | — | — |
| married → married | 1,834 | 334 | −1,025 | 1,149 |
| married → widowed | 1,149 | 683 | −3,577 | 2,279 |
| other change | −4,249 | 939 | 9,251 | 2,401 |
| *Health Status* | | | | |
| same | — | — | — | — |
| better | 18 | 301 | 1,087 | 1,184 |
| worse | −592 | 247 | −1,005 | 1,062 |
| *Children* | | | | |
| no | — | — | — | — |
| yes | 463 | 195 | −3,172 | 855 |
| Intercept | — | — | — | — |
| Number of observations = 21,224 | | | | |

[a]The standard errors have not been adjusted for repeated observations for the same person.

[b]Includes single to single, divorced to divorced, and widowed to widowed.

between the change in housing equity, on the one hand, and initial income versus housing equity, on the other.

Because of reporting errors, there is a tendency for those who report an unusually high level of income or home equity in one survey year to report a lower level in the next. In other words, errors in variables create a regression toward the mean. To correct for this, we estimate the change in housing equity for all homeowners, identifying separately those who move. Thus, for example, the estimated reduction in home equity for families who move and who report low income and high home equity in the first year of a two-year interval is the difference between the reduction for movers and the reduction for stayers; the regression toward the mean is netted out. The *mean* change in home equity for movers is shown in table 1.17.

Families with low income and high housing wealth reduce housing equity when they move. On the other hand, families with high income and low housing wealth, increase equity substantially at the time of the move. Overall, movers are as likely to increase as to decrease housing equity.

Homeowners apparently do not typically move to withdraw wealth from housing. They do not, in general, move to relieve a liquidity

**Table 1.17**    **Mean Change in Home Equity for Movers, by Income and Home Equity**

| Income | Housing Equity Quartile | | | |
|--------|------|------|------|------|
|        | Low | 2nd | 3rd | 4th |
| Low | $4,683 | $3,007 | $2,114 | −$16,377 |
| 2nd | 5,219 | 2,683 | 1,916 | −13,790 |
| 3rd | 5,393 | 1,381 | −4,236 | −9,479 |
| 4th | 8,396 | 9,375 | 4,218 | −4,503 |

constraint, although some apparently do. Indeed, there is a somewhat greater tendency for moves to be associated with high-income elderly who want to spend more on housing than with low-income families with high housing wealth who want to withdraw wealth from housing.

Like the housing equity of stayers, the equity of movers tends to increase from year to year before and after the move. Of course, the increase in home value in the absence of a move reflects the economy-wide trend in housing prices over the period of the RHS, not necessarily a conscious decision to increase saving through housing equity. The change at the time of a move presumably does reflect conscious intention. Nonhousing bequeathable wealth fell over time, usually more for movers than for stayers. In considering life-cycle theories of saving, housing equity is usually thought of jointly with other forms of saving, presumably to be consumed in old age. These data suggest that this view is not correct. Nonhousing bequeathable wealth is observed to fall with age. Most housing equity will apparently be left as a bequest, judging by the behavior of the RHS respondents through age 73.

This does not necessarily suggest that the reason housing equity is not consumed is in order to leave a bequest. Indeed the change in housing equity at the time of a sale by elderly persons without children is about the same as the change for those with children. Housing equity increases for about half of movers in each group. The same is true for the market value of housing. There is some evidence that nonhousing bequeathable wealth falls less for movers with children than for those without children. The differences are not substantial however. This suggests that the elderly may well be attached to their homes for reasons other than or in addition to the bequest motive.[15]

### 1.3.2    Moving and Rent

The rent of stayers typically declines over time, as shown in table 1.18. On the other hand, the median rent of movers usually increases. The initial rent of movers and stayers is about the same. An alternative description of the data is presented in appendix table 1.C. Like comparable tables for owners, it distinguishes movers and stayers in each

Table 1.18          Median Rent, by Stay versus Move and by Year,
                    Adjacent Year Renters[a]

| Year and Measure | Stay | Move |
|---|---|---|
| Median, 1969 | $ 140 | $ 132 |
| Median, 1971 | 134 | 134 |
| Median Change | −4.69 | 1.07 |
| % Change > 0 | 0.34 | 0.51 |
| Median, 1971 | 134 | 131 |
| Median, 1973 | 131 | 139 |
| Median Change | −6.36 | 5.89 |
| % Change > 0 | 0.34 | 0.58 |
| Median, 1973 | 131 | 136 |
| Median, 1975 | 121 | 135 |
| Median Change | −15.66 | −8.00 |
| % Change > 0 | 0.15 | 0.42 |
| Median, 1975 | 121 | 121 |
| Median, 1977 | 120 | 139 |
| Median Change | −4.66 | 4.77 |
| % Change > 0 | 0.35 | 0.56 |
| Median, 1977 | 132 | 132 |
| Median, 1979 | 120 | 125 |
| Median Change | −10.60 | −1.54 |
| % Change > 0 | 0.21 | 0.48 |

[a]All figures are in 1979 dollars. Sample: All renters in adjacent surveys.

two-year interval, but it also shows rents in each of the other years of the RHS as well. The respondents used in this table rented in each of the years. Median rents are graphed in figure 1.2. Those who do not move have declining rents. Thus there appears to be a substantial benefit to remaining in the same rental unit. Rent increases of stayers do not keep up with the rate of inflation. Indeed this apparent rent advantage to continuing renters may provide an incentive not to move.

The rent of movers increases at the time of the move, but typically declines in other years, reflecting the lower price faced by sitting tenants. For example, the rents of those who moved between 1971 and 1973 declined somewhat between 1969 and 1971, then increased sharply at the time of the move, and declined thereafter. Of course, both the movers and stayers in the 1969–71 period could have moved in subsequent or in earlier years.

### 1.3.3  User Cost

User cost provides a measure that is comparable for both owners and renters. It includes rent, mortgage payments, heat, electricity, gas, water, and trash removal. The change in user cost by tenure and move

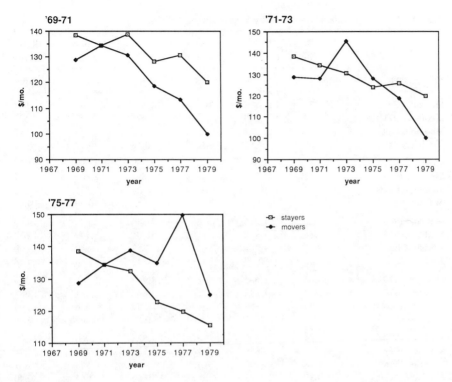

Fig. 1.2

type is shown in table 1.19.[16] The median change in the user cost of movers who own in both years is typically small and close to the change for nonmovers. Consistent with the rent data in section 1.3.2, the change in user cost for renters who move is usually positive and is always greater than the change for stayers. The median increase in user cost for those who move from owner-occupied to rental housing is in the neighborhood of $800 per year. Between 60 and 70 percent of the increases are positive for this group. The median change for those who move from rental to owner-occupied housing is negative in each interval, but much smaller than the increase for those who make the reverse move. Positive changes are almost as likely as negative ones.

User cost in each year of the survey is shown in figure 1.3 by move status in selected two-year intervals. It is easy to see that median user cost increases at the time of the move. In most other years user cost declined for both movers and stayers. Again, it is important to keep in mind that members of either group could have moved or stayed in intervals other than the one used for classification.

**Table 1.19    Annual User Cost by Tenure Change[a]**

| Year and Measure | Own to Own | | Rent to Rent | | Own to Rent | Rent to Own |
|---|---|---|---|---|---|---|
| | Stay | Move | Stay | Move | Move | Move |
| Median, 1969 | $ 931 | $1,188 | $1,663 | $1,616 | $1,544 | $1,901 |
| Median, 1971 | 1,577 | 1,574 | 1,936 | 1,936 | 2,217 | 1,523 |
| Median Change | 655 | 551 | 284 | 351 | 872 | − 167 |
| % Change > 0 | 0.81 | 0.63 | 0.77 | 0.68 | 0.68 | 0.46 |
| Median, 1971 | 1,542 | 1,642 | 1,905 | 1,799 | 1,692 | 2,194 |
| Median, 1973 | 1,512 | 1,397 | 1,849 | 1,862 | 2,801 | 2,107 |
| Median Change | − 13 | − 26 | − 74 | 21 | 715 | − 93 |
| % Change > 0 | 0.47 | 0.47 | 0.38 | 0.52 | 0.59 | 0.48 |
| Median, 1973 | 1,506 | 1,716 | 1,882 | 1,888 | 2,042 | 1,895 |
| Median, 1975 | 1,485 | 1,738 | 1,780 | 1,904 | 3,149 | 1,653 |
| Median Change | − 73 | 3 | − 152 | − 53 | 949 | − 39 |
| % Change > 0 | 0.42 | 0.50 | 0.29 | 0.47 | 0.66 | 0.48 |
| Median, 1975 | 1,462 | 1,605 | 1,813 | 1,767 | 1,749 | 2,239 |
| Median, 1977 | 1,492 | 1,738 | 1,803 | 1,869 | 2,381 | 1,885 |
| Median Change | 39 | 50 | − 28 | 53 | 758 | − 406 |
| % Change > 0 | 0.56 | 0.52 | 0.44 | 0.54 | 0.67 | 0.46 |
| Median, 1977 | 1,484 | 1,702 | 1,869 | 1,928 | 2,060 | 2,300 |
| Median, 1979 | 1,400 | 1,676 | 1,764 | 1,937 | 2,492 | 2,084 |
| Median Change | − 98 | − 55 | − 129 | − 32 | 550 | − 321 |
| % Change > 0 | 0.39 | 0.45 | 0.28 | 0.46 | 0.64 | 0.40 |

[a]All figures are in 1979 dollars. Sample: Families in the sample in adjacent years.

## 1.4   Summary and Conclusions

We have described the relationships between family attributes and moving and between moving and change in housing wealth. Moving is often associated with retirement and with precipitating shocks, such as the death of a spouse or by other changes in family status. Median housing wealth increases as the elderly age. Even when the elderly move, housing equity is as likely to increase as to decrease. (Although the RHS only follows persons through age 73, Garber [ch. 9, in this volume] reports no decline [in fact an increase] from age 70 through age 95 for noninstitutionalized households, based on the National Long-Term Care Survey.) The user cost of housing typically increases for both homeowners and renters when they move. Holding other attributes constant, families with high income and low housing wealth are as likely to move as those with low incomes and high housing wealth. The median housing equity of families in the first group increases when they move and the median of the second group decreases. Thus, the typical mover is not liquidity constrained, although apparently some are. High transaction costs associated with moving are apparently not

**Med. User Cost, Movers and Stayers**

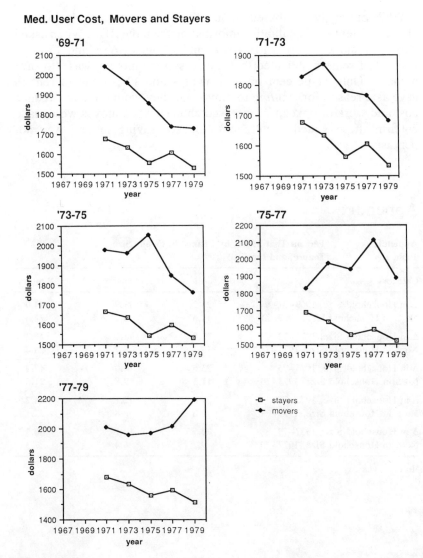

**Fig. 1.3**

the cause of the increase in housing wealth as the elderly age. Apparently, the absence of a well-developed market for reverse mortgages may be explained by a lack of demand for these financial instruments. The evidence suggests that the typical elderly family does not wish to reduce housing wealth to increase current consumption. For whatever reason, there is apparently a considerable attachment among homeowners to their habitual housing.

While our analysis is based on quantitative data, the conclusions are also consistent with qualitative information from the RHS. When asked why they moved, only 9 to 14 percent of homeowners and 15 to 17 percent of renters indicated that the reason for moving was "to save money." Only 11 percent of homeowners and 12 percent of renters gave as a reason for *wanting* to move that they would like to "reduce cost and work of upkeep." Observed choices when moves were made confirm these stated preferences; indeed, saving money was not pervasive.

## Appendix

**Appendix Table 1.A**  **Percent That Move, by Change in Family Size, Tenure, and Interval**

| Category | All | Owners[a] | Renters[a] |
|---|---|---|---|
| Δ in Household Size, 1969–71 | 23.2 | 11.9 | 44.0 |
| No Δ in Household Size, 1969–71 | 11.6 | 6.7 | 24.6 |
| Δ in Household Size, 1971–73 | 22.8 | 13.2 | 46.2 |
| No Δ in Household Size, 1971–73 | 13.1 | 8.7 | 25.4 |
| Δ in Household Size, 1973–75 | 23.5 | 14.0 | 42.9 |
| No Δ in Household Size, 1973–75 | 11.5 | 7.8 | 21.6 |
| Δ in Household Size, 1975–77 | 21.5 | 12.1 | 44.2 |
| No Δ in Household Size, 1975–77 | 10.6 | 6.8 | 22.1 |
| Δ in Household Size, 1977–79 | 20.5 | 12.1 | 40.5 |
| No Δ in Household Size, 1977–79 | 9.2 | 6.4 | 17.3 |

[a]In base year.

| Appendix | Median Housing Value, Equity, and Nonhousing Bequeathable |
|----------|----------------------------------------------------------|
| Table 1.B | Wealth, by Stay versus Move and by Year, Continuous |
| | Homeowners[a] |

| | Housing Value | | Housing Equity | | Bequeathable Wealth | |
|------|---------|---------|---------|---------|---------|---------|
| | Stay in | Move in | Stay in | Move in | Stay in | Move in |
| Year | * Years | * Years | * Years | * Years | * Years | * Years |
| 1969* | $29,699 | $35,639 | $25,740 | $29,699 | $27,349 | $44,023 |
| 1971* | 29,871 | 35,845 | 26,884 | 28,676 | 26,525 | 41,138 |
| 1973 | 32,667 | 40,017 | 28,094 | 32,667 | 24,097 | 40,709 |
| 1975 | 31,019 | 40,459 | 26,973 | 33,716 | 22,927 | 31,009 |
| 1977 | 32,939 | 38,330 | 29,945 | 35,934 | 21,261 | 31,168 |
| 1979 | 35,000 | 40,000 | 35,000 | 40,000 | 19,408 | 29,230 |
| | | | | | | |
| 1969 | 29,699 | 31,679 | 25,740 | 25,740 | 27,920 | 30,274 |
| 1971* | 30,244 | 31,364 | 26,884 | 26,884 | 26,834 | 30,729 |
| 1973* | 32,667 | 32,667 | 28,584 | 26,134 | 24,488 | 27,442 |
| 1975 | 32,367 | 32,367 | 27,160 | 26,973 | 23,148 | 27,647 |
| 1977 | 33,538 | 33,538 | 29,945 | 29,945 | 21,422 | 24,126 |
| 1979 | 35,000 | 35,000 | 35,000 | 33,000 | 19,358 | 23,684 |
| | | | | | | |
| 1969 | 29,699 | 31,679 | 25,740 | 25,938 | 27,349 | 36,801 |
| 1971 | 29,572 | 35,845 | 26,884 | 28,497 | 26,525 | 34,607 |
| 1973* | 32,667 | 32,667 | 28,584 | 28,584 | 24,052 | 31,690 |
| 1975* | 32,199 | 33,716 | 26,973 | 26,973 | 22,627 | 36,303 |
| 1977 | 33,538 | 35,634 | 29,945 | 29,945 | 20,898 | 29,284 |
| 1979 | 35,000 | 37,500 | 35,000 | 35,000 | 19,210 | 27,309 |
| | | | | | | |
| 1969 | 29,699 | 30,491 | 25,740 | 27,719 | 27,502 | 38,379 |
| 1971 | 29,572 | 32,261 | 26,884 | 28,676 | 26,601 | 35,439 |
| 1973 | 32,667 | 36,524 | 27,767 | 31,034 | 24,147 | 32,626 |
| 1975* | 31,019 | 33,716 | 26,973 | 32,367 | 22,927 | 33,716 |
| 1977* | 33,538 | 35,934 | 29,945 | 29,945 | 20,898 | 32,684 |
| 1979 | 35,000 | 39,418 | 35,000 | 35,000 | 19,280 | 28,937 |
| | | | | | | |
| 1969 | 29,699 | 33,659 | 25,740 | 27,125 | 27,309 | 45,206 |
| 1971 | 29,572 | 33,157 | 26,884 | 28,676 | 26,443 | 42,949 |
| 1973 | 32,667 | 32,667 | 28,003 | 30,707 | 23,948 | 38,710 |
| 1975 | 31,732 | 35,065 | 26,973 | 31,019 | 22,859 | 37,897 |
| 1977* | 32,939 | 35,934 | 29,945 | 35,934 | 20,898 | 36,373 |
| 1979* | 35,000 | 40,000 | 35,000 | 35,000 | 19,020 | 40,090 |

[a]All figures are in 1979 dollars.

| Appendix Table 1.C | Median Rent, by Stay versus Move and by Year, Continuous Renters[a] | |
|---|---|---|
| Year | Stay in * Years | Move in * Years |
| 1969* | $139 | $129 |
| 1971* | 134 | 134 |
| 1973 | 139 | 131 |
| 1975 | 128 | 119 |
| 1977 | 131 | 113 |
| 1979 | 120 | 100 |
| 1969 | 139 | 129 |
| 1971* | 134 | 128 |
| 1973* | 131 | 145 |
| 1975 | 124 | 128 |
| 1977 | 126 | 119 |
| 1979 | 120 | 100 |
| 1969 | 139 | 137 |
| 1971 | 134 | 134 |
| 1973* | 131 | 146 |
| 1975* | 121 | 148 |
| 1977 | 120 | 134 |
| 1979 | 110 | 127 |
| 1969 | 139 | 129 |
| 1971 | 134 | 134 |
| 1973 | 132 | 139 |
| 1975* | 123 | 135 |
| 1977* | 120 | 150 |
| 1979 | 116 | 125 |
| 1969 | 139 | 139 |
| 1971 | 134 | 131 |
| 1973 | 136 | 131 |
| 1975 | 128 | 115 |
| 1977* | 126 | 120 |
| 1979* | 115 | 125 |

[a]All figures are in 1979 dollars.

**Appendix**          **Median User Cost by Stay versus Move, by Classification**
**Table 1.D**         **Interval, All Owners and Renters[a]**

| Year | Stay in * Years | Move in * Years |
|------|-----------------|-----------------|
| 1969* | $1,138 | $1,663 |
| 1971* | 1,678 | 2,043 |
| 1973 | 1,633 | 1,960 |
| 1975 | 1,558 | 1,857 |
| 1977 | 1,610 | 1,739 |
| 1979 | 1,530 | 1,730 |
| 1969 | 1,129 | 1,544 |
| 1971* | 1,678 | 1,828 |
| 1973* | 1,633 | 1,870 |
| 1975 | 1,564 | 1,780 |
| 1977 | 1,607 | 1,707 |
| 1979 | 1,533 | 1,682 |
| 1969 | 1,142 | 1,544 |
| 1971 | 1,667 | 1,979 |
| 1973* | 1,633 | 1,960 |
| 1975* | 1,544 | 2,051 |
| 1977 | 1,594 | 1,847 |
| 1979 | 1,529 | 1,760 |
| 1969 | 1,152 | 1,544 |
| 1971 | 1,690 | 1,828 |
| 1973 | 1,633 | 1,976 |
| 1975* | 1,554 | 1,941 |
| 1977* | 1,588 | 2,113 |
| 1979 | 1,522 | 1,892 |
| 1969 | 1,142 | 1,782 |
| 1971 | 1,678 | 2,011 |
| 1973 | 1,633 | 1,960 |
| 1975 | 1,562 | 1,969 |
| 1977* | 1,594 | 2,016 |
| 1979* | 1,513 | 2,196 |

[a]All figures are in 1979 dollars.

# Notes

1. There may, of course, be response and coding errors in the data, and they may be concentrated among respondents reported to be in the "other" category.

2. According to the 1973 AHS, 23 percent of owners with heads aged 62 to 64 who moved changed to renting; 32 percent of renters who moved changed to owning. Of those aged 65 and older, the percentages were 39 and 15, respectively (see U.S. Department of Housing and Urban Development [1979], table a-7). Excluding the "other" category, apparently making the data more comparable with the AHS, the percentages by age based on the RHS are as follows:

| Age | Own→Rent | Rent→Own |
|-----|----------|----------|
| 62 | 17.5 | 25.1 |
| 63 | 23.0 | 21.9 |
| 64 | 16.6 | 28.2 |
| 65 | 20.0 | 21.4 |
| 66 | 25.8 | 17.9 |
| 67 | 19.1 | 19.0 |
| 68 | 28.1 | 12.2 |
| 69 | 19.6 | 9.5 |
| 70 | 31.6 | 11.3 |
| 71 | 25.9 | 20.0 |

Although the RHS samples families and the AHS samples structures, the data from the two surveys do not appear to be inconsistent.

3. The "same state" percentages in the tabulation exclude the "same city."

4. Income includes wages, capital income, pension income, and Social Security income. The income quartiles are: <$5,400, $5,400–$10,651, $10,651–$17,902, and $17,902+. The housing equity quartiles are: <$16,334; $16,334–$27,767; $27,767–$45,407; and $45,407+. The nonhousing wealth quartiles are: <$64,254; $64,254–$101,599; $101,599–$152,731; and $152,731+.

5. Respondents are defined as being retired if they report that they are retired or that they are partially retired but are neither working nor looking for work.

6. In the beginning of the ten-year RHS period, most of those who do not retire during a two-year interval are still working, while by the end of the period most who do not retire are already retired. The data in table 1.7 show that the probability of moving is about the same for both groups, judging from the percentages in the 1969–71 and 1977–79 intervals, for example—6.7 and 7.2, respectively.

7. To the extent that this progressive selection of stayers versus movers is important, a more formal analysis should account for it. It must also recognize that persons are observed in mid-tenure at the beginning of the survey: some have moved recently, while others have been in the same dwelling for many years, sometimes referred to as left censoring.

8. Strictly speaking, this is only true if a move is "nonabsorbing." In our case it is absorbing. The probit estimates, however, provide accurate descriptions of the hazard rates over the two-year intervals. See, for example, Hausman and Wise (1985).

9. See Cox and Miller (1965).

10. Other studies also report substantial increases in mobility associated with these demographic shocks. See Feinstein and McFadden (ch. 2, in this volume) who report the effects of both retirement and changes in family composition, and Merrill (1984) who reports the effects of retirement, also based on the RHS.

11. In addition, housing value and other wealth measures have been imputed when they are missing. To the extent that this introduces error in the measurements used here, the error should be less for bequeathable wealth, which is composed of several individually reported categories. We also calculated the change in the housing equity and housing value of movers based only on the reported values of those who responded to the relevant questions. The results were virtually the same as those obtained using imputations for the missing values. We are indebted to Michael Hurd for putting together a very complete and detailed asset tape from the RHS original data.

12. Merrill (1984) used only families in the sample in both 1969 and 1977.

13. The analysis based on adjacent survey years indicates the opposite.

14. An apparent anomaly in the data is that among the few homeowners who are reported to move to rental housing, there is no appreciable increase in nonhousing bequeathable wealth, although the medians are positive. Indeed, the sum of the change in housing wealth and the change in nonhousing bequeathable wealth is negative, at the median, for this group. In part, the moves are associated with the death of a husband, and we know from Hurd and Wise (ch. 6, in this volume) that substantial wealth is lost at the death of the husband. In addition, some wealth may be transferred to children. Symmetrically, there is an increase in the reported sum of the changes in these two categories among families who move from renting to owning. We have been unable to find a complete explanation.

15. See similar evidence in Hurd (1986) that pertains to nonhousing bequeathable wealth. On the surface at least, this evidence appears to be inconsistent with Bernheim, Shleifer, and Summers (1985).

16. Because of a change in the wording of some of the survey questions used to calculate user cost, the 1969 data are inconsistent with data for subsequent years. For this reason 1969 figures are deleted from the graphs in figure 1.3.

# References

Bernheim, B. Douglas. 1984. Dissaving after retirement: Testing the pure life-cycle hypothesis. National Bureau of Economic Research Working Paper no. 1409, Cambridge, Mass.: NBER.

Bernheim, B. Douglas, Andrei Shleifer, and Lawrence Summers. 1985. The strategic bequest motive. *Journal of Political Economy* 93, no. 6 (December): 1045–76.

Cox, D. R., and H. D. Miller. 1965. *The theory of stochastic processes.* New York: Wiley.

Diamond, Peter, and Jerry Hausman. 1984. Individual retirement and savings behavior. *Journal of Public Economics* 23 (February-March): 81–114.

Friedman, Benjamin, and Mark Warshawsky. 1985. The cost of annuities: Implications for saving behavior and bequests. National Bureau of Economic Research Working Paper no. 1682. Cambridge, Mass.: NBER.

Hausman, Jerry, and David Wise. 1985. Social Security, health status, and retirement. In *Pensions, labor, and individual choice,* ed. D. Wise. Chicago: University of Chicago Press.

Hurd, Michael. 1986. Savings and bequests. National Bureau of Economic Research Working Paper no. 1826. Cambridge, Mass.: NBER.

Hurd, Michael, and John Shoven. 1983. The economic status of the elderly. In *Financial aspects of the United States pension system,* ed. Z. Bodie and J. Shoven. Chicago: University of Chicago Press.

Manchester, Joyce. 1987. Reverse mortgages and their effects on consumption, savings, and welfare. Dartmouth College Working Paper 87-3.

Merrill, Sally R. 1984. Home equity and the elderly. In *Retirement and economic behavior,* ed. H. Aaron and G. Burtless. Washington, D.C.: Brookings Institution.

U.S. Department of Housing and Urban Development. 1979. *Annual housing survey: 1973.* Washington, D.C.: GPO.

Venti, Steven, and David Wise. 1986. Tax-deferred accounts, constrained choice, and estimation of individual savings. *Review of Economic Studies* 53: 579–601.

## Comment    James M. Poterba

Two issues have guided recent policy debates about housing and the elderly. The first concerns the higher incidence of substandard housing among elderly households than the population at large. The second concern, and the motivation for the current paper, is the possibility that some elderly households with low incomes have significant housing but they cannot use it to finance current consumption because of capital market imperfections. The existence of such households may justify government programs to promote or to provide home equity loans.

In this paper, Venti and Wise uncover a variety of stylized facts about the housing behavior of the elderly, particularly regarding financial matters. Their findings provide a useful background for policy discussions on both reverse annuity mortgages and home equity loans. Most of the chapter is devoted to an exploratory data analysis of the housing choices of elderly households in the Retirement History Survey (RHS). Related tabulations are reported in Merrill (1984). The most important finding is that reverse-annuity mortgages are of limited value

James M. Poterba is a Professor of Economics at the Massachusetts Institute of Technology and a Research Associate of the National Bureau of Economic Research.

as a policy tool for helping the indigent elderly, because most low-income elderly households have relatively little housing equity.

I agree with the majority of the conclusions drawn by the authors, but I am skeptical of three of their findings. My reservations, which arise principally from limitations of the RHS data set and not from the analysis, are detailed below.

*1. Tenure switching by elderly households.* Venti and Wise tabulate the probabilities of tenure transitions, conditional upon a move, and find relatively little evidence for movement from owner-occupation to rental accommodation. Their results, aggregating the "Rent" and "Other" categories from their table on page 12, are shown below:

| Previous Tenure | New Tenure | |
|---|---|---|
| | Own | Rent |
| Own | 0.78 | 0.22 |
| Rent | 0.17 | 0.83. |

A panel data set like the RHS is subject to attrition bias (nearly 20 percent of the sample households were lost between 1969 and 1979). Households that move, especially those that move significant distances, are particularly likely to disappear from the survey. The resulting oversampling of stayers and short distance movers, as well as the other sampling biases induced by data "cleaning" procedures that further reduce the sample size, may make the RHS sample unrepresentative of the elderly population at large.

These biases are difficult to evaluate. One natural check is to compare the RHS results with those from other cross-sectional household surveys. Tabulations from the 1973 Annual Housing Survey (AHS), reported in U.S. Department of Housing and Urban Development (1979, table A-7), indicate that owner-occupants aged 65+ who move are much more likely to switch to rental accommodations than the RHS data suggest. The AHS data are shown below:

| Previous Tenure | New Tenure | |
|---|---|---|
| | Own | Rent |
| Own | 0.61 | 0.39 |
| Rent | 0.15 | 0.85 |

The conditional probability that owners switch tenures given that they move ($\hat{P}_{OR}$) is twice as large as in the Venti-Wise data.

The two sets of transition probabilities may not be directly comparable however. The AHS estimates are transition rates over a one-year time span, while those from the RHS are necessarily separated by two years. This should not matter a great deal if most individuals experience at most one housing transition every few years. If elderly households tend to move from one area to another, however, and rent for a brief period after arriving in the new location until they find a suitable house for purchase, then the one- and two-year transition rates may show radically different patterns. This view implies that the one-year mobility rate should show a much greater propensity to enter the rental tenure than the longer-horizon transition rates. Further noncomparabilities arise because the RHS asks respondents only about their current behavior, while the AHS asks about behavior over a twelve-month period. Finally, the RHS respondents are younger than those covered by the AHS table, and the AHS data suggest that the conditional probability of tenure switching rises after age 65.

Data sets other than the 1973 AHS also suggest that the RHS results are unusual. Feinstein and McFadden (ch. 2, in this volume) estimated tenure transition rates in the Panel Survey of Income Dynamics and found $\hat{P}_{OR} = 0.373$, compared to 0.39 in the AHS and 0.22 in the RHS. Stahl's (ch. 3, in this volume) analysis of the Annual Housing Surveys for the 1970s and early 1980s also shows lower values of this probability and also indicates a trend with age. For 60 to 64 years olds, $\hat{P}_{OR} = 0.35$. For those ten years older, however, $\hat{P}_{OR} = 0.65$. This evidence suggests that the Venti-Wise estimates of tenure transition rates may understate tenure changes toward renting, but it does not dispute the general point that the incidence of all types of moves is very low for elderly households.

*2. The slope of the age-moving hazard.* The second aspect of behavior which the paper may not adequately capture is the age trajectory of the probability of moving. The authors conclude that moving rates exhibit little if any tendency to decline with age. This conclusion is limited, however, to the "young elderly" who appear in the RHS sample. The survey provides a detailed record of the housing choices of individuals in their sixties. Only one sample wave, 1979, includes a significant fraction of individuals in their seventies. Much of the policy concern, however, centers on the housing choices of the "extreme aged," those aged 80 and above, and on the mobility patterns of households in their seventies.

The limited evidence on mobility rates based on Census and other surveys suggests a decline after age 75. The U.S. Department of Commerce, Bureau of the Census (1979) calculated mobility rates for different age groups and found a falling mobility rate with age:

| Age Group | Moving Rate (3-Year horizon) |
|-----------|------------------------------|
| 55–64     | 0.059                        |
| 65–74     | 0.049                        |
| 75+       | 0.041                        |

The unconditional probability of moving declines by 50 percent between age 55 and age 75. Other survey evidence also bolsters the declining hazard view. Feinstein and McFadden (ch. 2) report that the moving hazard rate declines from age 55 to age 72, but turns up thereafter, and Stahl (ch. 3) finds a declining hazard over most age ranges.

*3. Downsizing decisions by elderly homeowners.* The most striking finding in this paper is that elderly homeowners do not reduce their housing equity when they move. The conclusion that those who do not move accumulate rather than decumulate equity is not surprising, especially given the rapid increase in real home prices during the 1970s. The finding that movers do not reduce their equity is more troubling. One could construct explanations of why movers might not experience changes in liquid assets. They may change tenures without selling their original house, or they may move to a new rental unit while their home is still on the market. Still other explanations could explain the small increase in liquid assets for movers. They may give the proceeds to their children, or they may transfer the entire house to a charity or another beneficiary. Medical emergencies may catalyze the decision to move and also place heavy financial burdens on the household, leading to a small net change in financial status. If this finding proves robust when examined using other data sets, it will constitute an important puzzle to be explained in future research on the economic behavior of the elderly.

Inferences about the trajectory of housing equity among elderly homeowners must be viewed with caution however. Some findings, such as the tendency of households that move within the owning tenure to increase their housing equity, may be due to data limitations rather than economic decisions. My skepticism arises in part from the rapid change in real house prices that occurred during the RHS sample period. The following table shows the percentage changes in the Census Bureau's "constant quality" new house price index divided by the GNP deflator between the second quarter of various RHS sample years:

| Years | Real House Price Change |
|-------|-------------------------|
| 1969–71 | − 3.3% |
| 1971–73 | + 3.9% |
| 1973–75 | + 1.5% |
| 1975–77 | + 7.1% |
| 1977–79 | + 13.5% |

Near the end of the sample, when the chances of downsizing should have been greatest, rapid real house price increases may confound the analysis.

Elderly homeowners may misperceive the value of their houses. In a rising market, they may undervalue their homes by substantial amounts. Figure 1.4 shows how this can bias the estimated effects of moving on housing equity. In the years prior to its move, the household reports home values along the dotted segment, although the actual value of the house is growing along the solid segment. When the household moves, it learns that its home is in fact worth $P_0$, and decides to downsize to a home valued at $P_1$. Perceived home value after the transition continues to grow more slowly than true values. Because the survey data on home equity is based on self-reported housing values, however, the measured change in home equity between the survey dates 1 and 2 will show an increase when the household moved. In fact, the household reduced its housing consumption through the move. The difficulty in analyzing estimated asset values arises from the coincidence of behavioral changes, such as moving, and the arrival of information that eliminates measurement error.

It is difficult to gauge the importance of these biases. Validation studies of self-reported asset values find substantial error rates. Broida's (1962) study of auto purchases and auto loans, for example, showed that 18 percent of the respondents in a 1955 Federal Reserve Board

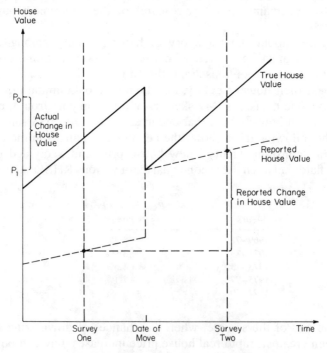

**Fig. 1.4**    Time paths of actual reported housing wealth

survey misreported their loan principal by more than 20 percent, while over a third made errors of more than 10 percent. I am not aware of any direct studies of the quality of housing data in wealth surveys. The bias of home equity changes is complicated by the tendency of households to undervalue their outstanding loans. An elderly homeowner who decides to sell his house may discover both that it is worth more than he thought and that he owes more than he thought. These biases suggest caution in interpreting results such as the absence of equity changes for homeowners who become renters.

Despite the three reservations just described, this paper provides a wealth of useful statistics on housing behavior by elderly households. In interpreting them, it is important to distinguish two questions: Why do elderly homeowners move so infrequently? Why do those homeowners with substantial equity stakes but low incomes fail to borrow against their houses to raise current consumption?

Many reasons could be advanced to explain elderly homeowners' reluctance to leave their homes. The transaction costs associated with moving are substantial, and for households with a relatively short time horizon, the present value of the gains from reoptimizing the housing bundle may be small. The tax code in force during the 1970s placed a sizeable capital gains tax burden on homeowners who realized accumulated gains on their homes; subsequent legislative changes have reduced this source of lock-in. Even the provisions of some welfare and medical assistance programs, which condition eligibility on non-housing wealth, may encourage elderly households to hold their wealth in the form of housing.

The greater puzzle is why households that have substantial accumulated equity in their homes, but low current income, do not seek ways to liquify their housing wealth. The available evidence on this question suggests that households (1) do not like to annuitize their houses and (2) are concerned about the bequests they leave. The results of the Buffalo Home Equity Loan Program, described in Weinrobe (1984), support models of bequest behavior such as those in Bernheim, Shleifer, and Summers (1985). The initial program in Buffalo permitted homeowners in low-income neighborhoods to obtain annuity payments collateralized by their house. The program was supported by a federal Community Development Block Grant, but despite substantial marketing and outreach efforts it did not command great interest among eligible homeowners. In a second stage of the program, households were allowed to apply for a single lump-sum payment instead of an annuity stream. Virtually all of the households that took advantage of the program after this choice was available opted for the single lump-sum payment. Although the actuarial value of the two plans has not yet been analyzed (Weinrobe 1984 is the most detailed discussion available), these results may suggest that household demand for annuities is simply not very large. Related evidence is provided by the "property tax circuit-breaker" programs that have been enacted in various states. Some programs, such as Oregon's, provide interest-free loans to qualified elderly homeowners that permit them to defer their property taxes until they die or sell their homes. Despite the financial attraction of this offer, Bowman (1980) reports that only a few hundred homeowners in Oregon took advantage of the program.

My final comment on this paper concerns whether the results are likely to apply to the elderly households that retire in the late 1980s and early 1990s. The last five years have witnessed dramatic growth in second mortgages and reverse annuity mortgages of various types. These mortgage instruments have grown from an $80 billion household liability at the beginning of 1982 to more than $300 billion at the beginning of 1987. Data on the demographic characteristics of households using second mortgages are not yet available, but they are likely to include households relatively late in the life cycle with significant accumulated housing equity. If these households take on new mortgages, they will reduce still further the potential of policies targeted at helping elderly homeowners by unlocking home equity.

## References

Bernheim, B. Douglas, Andrei Shleifer, and Lawrence Summers. 1985. The strategic bequest motive. *Journal of Political Economy* 93, no. 6 (December): 1045–76.

Bowman, John H. 1980. Property tax circuit breakers reconsidered: Continuing issues surrounding the popular program. *American Journal of Economics and Sociology* 39 (October): 355–70.

Broida, Arthur L. 1962. Consumer surveys as a source of information for social accounting: The problems. In *The flow-of-funds approach to social accounting: Appraisals, analysis, and applications.* NBER Studies in Income and Wealth, vol. 26. Princeton: Princeton University Press.

Merrill, Sally R. 1984. Home equity and the elderly. In *Retirement and economic behavior,* ed. H. Aaron and G. Burtless. Washington, D.C.: Brookings Institution.

U.S. Department of Commerce, Bureau of the Census. 1979. *Social and economic characteristics of the older population, 1978.* Washington, D.C.: GPO.

U.S. Department of Housing and Urban Development. 1979. *Annual housing survey: 1973. Housing characteristics of older Americans in the United States.* Washington, D.C.: GPO.

Weinrobe, Maurice. 1984. HELP comes to Buffalo: A review and analysis of the initial equity conversion experience. Clark University, Worcester, Massachusetts. Mimeo.

# 2 The Dynamics of Housing Demand by the Elderly: Wealth, Cash Flow, and Demographic Effects

Jonathan Feinstein and Daniel McFadden

## 2.1 Introduction

The stereotype of the housing problem of the elderly is the following case:

> Mrs. R. is a 74-year-old widow who continues to live alone in the four-bedroom family home. She has difficulty paying the utilities on this dwelling and has been unable to adequately maintain the property. Because of arthritis, she has increasing difficulty with the stairs. Mrs. R's house is fully paid for. If she were to sell it, she could easily afford the rent on an apartment in a nearby housing complex for the elderly. However, despite the urging of her children, she has resisted moving, claiming the alternative is "too expensive" and she is "not sure she would like it."

The main question we will address in this paper is whether this stereotype is accurate. Is there a significant elderly population living in housing that appears to be inappropriate in terms of physical needs and financial resources? Are the elderly constrained by illiquidity of assets and therefore forced to move to smaller properties or rentals to dissave? If so, does the market fail to provide alternatives, or through some imperfection does it create barriers to moving? Or, is lack of mobility a "rational" manifestation of tastes?

Jonathan Feinstein received his Ph.D. in economics from the Massachusetts Institute of Technology in 1987 and is currently an Assistant Professor of Economics at Stanford University's Graduate School of Business. Daniel McFadden is Elizabeth and James Killian Professor of Economics at the Massachusetts Institute of Technology and is a Research Associate of the National Bureau of Economic Research.

The authors thank Craig Alexander and Axel Börsch-Supan for their assistance.

The effects of policy interventions in the elderly housing market depend on the answers to these questions. If the stereotype is pervasive, then marketwide policies may be effective; otherwise, concentration on programs directed to individuals in trouble may be indicated. If the elderly face significant imperfections in the housing market, then initiatives that reduce imperfections by providing information, insurance, risk pooling, or licensing may help to reduce the imperfection. If tastes are the source of the problem, then the question is whether one can, or should, modify tastes through promotional campaigns. If intervention appears appropriate, should it be directed to programs that permit the elderly to stay on in their homes, such as reverse annuity mortgages and home care services? Or, is it better to encourage trading down, thus freeing larger dwellings for the market, by policies such as deferral of capital gains taxes, assistance in searching for housing, and reverse annuity mortgages applied to trade-downs?

This investigation concentrates on the effects of wealth, cash flow, and changes in household demographics on mobility and housing expenditure decisions of the elderly. We examine several issues. First, do mobility patterns suggest the presence of significant capital market imperfections that prevent elderly owners from life-cycle dissaving? Second, are moves closely associated with demographic shocks such as retirement, death of a spouse, or children leaving home, so that economic incentives (and policies that affect these incentives) would impact elderly households through rather narrow windows? Finally, do these variables collectively provide an adequate description of mobility among the elderly, or is there evidence of substantial remaining unexplained variation among households?

The remainder of the paper is organized as follows. Section 2.2 provides descriptive statistics of our data set, which is based on the PSID (Panel Study of Income Dynamics). Section 2.3 presents estimates of a series of models of mobility and changes in housing status among movers. Section 2.4 provides a test for the presence of unobserved heterogeneity among households. Section 2.5 presents some conclusions and section 2.6 a discussion of potential future research. An appendix provides some data details.

## 2.2  Some Descriptive Statistics

Using the PSID, we have summarized a few features of housing behavior of the elderly. We have used the first fifteen waves of the panel, from 1968 through 1982. We confine our attention to households that in 1968 had either head or wife over 50 years of age; there are 1,131 households meeting this condition. First, what is the mobility of the elderly, and how is it changing over time? Table 2.1 shows mobility

**Table 2.1**  **Crude Mobility versus Age**

| Age | Cases | Mobility Rate | Standard Deviation |
|---|---|---|---|
| 1968–72 | | | |
| 55–64 | 2,148 | 8.15% | 0.59% |
| 65–74 | 889 | 6.30% | 0.81% |
| 75+ | 236 | 3.81% | 1.25% |
| 1973–77 | | | |
| 55–64 | 2,635 | 9.11% | 0.56% |
| 65–74 | 1,762 | 6.75% | 0.60% |
| 75+ | 629 | 8.59% | 1.12% |
| 1978–82 | | | |
| 55–64 | 1,519 | 8.56% | 0.72% |
| 65–74 | 2,530 | 7.19% | 0.51% |
| 75+ | 1,185 | 8.02% | 0.79% |
| 1968–82 | | | |
| 55–64 | 6,302 | 8.65% | 0.35% |
| 65–74 | 5,181 | 6.89% | 0.35% |
| 75+ | 2,050 | 7.71% | 0.59% |

rates by age of head in each of three periods. Mobility rates decline from the 55–64 age bracket to the 65–74 age bracket, but rise (insignificantly) in the 75+ age bracket. Mobility appears to be slightly higher after 1972 than before; figure 2.1 shows the mobility rate of households with heads over 65 by year. Table 2.2 presents the pattern of tenure changes with moves for households with heads over 65. The "other" category in this table encompasses a variety of arrangements, such as living with relatives, living in a place of business, or living on a working

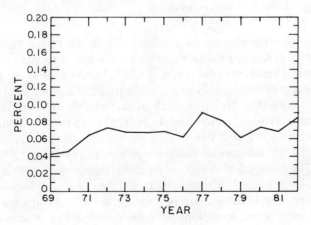

**Fig. 2.1**  Crude mobility rates, age 65+

**Table 2.2**    **Tenure Changes with Moves, Age 65+ (cell counts, percentages, and standard errors of percentages)**

| Move From | Move to | | | |
|---|---|---|---|---|
| | Own | Rent | Other | Total |
| Own | 141 | 59 | 25 | 225 |
| | 62.7% | 26.2% | 11.1% | 43.7% |
| | (3.2%) | (2.9%) | (2.1%) | (2.2%) |
| Rent | 34 | 191 | 11 | 236 |
| | 14.4% | 80.9% | 4.7% | 45.8% |
| | (2.3%) | (2.6%) | (1.4%) | (2.2%) |
| Other | 14 | 24 | 16 | 54 |
| | 25.9% | 44.4% | 29.6% | 10.5% |
| | (6.0%) | (6.8%) | (6.2%) | (1.4%) |
| Total | 189 | 274 | 52 | 515 |
| | 36.7% | 53.2% | 10.1% | |
| | (2.1%) | (2.2%) | (1.3%) | |

farm. The table shows 32.4 percent of moves result in tenure changes. There is a modest net flow from owning to the remaining categories. Thus, the crude evidence suggests only weak disaccumulation of real assets by exiting ownership. This pattern is consistent with that found by Merrill (1984) in the Retirement History Survey (RHS).

How pervasive is occupancy of "inappropriate" housing by the elderly? Merrill (1984) reports from RHS data the following median ratios for a sample who were between ages 66 and 71 in 1977, and who were homeowners in 1969, or 1977, or both:

| | |
|---|---|
| Home equity as a proportion of wealth | 0.763 |
| Ratio of shelter cost/income | 0.167 |
| Persons per room | 0.333 |

Consider the information on dwelling size in the PSID. Define, arbitrarily, excess size to be a dwelling with a number of rooms exceeding the number of residents plus three. Table 2.3 shows for three periods the proportion of households of each age living in dwellings of excess size. First, note that the proportion of households in large dwellings is substantial. While this may simply reflect tastes for consumption of housing services in a well-functioning market, it nevertheless indicates the potential for substantial transfers of housing services to younger families. The proportion in units of excess size increases with age. The pattern has not shifted substantially over time.

How pervasive is occupancy of "unaffordable" housing by the elderly? To answer this question, we have compared income with out-of-pocket housing costs. Income is measured as current after-tax. Out-

**Table 2.3**         **Households in Dwellings of "Excess" Size (cases, percentages, and standard errors of percentages)**

| Age | 1968–72 | 1973–77 | 1978–82 | 1968–82 |
|-----|---------|---------|---------|---------|
| 55–64 | 2,575 | 2,614 | 1,502 | 6,691 |
|  | 27.1% | 31.1% | 34.9% | 30.4% |
|  | (0.9%) | (0.9%) | (1.2%) | (0.6%) |
| 65–74 | 1,043 | 1,745 | 2,494 | 5,282 |
|  | 40.5% | 38.2% | 35.7% | 37.4% |
|  | (1.5%) | (1.2%) | (1.0%) | (0.7%) |
| 75+ | 277 | 627 | 1,162 | 2,066 |
|  | 39.7% | 41.0% | 38.1% | 39.2% |
|  | (2.9%) | (2.0%) | (1.4%) | (1.1%) |

*Note:* A dwelling is defined to be of "excess" size if the number of rooms less the family size exceeds 3.

of-pocket housing costs for homeowners are the sum of utility costs, mortgage payments, property taxes, and maintenance and insurance costs. Maintenance and insurance costs are imputed to equal 2 percent of house value. This is based on a maintenance rate of 1.5 percent of house value, obtained from unit expenditures given in the U.S. Bureau of the Census *Construction Reports* (Series C50). For renters, the housing cost variable is the sum of utility costs and rent. Construction of these variables is detailed in the appendix. Housing budget share is defined as the ratio of out-of-pocket housing costs to current after-tax income. Table 2.4 shows the average housing budget share for owners and renters in various age categories in three periods. This table excludes both households in "other" living arrangements and "poverty-level" households with disposable income below $5,000 in 1982 dollars. Renter budget shares are comparable to those for owners. (Remember that these are cash flow shares and do not reflect capital gains to owners.) For the entire 1968–82 period, there is a decline in budget share from the 55–64 age category to the 65–74 category, then a marginal increase to the 75+ age category. Over time, renter budget shares have been stable, while owner budget shares have increased.

Table 2.5 gives the distribution of the share of out-of-pocket housing costs in income by age bracket for homeowners and for renters. Note first that 8.8 percent of renters and 10.8 percent of owners have budget shares exceeding 0.4. For owners, there are mitigating factors, including capital gains in equity and the possibility of deferring maintenance. Nevertheless, there is an economically significant elderly population for whom financing shelter costs from cash flow is burdensome. Second, there is a clear pattern of an increasing proportion of high-burden households for owners. This is not the case for renters. Third, there

Table 2.4          Average Share of Out-of-pocket cost in After-Tax Income,
                   Households with $5,000 or More After-Tax Income (1982$)

| Age | Owners | | | Renters | | |
|---|---|---|---|---|---|---|
| | Share | Std Dev | Cases | Share | Std Dev | Cases |
| 1968–72 | | | | | | |
| 55–64 | 19.1% | 14.1% | 970 | 19.6% | 11.3% | 421 |
| 65–74 | 15.1% | 11.5% | 543 | 15.9% | 10.0% | 105 |
| 75+ | 16.0% | 11.5% | 125 | 18.4% | 10.4% | 31 |
| 1973–77 | | | | | | |
| 55–64 | 19.1% | 15.7% | 1,590 | 19.5% | 13.3% | 634 |
| 65–74 | 15.9% | 14.2% | 1,246 | 16.2% | 8.6% | 382 |
| 75+ | 14.9% | 13.1% | 459 | 17.6% | 13.2% | 115 |
| 1978–82 | | | | | | |
| 55–64 | 25.5% | 22.4% | 717 | 18.2% | 12.9% | 285 |
| 65–74 | 20.2% | 16.6% | 1,517 | 18.4% | 13.9% | 635 |
| 75+ | 19.5% | 14.9% | 785 | 21.4% | 17.8% | 263 |
| 1968–82 | | | | | | |
| 55–64 | 20.5% | 17.2% | 3,277 | 19.3% | 12.6% | 1,340 |
| 65–74 | 17.7% | 15.1% | 3,306 | 17.4% | 12.0% | 1,122 |
| 75+ | 17.7% | 14.2% | 1,369 | 20.1% | 16.2% | 409 |

is no evidence of increasing burden with age; the proportion of high-burden households in the 75+ age category is less than that for households in the 55–65 category.

The life-cycle theory of consumption implies that expenditures on housing services should be determined by lifetime wealth (and life-cycle demographics) rather than by current income or wealth composition, with transitory income fluctuations smoothed by asset changes. The operation of this theory requires good capital markets without credit rationing or wedges between buying and selling prices for assets. In particular, for individuals whose assets are primarily an owner-occupied dwelling, life-cycle planning would often require the market to finance dissaving by the elderly through borrowing secured by equity in the dwelling (e.g., reverse annuity mortgages). Alternatives are for the elderly to extract equity by trading-down to smaller owner-occupied housing, moving to a rental, or deferring maintenance and repair. On the other hand, bequest motives may encourage ownership as a convenient channel for holding assets.

Using the PSID data, we have constructed a measure of wealth from age-specific income and assets, observed future wage and transfer income during the period of the panel, and made projections of those income streams beyond the panel. The construction is detailed in the

**Table 2.5**    **Distribution of Share of Out-of-pocket Housing Cost in After-Tax Income**

| | | Owners | | | Renters | | |
|---|---|---|---|---|---|---|---|
| Period | Budget Share | 55–64 | 65–74 | 75+ | 55–64 | 65–74 | 75+ |
| 1968–72 | 0.0–0.2 | 49.1% | 61.7% | 60.0% | 39.7% | 58.1% | 48.4% |
| | 0.2–0.3 | 28.4% | 26.7% | 21.6% | 34.9% | 29.5% | 38.7% |
| | 0.3–0.4 | 12.3% | 7.2% | 11.2% | 14.0% | 8.6% | 3.2% |
| | 0.4–0.5 | 5.7% | 2.2% | 4.0% | 8.3% | 1.9% | 3.2% |
| | 0.5+ | 4.6% | 2.2% | 3.2% | 3.1% | 1.9% | 6.5% |
| | | 970 | 543 | 125 | 421 | 105 | 31 |
| 1973–77 | 0.0–0.2 | 50.8% | 61.8% | 66.9% | 44.5% | 51.6% | 56.5% |
| | 0.2–0.3 | 25.3% | 23.2% | 19.6% | 31.2% | 33.8% | 29.6% |
| | 0.3–0.4 | 13.0% | 8.5% | 6.1% | 14.4% | 10.7% | 5.2% |
| | 0.4–0.5 | 5.6% | 2.8% | 3.3% | 4.9% | 3.7% | 3.5% |
| | 0.5+ | 5.3% | 3.7% | 4.1% | 5.0% | 0.3% | 5.2% |
| | | 1590 | 1246 | 459 | 634 | 382 | 115 |
| 1978–82 | 0.0–0.2 | 37.4% | 45.7% | 48.8% | 54.0% | 52.8% | 46.4% |
| | 0.2–0.3 | 28.2% | 30.3% | 28.0% | 26.3% | 26.9% | 28.9% |
| | 0.3–0.4 | 11.7% | 11.5% | 12.6% | 9.8% | 12.1% | 13.7% |
| | 0.4–0.5 | 9.1% | 5.7% | 5.0% | 4.9% | 3.6% | 4.6% |
| | 0.5+ | 13.7% | 6.7% | 5.6% | 4.9% | 4.6% | 6.5% |
| | | 717 | 1517 | 785 | 285 | 635 | 263 |
| 1968–82 | 0.0–0.2 | 47.3% | 54.4% | 55.9% | 45.0% | 52.9% | 49.4% |
| | 0.2–0.3 | 26.8% | 27.0% | 24.6% | 31.3% | 29.5% | 29.8% |
| | 0.3–0.4 | 12.5% | 9.7% | 10.3% | 13.3% | 11.3% | 10.5% |
| | 0.4–0.5 | 6.4% | 4.1% | 4.3% | 6.0% | 3.5% | 4.2% |
| | 0.5+ | 7.0% | 4.8% | 4.9% | 4.4% | 2.9% | 6.1% |
| | | 3277 | 3306 | 1369 | 1340 | 1122 | 409 |

appendix. Table 2.6 shows mobility rates classified by wealth and age categories. There is no uniform pattern of mobility shifts with age within a wealth category. The table indicates sharply decreasing mobility with increasing wealth for renters, but relatively little effect of wealth on owner mobility. With owners concentrated in higher wealth brackets, the mobility variation with wealth for all households combined is a correlate of the differences of mobility between owners and renters. To a considerable extent, tenure choice is endogenously related to the propensity to move, with the transactions costs of ownership encouraging renting by highly mobile households, and the lower costs of moving encouraging more frequent "fine tuning" of housing consumption by renters. Self-selection into the population of owners is likely to yield low-wealth households that have a low propensity to move. These results indicate that association of wealth and mobility in the elderly population as a whole operates primarily through tenure choice.

Table 2.6    **Mobility by Wealth and Age (rates and standard deviations)**

| Wealth | Age 55–64 | Age 65–74 | Age 75+ |
|---|---|---|---|
| All households | | | |
| 0–42K | 13.32% | 11.01% | 11.92% |
| | (0.93%) | (0.85%) | (1.32%) |
| 42–90K | 10.55% | 6.11% | 8.75% |
| | (0.84%) | (0.67%) | (1.17%) |
| 90–186K | 6.38% | 5.12% | 4.08% |
| | (0.60%) | (0.56%) | (0.80%) |
| 186K+ | 6.07% | 5.12% | 3.98% |
| | (0.54%) | (0.69%) | (1.23%) |
| Owners | | | |
| 0–42K | 3.79% | 2.48% | 4.59% |
| | (0.99%) | (0.71%) | (1.24%) |
| 42–90K | 5.81% | 2.43% | 4.04% |
| | (0.86%) | (0.51%) | (0.96%) |
| 90–186K | 4.83% | 3.96% | 3.47% |
| | (0.60%) | (0.53%) | (0.78%) |
| 186K+ | 5.19% | 4.72% | 3.43% |
| | (0.53%) | (0.69%) | (1.19%) |
| Renters | | | |
| 0–42K | 16.17% | 15.92% | 17.95% |
| | (1.25%) | (1.34%) | (2.51%) |
| 42–90K | 15.70% | 15.76% | 20.98% |
| | (1.57%) | (2.07%) | (3.40%) |
| 90–186K | 10.06% | 11.24% | 9.52% |
| | (1.59%) | (2.37%) | (3.70%) |

The existence of substantial assets other than an owner-occupied dwelling should facilitate decumulation of wealth and reduce the need for owners to downsize their houses or switch tenure. Table 2.7 shows mobility rates classified by wealth and liquidity, where a household is classified as "liquid" if it has after-tax income above $10,000 or assets (other than an owner-occupied dwelling) exceeding $20,000 in 1982 dollars. Mobility rates are significantly elevated for renters with less than $90,000 in wealth; there is no consistent pattern of declining mobility with increasing liquidity.

If life-cycle theory applies, and the elderly are able directly or indirectly to dissave at rates that depend only on wealth, then mobility rates given wealth should be independent of current income and the composition of wealth. Then, in particular, mobility should be independent of the liquidity of the household. Table 2.7 shows no significant decline for liquid versus nonliquid households when wealth is held constant.

**Table 2.7**     **Mobility by Wealth and Liquidity (age 65 +, rates and standard deviations)**

| Wealth | Illiquid | Liquid |
|---|---|---|
| All households | | |
| 0–42K | 12.52% | 10.64% |
| | (0.65%) | (1.16%) |
| 42–90K | 8.79% | 8.14% |
| | (0.72%) | (0.68%) |
| 90–186K | 4.95K | 5.64% |
| | (0.79%) | (0.41%) |
| 186K + | 5.67% | 5.60% |
| | (1.33%) | (0.43%) |
| Owners | | |
| 0–42K | 3.80% | 2.49% |
| | (0.67%) | (0.87%) |
| 42–90K | 4.54% | 3.39% |
| | (0.65%) | (0.56%) |
| 90–186K | 4.07% | 4.26% |
| | (0.81%) | (0.40%) |
| 186K + | 4.91% | 4.90% |
| | (1.33%) | (0.42%) |
| Renters | | |
| 0–42K | 16.12% | 17.06% |
| | (0.95%) | (2.04%) |
| 42–90K | 17.03% | 16.01% |
| | (1.76%) | (1.59%) |
| 90–186K | 8.39% | 10.96% |
| | (2.32%) | (1.46%) |
| 186K + | 9.68% | 12.70% |
| | (5.31%) | (2.13%) |

For households with head aged 65 +, table 2.8 shows mobility by current income and asset class for various wealth classes. The evidence suggests no variation in mobility rates with income or wealth composition once wealth is fixed. Thus, these data are generally consistent with the life-cycle theory and suggest that liquidity constraints on the elderly are not pervasive.

## 2.3 Simple Models of Elderly Housing Dynamics

In this section, we estimate simple models of a rational life-cycle household facing the decision of whether to move and, if moving, whether to "downsize" to a smaller or less expensive dwelling. Economic theory indicates that the consumer will choose lifetime consumption profiles, including choice of housing, by solving a dynamic programming problem to optimize an intertemporal utility function

Table 2.8        Mobility Rates by Income and Wealth Composition, Given Wealth
                 Level (Age 65+)

| Wealth | Income Class | Liquid Asset Class | Cases | Mobility | Standard Error |
|--------|--------------|--------------------|-------|----------|----------------|
| 0–42K | <$5K | <$10K | 110 | 16.36% | 3.53% |
| | >$5K | <$10K | | | |
| | <$5K | >$10K | 2,681 | 15.07% | 0.69% |
| | >$5K | >$10K | 1,305 | 16.17% | 1.02% |
| 42–90K | <$5K | <$10K | 463 | 10.37% | 1.42% |
| | >$5K | <$10K | | | |
| | <$5K | >$10K | 2,522 | 9.16% | 0. 57% |
| | >$5K | >$10K | 533 | 8.82% | 1.23% |
| 90–186K | <$5K | <$10K | 1,110 | 5.86% | 0.70% |
| | >$5K | <$10K | 106 | 7.55% | 2.57% |
| | <$5K | >$10K | 2,609 | 6.44% | 0.48% |
| | >$5K | >$10K | 458 | 6.55% | 1.16% |
| 186K+ | <$5K | <$10K | 1,443 | 6.31% | 0.64% |
| | >$5K | <$10K | 154 | 9.74% | 2.39% |
| | <$5K | >$10K | 1,904 | 6.83% | 0.58% |
| | >$5K | >$10K | 428 | 8.18% | 1.32% |

subject to intertemporal budget constraints whose structure depends
on the capital market. Henderson and Ioannides (1986) have developed
a model with this structure; related models have been proposed by
Artle and Varaiya (1978) and Hu (1980). In principle, these models can
explain joint choice of shelter consumption levels, moving, and tenure.
In practice, the models are intractable except for special cases, such
as stationarity assumptions that allow application of renewal theory.
Consequently, these models must be used primarily to motivate the
qualitative features of empirical demand models. This problem is particularly acute when the assumption of a perfect capital market is re-
laxed to permit liquidity constraints and wedges between borrowing
and lending rates.

    Consider the decision to move. The life-cycle model suggests that
in each period the household starts from a state described by wealth
(measured as the sum of home equity, other assets, and the expected
present value of future income flows), characteristics of current dwelling, and demographic characteristics. For these state variables, the
household calculates the present value of remaining utility for optimal
consumption plans with and without a current period move, taking into
account the cost of a move. A move is made if it yields the higher
expected utility. In a perfect capital market, the consumer's intertemporal consumption plans, including move decisions, depend only on
total wealth, not on its composition. (We abstract from the implications
of portfolio composition for risk.) In particular, cash flow or holdings

of liquid assets should affect consumption decisions once the effects of wealth are taken into account only if there are capital market imperfections. Capital market failure is most likely for low-income households with limited assets other than home ownership. Welfeld and Struyk (1978) have pointed out that a significant number of elderly households below the poverty line have this wealth configuration. The efficacy of the policy initiative to promote reverse annuity mortgages depends on whether liquidity constraints are in fact binding on these households.

In addition to wealth, and possibly cash flow and liquidity measures, the life-cycle model suggests that housing choice behavior will depend on demographic characteristics of the household, possibly interacting with features of the dwelling. Changes in household composition that alter the need for housing services should be important, as should retirement decisions that relax locational constraints. An interesting question for policy is whether these demographic changes affect mobility only over a limited period of time, giving only a narrow window in which programs to influence the destination of moves can be effective. The life-cycle model also suggests that housing choices will be sensitive to prices, in particular to the comparison of the expected stream of net cost savings from a move with the direct and indirect moving costs. Housing prices are difficult to construct for the full panel of elderly households in the PSID, and analysis of their effect is left for future research.

An econometric model that captures the qualitative features of the life-cycle consumer model can be defined in terms of the marginal probability that a household will move in a year times the conditional probability, given a move, that various alternatives are chosen. The marginal probability of a move is a function of the variables described above and, in general, can depend on previous state, including dwelling size, shelter expenditure, tenure, and dwelling type. The alternatives available, given a move, range in principle over the full set of features entering the description of the household's state. In particular, the set of alternatives includes both discrete variables, such as tenure, dwelling type, and number of rooms, and continuous variables, such as shelter expenditure. The current analysis will be limited to one aspect of dwelling choice, an indicator for changes in shelter expenditure. This permits us to examine the phenomenon of "downsizing" to extract equity or reduce shelter cost. Other aspects of choice among housing alternatives will be left for future research which will examine the effects of housing prices on choices. It will be of particular interest to estimate fully specified models for transitions between alternative states that can be used in dynamic policy simulation of the housing behavior of the elderly.

In addition to dependence on demographic and housing state of mobility probabilities and conditional probabilities for choice among housing alternatives, there may be unobserved variations across households in tastes for moving, a "mover-stayer" effect. The combination of dependence on previous state and population heterogeneity creates the econometrically difficult "initial values problem" discussed by Heckman (1981). In addition, statistical dependence across states induced by the heterogeneity makes it necessary to model the probabilities of entire panel decision sequences, which may be computationally burdensome. Further, the effect of heterogeneity is to bias estimates of durations of spells between moves because of "self-selection" over time of households more resistant to moving.

In this paper, we do not attempt to deal with unobserved heterogeneity. We instead assume housing choice behavior can be modeled as an independent Bernoulli process over years (with time-dependent explanatory variables). This simplistic modeling assumption permits us to examine some of the qualitative features predicted by the life-cycle model that are not particularly sensitive to the time profile of mobility rates for a single household. However, it should be noted that the resulting estimated models are likely to be badly biased for describing features that depend critically on time dependence, such as duration of spells between moves or number of moves. Some sense of the quality of the assumption of no unobserved heterogeneity can be obtained by examining the numbers of multiple moves made in the PSID panel. Table 2.9 compares the observed number of moves with the numbers predicted by two simple models. The observed counts display the clas-

**Table 2.9        Independent Bernoulli Model of Number of Moves**

| Number of Moves | Observed | Predicted, Model 1 | Predicted, Model 2 |
|---|---|---|---|
| 0 | 388 | 146 | 385 |
| 1 | 239 | 322 | 221 |
| 2 | 170 | 330 | 199 |
| 3 | 123 | 208 | 118 |
| 4 | 72 | 90 | 62 |
| 5 | 42 | 29 | 44 |
| 6 | 34 | 7 | 39 |
| 7 | 38 | 1 | 31 |
| 8 | 11 | 0 | 20 |
| 9 | 9 | 0 | 10 |
| 10 | 3 | 0 | 3 |
| 11 | 4 | 0 | 1 |
| 12–14 | 0 | 0 | 0 |
| Total | 1,133 | 1,133 | 1,133 |

*Notes:* Model 1: Bernoulli model with mobility rate 13.6 percent (maximum likelihood estimate), goodness-of-fit statistic 971 (chi-square with 12 degrees of freedom).

Model 2: Mixture of 0.238 "stayers," 0.61 with mobility rate 12.0 percent, 0.152 with mobility rate 42.4 percent (minimum chi-square estimates), goodness-of-fit statistic 14.7 (chi-square with 8 degrees of freedom).

sic long-tail characteristic of heterogeneity. Model 1 is a homogeneous Bernoulli model, estimated by maximum likelihood. A goodness-of-fit test strongly rejects the Bernoulli model. Model 2 is a mixture of stayers and two Bernoulli populations, one with a mobility rate of 12 percent and the second with a mobility rate of 42.4 percent, with the mixing probabilities and mobility rates fitted by minimum chi-square. This model is accepted by a goodness-of-fit test at the 95 percent significance level. This model corresponds very roughly to a population of "owners" who are either stayers or have the 12 percent mobility rate, and a population of "renters" with the 42.4 percent mobility rate. Neither model is a good test for unobserved heterogeneity in the PSID sample, since variation in explanatory variables, which will also tend to produce rejections of simple Bernoulli models, is not accounted for. However, the very poor fit of Model 1 and the significant fraction of stayers in Model 2 suggest that unobserved heterogeneity is likely to be significant. Later in this paper, we carry out a more precise Lagrange Multiplier test for the presence of unobserved heterogeneity.

Consider first the marginal move decision. Under the assumptions set out above, this can be independently modeled as a discrete choice for each household and each period of observation. We assume a probit functional form. We fit this model to the pooled PSID data, beginning with lagged wealth (the household's assets as of last period) and head age as explanatory variables, and then adding variables that may enter if liquidity constraints are binding or if demographics influence consumption decisions. Table 2.10 shows that wealth has a significant

**Table 2.10**     **Independent Trials Probit Model of Mobility, Wealth Effects**

|  | Model 1 | Model 2 |
|---|---|---|
| Constant | 3.57 | 3.29 |
|  | (1.00) | (1.03) |
| HEADAGE | − .13* | − .125* |
|  | (.029) | (.03) |
| HEADAGE2($\times$ 10−3) | .89* | .836* |
|  | (.21) | (.214) |
| WEALTHLAG ($\times$ 10−6) | − .957* | − 1.01* |
|  | (.125) | (.133) |
| $\Delta$WEALTHLAG ($\times$ 10−6) |  | .016 |
|  |  | (.286) |
| Log likelihood | − 3,593 | − 3,422 |
| # Observations | 13,229 | 12,528 |
| Mobility rate | 7.85% | 7.91% |

*Denotes significant at the 5% level.
Standard errors are in parentheses.

negative effect on mobility. Mobility falls with age of head until age 74, then increases. Mobility is insensitive to changes in wealth.

Table 2.11 introduces cash flow and an indicator for liquidity to test for the significance of capital market imperfections that introduce liquidity constraints. The new variables are LIQLAG, indicating either that last period's after-tax income was above $10,000 or that nondwelling assets were above $20,000, in 1982 dollars, as of last period, and CASHLAG, measuring after-tax income of the head and spouse last period, and CASHOTHERLAG, measuring after-tax income of other household members last period. (These variables are lagged, as is the wealth variable, to avoid simultaneity biases in estimation.) The LIQLAG variable is found to have a significant effect on mobility rates, with mobility falling for liquid households; CASHLAG and CASH-OTHERLAG are insignificant. This provides mixed evidence that capital market imperfections may be a quantitatively significant constraint on behavior in the elderly population. However, there is some confounding of the effects of liquidity when owners and renters who face different moving costs are pooled. If liquidity is positively associated with ownership, and hence lower mobility due to higher moving costs, then LIQLAG will display a negative coefficient for this reason and may not represent capital market imperfections. A significant liquidity

**Table 2.11        Independent Trials Probit Model of Mobility, Cash Flow Effects**

|  | Model 1 | Model 2 |
|---|---|---|
| Constant | 3.44 | 3.43 |
|  | (1.01) | (1.01) |
| WEALTHLAG ($\times$ 10–6) | –.899* | –.903* |
|  | (.148) | (.148) |
| HEADAGE | –0.129* | –.129* |
|  | (.029) | (.029) |
| HEADAGE2 ($\times$ 10–3) | .869* | .867* |
|  | (.210) | (.210) |
| LIQLAG | –.114* | –.114* |
|  | (0.041) | (0.041) |
| CASHLAG ($\times$ 10–6) | 2.02 | 2.05 |
|  | (1.69) | (.169) |
| CASHOTHERLAG ($\times$ 10–6) |  | –2.54 |
|  |  | (4.95) |
| Log likelihood | –3589 | –3589 |
| # Observations | 13,229 | 13,229 |
| Mobility rate | 7.85% | 7.85% |

*Denotes significant at the 5% level.
Standard errors are in parentheses.

effect for owners or renters separately would be stronger evidence for capital market problems.

Table 2.12 introduces family composition effects, including a dummy variable that indicates that a wife who was present in one of the previous two periods has now gone (WIFEGONE), the number of persons who have moved out of the household since the previous period (MOVE-OUT), the number of persons who have moved in (MOVEIN), and the change in the number of children living at home (ΔCHILDREN). As in the earlier models, wealth and head age are significant, as are LIQLAG and CASHLAG. The demographic shocks of a wife disappearing or

**Table 2.12**    **Independent Trials Probit Model of Mobility, Family Composition and Retirement Effects**

|  | Model 1 |
|---|---|
| Constant | 3.45 |
|  | (1.06) |
| WEALTHLAG (× 10–6) | −.759* |
|  | (.166) |
| HEADAGE | −.135* |
|  | (.031) |
| HEADAGE2 (× 10–3) | .934* |
|  | (.220) |
| LIQLAG | −.135* |
|  | (.043) |
| CASHLAG (× 10–6) | 1.41 |
|  | (1.81) |
| CASHOTHERLAG (× 10–6) | −5.74 |
|  | (5.12) |
| WIFEGONE | .349* |
|  | (.071) |
| MOVEOUT | .076* |
|  | (.039) |
| MOVEIN | .334* |
|  | (.046) |
| HEADRETDUM | .198* |
|  | (.057) |
| WIFERETDUM | .271* |
|  | (.055) |
| ΔCHILDREN | −.170* |
|  | (.051) |
| Log likelihood | −3,339 |
| # Observations | 12,524 |
| Mobility rate | 7.91% |

*Denotes significant at the 5% level.
Standard errors are in parentheses.

individuals moving into the household significantly increase mobility, as does a decrease in the number of children living at home. Positive values of the variable MOVEOUT usually occur because the husband disappears, the wife is gone, or a child moves out. Since the latter two events are captured by the WIFEGONE and ΔCHILDREN variables, the coefficient on MOVEOUT primarily reflects the event of the husband disappearing. This event also increases mobility, but not significantly.

Merrill (1984) found that the event of retiring had a significant effect on mobility in the RHS, with a peak several years after retirement. Table 2.12 includes dummy variables indicating whether the head or the wife have retired within the past three years. Both husband and wife retirement dummies are found to significantly increase mobility. Hence, there appears to be a window of relatively high mobility for several years after retirement, as households optimize after being freed of the locational constraints imposed by workplace.

The preceding models do not distinguish tenure state as a factor influencing mobility. Since moving costs are considerably higher for owners than for renters, one expects the former group to have lower transition probabilities. Table 2.13 shows the basic model of mobility dependence on head age and wealth, estimated separately for owners

Table 2.13    **Independent Trials Probit Model of Mobility, Wealth and Cash Flow Effects by Owner/Renter**

|  | Owners | Renters |
|---|---|---|
| Constant | 3.22 | 1.39 |
|  | (1.46) | (1.57) |
| WEALTHLAG ($\times$ 10-6) | $-.0778$ | $-.311$ |
|  | (.157) | (.289) |
| HEADAGE | $-.143*$ | $-.0646$ |
|  | (.042) | (.046) |
| HEADAGE2 ($\times$ 10-3) | 1.03* | .406 |
|  | (.301) | .328 |
| LIQLAG | .003 | $-.032$ |
|  | (.060) | (.071) |
| CASHLAG ($\times$ 10-6) | .481 | 4.32 |
|  | (2.02) | (3.76) |
| CASHOTHERLAG ($\times$ 10-6) | 1.05 | 7.09 |
|  | (6.20) | (9.04) |
| Log likelihood | $-1666$ | $-1477$ |
| # Observations | 9096 | 3597 |
| Mobility rate | 4.51% | 14.37% |

*Denotes significant at the 5% level.
Standard errors are in parentheses.

and for renters. In these models, head age remains significant for owners, with mobility minimized at age 70. For renters, mobility declines (insignificantly) until age 83. Wealth is not significant for either owners or renters. Of course, this does not indicate wealth has an insignificant effect on the dynamics of rental housing demand, since tenure choice is endogenous, and wealth is likely to strongly influence tenure choice conditioned on moves. The variables called CASHLAG, LIQLAG, and CASHOTHERLAG measuring liquidity are found to be insignificant for both owners and renters. This supports the view that the significance found in table 2.12 for these variables is due to their correlation with moving costs through the association of liquidity and ownership. While this conclusion should be interpreted with caution in light of the issues of endogeneity of tenure choice and population heterogeneity, it has a potentially important policy implication that programs such as reverse annuity mortgages, designed to allow the elderly to extract equity from their homes, are unlikely to be utilized by most of the elderly population.

Table 2.14 estimates separately for owners and renters the model including family composition effects. The pattern of effects is similar to that observed in table 2.12 estimated on owners and renters together, except that wealth and cash flow effects are both insignificant. The effects of family composition changes are similar for owners and renters.

Estimates of tenure choice of movers are given separately in table 2.15 for previous owners and for previous renters. The effect of liquidity constraints or low cash income is to discourage ownership, but the effects are statistically insignificant. Increasing wealth increases ownership for both previous owners and renters, as does a family composition change increasing household size. Retirement of the head significantly discourages ownership by previous owners.

Next consider the conditional probability of changing consumption of housing services, given a move. We consider first a categorical variable (RECOST) that indicates whether expenditures on shelter fall more than 5 percent ($-1$) or not (0). Table 2.16 gives the results of estimation, separately for owners and renters. Wealth has a weak positive effect on maintaining expenditures by owners. The variable LIQLAG has a significant negative effect among renters, and both LIQLAG and CASHLAG are insignificant among owners. HEADAGE is statistically insignificant, as are the family composition variables.

Second, consider the conditional probability of reducing dwelling size, measured relative to family size, given a move. The dependent variable (DEXSIZE) is categorical, indicating whether number of rooms minus family size falls with the move ($-1$) or not (0). Table 2.17 gives the estimates. Wealth is again insignificant. Many of the family composition variables are significant for both owners and renters, while

Table 2.14          Independent Trials Probit Model of Mobility, Family Composition
                    and Retirement Effects, by Owner/Renter

|  | Owners | Renters |
|---|---|---|
| Constant | 3.59 | 1.13 |
|  | (1.53) | (1.67) |
| WEALTHLAG (× 10–6) | .149 | −.374 |
|  | (.159) | (.378) |
| HEADAGE | −.162* | −.0625 |
|  | (.044) | (.048) |
| HEADAGE2 (× 10–3) | 1.19* | .410 |
|  | (.315) | (.346) |
| LIQLAG | −1.21 × 10–3 | −.0411 |
|  | (.063) | (.073) |
| CASHLAG (× 10–6) | −1.91 | 4.47 |
|  | (2.14) | (4.16) |
| CASHOTHERLAG (× 10–6) | 1.18 | 2.93 |
|  | (6.44) | (9.21) |
| WIFEGONE | .337* | .547* |
|  | (.096) | (.125) |
| MOVEOUT | .119* | .0196 |
|  | (.055)* | (.063) |
| MOVEIN | .270* | .375* |
|  | (.069) | (.073) |
| HEADRETDUM | .319* | .140 |
|  | (.073) | (.114) |
| WIFERETDUM | .274* | .251* |
|  | (.077) | (.089) |
| ΔCHILDREN | −.134 | −.205 |
|  | (.074) | (.083) |
| Log likelihood | −1,542 | −1,372 |
| # Observation | 8,600 | 3,416 |
| Mobility rate | 4.55% | 14.43% |

*Denotes significant at the 5% level.
Standard errors are in parentheses.

the retirement dummies are insignificant. Among the lagged liquidity
variables, LIQLAG is positive and significant among owners and insignificant among renters, while CASHLAG is insignificant.

Finally, consider changes in equity given a move. We consider a
categorical variable (DEQUITY) that indicates whether equity falls
(−1) or not (0). Table 2.18 gives the estimation results for owners.
Wealth is again insignificant; the estimates indicate no significant effect
of liquidity, suggesting either that most owners have sufficient cash
flow or liquid assets to make extraction of equity unnecessary, or that
existing capital markets provide adequate opportunities for extracting
equity. Demographic and retirement variables are insignificant.

**Table 2.15** **Tenure Choice, Dependent Variable: Owner**

| | Model 1 (OWNLAG = 1) | Model 2 (RENTLAG = 1) |
|---|---|---|
| Constant | −4.08 | 4.22 |
| | (4.50) | (4.35) |
| HEADAGE | .118 | −.152 |
| | (.131) | (.128) |
| HEADAGE2 (× 10−3) | −.902 | .984 |
| | (.931) | (.925) |
| WEALTHLAG (× 10−6) | 2.07* | 3.63* |
| | (.673) | (.958) |
| LIQLAG | .318 | .298 |
| | (.192) | (.190) |
| CASHLAG (× 10−6) | 2.26 | .966 |
| | (8.01) | (9.80) |
| WIFEGONE | −.075 | −.620 |
| | (.254) | (.333) |
| MOVEOUT | −.280 | .117 |
| | (.158) | (.142) |
| MOVEIN | .593* | .282* |
| | (.210) | (.139) |
| HEADRETDUM | −.620* | .224 |
| | (.231) | (.269) |
| WIFERETDUM | .139 | −.111 |
| | (.222) | (.234) |
| ΔCHILDREN | −.281 | 0.054 |
| | (.208) | (.183) |
| Log likelihood | −221 | −199 |
| # Observations | 391 | 493 |
| % Owner | 65 | 18 |

*Denotes significant at the 5% level.
Standard errors are in parentheses.

The effects of age on mobility of owners and renters are summarized in figure 2.2; the mobility of owners rises after age 70, while the mobility of renters falls until age 79. Given a move, the probability that a former owner or renter becomes an owner is given in figure 2.3. The probability of ownership falls steadily with age for owners, and is nearly constant for renters. Figure 2.4 gives the probabilities that when an owner moves, the adjustment maintains the level of expenditures on housing, excess size of housing, and equity in housing. The probability of maintaining housing costs rises with age, while the probability of maintaining excess rooms falls. The probability of maintaining equity falls after age 71. Figures 2.2, 2.3, and 2.4 are calculated for a "standard" low-income household with wealth of $10,000, cash income of $5,000, and population

Table 2.16    **Changes in Shelter Cost Among Movers (independent probit, dependent variable is −1 if shelter cost falls more than 5 percent, 0 otherwise)**

|  | Owners | Renters |
|---|---|---|
| Constant | 1.70 | .115 |
|  | (4.27) | (3.66) |
| WEALTHLAG (× 10−6) | .327 | −.836 |
|  | (.469) | (.900) |
| HEADAGE | −.0673 | $5.51 \times 10-3$ |
|  | (.124) | (.107) |
| HEADAGE2 (× 10−3) | .550 | −.0861 |
|  | (.887) | (.776) |
| LIQLAG | .152 | −3.51* |
|  | (.179) | (.159) |
| CASHLAG (× 10−6) | 6.06 | 18.2 |
|  | (6.36) | (9.56) |
| WIFEGONE | −.188 | −.184 |
|  | (.240) | (.229) |
| MOVEOUT | −.0251 | −.172 |
|  | (.143) | (.124) |
| MOVEIN | .236 | .157 |
|  | (.169) | (.122) |
| HEADRETDUM | −.0256 | −.256 |
|  | (.189) | (.233) |
| WIFERETDUM | −.191 | −.228 |
|  | (.202) | (.182) |
| ΔCHILDREN | .0413 | −.226 |
|  | (.186) | (.160) |
| Log likelihood | −263 | −334 |
| # Observations | 389 | 493 |
| Pct down | 47.6 | 48.3 |

*Denotes significant at the 5% level.
Standard errors are in parentheses.

averages for other variables; the models used are in tables 2.13, 2.16, 2.17, and 2.18.

The mobility of owners varies little with income or wealth, increasing from 0.041 to 0.042 as income rises from $5,000 to $40,000 with wealth fixed at $10,000, and falling from 0.041 to 0.040 as wealth increases from $10,000 to $140,000 with income fixed at $5,000. The mobility of renters increases sharply with income and decreases with wealth, as shown in figure 2.5. In particular, mobility is high for renters with low liquidity. The wealth categories in this figure are $10,000 for "lo W," $70,000 for "mid W," and $140,000 for "hi W." The last wealth level is near the sample median, so these categories all apply to relatively poor families.

**Table 2.17**    **Changes in Number of Excess Rooms Among Movers (independent probit, dependent variable is −1 if number of rooms − family size falls, 0 otherwise)**

|  | Owners | Renters |
|---|---|---|
| Constant | −3.23 | 9.36 |
|  | (4.55) | (4.01) |
| WEALTHLAG (× 10−6) | .560 | −.710 |
|  | (.583) | (.930) |
| HEADAGE | .100 | −.246* |
|  | (.132) | (.117) |
| HEADAGE2 (× 10−3) | −.835 | 1.65 |
|  | (.945) | (.846) |
| LIQLAG | .395* | −6.51 × 10−3 |
|  | (.190) | (.168) |
| CASHLAG (× 10−6) | 2.07 | 8.93 |
|  | (7.02) | (10.2) |
| WIFEGONE | −.639* | −.527* |
|  | (.262) | (.239) |
| MOVEOUT | .291 | .375* |
|  | (.181) | (.146) |
| MOVEIN | −.470 | −.413* |
|  | (.248) | (.137) |
| HEADRETDUM | −.177 | −.129 |
|  | (.193) | (.238) |
| WIFERETDUM | .128 | .117 |
|  | (.208) | (.193) |
| ΔCHILDREN | −.331 | −.153 |
|  | (.281) | (.208) |
| Log likelihood | −237 | −291 |
| # Oberservations | 375 | 480 |
| Pct down | 47.5% | 33.5% |

*Denotes significant at the 5% level.

Standard errors are in parentheses.

Ownership rates given moves rise with income, particularly for low-wealth families, as figures 2.6 and 2.7 show for owners and renters, respectively. Figure 2.8 gives the probability that the result of a move by a previous owner is housing costs as high as experienced previously; these probabilities rise with income and wealth and are particularly sensitive to low liquidity. Figure 2.9 shows that the probability that a previous owner chooses an "excess size" dwelling after a move is relatively insensitive to wealth and income, except that low-liquidity households have a much lower probability of maintaining excess size. Figure 2.10 shows that the probability of maintaining equity after a move by a previous owner rises sharply with income, and at low incomes is quite sensitive to wealth.

| Table 2.18 | Changes in Equity Among Movers Who were Owners (independent probit, dependent variable is $-1$ if equity falls, 0 otherwise) | |
|---|---|---|
| | Constant | $-5.69$ |
| | | (4.72) |
| | WEALTHLAG ($\times$ 10-6) | .421 |
| | | (.476) |
| | HEADAGE | .141 |
| | | (.137) |
| | HEADAGE2 ($\times$ 10-3) | $-.993$ |
| | | (9.81) |
| | LIQLAG | .110 |
| | | (.194) |
| | CASHLAG ($\times$ 10-6) | 14.2* |
| | | (6.56) |
| | WIFEGONE | $-.170$ |
| | | (.270) |
| | MOVEOUT | $-.370$ |
| | | (.193) |
| | MOVEIN | $-.00257$ |
| | | (.187) |
| | HEADRETDUM | .0566 |
| | | (.192) |
| | WIFERETDUM | $-.0692$ |
| | | (.210) |
| | ΔCHILDREN | .190 |
| | | (.252) |
| | Log likelihood | $-229$ |
| | # Observations | 391 |
| | Pct down | 68.0 |

*Denotes significant at 5% level.
Standard errors are in parentheses.

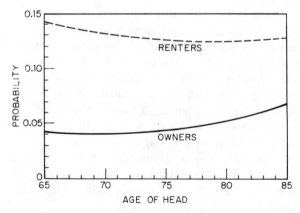

**Fig. 2.2**    Mobility vs. age

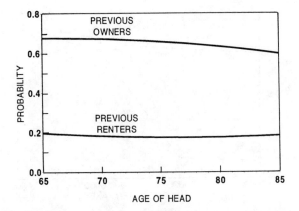

**Fig. 2.3**        Ownership given move

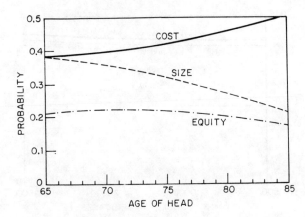

**Fig. 2.4**        Adjustments given move

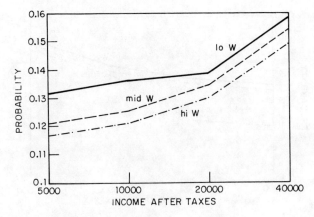

**Fig. 2.5**        Mobility of renters (W = wealth)

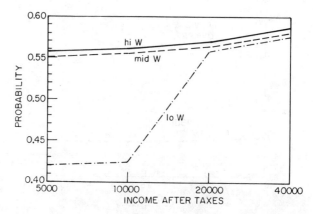

**Fig. 2.6**     Ownership given owner move (W = wealth)

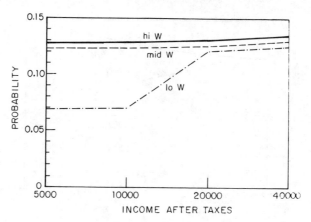

**Fig. 2.7**     Ownership given renter move (W = wealth)

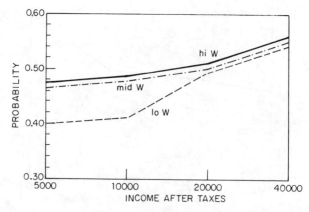

**Fig. 2.8**     Cost maintained given move (W = wealth)

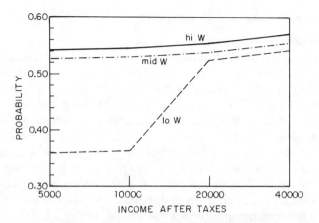

**Fig. 2.9**          Excess size maintained given move (W = wealth)

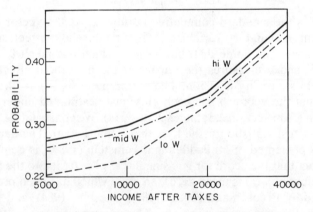

**Fig. 2.10**          Equity maintained given move (W = wealth)

In sum, these figures suggest that there are economically significant effects of low liquidity leading to downsizing, relative reductions in shelter cost, and extraction of equity. This behavior would be expected from poor households faced with difficult budget choices requiring trade-offs between shelter costs and nonhousing consumption. The absence of a significant effect of low liquidity on mobility suggests that the moves of most elderly homeowners are the result of noneconomic causes and not forced by economic pressure. There do appear to be significant economic pressures on low-liquidity renters to move and reduce shelter costs. These may well involve substantial welfare losses; our results give no indication that this is a result of a market failure calling for policy measures beyond distributional policy.

## 2.4    Test for Unobserved Heterogeneity

As mentioned above, all of the models in this paper have been estimated under the assumption that there are no unobserved household effects. If such effects are present, they invalidate our assumption that the conditional probability of a household moving in any particular year is independent of that household's prior mobility decisions (though it may depend upon previous year household characteristics through time-dependent explanatory variables). Since estimating models which allow for unobserved household effects are quite complicated and computer intensive, we have developed a Lagrange Multiplier test for the presence of unobserved effects which is based on the estimates derived from models which assume no such effects. We assume a normal random effects formulation in which the probability of a move in period $t$ by household $n$ may be written:

$$P_{tn} = F(x_{tn}b + z_n g),$$

where $F$ is the standard cumulative normal, $x_{tn}$ is the vector of time-dependent explanatory variables, $z_n$ is the household effect, assumed to be drawn from some distribution $q(z)$ which has mean 0 and unit variance, and $g$ measures the impact of the household effect on the household's mobility decision. The null hypothesis is $g = 0$. It is assumed that the vector $b$ has been previously estimated under this assumption (as in section 2.3, tables 2.10–2.14). We construct a Lagrange Multiplier test statistic for the hypothesis that $g = 0$. The derivation, which is presented in McFadden and Feinstein (1987), is complicated by the fact that the score for $g$ is singular at $g = 0$ (due to the fact that the distribution $q(z)$ is mean zero), an issue which has been previously discussed by Breusch and Pagan (1980), Chesher (1984), and Lee and Chesher (1986) in other contexts. The appropriate test is therefore based on the second derivative of the log likelihood function. The test statistic is:

$$LM2 = [\Sigma_n lm_n]^2/N[C_N - B_N'A_N^{-1}B_N],$$
$$lm_n = -\Sigma_t a_{tn}d_{tn}h_{tn}m_{tn} + 2\Sigma_t \Sigma_{s>t} d_{tn}d_{sn}h_{tn}h_{sn}m_{tn}m_{sn},$$
$$a_{tn} = x_{tn}b,$$
$$d_{tn} = 1 \text{ if the household moves, } -1 \text{ if not,}$$
$$h_{tn} = f[d_{tn}(x_{tn}b)]/F[d_{tn}(x_{tn}b)],$$
$$m_{tn} = 1 \text{ if data is present, } 0 \text{ if it is missing,}$$
$$c_n = \Sigma_t x_{tn}d_{tn}h_{tn},$$
$$A_N = (1/N)\Sigma_n c_nc_n',$$
$$B_N = (1/N)\Sigma_n c_n lm_n,$$
$$C_N = (1/N)\Sigma_n lm_n^2,$$

where there are $N$ individuals (1,131 in our case) and $T$ time periods (15 in our case). LM2 is asymptotically distributed as chi-squared with 1 degree of freedom.

We have calculated LM2 for the model of table 2.12. The calculated value far exceeds the 5 percent critical value and decisively rejects the null of no heterogeneity. This finding indicates that future efforts to model elderly mobility must come to grips with the statistical issues involved in estimating models which allow for household effects.

## 2.5 Conclusions

This paper has given a preliminary analysis of the effects of wealth, cash flow, and demographic shocks on decisions of the elderly on whether to move, whether to adjust housing consumption up or down when moving, and whether to extract equity when moving from an owner-occupied dwelling. The analysis of price effects has been left for future research. The current paper makes the simplistic assumption of no unobserved heterogeneity. Consequently, the resulting models are unlikely to be reliable predictors of the life-cycle dynamics of mobility of the elderly. In particular, the models are unlikely to predict accurately the number of moves or the durations of spells between moves for households observed through time. However, it is more reasonable to use these models to draw conclusions on the qualitative impacts of wealth, cash flow, and demographic shocks on mobility and housing consumption levels.

The models suggest that with the possible exception of downsizing decisions by renters, conditioned on a decision to move, there is no evidence that housing choice behavior is affected by capital market imperfections. Wealth has a generally strong effect on housing choices, as predicted by the life-cycle model. Mobility and consumption level decisions are both strongly influenced by some demographic shocks, notably recent retirement or changes in household size or composition (e.g., disappearance of husband or wife).

We have also calculated the changes in mobility rates associated with changes in various explanatory variables. Table 2.19 shows mobility rates by age of head for the model given in table 2.12, with all other explanatory variables set to sample means. (Note that this is not the same as calculating the sample average of the individual household probabilities, with ages varied parametrically and remaining variables set to actual values for the household, since the probit model is non-linear.) Mobility falls with age until age 72, and then rises slightly.

Table 2.20 shows the effects on mobility of different wealth levels and demographic shocks. These calculations again use the model in

**Table 2.19**    **Projected Mobility Rates: Effect of Head Age**

| Head Age | Probability of a Move (%) (in a given year)* | Head Age | Probability of a Move (%) (in a given year)* |
|----------|----------------------------------------------|----------|----------------------------------------------|
| 55 | 11.0 | 69 | 6.8 |
| 56 | 11.0 | 70 | 6.8 |
| 57 | 10.0 | 71 | 6.7 |
| 58 | 9.5 | 72 | 6.7 (minimum) |
| 59 | 9.1 | 72 | 6.7 |
| 60 | 8.7 | 73 | 6.7 |
| 61 | 8.4 | 74 | 6.8 |
| 62 | 8.1 | 75 | 6.9 |
| 63 | 7.8 | 76 | 7.0 |
| 64 | 7.6 | 77 | 7.1 |
| 65 | 7.4 | 78 | 7.3 |
| 66 | 7.2 | 79 | 7.5 |
| 67 | 7.0 | 80 | 7.7 |
| 68 | 6.9 | | |

*Based on model of table 2.12. All other variables evaluated at their sample means.

**Table 2.20**    **Projected Mobility Rates: Effects of Wealth and Family Composition**

| | Probability of a Move (%) (in a given year)* |
|---|---|
| Wealth | |
| $10,000 | 9.1 |
| $70,000 | 8.4 |
| $140,000 (mean) | 7.6 |
| $200,000 | 6.9 |
| $300,000 | 6.0 |
| WIFEGONE | |
| = 0 (base) | 7.3 |
| = 1 (wife left in last 2 years | 13.5 |
| MOVEIN | |
| = 0 | 7.2 |
| = 1 (1 person) | 12.9 |
| MOVEOUT | |
| = 0 | 7.5 |
| = 1 (1 person) | 8.6 |
| ΔCHILDREN | |
| = 0 | 7.5 |
| = 1 (1 child leaves) | 10.2 |
| Retirement | |
| Of neither | 7.1 |
| Of person 1 only | 10.3 |
| Of person 2 only | 11.6 |
| Of both | 16.0 |

*Based on model of table 2.12. All other variables evaluated at their sample means.

table 2.12 and set all remaining variables to sample means. The demographic shocks of disappearance of the wife or individuals moving into the household have a substantial effect on mobility, as does recent retirement. The other demographic variables, changes in number of children and persons moving out, have modest effects. While wealth is an important determinant of mobility, small changes in wealth have small mobility effects.

In summary, we conclude from the analysis of housing behavior for the elderly completed to date that this population group does not appear to be substantially disadvantaged by capital market imperfections that limit the ability to extract equity or dissave, and that mobility is strongly concentrated in windows opened by demographic shocks, particularly recent retirement or recent changes in family composition.

## 2.6  Future Research

This paper is an initial progress report in a multiyear program of research into the dynamics of housing behavior of the elderly. Future research plans can be divided into extensions of the simple mobility and housing consumption level models described above to incorporate population heterogeneity and model other aspects of choice of housing state, and extensions to incorporate the effects of price and health.

Extensions of the analysis of the effects of wealth, demographics, and liquidity will concentrate, first, on removing the assumption of unobserved population homogeneity. Parametric and "nonparametric" models with heterogeneity will be estimated. To manage the computational problems, McFadden's method of simulated moments estimation will be used. We do not have a fully satisfactory method for handling the initial values problem when both unobserved heterogeneity and state dependence are present, but we propose to employ a nonparametric ("flexible") estimator for the initial value distribution, with dimensionality restricted by plausible conditional independence assumptions.

A second part of these extensions will concentrate on refining the explanatory variables, particularly the lag structure of demographic shocks, the description of the housing state, and nonlinearities in the effects of wealth and wealth composition. The third part will concentrate on developing a complete transition model between housing states, including tenure choice and housing consumption level, measured by real expenditure and dwelling size. These extensions will be limited by the PSID data.

The final area of future research will concentrate on the effects of housing prices and the effects of health. The PSID does not provide adequate information to construct housing prices. Henderson and Ioannides (1986) confine attention to PSID households living in identifiable

SMSAs and use Annual Housing Survey data to calculate housing prices in these locations. We have not done this because it would substantially reduce the smaller sample of elderly households. We will instead use hedonic price equations estimated from Annual Housing Survey data. Health status is also poorly measured in the PSID. We will attempt to use limited data on hospitalization, which is available in only one year, and self-rated level of disability.

# Appendix
## Description of the Data

Our primary data source is the first fifteen waves of the PSID study, from 1968 to 1982. We restrict ourselves to elderly households, defined as those households which satisfy at least one of the following criteria:

(1) The head of household, or "wife" (a term which refers to both spouses by marriage and cohabitors), or both are aged 50 or above in 1968.
(2) The identity of the head of household, or "wife," or both changes during the years 1969–82, and the new head, or "wife," or both were aged 50 or above in 1968.

There are 1,901 households that fulfill at least one of these criteria. Of these, 770 are "split-offs," and most of these split-offs refer to young persons who leave a family in which the parents satisfy either criterion (1) or (2): 668 refer to households for whom, once the split-off occurs, the new head is aged 30 or less, and another 60 refer to households whose new head is aged 30 to 50. We eliminate all split-offs, which leaves us with 1,131 observations.

We have used the PSID variables to construct a number of additional variables, which we now describe. An important variable in our models is the present discounted value of household wealth, which is our measure of permanent income. Set $PERM_{it}$ to be household $i$'s present discounted wealth as of year $t$, $t = 1968, \ldots, 1982$. $PERM_{it}$ is defined to be:

$$PERM_{it} = \sum_{s=t}^{1982} (Y1_{is} + Y2_{is})/\text{DISCOUNT}(t,s)$$

$$+ \sum_{s=1983}^{1988} (Y1PROJ_{is} + Y2PROJ_{is})/\text{DISCOUNT}(t,s)$$

$$+ ASSET_{it} + EQUITY_{it} ,$$

where the first term refers to the future horizon up to the end of the PSID data, 1982; the second term refers to an extension of the household's horizon to 1988, using projections based on the PSID of earlier years; and the last two terms to the household's financial assets and home equity in year $t$. $Y1$ and $Y1PROJ$ refer to the household head, and $Y2$ and $Y2PROJ$ to the "wife" (if there is no "wife," $Y2$ and $Y2PROJ$ are zero).

$Y1_{is}$ and $Y2_{is}$ are constructed as follows. If the head is working in year $s$ ($s < 1983$), $Y1_{is}$ is his wage income; similarly for $Y2_{is}$. If both head and wife are retired, $Y1_{is}$ and $Y2_{is}$ each equal one half of the household's total retirement income. If the head is working and the wife is retired, $Y1_{is}$ is the head's wage income and $Y2_{is}$ is the household's total retirement income; similarly if the head is retired and the wife working.

$Y1PROJ_{is}$ and $Y2PROJ_{is}$ are constructed as follows. If the head retires prior to 1982, $Y1PROJ_{is}$ is his retirement income as of 1982; and similarly for the wife (if both are retired each of these is one half of total retirement income as of 1982). If the head has not retired as of 1982, he is assumed to retire at age 70, or, if above age 70 as of 1983, at 1983. Until age 70, $Y1PROJ_{is}$ is equal to his wage income as of 1982; after age 70, $Y1PROJ_{is}$ is 0.35 of his wage income. Similarly for the wife.

To construct a measure of financial assets, $ASSET_{it}$, we add up the separate asset income measures for business income, farm income, garden income, roomer income, and interest, dividends, and rental income provided by the PSID, and divide by year $t$'s treasury bill rate (described below), which provides a measure of the wealth generating the year $t$ asset income. $EQUITY_{it}$ is just house value minus the outstanding mortgage.

Finally, $DISCOUNT(t,s)$ is the discount rate: for $s < 1983$, it is the nominal rate on treasury bills, while for $s > 1983$, it is the nominal T-bill rate minus the consumer price index (to allow for the fact that real income post-1982 is in 1982 dollars). Some ambiguity attaches to the choice of DISCOUNT, as arguments can be made for choosing it to be the real rather than the nominal rate; however, we have felt that the majority of nonwage income is likely to derive from bank accounts, in which case the nominal rate is appropriate. (Source for these numbers is the Data Resources Inc. publication, *Review of the U.S. Economy*.)

Our measure of cash flow income, $CASH_{it}$, is defined to be the household's gross year $t$ income, which includes husband and wife's taxable income, the taxable income of other household members, husband and wife's transfer income, the transfer income of other household members, husband and wife's Social Security income, and the Social Security income of other household members; minus the husband and wife's federal taxes and the federal taxes of other household members.

Shelter costs are the sum of property taxes, mortgage payments, utilities, 2 percent of the house value (for maintenance; source for this value is the *U.S. Statistical Abstract*), and rent. The share of cash flow income devoted to shelter costs is this sum divided by $CASH_{it}$.

# References

Artle, R., and P. Varaiya. 1978. Life cycle consumption and homeownership. *Journal of Economic Theory* 18, 38–58.

Breusch, T. S., and A. R. Pagan. 1980. The Lagrange Multiplier Test and its applications to model specification in econometrics. *Review of Economic Studies* 57: 239–53.

Chesher, A. 1984. Testing for neglected heterogeneity. *Econometrica* 52: 865–72.

Heckman, J. 1981. The incidental parameters problem and the problem of initial conditions in estimating a discrete time-discrete data stochastic process. In *Structural analysis of discrete data with econometric applications*, ed. C. Manski and D. McFadden. Cambridge, Mass.: MIT Press.

Henderson, J., and Y. Ioannides. 1986. Tenure choice and the demand for housing. *Economica* 53:231–46.

Hu, S. C. 1980. Imperfect capital markets, demand for durables, and the consumer lifetime allocation process. *Econometrica* 48:577–94.

Institute for Social Research. 1985. *A panel study of income dynamics: Procedures and tape codes, 1983 interviewing year.* Ann Arbor: Mich.: The University of Michigan.

Lee, L. F., and A. Chesher. 1986. Specification testing when score test statistics are identically zero. *Journal of Econometrics* 31:121–49.

McFadden, D., and J. Feinstein. 1987. Lagrange Multiplier Test for random subject effects in discrete panel data. Mimeo.

Merrill, S. 1984. Home equity and the elderly. In *Retirement and economic behavior*, ed. H. Aaron and G. Burtless. Washington, D.C.: Brookings Institution.

Struyk, R., and B. Soldo. 1980. *Improving the elderly's housing.* Cambridge, Mass.: Ballinger Publishing Company.

Welfeld, I., and R. Struyk. 1978. Housing options for the elderly. *Occasional Papers in Housing and Community Affairs,* vol. 3. Washington, D.C.: U.S. Department of Housing and Urban Development.

# Comment     Yannis M. Ioannides

The paper by Jonathan Feinstein and Daniel McFadden does an admirable job in addressing two key issues associated with the dynamics

Yannis M. Ioannides is Professor of Economics at Virginia Polytechnic Institute and State University and a Research Associate of the National Bureau of Economic Research.

of housing decisions by the elderly. One is the determinants of the propensity to move. The second is how households adjust their housing consumption when they do move. The nature of the housing commodity and the reality of housing markets make it very likely that these two issues are very much related.

Many commonly held beliefs about the housing behavior of the elderly are explained by the econometric models in this paper. The authors conclude that they found no evidence that housing decisions by the elderly are constrained by imperfections in the capital market. Their results confirm the predictions of the life-cycle theory model that wealth is an important determinant of housing decisions, and that mobility and consumption level changes are prompted by retirement and by changes in household composition.

This comment addresses some primarily methodological issues. I argue that a more general analysis of the propensity to move jointly with housing consumption changes would improve our understanding of the behavior of the elderly and could be easily implemented. Furthermore, I direct attention to some implications of portfolio-theoretic considerations within the life-cycle model. This would help to strengthen the authors' conclusions regarding the impact of capital market imperfections.

Life-cycle theory suggests that households form a lifetime investment plan together with a consumption plan. Stylized facts about the path of income over time would imply that households save the excess of income receipts over desired expenditures earlier in life and invest them in a portfolio of assets. Later on in life, households decumulate by liquidating assets. The actual extent of decumulation depends critically on the bequest motive. The time pattern of accumulation may be affected critically by changes in life-cycle characteristics (e.g., when children or other dependents leave the household, or the death of a spouse).

Certain nontrivial characteristics of housing require modifications of the standard life-cycle model. Some such modifications are necessary for a deep understanding of the particular problems and circumstances of the elderly. In order to change the quantity and quality of services generated by a particular dwelling unit, one may either have to move or to modify structurally an existing unit. In both those cases, costs are involved which may contain a fixed component, and the optimal adjustment is complicated by the lumpiness of housing. Another factor which complicates the analysis of housing decisions is that the amount of housing owned by households may reflect investment motives, too. The inflationary experiences of the 1970s and the early 1980s have shown that housing performed well with respect to inflation adjustment, and thus its attractiveness as an asset has been well deserved. Yet, it must be emphasized that there is a substantial geographical variation in the performance of housing as an inflation hedge, which may in fact be important in the context of housing decisions by the elderly.

It is well known that a dynamic programming formulation of households' life-time allocation decisions which explores the above features quickly becomes intractable. This is recognized in the paper. The only way analysis can proceed further is to work with reduced forms. This is, in fact, what the authors pursue. In particular, the paper investigates separately the households' propensity to move per unit of time and their choice of whether to reduce or increase their consumption of housing when moves occur. A number of difficulties are inherent in this separation, which researchers familiar with these issues are well aware of. Even so, discussing them further here may be helpful in interpreting the results in the paper.

I will start with the authors' analysis of the propensity to move. The authors use a Bernoulli model to analyze the propensity to move per year. This model implies that the duration of stay in a given dwelling and for a given set of characteristics of the household is geometrically distributed. (If time were continuous, it would be exponentially distributed.) It is straightforward to show that for the geometric distribution, the hazard rate (i.e., the probability of moving in a particular period given that no move has already taken place) is constant over time. However, it is well known that with heterogeneity and duration dependence, the hazard rate may be an increasing or a decreasing function of duration. Forcing a constant hazard rate on duration data makes it quite likely that important dynamic relationships are being missed. It is not surprising, therefore, that the hypothesis of a constant hazard rate can be easily rejected.

More general models for the propensity to move characterized by a richer dynamic structure may be easily utilized, especially since reduced forms are used anyway (Heckman 1981). An alternative way to easily introduce heterogeneity, duration, and state dependence would be to look at mobility through the duration of residence spells. Prior experience from applications of such an approach and the richness of the PSID data are quite encouraging (see Henderson and Ioannides 1988; Ioannides 1987; Rosenthal 1986). Competing risks models, which are also reduced form, may also be applied fruitfully (Pickles and Davies 1985). In contrast, the attractiveness of the model underlying the Feinstein-McFadden formulation is that mobility in effect follows from comparing every period's utilities from different alternative courses of action. In fact, it is important to direct attention to the remarkably good fit obtained by Model 2, table 2.9. The authors' reduced-form model seems to perform quite well.

I will now discuss results reported in the paper regarding changes in housing consumption among elderly movers. It would, of course, be desirable to have a full model of the demand for housing by the elderly, but that requires availability of housing price data. The authors state they wish to investigate only whether significant changes in housing consumption take place when elderly do change residences. Such changes may take the form of changes in mode (owners becoming renters and vice versa) or of changes in the quantity of housing services consumed. Both kinds of changes may coexist. The latter are emphasized, and the corresponding results are reported in tables 2.15 and 2.16. A probit model for the changes in housing expenditure as a function of wealth, of various socioeconomic characteristics, and of two measures of liquidity constraints gives similar results to those obtained by Venti and Wise (ch. 1, in this volume). This is all the more interesting and significant because key wealth variables—like earned income wealth and, especially, financial wealth—had to be constructed by the authors from other data available in the PSID. Assets data are readily available in the Retirement History Survey (RHS), which is the data used by Venti and Wise. (Further work in the future along such lines can take advantage of the availability of assets data within the PSID, starting from the 1984 wave of interviews).

There is, of course, no unambiguous way to define what constitutes substantial change in shelter costs or dwelling size. The authors' arbitrary, and yet reasonable, definitions for such changes do throw light on the underlying question about the behavior of the elderly. The relative magnitudes of such changes must be related to typical magnitudes of transactions costs associated with these changes. While realtor fees and moving costs may be estimated with some accuracy, there is no clue as to how to account for the nonpecuniary costs of moving. Thus, observed reluctance by the elderly to downsize their dwelling units may, in principle, be interpreted as large perceived transactions costs.

However, large perceived transactions costs are not the whole story. In adjusting their housing expenditure after substantial changes in socioeconomic characteristics relevant to housing demand, households are motivated by the dual role of housing as a consumer durable and an investment good. That is, within a life-cycle theory model, we could consider the quantity of housing stock desired for consumption purposes $(h_C)$ and, separately, the amount of housing stock desired for portfolio purposes $(h_I)$ (Henderson and Ioannides 1983). For a number of reasons which are characteristic of housing markets, such as transactions costs and moral hazard, households may have an incentive to equate $h_C$ to $h_I$. However, in general, households that want to have $h_C > h_I$ would rent the respective amount of housing services. On the other hand, those who desire $h_C < h_I$ would typically use part of the housing stock they own to produce housing services for their own consumption.

I will now utilize these considerations to examine whether the behavior of the elderly, as portrayed by the paper, does conform to the prediction of life-cycle theory. In particular, since the desire to adjust housing consumption does indeed constitute a primary impetus to move, do elderly households change their holdings of housing when they do move in the direction predicted by the life-cycle model, as augmented by the above considerations peculiar to housing? Some of the special circumstances of the elderly allow us to test, in a somewhat unique fashion, some key predictions of the theory. Elderly who are close to retirement (or have already retired) operate with considerably reduced uncertainty with respect to income. They are also forced to consider the composition of their wealth portfolios, within which housing figures prominently.

A key prediction of the theory is that households should decumulate later in life by liquidating some of their wealth. Thus, as wealth decreases with age, so should its housing component—unless, of course, housing behaves in an extraordinary way within wealth portfolios. The amount of housing stock desired for consumption purposes, on the other hand, should not vary very much with age. To the extent that many households find it attractive to equate $h_C$ to $h_I$, the resulting decrease in housing stock held, $h^* = h_C = h_I$, is not as pronounced as decumulation of wealth required by the life-cycle model. Therefore, failure to sell and move into smaller quarters, which is what we typically observe, is not inconsistent with perfect capital markets as long as one recognizes certain characteristic rigidities of housing. Furthermore, the above observation along with a bequest motive may make $h^*$ completely invariant with age (see figure 2.11). Nonpecuniary transactions costs contribute further to this noted tendency. The authors' conclusions are thus strengthened by this argument.

The probit model of choosing whether to downsize or upsize would be much more revealing if price comparisons had also been included. Furthermore, because several of the determinants of changes in shelter costs may also contribute to the decision of whether or not to change mode, a bivariate probit model would be a simple way to model those joint discrete decisions.

Finally, I would like to direct attention to the test for unobserved heterogeneity conducted in section 2.4. This test is novel and very powerful, as it tests a particular hypothesis—in the present case, the Bernoulli model for households' propensity to move—against a random effects alternative with an *arbitrary* distribution. Models involving time

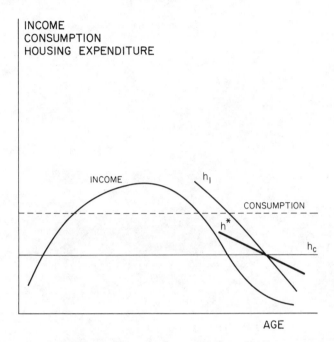

**Fig. 2.11**          Housing and wealth

processes (or duration data) are typically very complicated. Therefore such a simple test is a most welcome addition to our arsenal.

To conclude, I should emphasize that all-in-all the paper does an impressive job of illuminating housing decisions of the elderly by striking a remarkable economy between data utilization and complexity of econometric modeling.

## References

Heckman, James J. 1981. *Structural analysis of discrete data with econometric applications,* ed. C. Charles and D. McFadden, ch. 4. Cambridge, Mass.: MIT Press.

Henderson, J. Vernon, and Yannis M. Ioannides. 1983. A model of housing tenure choice. *American Economic Review* 73 (March): 98–113.

———. 1988. Dynamic aspects of consumer decisions in housing markets. *Journal of Urban Economics,* forthcoming.

Ioannides, Yannis M. 1987. Residential mobility and housing tenure choice. *Regional Science and Urban Economics* 17 (2):265–87.

Pickles, A. R., and B. Davies. 1985. The longitudinal analysis of housing careers. *Journal of Regional Science* 25 (1):85–101.

Rosenthal, Stuart S. 1986. A residence time model of housing markets. Working Paper Series, no. 65, Board of Governors of the Federal Reserve System.

# 3 Housing Patterns and Mobility of the Aged: The United States and West Germany

Konrad Stahl

## 3.1 Introduction

Most industrialized nations have experienced steep increases in household expenditures on housing and on the consumption of housing services as measured, for example, in floor space or in complementary land. While the better portion of this increase is undoubtedly attributable to secular increases in real income, leading to both increases in housing consumption per household of given size and to increased household formation, there appears to be a somewhat less obvious cause embedded in the changing demographic structure of these nations' populations. Particularly in the United States and West Germany (F.R.G.), we observe an increasing elderly population, and concomitant to this is an apparent "ratchet effect" in housing consumption: income decreases due to the retirement of the primary wage earner or due to his (or her) death often do not result in a decrease in the related household's housing consumption. Rather, the established household consumption pattern is sustained, despite the decrease in income. If elderly households would like to decrease their housing consumption but face impediments to mobility, there may be an "overconsumption" of housing services.

In addressing this issue, the following research questions ought to be attacked: First, is there indeed an "overconsumption" of housing services among the aged? Does the "ratchet effect" possibly result

Konrad Stahl is a Professor of Economics at the University of Mannheim, West Germany.

The author is indebted to David Ellwood, Henry Pollakowski, and especially Axel Börsch-Supan for useful comments. This research was sponsored by National Science Foundation grant no. SES-8511118.

from the elderly's inability to adjust housing consumption to their current preferences, typically via a move? What are the causes of, or impediments to, their mobility? In particular, to what extent are their moving decisions conditioned on events such as the retirement or death of the primary wage earner?

Studying these questions within an internationally comparative context, such as the U.S. vis-à-vis the F.R.G., may be helpful for several reasons. First, the age distribution of the West German population today has a high share of aged very similar to that predicted for the U.S. population around the year 2,000, so an analysis of the present situation in the F.R.G. may yield predictions of what will happen in the U.S. in the future. Second, the two nations' housing policies, while broadly similar, differ in substantive details (McGuire 1981).

Earlier research collected in Stahl and Struyk (1985) suggests that there are unexpectedly large cross-country differences in key housing market indicators, such as housing costs, quantity of housing consumed, or ownership and mobility rates, some of which may be related to behavioral differences rather than differences in policy. While broadly comparable, the micro databases presently at hand lack the sensitivity needed to separate out these differences. To be more specific, two comparable sets of microdata are currently available. The first, the Annual Housing Survey of 1978 (AHS) for the U.S. and the One Percent Housing Sample of 1978 (WS) for the F.R.G., consists of cross-sectional data. While comparable in some key variables, difficulties arise from cross-nationally incompatible definitions of other variables, or from the lack of records on some important housing market features in one or the other of the data sets.[1]

The second set of data bases consists of the Panel Survey on Income Dynamics (PSID) for the U.S. and the Socio-Economic Panel (SÖP) for the F.R.G. Here comparability is virtually not an issue since the SÖP is a close to perfect copy of the PSID. However, only the first wave (1983) of the SÖP was available to us for analysis. While this first wave contains a large number of restrospective questions, questions important to an analysis of the problems at hand date back not more than one year; so we are left with subsamples of households experiencing the relevant events that are too small for our analysis.[2]

Given the present limitations of the data bases, our approach is more or less descriptive rather than structural. A discussion of the data base is presented in section 3.2. In section 3.3 we pursue some descriptive statistical work on these data by comparing the structure of elderly households, their housing consumption patterns, and their adjustment. In section 3.4 we discuss the results of a series of simple binomial logit and ordinary least-squares estimates relating mobility and movers' and stayers' housing consumption to household and housing characteristics. Section 3.5 contains a summary of the results and some conclusions for further analysis.

## 3.2    Data, Samples, and Variables

The first pair of data bases used here, the AHS for the U.S. and the WS for the F.R.G., are broadly described and compared in Schneider, Stahl, and Struyk (1985). A description of the PSID up to wave 14 can be found in Institute for Social Research (1982), while the SÖP (wave 1983) is described in Infratest (1985). Since only circumstantial information is extracted from the PSID and the SÖP, this section concentrates on our use of the AHS and WS.

We selected from both the AHS and the WS the observations containing original[3] information for the variables used. To be selected, an observation had to include the following information:

1. *Household type,* consisting of a composite of the *number of adults,* their *marital relationship,* the *number of children,* and, in single adult households, this person's *sex.*
2. *Age of the head of household.*
3. *Household income*[4].
4. *Work/retirement status* of the head of household.
5. *Date of move* into the presently occupied unit.
6. *Pre-move tenure status of the household.*
7. *Post-move tenure status of the household.* Subletting persons were excluded.
8. *Type of living quarters.* Only households living in permanent units were included, not those living in mobile homes, transient hotels, second dwelling units, or institutions.[5]
9. *Subsidized housing units.* To avoid the effects of subsidies on housing consumption and in particular on mobility rates, we excluded U.S. households residing in public housing or receiving rent subsidies, as well as the sizeable portion of their West German counterparts living in subsidized social housing and/or receiving housing allowances.
10. *Location type.* Only urban and rural locations were distinguished.

After excluding unusable observations, we were left with an AHS file containing 18,433 out of an original 66,000 cases weighed for national representativity, and a WS file with 57,727 out of over 245,000 unweighted cases (see table 3.1). Both files should be representative for the "free market," "immobile housing" portions of the two nations' housing sectors. The households contained in this set were stratified by (at most) seven attributes, namely, household type, age of head of household, household income, work/retirement status, pre- or

Table 3.1        Comparison of Data and Samples

| Sample Attributes | U. S. | F. R. G. |
|---|---|---|
| Data source | Annual Housing Survey (National), 1978 | One-percent Dwelling Sample, 1978 |
| | U. S. Department of Commerce, Bureau of the Census | Statistisches Bundesamt |
| Dates of interviews | From October 1978 to January 1979 | From April to May 1978 |
| Number of original interviews | 66,472 | 245,422 |
| Exposure rate | Urban 0.07 (1/1,472) | 1.0 |
| | Rural 0.14 (1/736) | |
| Number of cases remaining after selection procedure | 18,433 (244,046)[a] | 57,727 |
| Number of strata | 320 | 320 |

[a]Weighted sum to correct for sample stratification. The sum represents 1 percent of the U. S. population.

post-move tenure status, and location type. Table 3.1 summarizes the file characteristics. The details for the stratification are summarized in table 3.2.

## 3.3 Descriptive Statistics

This section provides preliminary answers to the questions raised in section 3.1. We will first compare the household structure of the aged cross-nationally to control for behavioral differences due to differences in this structure. We then examine the levels of housing consumption of the aged and the extent possible overconsumption is reduced by voluntary moves. In passing, we look finally at event histories linking retirement and mobility. The data referred to are summarized from the AHS and the WS.

As mentioned before, on average the German population is much older than the American one. In 1978 the share of U.S. households with the head of household aged 55 years or older was 35.6 percent, while in the F.R.G. it was 42.2 percent. Table 3.3 provides information on the elderly's attributes in the two countries. It also singles out information on the portion of households with a retired head.

Let us begin by considering the aged households in toto. Several features are striking. First, 75 percent of the aged West German households have a retired head, as compared to only 62.5 percent in the U.S. Second, ownership rates differ widely: 75 percent of the elderly American households are owners compared to only 52 percent of the West German ones. While the West German aged heads of household are still somewhat older on average, the age distributions of household

**Table 3.2**          **Comparison of Variables**

| Variable Categories | U. S. | F. R. G. |
|---|---|---|
| Type of household | single male, single female, 2+ Persons (married), 2+ Persons (unmarried), 3+ Persons (including married couple) | |
| Age of head of household | 55–59, 60–64, 65–69, 70–74, 75–79, 80+ years | |
| Work/retirement status of head of household[a] | partially or fully employed/retired | |
| Pre-move tenure status | partially imputed pre-move-percent of owner[b] | |
| Post-move tenure status | owner/renter | |
| Household income[c] quartiles | (monthly gross) | (monthly net) |
| Lowest | Below $230 | Below DM 698 |
| Second | $230–$382 | DM 699–DM 942 |
| Third | $383–$673 | DM 943–DM 1,297 |
| Highest | $674– | DM 1,298– |
| Location | | |
| Urban | Inside SMSA or place with 20,000 or more inhabitants | Place with 100,000 or more inhabitants or inside suburban area of high population density |
| Rural | All other areas | All other areas |
| Mover | Household moved between September 1976 and August 1978 | Household moved in 1976 or 1977 |

[a]While in the WS this status is well defined, there is no clearly distinguishable retirement status in the AHS. We defined as "retired" all heads of households with age 55+ years and no salary income.

[b]Only 70 percent of the West German and 57 percent of the American movers reported on their pre-move housing status. In order to keep the nonreporting households' records in the analysis, we imputed their pre-move status from the reported cases in the same stratum.

[c]Since the aged are the focus of our analysis, the quartiles were formed on the basis of incomes of households with heads 55+ years old. The table gives quartiles for single person households' monthly income, standardized by the West German minimum guaranteed income index. For the U. S. population that index was converted using the mean 1977 exchange rate of 2.186 DM = $1.

heads do not differ much. By contrast, there are sharper differences in household types: the share of single female households is much larger in the F.R.G. than in the U.S.

Turning to the *retired* among these households, we observe that relative to the income distribution of all the aged, a higher share of American households with retired heads belongs to the lower income quartiles. Observe also that in contrast to the overall figures on

Table 3.3    **Characteristics of American and West German Households**

| | All Households with Age of Head 55+ | | | |
| | All Households = 100 % | | Households with Retired Head = 100 % | |
| | U.S. | F.R.G. | U.S. | F.R.G. |
|---|---|---|---|---|
| Income quartile | | | | |
| Lowest | 24.2 | 25.9 | 31.1 | 28.4 |
| Second | 25.2 | 23.4 | 30.4 | 24.8 |
| Third | 25.1 | 27.5 | 23.4 | 28.0 |
| Highest | 25.5 | 23.2 | 15.1 | 18.8 |
| Work/retirement status of Head | | | | |
| Working | 37.4 | 24.9 | | |
| Retirement | 62.6 | 75.1 | | |
| Age of head | | | | |
| 55–59 years | 23.0 | 19.8 | 10.1 | 6.2 |
| 60–64 years | 20.6 | 16.7 | 14.5 | 15.1 |
| 65–69 years | 19.6 | 22.8 | 22.6 | 27.8 |
| 70–74 years | 15.4 | 19.2 | 20.9 | 24.0 |
| 75–79 years | 11.0 | 13.1 | 16.0 | 16.4 |
| 80+ years | 10.4 | 8.3 | 15.8 | 10.5 |
| Household type | | | | |
| Single male | 7.9 | 6.4 | 8.8 | 7.0 |
| Single female | 27.2 | 35.6 | 33.2 | 41.2 |
| 2 Persons (married) | 36.5 | 34.1 | 34.7 | 33.7 |
| 2+ persons (unmarried) | 11.7 | 8.5 | 12.5 | 9.0 |
| 3+ persons (married) | 16.8 | 15.4 | 10.8 | 9.0 |
| Tenure | | | | |
| Owner | 74.9 | 52.2 | 72.2 | 48.9 |
| Renter | 25.1 | 47.8 | 27.8 | 51.1 |

*Source:* AHS 1978 (U.S.), WS 1978 (F.R.G.).

retirement, the share of early retired household heads is higher in the U.S. than in the F.R.G. Figure 3.1 shows that some 25 percent of U.S. male heads of households aged 55–59 are retired, as compared to only 15 percent of their West German counterparts. In the higher age brackets, however, male retirement in the F.R.G. exceeds that in the U.S. The likely cause of this pattern is that the retirement behavior, at least of the male population, is more strongly influenced by institutional factors in the F.R.G. than in the U.S.

Table 3.4 highlights cross-national differences in the income distributions of owners and renters. Observe in particular that American renters among the elderly are substantially poorer than West German

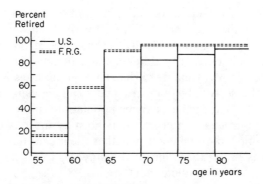

**Fig. 3.1**    Percentage retired of American and West German households. All households with male head aged 55 + .
*Source:* AHS 1978 (U.S.), WS 1978 (F.R.G.).

**Table 3.4**    **Characteristics of American and West German Households**

|  | All Households with Age of Head 55 + * | | | |
|---|---|---|---|---|
|  | Homeowners | | Renters | |
|  | U.S. | F.R.G. | U.S. | F.R.G. |
| Income quartile |  |  |  |  |
| Lowest | 22.0 | 27.1 | 30.8 | 24.5 |
| Second | 23.6 | 23.4 | 29.7 | 23.4 |
| Third | 26.4 | 26.0 | 21.2 | 29.0 |
| Highest | 27.9 | 23.4 | 18.2 | 23.0 |

*Source:* AHS 1978 (U.S.), WS 1978 (F.R.G.).
*All households = 100%

ones. In part, this may reflect the greater share of West German households who rent, but it may also be due to the preferential tax treatment given to U.S. homeowners which encourages high-income Americans to become owner-occupants.

In summary, we observe substantive cross-country differences in the share of the aged, their retirement status, their tenure status, and their income distributions. All these differences should affect housing consumption and its adjustment over time. In particular, we expect that because of the lower ownership rate and the higher proportion of retired heads in virtually each age stratum, the older West German population is much more prone to an adjustment in its housing consumption pattern than the American one.

Before we address this hypothesis, let us now turn to the question of housing "overconsumption" by the aged. As of now, data revealing the preferences of aged households for alternative housing bundles are not yet available for Germany. Such data are necessary to determine whether or not the aged are inhibited by the transactions costs of moving from adjusting (downward) the quantity of housing services consumed to their current preferences and incomes. Currently only indirect indicators are available to shed light on this question. One such indicator may be derived by comparing per capita housing consumption of the aged with that of the younger population; another, by looking at the relative burdens of housing costs born by these two population strata; and a third, by finding out whether the recent movers' housing consumption is lower than that of the stayers. In all these cases we have to account for possible cohort effects.

Tables 3.5A and 3.5B compare housing consumption patterns of households by age for owners and renters, respectively. Turning to the owners first, we observe in both countries a higher consumption of housing among older households as measured in rooms per head. Earlier research suggests that cohort effects emphasize this pattern. Fähn-

**Table 3.5A**        **Owners' Consumption (rooms per head)**

|  | U.S. | | F.R.G. | |
|---|---|---|---|---|
|  | Head of Household with Age | | Head of Household with Age | |
|  | below 55 | 55+ | below 55 | 55+ |
| Income quartile |  |  |  |  |
| Lowest | 1.4 | 2.7 | 1.4 | 2.8 |
| Second | 1.7 | 3.2 | 1.7 | 2.6 |
| Third | 2.1 | 3.3 | 1.9 | 2.8 |
| Highest | 3.3 | 3.6 | 2.4 | 3.0 |
| Age of head of household |  |  |  |  |
| −54 years | 2.0 |  | 1.8 |  |
| 55–59 years |  | 2.7 |  | 2.4 |
| 60–64 years |  | 3.0 |  | 2.7 |
| 65–69 years |  | 3.3 |  | 2.8 |
| 70–74 years |  | 3.5 |  | 3.0 |
| 75–79 years |  | 3.7 |  | 3.1 |
| 80+ years |  | 3.8 |  | 3.3 |
| Household type |  |  |  |  |
| Single male | 5.1 | 5.0 | 4.2 | 4.3 |
| Single female | 5.1 | 5.2 | 4.2 | 4.2 |
| 2 persons (married) | 2.9 | 2.8 | 2.5 | 2.4 |
| 2+ persons (unmarried) | 2.1 | 2.4 | 2.2 | 2.4 |
| 3+ persons (married) | 1.6 | 1.8 | 1.5 | 1.7 |
| Location |  |  |  |  |
| Urban | 2.1 | 3.2 | 1.8 | 2.8 |
| Rural | 1.9 | 3.3 | 1.8 | 2.8 |

*Source:* AHS 1978 (U.S.), WS 1978 (F.R.G.).

Table 3.5B        **Renters' Consumption (rooms per head)**

|  | U.S. | | F.R.G. | |
|---|---|---|---|---|
|  | Head of Household with Age | | Head of Household with Age | |
|  | below 55 | 55+ | below 55 | 55+ |
| Income quartile | | | | |
| Lowest | 1.4 | 2.4 | 1.4 | 2.6 |
| Second | 1.8 | 2.6 | 1.6 | 2.6 |
| Third | 2.3 | 2.8 | 2.0 | 2.7 |
| Highest | 2.8 | 3.0 | 2.3 | 2.8 |
| Age of head of household | | | | |
| −54 years | 2.0 | | 1.9 | |
| 55–59 years | | 2.5 | | 2.4 |
| 60–64 years | | 2.6 | | 2.6 |
| 65–69 years | | 2.7 | | 2.7 |
| 70–74 years | | 2.7 | | 2.7 |
| 75–79 years | | 2.8 | | 2.8 |
| 80+ years | | 2.8 | | 2.8 |
| Household type | | | | |
| Single male | 3.1 | 2.8 | 2.9 | 3.3 |
| Single female | 3.3 | 3.4 | 3.0 | 3.3 |
| 2 persons (married) | 2.0 | 2.0 | 2.0 | 2.0 |
| 2+ persons (unmarried) | 1.6 | 1.9 | 1.7 | 1.9 |
| 3+ persons (married) | 1.2 | 1.3 | 1.3 | 1.4 |
| Location | | | | |
| Urban | 2.2 | 2.6 | 1.9 | 2.7 |
| Rural | 2.0 | 2.9 | 1.8 | 2.7 |

*Source:* AHS 1978 (U.S.), WS 1978 (F.R.G.).

rich, Gabriel, and Stahl (1988) show that life-cycle housing consumption patterns are strongly influenced by time-dependent increases in housing consumption. Comparing housing consumption cross-sectionally, differentiated by age of head of household, we observe a relatively lower consumption of the now aged, having started their housing consumption career earlier in real time.

At any rate, the difference in housing consumption of young and elderly households is more dramatic in the U.S., and, compared to the F.R.G., there is a greater narrowing of the difference as income rises. This may be due to cross-national differences in retirement schemes, worth further research, that lead to income decreases at retirement that are sharper in the U.S. than in the F.R.G.

Table 3.5A also reveals that, in contrast to the younger households, the elderly owners' housing consumption per head is nearly independent of (household-size adjusted) income. It follows that the difference between the younger and the older households' consumption tends to decrease with income. Differentiating further by age of the elderly, we observe, as expected, that this difference increases with the increasing age of the households' heads. Between owners younger than 55 and older than 80, we find a difference in consumption per head of more than 1.5 rooms. As expected, consumption per head is maximal among the single-person household strata. Surprisingly, we observe in both countries virtually no urban-rural differences in consumption per head.

Table 3.5B, comparing renters' consumption by age, reveals the same general patterns detected for the owners but the difference between old and young is not nearly as large as in the owners' case. The same holds for increases in consumption with increasing age. Observe finally that the aged renters' housing consumption is nearly independent of (household-size adjusted) purchasing power.

Comparing owners' and renters' consumption patterns, we observe that in both countries there is virtually no difference between these two groups' consumption in the age bracket 55–59, but that this difference grows quite drastically for owners with increasing age of the household head. While among the household types, the single female renter households' consumption is again largest, it is also dominated by the owners' consumption in this stratum. Observe finally again that the urban-rural differences are quite marginal.

How do these large differences in housing consumption between the young and the aged relate to differences in housing costs? Unfortunately, the West German survey did not record the costs of owning a home in enough detail to allow a cross-national comparison.[6] In relating the renters' costs to income, we faced the additional problem that income data from the two countries are incompatible. Nevertheless, the figures on the rent-to-income ratios provided in table 3.6, should be indicative. After controlling for household-size effects through household-size-specific income weights, we observe that the rent-to-income ratios are perceivably larger for the aged only among the high-income retired renters in the U.S. and among the low-income nonretired in the F.R.G.

Summarizing our comparisons of younger and older households' consumption patterns, we find that especially the older lower-income owners do consume substantially more housing services per head. While this also holds to a lesser degree for the renters, it is by no means reflected in the renters' expenditures as a proportion of income. These tend to be lower for the aged, especially in the lower-income strata.

Let us turn finally to the questions of whether mobility of the aged, in particular of the retired, results in decreases in the quantity of housing services consumed, and if so, to what events mobility is related. Again, we have no cross-nationally comparable evidence on the direct consumption effects of housing mobility, so we resort to a comparison

Table 3.6          Rent-to-Income Ratios by Income Quartile

|  | Not Retired | | Retired | |
|---|---|---|---|---|
|  | Head of Household with Age | | Head of Household with Age | |
|  | below 55 | 55+ | below 55 | 55+ |
| U.S.* | | | | |
| Lowest | 27.1 | 25.6 | 38.1 | 34.1 |
| Second | 22.6 | 21.5 | 33.7 | 34.5 |
| Third | 21.8 | 21.5 | 26.3 | 29.0 |
| Highest | 15.8 | 15.0 | 14.0 | 20.3 |
| F.R.G.** | | | | |
| Lowest | 22.2 | 26.3 | 26.0 | 25.6 |
| Second | 16.9 | 17.7 | 17.4 | 19.0 |
| Third | 15.8 | 15.7 | 15.7 | 16.6 |
| Highest | 13.3 | 13.2 | 14.1 | 14.0 |

*Source: AHS 1978 (U.S.); the ratio of annual rent net of utilities to household gross annual income is reported.
**Source: WS 1978 (F.R.G.); the ratio of annual rent net of utilities to household annual income net of taxes is reported.

of the aged stayers' versus the movers' housing consumption patterns. While this comparison is problematic due to unobserved heterogeneity, it is the best we can perform with the data currently available. Additionally, we can report on the tenure status adjustments made with a move.

Table 3.7 gives stayers' and movers' room consumption per head. We observe that, on average, the recent movers among the aged consume less housing services. The reduction is larger for the American than the West German households, especially for those with retired heads. In both countries, the difference increases with increasing age of head, but again more strongly so in the U.S. than in the F.R.G.[7]

However, less consumption of housing services measured in rooms per head is not accompanied by a decrease in the rent-to-income ratio, as shown in table 3.8. In both countries this ratio is substantially higher for recent movers. The increase is higher in the F.R.G. across all income groups, possibly due to higher tenure discounts as a result of regulatory intervention in the housing market.[8] The stratification by age shows that the burden of rent relative to income increases across all household age strata.[9]

What are the proportions of households with elderly heads venturing such a move? Table 3.9 reveals dramatic cross-country differences in mobility rates that run counter to the expectations raised earlier. American elderly households are more mobile on average by several orders

**Table 3.7**               **Housing Consumption of Stayers and Movers (rooms per head)**

| | All Households with Age of Head 55+ | | | |
| | U.S. | | F.R.G. | |
| | Stayer | Mover | Stayer | Mover |
|---|---|---|---|---|
| Income quartile | | | | |
| Lowest | 2.6 | 2.3 | 2.7 | 2.6 |
| Second | 3.1 | 2.5 | 2.6 | 2.5 |
| Third | 3.2 | 2.8 | 2.7 | 2.6 |
| Highest | 3.6 | 3.1 | 2.9 | 2.7 |
| Work/retirement status | | | | |
| Working | 2.9 | 2.7 | 2.4 | 2.3 |
| Retired | 3.3 | 2.7 | 2.8 | 2.7 |
| Age of head of household | | | | |
| 55–59 years | 2.7 | 2.6 | 2.4 | 2.4 |
| 60–64 years | 3.0 | 2.6 | 2.7 | 2.6 |
| 65–69 years | 3.2 | 2.8 | 2.8 | 2.6 |
| 70–74 years | 3.3 | 2.7 | 2.9 | 2.7 |
| 75–79 years | 3.5 | 2.7 | 2.9 | 2.7 |
| 80+ years | 3.6 | 2.8 | 3.0 | 2.8 |

*Source:* AHS 1978 (U.S.), WS 1978 (F.R.G.).

**Table 3.8**               **Rent-to-Income Ratios of Stayers and Movers**

| | All Renters with Age of Head 55+ | | | |
| | U.S.* | | F.R.G.** | |
| | Stayer | Mover | Stayer | Mover |
|---|---|---|---|---|
| Income quartile | | | | |
| Lowest | 31.9 | 35.1 | 25.2 | 30.3 |
| Second | 31.7 | 33.8 | 18.4 | 22.8 |
| Third | 25.1 | 27.6 | 16.1 | 20.0 |
| Highest | 16.2 | 18.9 | 13.5 | 17.1 |
| Age of head of household | | | | |
| 55–59 years | 22.1 | 27.1 | 16.2 | 20.7 |
| 60–64 years | 23.1 | 27.5 | 17.7 | 22.7 |
| 65–69 years | 27.3 | 31.3 | 18.3 | 23.1 |
| 70–74 years | 29.2 | 31.2 | 19.0 | 23.4 |
| 75–79 years | 30.8 | 32.5 | 18.9 | 24.0 |
| 80+ years | 32.0 | 38.3 | 18.7 | 22.8 |

*Source:* AHS 1978 (U.S.); the ratio of annual rent net of utilities to household gross annual income is reported.

**Source:* WS 1978 (F.R.G.); the ratio of annual rent net of utilities to household annual income net of taxes is reported.

**Table 3.9**         **Mobility Rates[a] of American and West German Households**

| | All Households with Age of Head 55 + | | | |
| | Homeowners | | Renters | |
| | U.S. | F.R.G. | U.S. | F.R.G. |
|---|---|---|---|---|
| All households | 6.5 | 2.5 | 27.3 | 8.9 |
| Retired only | 6.3 | 2.2 | 26.1 | 8.8 |
| Age of head | | | | |
| 55–59 years | 8.6 | 3.2 | 35.5 | 10.8 |
| 60–64 years | 7.5 | 3.0 | 32.0 | 11.7 |
| 65–69 years | 6.9 | 3.0 | 28.5 | 10.4 |
| 70–74 years | 5.1 | 1.7 | 25.2 | 8.1 |
| 75–79 years | 4.0 | 1.1 | 21.0 | 6.2 |
| 80+ years | 2.9 | 1.1 | 16.1 | 4.7 |

*Source:* AHS 1978 (U.S.), WS 1978 (F.R.G.).
[a]Movers in the two-year period 1976 and 1977.

of magnitude. The differences are especially dramatic in absolute terms among the renters. While, as expected, the mobility rates decline with increasing age of the household head, the differences in mobility rates decline only in absolute rather than in relative terms. Note in passing that the aged owners' mobility rates tend to increase, and those of the renters to decrease, with income.

The tenure status adjustments associated with the elderly's moves are recorded in table 3.10. Most of them, namely 77.5 percent in the

**Table 3.10**         **Tenure Status Changes of Movers, by Income Quartile (percent)**

| | All Movers with Age of Head 55 + | | | | | | |
| | O-O[a] | | O-R | | R-O | | R-R |
|---|---|---|---|---|---|---|---|
| U.S. | | | | | | | |
| Lowest | 13.4 | | 16.0 | | 23.3 | | 35.6 |
| Second | 19.4 | | 26.7 | | 23.0 | | 31.3 |
| Third | 22.8 | | 26.4 | | 25.8 | | 15.4 |
| Highest | 44.4 | | 30.9 | | 27.9 | | 17.6 |
| Overall  100 % = | 34.3 | + | 14.6 | + | 8.0 | + | 43.1 |
| F.R.G. | | | | | | | |
| Lowest | 24.0 | | 28.6 | | 14.6 | | 25.3 |
| Second | 18.8 | | 19.6 | | 15.2 | | 24.4 |
| Third | 28.8 | | 29.2 | | 29.5 | | 27.8 |
| Highest | 28.4 | | 22.6 | | 40.7 | | 22.5 |
| Overall  100 % = | 7.9 | + | 6.4 | + | 12.6 | + | 73.1 |

*Source:* AHS 1978 (U.S.), WS 1978 (F.R.G.).
[a]"O" stands for Owner, "R" stands for Renter.

U.S. and 81 percent in the F.R.G., are status preserving. However, while in the U.S. some 34 percent (43 percent) of the movers preserve the owner (renter) status, respectively, renter status preservation outweighs with 73 percent all other status adjustments in the F.R.G. Furthermore, owner status preservation in the U.S. is concentrated more in the higher income strata, and renter status preservation in the lower income strata.[10]

The status change from owning to renting is most interesting. With 14.6 percent of all moves (63 percent of which are exercised by the retired), it occurs in the U.S. more than twice as often than in West Germany. Almost the converse is true for the reverse status change. While still 12.6 percent of all elderly movers in West Germany change from renting to owning, only 8 percent of the corresponding U.S. population do so. Observe finally that the status adjustment patterns are clearly income dependent in the expected way, but much more so in the U.S. than in the F.R.G.

Let us summarize the evidence presented so far. First, we have seen that the aged consume more housing services per head than their younger counterparts, if measured in rooms per head; this result prevails especially among the homeowners, in the single-person household strata, among the very old, and somewhat surprisingly in the groups with lower household-size-adjusted income. However, this high level of consumption was associated with an increase in the housing cost burden only for the high-income retired in the U.S., and for the low-income nonretired in the F.R.G. Unfortunately, we have no comparative evidence for the owners' cost burden. The fact that high levels of housing consumption is concentrated among the low-income, single-person households may result from relatively low out-of-pocket costs and an underestimation of the opportunity costs of holding that large a housing bundle.

Second, we showed that moves among the aged lead to a reduction in housing consumption per head. Again, this reduction is on average accompanied by an increase in the rent-to-income ratio. While most of these moves are tenure-status preserving, there is a not unsubstantial portion of moves from owner to renter status.

However, these moves take place at rates that dramatically differ across the two countries. Overall, the U.S. aged are more mobile by several orders of magnitude. The cross-country difference in mobility rates is especially evident among renters. Clearly, all this evidence is taken from cross-sectional data and is therefore partial. In particular, it is only partially controlled for heterogeneity.

Of immediate concern now would be an analysis of the causes and impediments of the elderly's mobility. From the one wave of the SÖP available to us so far, we could only extract the comparative event history diagrams contained in figures 3.2 and 3.3 that relate the house-

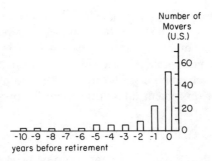

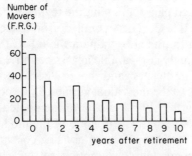

**Fig. 3.2**    Retirement of head of household and decision to move. All households with retired head. *Source:* PSID Wave 14 (U.S.), SÖP Wave 1 (F.R.G.).

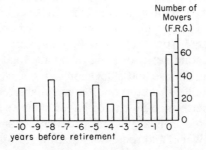

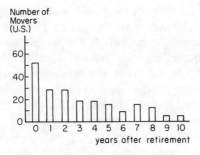

**Fig. 3.3**    Retirement of head of household and decision to move. All households with retired head. *Source:* PSID Wave 14 (U.S.), SÖP Wave 1 (F.R.G.).

hold's last move to the head of household's retirement. In both West Germany and the United States, households are more likely to move in the year of retirement than in the years before or after retirement. While post-retirement mobility rates in West Germany return to their pre-retirement levels, mobility rates in the United States remain higher in the years after retirement than in the years before retirement.

### 3.4 Multivariate Analysis

We now present the results of simple ordinary least squares (OLS) estimates and binary logit estimates. The first set consisting of OLS estimates serves to determine the simultaneous impact of household and tenure characteristics, location, and mobility on housing consumption. The second set consisting of binary logit estimates determines the individual household's decision to move as a function of the very same household, location, and tenure characteristics. Both sets of estimates are performed on choice-based samples of recent movers and stayers sampled in nearly equal proportions and presented in a form pooled for owners and renters, and stratified by mode of tenure. Because of the limitations in exactly comparable data, the models are quite simple and provide only a summary description of the mobility process rather than a structural analysis of the aged's' housing consumption and mobility.

In the first set of estimates we relate housing consumption as measured in rooms per head to a set of dummy variables, referring to the household characteristics, household type, age of head of household, household-size-adjusted income, tenure status (in the pooled model), location, and finally to the event of a move during the last two years. The omitted category for the dummies is the married couple without children, age of head 65–69, income in the lowest quartile, living in an urban area, who did not move during the two years preceding the survey.

The estimates are presented in table 3.11. Three pairs of estimates are shown, with each pair containing the results of the same model for the U.S. and the F.R.G. The overall performance of the models is substantially better for the U.S. than for the F.R.G. Mean consumption of the elderly is roughly comparable across countries, with a somewhat smaller difference in owners' and renters' consumption in the F.R.G. than in the U.S. As to the individual variables, the coefficient on home-ownership turns out highly significant in the pooled model and carries the expected sign. By contrast, in none of the models does the retirement status per se have an effect on housing consumption. The effect of the adjusted incomes on consumption per head is generally as expected. It is typically (throughout) significant for the higher (highest) income quartiles.[11]

**Table 3.11        OLS Estimates[a] on Room Consumption per Head**

| | All Households with Age of Head 55 + | | | | | |
|---|---|---|---|---|---|---|
| | Pooled | | Homeowners | | Renters | |
| Independent[b] Variables | U.S. | F.R.G. | U.S. | F.R.G. | U.S. | F.R.G. |
| Percentage of homeowners | 0.82 | 0.56 | | | | |
| | (12.04) | (8.31) | | | | |
| Percentage of retired | 0.06 | −0.12 | 0.12 | −0.06 | −0.03 | −0.17 |
| | (0.87) | (−1.28) | (1.51) | (−0.45) | (−0.25) | (−1.38) |
| Percentage of movers | −0.26 | −0.12 | −0.23 | −0.19 | −0.12 | −0.04 |
| | (−4.28) | (−1.85) | (−3.41) | (−1.71) | (−1.20) | (−0.49) |
| Income Quartile | | | | | | |
| Second | 0.04 | 0.17 | 0.17 | 0.11 | −0.04 | 0.17 |
| | (0.50) | (1.93) | (1.89) | (0.84) | (−0.29) | (1.47) |
| Third | 0.20 | 0.19 | 0.40 | 0.19 | −0.05 | 0.15 |
| | (2.42) | (1.94) | (4.07) | (1.37) | (−0.34) | (1.13) |
| Highest | 0.64 | 0.52 | 0.85 | 0.58 | 0.27 | 0.46 |
| | (7.01) | (5.68) | (8.29) | (4.32) | (1.68) | (3.65) |
| Age of head of household | | | | | | |
| 55–59 years | −0.01 | −0.13 | 0.00 | −0.05 | 0.09 | −0.18 |
| | (−0.14) | (−1.22) | (0.04) | (−0.32) | (0.62) | (−1.22) |
| 60–64 years | −0.05 | −0.05 | 0.00 | 0.08 | 0.06 | −0.17 |
| | (−0.52) | (−0.51) | (−0.02) | (0.62) | (0.41) | (−1.43) |
| 70–74 years | −0.08 | −0.05 | −0.04 | −0.11 | −0.07 | −0.05 |
| | (−0.84) | (−0.56) | (−0.35) | (−0.71) | (−0.45) | (−0.39) |
| 75–79 years | −0.08 | 2.64 | 0.04 | −0.30 | −0.16 | 0.18 |
| | (−0.73) | (0.26) | (0.30) | (−1.78) | (−0.98) | (1.47) |
| 80+ years | 0.17 | −0.09 | 0.26 | −0.09 | −0.05 | −0.03 |
| | (1.40) | (−0.67) | (1.88) | (−0.47) | (−0.26) | (−0.16) |
| Household type | | | | | | |
| Single male | 1.40 | 1.16 | 2.26 | 2.19 | 0.51 | 0.74 |
| | (13.48) | (9.21) | (16.50) | (9.82) | (3.42) | (4.81) |
| Single female | 1.87 | 1.43 | 2.24 | 1.55 | 1.35 | 1.31 |
| | (24.90) | (19.40) | (24.93) | (12.84) | (11.34) | (14.08) |
| 2+ persons (unmarried) | −1.34 | −0.10 | −1.55 | −0.16 | −1.32 | −0.08 |
| | (−12.92) | (−0.91) | (−12.78) | (−1.03) | (−7.82) | (−0.49) |
| 3+ persons (married) | −1.75 | −0.65 | −1.77 | −0.73 | −1.51 | −0.50 |
| | (−19.69) | (−6.53) | (−19.13) | (−5.79) | (−8.08) | (−3.20) |
| Location | | | | | | |
| Rural | 0.20 | 0.10 | 0.10 | 0.01 | 0.46 | 0.17 |
| | (3.36) | (1.58) | (1.50) | (0.07) | (4.31) | (2.11) |
| Intercept | 1.72 | 1.82 | 2.27 | 2.35 | 2.05 | 1.90 |
| | (13.80) | (13.53) | (16.77) | (12.69) | (10.11) | (10.68) |
| Number of observations | 1,190 | 1,070 | 764 | 428 | 426 | 642 |
| Corrected R-square | 0.68 | 0.41 | 0.77 | 0.50 | 0.57 | 0.37 |
| Standard error of regression | 0.94 | 0.96 | 0.85 | 0.92 | 0.91 | 0.95 |
| Dependent variable mean | 2.60 | 2.69 | 2.71 | 2.74 | 2.41 | 2.66 |

*Source:* AHS 1978 (U.S.), WS 1978 (F.R.G.).

[a]The entries in the table are the regression coefficients. The numbers in parentheses are the values of the $t$-statistics for the coefficients. The base group (or omitted category) for the dummy variables is a married couple without children, with age of head of household 65–69 years, within the lowest income quartile, and living in an urban area.

[b]The dependent variable is the number of rooms per head.

One may be surprised that after controlling for other household characteristics, the household head's age is hardly of impact on the per capita consumption of housing. Apparently most of the age effect is absorbed by household type as a covariate. This comes up quite well in all estimates, and, as expected, with a positive sign for the single person, and a negative one for the large households. Location has also the expected effect, with increased consumption in non-urban regions within both the pooled and the renter models. The effect is insignificant in both countries' owner models. It is finally interesting to observe that in both countries mobility has a sizeable negative impact on per capita housing consumption in the pooled and owner-occupant models. Its impact has the correct sign, but it is smaller and insignificant in the renter models. This lends some support to the conclusion drawn earlier that especially the owners among the movers on average downscale their housing consumption.

The second and final set of estimates relates the household and tenure characteristics used heretofore to the individual household's moving decisions. We again used for each country a model pooling by mode of tenure, and then two models separately for owners and renters. The results are presented in table 3.12. In both countries ownership contributes, as expected, strongly negatively to mobility, an effect due to the large differences in the transactions costs of moving. In fact, the effect dominates all other influences by several orders of magnitude. Yet it is surprisingly much smaller in the F.R.G., possibly reflecting renters' transactions costs of moving that in the F.R.G. are closer to those of the owners because of institutional and market rigidities.

The cross-country differences extend to the influence of retirement on mobility. In the U.S., it is strongly and significantly positive in both

**Table 3.12**     **Binary Logit Estimates[a] of Household Mobility**

| | All Households with Age of Head 55 + | | | | | |
| | Pooled | | Homeowners | | Renters | |
| Independent[b] Variables | U.S. | F.R.G. | U.S. | F.R.G. | U.S. | F.R.G. |
|---|---|---|---|---|---|---|
| Percentage of homeowners | −1.83 | −1.20 | | | | |
| | (−11.82) | (−7.68) | | | | |
| Percentage of retired | 0.59 | −0.42 | 0.91 | −0.33 | −0.29 | −0.35 |
| | (3.53) | (−2.05) | (4.47) | (−0.98) | (−0.93) | (−1.34) |
| Income Quartile | | | | | | |
| Second | 0.45 | −0.10 | 0.31 | 0.12 | 0.58 | −0.30 |
| | (2.50) | (−0.46) | (1.30) | (0.31) | (1.93) | (−1.14) |

**Table 3.12**     (*continued*)

| Independent[b] Variables | All Households with Age of Head 55+ | | | | | |
| | Pooled | | Homeowners | | Renters | |
| | U.S. | F.R.G. | U.S. | F.R.G. | U.S. | F.R.G. |
|---|---|---|---|---|---|---|
| Third | 0.34 | 0.09 | 0.43 | 0.64 | −0.03 | −0.20 |
| | (1.70) | (0.41) | (1.68) | (1.64) | (−0.09) | (−0.71) |
| Highest | 0.51 | 0.17 | 0.71 | 1.07 | −0.19 | −0.29 |
| | (2.41) | (0.81) | (2.64) | (2.88) | (−0.51) | (−1.07) |
| Age of head of household | | | | | | |
| 55–59 years | 0.83 | −0.09 | 0.91 | −0.20 | 0.52 | −0.03 |
| | (3.88) | (−0.36) | (3.44) | (−0.50) | (1.43) | (−0.10) |
| 60–64 years | 0.37 | −0.31 | 0.42 | −0.97 | 0.19 | 0.03 |
| | (1.78) | (−1.51) | (1.62) | (−2.60) | (0.55) | (0.11) |
| 70–74 years | −0.11 | −0.58 | −0.33 | −0.71 | 0.35 | −0.55 |
| | (−0.51) | (−2.75) | (−1.09) | (−1.64) | (0.92) | (−2.20) |
| 75–79 years | −0.46 | −0.67 | −0.73 | −0.43 | −0.11 | −0.66 |
| | (−1.76) | (−2.91) | (−1.86) | (−0.89) | (−0.28) | (−2.45) |
| 80+ years | −0.53 | −0.81 | −0.51 | −0.73 | −0.31 | −0.85 |
| | (−1.86) | (−2.66) | (−1.32) | (−1.22) | (−0.71) | (−2.40) |
| Household type | | | | | | |
| Single male | −0.20 | 0.29 | −1.14 | −1.80 | 0.58 | 0.75 |
| | (−0.81) | (1.04) | (−2.46) | (−1.70) | (1.51) | (2.27) |
| Single female | −0.24 | 0.05 | −0.40 | −0.17 | 0.05 | 0.16 |
| | (−1.37) | (0.32) | (−1.64) | (−0.50) | (0.18) | (0.82) |
| 2+ persons (unmarried) | 0.27 | −0.15 | 0.48 | 0.10 | 0.21 | −0.24 |
| | (1.09) | (−0.57) | (1.58) | (0.24) | (0.49) | (−0.70) |
| 3+ persons (married) | −0.11 | −0.05 | 0.01 | 0.17 | −0.51 | −0.19 |
| | (−0.56) | (−0.21) | (0.06) | (0.52) | (−1.15) | (−0.58) |
| Location | | | | | | |
| Rural | 0.12 | 0.19 | 0.14 | 0.05 | −0.03 | 0.27 |
| | (0.86) | (1.32) | (0.86) | (0.20) | (−0.10) | (1.56) |
| Intercept | 0.20 | 0.31 | −1.86 | −1.16 | 0.75 | 0.36 |
| | (0.70) | (1.06) | (−5.14) | (−2.32) | (1.59) | (0.96) |
| Number of observations | 1,190 | 1,070 | 764 | 428 | 426 | 642 |
| Mover | 558 | 381 | 256 | 93 | 124 | 288 |
| Non-mover | 632 | 689 | 508 | 335 | 302 | 354 |
| Percent correctly predicted | 69.50 | 66.26 | 69.11 | 78.74 | 70.66 | 59.03 |
| Log likelihood | | | | | | |
| Initial | −824.85 | −741.67 | −529.56 | −296.67 | −295.28 | −445.00 |
| At convergence | −717.85 | −648.24 | −454.63 | −208.92 | −248.34 | −426.60 |

*Source:* AHS 1978 (U.S.), WS 1978 (F.R.G.).

[a]The entries in the table are the regression coefficients. The numbers in parentheses are the values of the $t$-statistics for the coefficents. The base group (or omitted category) for the dummy variables is a married couple without children, with age of head of household 65–69 years, within the lowest income quartile, and living in an urban area.

[b]The dependent variable indicates whether the household has moved or not (1 resp. 0).

the pooled and the owner models, but significant and strongly negative in the pooled model for West Germany, and also negative (but insignificant) in the other models.[12] The effect of income on mobility is also quite different in the pooled models. In the U.S. model, increasing incomes have a generally positive effect on mobility. This is not the case in the F.R.G. model where that influence is ineffective. By contrast, increasing income tends to exercise a positive influence on owners' mobility in both countries, which lends additional, if only partial, support to the argument presented by Feinstein and McFadden (ch. 2, in this volume) and Venti and Wise (ch. 1, in this volume) that owners' moves tend not to be influenced by liquidity constraints.

The household head's age should influence mobility in two ways. On the one hand, one expects a decreasing tendency to move with increasing age; on the other hand, moves may be conditioned on the retirement decision, resulting in higher mobility of the reference household relative to its younger peers. Indeed, the pattern of influence is quite unclear for the age groups younger than the reference age. By contrast, for the age groups above that age we generally observe a negative impact on mobility.

After controlling for other household characteristics, the influence of household type on mobility is very weak in both countries. This is not surprising, given that mobility differentials are absorbed by age as a covariate to household type.

### 3.5  Summary and Conclusions

While our analysis herein is largely descriptive, it nevertheless develops some fairly clear patterns extending across both countries. First, in both countries the aged consume more housing services per head (according to our rough measure) than their younger counterparts. The difference is largest for small households with low incomes in the U.S. It is generally not accompanied by a comparable difference in the (renters') housing costs burden, which for most household strata decreases rather than increases with age.

Second, the aged movers consume less housing services than the stayers. This is especially the case for the (former) owners. In the rental sector, however, the reduction in the quantity of housing services consumed by the movers is almost never matched by a decrease in rent relative to income spent after a move. On average, the increase in the cost burden is sharper for the West German than for the American households.

This may be one clue to the lower mobility rates of West German aged renters relative to their American counterparts. It is most likely that tenure discounts—which in West Germany are to some extent enforced by a national tenants' protection legislation—are responsible for large differences in rent levels between occupied and vacant stock, and they thereby impede especially the elderly's mobility. Although smaller, there are also perceivable differences between the elderly stayers' and movers' rent-to-income ratios in the U.S. Any reduction in this difference should be of positive effect on the aged's mobility, and thereby on the downward adjustment of housing services consumed. This effect should directly extend to owners contemplating a status change backward to renting. The low mobility of elderly owners in both countries may be largely due to the relatively low out-of-pocket costs of owning and the low perceived opportunity costs of holding their property. If this is true, then a decrease in the costs of renting should decrease the opportunity costs of moving.

The most notable difference arising from our cross-country comparison of the housing market participation by the elderly is that despite a lower ownership rate and a higher proportion of retired heads, the West German elderly are decidely less mobile overall than the American ones. The causes and consequences of this difference should be worth further analysis as comparable panel data become available. Of particular interest should be the determination of whether these differences are largely behavioral or due to cross-country policy differentials.

Moves are only one form of adjustment in housing consumption. Of equal interest are adjustments-in-place via unit subdivision or subletting, or the intrafamily, in-place formation of new households. These more subtle changes are unobserved in the present data set, but they can be discerned and related to behavioral and policy descriptors within successive waves of the PSID and the SÖP. Their analysis should increase our understanding of the elderly's housing market behavior.

# Notes

1. Examples in point are the incompatible recordings of household income, housing quality characteristics, and premove housing conditions.
2. We should emphasize, however, that there will be room for interesting cross-country analyses as successive waves of the SÖP are made available.
3. All cases containing adjusted or imputed data were deleted. The exception was information on item 6, below.
4. As mentioned before, household incomes are incompatibly defined in the two surveys. In the AHS, household members' gross annual incomes from different sources are reported in detail, while the WS reports household income net of taxes. Using income quartiles, we chose to emphasize the households' relative position within the national personal income distribution, and this way established cross-national comparability. To obtain comparability across house-

hold sizes, we weighted incomes by a household-size-specific index of minimum guaranteed income (*Sozialhilfesatz*) constructed for West Germany.

5. Unfortunately, neither survey includes information on individuals living in retirement homes, which would have been most interesting for our analysis.

6. Using panel data, Feinstein and McFadden (ch. 2, in this volume) and Venti and Wise (ch. 1, in this volume) analyze in detail the relationship between the owners' housing consumption adjustment and adjustment in out-of-pocket costs as well as in income and wealth.

7. For the U.S., several authors give direct evidence on mobility-related housing consumption adjustments of the elderly. While tabulations from different data sets arranged by Struyk (1980) and Pollakowski (1985) reveal that among the elderly some smaller share also moves into larger units, Struyk's multivariate analysis shows that both tenure groups downsize their housing consumption with a move (see also Struyk 1986). Börsch-Supan and Pollakowski (1988) also infer from a longitudinal discrete choice model of housing tenure and size that older age and retirement have a significant effect on the choice of small dwellings. Thus, while cohort effects might have an influence on the magnitude of downsizing as reported in table 3.7, accounting for them should not turn around the size effect of moving. See also the multivariate analysis in section 3.4, below.

8. Throughout the F.R.G., tenants' protection legislation constrains the upward adjustment of rents in occupied units.

9. In contrast to this picture, Struyk's (1980) multivariate analysis of panel data suggests that, on relocation, the elderly renters adjust their expense-to-income ratio downward. Furthermore, this adjustment increases with income. For homeowners, the change in this ratio increases with base year income for annual (1973) incomes up to $5,600, and decreases thereafter.

10. Controlling for moves into dependent status in Feinstein and McFadden (ch. 2, this volume) and Venti and Wise (ch. 1, this volume), respectively, the rate of status preserving moves reported here for the owners is higher by 3 percent surprisingly lower by 13.5 percent, respectively; for the renters, lower by 5 percent and higher by 4 percent, respectively. Evidence communicated by James Poterba suggests that the share of owners'-status-preserving moves is too high in Venti and Wise.

11. Earlier estimates on the basis of unadjusted household incomes yielded insignificant parameters, as is typical of the literature.

12. The same cross-country difference was found in earlier, technically quite different estimates.

# References

Börsch-Supan, A., and H. Pollakowski. 1988. Estimating housing consumption adjustments from panel data. *Journal of Urban Economics,* forthcoming.

Fähnrich, E., J. Gabriel, and K. Stahl. 1988. *Prognosemodell regionaler Wohnungsnachfrage.* Baden-Baden: Nomos, forthcoming.

Infratest. 1985. *Das Sozio-Ökonomische Panel, Welle 1, Methodenbericht zur Haupterhebung.* Munich: Infratest Wirtschaftsforschung GmbH.

Institute for Social Research. 1982. *A panel study on income dynamics: Procedures and tape codes, 1981 interviewing year, wave XIV,* A Supplement. Ann Arbor, Mich.: University of Michigan.

McGuire, Chester C. 1981. *International housing policies: A comparative analysis*. Lexington, Mass.: D.C. Heath Co.

Pollakowski, H. O. 1985. Housing mobility and demand. Cambridge, Mass.: Joint Center for Housing Studies. Mimeo.

Schneider, W., K. Stahl, and R. Struyk. 1985. Residential mobility in the United States and the Federal Republic of Germany. *In U.S. and West German housing markets: Comparative economic analyses,* ed. K. Stahl and R. Struyk, 23–54. Washington, D.C.: The Urban Institute Press.

Stahl, K., and R. Struyk, eds. 1985. *U.S. and West German housing markets: Comparative economic analyses.* Washington, D.C.: The Urban Institute Press.

Struyk, R. 1980. Housing adjustments of relocating elderly households. *The Gerontologist* 20 no. 1 (February): 45–55.

Struyk, R. 1986. The economic behaviour of the elderly in housing markets. Washington, D.C.: The Urban Institute. Mimeo.

# Comment    Henry O. Pollakowski

Konrad Stahl has provided us with a thorough examination of comparative U.S. and West German housing consumption and mobility among the elderly. Drawing on two large cross-sectional data bases—the U.S. Annual Housing Survey and the West German One Percent Housing Sample—he has provided us with a wealth of comparable information not previously available. He also wisely points out numerous limitations of the analysis, including comparability of data, institutional differences, possible underlying behavioral differences, and the lack of panel data.

Stahl points out that an important reason for such a comparative study is the possibility of identification of policy effects that are not otherwise identifiable. There are some important differences in the two countries' housing policies, and the hope is that a careful comparative analysis would allow for identification of policy effects. As is pointed out by Stahl, however, large differences in key housing market indicators exist between the United States and West Germany, and some of these differences may be related to behavioral differences instead of policy differences.

This point is worth pursuing further, since a primary justification for further work of this type is the possible identification of policy impacts. Use of this type of analysis for policy purposes requires the assumption of fundamentally similar behavior. It is thus useful to review the differences in housing market settings and outcomes between the two countries.

Henry O. Pollakowski is a Research Associate of the Joint Center for Housing Studies of Massachusetts Institute of Technology and Harvard University.

As summarized in Stahl and Struyk (1985), a number of factors lead to more sluggish housing market behavior in general in West Germany. The price of newly constructed dwelling units is much higher in West Germany, financing is more difficult, and, not surprisingly, the home-ownership rate is lower. The most important indicator of the greater sluggishness of the West German housing market, of course, is the much lower mobility rate.

Stahl finds that the mobility rate among the West German elderly is much lower than that for the U.S. elderly. This reflects the difference in mobility rates between the two countries for households of all ages. It is interesting to note that this difference in elderly mobility rates persists even though a presumably important factor in explaining the difference—job mobility—is of much less importance for the elderly.

What other considerations, then, should we look to to explain the large difference in elderly mobility behavior between the two countries? Again, as summarized in Stahl and Struyk (1985), several matters should be noted. Among renters, the possible effect of extensive eviction controls in West Germany must be considered. Among owners, the effect of the West German system of housing finance should be examined. The favorable terms obtained from thrift institutions in West Germany, which include long-term savings contracts, are typically lost when a household moves. (A larger proporiton of the elderly than of the entire population of homeowners, however, have no mortgage debt.) In addition, most West German homeowners have designed and built their own houses. This consideration would seem to operate more strongly in the case of the elderly, since on average they have been in their homes for a longer time than younger individuals, increasing the degree of attachment. Transaction costs are much higher in West Germany than in the U.S., and this would appear to affect the elderly more than the nonelderly. Search costs are higher, since the lower turnover rate leads to fewer vacancies at any given point in time. Also, actual relocation costs are higher because units in West Germany are usually exchanged without kitchen appliances and closets.

Sufficient panel data for West Germany were not available at the time this work was done, and Stahl points out numerous advantages of using panel data for this type of analysis. It should be added that important leads and lags exist in the process of housing consumption adjustment, and panel data are well suited for dealing with these. When comparing the housing of different age groups, the possibility that cohort effects are confounding the results must be considered. For his measure of housing consumption—rooms per head—he argues persuasively, however, that if cohort effects were properly accounted for, the result of the elderly consuming more housing would be even stronger.

Stahl finds that the elderly, especially elderly owners, consume more housing as measured in rooms per head, and that some striking differences exist between the elderly populations in terms of this measure. It is important to point out that to an important degree this result rests on the different distributions of the nonelderly and elderly populations by household type. Within each household type, consumption in terms of rooms per head is broadly similar for the nonelderly and the elderly. The elderly, however, are considerably more likely to be found in smaller households. This brings us back to evaluating the policy issue involving "overconsumption." Are younger single-person owner households "overconsuming"? The issue is an important one: Stahl does present results consistent with elderly movers choosing smaller dwellings. However, this similarity of the nonelderly and the elderly in terms of consumption by household type should be borne in mind in discussing how far the downsizing process can reasonably be expected to go.

The regression results are carefully done and provide several useful findings. Microdata are employed, and choice-based sampling is employed to make most economical use of the data.

The regression results explaining room consumption per head are interesting. Note that, especially for the pooled sample, the effects of income are remarkably similar in the U.S. and West Germany. Not surprisingly, some of the most pronounced results are obtained for the effect of household type on housing consumption. In particular, the one-person household dummies have a strong positive effect on consumption.

Turning to the logit estimates of household mobility, we note that homeownership has a greater negative effect on mobility in the U.S. than in West Germany. This is at least consistent with the West German financial disincentives to mobility being less important for the elderly. A further striking result is that percentage retired has opposite and significant effects in the two countries. In the U.S., mobility is enhanced by being retired (although only for homeowners), while in West Germany it is retarded (although here the result is strongest for renters). There is a positive effect of income on mobility for the eldelry in the U.S., but not for West Germany. Once past the age of 70, the (negative) effects of age are quite similar for the pooled samples.

Residential mobility should be viewed as the most extreme manner in which an elderly household can adjust its housing consumption. Given the high transaction costs of moving, an elderly household may instead choose to sublet part of its dwelling. An elderly household may also alter its dwelling to make it more convenient, although this adjustment will probably not have a negative effect on its housing consumption. Assessment of data required for further work in this area should take into consideration these other possible adjustments.

In assessing the issue of the elderly making housing available for younger households, the fact that the housing of the elderly is locationally fixed should be borne in mind. The value of housing freed up by the elderly depends on its location. In the U.S., for example, substantial amounts of housing in older northeastern cities are occupied by elderly persons, while substantial demand by younger households with children occurs in more suburban locations in the South or West.

## Reference

Stahl, Konrad, and Ray Struyk, eds. 1985. *U.S. and West German housing markets: Comparative economic analysis*. Washington, D.C.: The Urban Institute Press.

# 4    Household Dissolution and the Choice of Alternative Living Arrangements Among Elderly Americans

Axel Börsch-Supan

## 4.1    Introduction

A significant segment of the housing market is governed by choices and decisions made by the elderly. The importance of this segment will be even greater in the future because the share of elderly Americans in the total population will be steadily increasing. For the elderly, housing choices are more complex than the choice of housing expenditure, dwelling size, tenure, etc., of their own dwelling. In particular for the older elderly, a potential alternative to living independently is to live in one household with their adult children or to share accommodations with other elderly. The decision to dissolve the household, and the consequent choice of living arrangements, is the focus of this paper.

The choice of living arrangements is an important aspect of the well-being of the elderly and the economics of aging because of its side-effects in the provision of care and the physical environment that this choice implies. Sharing accommodations, in particular with adult children, will not only provide housing but also some degree of medical care and social support for the elderly. If elderly persons perceive sharing accommodations as an inferior housing alternative and remain living independently as long as their physical and economic means allow, this social support and a larger amount of medical care have to be picked up by society at large rather than the family or close friends.

Axel Börsch-Supan is Assistant Professor of Public Policy at the John F. Kennedy School of Government, Harvard University; Assistant Professor at the University of Dortmund (West Germany); and Faculty Research Fellow of the National Bureau of Economic Research.

Mike Tamada and Winston Lin provided valuable research assistance. Helpful comments by John Quigley and Angus Deaton were appreciated. Financial support was received from the National Institutes of Health, Institute on Aging, grant no. 1-P01-AGO5842-01.

Household dissolution decisions also have obvious consequences for the intergenerational distribution of housing. In particular, in times of tight housing market conditions with very high housing prices for newly developed units, the elderly's willingness to move out of the family home is an important parameter in the supply of more affordable existing homes. There is also the subtle question of intergenerational equity when the elderly are perceived as being "overhoused," that is, living in houses that are relatively more spacious than those of younger families with children.

This paper studies the economic and demographic determinants of the elderly's decision to continue living independently or to choose some kind of shared accommodations. The main questions being asked are:

- How many elderly live independently? Does this percentage exhibit a similar development as in the nonelderly population?
- Who are the elderly living independently? Are they younger, are they wealthier?
- How many elderly live with their children? If so, do they head the household, or are they "received" by their children?
- How many distantly related and unrelated elderly share accommodations?
- Are economic conditions (income, housing prices) important determinants for the choice between living independently or sharing accommodations? Or is the decision to give up an independent household simply determined by age and health?
- Do only the less wealthy and older elderly "seek refuge" in their childrens' homes?
- Who are the "hosts" for subfamilies? Do they tend to be richer (because they can afford supplying extra shelter) or do they tend to be poorer (because they cannot afford privacy)?

The paper is organized in three parts. We first contrast living arrangements of elderly Americans with the population under the age of 65 years, describe the changes from 1974 to 1983, and compare housing choices in SMSAs with those in nonmetropolitan areas and study regional variations. Our main result in this descriptive analysis is the discrepancy of the trends of household formation/dissolution between the elderly and the younger population; after a steady decline in the 1970s, who observe a rapid increase in the rate of "doubled-up" young families in the beginning of the 1980s. No such development can be found among elderly Americans. The proportion of the elderly living independently steadily increases in our sample period from 1974 to 1983.

In the second part, we estimate a formal choice model among living independently and six categories of alternative living arrangements. The main finding is the predominance of demographic determinants as opposed to economic explanations. This is not too surprising, but somewhat frustrating for an economist. To our relief, the data indicate a growing importance of income in this choice. We also discover a striking difference in the importance of income between the poor elderly and the well-to-do.

Finally, we employ these estimation results to explain the discrepancy in the development of household formation/dissolution between the young and the elderly.

## 4.2  Data and Household Decomposition

Our analysis is based on the Linked National Sample, 1974 to 1983, of the Annual Housing Survey, now called American Housing Survey (AHS). Our primary reason for employing the AHS is its very large sample size that allows us to make inferences about infrequent choices and to conduct subgroup analyses. The careful recording of household composition makes it possible to detect elderly living as subfamilies or as "secondary individuals" in households headed by their children or other younger persons. Another important advantage of the AHS for the study of housing decisions is its inclusion of structural housing characteristics that allow a precise definition of housing prices. Data sets such as the Panel Study of Income Dynamics (PSID) and the Retirement History Survey (RHS) allow only the construction of simple expenditure measures uncorrected for quality differences.

However, it should be pointed out that the AHS has also several severe shortcomings. Though the dwelling units are linked over time, the households or individuals living in these units are not. This prevents any dynamic analysis without stringent assumptions on the transition probabilities. The analysis in this paper is strictly cross-sectional and static; a limited dynamic version of the model in the second part of this paper is the subject of a sequel to this paper. The AHS does not contain a systematic record of the functional health status of the elderly.[1] We will depend on age as an indicator for health also, relying on the fact that age-specific medical cost and hospitalization patterns have been relatively stable for the last two decades (see Poterba and Summers 1985). Finally, the AHS includes all elderly that live in regular housing units but not the institutionalized population. Hence, the choice among alternative living arrangements excludes the choice of the continuum between congregate housing and nursing homes, alternatives that are becoming increasingly popular.[2]

Therefore, most housing data are collected on a household level, with much information about individual household members subsumed in a household total. This is the case in the Census, to some degree in the PSID, and in the AHS. However, once one realizes that many elderly do not live independently, and that the choice between living independently and sharing accommodations is an important decision, one must veiw households as an outcome of such decisions rather than an exogenously given sampling unit. If the alternative living arrangements are endogenous, the primary decision unit in housing choice analysis must be smaller than the household, and a fairly narrow definition of a family is more appropriate. A suitable decision unit is the (family-) nucleus, defined as follows:

A nucleus consists of a married couple or a single individual with all their own children below age 18.

Households are formed as an outcome of living arrangement decisions made by individual nuclei. In many cases, the household is formed by only one nucleus. Typical examples of multi-nuclei households are elderly parents in the household of their children, adult children still living in the household of their parents, or roommates. We can distinguish four types of households:

(1) Households consisting of only one nucleus.
(2) Households composed of nuclei with family relations (in this household type, child-parent relationships are of particular interest).
(3) Households composed of nuclei without family relations.
(4) Complex households, that is, a combination of the latter two types.

Therefore, our first step in analyzing the data is to create a data base in which the appropriate decision unit, the nucleus, is the sampling unit. This is achieved by detecting elderly subfamilies in existing households and splitting up households of type (2) through (4) into several nuclei. This household decomposition is based on the demographic and financial information on individual household members available in the AHS. Variables like income, nucleus size, etc., are apportioned accordingly.[3]

Our analysis will be based on 19,154 elderly nuclei. A nucleus is considered elderly if at least one person in the nucleus is above the age of 65 years. For some comparisons, we also use a "control sample" of 19,938 younger nuclei. These samples were drawn as follows. The original AHS data base consists of dwellings that are tracked through nine cross-sections from 1974 through 1983 (with the exception of 1982). First, we systematically sampled every fourth dwelling from the original AHS. Of those, every dwelling in which at least one elderly person lived was sampled, and every fourth of the remaining dwellings. We then decomposed each household according to the above rules into nuclei—cross section by cross section.

As was already mentioned, this analysis does not attempt to track individual nuclei over time. Because the AHS cross-sections are linked across time by dwelling only, households will appear and vanish in the sample whenever they move. Hence, only a panel of stayer households could be constructed. Tracking nuclei over time introduces additional difficulties, because nuclei must be identified in each cross section and then be matched over time. This matching is nontrivial because of demographic changes (death or institutionalization) that are confounded by the frequent occurrence of unreliable demographic data. Because we treat observations of the same nucleus in separate years as independent observations, the above 19,154 nuclei should more precisely be termed "nucleus-years." We estimate that the elderly sample contains approximately 5,000 different nuclei.

### 4.3 Living Arrangements

We will describe the choice of an elderly nucleus among the following seven types of living arrangements:

- Living independently (denoted by INDEP).
- Parents living in one household with their adult children either as head of this joint household (denoted by PARE-H) or as subfamily in the household headed by the adult child (denoted by PARE-S).
- Living with relatives other than adult children either as head of this joint household (denoted by DREL-H) or as subfamily in the household headed by the distant relative (denoted by DREL-S).
- Living with unrelated persons either as head of this joint household (denoted by NREL-H) or as subfamily in the household headed by the nonrelative (denoted by NREL-S)[4]

These seven types of living arrangements for the elderly are depicted in figure 4.1. Note that for elderly who do not live independently we distinguish not only among three different relations to the other household members (PARE, DREL, NREL), but also between two headship categories (HEAD and SUBF). This is important because elderly who dissolve their own household in order to live in their adult childrens' household are living in an entirely different situation than elderly who stay in their family home but provide shelter for some of their adult children. In the first case, an explicit decision to move and to dissolve the elderly's household has to be made, and the elderly person gives up the economically important function as a homeowner (or, more

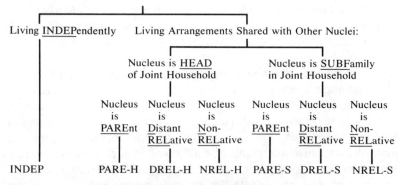

**Fig. 4.1**        Alternative living arrangements

rarely, as a renter) to become a subletee. In the second case, the elderly person avoids the important psychic and physical moving costs and keeps the status as homeowner.

For the younger nuclei, two additional living arrangements become relevant:

- Adult children living in one household with their parents either as head of this joint household (denoted by CHIL-H) or as subfamily in the household headed by the parent (denoted by CHIL-S).

Table 4.1 presents the proportions in which these living arrangements are chosen by the elderly. The data are stratified by year of cross section (1974 through 1983, except for 1982), by the four census regions (Northeast, Midwest, South, and West), and by whether the dwelling is located in an SMSA or a nonmetropolitan area. For comparison, table 4.2 presents the same proportions for younger nuclei. Based on more than 19,000 observations, the entries have a standard deviation of less than 0.36 percentage points.

More than two-third of all elderly nuclei live independently, that is, either as a married couple or as a single person forming a household. This proportion increases steadily from 1974 to 1983. More detailed tabulations show that about 32.5 percent of all elderly nuclei are elderly living together with their spouses, and about 38.5 percent are elderly living alone. Almost all of the increase in independent elderly nuclei is generated by an increase in the single-person nuclei. A continuation of this trend will have serious consequences in the delivery of health care and social support, because the elderly seem to become increasingly isolated and detached from their traditional source of medical and social support.

The percentage of elderly living independently is highest in the West and Midwest regions of the United States, lowest in the Northeast,

**Table 4.1**              **Observed Frequencies of Living Arrangements (percentages of elderly nuclei)**

|         | INDEP | PARE-H | PARE-S | DREL-H | DREL-S | NREL-H | NREL-S |       |
|---------|-------|--------|--------|--------|--------|--------|--------|-------|
| *Year*  |       |        |        |        |        |        |        |       |
| 1974    | 69.3  | 11.4   | 6.4    | 5.0    | 4.8    | 1.9    | 1.2    | 100.0 |
| 1975    | 70.4  | 11.8   | 5.9    | 4.6    | 4.4    | 1.8    | 1.2    | 100.0 |
| 1976    | 70.5  | 11.8   | 6.1    | 4.8    | 3.9    | 1.6    | 1.2    | 100.0 |
| 1977    | 70.5  | 12.4   | 5.7    | 4.9    | 3.9    | 1.5    | 1.1    | 100.0 |
| 1978    | 71.5  | 11.7   | 5.4    | 5.0    | 3.5    | 1.4    | 1.4    | 100.0 |
| 1979    | 71.5  | 11.2   | 5.3    | 4.9    | 3.9    | 1.5    | 1.6    | 100.0 |
| 1980    | 71.3  | 11.8   | 4.8    | 5.0    | 3.9    | 1.7    | 1.5    | 100.0 |
| 1981    | 71.5  | 12.5   | 4.1    | 4.4    | 4.3    | 1.9    | 1.4    | 100.0 |
| 1983    | 73.0  | 12.3   | 4.5    | 4.4    | 3.0    | 1.8    | 1.1    | 100.0 |
|         | 71.1  | 11.9   | 5.4    | 4.8    | 3.9    | 1.7    | 1.3    | 100.0 |
| *Region* |      |        |        |        |        |        |        |       |
| Northeast | 64.6 | 13.8  | 6.7    | 6.1    | 5.2    | 1.8    | 1.7    | 100.0 |
| Midwest | 74.5  | 9.3    | 5.0    | 4.3    | 3.5    | 2.0    | 1.4    | 100.0 |
| South   | 71.0  | 13.2   | 4.9    | 5.1    | 4.0    | 1.0    | .7     | 100.0 |
| West    | 74.8  | 10.5   | 5.0    | 2.9    | 2.7    | 2.4    | 1.7    | 100.0 |
|         | 71.1  | 11.9   | 5.4    | 4.8    | 3.9    | 1.7    | 1.3    | 100.0 |
| *Urban* |       |        |        |        |        |        |        |       |
| SMSA    | 68.5  | 12.7   | 6.3    | 5.1    | 3.9    | 2.0    | 1.4    | 100.0 |
| NON-SMSA | 75.0 | 10.5   | 3.8    | 4.3    | 3.9    | 1.2    | 1.1    | 100.0 |
|         | 71.1  | 11.9   | 5.4    | 4.8    | 3.9    | 1.7    | 1.3    | 100.0 |

and is much higher in rural areas as compared to metropolitan areas. The latter result is surprising and in contrast to common beliefs about rural and nonrural living arrangements.

The growing number of independent nuclei is particularly significant because it is not typical for the population at large. Comparing the trend among elderly nuclei with the development among younger nuclei (first column in tables 4.1 and 4.2) yields a striking result: there is a large discrepancy in the development of household formation and dissolution between the elderly and the young. Whereas the percentage of all elderly nuclei living independently rises from 69.3 percent in 1974 to 73.0 percent in 1983, the percentage of nuclei in the younger part of the population that lives independently fluctuates around 55 percent throughout the second half of the 1970s and then markedly declines to 52.4 percent in 1983.

How does this discrepancy come about? In particular, why is there no increase in alternative living arrangements in the early 1980s? This question will be the focus of the balance of this paper. Before discussing potential explanations, we will analyze the importance of the six dependent living arrangements.

**Table 4.2**  Observed Frequencies of Living Arrangements (percentages of young nuclei)

| | INDEP | PARE-H[a] | CHIL-H | CHIL-S | DREL-H | DREL-S | NREL-H | NREL-S | |
|---|---|---|---|---|---|---|---|---|---|
| *Year* | | | | | | | | | |
| 1974 | 55.7 | 13.5 | 1.7 | 20.0 | 3.3 | 3.7 | 1.0 | 1.7 | 100.0 |
| 1975 | 55.2 | 13.3 | 1.5 | 19.9 | 3.9 | 4.3 | .9 | 1.5 | 100.0 |
| 1976 | 55.5 | 12.6 | 1.9 | 19.4 | 4.2 | 4.5 | .9 | 1.5 | 100.0 |
| 1977 | 55.3 | 12.5 | 1.4 | 19.5 | 4.0 | 5.1 | 1.2 | 1.7 | 100.0 |
| 1978 | 54.5 | 12.4 | .9 | 20.0 | 4.0 | 4.9 | 1.7 | 2.6 | 100.0 |
| 1979 | 55.3 | 12.1 | .8 | 20.1 | 4.4 | 5.0 | 1.2 | 1.7 | 100.0 |
| 1980 | 54.1 | 12.0 | .9 | 19.2 | 4.7 | 5.5 | 1.7 | 2.8 | 100.0 |
| 1981 | 53.4 | 11.4 | 1.0 | 19.9 | 4.9 | 5.9 | 1.8 | 2.8 | 100.0 |
| 1983 | 52.4 | 12.9 | 1.0 | 20.8 | 4.4 | 5.1 | 1.8 | 2.5 | 100.0 |
| | 53.5 | 12.6 | 1.2 | 19.8 | 4.2 | 4.9 | 1.3 | 2.1 | 100.0 |
| *Region* | | | | | | | | | |
| Northeast | 50.2 | 14.2 | 1.9 | 23.8 | 3.4 | 3.8 | 1.4 | 1.9 | 100.0 |
| Midwest | 53.5 | 12.4 | 1.3 | 20.8 | 4.7 | 5.3 | 1.0 | 1.5 | 100.0 |
| South | 57.4 | 12.3 | .9 | 19.2 | 3.6 | 4.4 | 1.3 | 1.9 | 100.0 |
| West | 56.5 | 11.3 | 1.1 | 15.2 | 5.3 | 6.4 | 1.8 | 3.3 | 100.0 |
| | 53.5 | 12.6 | 1.2 | 19.8 | 4.2 | 4.9 | 1.3 | 2.1 | 100.0 |
| *Urban* | | | | | | | | | |
| SMSA | 52.0 | 12.8 | 1.4 | 20.8 | 4.5 | 5.4 | 1.5 | 2.4 | 100.0 |
| NON-SMSA | 59.8 | 12.1 | .9 | 17.9 | 3.5 | 3.8 | 1.1 | 1.5 | 100.0 |
| | 53.5 | 12.6 | 1.2 | 19.8 | 4.2 | 4.9 | 1.3 | 2.1 | 100.0 |

[a]About 0.4 percent of nuclei in PARE-S are included in PARE-H.

Living together with one's own adult children is the most important alternative living arrangement. Of the 28.9 percent of those elderly nuclei who share accommodations with other nuclei, about 60 percent live in the same household as their adult children do. In most of these cases, the elderly nucleus is household head, not the adult child. Corresponding to the increasing proportion of elderly living independently (especially living alone), parent-child households decline as alternative living arrangements. However, the relative importance of being head or subfamily in an elderly parent–adult child household shifts dramatically (columns PARE-H and PARE-S): in 1974, about 64 percent of all elderly parent–adult child households were headed by the elderly; in 1983, more than 73 percent. The percentage of parent-child nuclei is lower in the Midwest and the West, and markedly lower in nonmetropolitan areas as compared to SMSAs.

The third and fourth columns in table 4.2 (labeled CHIL-H and CHIL-S) represent the mirror image of elderly parent–adult child households, now relative to the living arrangements chosen by younger nuclei. Column three displays again the decline in headship rates of adult children in parent-children households. Note that the proportion of both elderly parent–adult child living arrangements among all living arrangements chosen by younger nuclei households stays approximately constant as opposed to the relative decline of this choice among elderly nuclei—reflecting the changing age distribution in the United States toward a higher proportion of elder Americans and a relatively declining "supply" of younger nuclei for joint households.

About 8.7 percent of all elderly nuclei live doubled-up with relatives other than their own children (categories DREL-H and DREL-S). This percentage exhibits a similar declining trend as parent-child households, from 9.8 percent in 1974 to 7.4 percent in 1983. Again, this trend is in striking contrast to the younger population in which the relative share of this kind of living arrangement increases from 7.0 percent in 1974 to 9.5 percent in 1983.

Only a very small percentage of elderly nuclei (3.0 percent) share a household with nonrelated household members (living arrangements NREL-H and NREL-S in tables 4.1 and 4.2). This percentage is more or less stable in 1974–83 and is slightly lower than the corresponding percentage in younger households (3.4 percent), where we observe a distinct increase from about 2.5 percent in 1974–76 to about 4.5 percent in the early 1980s.

## 4.4    Determinants of Living Arrangements

Who are the nuclei who live alone, and who are the nuclei who share accommodations? In this section, we will collect descriptive statistics of the most important financial and demographic characteristics by living arrangement: income, age, marital status, sex, and size of the nucleus. These variables, among others, will influence the demand for housing of each nucleus where housing choices are understood to also include the way in which accommodations are shared with other nuclei. In the case of shared accommodations, these variables will also influence the "supply" of living arrangements by the head nuclei. Short of formulating some kind of demand-supply relationship of household formulation,[5] we will display some of these variables not only by nucleus (as a determinant of demand), but also by each nucleus's respective head nucleus (as a determinant of supply).

We will first concentrate on demand. Tables 4.3 and 4.4 tabulate the income of each nucleus. Average nucleus income for elderly is $11,150 compared to $15,450 for nonelderly nuclei. (These dollar amounts correspond to 1980 figures, and are deflated with the Consumer Price Index.) The respective household incomes are $14,100 for the elderly population and $22,450 for the nonelderly. The income of the elderly is 87 percent transfer income; in turn, 80.1 percent of nonelderly nuclei earn salary or wages as their predominant income source.

Table 4.3     Income of Nuclei by Living Arrangements (elderly nuclei; hundred 1980 dollars)

|  | INDEP | PARE-H | PARE-S | DREL-H | DREL-S | NREL-H | NREL-S | |
|---|---|---|---|---|---|---|---|---|
| *Year* | | | | | | | | |
| 1974 | 113.6 | 115.4 | 52.6 | 95.5 | 54.7 | 105.8 | 1.3 | 104.7 |
| 1975 | 114.5 | 111.4 | 52.3 | 102.2 | 44.9 | 119.7 | .0 | 105.6 |
| 1976 | 116.6 | 119.7 | 55.3 | 82.1 | 52.6 | 110.6 | 1.4 | 107.6 |
| 1977 | 118.2 | 115.7 | 54.0 | 96.1 | 59.4 | 104.2 | 35.2 | 109.8 |
| 1978 | 120.2 | 131.1 | 46.2 | 91.5 | 53.2 | 96.6 | 48.7 | 112.3 |
| 1979 | 116.9 | 128.7 | 49.3 | 71.8 | 52.6 | 82.7 | 65.9 | 108.6 |
| 1980 | 116.2 | 141.9 | 45.8 | 89.1 | 50.5 | 121.9 | 48.6 | 111.0 |
| 1981 | 128.1 | 155.0 | 48.0 | 88.4 | 44.9 | 89.7 | 51.5 | 121.1 |
| 1983 | 128.3 | 152.7 | 54.2 | 102.4 | 52.8 | 91.3 | 78.3 | 123.4 |
| | 119.1 | 130.2 | 51.1 | 90.9 | 51.7 | 102.9 | 38.3 | 111.5 |
| *Region* | | | | | | | | |
| Northeast | 123.2 | 148.7 | 41.8 | 104.5 | 59.0 | 103.6 | 56.8 | 115.3 |
| Midwest | 111.8 | 119.3 | 57.1 | 91.7 | 45.6 | 91.5 | 25.8 | 105.0 |
| South | 110.6 | 109.6 | 50.0 | 72.9 | 48.9 | 99.2 | 32.6 | 102.4 |
| West | 141.3 | 161.8 | 61.7 | 111.2 | 52.4 | 120.1 | 31.8 | 133.9 |
| | 119.1 | 130.2 | 51.1 | 90.9 | 51.7 | 102.9 | 38.3 | 111.5 |
| *Urban* | | | | | | | | |
| SMSA | 129.3 | 148.9 | 50.7 | 98.6 | 50.7 | 115.0 | 34.5 | 120.5 |
| NON-SMSA | 104.7 | 95.0 | 52.1 | 76.9 | 53.2 | 72.6 | 46.2 | 97.4 |
| | 119.1 | 130.2 | 51.1 | 90.9 | 51.7 | 102.9 | 38.3 | 111.5 |

**Table 4.4**            **Income of Nuclei by Living Arrangements (young nuclei; hundred 1980 dollars)**

|  | INDEP[a] | CHIL-H | CHIL-S | DREL-H | DREL-S | NREL-H | NREL-S |
|---|---|---|---|---|---|---|---|
| *Year* |  |  |  |  |  |  |  |
| 1974 | 191.1 | 184.6 | 35.9 | 136.0 | 23.4 | 124.4 | 11.9 | 148.3 |
| 1975 | 198.0 | 214.1 | 40.0 | 142.7 | 25.1 | 120.9 | 7.6 | 153.6 |
| 1976 | 200.2 | 237.0 | 38.7 | 132.9 | 31.0 | 104.7 | 10.2 | 155.2 |
| 1977 | 198.2 | 209.1 | 37.1 | 158.5 | 80.5 | 109.1 | 53.2 | 155.9 |
| 1978 | 201.2 | 238.1 | 43.4 | 158.3 | 76.9 | 139.7 | 59.1 | 157.5 |
| 1979 | 204.7 | 155.4 | 45.5 | 141.6 | 76.2 | 141.5 | 75.0 | 160.1 |
| 1980 | 202.7 | 148.0 | 41.8 | 140.4 | 78.9 | 139.8 | 59.3 | 156.5 |
| 1981 | 205.7 | 186.9 | 37.5 | 122.2 | 67.9 | 147.4 | 67.0 | 155.0 |
| 1983 | 197.1 | 174.6 | 31.8 | 136.1 | 70.9 | 123.4 | 56.3 | 148.5 |
|  | 199.7 | 199.1 | 39.1 | 140.9 | 61.1 | 130.1 | 48.1 | 154.5 |
| *Region* |  |  |  |  |  |  |  |
| Northeast | 192.8 | 215.4 | 42.6 | 158.6 | 69.6 | 133.7 | 53.0 | 148.2 |
| Midwest | 204.7 | 187.8 | 41.5 | 139.6 | 58.9 | 132.5 | 47.9 | 156.6 |
| South | 186.6 | 182.9 | 36.9 | 134.2 | 56.9 | 121.4 | 55.8 | 147.1 |
| West | 221.5 | 210.9 | 32.8 | 137.8 | 63.5 | 135.4 | 38.1 | 170.5 |
|  | 199.7 | 199.1 | 39.1 | 140.9 | 61.1 | 130.1 | 48.1 | 154.5 |
| *Urban* |  |  |  |  |  |  |  |
| SMSA | 209.4 | 212.2 | 38.6 | 149.2 | 65.3 | 138.1 | 47.8 | 158.5 |
| NON-SMSA | 182.3 | 159.8 | 40.4 | 119.1 | 49.3 | 108.1 | 49.0 | 146.6 |
|  | 199.7 | 199.1 | 39.1 | 140.9 | 61.1 | 130.1 | 48.1 | 154.5 |

[a]INDEP category includes PARE-H category.

The row averages in the last columns of tables 4.3 and 4.4 indicate the income development from 1974 to 1983. Real income of elderly nuclei went up almost steadily from $10,470 to $12,340, essentially due to doubly indexed transfer income. This is in stark contrast to the general real income development. Real income of nonelderly nuclei essentially stayed constant in our sample period—it increased from 1974 to 1979, then decreased rapidly back to the 1974 level. If household formation is income elastic, the diverging income distribution is a formidable explanation for the discrepancy in household formation trends between the young and the elderly. The choice model in section 4.5 will try to estimate this elasticity.

The intergenerational income distribution also exhibits some interesting regional variation: for both elderly and nonelderly, income is highest in the West and higher in urban than in nonmetropolitan areas. In the Northeast, where income of young nuclei is below the national average, elderly nuclei receive an above-average real income.

Not surprisingly, there is a large income gap between nuclei living as head and nuclei living as subfamilies. Head elderly nuclei generally earn more than twice as much as subfamilies. However, this difference in income between subfamilies and head nuclei is less pronounced among elderly than among younger nuclei (table 4.4). Headship clearly has a strongly positive income elasticity. Among younger nuclei, nuclei living in any kind of shared accommodations have lower incomes than nuclei living independently. Not only headship but also living independently has a positive income elasticity for younger nuclei. This is not necessarily the case with elderly nuclei. Elderly parents who head a joint household with their adult children exhibit larger average incomes than those living independently, and their income rose dramatically from 1974 to 1983. Hence, we observe not only an increasing share of elderly who live as heads of two-generation households (table 4.1), but also that these elderly are very different from the nuclei we would most likely expect to "double-up."

The above observation may be attributable to the demand for or the supply of shared housing opportunities. The stratification by region and urbanization in table 4.3 may yield some clues to help us separate demand from supply: in metropolitan areas, in the Northeast, and in the West—where housing prices rose most during the late 1970s and early 1980s—this income gap is largest; in nonmetropolitan areas and in the South—areas less affected by housing market pressures—it is reversed. Elderly parents with an existing family home owned free and clear seem to provide an increasing amount of housing for the younger generation. Hence, this development may be a supply effect on the part of the elderly and a demand effect on the part of the younger generation.

This finding would also indicate that the supply elasticity for shared accommodations is positive, because those parents who are "host" for the younger generation appear to be wealthier than average. In general, we may distinguish two contradictory hypotheses about the supply elasticity for shared housing. In addition to the hypothesis that only a wealthy nucleus can afford being a "host" for another nucleus (positive income elasticity of supply), it may also be reasoned that only poor nuclei will offer to share accommodations with other nuclei, since in this way they can save on housing costs by splitting them with the "guest" nucleus (negative income elasticity of supply).

Table 4.5 sheds some light on this question. It tabulates the income of the head nucleus by the living arrangement of each nucleus. Hence, columns referring to head nuclei (labeled INDEP or ending in -H) are identical to table 4.3, whereas columns referring to subfamilies (labels ending with -S) now indicate the income of the respective head nucleus.

For distant relatives and nonrelatives living with each other, incomes are roughly comparable (the yearly averages for these living arrangements are based on cells with 25 to 150 observations and carry large standard deviations). Income of both host and guest nuclei are markedly

**Table 4.5**      **Income of Head by Living Arrangement of Nucleus (head nuclei of elderly nuclei; thousand 1980 dollars)**

|           | INDEP | PARE-H | PARE-S | DREL-H | DREL-S | NREL-H | NREL-S |
|-----------|-------|--------|--------|--------|--------|--------|--------|
| *Year*    |       |        |        |        |        |        |        |
| 1974      | 113.6 | 115.4  | 179.7  | 95.5   | 102.8  | 105.8  | 151.9  | 116.9 |
| 1975      | 114.5 | 111.4  | 210.4  | 102.2  | 106.4  | 119.7  | 84.2   | 118.5 |
| 1976      | 116.6 | 119.7  | 220.0  | 82.1   | 95.8   | 110.6  | 64.8   | 120.1 |
| 1977      | 118.2 | 115.7  | 226.5  | 96.1   | 106.1  | 104.2  | 66.4   | 121.7 |
| 1978      | 120.2 | 131.1  | 217.8  | 91.5   | 97.7   | 96.6   | 62.4   | 123.4 |
| 1979      | 116.9 | 128.7  | 189.5  | 71.8   | 90.1   | 82.7   | 80.6   | 117.7 |
| 1980      | 116.2 | 141.9  | 202.9  | 89.1   | 100.1  | 121.9  | 94.5   | 121.2 |
| 1981      | 128.1 | 155.0  | 198.6  | 88.4   | 97.3   | 89.7   | 92.3   | 130.1 |
| 1983      | 128.3 | 152.7  | 162.2  | 102.4  | 113.0  | 91.3   | 85.3   | 130.1 |
|           | 119.1 | 130.2  | 201.4  | 90.9   | 100.9  | 102.9  | 86.5   | 122.1 |
| *Region*  |       |        |        |        |        |        |        |
| Northeast | 123.2 | 148.7  | 207.4  | 104.5  | 85.7   | 103.6  | 109.6  | 128.7 |
| Midwest   | 111.8 | 119.3  | 197.6  | 91.7   | 107.4  | 91.5   | 63.5   | 114.7 |
| South     | 110.6 | 109.6  | 188.1  | 72.9   | 96.3   | 99.2   | 69.5   | 111.4 |
| West      | 141.3 | 161.8  | 221.5  | 111.2  | 142.9  | 120.1  | 96.7   | 145.4 |
|           | 119.1 | 130.2  | 201.4  | 90.9   | 100.9  | 102.9  | 86.5   | 122.1 |
| *Urban*   |       |        |        |        |        |        |        |
| SMSA      | 129.3 | 148.9  | 215.2  | 98.6   | 108.7  | 115.0  | 92.1   | 134.0 |
| NON-SMSA  | 104.7 | 95.0   | 166.1  | 76.9   | 88.7   | 72.6   | 74.9   | 103.5 |
|           | 119.1 | 130.2  | 201.4  | 90.9   | 100.9  | 102.9  | 86.5   | 122.1 |

lower than average. In these cases the distinction between supply and demand for shared living arrangements may be as artificial as the distinction between head nuclei and subfamilies, and we observe the generally declining tendency to double-up when income is increasing.

The situation is quite different among elderly parent–adult children households. If elderly parents live in the same household as their children, and the children are head of the household, then the children have a markedly higher income ($20,140, third column of table 4.5, roughly corresponding to the income in the second column of table 4.4, its mirror image) than the average income of young nuclei ($15,450). Conversely, if elderly parents head a two-generation household, they earn more than the average elderly nucleus ($13,020 versus $11,150). This pattern is true in all of the four census regions and in metropolitan and nonmetropolitan areas alike. This finding rejects the hypothesis of a negative income elasticity of supply of living arrangements when two-generation households are concerned.

Stated differently, economic considerations such as saving housing costs may well play a role when distantly related or unrelated nuclei double-up. Not only the demand but also the supply elasticity declines with income. The mechanisms that create two-generation households seem more complicated. Income clearly indicates which nucleus plays the headship role. The data include elderly parents who provide housing for adult children constrained by the housing affordability crisis in the late 1970s and early 1980s, and we observe adult children with above-average income who provide housing for their elderly parents. To study the economic incentives in these two-generation households more carefully, we would need to know the elderly parents' health status.

Tables 4.6 through 4.9 present the main demographic determinants of the choice among living arrangements: age, nucleus size, and sex of nucleus head, relevant mostly for single elderly nuclei.[6]

The last column of table 4.6 reflects the aging of the American population. Average age increased from 69.2 years to 69.8 years in the decade considered. It is important to realize that this change is more pronounced in the category of elderly who live independently. Once again, this points out the increasing burden of social support and health care that has to be borne by society at large rather than the immediate family. Table 4.7 displays the corresponding age profile: only after age 75 does the proportion of elderly Americans living independently decline with a corresponding increase of living arrangements within the immediate or more distant family.

**Table 4.6**     **Average Age of Nuclei by Living Arrangements (elderly nuclei; years)**

|  | INDEP | PARE-H | PARE-S | DREL-H | DREL-S | NREL-H | NREL-S |
|---|---|---|---|---|---|---|---|
| *Year* | | | | | | | |
| 1974 | 68.7 | 66.2 | 77.8 | 67.9 | 72.2 | 68.8 | 70.7 | 69.2 |
| 1975 | 68.8 | 66.2 | 75.8 | 68.6 | 72.2 | 69.1 | 71.2 | 69.1 |
| 1976 | 69.1 | 66.4 | 75.8 | 67.9 | 72.3 | 71.0 | 71.3 | 69.3 |
| 1977 | 69.3 | 66.2 | 76.8 | 68.6 | 71.8 | 70.2 | 70.6 | 69.4 |
| 1978 | 69.3 | 66.8 | 77.0 | 68.4 | 72.1 | 70.0 | 71.5 | 69.5 |
| 1979 | 69.5 | 66.5 | 76.8 | 69.2 | 72.5 | 70.7 | 72.9 | 69.7 |
| 1980 | 69.6 | 66.2 | 77.2 | 68.6 | 72.8 | 68.4 | 71.2 | 69.6 |
| 1981 | 69.6 | 66.8 | 77.6 | 68.4 | 71.9 | 68.3 | 71.2 | 69.6 |
| 1983 | 70.0 | 65.5 | 77.4 | 69.3 | 72.0 | 69.8 | 71.0 | 69.8 |
|  | 69.3 | 66.3 | 76.8 | 68.5 | 72.2 | 69.5 | 71.3 | 69.5 |
| *Region* | | | | | | | |
| Northeast | 69.6 | 66.1 | 75.4 | 69.2 | 72.2 | 67.8 | 71.1 | 69.6 |
| Midwest | 70.0 | 67.7 | 77.6 | 68.7 | 74.4 | 70.5 | 72.1 | 70.3 |
| South | 68.7 | 66.2 | 76.9 | 68.6 | 71.2 | 68.5 | 71.7 | 68.9 |
| West | 69.1 | 64.9 | 78.3 | 66.0 | 70.8 | 71.0 | 70.3 | 69.2 |
|  | 69.3 | 66.3 | 76.8 | 68.5 | 72.2 | 69.5 | 71.3 | 69.5 |
| *Urban* | | | | | | | |
| SMSA | 69.2 | 66.0 | 77.0 | 68.0 | 72.1 | 70.3 | 71.1 | 69.4 |
| NON-SMSA | 69.4 | 66.9 | 76.5 | 69.6 | 72.4 | 67.5 | 71.9 | 69.5 |
|  | 69.3 | 66.3 | 76.8 | 68.5 | 72.2 | 69.5 | 71.3 | 69.5 |

**Table 4.7**     Frequency of Living Arrangements by Age (percentage of elderly nuclei)

| Age | INDEP | PARE-H | PARE-S | DREL-H | DREL-S | NREL-H | NREL-S | |
|---|---|---|---|---|---|---|---|---|
| < 65 | 68.3 | 21.9 | 1.1 | 5.1 | 1.9 | 1.0 | .7 | 100.0 |
| 66–70 | 72.8 | 12.2 | 2.8 | 5.1 | 3.7 | 2.2 | 1.2 | 100.0 |
| 71–75 | 77.9 | 6.5 | 3.2 | 5.1 | 3.6 | 2.4 | 1.2 | 100.0 |
| 76–80 | 74.1 | 5.5 | 8.2 | 4.7 | 4.1 | 1.4 | 1.9 | 100.0 |
| > 80 | 58.9 | 8.8 | 18.1 | 3.1 | 8.0 | 1.1 | 2.0 | 100.0 |

**Table 4.8**     Size of Nucleus by Living Arrangements (elderly nuclei; number of persons)

| Year | INDEP | PARE-H | PARE-S | DREL-H | DREL-S | NREL-H | NREL-S | |
|---|---|---|---|---|---|---|---|---|
| 1974 | 1.6 | 1.7 | 1.0 | 1.6 | 1.1 | 1.2 | 1.0 | 1.5 |
| 1975 | 1.6 | 1.7 | 1.1 | 1.5 | 1.0 | 1.3 | 1.0 | 1.5 |
| 1976 | 1.5 | 1.7 | 1.1 | 1.4 | 1.1 | 1.3 | 1.0 | 1.5 |
| 1977 | 1.5 | 1.7 | 1.1 | 1.5 | 1.1 | 1.2 | 1.0 | 1.5 |
| 1978 | 1.5 | 1.7 | 1.0 | 1.5 | 1.1 | 1.3 | 1.0 | 1.5 |
| 1979 | 1.5 | 1.7 | 1.1 | 1.5 | 1.1 | 1.2 | 1.0 | 1.5 |
| 1980 | 1.5 | 1.7 | 1.0 | 1.5 | 1.0 | 1.3 | 1.0 | 1.5 |
| 1981 | 1.5 | 1.7 | 1.0 | 1.4 | 1.1 | 1.2 | 1.0 | 1.5 |
| 1983 | 1.5 | 1.7 | 1.1 | 1.4 | 1.1 | 1.1 | 1.0 | 1.5 |
| | 1.5 | 1.7 | 1.0 | 1.5 | 1.1 | 1.2 | 1.0 | 1.5 |

The columns in table 4.6 represent the relation between multi-nuclei living arrangements and age. Subfamilies tend to be older than head nuclei, a finding that may be explained by the health status of older and therefore more dependent nuclei. In the case of elderly parents living in the home of their adult children, the age of the parent nucleus is particularly high (76.8 years).[7] This relates back to the discussion of the role of income in forming two-generation households and the importance of the elderly parent's health status in that decision.

Surprising, however, is the fact that elderly parents who head a joint household with their adult children are not only younger than average nuclei, but also became even more so in the time from 1974 to 1983. It is interesting to relate this finding to the ownership rates in table 4.10. These ownership rates represent the percentage of nuclei who live in a dwelling that is owned by the head nucleus rather than rented. The second and third columns in table 4.10 show that the average ownership rates of a two-generation family home are virtually unchanged in our sample period. However, the proportion of family homes owned by the elderly parent increases, whereas the proportion of homes owned by the younger generation declines.

**Table 4.9**          Sex of Nucleus-Head by Living Arrangement (elderly nuclei; percent female)

|  | INDEP | PARE-H | PARE-S | DREL-H | DREL-S | NREL-H | NREL-S |
|---|---|---|---|---|---|---|---|
| *Year* | | | | | | | |
| 1974 | 38.6 | 37.1 | 79.7 | 38.9 | 66.7 | 47.6 | 52.0 | 42.7 |
| 1975 | 38.4 | 36.3 | 77.6 | 42.8 | 73.1 | 55.2 | 38.5 | 42.5 |
| 1976 | 39.3 | 37.0 | 76.5 | 50.5 | 64.4 | 50.0 | 44.4 | 43.1 |
| 1977 | 39.8 | 35.0 | 79.5 | 42.6 | 61.2 | 54.8 | 47.8 | 42.7 |
| 1978 | 39.5 | 36.2 | 82.5 | 37.1 | 67.6 | 63.3 | 48.3 | 42.8 |
| 1979 | 39.7 | 35.1 | 79.7 | 45.2 | 66.7 | 66.7 | 48.6 | 43.2 |
| 1980 | 41.5 | 35.2 | 84.0 | 43.6 | 68.6 | 63.1 | 42.4 | 44.4 |
| 1981 | 43.6 | 39.9 | 85.3 | 52.5 | 73.1 | 60.0 | 38.5 | 46.7 |
| 1983 | 41.5 | 34.5 | 80.6 | 53.5 | 66.2 | 53.7 | 46.2 | 44.0 |
|  | 40.2 | 36.2 | 80.2 | 45.0 | 67.5 | 56.8 | 45.2 | 43.5 |
| *Region* | | | | | | | |
| Northeast | 43.0 | 30.3 | 85.0 | 47.0 | 70.3 | 50.0 | 55.0 | 46.1 |
| Midwest | 43.1 | 43.1 | 83.7 | 46.1 | 77.4 | 63.6 | 20.0 | 46.5 |
| South | 39.1 | 39.8 | 70.8 | 46.8 | 62.3 | 69.7 | 45.7 | 42.5 |
| West | 34.1 | 28.7 | 83.9 | 30.1 | 55.2 | 44.2 | 63.0 | 37.2 |
|  | 40.2 | 36.2 | 80.2 | 45.0 | 67.5 | 56.8 | 45.2 | 43.5 |
| *Urban* | | | | | | | |
| SMSA | 40.1 | 35.7 | 82.5 | 45.6 | 68.0 | 62.1 | 47.9 | 44.2 |
| NON-SMSA | 40.3 | 37.1 | 74.3 | 43.8 | 66.8 | 43.5 | 39.5 | 42.5 |
|  | 40.2 | 36.2 | 80.2 | 45.0 | 67.5 | 56.8 | 45.2 | 43.5 |

Furthermore, the age profiles in the second and third columns of table 4.10 show the reversal of roles with increasing age, the crucial age being 75 years, after which more elderly become subfamilies rather than heads and at which the rate of independently living elderly nuclei peaks. Except for the small category of NREL-S, the attractiveness

**Table 4.10**          Ownership Rates of Head Nuclei by Living Arrangements (elderly nuclei; percent homeowners)

| Year | INDEP | PARE-H | PARE-S | DREL-H | DREL-S | NREL-H | NREL-S |
|---|---|---|---|---|---|---|---|
| 1974 | 70.3 | 79.0 | 89.1 | 75.9 | 67.6 | 61.9 | 68.0 | 72.5 |
| 1975 | 70.2 | 78.5 | 83.2 | 78.6 | 69.9 | 65.8 | 69.2 | 72.2 |
| 1976 | 70.1 | 75.9 | 83.8 | 78.5 | 72.4 | 66.7 | 55.6 | 71.9 |
| 1977 | 71.4 | 75.9 | 82.9 | 84.2 | 80.0 | 67.7 | 60.9 | 73.4 |
| 1978 | 71.0 | 79.3 | 83.3 | 86.7 | 74.3 | 70.0 | 62.1 | 73.4 |
| 1979 | 70.8 | 78.3 | 84.1 | 83.7 | 77.4 | 54.6 | 54.3 | 72.7 |
| 1980 | 71.5 | 79.7 | 84.9 | 80.0 | 72.1 | 57.9 | 57.6 | 73.1 |
| 1981 | 70.7 | 83.3 | 86.7 | 76.2 | 74.4 | 62.9 | 61.5 | 73.0 |
| 1983 | 73.6 | 84.7 | 83.5 | 74.3 | 76.5 | 61.0 | 65.4 | 75.2 |
|  | 71.1 | 79.4 | 84.6 | 79.9 | 73.5 | 63.0 | 61.2 | 73.0 |

of all other living arrangements also strongly declines after the age of 75. In passing, note the low ownership rates of living arrangements among nonrelatives. All age patterns exhibit little variation across regions and degree of urbanization (see table 4.6).

Tables 4.8 and 4.9 shed more light on the demographic characteristics of living arrangements, particularly two-generation households. Elderly living in the household headed by their adult children are almost always single and mostly female, whereas elderly parents who are heads in a two-generation household are more often but by no means exclusively couples. Living arrangements with nonrelatives are most frequently chosen by single male elderly persons, particularly in the Midwest.

### 4.5    A Multinomial Logit Model of the Choice among Living Arrangements

The descriptive analysis in section 4.4 pointed out some important changes in the way elderly Americans live. In addition to the intergenerational shift in ownership patterns among two-generation households, the most striking change is the unexpectedly large increase in the proportion of elderly Americans living independently as opposed to the reversal of headship rates in the younger population.

What factors are generating the difference in household formation/dissolution patterns between the elderly and the young? There are two primary hypotheses. The first could be termed the "inertia hypothesis." Low mobility, caused by relatively higher monetary and nonmonetary moving costs for the elderly, creates a slow adaptation of housing patterns to a changing economic environment among the elderly. Market forces that may induce trends in the general market will only very slowly shift consumption patterns of the elderly. With an increasing share of the population becoming elderly, the proportion of elderly living independently among all households will rise. A relatively decreasing "supply" of younger households because of the change in the age distribution will also increase the proportion of elderly living independently among all elderly nuclei.

The second, the "income distribution hypothesis," rests on the observation that the economic environment has actually changed much less for the elderly than for the younger population. Whereas real income rose in the 1970s and then sharply declined in the beginning of the 1980s for younger families, this was not the case for the elderly. The same holds for housing prices. Housing prices were rising drastically at the beginning of the 1980s, but most elderly were already sitting in houses owned free and clear that appreciated during that period but without a proportional increase in cash costs.

To distinguish between both hypotheses, we need to estimate the price and income elasticities of the proportions in which living arrangements are chosen, as well as to contrast these elasticities with the influence of demographic variables. We will estimate a variant of the multinomial logit model describing the choice among the seven alternative living arrangements introduced in section 4.3 and depicted in figure 4.1.

We consider the most frequent choice of living independently as the base category and measure the attractiveness of the remaining six choices relative to this category. We postulate that the attractiveness or (dis-)-utility of each alternative relative to living independently can be decomposed into three additive components. The first component describes the (dis-)utility of sharing accommodations either as head of the joint household (denoted by HEAD) or as subfamily (denoted by SUBF). The second component describes the attractiveness of the partners, that is the (dis-)utility an elderly nucleus receives from living with distant relatives (denoted by DREL) or with unrelated persons (denoted by NREL). Living as elderly parents with adult children (denoted by PARE) serves as the base category for shared living arrangements.

These utility components are a deterministic function $v$ of regional housing prices (denoted by PRI), nucleus income (INC), age of nucleus members (AGE), the size of the nucleus (PER), and the sex of the nucleus head (SEX), comprised in the vector $\mathbf{X}$. In addition, a random utility component $\mu_i$ represents all unmeasurable factors that characterize each alternative. Using the symbols in figure 4.1, total (dis-)utility $u_i$ becomes:

$$
\begin{aligned}
(1) \quad u_{\text{PARE}-\text{H}} - u_{\text{INDEP}} &= v_{\text{HEAD}}(\mathbf{X}) & &+ \mu_1, \\
u_{\text{DREL}-\text{H}} - u_{\text{INDEP}} &= v_{\text{HEAD}}(\mathbf{X}) + v_{\text{DREL}}(\mathbf{X}) + \mu_2, \\
u_{\text{NREL}-\text{H}} - u_{\text{INDEP}} &= v_{\text{HEAD}}(\mathbf{X}) + v_{\text{NREL}}(\mathbf{X}) + \mu_3, \\
u_{\text{PARE}-\text{S}} - u_{\text{INDEP}} &= v_{\text{SUBF}}(\mathbf{X}) & &+ \mu_4, \\
u_{\text{DREL}-\text{S}} - u_{\text{INDEP}} &= v_{\text{SUBF}}(\mathbf{X}) + v_{\text{DREL}}(\mathbf{X}) + \mu_5, \\
u_{\text{NREL}-\text{S}} - u_{\text{INDEP}} &= v_{\text{SUBF}}(\mathbf{X}) + v_{\text{NREL}}(\mathbf{X}) + \mu_6.
\end{aligned}
$$

We assume that the $\mu_i$ are mutually independent and logistically distributed and specify functions $v$ linear in the explanatory variables. Hence, the probability of choosing the alternative with the highest attractiveness is of the familiar multinomial logit form (McFadden 1973).

Several comments are appropriate concerning the choice of this model. First, all explanatory variables are nucleus-specific, but not alternative-specific. An alternative model commonly used in this situation is the logit model with alternative-specific coefficients, where for each relative utility component

(2)    $u_i - u_{\text{INDEP}} = \mathbf{X}'\beta_i + \mu_i,$

$$i = 1, \ldots, 6 \text{ or PARE-H}, \ldots, \text{NREL-S.}$$

Our specification simply economizes on the number of parameters by imposing a set of linear restrictions on the $\beta_i$:

(3)    $\beta_1 - \beta_2 = \beta_4 - \beta_5,$ and $\beta_1 - \beta_3 = \beta_4 - \beta_6.$

In addition, these restrictions reflect a nonhierarchical pattern of similarities among the alternatives.

Second, it would be desirable to allow for a more flexible specification of the distribution of the unobserved utility components $\mu_i$. After excluding a general multivariate normal distribution because of its computational intractability, an obvious choice is the generalized extreme value distribution leading to the nested multinomial logit (NMNL) model. However, the NMNL model is not identified in the context of explanatory variables that do not vary across alternatives.[8]

Finally, the data include repeated observations of the same nucleus but treat each observation independently. This assumption requires that all nucleus-specific time-invariant utility components be included in the explanatory variables. We are well aware that if in fact the unobserved characteristics $\mu_i$ correlate over time, the logit model will produce inconsistent estimates. It is possible to correct for this potential inconsistency by conditioning on the time-invariant, unobserved nucleus characteristics (Chamberlain 1980). However, with nine cross sections, this approach is prohibitively costly. Little is known about the magnitude of this bias in the coefficients.[9] The longitudinal nature of the data will also deflate the standard errors. Assuming essentially unbiased estimates, the correct standard errors should be approximately twice as large as reported.[10]

Table 4.11 presents parameter estimates of the choice model. The estimates are based on a choice-based subsample of all 19,154 nuclei. The subsample includes all nuclei that live with nonrelatives, a 0.05 percent random sample of independent nuclei, and intermediate-sized random sample of nuclei in other living arrangements. The subsample includes 3,081 nuclei and substantially economizes the estimation, while including a sufficiently large number of observations for each living arrangement to guarantee reliable estimation results. To correct for the case-controlled or choice-based subsampling, the estimation procedure re-weights each observation. The weights (the ratio of the percentage of each alternative in the original sample over the percentage in the subsample) vary by income class and cross section. The estimation approach is a slight generalization of the weighted exogenous sampling maximum likelihood (WESML) estimator proposed by Manski and Lerman (1977).[11]

A striking result in table 4.11 is the predominance of demographic variables relative to economic determinants. The coefficients measuring housing prices are insignificant, the income elasticities are surprisingly small. In contrast, age, nucleus size, and sex of single person nuclei determine most of the observed variation in choices among living arrangements. The overall fit, measured as the ratio of optimal over diffuse likelihood value, is quite satisfactory.

We will first discuss the age variables. Nucleus age refers to the average age of nucleus head and spouse; its sample mean is about 70 years. To be able to capture the important differences in housing choices before and after age 75 discovered in table 4.7, we include age linearly (measured in years) as well as quadratically (measured in squared years divided by 100). The probability of living as a subfamily increases with

**Table 4.11          Multinomial Logit Estimates of Living Arrangement Choices**

| Variable | Utility Component | Estimate | Std. Error | t-Statistic |
|---|---|---|---|---|
| Price | Subfamily | −.0185 | .0266 | −.69 |
| Price | Head | −.0043 | .0233 | −.18 |
| Price | Distant relative | .0274 | .0212 | 1.29 |
| Price | Non-relative | .0197 | .0262 | .75 |
| Income | Subfamily | −.1061 | .0177 | −5.97 |
| Income | Head | −.0013 | .0044 | −.31 |
| Income | Distant relative | −.0421 | .0079 | −5.27 |
| Income | Non-relative | −.0208 | .0095 | −2.17 |
| Age | Subfamily | −.0300 | .0125 | −2.39 |
| Age sq. | Subfamily | .0521 | .0126 | 4.11 |
| Age | Head | −.0691 | .0124 | −5.53 |
| Age sq. | Head | .0374 | .0138 | 2.70 |
| Age | Distant relative | .0616 | .0121 | 5.07 |
| Age sq. | Distant relative | −.0671 | .0124 | −5.40 |
| Age | Non-relative | .1136 | .0137 | 8.24 |
| Age sq. | Non-relative | −.1144 | .0145 | −7.89 |
| Persons | Subfamily | −1.8548 | .2159 | −8.58 |
| Persons | Head | .6145 | .1433 | 4.28 |
| Persons | Distant relative | −.7961 | .1826 | −4.35 |
| Persons | Non-relative | −2.5076 | .2248 | −11.15 |
| Female | Subfamily | −.0075 | .1607 | −.04 |
| Female | Head | .4760 | .1732 | 2.74 |
| Female | Distant relative | −.4730 | .1543 | −3.06 |
| Female | Non-relative | −1.2829 | .1497 | −8.56 |
| Log likelihood at optimum | −3,159.5 | | | |
| Log likelihood at zero | −5,995.3 | | | |
| Number of observations | 3,081 | | | |

*Note:* Estimates are obtained by weighted exogenous sampling maximum likelihood (WESML). Standard errors are not corrected for intertemporal correlations.

old age; correspondingly, headship rates decline. However, at ages below 75 years, becoming one year older still decreases the log-odds of being a subfamily rather than living independently. The probabilities of the HEAD alternatives decline uniformly in the relevant age range, whereas the tendency to move as an elderly parent to a home headed by an adult child increases steadily. All these patterns correspond to simple intuition and the tabulations in section 4.4. We will compute these predicted age profiles in more detail below.

The variable PER (persons) represents the number of persons in the nucleus, therefore also the marital status of its head (PER = 1, if the elderly person is widowed, divorced, or never married, in general PER = 2 otherwise).[12] Not surprisingly, elderly couples strongly prefer to live independently. If they share housing, they prefer to head the joint household, other things being equal. They regard doubling-up with nonrelatives as a strongly inferior alternative. The odds of preferring such a living arrangement are about 12 times lower than for single elderly.

The variable FEM (female) indicates that the head of the nucleus is female which is relevant for one-person nuclei. After correcting for differences in income and age between single male and single female elderly, males are much more likely to live together with nonrelated persons in one household; the odds of their choosing this alternative being 3.6 times higher than among female persons.

Of the economic variables, PRI (price) denotes a housing price index of owner-occupied housing computed by Brown and Yinger (1986). The index represents after-tax user cost of a typical single-family home and includes historical appreciation as well as the federal income tax advantages of homeownership for the relevant income range. Because of the very large ownership rates, an owner-oriented price index seems to be the most appropriate index of housing costs for the elderly. The index is computed from AHS tabulations. The index is not SMSA-specific and varies only by the four census regions: Northeast, Midwest, South, and West. However, regional and intertemporal price variation is very large because the second half of the sample period encompasses the rapid rise in housing costs, starting in the West, then picking up in the remainder of the United States. In spite of this dramatic change in housing prices, virtually no price effect can be found in our estimation.

The variable INC (income) represents the nucleus's currrent income, measured in $1,000 per year deflated by the Consumer Price Index with base year 1980. Its sample mean is about 10.0. The estimated coefficients indicate a precisely measured, but surprisingly small, income effect in favor of living independently. The log-odds ratio of choosing to live as a subfamily rather than independently decreases by 0.1061 for an income increase of $1,000. At first sight, these results seem to reject the "income distribution hypothesis" in favor of the notion that housing consumption of the elderly is very inert. Even if the income of the elderly had declined as much as in the general population, the lack of responsiveness of household dissolution decisions to income changes would have predicted an essentially unchanged housing consumption pattern.

Because the author of this paper is an economist, not a demographer, the paper would have ended at this point. However, believing in economics after all, we reestimated the model in two different ways. First, the sample was stratified into three income classes and each income class estimated separately. Second, the pooled cross sections were decomposed into an early sample period (1974–76), a middle period (1977–79), and a late period (1980–83).

Table 4.12 presents the results stratified by income class. The lower income class extends to $5,000 per year, and the upper income class begins with a yearly income in excess of $10,000.

Quite clearly, there are very strong differences between the income classes. The statistical hypothesis that the estimated relationships are homogenous with respect to income class can easily be rejected.[13] Whereas the coefficients for housing prices and demographic variables are essentially stable, most of this difference can be found in the income variable. Low-income nuclei are highly income responsive, about 5 times as much as was estimated in the pooled regression in table 4.11. Income responses among the other two income groups are essentially insignificant, while a perverse sign characterizes the middle-income group.[14] Low-income elderly comprise almost half of the sample (1,404 out of 3,081). Hence, the aggregation error in table 4.11 is considerable, and we will use this disaggregate model for the applications in section 4.6.

The result of high income elasticities among the poor elderly corresponds to earlier findings that predicted very elastic household formation rates for single elderly women participating in a general housing allowances program (Börsch-Supan 1986). It also revives the hypothesis that without the double indexation of Social Security income the United States may have experienced a much larger incidence of doubling-up among the elderly than was actually the case. For more affluent elderly, economic considerations appear to be irrelevant in the decision about living arrangements.

We performed a second sample stratification to investigate whether tastes have changed from 1974 to 1983, reestimating the model separately for the periods 1974–76, 1977–79, and 1980–83. This decomposition also alleviates the econometric problems of pooling cross sections in the presence of unobserved nucleus-specific but time-

**Table 4.12**    **Multinomial Logit Estimates After Income Stratification**

| Variable | Income < $5,000 | | $5,000 – $10,000 | | Income > $10,000 | |
|---|---|---|---|---|---|---|
| | Estimate | t-Stat. | Estimate | t-Stat. | Estimate | t-Stat. |
| PRI*SUBF | −.0074 | −.18 | −.0299 | −.60 | −.0107 | −.23 |
| PRI*HEAD | −.0230 | −.55 | −.1036 | −2.08 | .0717 | 2.02 |
| PRI*DREL | .0286 | .92 | .0797 | 1.67 | .0037 | .10 |
| PRI*NREL | .0409 | 1.03 | .0284 | .54 | −.0086 | −.19 |
| INC*SUBF | −.5191 | −7.26 | .1701 | 2.15 | −.0162 | −1.18 |
| INC*HEAD | −.1186 | −1.56 | .1765 | 2.26 | −.0115 | −1.84 |
| INC*DREL | −.0799 | −1.69 | −.0755 | −1.05 | −.0173 | −1.93 |
| INC*NREL | −.2780 | −4.80 | −.1123 | −1.42 | .0112 | 1.13 |
| AGE*SUBF | .0168 | .86 | −.1489 | −5.47 | −.1068 | −3.76 |
| AG²*SUBF | .0204 | 1.12 | .1534 | 6.04 | .1370 | 4.45 |
| AGE*HEAD | −.0812 | −4.06 | −.0911 | −2.88 | .0005 | .02 |
| AG²*HEAD | .0617 | 3.06 | .0475 | 1.50 | −.0600 | −2.09 |
| AGE*DREL | .0550 | 3.47 | .0682 | 2.33 | .0761 | 2.69 |
| AG²*DREL | −.0645 | −4.12 | −.0721 | −2.58 | −.0669 | −2.22 |
| AGE*NREL | .1381 | 6.70 | .0871 | 2.80 | .0537 | 1.89 |
| AG²*NREL | −.1380 | −6.88 | −.0853 | −2.87 | −.0223 | −.73 |
| PER*SUBF | −2.1678 | −5.70 | −1.2889 | −3.39 | −1.9998 | −5.10 |
| PER*HEAD | .7366 | 2.61 | .5017 | 1.90 | .4561 | 1.88 |
| PER*DREL | −.4670 | −1.71 | −.8342 | −2.99 | −1.6117 | −4.58 |
| PER*NREL | −2.4771 | −5.49 | −1.6769 | −4.54 | −3.0806 | −7.81 |
| FEM*SUBF | −.2018 | −.87 | .6367 | 2.01 | .1913 | .54 |
| FEM*HEAD | .4550 | 1.64 | .7059 | 2.16 | .1121 | .32 |
| FEM*DREL | −.3232 | −1.61 | −.8141 | −2.77 | −.7886 | −2.13 |
| FEM*NREL | −1.2613 | −6.45 | −1.1145 | −3.40 | −1.2541 | −3.63 |
| Log likelihood at optimum | −1702.4 | | −729.6 | | −633.4 | |
| Log likelihood at zero | −2732.1 | | −1562.6 | | −1700.7 | |
| Number of observations | 1404 | | 803 | | 874 | |

*Note:* See table 4.11.

invariant utility components. Estimated coefficients are presented in table 4.13. The results are qualitatively unchanged from table 4.11, and the likelihood ratio test version of the Chow-test is insignificant. If any at all, the income elasticities show a rising tendency both in terms of magnitude and significance. The stability of the results is a fair indication that the potential inconsistency of the logit results may not be a severe problem in this data set.

## 4.6  Simulations and Applications of the Model

What do the magnitudes of the estimated coefficients imply? How do living arrangement decisions vary by age and income? Are the estimated income effects sufficiently large to explain the discrepancy

**Table 4.13**    **Multinomial Logit Estimates for Three Time Periods**

| | 1974–76 | | 1977–79 | | 1980–83 | |
|---|---|---|---|---|---|---|
| Variable | Estimate | t-Stat. | Estimate | t-Stat. | Estimate | t-Stat. |
| PRI*SUBF | .0193 | .31 | .0273 | .54 | −.0134 | −.17 |
| PRI*HEAD | .0335 | .57 | .0094 | .22 | −.1055 | −1.54 |
| PRI*DREL | .0863 | 1.68 | −.0214 | −.56 | .1085 | 1.78 |
| PRI*NREL | .0108 | .17 | −.0532 | −1.15 | .1306 | 1.68 |
| INC*SUBF | −.0923 | −2.87 | −.0988 | −3.41 | −.1275 | −4.43 |
| INC*HEAD | −.0065 | −.91 | −.0088 | −1.05 | .0095 | 1.23 |
| INC*DREL | −.0204 | −1.66 | −.0440 | −2.96 | −.0714 | −4.37 |
| INC*NREL | −.0415 | −1.42 | −.0047 | −.32 | −.0238 | −1.69 |
| AGE*SUBF | −.0472 | −2.04 | −.0143 | −.66 | −.0365 | −1.52 |
| AG²*SUBF | −.0737 | 3.22 | .0399 | 1.81 | .0464 | 2.03 |
| AGE*HEAD | −.0865 | −3.82 | −.0779 | −3.46 | −.0401 | −1.77 |
| AG²*HEAD | −.0539 | 2.22 | .0509 | 1.99 | .0073 | .31 |
| AGE*DREL | .0682 | 2.61 | .0520 | 2.74 | .0585 | 2.80 |
| AG²*DREL | −.0771 | −3.19 | −.0577 | −2.72 | −.0612 | −2.91 |
| AGE*NREL | .1207 | 5.19 | .0868 | 3.38 | .1216 | 4.81 |
| AG²*NREL | −.1255 | −5.18 | −.0858 | −3.17 | −.1225 | −4.78 |
| PER*SUBF | −1.8601 | −4.42 | −2.3011 | −6.20 | −1.3585 | −3.98 |
| PER*HEAD | .8139 | 2.85 | .6307 | 2.60 | .5294 | 2.27 |
| PER*DREL | −1.0270 | −2.13 | −.5433 | −2.50 | −.9856 | −3.60 |
| PER*NREL | −2.2964 | −6.23 | 2.2766 | −5.16 | −2.9720 | −7.61 |
| FEM*SUBF | .0257 | .09 | −.1337 | −.46 | .2011 | .73 |
| FEM*HEAD | .6700 | 2.12 | .3791 | 1.23 | .4587 | 1.56 |
| FEM*DREL | −.4467 | −1.45 | −.4575 | −1.84 | −.6428 | −2.41 |
| FEM*NREL | −1.4096 | −5.38 | −.9965 | −3.86 | −1.4841 | −5.41 |
| Log likelihood at optimum | −1101.0 | | −1045.4 | | −998.5 | |
| Log likelihood at zero | −2027.6 | | −2006.2 | | −1961.5 | |
| Number of observations | 1042 | | 1031 | | 1008. | |

*Note:* See table 4.11

between declining headship rates among young nuclei and a rising proportion of elderly living independently in the early 1980s? We will try to answer these questions by evaluating predicted choice probabilities generated by the multinomial logit models in table 4.12 in various scenarios.

Table 4.14 presents predicted age profiles for the three income classes. Clearly, poorer elderly not only have a lower tendency to live independently but also give up this status earlier than elderly with higher incomes. The reversal in the choice probability of living independently occurs at 70.5 years for elderly nuclei with yearly incomes below $5,000, at 75.5 years for the middle-income group, and at 78.5 years for those elderly nuclei who receive more than $10,000 yearly.

**Table 4.14**      **Household Dissolution of Elderly Americans by Age and Income**

| Age | INDEP | PARE-H | PARE-S | DREL-H | DREL-S | NREL-H | NREL-S |
|---|---|---|---|---|---|---|---|
| | | | *Nuclei with income < $5,000* | | | | |
| 60 | 69.0 | 11.0 | 3.1 | 10.9 | 3.0 | 2.3 | .6 |
| 65 | 69.8 | 10.9 | 3.8 | 9.5 | 3.3 | 1.9 | .7 |
| 70 | 70.1 | 11.1 | 4.8 | 8.2 | 3.6 | 1.5 | .7 |
| 75 | 69.9 | 11.5 | 6.0 | 7.1 | 3.7 | 1.2 | .6 |
| 80 | 69.1 | 12.2 | 7.6 | 6.0 | 3.7 | .8 | .5 |
| 85 | 67.6 | 13.2 | 9.5 | 5.0 | 3.6 | .6 | .4 |
| 90 | 65.2 | 14.6 | 12.0 | 4.1 | 3.4 | .4 | .3 |
| 95 | 61.9 | 16.3 | 14.9 | 3.4 | 3.1 | .2 | .2 |
| | | | *Nuclei with income $5,000 − $10,000* | | | | |
| 60 | 73.2 | 12.3 | 1.6 | 8.6 | 1.1 | 2.8 | .4 |
| 65 | 76.2 | 10.9 | 2.1 | 6.8 | 1.3 | 2.3 | .4 |
| 70 | 78.3 | 9.8 | 2.8 | 5.3 | 1.5 | 1.8 | .5 |
| 75 | 79.2 | 8.9 | 4.2 | 4.0 | 1.9 | 1.3 | .6 |
| 80 | 78.5 | 8.1 | 6.4 | 2.9 | 2.3 | 1.0 | .8 |
| 85 | 75.7 | 7.3 | 10.4 | 2.0 | 2.9 | .7 | 1.0 |
| 90 | 69.5 | 6.4 | 17.4 | 1.4 | 3.7 | .4 | 1.2 |
| 95 | 58.9 | 5.4 | 28.9 | .8 | 4.4 | .3 | 1.4 |
| | | | *Nuclei with income > $10,000* | | | | |
| 60 | 73.6 | 16.9 | .7 | 6.8 | .3 | 1.6 | .1 |
| 65 | 79.6 | 12.6 | 1.1 | 4.9 | .4 | 1.4 | .1 |
| 70 | 84.3 | 8.9 | 1.7 | 3.2 | .6 | 1.1 | .2 |
| 75 | 87.3 | 6.0 | 2.7 | 1.9 | .9 | .8 | .4 |
| 80 | 87.9 | 3.8 | 4.7 | 1.1 | 1.3 | .6 | .7 |
| 85 | 85.3 | 2.2 | 8.2 | .5 | 2.0 | .4 | 1.4 |
| 90 | 78.2 | 1.2 | 14.7 | .2 | 2.8 | .2 | 2.6 |
| 95 | 65.1 | .6 | 25.4 | .1 | 3.9 | .1 | 4.8 |

*Note:* All predictions are based on the disaggregate model in table 4.12.

Once they dissolve their households, the upper-income classes are more likely to be received by their adult children or by more distant relatives. The pattern is different for poorer elderly among whom a large proportion stays head of a two-generation household. As opposed to the low-income strata, elderly nuclei with incomes above $5,000 become increasingly likely to also be received by distant or unrelated persons. However, this trend is statistically insignificant.

Which living arrangements would elderly Americans have chosen in the absence of the rise in real income generated by Social Security indexation? Table 4.15 presents estimated changes that would have occurred if the income of elderly nuclei had exhibited a similar development as the income of younger nuclei. Using the observed income at 1974, we computed the hypothetical elderly's income by using an income index calculated from the sample of young nuclei. Columns 1 and 3 display the changes between this and the baseline prediction for

Table 4.15    Predicted Proportions of Nuclei Living Independently if Income
of Elderly had Developed as General Income (changes;
percentage points)

| | Low Income Elderly | | All Elderly Nuclei | | Young Nuclei |
|---|---|---|---|---|---|
| | Predicted Change Versus Baseline | Predicted Change Versus Prev. Year | Predicted Change Versus Prev. Year | Predicted Change Versus Prev. Year | Actual Change Versus Prev. Year |
| 1974 | .0 | .0 | .0 | .0 | .0 |
| 1975 | −1.1 | −.9 | −.4 | −.3 | −.5 |
| 1976 | −1.2 | .3 | −.4 | .1 | .3 |
| 1977 | −1.3 | .2 | −.4 | .1 | −.2 |
| 1978 | −.8 | 1.0 | −.2 | .3 | −.8 |
| 1979 | −.6 | −.5 | −.2 | −.2 | .8 |
| 1980 | −2.2 | −1.2 | −.7 | −.4 | −1.2 |
| 1981 | −3.6 | .3 | −1.1 | .1 | −.7 |
| 1983 | −4.8 | −.7 | −1.4 | −.2 | −1.0 |

*Note:* The entries in columns 1 and 3 represent the differences between baseline prediction (using the elderly's actual income) and alternative prediction (deflating the elderly's income at the rate of the general income develpment). The entries in columns 2
and 4 represent the yearly changes of the alternative prediction. Column 5 represents
the yearly changes of the actual proportions among young nuclei (table 4.2). All predictions are based on the disaggregate model in table 4.12.

nuclei with income below $5,000 and for all nuclei. The differences are
substantial for poor nuclei, but they are not large enough to explain a
similar decrease in headship rates among all elderly as was observed
among young nuclei. This is indicated in columns 2, 4, and 5, which
compare the yearly changes in the proportion of elderly living independently with the actural changes in this category among the young
nuclei.

We conclude that the divergence in the income development substantially contributed to the steady increase in the proportion of elderly
living independently, but that this explanation in itself is not sufficient
to account for the entire discrepancy in choosing living arrangements
between young and elderly Americans.

### 4.7    Summary of Conclusions

1. About a third of all nuclei with at least one elderly person do not
live independently. As opposed to an increase in the proportion of
doubled-up households in the general population in the early 1980s,
this percentage has fallen among elderly Americans.

2. The emerging discrepancy in living arrangement choices between
young and elderly can only partially be explained by the discrepancy

in the income development from 1974 to 1983. The residual may be attributed to inertia due to low mobility and slow adaptation to economic changes.

3. More than 17 percent of all elderly nuclei live with their adult children. In most of these cases, the parents head the common household. If the children are household heads, the parents are usually single and old with a small income.

4. Within these two-generation households, important intergenerational changes occurred from 1974 to 1983. An increasing percentage of these households are headed by the parent generation rather than the adult child. We speculate that this development can be attributed to the housing affordability crisis among young first-time home buyers.

5. Few elderly live with distant relatives (the proportion is less than 9 percent), and very few elderly share the household with nonrelatives (about 3 percent).

6. The choice probabilities among living arrangements are predominantly determined by demographic variables. There is no evidence that they respond to an aggregate price index of owner-occupied housing.

7. The "demand elasticity for shared accommodations" with respect to income is strongly negative for elderly with low incomes. However, for elderly nuclei with yearly incomes in excess of $5,000, the income elasticity is insignificant after correcting for demographic variables.

8. In elderly parents–adult children households, there is some evidence that the corresponding "supply elasticity for shared accommodations" with respect to income is positive: children who "receive" their parents have about twice than average nucleus income.

# Notes

1. The 1978 National Sample contains a supplement on disabilities.

2. The AHS can be augmented with data from the National Nursing Home Survey. This is a subject for further research.

3. The creation of this data base is a large, mostly mechanical task that is not particularly glamorous but devoured most of the work for this paper.

4. Complex households are assigned to the above categories in the stated order.

5. See Becker's (1981) treatise or the paper by Ermisch (1981).

6. If the nucleus consists of a married couple, age refers to the average age of husband and spouse. Sex of nucleus head is a somewhat ambiguous concept because the head of a nucleus is only well defined in the trivial case of one-person nuclei or self-reported in one-nuclei households. Otherwise, we assigned the head status to the male.

7. A table similar to table 4.5 indicates that the corresponding age of the receiving child nucleus is quite young (52.8 years).

8. There is no variation in the inclusive values to identify the dissimilarity parameters.

9. See Börsch-Supan and Pollakowski (1988) for an application and sensitivity analysis using a panel of three cross sections.

10. The 3,081 observations in the estimation sample represent between 700 and 800 different nuclei.

11. See McFadden, Winston, and Börsch-Supan (1985) for details, including a derivation of the appropriate asymptotic covariance matrix. The WESML estimation approach is not necessary to consistently estimate the coefficients in the MNL model. Inclusion of alternative specific constants would serve the same purpose. However, these constants are highly collinear with PER and FEM, which makes the WESML approach more attractive.

12. There are some cases of elderly nuclei with own children under age 18.

13. The likelihood ratio test statistic is 188.2 [the log likelihood of the constrained estimation is 3159.5 (table 4.11); the likelihood of the unconstrained model (table 4.12) is 3065.4]. The chi-squared value for 50 degrees of freedom at 0.99 confidence is 76.2.

14. Note that the reported standard errors ignore intertemporal correlations. Correct standard errors are approximately twice as large.

# References

Becker, G. S. 1981. *A treatise on the family*. Cambridge, Mass.: Harvard University Press.

Börsch-Supan, A. 1986. Household formation, housing prices, and public policy impacts. *Journal of Public Economics* 25: 145–64.

Börsch-Supan, A., and H. Pollakowski. 1988. Estimating housing consumption adjustments from panel data. *Journal of Urban Economics*, forthcoming.

Brown, H. J., and J. M. Yinger. 1986. *Homeownership and housing affordability in the United States: 1963–1986*. Joint Center of Housing Studies of MIT and Harvard University. Mimeo.

Chamberlain, G. 1980. Analysis of covariance with qualitative data. *Review of Economic Studies* 47: 225–38.

Ermisch, J. 1981. An econometric theory of household formation. *Scottish Journal of Political Economy* 28: 1–19.

Manski, C. F., and S. R. Lerman. 1977. The estimation of choice probabilities from choice based samples. *Econometrica* 45: 1977–88.

McFadden, D. 1973. Conditional logit analysis of qualitative choice behavior. In *Frontiers in econometrics*, ed. P. Zarembka, 105–42. New York: Academic Press.

McFadden, D., C. Winston, and A. Börsch-Supan. 1985. Joint estimation of freight transportation decisions under non-random sampling. In *Analytical studies in transport economics*, ed. A. Daughety, 137–57. Cambridge: Cambridge University Press.

Poterba, J. M., and L. H. Summers. 1985. Public policy implications of declining old-age mortality. Paper prepared for Brookings Institution Conference on Retirement and Aging.

# Comment    John M. Quigley

There is much to applaud in Axel Börsch-Supan's careful empirical analysis of the household and housing choices of the elderly. First is the explicit recognition of the endogeneity of the household itself. Second is the demonstration that the decision to combine adults to form a household is amenable to economic analysis. To those of you who have seen undergraduates doubling, tripling, or living in communes in high-rent cities like Boston this may not be implausible. This way of looking at households is, however, almost totally foreign to those public officials charged with forecasting future housing or construction needs. These analyses, undertaken by HUD, by the FHLBB, even by the Federal Reserve, typically take projected age distributions of the population and mechanically transform them to numbers of households— which are then compared to numbers of available dwellings.

The third striking feature of the paper is the endogeneity of the household head in extended families. When the elderly member has the highest income, he or she is the head of the extended family. When the child has the money, the child is the head. It has become an awkward thing to unravel male-female, husband-wife, from head-spouse on questionnaire data, and apparently will become more so as incomes within households get more equal.

Fourth, the statistical methodology employed by Börsch-Supan is unambiguously appropriate to this problem. In several of the papers discussed at this conference, considerable attention was paid to reducing the information conveyed by an important measurement, for example, by converting a continuous measure of household income or hours worked into a binary variable measuring poverty or retirement status. This paper avoids these complications.

The paper's substantive conclusions are that an elderly person's choice of living conditions—independence, living with children, etc.— is sensitive to the age and sex of that householder and to whether the person's spouse is still living. At incomes less than $5,000, household choice is also responsive to income; for the lower half of the income distribution of the elderly, annual income matters a lot. Axel finds the irrelevance of housing price (the user cost of housing capital) to these choice surprising. I find it less so since such a large fraction of the elderly are homeowners with clear title and no mortgage payments. Using the Panel Study of Income Dynamics (PSID) data, I discovered recently that less than 50 percent of younger households with

John M. Quigley is Professor of Economics and Public Policy at the University of California, Berkeley.

outstanding mortgages were able to compute the components of user cost in a consistent manner. For example, the outstanding mortgage balance, the monthly payment, and the mortgage term were internally inconsistent and yielded implausible interest rates for a great many households.

Despite the lack of statistical significance of the price term in the logit models, the tabulations reported in the paper suggest that, over time, as interest rates rose and housing prices increased, a larger fraction of elderly households took in their children as subtenants. Anecdotal evidence from elsewhere under a variety of different institutions supports this kind of effect. For example, in Budapest, where price controls and a stagnant supply have made the shadow prices of rental housing very large, elderly renters routinely take in young households as subtenants, providing shelter or assigning them the right to assume rental contracts in return for household help and private nursing care (Hårsman and Quigley 1988). The socialist alternative.

The real problems I see with this paper do not arise from Axel's clear and careful analysis, but rather from his choice of data set. The decision to use the Annual Housing Survey (AHS) locks the analyst into three sets of data problems. First, the AHS is a sample of dwelling units. As such it excludes intermediate care facilities, nursing homes, and various kinds of congregate facilities. There is simply no way to describe these alternatives or to use the generic utility indicators, which have been so carefully estimated, to simulate the effects of policy changes (or merely income or price changes) upon the propensity to choose these unexplored options. The importance of these options is growing. Garber's paper (ch. 9, in this volume) suggests that 5 percent of the elderly live in congregate facilities, making it the second or third most likely living arrangement. It's surely the most expensive.

Second, the AHS contains not a scrap of information on the health status of the elderly. Casual empiricism applied to the elderly of the middle class—my own family stories and those of virtually everyone I know—suggests that the independence of the elderly in their living condition is as fragile as an arthritic hip or a burst blood vessel. Of course, this is consistent with Axel's finding that the income elasticity of choice among middle-class elderly households is low. But this latter description is way off point.

Third, the pooling of a decade's worth of data on a panel of dwelling units—to achieve sufficiently large samples for the rarer alternatives— is quite dangerous. Since the sampling frame is dwelling units, a panel of "stayers" is mixed with a sample of "movers," causing serious problems in inference and interpretation. This problem is not merely the inaccurate degrees of freedom and misleading standard errors noted by the author. It is well known that the probability of "staying" at

$t + 1$ is higher for those who have "stayed" at $t$. This individual-specific but unobserved heterogeneity could be accounted for, as Axel notes, but only by poaching on the Rust computer budget. But there's another problem here that arises because the attachment to residential amenities and "neighborhood" increases as households remain stayers. I've recently tried to sort out these effects, estimating mobility models from the PSID. It appears that, even when unobserved heterogeneity is controlled for, in the Heckman-Flynn sense, the mobility hazard is at least inversely proportional to duration (Quigley 1987). This is quite consistent with the arguments of Dynarski (1985) about the increasing importance of neighborhood attributes and amenity (or, in the terminology of Venti and Wise, of nonmonetary transactions costs which increase with duration). It would be very hard to address duration effects or the timing of choices within the framework Börsch-Supan has chosen.

These problems are unfortunate; they limit the applicability of the specific findings of an otherwise interesting and creative effort. One can believe the cross-sectional descriptive results presented and still doubt the conclusions about the causal effects of income and price upon the household choices of the elderly.

## References

Dynarski, Mark. 1985. Housing demand and disequilibrium. *Journal of Urban Economics* 17(January):42–57.

Hårsman, Björn, and John Quigley. 1988. Housing markets and housing institutions: An international comparison. Center for Real Estate and Urban Economics, University of California, Berkeley. Mimeo.

Quigley, John M. 1987. Interest rate variations, mortgage prepayments and household mobility. *Review of Economics and Statistics* 69(4):636–43.

# 5     How Much Care Do the Aged Receive from Their Children? A Bimodal Picture of Contact and Assistance

Laurence J. Kotlikoff and John N. Morris

## 5.1   Introduction

This paper presents some preliminary findings about contact between the aged and their children based on a new survey of the aged and their children, entitled The Hebrew Rehabilitation Center for the Aged–NBER (HRC-NBER) Child Survey. Data on extended families are quite limited. The HRC-NBER Child Survey represents one of the few attempts to collect economic and demographic data on the elderly and their children. While these data will be used in future research to test structural models of living arrangements, the purposes of the current paper are to describe the survey and to examine contact between the elderly and their children.

The HRC-NBER Child Survey collects information on the children of elderly individuals residing in Massachusetts. Since 1982 The Hebrew Rehabilitation Center for the Aged has been conducting a panel survey of the elderly in Massachusetts, which we will refer to as the HRCA Elderly Survey. The original sample of 5,000 elderly individuals in the HRCA Elderly Survey was randomly drawn based on Massachusetts police records which record the ages and addresses of Massachusetts residents. The initial sample included only the noninstitutionalized elderly, but each subsequent survey has followed the noninstitutionalized elderly to their institutions if they became institutionalized. The primary purpose of the HRCA Elderly Survey

Laurence J. Kotlikoff is a Professor of Economics and Chairman of the Department of Economics at Boston University and a Research Associate of the National Bureau of Economic Research. John N. Morris is the Associate Director of the Department of Social Gerontological Research at the Hebrew Rehabilitation Center for the Aged.

The authors thank The National Institute of Aging for research support via grant no. 1PO1AG05842-01 is to collect information on the living arrangements, health status, and helpers of the elderly. In the most recent and still ongoing reinterview of the elderly we added additional economic questions as well as questions about children. We also requested permission to interview the children of the elderly.

In the HRC-NBER Child Survey we are interviewing one child of each of the elderly in the HRCA Elderly Survey who had children and who granted permission for the interview. The child contacted is not randomly selected from the set of children of the elderly; we felt it was most appropriate to let the elderly tell us which of their children they were willing to let us contact. To date we have completed 399 child surveys. Each child survey asks questions about the child, the child's spouse, and the child and spouse's children. It also asks about the elderly parents and about the child's siblings.

The elderly in the HRCA panel are now quite old, and over two fifths have health problems or difficulties in performing daily activities. Hence, the combination of panel data on the elderly and data on their children from the child survey provide a unique opportunity to examine the behavior of the extended family for a sample of elderly, many of whom appear to need assistance of one kind or another.

Section 5.2 briefly discusses the child survey. Section 5.3 presents data from 2,354 HRC elderly reinterviews that were completed between June 1986 and June 1987. Section 5.4 presents some preliminary findings from the initial 399 respondents in our child survey.

## 5.2    A Description of The HRC-NBER Child Survey

The HRC-NBER Child Survey is a telephone interview survey roughly 45 minutes in length. Interviews with the child's spouse were conducted if the child was unavailable. The current survey is the product of three small pretests. Our primary objective in conducting the pretests was to find a sequence of questions about siblings' income and net wealth positions that would elicit a high response rate. The respondents in our child survey appear to know, within a range, how much income their siblings receive and the amount of their siblings' net wealth. But if one asks them straight off about their siblings' resources, their inclination is to say "I don't know." "I don't know" appears really to mean "I don't know precisely." Hence, to elicit the admittedly imprecise, but potentially still quite useful information about siblings, the respondent needs to be coaxed a bit by first asking much broader questions.

The sequence of questions about income (net wealth) that worked best involves first asking the child whether the sibling owns a home and, if so, its market value. Next we ask the child to rank his and his spouse's combined income (net wealth) relative to the combined incomes (net wealth) of his siblings and their spouses. Next we ask how much larger or smaller each sibling's and sibling's spouse's combined income (net wealth) is relative to the combined income (net wealth) of the child and his spouse. The response rate to these questions is about 75 percent.

The response rates to other questions in the survey, including other questions about siblings, are closer to 100 percent. In the case of siblings, these other questions include age, geographic location, marital status, number of young children, work and health status, occupation, industry, education, and grades in high school. Most of these questions are repeated for the sibling's spouse. In addition, the child was asked to indicate the frequency of contact between the sibling and his spouse and the child's parent(s), the amount of time the sibling and his spouse spent helping the child's parent(s), and the amount of financial assistance the sibling and his spouse give to or receive from the child's parent(s).

The child is also asked about his parents' health status as well as their income and net wealth. Since we have information directly from the parent(s) on these and other questions, we are in a position to compare the responses of the child to those of the parent(s).

## 5.3 Some Findings on Child-Parent Contact from the 1986–87 HRCA Elderly Survey

In the 1986–87 HRCA Elderly Survey, we asked the elderly questions about their children, including their geographic location, their contact with the elderly parent(s), their time spent helping the elderly parent(s), and the amount of financial support they give to or receive from the elderly parent(s).

Table 5.1 presents the distribution by age, sex, and vulnerability status of the 1986–87 sample of elderly that has been surveyed to date. The elderly respondent is designated vulnerable if he or she has problems of low fatigue or physical function or has difficulties in performing chores such as preparing meals or shopping. The sample is clearly quite old. Less than 10 percent of the total 2,354 respondents are under age 70. A total of 14.4 percent are 90 or older. Over two thirds of the respondents are elderly women. The female respondents tend to be somewhat older than the male respondents.

Table 5.2 enumerates parents by the number of their children. The table distinguishes the elderly respondents by their marital status and the children by their sex. Of the 2,354 elderly in the sample, over one

**Table 5.1**    **Age and Vulnerable Status of Elderly**

|  | Male Elderly | | Female Elderly | | Total | |
|---|---|---|---|---|---|---|
| *Less than 70* | 91 | (13.1) | 115 | (6.9) | 206 | (8.8) |
| *Age 70–74* | 73 | (10.5) | 150 | (9.0) | 223 | (9.5) |
| Nonvulnerable | 68 | (9.8) | 118 | (7.1) | 186 | (7.9) |
| Vulnerable | 5 | (0.7) | 32 | (1.9) | 37 | (1.6) |
| *Age 75–79* | 63 | (9.1) | 139 | (8.4) | 202 | (8.6) |
| Nonvulnerable | 50 | (7.2) | 91 | (5.5) | 141 | (6.0) |
| Vulnerable | 13 | (1.9) | 48 | (2.9) | 61 | (2.6) |
| *Age 80–84* | 246 | (35.2) | 518 | (31.2) | 764 | (32.5) |
| Nonvulnerable | 184 | (26.5) | 300 | (18.1) | 484 | (20.6) |
| Vulnerable | 62 | (8.9) | 218 | (13.1) | 280 | (11.9) |
| *Age 85–89* | 154 | (22.2) | 467 | (28.1) | 621 | (26.4) |
| Nonvulnerable | 97 | (14.0) | 195 | (11.8) | 292 | (12.4) |
| Vulnerable | 57 | (8.2) | 272 | (16.4) | 329 | (14.0) |
| *Age 90–94* | 50 | (7.2) | 202 | (12.2) | 252 | (10.7) |
| Nonvulnerable | 22 | (3.2) | 51 | (3.1) | 73 | (3.1) |
| Vulnerable | 28 | (4.0) | 151 | (9.1) | 179 | (7.6) |
| *Age 95 +* | 18 | (2.6) | 68 | (4.1) | 86 | (3.7) |
| Nonvulnerable | 5 | (0.7) | 9 | (0.5) | 14 | (0.6) |
| Vulnerable | 13 | (1.9) | 59 | (3.6) | 72 | (3.1) |
| *Total* | 695 | (100.0) | 1,659 | (100.0) | 2,354 | (100.1) |

Figures in parentheses are column percents.
HRCA Elderly Survey.

fifth, 22.4 percent, have no children. Another 19.8 percent have only one child. Slightly under half have two, three, or four children, and less then 10 percent have five or more children.

Elderly couples are more likely to have children than the single elderly. This reflects both the fact that some of the single elderly never married and that parent and child life spans are positively correlated. Only 13.2 percent of elderly couples have no children, compared with over a quarter of single males and single females.

Daughters are often viewed as more important providers of care to the elderly than sons. In total, 40.5 percent of the sample have no daughters, and one half of the sample have either no daughters or just one daughter; 43.5 percent of single elderly males in the sample have no daughters. The comparable figures for single elderly females and elderly couples are 44.4 percent and 31.1 percent, respectively.

Table 5.3 repeats table 5.2 for the vulnerable sample. Of the 2,354 elderly respondents, 985 are vulnerable. The distribution of vulnerable elderly by number and sex of children is quite similar to that of the nonvulnerable.

Table 5.4 examines the geographic location of children. Fewer than one fifth of the elderly live with their children. One third of the elderly

**Table 5.2**    **Demographic Composition of Extended Families, Number of Elderly Parents with Specified Children**

| | Single Males | | Single Females | | Married | | Total | |
|---|---|---|---|---|---|---|---|---|
| Zero children | 70 | (26.0) | 369 | (26.0) | 88 | (13.2) | 527 | (22.4) |
| One child | 60 | (22.3) | 292 | (20.6) | 114 | (17.1) | 466 | (19.8) |
| 1 son | 29 | (10.8) | 153 | (10.8) | 52 | (7.8) | 234 | (9.9) |
| 1 daughter | 31 | (11.5) | 139 | (9.8) | 62 | (9.3) | 232 | (9.9) |
| Two children | 55 | (20.4) | 313 | (22.1) | 198 | (29.8) | 566 | (24.0) |
| 2 sons | 13 | (4.8) | 76 | (5.4) | 45 | (6.7) | 134 | (5.7) |
| 2 daughters | 10 | (3.7) | 76 | (5.4) | 45 | (6.7) | 131 | (5.6) |
| 1 son, 1 daughter | 32 | (11.9) | 161 | (11.4) | 108 | (16.2) | 301 | (12.8) |
| Three children | 40 | (14.9) | 206 | (14.5) | 147 | (22.0) | 393 | (16.7) |
| 3 sons | 4 | (1.5) | 26 | (1.8) | 19 | (2.8) | 49 | (2.1) |
| 3 daughters | 5 | (1.9) | 20 | (1.4) | 26 | (3.9) | 51 | (2.2) |
| 2 sons and 1 daughter | 16 | (5.9) | 67 | (4.7) | 52 | (7.8) | 135 | (5.7) |
| 2 daughters and 1 son | 15 | (5.6) | 93 | (6.6) | 50 | (7.5) | 158 | (6.7) |
| Four children | 26 | (9.7) | 110 | (7.8) | 60 | (9.0) | 196 | (8.3) |
| 4 sons | 1 | (0.4) | 3 | (0.2) | 4 | (0.6) | 8 | (0.3) |
| 4 daughters | 2 | (0.1) | 13 | (0.9) | 4 | (0.6) | 19 | (0.8) |
| 3 sons and 1 daughter | 6 | (2.2) | 22 | (1.6) | 17 | (2.5) | 45 | (1.9) |
| 3 daughters and 1 son | 6 | (2.2) | 34 | (2.4) | 15 | (2.2) | 55 | (2.3) |
| 2 sons and 2 daughters | 11 | (4.1) | 38 | (2.7) | 20 | (3.0) | 69 | (2.9) |
| Five or more children | 18 | (6.7) | 128 | (9.0) | 60 | (9.0) | 206 | (8.8) |
| All sons | 0 | (0.0) | 2 | (0.1) | 0 | (0.0) | 2 | (0.1) |
| All daughters | 0 | (0.0) | 1 | (0.1) | 3 | (0.4) | 4 | (0.2) |
| Some sons and daughters | 18 | (6.7) | 125 | (8.8) | 57 | (8.5) | 200 | (8.5) |
| Total | 269 | (100.0) | 1,418 | (100.0) | 667 | (100.0) | 2,354 | (100.0) |

Figures in parentheses are column percents.
HRCA Elderly Survey.

have either no children or no children who live within 1 hour. Of those elderly who have children but are not living with any of them, only 44.6 percent have more than one child within 1 hour. These numbers suggest a rather limited ability of the children of a sizeable minority of elderly to provide direct care for the elderly.

Surprisingly, the figures for vulnerable elderly reported in table 5.5 are quite similar. Despite their health problems, the vulnerable elderly are only slightly more likely to live with or near their children than the nonvulnerable elderly.

The next two tables, 5.6 and 5.7, consider in more detail the living arrangements of the entire sample of the elderly and the subsample of vulnerable elderly. Only 13.1 percent of all the elderly and only 15.9 percent of the vulnerable elderly live with their children. The majority of single elderly and over 40 percent of the single vulnerable elderly live completely by themselves. Only 11.8 percent of the elderly sample

**Table 5.3**    **Demographic Composition of Extended Families with Vulnerable Parents, Number of Vulnerable Elderly Parents with Specified Children**

|  | Single Males | | Single Females | | Married | | Total | |
|---|---|---|---|---|---|---|---|---|
| *Zero children* | 27 | (27.3) | 175 | (23.9) | 22 | (14.4) | 224 | (22.7) |
| *One child* | 23 | (23.2) | 149 | (20.3) | 27 | (17.6) | 199 | (20.2) |
| 1 son | 12 | (12.1) | 77 | (10.5) | 16 | (10.5) | 105 | (10.7) |
| 1 daughter | 11 | (11.1) | 72 | (9.8) | 11 | (7.2) | 94 | (9.5) |
| *Two children* | 20 | (20.2) | 152 | (20.7) | 49 | (32.0) | 221 | (22.4) |
| 2 sons | 3 | (3.0) | 32 | (4.4) | 11 | (7.2) | 46 | (4.7) |
| 2 daughters | 5 | (5.1) | 44 | (6.0) | 10 | (6.5) | 59 | (6.0) |
| 1 son, 1 daughter | 12 | (12.1) | 76 | (10.4) | 28 | (18.3) | 116 | (11.8) |
| *Three children* | 15 | (15.2) | 117 | (16.0) | 31 | (20.3) | 163 | (16.5) |
| 3 sons | 0 | (0.0) | 16 | (2.2) | 3 | (2.0) | 19 | (1.9) |
| 3 daughters | 3 | (3.0) | 14 | (1.9) | 5 | (3.3) | 22 | (2.2) |
| 2 sons and 1 daughter | 7 | (7.1) | 35 | (4.8) | 12 | (7.8) | 54 | (5.5) |
| 2 daughters and 1 son | 5 | (5.1) | 52 | (7.1) | 11 | (7.2) | 68 | (6.9) |
| *Four children* | 8 | (8.1) | 63 | (8.6) | 9 | (5.9) | 80 | (8.1) |
| 4 sons | 0 | (0.0) | 3 | (0.4) | 2 | (1.3) | 5 | (0.5) |
| 4 daughters | 0 | (0.0) | 7 | (1.0) | 0 | (0.0) | 7 | (0.7) |
| 3 sons and 1 daughter | 3 | (3.0) | 11 | (1.5) | 3 | (2.0) | 17 | (1.7) |
| 3 daughters and 1 son | 2 | (2.0) | 17 | (2.3) | 2 | (1.3) | 21 | (2.1) |
| 2 sons and 2 daughters | 3 | (3.0) | 25 | (3.4) | 2 | (1.3) | 30 | (3.0) |
| *Five or more children* | 6 | (6.1) | 77 | (10.5) | 15 | (9.8) | 98 | (9.9) |
| All sons | 0 | (0.0) | 0 | (0.0) | 0 | (0.0) | 0 | (0.0) |
| All daughters | 0 | (0.0) | 1 | (0.1) | 1 | (0.7) | 2 | (0.2) |
| Some sons and daughters | 6 | (6.1) | 76 | (10.4) | 14 | (9.2) | 96 | (9.7) |
| *Total* | 99 | (100.0) | 733 | (100.0) | 153 | (100.0) | 985 | (100.0) |

Figures in parentheses are column percents.
HRCA Elderly Survey.

**Table 5.4**    **Geographic Location of Children**

|  | Single Males | | Single Females | | Married | | Total | |
|---|---|---|---|---|---|---|---|---|
| Zero children | 70 | (26.0) | 369 | (26.0) | 88 | (13.2) | 527 | (22.4) |
| Lives with child/children | 57 | (21.2) | 264 | (18.6) | 100 | (15.0) | 421 | (17.9) |
| Zero children within 1 hour | 26 | (9.7) | 131 | (9.2) | 98 | (14.7) | 255 | (10.8) |
| 1 child within 1 hour | 52 | (19.3) | 311 | (21.9) | 157 | (23.5) | 520 | (20.1) |
| 2 children within 1 hour | 41 | (15.2) | 188 | (13.3) | 127 | (19.0) | 356 | (15.1) |
| 3 children within 1 hour | 14 | (5.2) | 88 | (6.2) | 59 | (8.8) | 161 | (6.8) |
| 4 children within 1 hour | 4 | (1.5) | 29 | (2.0) | 20 | (3.0) | 53 | (2.3) |
| 5 or more children within 1 hour | 5 | (1.9) | 38 | (2.7) | 18 | (2.7) | 61 | (2.6) |
| Total | 269 | (100.0) | 1,418 | (100.0) | 667 | (100.0) | 2,354 | (100.0) |

Figures in parentheses are column percents.
HRCA Elderly Survey.

**Table 5.5**         **Geographic Location of Children of Vulnerable Elderly**

| | Single Males | | Single Females | | Married | | Total | |
|---|---|---|---|---|---|---|---|---|
| Zero children | 27 | (27.3) | 175 | (23.9) | 22 | (14.4) | 224 | (22.7) |
| Lives with child/children | 21 | (21.2) | 145 | (19.8) | 25 | (16.3) | 193 | (19.4) |
| Zero children within 1 hour· | 7 | (7.1) | 57 | (7.8) | 23 | (15.0) | 87 | (8.8) |
| 1 child within 1 hour | 20 | (20.2) | 159 | (21.7) | 34 | (22.2) | 213 | (21.6) |
| 2 children within 1 hour | 15 | (15.2) | 102 | (13.9) | 30 | (19.6) | 147 | (14.9) |
| 3 children within 1 hour | 5 | (5.1) | 50 | (6.8) | 10 | (6.5) | 65 | (6.6) |
| 4 children within 1 hour | 1 | (1.0) | 18 | (2.5) | 4 | (2.6) | 23 | (2.3) |
| 5 or more children within 1 hour | 3 | (3.0) | 27 | (3.7) | 5 | (3.3) | 35 | (3.6) |
| Total | 99 | (100.0) | 733 | (100.0) | 153 | (100.0) | 985 | (100.0) |

Figures in parentheses are column percents. HRCA Elderly Survey.

**Table 5.6**         **Living Arrangements of Elderly**

| | Single Males | | Single Females | | Married | | Total | |
|---|---|---|---|---|---|---|---|---|
| Lives alone | 151 | (56.1) | 839 | (59.2) | 25 | (3.7) | 1,015 | (43.1) |
| Lives with children | 55 | (20.4) | 246 | (17.3) | 8 | (1.2) | 309 | (13.1) |
| Lives in nursing home/ institution | 31 | (11.5) | 225 | (15.9) | 21 | (3.1) | 277 | (11.8) |
| Lives with other relatives/ friends | 17 | (6.3) | 67 | (4.7) | 0 | (0.0) | 84 | (3.6) |
| Lives in retirement community | 1 | (0.4) | 10 | (0.7) | 3 | (0.4) | 14 | (0.6) |
| Other | 14 | (5.2) | 31 | (2.2) | 610 | (91.5) | 655 | (27.8) |
| Total | 269 | | 1,418 | | 667 | | 2,354 | |

Figures in parentheses are column percents. HRCA Elderly Survey.

**Table 5.7**         **Living Arrangements of the Vulnerable Elderly**

| | Single Males | | Single Females | | Married | | Total | |
|---|---|---|---|---|---|---|---|---|
| Lives alone | 39 | (39.4) | 330 | (45.0) | 5 | (3.3) | 374 | (38.0) |
| Lives with children | 20 | (20.2) | 136 | (18.6) | 1 | (0.7) | 157 | (15.9) |
| Lives in nursing home/ institution | 30 | (30.3) | 221 | (30.2) | 21 | (13.7) | 272 | (27.6) |
| Lives with other relatives/ friends | 3 | (3.0) | 27 | (3.7) | 0 | (0.0) | 30 | (3.0) |
| Lives in retirement community | 0 | (0.0) | 5 | (0.7) | 1 | (0.7) | 6 | (0.6) |
| Other | 7 | (7.1) | 14 | (1.9) | 125 | (81.7) | 146 | (14.8) |
| *Total* | 99 | | 733 | | 153 | | 9,854 | |

Figures in parentheses are column percents.
HRCA Elderly Survey.

are institutionalized, while over one fourth of the vulnerable elderly are institutionalized. Taken together, these tables suggest only a modest amount of support by children in the form of living with their elderly and often vulnerable parents.

Tables 5.8, 5.9, and 5.10 consider contact with children of the entire elderly sample and the vulnerable elderly sample, respectively. The

**Table 5.8    Contact of Elderly with Children**

| | Single Males | | Single Females | | Married | | Total | |
|---|---|---|---|---|---|---|---|---|
| *Zero Children* | 70 | (26.2) | 369 | (26.2) | 88 | (13.3) | 527 | (22.5) |
| *One Child* | 59 | (22.1) | 290 | (20.6) | 112 | (17.6) | 461 | (19.7) |
| Lives with child | 13 | (4.9) | 47 | (3.3) | 14 | (2.1) | 74 | (3.2) |
| Daily | 11 | (4.1) | 77 | (5.5) | 32 | (4.8) | 120 | (5.1) |
| Once or more a week | 20 | (7.5) | 112 | (7.9) | 42 | (6.4) | 174 | (7.4) |
| Once or more a month | 6 | (2.2) | 30 | (2.1) | 20 | (3.0) | 56 | (2.4) |
| One or more a year | 6 | (2.2) | 18 | (1.3) | 4 | (0.6) | 28 | (1.2) |
| Never, almost never | 3 | (1.1) | 6 | (2.1) | 0 | (0.0) | 9 | (0.4) |
| *Two Children* | 54 | (20.2) | 311 | (22.0) | 195 | (29.5) | 560 | (23.9) |
| Lives with child | 11 | (4.1) | 61 | (4.3) | 31 | (4.7) | 103 | (4.4) |
| Daily | 22 | (8.2) | 100 | (7.1) | 52 | (7.9) | 174 | (7.4) |
| Once or more a week | 15 | (5.6) | 120 | (8.5) | 92 | (13.9) | 227 | (9.7) |
| Once or more a month | 4 | (1.5) | 24 | (1.7) | 12 | (1.8) | 40 | (1.7) |
| One or more a year | 1 | (0.4) | 5 | (0.4) | 7 | (1.1) | 13 | (0.6) |
| Never, almost never | 1 | (0.4) | 1 | (0.1) | 1 | (0.2) | 3 | (0.1) |
| *Three Children* | 40 | (15.0) | 205 | (14.5) | 147 | (22.3) | 392 | (16.8) |
| Lives with child | 15 | (5.6) | 55 | (3.9) | 23 | (3.5) | 93 | (4.0) |
| Daily | 6 | (2.2) | 80 | (5.7) | 44 | (6.7) | 130 | (5.6) |
| Once or more a week | 15 | (5.6) | 62 | (4.4) | 70 | (10.6) | 147 | (6.3) |
| Once or more a month | 4 | (1.5) | 7 | (0.5) | 10 | (1.5) | 21 | (0.9) |
| Once or more a year | 0 | (0.0) | 1 | (0.1) | 0 | (0.0) | 1 | (0.0) |
| Never, almost never | 0 | (0.0) | 0 | (0.0) | 0 | (0.0) | 0 | (0.0) |
| *Four Children* | 26 | (9.7) | 109 | (7.7) | 58 | (8.8) | 193 | (8.3) |
| Lives with child | 8 | (3.0) | 34 | (2.4) | 12 | (1.8) | 54 | (2.3) |
| Daily | 8 | (3.0) | 41 | (2.9) | 18 | (2.7) | 67 | (2.9) |
| Once or more a week | 9 | (3.4) | 32 | (2.3) | 26 | (3.9) | 67 | (2.9) |
| Once or more a month | 1 | (0.4) | 2 | (0.1) | 1 | (0.2) | 4 | (0.2) |
| Once or more a year | 0 | (0.0) | 0 | (0.0) | 1 | (0.2) | 1 | (0.0) |
| Never, almost never | 0 | (0.0) | 0 | (0.0) | 0 | (0.0) | 0 | (0.0) |
| *Five or More Children* | 18 | (6.7) | 127 | (9.0) | 60 | (9.1) | 205 | (8.8) |
| Lives with child | 7 | (2.6) | 54 | (3.8) | 16 | (2.4) | 77 | (3.3) |
| Daily | 3 | (1.1) | 47 | (3.3) | 20 | (3.0) | 70 | (3.0) |
| Once or more a week | 7 | (2.6) | 23 | (1.6) | 19 | (2.9) | 49 | (2.1) |
| Once or more a month | 0 | (0.0) | 3 | (0.2) | 4 | (0.6) | 7 | (0.3) |
| Once or more a year | 1 | (0.4) | 0 | (0.0) | 1 | (0.2) | 2 | (0.1) |
| Never, almost never | 0 | (0.0) | 0 | (0.0) | 0 | (0.0) | 0 | (0.0) |
| *Total* | 267 | (100.0) | 1,411 | (100.0) | 660 | (100.0) | 2,338 | (100.0) |

Figures in parentheses are column percents.
HRCA Elderly Survey.

question in the HRCA Elderly Survey on contact is, "How often do you hear from your child?" The elderly respondent was asked this question about each of his (her) children. The tables consider the extent of contact between the elderly parent and the child who is designated as most in contact with the elderly parent.

**Table 5.9    Contact of Vulnerable Elderly with Children**

|  | Single Males | | Single Females | | Married | | Total | |
|---|---|---|---|---|---|---|---|---|
| *Zero Children* | 27 | (27.6) | 175 | (24.0) | 22 | (14.5) | 224 | (22.9) |
| *One Child* | 23 | (23.5) | 147 | (20.2) | 27 | (17.8) | 197 | (20.1) |
| Lives with child | 4 | (4.1) | 23 | (3.2) | 2 | (1.3) | 29 | (3.0) |
| Daily | 4 | (4.1) | 39 | (5.4) | 8 | (5.3) | 51 | (5.2) |
| Once or more a week | 9 | (9.2) | 54 | (7.4) | 10 | (6.6) | 73 | (7.5) |
| Once or more a month | 2 | (2.0) | 14 | (1.9) | 6 | (3.9) | 22 | (2.2) |
| Once or more a year | 3 | (3.1) | 12 | (1.6) | 1 | (0.7) | 16 | (1.6) |
| Never, almost never | 1 | (1.0) | 5 | (0.7) | 0 | (0.0) | 6 | (0.6) |
| *Two Children* | 19 | (19.4) | 151 | (20.7) | 48 | (31.6) | 218 | (22.3) |
| Lives with child | 5 | (5.1) | 34 | (4.7) | 11 | (7.2) | 50 | (5.1) |
| Daily | 9 | (9.2) | 45 | (6.2) | 12 | (7.9) | 66 | (6.7) |
| Once or more a week | 3 | (3.1) | 60 | (8.2) | 21 | (13.8) | 84 | (8.6) |
| Once or more a month | 0 | (0.0) | 8 | (1.1) | 1 | (0.7) | 9 | (1.0) |
| Once or more a year | 1 | (1.0) | 4 | (0.5) | 3 | (2.0) | 8 | (0.8) |
| Never, almost never | 1 | (1.0) | 0 | (0.0) | 0 | (0.0) | 1 | (0.1) |
| *Three Children* | 15 | (15.3) | 116 | (15.9) | 31 | (20.4) | 162 | (16.6) |
| Lives with child | 6 | (6.1) | 33 | (4.5) | 4 | (2.6) | 43 | (4.4) |
| Daily | 4 | (4.1) | 43 | (5.9) | 7 | (4.6) | 54 | (5.5) |
| Once or more a week | 3 | (3.1) | 35 | (4.8) | 18 | (11.8) | 56 | (5.7) |
| Once or more a month | 2 | (2.0) | 4 | (0.5) | 2 | (1.3) | 8 | (0.8) |
| Once or more a year | 0 | (0.0) | 1 | (0.1) | 0 | (0.0) | 1 | (0.1) |
| Never, almost never | 0 | (0.0) | 0 | (0.0) | 0 | (0.0) | 0 | (0.0) |
| *Four Children* | 8 | (8.2) | 62 | (8.5) | 9 | (5.9) | 79 | (8.1) |
| Lives with child | 1 | (1.0) | 19 | (2.6) | 4 | (2.6) | 24 | (2.5) |
| Daily | 3 | (3.1) | 19 | (2.6) | 4 | (2.6) | 26 | (2.7) |
| Once or more a week | 4 | (4.1) | 23 | (3.2) | 0 | (0.0) | 27 | (2.8) |
| Once or more a month | 0 | (0.0) | 1 | (0.1) | 1 | (0.7) | 2 | (0.2) |
| Once or more a year | 0 | (0.0) | 0 | (0.0) | 0 | (0.0) | 1 | (0.0) |
| Never, almost never | 0 | (0.0) | 0 | (0.0) | 0 | (0.0) | 0 | (0.0) |
| *Five or More Children* | 6 | (6.1) | 77 | (10.6) | 15 | (9.9) | 98 | (10.0) |
| Lives with child | 3 | (3.1) | 29 | (4.0) | 3 | (2.0) | 35 | (3.6) |
| Daily | 0 | (0.0) | 26 | (3.6) | 5 | (3.3) | 31 | (3.2) |
| Once or more a week | 3 | (3.1) | 20 | (2.7) | 6 | (3.9) | 29 | (3.0) |
| Once or more a month | 0 | (0.0) | 2 | (0.3) | 0 | (0.0) | 2 | (0.2) |
| Once or more a year | 0 | (0.0) | 0 | (0.0) | 1 | (0.7) | 1 | (0.0) |
| Never, almost never | 0 | (0.0) | 0 | (0.0) | 0 | (0.0) | 0 | (0.0) |
| *Total* | 98 | (100.0) | 728 | (100.0) | 152 | (100.0) | 978 | (100.0) |

Figures in parentheses are column percents.
HRCA Elderly Survey.

Table 5.10    **Contact of Institutionalized and Noninstitutionalized Elderly with Children**

| | Institutionalized | | Noninstitutionalized | |
|---|---|---|---|---|
| | Male Elderly | Female Elderly | Male Elderly | Female Elderly |
| *Zero Children* | 14 (33.3) | 62 (25.7) | 110 (17.1) | 341 (24.2) |
| *One Child* | 7 (16.7) | 64 (26.6) | 130 (20.2) | 260 (18.4) |
| Lives with child | 0 (0.0) | 0 (0.0) | 20 (3.1) | 53 (3.8) |
| Daily | 0 (0.0) | 12 (5.0) | 32 (5.0) | 77 (5.5) |
| Once or more a week | 4 (9.5) | 35 (14.5) | 48 (7.4) | 87 (6.2) |
| Once or more a month | 1 (2.4) | 7 (2.9) | 21 (3.3) | 27 (1.9) |
| Once or more a year | 2 (4.8) | 8 (3.3) | 6 (0.9) | 12 (0.9) |
| Never, almost never | 0 (0.0) | 2 (0.8) | 3 (0.5) | 4 (0.3) |
| *Two Children* | 7 (16.7) | 47 (19.5) | 166 (25.7) | 340 (24.1) |
| Lives with child | 0 (0.0) | 0 (0.0) | 29 (4.5) | 74 (5.2) |
| Daily | 1 (2.4) | 10 (4.1) | 49 (7.6) | 114 (8.1) |
| Once or more a week | 4 (9.5) | 33 (13.7) | 70 (10.9) | 120 (8.5) |
| Once or more a month | 0 (0.0) | 3 (1.2) | 12 (1.9) | 25 (1.8) |
| Once or more a year | 1 (2.4) | 1 (0.4) | 5 (0.8) | 6 (0.4) |
| Never, almost never | 1 (2.4) | 0 (0.0) | 1 (0.2) | 1 (0.1) |
| *Three Children* | 4 (9.5) | 38 (15.8) | 126 (19.5) | 224 (15.9) |
| Lives with child | 0 (0.0) | 0 (0.0) | 34 (5.3) | 59 (4.2) |
| Daily | 1 (2.4) | 3 (1.2) | 27 (4.2) | 99 (7.0) |
| Once or more a week | 2 (4.8) | 31 (12.9) | 56 (8.7) | 58 (4.1) |
| Once or more a month | 1 (2.4) | 3 (1.2) | 9 (7.1) | 8 (0.6) |
| Once or more a year | 0 (0.0) | 1 (0.4) | 0 (0.0) | 0 (0.0) |
| Never, almost never | 0 (0.0) | 0 (0.0) | 0 (0.0) | 0 (0.0) |
| *Four Children* | 5 (11.9) | 16 (6.6) | 64 (9.9) | 108 (7.7) |
| Lives with child | 0 (0.0) | 0 (0.0) | 16 (2.5) | 38 (2.7) |
| Daily | 2 (4.8) | 3 (1.2) | 23 (3.6) | 39 (2.8) |
| Once or more a week | 3 (7.1) | 11 (4.6) | 23 (3.6) | 30 (2.1) |
| Once or more a month | 0 (0.0) | 2 (0.8) | 1 (0.2) | 1 (0.1) |
| Once or more a year | 0 (0.0) | 0 (0.0) | 1 (0.2) | 0 (0.0) |
| Never, almost never | 0 (0.0) | 0 (0.0) | 0 (0.0) | 0 (0.0) |
| *Five or More Children* | 5 (11.9) | 14 (5.8) | 49 (7.6) | 137 (9.7) |
| Lives with child | 0 (0.0) | 0 (0.0) | 17 (2.6) | 60 (4.3) |
| Daily | 0 (0.0) | 3 (1.2) | 15 (2.3) | 52 (3.7) |
| Once or more a week | 4 (9.5) | 11 (4.6) | 13 (2.0) | 21 (1.5) |
| Once or more a month | 0 (0.0) | 2 (0.0) | 3 (0.5) | 4 (0.3) |
| Once or more a year | 1 (2.4) | 0 (0.0) | 1 (0.2) | 0 (0.0) |
| Never, almost never | 0 (0.0) | 0 (0.0) | 0 (0.0) | 0 (0.0) |
| *Total* | 42 (100.0) | 241 (100.0) | 645 (100.0) | 1,410 (100.0) |

Figures in parentheses are column percents.
HRCA Elderly Survey.

There are a number of interesting features in these tables. First, there are a few elderly parents who have no contact or very little contact with their children. Of the 1,410 elderly with children, but not living with children, 67 reported no contact or only yearly contact with the most attentive child. The sum of these parents who are either estranged from their children or have very little contact plus those with no children is just under one quarter of the total elderly sample. The corresponding figure for the vulnerable elderly is 26.3 percent.

A second interesting feature of these tables is the large fraction of elderly with children who either live with a child or have daily or weekly contact with the child who is designated as having maximum contact. Of the 1,811 elderly with children, 1,526 have immediate, daily, or weekly contact. The corresponding fraction for the vulnerable elderly contained in table 5.9 is quite similar.

Table 5.10 distinguishes the extent of contact with children between the institutionalized and noninstitutionalized elderly. The table indicates that almost one third of the institutionalized elderly either have no children or have very little contact with their children. For the noninstitutionalized the figure is less than one quarter.

The HRCA Elderly Survey also asks the elderly respondents about time spent talking on the phone or visiting with their family during the previous week. Tables 5.11A,B,C provides the responses to this question cross-tabulated by the number of children, income, vulnerable status, and, given vulnerability, whether the elderly respondent is institutionalized. The poor–not poor distinction is based on whether the elderly respondent's income is less than or greater than $5,000. The table indicates that just under 4 percent of those elderly who have children, but who do not live with their children, report no contact with family in the previous week. Another 10 percent of this group reported little telephone contact. At the other extreme, over half of the elderly living apart from their children reported considerable contact with their children in the previous week.

The institutionalized vulnerable elderly with children, according to Table 5.11C, indicate less contact with their families than the rest of the elderly. One quarter of the institutionalized with children reported no contact or little contact in the week preceding the survey. According to this table there is no indication that families provide less assistance in the form of shared housing or have less contact with the poor elderly as compared with the nonpoor elderly.

The next tables, 5.12A,B,C, examine, respectively, differences in contact among the children of the elderly, the vulnerable elderly, and the institutionalized elderly. The first row of table 5.12A indicates that there are 462 children who have no siblings. Of these, 16 percent live with their parents, 63.9 percent talk daily or weekly with their parents,

**Table 5.11A    Contact with Family Last Week, Nonvulnerable, Noninstitutionalized Elderly**

| | Single Males | | Single Females | | Married | |
|---|---|---|---|---|---|---|
| | Poor | Not Poor | Poor | Not Poor | Poor | Not Poor |
| *Zero children* | 2 (20.0) | 27 (24.8) | 19 (25.0) | 104 (25.8) | 1 (12.5) | 42 (12.4) |
| *Lives with child/children* | 4 (40.0) | 21 (19.3) | 26 (34.2) | 61 (15.1) | 3 (37.5) | 52 (15.3) |
| *No contact* | 1 (10.0) | 5 (4.6) | 0 (0.0) | 6 (1.5) | 0 (0.0) | 6 (1.8) |
| 1 child | 1 (10.0) | 2 (1.8) | 0 (0.0) | 3 (0.7) | 0 (0.0) | 3 (0.9) |
| 2 children | 0 (0.0) | 2 (1.8) | 0 (0.0) | 3 (0.7) | 0 (0.0) | 0 (0.0) |
| 3 children | 0 (0.0) | 1 (1.0) | 0 (0.0) | 0 (0.0) | 0 (0.0) | 1 (0.3) |
| 4 children | 0 (0.0) | 0 (0.0) | 0 (0.0) | 0 (0.0) | 0 (0.0) | 2 (0.6) |
| 5 children | 0 (0.0) | 0 (0.0) | 0 (0.0) | 0 (0.0) | 0 (0.0) | 0 (0.0) |
| *Little contact* | 2 (20.0) | 9 (8.3) | 2 (2.6) | 24 (6.0) | 0 (0.0) | 13 (3.8) |
| 1 child | 0 (0.0) | 2 (1.8) | 0 (0.0) | 15 (3.7) | 0 (0.0) | 3 (0.9) |
| 2 children | 0 (0.0) | 2 (1.8) | 1 (1.3) | 6 (1.5) | 0 (0.0) | 6 (1.8) |
| 3 children | 0 (0.0) | 3 (2.8) | 1 (1.3) | 1 (0.2) | 0 (0.0) | 3 (0.9) |
| 4 children | 1 (10.0) | 1 (0.9) | 0 (0.0) | 0 (0.0) | 0 (0.0) | 1 (0.3) |
| 5 children | 1 (10.0) | 1 (0.9) | 0 (0.0) | 2 (0.5) | 0 (0.0) | 0 (0.0) |
| *Some contact* | 0 (0.0) | 15 (13.8) | 7 (9.2) | 69 (17.1) | 1 (12.5) | 60 (17.6) |
| 1 child | 0 (0.0) | 2 (1.8) | 2 (2.6) | 19 (4.7) | 1 (12.5) | 11 (3.2) |
| 2 children | 0 (0.0) | 6 (5.5) | 2 (2.6) | 31 (7.7) | 0 (0.0) | 22 (6.5) |
| 3 children | 0 (0.0) | 5 (4.6) | 2 (2.6) | 11 (2.7) | 0 (0.0) | 18 (5.3) |
| 4 children | 0 (0.0) | 2 (1.8) | 0 (0.0) | 6 (1.5) | 0 (0.0) | 5 (1.5) |
| 5 children | 0 (0.0) | 0 (0.0) | 1 (1.3) | 2 (0.5) | 0 (0.0) | 4 (1.2) |
| *Considerable contact* | 1 (10.0) | 32 (29.4) | 22 (28.9) | 139 (34.5) | 3 (37.5) | 167 (49.1) |
| 1 child | 1 (10.0) | 8 (7.3) | 10 (13.2) | 29 (7.2) | 1 (12.5) | 23 (6.8) |
| 2 children | 0 (0.0) | 10 (9.2) | 5 (6.6) | 54 (13.4) | 0 (0.0) | 58 (17.0) |
| 3 children | 0 (0.0) | 6 (5.5) | 4 (5.3) | 27 (6.7) | 1 (12.5) | 43 (12.6) |
| 4 children | 0 (0.0) | 6 (5.5) | 2 (2.6) | 14 (3.5) | 1 (12.5) | 23 (6.7) |
| 5 children | 0 (0.0) | 2 (1.8) | 1 (1.3) | 15 (3.7) | 0 (0.0) | 20 (5.9) |
| *Total* | 10 | 109 | 76 | 403 | 8 | 340 |

Figures in parentheses are row percents.
HRCA Elderly Survey.

**Table 5.11B    Contact with Family Last Week, Vulnerable, Noninstitutionalized Elderly**

| | Single Males | | Single Females | | Married | |
|---|---|---|---|---|---|---|
| | Poor | Not Poor | Poor | Not Poor | Poor | Not Poor |
| *Zero children* | 2 (25.0) | 9 (20.5) | 17 (15.5) | 70 (23.0) | 1 (33.3) | 13 (14.1) |
| *Lives with child/children* | 3 (37.5) | 13 (29.5) | 46 (41.8) | 75 (24.7) | 0 (0.0) | 17 (18.5) |
| *No contact* | 0 (0.0) | 2 (4.5) | 1 (0.9) | 5 (1.6) | 0 (0.0) | 2 (2.2) |
| 1 child | 0 (0.0) | 2 (4.5) | 0 (0.0) | 3 (1.0) | 0 (0.0) | 0 (0.0) |
| 2 children | 0 (0.0) | 0 (0.0) | 0 (0.0) | 2 (0.6) | 0 (0.0) | 1 (1.1) |
| 3 children | 0 (0.0) | 0 (0.0) | 0 (0.0) | 0 (0.0) | 0 (0.0) | 1 (1.1) |
| 4 children | 0 (0.0) | 0 (0.0) | 1 (0.9) | 0 (0.0) | 0 (0.0) | 0 (0.0) |
| 5 children | 0 (0.0) | 0 (0.0) | 0 (0.0) | 0 (0.0) | 0 (0.0) | 1 (1.1) |
| *Little contact* | 0 (0.0) | 3 (6.8) | 5 (4.5) | 14 (4.6) | 0 (0.0) | 5 (5.4) |
| 1 child | 0 (0.0) | 1 (2.3) | 1 (0.9) | 6 (2.0) | 0 (0.0) | 1 (1.1) |
| 2 children | 0 (0.0) | 1 (2.3) | 3 (2.7) | 4 (1.3) | 0 (0.0) | 1 (1.1) |
| 3 children | 0 (0.0) | 1 (2.3) | 1 (0.9) | 1 (0.3) | 0 (0.0) | 2 (2.2) |
| 4 children | 0 (0.0) | 0 (0.0) | 0 (0.0) | 1 (0.3) | 0 (0.0) | 0 (0.0) |
| 5 children | 0 (0.0) | 0 (0.0) | 0 (0.0) | 2 (0.7) | 0 (0.0) | 1 (1.1) |
| *Some contact* | 3 (37.5) | 7 (15.9) | 14 (12.7) | 40 (13.2) | 1 (33.3) | 21 (22.8) |
| 1 child | 2 (25.0) | 4 (9.1) | 5 (4.5) | 16 (5.3) | 0 (0.0) | 5 (5.4) |
| 2 children | 1 (12.5) | 2 (4.5) | 7 (6.4) | 8 (2.6) | 1 (33.3) | 11 (12.0) |
| 3 children | 0 (0.0) | 1 (2.3) | 0 (0.0) | 7 (2.3) | 0 (0.0) | 4 (4.3) |
| 4 children | 0 (0.0) | 0 (0.0) | 2 (1.8) | 4 (1.3) | 0 (0.0) | 0 (0.0) |
| 5 children | 0 (0.0) | 0 (0.0) | 0 (0.0) | 5 (1.6) | 0 (0.0) | 1 (1.1) |
| *Considerable contact* | 0 (0.0) | 10 (22.7) | 27 (24.5) | 100 (32.9) | 1 (33.3) | 34 (37.0) |
| 1 child | 0 (0.0) | 2 (4.5) | 9 (8.2) | 15 (4.9) | 0 (0.0) | 8 (8.7) |
| 2 children | 0 (0.0) | 5 (11.4) | 5 (4.5) | 30 (9.9) | 0 (0.0) | 10 (10.9) |
| 3 children | 0 (0.0) | 2 (4.5) | 6 (5.5) | 24 (7.9) | 0 (0.0) | 9 (9.8) |
| 4 children | 0 (0.0) | 1 (2.3) | 3 (2.7) | 13 (4.3) | 0 (0.0) | 2 (2.2) |
| 5 children | 0 (0.0) | 0 (0.0) | 4 (3.6) | 18 (5.9) | 1 (33.3) | 5 (5.4) |
| *Total* | 8 | 44 | 110 | 304 | 3 | 92 |

Figures in parentheses are row percents.
HRCA Elderly Survey.

**Table 5.11C  Contact with Family Last Week, Institutionalized Elderly**

| | Single Males | | Single Females | | Married | |
|---|---|---|---|---|---|---|
| | Poor | Not Poor | Poor | Not Poor | Poor | Not Poor |
| *Zero children* | 2 (66.7) | 3 (17.6) | 13 (19.4) | 13 (16.7) | 1 (16.7) | 3 (33.0) |
| *Lives with child/children* | 0 (0.0) | 1 (5.9) | 0 (0.0) | 0 (0.0) | 0 (0.0) | 0 (0.0) |
| *No contact* | 0 (0.0) | 2 (11.8) | 4 (6.0) | 3 (3.8) | 1 (16.7) | 2 (20.0) |
| 1 child | 0 (0.0) | 1 (5.9) | 3 (4.5) | 1 (1.3) | 1 (16.7) | 2 (20.0) |
| 2 children | 0 (0.0) | 0 (5.9) | 1 (1.5) | 2 (2.6) | 0 (0.0) | 0 (0.0) |
| 3 children | 0 (0.0) | 0 (0.0) | 0 (0.0) | 0 (0.0) | 0 (0.0) | 0 (0.0) |
| 4 children | 0 (0.0) | 0 (0.0) | 0 (0.0) | 0 (0.0) | 0 (0.0) | 1 (10.0) |
| 5 children | 0 (0.0) | 0 (0.0) | 0 (0.0) | 0 (0.0) | 0 (0.0) | 0 (0.0) |
| *Little contact* | 0 (0.0) | 2 (11.8) | 11 (16.4) | 9 (11.5) | 0 (0.0) | 1 (10.0) |
| 1 child | 0 (0.0) | 1 (5.9) | 5 (7.5) | 3 (3.8) | 0 (0.0) | 0 (0.0) |
| 2 children | 0 (0.0) | 1 (5.9) | 2 (3.0) | 2 (2.6) | 0 (0.0) | 0 (0.0) |
| 3 children | 0 (0.0) | 0 (0.0) | 1 (1.5) | 4 (5.1) | 0 (0.0) | 0 (0.0) |
| 4 children | 0 (0.0) | 0 (5.9) | 1 (1.5) | 0 (0.0) | 0 (0.0) | 1 (10.0) |
| 5 children | 0 (0.0) | 0 (0.0) | 2 (3.0) | 0 (0.0) | 0 (0.0) | 0 (0.0) |
| *Some contact* | 0 (0.0) | 3 (17.6) | 19 (29.2) | 36 (28.4) | 1 (16.7) | 2 (20.0) |
| 1 child | 0 (0.0) | 1 (5.9) | 5 (7.5) | 11 (14.1) | 0 (0.0) | 0 (0.0) |
| 2 children | 0 (0.0) | 1 (5.9) | 6 (9.0) | 11 (14.1) | 1 (16.7) | 1 (10.0) |
| 3 children | 0 (0.0) | 0 (0.0) | 4 (6.0) | 10 (12.8) | 0 (0.0) | 1 (10.0) |
| 4 children | 0 (0.0) | 1 (5.9) | 3 (4.5) | 3 (3.8) | 0 (0.0) | 0 (0.0) |
| 5 children | 0 (0.0) | 0 (0.0) | 1 (1.5) | 1 (1.3) | 0 (0.0) | 0 (0.0) |
| *Considerable contact* | 1 (33.3) | 6 (35.3) | 19 (28.4) | 15 (19.5) | 3 (50.0) | 2 (20.0) |
| 1 child | 0 (0.0) | 1 (5.9) | 6 (9.2) | 6 (7.7) | 0 (0.0) | 1 (10.0) |
| 2 children | 0 (0.0) | 1 (5.9) | 3 (4.6) | 3 (3.8) | 1 (16.7) | 0 (0.0) |
| 3 children | 0 (0.0) | 2 (11.8) | 8 (11.9) | 1 (1.3) | 1 (16.7) | 0 (0.0) |
| 4 children | 0 (33.3) | 1 (5.9) | 0 (0.0) | 2 (2.6) | 0 (0.0) | 0 (0.0) |
| 5 children | 0 (0.0) | 1 (5.9) | 2 (3.1) | 3 (3.8) | 1 (16.7) | 1 (10.0) |
| *Total* | 3 | 17 | 67 | 78 | 6 | 10 |

Figures in parentheses are row percents.
HRCA Elderly Survey.

**Table 5.12A**  Differences in Contact Among Children Of Elderly

| | Total Number of Children | Live with Parent | Talk with Parent Daily | Talk with Parent at Least Weekly | Talk with Parent at Least Monthly | Talk with Parent at Least Yearly | Talk with Parent Never/Almost Never |
|---|---|---|---|---|---|---|---|
| 1 child | 462 | 74 (16.0) | 121 (26.2) | 174 (37.7) | 56 (12.1) | 28 (6.1) | 9 (1.9) |
| 2 children | 1,113 | 110 (9.9) | 250 (22.5) | 486 (43.7) | 175 (15.7) | 74 (6.6) | 18 (1.6) |
| 3 children | 1,167 | 109 (9.3) | 244 (20.9) | 502 (43.0) | 217 (18.6) | 79 (6.8) | 16 (1.4) |
| 4 children | 751 | 61 (8.1) | 133 (17.7) | 329 (43.8) | 140 (18.6) | 72 (9.6) | 16 (2.1) |
| 5 or more children | 1,195 | 93 (7.8) | 190 (15.9) | 554 (46.4) | 230 (19.2) | 112 (9.4) | 16 (1.3) |

Figures in parentheses are row percents.

HRCA Elderly Survey.

**Table 5.12B**  Differences in Contact among Children of Vulnerable Elderly

| | Total Number of Children | Live with Parent | Talk with Parent Daily | Talk with Parent at Least Weekly | Talk with Parent at Least Monthly | Talk with Parent at Least Yearly | Talk with Parent Never/Almost Never |
|---|---|---|---|---|---|---|---|
| 1 child | 197 | 29 (14.7) | 51 (25.9) | 73 (37.1) | 22 (11.2) | 16 (8.1) | 6 (3.0) |
| 2 children | 433 | 53 (12.2) | 100 (23.1) | 175 (40.2) | 55 (12.7) | 40 (9.2) | 10 (2.3) |
| 3 children | 486 | 50 (10.3) | 99 (20.4) | 179 (36.8) | 84 (17.3) | 62 (12.8) | 12 (2.5) |
| 4 children | 306 | 26 (8.5) | 47 (15.4) | 114 (37.3) | 67 (21.9) | 42 (13.7) | 10 (3.3) |
| 5 or more children | 597 | 39 (6.5) | 79 (13.2) | 287 (48.1) | 108 (18.1) | 72 (12.1) | 12 (2.0) |

Figures in parentheses are row percents.

HRCA Elderly Survey.

**Table 5.12C**     **Differences in Contact Among Children of Institutionalized Elderly**

| | Total Number of Children | Live with Parent | Talk with Parent Daily | Talk with Parent at Least Weekly | Talk with Parent at Least Monthly | Talk with Parent at Least Yearly | Talk with Parent Never/Almost Never |
|---|---|---|---|---|---|---|---|
| 1 child | 70 | 0 (0.0) | 11 (15.7) | 39 (55.7) | 8 (11.4) | 10 (14.3) | 2 (2.9) |
| 2 children | 105 | 0 (0.0) | 14 (13.3) | 51 (48.6) | 19 (18.1) | 17 (16.2) | 4 (3.9) |
| 3 children | 124 | 0 (0.0) | 4 (3.2) | 66 (53.2) | 22 (17.7) | 23 (18.5) | 9 (8.8) |
| 4 children | 76 | 0 (0.0) | 5 (6.6) | 25 (32.9) | 15 (19.7) | 26 (34.2) | 5 (6.6) |
| 5 or more children | 111 | 0 (0.0) | 3 (2.7) | 76 (68.5) | 13 (11.7) | 16 (14.4) | 3 (2.7) |

Figures in parentheses are row percents.

HRCA Elderly Survey.

and 8 percent talk yearly or very rarely. Note that only children are in somewhat more contact with their parent(s) on average than children with one or more siblings; the percentage of only children who have at least weekly contact with their parents is 79.9 percent, compared with 70.1 percent for children who have four or more siblings. Apparently, children in such larger families can share the burden of contact, to the extent it is a burden, and each child doesn't feel the need to engage in as much contact. Interestingly, close to one tenth of children are reported by their parents to have no or very little contact over the course of the year.

The figures in table 5.12B for contact of children of the vulnerable elderly suggest a quite similar degree of child-parent contact. In contrast, children of the institutionalized elderly have less contact with their parents than other children. According to table 5.12C, over 17 percent have no contact or very little contact over the course of the year with their institutionalized parent(s).

Tables 5.13 and 5.14 document the fact that financial transfers from children to parents and from parents to children are quite rare, even in the case of parents who are very poor. The income categories "very poor," "poor," "middle," and "rich" correspond, respectively, to income levels of zero to $5000, $5000 to $10,000, $10,000 to $40,000, and

**Table 5.13    Monthly Financial Help from Children to Parent**

|  | Very Poor Parents | Poor Parents | Middle Parents | Rich Parents |
|---|---|---|---|---|
| *One child* | | | | |
| Number | 78 | 172 | 76 | 0 |
| Number receiving help | 2 | 2 | 2 | 0 |
| Average amount of help | 255.0 | 740.0 | 460.0 | 0 |
| *Two children* | | | | |
| Number | 57 | 212 | 141 | 10 |
| Number receiving help | 4 | 7 | 5 | 0 |
| Average amount of help | 595.0 | 371.0 | 204.0 | 0 |
| *Three children* | | | | |
| Number | 45 | 137 | 100 | 11 |
| Number receiving help | 0 | 4 | 1 | 0 |
| Average amount of help | 0 | 76.0 | 60.0 | 0 |
| *Four children* | | | | |
| Number | 25 | 70 | 50 | 2 |
| Number receiving help | 1 | 2 | 2 | 0 |
| Average amount of help | 120.0 | 38.0 | 170.0 | 0 |
| *Five or more children* | | | | |
| Number | 30 | 92 | 41 | 0 |
| Number receiving help | 3 | 6 | 2 | 0 |
| Average amount of help | 13.0 | 80.0 | 26.2 | 0 |

HRCA Elderly Survey.

**Table 5.14          Monthly Financial Help to Children from Parent**

|  | Very Poor Parents | Poor Parents | Middle Parents | Rich Parents |
|---|---|---|---|---|
| *One child* | | | | |
| Number | 78 | 172 | 76 | 0 |
| Number giving help | 1 | 2 | 2 | 0 |
| Average amount of help | 40.0 | 116.0 | 155.0 | 0 |
| *Two children* | | | | |
| Number | 57 | 212 | 141 | 10 |
| Number giving help | 3 | 4 | 3 | 1 |
| Average amount given | 42.0 | 1,423.0 | 1,108.3 | 1,000.0 |
| *Three children* | | | | |
| Number | 45 | 137 | 100 | 11 |
| Number giving help | 2 | 1 | 4 | 2 |
| Average amount of help | 62.0 | 160.0 | 229.0 | 326.0 |
| *Four children* | | | | |
| Number | 25 | 70 | 50 | 2 |
| Number giving help | 1 | 1 | 2 | 0 |
| Average amount of help | 240.0 | 63.0 | 1,605.0 | 0 |
| *Five or more children* | | | | |
| Number | 30 | 92 | 41 | 0 |
| Number giving help | 1 | 3 | 2 | 0 |
| Average amount of help | 20.0 | 168.0 | 48.2 | 0 |

HRCA Elderly Survey.

above $40,000. The tables consider only those parent(s) who have children but live apart from their children.

Of the 1,349 parents listed in table 5.13, only 44, 3.26 percent, report receiving regular monthly financial help from their children. Of the 235 very poor parents, only 10 (4.25 percent) report receiving transfers. These figures are surprising; what is even more surprising is that even in cases where there are a large number of children, there are few transfers to poor or very poor parents.

Of the 1,349 parents listed in table 5.14, 35 report they provide regular monthly help to one or more of their children. Rich parents are more likely to provide such transfers, but there are also 8 cases of very poor parents transferring to their children.

## 5.4   Some Preliminary Findings from the HRC-NBER Child Survey

Table 5.15A considers the telephone contact between the 399 children we have interviewed to date in the HRC-NBER Child Survey and their parent who is a respondent in the HRCA Elderly Survey. Of the 399 children, 87 live with their parent, 76 reported daily telephone contact, 127 reported weekly telephone contact, 48 reported monthly telephone contact, and 61 (15.3 percent) reported no telephone contact in the

**Table 5.15A          Child Respondent Telephone Contact Last Month with Parents**

|  | All Children | | Children with Vulnerable Parents | | Children with Institutionalized Parents | |
|---|---|---|---|---|---|---|
| Lives with parent | 87 | (21.8) | 38 | (27.7) | 0 | (0.0) |
| Several times a day | 17 | (4.3) | 4 | (2.9) | 0 | (0.0) |
| Daily | 59 | (14.8) | 16 | (11.7) | 0 | (0.0) |
| 3–6 times a week | 54 | (13.5) | 12 | (8.8) | 2 | (4.7) |
| Twice a week | 36 | (9.0) | 7 | (5.1) | 2 | (4.7) |
| Once a week | 37 | (9.3) | 9 | (6.6) | 3 | (7.0) |
| 2–3 times a month | 37 | (9.3) | 6 | (4.4) | 0 | (0.0) |
| Once a month | 11 | (2.8) | 2 | (1.5) | 1 | (2.3) |
| No contact last month | 61 | (15.3) | 43 | (31.4) | 34 | (79.1) |
| Total | 399 | (100.0) | 137 | (100.0) | 42 | (100.0) |

Figures in parentheses are column percents.
HRC/NBER Child Survey.

previous month. Of the 137 children with vulnerable parents, the no telephone contact percentage is 31.4 percent. It is a surprising 79.1 percent for the children of the institutionalized.

Table 5.15B repeats the analysis of table 5.15A but includes the siblings of the 399 children. Of the total of 1,055 children of the 399 HRCA elderly respondents, 12.4 percent live with their parents, 13 percent have daily telephone contact, 32.3 percent had weekly telephone contact in the previous month. Again, there is evidence of less contact with the vulnerable and institutionalized elderly. Over one third

**Table 5.15B          Child Respondent and Sibling Telephone Contact Last Month with Parents**

|  | All Children | | Children with Vulnerable Parents | | Children with Institutionalized Parent | |
|---|---|---|---|---|---|---|
| Lives with parent | 131 | (12.4) | 54 | (14.5) | 0 | (0.0) |
| Several times a day | 24 | (2.3) | 6 | (1.6) | 0 | (0.0) |
| Daily | 113 | (10.7) | 39 | (10.5) | 1 | (0.9) |
| 3–6 times a week | 106 | (10.0) | 30 | (8.0) | 2 | (1.8) |
| Twice a week | 80 | (7.6) | 19 | (5.1) | 3 | (2.7) |
| Once a week | 155 | (14.7) | 41 | (11.0) | 4 | (3.6) |
| 2–3 times a month | 134 | (12.7) | 21 | (5.6) | 4 | (3.6) |
| Once a month | 99 | (9.4) | 32 | (8.6) | 5 | (4.5) |
| No contact last month | 213 | (20.1) | 131 | (35.1) | 90 | (81.8) |
| Total | 1,055 | (100.0) | 373 | (100.0) | 109 | (100.0) |

Figures in parentheses are column percents.
HRC/NBER Child Survey.

of the children of the vulnerable elderly and over four fifths of the
children of the institutionalized elderly are reported to have had no
telephone contact with their parent(s) in the previous month.

Tables 5.16A and 5.16B repeat the contact calculations of tables
5.15A and 5.15B but consider time spent with the elderly parent in the
previous month. Table 5.16B indicates that over a quarter of all children
spent zero hours with their elderly parent. In contrast almost a quarter
of children, including those living with their parent(s), spent over 30
hours in the previous month with their parents.

**Table 5.16A**     **Child Respondent Contact Last Month with Parents**

|  | All Children | | Children with Vulnerable Parents | | Children with Institutionalized Parents | |
| --- | --- | --- | --- | --- | --- | --- |
| Lives with parent | 87 | (21.8) | 38 | (27.7) | 0 | (0.0) |
| 0 hours | 52 | (13.0) | 10 | (7.2) | 3 | (6.8) |
| 1–5 hours | 28 | (7.0) | 7 | (5.1) | 5 | (11.4) |
| 5–10 hours | 51 | (12.8) | 18 | (13.0) | 10 | (22.7) |
| 10–20 hours | 66 | (16.5) | 29 | (21.0) | 12 | (27.3) |
| 20–30 hours | 35 | (8.8) | 12 | (8.7) | 4 | (9.1) |
| 30–40 hours | 27 | (6.8) | 9 | (6.5) | 1 | (2.3) |
| 40–50 hours | 14 | (3.5) | 5 | (3.6) | 4 | (9.1) |
| 50+ hours | 39 | (9.8) | 10 | (7.2) | 4 | (9.1) |
| Total | 399 | (100.0) | 138 | (100.0) | 44 | (100.0) |

Figures in parentheses are column percents.
HRC/NBER Child Survey.

**Table 5.16B**     **Child Respondent and Sibling Contact Last Month with Parents**

|  | All Children | | Children with Vulnerable Parents | | Children with Institutionalized Parents | |
| --- | --- | --- | --- | --- | --- | --- |
| Lives with parent | 131 | (12.5) | 54 | (14.9) | 0 | (0.0) |
| 0 hours | 296 | (28.2) | 87 | (24.0) | 24 | (25.0) |
| 1–5 hours | 157 | (15.0) | 61 | (16.8) | 21 | (21.8) |
| 5–10 hours | 139 | (13.3) | 44 | (12.2) | 19 | (19.8) |
| 10–20 hours | 147 | (14.0) | 63 | (17.4) | 20 | (20.8) |
| 20–30 hours | 60 | (5.7) | 18 | (4.9) | 4 | (4.2) |
| 30–40 hours | 41 | (3.9) | 14 | (3.9) | 1 | (1.0) |
| 40–50 hours | 17 | (1.6) | 6 | (1.7) | 4 | (4.2) |
| 50+ hourse | 60 | (5.7) | 15 | (4.1) | 3 | (3.1) |
| Total | 1,048 | (100.0) | 362 | (100.0) | 96 | (100.0) |

Figures in parentheses are column percents.
HRC/NBER Child Survey.

Table 5.17 examines the 230 of the 399 parents who received five or more hours last month in assistance from their children and for whom we have information about each of their children's income. The "low" and "high" income distinction is based on income below and above $20,000. These data suggest that most of the elderly are receiving some child time, and that some of this child time is provided by high-income children to low-income parents.

Tables 5.18, 5.19, and 5.20 cross-tabulate parent and child income levels for cases with complete child and parent income information. Table 5.18 considers all parents, table 5.19 considers only the vulnerable elderly cases, and table 5.20 classifies parents based on their Medicaid status and institutionalization status. These very preliminary data sug-

| Table 5.17 | **Number of Parents Who Received Five or More Hours of Child/ Children Time Last Month by Child Income** | | | | | | | |
|---|---|---|---|---|---|---|---|---|
| | Parental Income Level | | | | | | | |
| | Very Poor | | Poor | | Middle | | Rich | |
| | Nonvul. | Vul. | Nonvul. | Vul. | Nonvul. | Vul. | Nonvul. | Vul. |
| *One Child* | 1 | 5 | 17 | 12 | 16 | 5 | 0 | 0 |
| Low income | 0 | 2 | 11 | 4 | 15 | 5 | 0 | 0 |
| High income | 1 | 3 | 6 | 8 | 1 | 0 | 0 | 0 |
| *Two Children* | 4 | 5 | 22 | 6 | 23 | 3 | 1 | 0 |
| Both low | 0 | 2 | 4 | 3 | 2 | 0 | 0 | 0 |
| Both high | 3 | 2 | 12 | 2 | 14 | 1 | 0 | 0 |
| 1 high, 1 low | 1 | 1 | 6 | 1 | 7 | 2 | 1 | 0 |
| *Three Children* | 1 | 4 | 10 | 14 | 18 | 8 | 2 | 0 |
| All low | 0 | 1 | 0 | 0 | 1 | 1 | 0 | 0 |
| All high | 0 | 1 | 4 | 8 | 8 | 1 | 1 | 0 |
| 1 low, 2 high | 1 | 1 | 4 | 4 | 8 | 5 | 1 | 0 |
| 2 low, 1 high | 0 | 1 | 2 | 2 | 1 | 1 | 0 | 0 |
| *Four Children* | 0 | 2 | 6 | 4 | 9 | 3 | 1 | 0 |
| All low | 0 | 1 | 1 | 1 | 0 | 0 | 0 | 0 |
| All high | 0 | 0 | 2 | 1 | 4 | 2 | 0 | 0 |
| 1 low, 3 high | 0 | 0 | 1 | 1 | 4 | 0 | 1 | 0 |
| 2 low, 2 high | 0 | 0 | 2 | 1 | 1 | 1 | 0 | 0 |
| 3 low, 1 high | 0 | 1 | 0 | 0 | 0 | 0 | 0 | 0 |
| *Five Children* | 0 | 3 | 11 | 3 | 10 | 1 | 0 | 0 |
| All low | 0 | 0 | 0 | 0 | 0 | 0 | 0 | 0 |
| All high | 0 | 0 | 2 | 0 | 4 | 1 | 0 | 0 |
| Some low and Some high | 0 | 3 | 9 | 3 | 6 | 0 | 0 | 0 |
| *Total* | 6 | 19 | 66 | 39 | 76 | 20 | 4 | 0 |

HRCA Elderly Survey.

Table 5.18    **Parent vs. Child Income**

|  | Parental Income Level | | | |
|---|---|---|---|---|
|  | Very Poor | Poor | Middle | Rich |
| *One Child* | 16 | 48 | 32 | 0 |
| Low income | 8 | 21 | 2 | 0 |
| High income | 8 | 27 | 30 | 0 |
| *Two Children* | 13 | 38 | 31 | 2 |
| Both low | 3 | 8 | 2 | 0 |
| Both high | 7 | 21 | 18 | 0 |
| 1 high, 1 low | 3 | 9 | 11 | 2 |
| *Three Children* | 6 | 30 | 32 | 3 |
| All low | 2 | 3 | 2 | 0 |
| All high | 1 | 14 | 12 | 1 |
| 1 low, 2 high | 2 | 8 | 15 | 2 |
| 2 low, 1 high | 1 | 5 | 3 | 0 |
| *Four Children* | 3 | 14 | 14 | 1 |
| All low | 1 | 3 | 0 | 0 |
| All high | 1 | 4 | 7 | 0 |
| 1 low, 3 high | 0 | 3 | 4 | 1 |
| 2 low, 2 high | 0 | 3 | 2 | 0 |
| 3 low, 1 high | 1 | 0 | 1 | 0 |
| *Five Children* | 4 | 16 | 11 | 0 |
| All low | 1 | 0 | 0 | 0 |
| All high | 0 | 2 | 5 | 0 |
| Some low and |  |  |  |  |
| Some high | 3 | 14 | 6 | 0 |
| *Total* | 42 | 146 | 120 | 6 |

HRCA Elderly Survey.

gest that most poor and most very poor parents have one or more children with incomes above $20,000.

## 5.5 Preliminary Conclusions

While our findings are preliminary and will be updated and expanded as we receive more data, the tables above suggest that a significant minority of the elderly, many of whom need assistance with the activities of daily living, have either no children or are not in contact with their children. Contact between children and the vulnerable elderly appears to be less than that between children and the nonvulnerable elderly, and the amount of contact between children and the institutionalized elderly seems the least of all. In addition, although many of the parents in our data are very poor, financial support from children to parents, other than in the form of shared housing, is uncommon. The impression given by these data is that many of the elderly are very

Table 5.19          Vulnerable Parent vs. Child Income Levels

|  | Very Poor | Poor | Middle | Rich |
|---|---|---|---|---|
|  | | Parental Income Level | | |
| *One Child* | 9 | 19 | 7 | 0 |
| Low income | 4 | 12 | 0 | 0 |
| High income | 5 | 7 | 7 | 0 |
| *Two Children* | 8 | 10 | 4 | 0 |
| Both low | 3 | 4 | 0 | 0 |
| Both high | 3 | 5 | 1 | 0 |
| 1 high, 2 low | 2 | 1 | 3 | 0 |
| *Three Children* | 5 | 19 | 8 | 0 |
| All low | 2 | 3 | 1 | 0 |
| All high | 1 | 10 | 1 | 0 |
| 1 low, 2 high | 1 | 4 | 5 | 0 |
| 2 low, 1 high | 1 | 2 | 1 | 0 |
| *Four Children* | 3 | 7 | 3 | 0 |
| All low | 1 | 2 | 0 | 0 |
| All high | 1 | 2 | 2 | 0 |
| 1 low, 3 high | 0 | 1 | 0 | 0 |
| 2 low, 2 high | 0 | 2 | 1 | 0 |
| 3 low, 1 high | 1 | 0 | 0 | 0 |
| *Five Children* | 4 | 4 | 1 | 0 |
| All low | 1 | 0 | 0 | 0 |
| All high | 0 | 0 | 1 | 0 |
| Some low and Some high | 3 | 4 | 0 | 0 |
| *Total* | 29 | 59 | 23 | 0 |

HRCA Elderly Survey.

well cared for by their children, while a significant minority either have no children or have no children who provide significant time or care. Some of the findings for this sample are striking:

(1) Over a fifth of the elderly have no children.
(2) Over one half of the elderly either do not have a daughter or do not have a daughter who lives within an hour of them.
(3) Over half of single elderly males and females and over two fifths of vulnerable single elderly males and females live completely alone.
(4) Of the elderly who have children, fewer than a quarter live with their children.
(5) A small fraction of elderly with children hear from them at most on a yearly basis.
(6) Almost 10 percent of the children of the elderly have at most yearly contact.

**Table 5.20**          **Institutionalized Parent vs. Child Income Levels**

| | Parental Income Level | | | |
|---|---|---|---|---|
| | Very Poor | Poor | Middle | Rich |
| *One Child* | 5 | 6 | 2 | 0 |
| Low income | 3 | 1 | 2 | 0 |
| High income | 2 | 5 | 0 | 0 |
| *Two Children* | 2 | 4 | 0 | 0 |
| Both low | 1 | 2 | 0 | 0 |
| Both high | 1 | 2 | 0 | 0 |
| 1 high, 1 low | 0 | 0 | 0 | 0 |
| *Three Children* | 3 | 4 | 1 | 0 |
| All low | 1 | 1 | 0 | 0 |
| All high | 1 | 2 | 0 | 0 |
| 1 low, 2 high | 0 | 0 | 1 | 0 |
| 2 low, 1 high | 1 | 1 | 0 | 0 |
| *Four Children* | 1 | 2 | 1 | 0 |
| All low | 0 | 0 | 0 | 0 |
| All high | 0 | 0 | 1 | 0 |
| 1 low, 3 high | 0 | 0 | 0 | 0 |
| 2 low, 2 high | 0 | 2 | 0 | 0 |
| 3 low, 1 high | 1 | 0 | 0 | 0 |
| *Five Children* | 1 | 0 | 0 | 0 |
| All low | 0 | 0 | 0 | 0 |
| All high | 0 | 0 | 0 | 0 |
| Some low and | | | | |
| Some high | 1 | 0 | 0 | 0 |
| *Total* | 12 | 16 | 4 | 0 |

HRCA Elderly Survey.

(7) Financial assistance from children to the elderly, even in cases where the elderly are quite poor, is extremely rare.

(8) In a typical month, over a quarter of elderly who have children do not physically spend time with their children.

# 6 The Wealth and Poverty of Widows: Assets Before and After the Husband's Death

Michael D. Hurd and David A. Wise

The elderly have experienced substantial absolute and relative gains in real income in the past fifteen years.[1] But while the financial status of the average elderly person has improved, many are still in poverty; in particular, single older persons are often poor. Because of measurement error and variation in yearly income, there is considerable movement into and out of poverty from year to year.[2] But even if one adjusts for the difference between permanent poverty and transitory poverty, the high incidence of poverty among the single elderly is a cause for social concern. While some work has been done on the events surrounding the transition of the elderly into poverty,[3] our knowledge of the course of income and wealth as the elderly age is limited.

We first document in this paper the income and wealth status of the elderly, showing that widows and other single elderly are much more likely to be poor than those who are married. Then we seek to explain why the single elderly are poor, with emphasis on widows. We do this by tracing back over time their financial status, concentrating on the variation in income and wealth. In particular, we concentrate on the wealth of widows when they were married and how it changed when their husbands died. The analysis is based on data from the Retirement History Survey.

Michael D. Hurd is a Professor of Economics at the State University of New York, Stony Brook, and a Research Associate of the National Bureau of Economic Research. David A. Wise is John F. Stambaugh Professor of Political Economy at the John F. Kennedy School of Government, Harvard University, and a Research Associate of the National Bureau of Economic Research.

The authors are grateful to the Commonwealth Fund for financial support and to Tom Prusa for excellent research assistance. John Shoven provided very useful comments on the paper.

177

We find that about 30 percent of widows and other single elderly are poor by standard definitions; only about 8 or 9 percent of married elderly are poor. Although the widows of prior families who were poor are very likely to be poor, more than three quarters of poor widows were not poor before the husband's death. When the husbands in this group died, enough family wealth was lost that the widows became poor. We find that a good deal of family wealth is lost when the husband dies. Private pension income falls substantially at the husband's death. Other resources do not compensate for this wealth decline. Life insurance is rarely large enough to maintain the economic status of widows. Poor widows typically had little housing wealth when they were married. Thus, poor widows do not live in expensive homes with substantial wealth trapped in housing. In short, in families with modest means the loss in wealth when the husband dies is likely to leave the widow in poverty.

The conclusions reached in the paper are based on a large number of calculations, some of them in the form of detailed tables. To facilitate exposition, we have included in the paper itself only summary tables or illustrative excerpts from the more extensive tables. We begin in section 6.1 with documentation of the wealth and poverty status of the elderly. We then consider the circumstances that led to the disproportionate poverty of widows.

### 6.1 Wealth, Income, and Poverty Status

In this section we discuss our data and give some wealth and income measures for the elderly population studied. Finally, we offer several definitions of the poverty level. One of them is quite close to the official U.S. Bureau of Labor Statistics definition; using that definition we find fractions in poverty similar to those found in the official statistics. Other, more inclusive, definitions reduce the fraction in poverty substantially.

### 6.1.1  Data

Our data come from the Longitudinal Retirement History Survey (RHS). The RHS is a self-weighting sample of heads of households who were born in 1905–11. The heads were initially interviewed in 1969, and either they or their survivors were reinterviewed every two years through 1979. Of the original sample, about 63 percent were married couples, about 21 percent widows (original widows), and 16 percent singles. Over the ten years of the survey, many husbands died: by 1979 about 15 percent of the sample are surviving spouses.

The survey collected extensive data on the income, assets, work behavior, and health of the households. We have aggregated more than forty income and asset categories into our income and wealth measures. No single wealth or income measure is completely satisfactory in assessing the economic status of widows; therefore we use a number of measures.

One measure we call bequeathable wealth. Roughly speaking it is the sum of stocks of wealth except housing equity. The main components are savings accounts, stocks and bonds, equity in a business, property, loans receivable, all net of debt. The reasoning behind our use of this wealth measure is that it gives the amount of wealth, other than housing, that may be inherited by a widow; it measures liquidity better than other wealth aggregates; and changes in its level are probably the best measure of desired wealth change. We also study housing wealth, which is the estimated market value of the house less debts on the house. Because it is costly to vary consumption of housing services, housing wealth is less useful as a measure of desired wealth change. It is, of course, useful in understanding economic well-being.

Social Security wealth is the expected present value of future Social Security payments. Annuity wealth is the expected present value of future pension payments. The other income and wealth measures we use are direct responses from the questionnaire.

The value that we place on Medicare/Medicaid services is the per person value transferred into the Medicare/Medicaid system.[4] Our thinking is that it represents the cost of a fair medical insurance policy which is given each year to those eligible. Whether the insurance is valued at its true cost by those who use the services is another question. The value of the services to users who pay very little for them is likely to be much less than the cost of providing them. On the other hand, a large fraction of persons covered by Medicare/Medicaid would be willing to pay much more for the coverage than this cost. Many of these would be unable to purchase such insurance in the private market at the per person value of transfers, and for many it would be unavailable at any price. Thus the average value of such insurance to its recipients may be more or less than its cost. Because of these ambiguities we offer several wealth measures that exclude Medicare/Medicaid.

In our discussion of wealth we usually refer to medians rather than means. This is because the wealth of the elderly is highly skewed; the means may give a misleading impression of the situation of most of the elderly. The drawback is that one cannot sum the medians of the individual components to obtain an aggregate median.

### 6.1.2   Wealth and Income

As shown in table 6.1, widows have much less wealth and income than married couples. The mean of (nonhousing) bequeathable wealth for married couples is about $58,000 in 1979, but little more than $21,000

Table 6.1          Wealth and Income by Marital Status and by Wealth and Income
                   Category, 1979[a]

| Category | Married | | Single | | Widowed | |
|---|---|---|---|---|---|---|
| | Mean | Median | Mean | Median | Mean | Median |
| *Wealth* | | | Wealth | | | |
| Bequeathable | 57,953 | 22,411 | 17,973 | 5,084 | 21,461 | 5,745 |
| Housing | 35,630 | 30,000 | 11,267 | 0 | 20,020 | 12,000 |
| Social Security | 58,372 | 60,413 | 26,067 | 25,979 | 26,411 | 27,784 |
| Pension | 16,064 | 4,447 | 10,191 | 0 | 6,588 | 0 |
| Medicare/Medicaid | 23,422 | 23,584 | 11,959 | 12,408 | 12,344 | 12,408 |
| Human Capital | 6,198 | 0 | 926 | 0 | 1,862 | 0 |
| Other | 1,188 | 0 | 1,011 | 0 | 1,064 | 0 |
| *Income* | | | Income | | | |
| Capital Income | 2,631 | 45 | 898 | 69 | 1,079 | 73 |
| Wages | 3,050 | 0 | 854 | 0 | 925 | 0 |
| Housing | 1,069 | 900 | 338 | 0 | 601 | 360 |
| Social Security | 4,690 | 4,926 | 2,746 | 2,772 | 2,732 | 2,892 |
| Pension | 2,605 | 729 | 1,513 | 0 | 936 | 0 |
| Medicare/Medicaid | 1,662 | 1,513 | 1,080 | 1,246 | 795 | 1,246 |
| Other | 176 | 0 | 141 | 0 | 152 | 0 |

[a]Figures are in 1979 dollars.

for widows and only $18,000 for other single persons. The medians are
much smaller. Half of widows, for example, have less than $6,000 in
financial savings. Widows have much less wealth in other categories
as well. Their median housing value is only $12,000, compared to $30,000
for couples. More than half have no pension income. The average of
pension income is just $936 compared to $2,605 for couples. As we
shall see, this difference reflects the fact that many private pensions
do not have survivorship rights; but, in addition, the husbands who
died during the survey years began with smaller pensions than the
husbands who survived during the survey years.

   Human capital is the expected discounted value of future labor earnings. At the advanced ages of the RHS population in 1979, the stock
is not very important even though earnings are about 19 percent of the
income of couples and 13 percent of widows' income.

   By far the largest source of income for widows is Social Security:
their average benefits are $2,732 per year, somewhat more than half of
the mean level of benefits received by couples. A substantial proportion
of income for both couples and widows is in the form of medical care
provided through Medicare or Medicaid. For widows, we estimate its
average value to be about 11 percent of all income.

Data for the other survey years show a pattern very similar to that for 1979, except that Medicare/Medicaid income was much lower in the earlier years. Because eligibility for these programs does not begin until age 65, most of the elderly did not have Medicare/Medicaid income in earlier years.

### 6.1.3 Poverty

Poverty levels were originally determined by considering the cost of goods and services that would be necessary to maintain a minimum acceptable standard of living. Goods and services include such items as housing and health care. In practice, the poverty level is usually defined by the income necessary to buy these goods and services. If some goods and services are provided through owner-occupied housing or through social insurance, less current income is required to maintain this standard of living, and the definition of a poverty level becomes ambiguous. In principle, the income definition used should correspond to the services included in the market basket used to determine the poverty income level. The ambiguity is especially acute for the elderly; 70 percent live in houses that they own, and many receive large amounts of health care covered by Medicare or Medicaid. Because there is no single unambiguous way to account for these services, we have elected to present estimates of the proportions of persons in poverty based on several income definitions that are progressively more inclusive. The first includes all standard measures of income; the second adds car services and subtracts interest payments on some forms of debt; the third adds the value of housing services from owner-occupied housing; and the fourth adds the annual value of Medicare/Medicaid coverage.[5] In evaluating the change in the financial status of the elderly over time, the latter addition is especially important although difficult to measure precisely.

The mean and median levels of income by these definitions, together with the proportion below the poverty line, are shown in table 6.2 for 1979 and for 1969.

Almost 37 percent of widows were poor in 1979, according to the most limited income definition. Fewer than 10 percent of married couples were poor by this measure. The median income of widows was only 42 percent of the median for couples. Adding the transportation services from owned cars and adjusting for debt servicing (B) changes these numbers very little. Including the cost of renting owner-occupied housing does reduce somewhat the percent below the poverty line.[6] For example, the proportion of widows with incomes below the poverty line is reduced from 36.7 percent to 29.6 percent. We will show below that most widows with low income and total wealth also have little housing wealth. This means that most could not improve their financial

Table 6.2    Mean and Median Income and Percent below the Poverty Line, by Marital Status and Income Definition, 1969 and 1979

| Income Definition[a] | | Married | Single | Widowed |
|---|---|---|---|---|
| | | 1969 ($) | | |
| (A) | Mean | 10,037 | 4,295 | 3,622 |
| | Median | 8,350 | 3,490 | 2,762 |
| | Percent below poverty line | 7.26 | 30.99 | 35.11 |
| (B) | Mean | 10,072 | 4,315 | 3,635 |
| | Median | 8,371 | 3,474 | 2,783 |
| | Percent below poverty line | 7.20 | 30.92 | 34.97 |
| (C) | Mean | 10,462 | 4,451 | 3,847 |
| | Median | 8,735 | 3,601 | 3,008 |
| | Percent below poverty line | 6.27 | 29.76 | 31.73 |
| (D) | Mean | 10,473 | 4,451 | 3,847 |
| | Median | 8,748 | 3,601 | 3,008 |
| | Percent below poverty line | 6.24 | 29.76 | 31.73 |
| | | 1979 ($) | | |
| (A) | Mean | 13,056 | 6,130 | 5,780 |
| | Median | 9,998 | 4,425 | 4,248 |
| | Percent below poverty line | 9.56 | 35.92 | 36.71 |
| (B) | Mean | 13,152 | 6,152 | 5,825 |
| | Median | 10,093 | 4,439 | 4,280 |
| | Percent below poverty line | 9.32 | 36.03 | 36.36 |
| (C) | Mean | 14,221 | 6,490 | 6,425 |
| | Median | 11,035 | 4,805 | 4,985 |
| | Percent below poverty line | 7.38 | 33.22 | 29.62 |
| (D) | Mean | 15,884 | 7,571 | 7,220 |
| | Median | 12,746 | 5,978 | 5,790 |
| | Percent below poverty line | 2.81 | 13.85 | 17.09 |

[a]Income category definitions are as follows:
(A) includes: Business services/debt, real property services/debt, interest income, wages, Social Security income, SSI, pension income (all forms), income from relatives, workman's compensation, unemployment insurance, AFDC, state cash sickness, income from other public assistance, income from non-Social Security disability, income from private welfare, and income from other private individuals.
(B) includes: (A) + car services and interest on the following debt: car, medical, store, bank, and private.
(C) includes: (B) + housing services/debt.
(D) includes: (C) + Medicare/Medicaid income.

position significantly by converting their housing wealth into current consumption, say by means of a reverse mortgage. Most have little to mortgage: as we reported in table 6.1, median housing wealth was only $12,000. Other single elderly have even less housing wealth, as indicated by the very small reduction in the percent below the poverty line when housing services are counted as income.

Judging by economic theory, our income measure (C) is probably more accurate than (A) or (B): it adds to the usual kinds of income flows from nonfinancial assets. Although there is some difference in income levels from measure (A), the general impression is the same: many more widows and singles than couples are poor. Of course, it is difficult to compare incomes across family sizes as one does not know the right correction for economies of scale. The official poverty scale for the elderly suggests that a single person requires about 79 percent of the income of a couple. The Social Security survivorship rights of a widow suggest a widow requires about 67 percent of the income of a couple. Whichever is correct, it is clear that widows have considerably less, about 45 percent according to (C). Thus, even if there are economies of scale in household production and consumption, at the median widows are considerably poorer than couples.

Counting as income our rather crude measure of the cost of medical care, however, has a very substantial effect on the number of elderly that are classified as poor. The percent of poor widows is reduced from 29.6 to 17.1 by adding the cost of medical care to income. Counting housing services and medical care more than halves the percent of poor widows. The reduction is even greater for single persons, from 35.9 to 13.9 percent. While almost 10 percent of married couples are counted as poor by the standard definition of income, fewer than 3 percent are below the poverty line when medical care and housing services are counted as income. These large changes in the fraction in poverty underscore two important points.

First, it is clear from a comparison of the 1979 with the 1969 numbers that accounting for Medicare/Medicaid can have a substantial effect on the poverty status of the elderly. This happens mainly because we included in (D) an income flow from Medicare/Medicaid only if an individual was eligible. But because the age of eligibility is 65, almost no one had an income flow from Medicare/Medicaid in 1969. By 1979 most of the sample were eligible (except young widows). In addition, benefits under Medicare/Medicaid increased faster than the Consumer Price Index, so the imputed income from the medical programs increased faster than the poverty cutoff. Nonetheless, although there can be dispute about how to measure precisely the benefits from the medical programs, these programs were intended to help the elderly population and by these measures they have done just that.

Second, it is evident from the 1979 numbers that relatively small changes in income can have a large effect on the proportion below the poverty line. For example, a $2,748 increase in income for married couples removes from the poverty roles 70 percent of those who would otherwise be there. This sensitivity to definition indicates, of course, that the incomes of many of the poorest elderly are close to the poverty line.

To avoid confusion, all of the calculations below are based on income definition (A). In addition, all money values are in 1979 dollars. For simplicity, we have not reported sample sizes in the tabulations; differences and other patterns that are revealed in the data should be taken to be statistically significant, however.

## 6.2    The Husband's Death and the Inducement of Poverty

The death of a woman's husband increases very substantially the likelihood that she is poor. This is shown in the first panel of table 6.3.

The classification in the table is based on the transition between 1973 and 1975. A couple is classified in the first column if the husband and wife were alive in 1973 and in 1975; a couple is classified in the second column if the husband died between 1973 and 1975. The last two columns pertain to singles and widows, respectively. The data for the groups with no change in marital status provide a control for economymide trends that may have affected the changes in poverty rates from one year to the next. About 8 percent of couples are poor. In particular, 8 or 9 percent of couples prior to the death of the husband are poor (column 2).[7] But when the husband dies, 42 percent of the widows are poor.

The table also highlights the strong relationship between the prior income of the couple and the poverty status of the widow. If the couple

**Table 6.3**         **Percent Poor, by Marital Transition, 1973 → 1975[a]**

| Year | Couple → Couple | Couple → Widow | Single → Single | Widow → Widow |
|------|------|------|------|------|
| | Total Sample | | | |
| 1971 | 8 | 8 | 30 | 28 |
| 1973 | 8 | 9 | 29 | 33 |
| 1975 | 7 | 42 | 29 | 24 |
| | Poor in 1973 | | | |
| 1971 | 50 | 50 | 72 | 48 |
| 1973 | 100 | 100 | 100 | 100 |
| 1975 | 51 | 85 | 78 | 50 |
| | Not Poor in 1973 | | | |
| 1971 | 4 | 4 | 12 | 19 |
| 1973 | 0 | 0 | 0 | 0 |
| 1975 | 4 | 37 | 9 | 11 |

[a]The entries are percents. The husbands in the couple-to-widow category died between 1973 and 1975. The data for 1971 are shown for comparison.

was poor prior to the death of the husband, fully 85 percent of the widows are poor; if the couples was not poor, 37 percent of the widows are subsequently poor. Notice that if the husband had not died, only about 50 percent of the couples who were poor in 1973 would be expected to be poor in 1975, as compared with 85 percent if the husband dies.

In demonstrating the enormous movement in and out of poverty, these data also highlight a difficulty in using income as a measure of permanent poverty status. About 50 percent of couples who were poor in 1973 were not poor two years earlier in 1971; about 50 percent were not poor two years later. Of the continuing widows who were poor in 1973, only about 50 percent were poor in 1971. More detailed data show that poverty of widows and singles is more likely than poverty of married couples to persist. But this conclusion is very sensitive to the way that poverty is defined.[8]

Instead of income, suppose that poverty is defined by wealth. Our wealth poverty line is chosen so that the same proportion of households has total wealth below this cutoff as the proportion that has income below the official income-based poverty line. In addition, we distinguish surviving spouse widows from original widows. The husbands of surviving spouse widows died during the RHS survey years; heads of households who were already widows when the survey began are called original widows. Using these definitions, we find the prevalence and persistence of poverty as shown in table 6.4.

Note that the percent of surviving spouses poor in 1969 pertains to the poverty status of these widows when they were married; all were married when the survey began. Original widows are the most likely to be poor.[9] They have been widowed the longest and presumably their husbands died at the youngest ages. The poverty status of original widows and singles is by far the most persistent, based on the usual income definition. But this conclusion is much less obvious if poverty is based on wealth. The poverty status of all groups is much more permanent based on the wealth definition. This is particularly true for married couples and surviving spouses, who appeared to have the greatest fluctuation in financial status based on the income definition.

## 6.3 Causes of Poverty

We have shown above that the death of the husband in itself induces poverty. To understand how widows come to be poor, we consider their financial position prior to widowhood and how it changed when their husbands died. We also consider other prior attributes, such as health status and the age of the husband at his death, which may be considered proximate causes of poverty. It will help at this point to outline how we shall proceed:

**Table 6.4**     **Percent Poor and Persistence, by Poverty Definition and Marital Status[a]**

| 1979 Marital Status | Percent Poor in 1979, Income Definition | Percent Of Total Poor in 1979, Income Definition | Percent Also Poor in 1969, Income Definition | Percent Also Poor in 1969, Wealth Definition |
|---|---|---|---|---|
| Married | 10 | 20 | 32 | 72 |
| Surviving Spouse | 34 | 21 | 21 | 60 |
| Original Widow | 45 | 39 | 60 | 82 |
| Single | 36 | 20 | 61 | 77 |

[a]The last two columns show the percent of those who were poor in 1979 who were also poor in 1969. Surviving spouses in 1979 were married in 1969.

- We show first that the husband's death is associated with less prior accumulation of wealth; mortality is associated with differential wealth.
- Loss of wealth when the husband dies is then described in detail. It is shown that the prior households of poor widows had much less wealth than the prior households of nonpoor widows. And a larger proportion of the wealth of poor widow households was lost at the husband's death.
- Next it is shown that transfer of wealth to children when the husband dies does not explain the loss of wealth at his death.
- The relationship of earnings to wealth accumulation for poor and nonpoor widows is then explored, albeit in a rather crude fashion, and the potential effect of health on savings is investigated. The households of poor widows apparently accumulated much less wealth per dollar of earned income than the households of nonpoor widows. The husbands in the prior households of widows also had poorer health than the husbands in the continuing couple households. In addition, the husbands of poor widows had poorer health in prior years than the husbands of nonpoor widows.
- Finally, there is a brief discussion of the extent of support from children. It is very limited, but greater for poor than for nonpoor widows.

### 6.3.1 Differential Mortality

The early death of the husband is itself associated with less prior wealth accumulation. Table 6.5 gives total wealth in earlier survey years by change in marital status between 1977 and 1979. This table presents convincing evidence of some differential wealth by mortality of husbands. The striking fact is that in every year the prior couples of surviving spouses had less wealth than continuing couples, not only in the year just before the husband's death, but even several years before. In this case, they had 7 percent less in 1969, 10 percent in 1973, and 8 percent in 1977; and then 35 percent less after the husband's death. The fact that the households in which the husband died always had

**Table 6.5**     **Median Total Wealth, by Marital Transition 1977 → 1979[a]**

| Year | Couple → Couple | Couple → Widow | Single → Single | Widow → Widow |
|------|------|------|------|------|
| 1969 | $120,919 | $112,021 | $45,797 | $99,380 |
| 1973 | 150,962 | 136,582 | 62,488 | 109,581 |
| 1977 | 144,683 | 132,821 | 54,152 | 80,932 |
| 1979 | 134,953 | 87,878 | 46,807 | 73,312 |

[a]The column categories are defined by change in marital status between 1977 and 1979. The entries are in 1979 dollars.

lower wealth suggests that the lower wealth is not caused by medical expenses in the year or so before the husband's death. It suggests that lifetime health differences lead to low lifetime earnings and to early mortality. Data on health status presented below tend to support this hypothesis. Such differential wealth apparently contributes to the poverty of widows. We can speculate that the differential mortality is due to lifetime differences in health: earlier in life earnings were lower because of health differences, and later in life the health differences caused earlier death.

We have shown above that original widows are the most likely to be poor. And given that households in which the husband later died had less wealth, prior to his death, than households in which both the husband and wife lived, one might expect that surviving spouse widows would be more likely to be poor the younger the husband was when he died. The evidence is not consistent with this presumption, however. As table 6.6 shows for widows in 1979, there is essentially no relationship between the percent who are poor and the age of the husband at his death. There is also no relationship between the proportion of widows who are poor and the number of years since the husband's death.

### 6.3.2  Wealth Loss When the Husband Dies

It is clear from the data above that a widow is much more likely to be poor if the prior couple was poor than if the prior couple was not poor. We consider that question in more detail in this section. In particular, we consider the change in wealth when the husband dies. One common explanation for the high incidence of poverty among widows is that the husband's death consumes a large fraction of the family's wealth, for medical or funeral expenses for example. Table 6.7 verifies substantial wealth loss at the husband's death. In this table, we classify according to poverty status in 1977 and consider wealth in 1977 and in 1975. We again present data for those who had no change in marital status during this period, as well as the data for widows in 1977 whose

**Table 6.6**          **Percent Poor Widows in 1979 by Age of the Husband at His Death**

| Age | Percent Poor |
|-----|--------------|
| 59  | 32           |
| 61  | 36           |
| 63  | 34           |
| 65  | 33           |
| 67  | 37           |
| 69  | 36           |
| 71  | 30           |

**Table 6.7**          **Median Wealth in 1975 and 1977, by Marital Transition 1975 →  1977, Wealth Category, and 1977 Poverty Status[a]**

| Wealth Category | Couple → Couple | Couple → Widow | Single → Single | Widow → Widow |
|---|---|---|---|---|
| | Poor in 1977 | | | |
| Total | $65,556 | $85,433 | $29,780 | $47,250 |
| | 62,941 | 54,159 | 29,590 | 48,043 |
| Bequeathable | 1,348 | 4,389 | 281 | 1,187 |
| | 1,677 | 3,139 | 240 | 772 |
| Life Insurance | 1,349 | 3,372 | 539 | 674 |
| | 1,198 | 1,198 | 0 | 898 |
| Annuity | 4,709 | 9,804 | 1,551 | 3,433 |
| | 2,468 | 1,359 | 789 | 1,975 |
| Social Security | 46,584 | 53,981 | 23,623 | 32,953 |
| | 45,129 | 35,310 | 24,303 | 33,881 |
| Housing | 6,743 | 12,138 | 0 | 7,642 |
| | 8,624 | 11,978 | 0 | 4,212 |
| | Not Poor in 1977 | | | |
| Total | 149,844 | 129,353 | 70,051 | 95,334 |
| | 150,851 | 92,939 | 71,549 | 100,563 |
| Bequeathable | 17,532 | 11,005 | 8,698 | 12,542 |
| | 17,755 | 15,810 | 8,795 | 13,205 |
| Life Insurance | 6,743 | 6,237 | 1,349 | 1,349 |
| | 5,151 | 1,198 | 1,198 | 1,198 |
| Annuity | 21,704 | 23,292 | 19,631 | 10,399 |
| | 25,061 | 14,938 | 21,550 | 12,211 |
| Social Security | 70,542 | 69,484 | 35,858 | 43,261 |
| | 69,807 | 44,552 | 35,943 | 44,631 |
| Housing | 26,973 | 21,915 | 0 | 21,578 |
| | 29,945 | 21,956 | 0 | 21,560 |

[a]The first of the two entries in each category pertains to 1975 (when the husband in the couple-to-widow category was living) and the second entry to 1977 (after he had died). The entries are in 1979 dollars.

husbands were alive in 1975. The first number of each category pertains to 1975 and the second number to 1977.

This table makes it clear that poor widows had much less wealth when their husbands were living than nonpoor widows had. In addition, a substantial portion of the prior couple's wealth was dissipated with the husband's death. Poor widows had 37 percent less wealth after the husband's death and nonpoor widows 28 percent less. But even had the poor widows lost the same percentage, more would have been poor in 1977; one reason they are poor is that they were more likely to have come from poor families.

The major differences are in housing wealth, nonhousing bequeathable wealth, and annuity wealth. Bequeathable wealth of poor widows fell to $3,139 after the husband's death: they had almost no private financial resources at the median except for housing wealth. Housing and bequeathable wealth are, except for life insurance, the forms of wealth in which private savings is held. Social savings through Social Security is more evenly distributed.

In fact the levels of Social Security wealth in 1975 were much closer than other forms of wealth. Social Security wealth fell by about 35 percent for both groups. To the extent that Social Security wealth is proportional to Social Security benefits for people of the same sex and age, and Social Security benefits are related to lifetime earnings, the similarity of Social Security wealth indicates that the two groups of widows came from families whose lifetime earnings were not widely different. Of course, the progressivity of the Social Security benefit schedule dampens earnings differences; nonetheless, the differences between Social Security wealth, on the one hand, and bequeathable wealth and housing wealth, on the other hand, suggest that part of the cause of poverty is a failure of the family to accumulate assets during the working life. These data do not, of course, indicate why some families accumulated assets and others did not; but differential mortality, emphasized below, is consistent with the hypothesis that health was different during the working life. That, in turn, suggests that medical expenditures may have been greater during the working life. Of course, it is certainly possible that rather small lifetime earnings differences lead to large ex post differences in assets at retirement.

Possibly the most striking result is that the private annuity wealth of poor widows was virtually eliminated at the death of the husband, declining from $9,804 to $1,359. On the other hand, widows who were not poor had much more annuity wealth when married and lost much less of it when the husband died, 36 percent instead of 86 percent. Presumably recent legislation will reduce very substantially this kind of wealth loss when a spouse dies.

Neither group had much life insurance, although widows who were not poor had about twice as much as those who were poor. Apparently the life insurance collected by nonpoor widows led to the increase in bequeathable wealth, whereas the bequeathable wealth of poor widows fell at the death of the husband. Whatever the interpretation of the reported face value of life insurance, the table makes it clear that life insurance was not sufficient to make up for the loss in other wealth.

In summary: If the husband in a household dies, the probability that the household is poor typically increases from less than 10 percent to more than 35 percent. We find that households in which the husband died accumulated less wealth than households in which both the husband and wife survived. This effect is especially pronounced for personal savings. The prior couples of poor widows accumulated much less wealth than the prior couples of nonpoor widows. A large fraction of the wealth of the couple is dissipated when the husband dies, and the loss of wealth is greater for poor than for nonpoor widows. In the next sections, we explore further the potential reasons for the lower prior household wealth of widows and the particularly low prior wealth of poor widows.

### 6.3.3  Transfer of Wealth to Children?

An explanation for the wealth decline at the husband's death is that children receive inheritances. In table 6.8 we give data that allow an informal test of that hypothesis and that also confirm the differential mortality by wealth. Again the table differentiates households according to whether the husbands died in the 1977–79 interval; wealth of the households is shown back to 1969 by that classification. In this table, however, only housing wealth and nonhousing bequeathable wealth are shown, that is, wealth that could be passed on to children. Once again we see differential mortality and wealth loss at the husband's

**Table 6.8**    **Median Housing and Nonhousing Bequeathable Wealth, by Change in Marital Status 1977 → 1979, and by Year and Whether the Household Had Children[a]**

| Year | Couple → Couple | Couple → Widow | Single → Single | Widow → Widow |
|------|------|------|------|------|
| | Total Sample | | | |
| 1969 | $38,743 | $31,814 | $10,022 | $27,261 |
| 1973 | 43,303 | 36,754 | 9,650 | 31,623 |
| 1977 | 48,763 | 47,236 | 10,604 | 31,598 |
| 1979 | 51,213 | 45,046 | 9,342 | 29,159 |
| | Households with Children | | | |
| 1969 | 37,004 | 32,235 | 4,493 | 26,334 |
| 1973 | 42,434 | 36,754 | 4,358 | 31,426 |
| 1977 | 47,903 | 47,455 | 3,856 | 31,574 |
| 1979 | 50,193 | 45,439 | 3,472 | 28,480 |
| | Households without Children | | | |
| 1969 | 49,706 | 25,603 | 16,224 | 34,936 |
| 1973 | 53,337 | 31,347 | 14,802 | 36,585 |
| 1977 | 55,509 | 37,359 | 16,041 | 32,580 |
| 1979 | 59,157 | 34,340 | 15,250 | 32,222 |

[a]The column categories are defined by change in marital status between 1977 and 1979. The entries are in 1979 dollars.

death. The wealth difference extends back to 1969, at least eight years before the husband's death. We can see that the wealth differential in the year or two before the husband's death is due to a permanent differential, not one caused by sharp wealth declines that would be associated with high medical expenses in the three or four years just preceding the husband's death.

The middle and last panels give wealth changes according to whether the household has children.[10] We see that, if anything, there was more wealth destruction in the households without children than in those with children. This pattern is also found in the other years. Thus it seems unlikely that the wealth decline is due to the transfer of wealth to children. The table also shows that couples with children have substantially less wealth than couples without children. We explore this issue further below, but note now that raising children substantially decreases the retirement assets of households.

One anomaly of the data for this year is that there appears in some years to be little differential mortality in families with children. In comparisons for all other two-year periods differential mortality is revealed. Indeed, the association between early death and the accumulation of personal savings is much more pronounced than the relationship for all wealth, including government-directed savings—Social Security—and saving through firm pension plans. The data typically look like those in table 6.8 for households without children.

### 6.3.4  Prior Earnings, Wealth Accumulation, and Health

The data on Social Security wealth suggest that continuing couples had somewhat greater wage earnings over their lifetimes than the prior couples of widows, 2 to 7 percent more depending on the year for which the calculation is made. Table 6.9 shows prior Social Security wealth, housing and other bequeathable wealth, and total wealth of couples, by change in marital status in the 1975–77 interval. Those who became widows during that period are distinguished by whether they were poor in 1977.

Prior couples of widows had about 3 percent less Social Security wealth in 1969 than continuing couples; they had about 8 percent less in 1975. The 1969 prior Social Security wealth of poor widows was about 21 percent less than that of nonpoor widows; 1975 Social Security wealth was about 22 percent less.

Differences in wealth accumulation were much greater. If Social Security wealth is taken as an index of earnings and other wealth as an index of savings, households in which the husband died saved much less than households in which the husband did not die. And households in which the death of the husband left a poor widow saved very much less than those in which the widow was not poor. Thus this admittedly

**Table 6.9**    **Median Social Security versus Other Wealth by Marital Transition 1975 → 1977[a]**

| Year | Couple → Couple | Couple → Widow | Couple → Not Poor Widow | Couple → Poor Widow |
|------|-----------------|----------------|-------------------------|---------------------|
| | | Social Security Wealth | | |
| 1969 | $49,725 | $48,021 | $51,368 | $40,565 |
| 1975 | 69,414 | 63,741 | 69,484 | 53,981 |
| 1977 | 68,176 | 40,374 | 44,552 | 35,310 |
| | | Bequeathable Plus Housing Wealth | | |
| 1969 | 39,581 | 23,096 | 32,201 | 15,196 |
| 1975 | 46,847 | 26,973 | 35,065 | 14,363 |
| 1977 | 49,427 | 30,722 | | 16,093 |
| | | Total Wealth | | |
| 1969 | 121,933 | 97,627 | 114,143 | 72,066 |
| 1975 | 144,527 | 110,492 | 129,353 | 85,433 |
| 1977 | 145,867 | 78,696 | 92,939 | 54,159 |
| | | Ratio: Bequeathable Plus Housing Wealth to SS | | |
| 1969 | 0.80 | 0.48 | 0.63 | 0.37 |
| | | Ratio: Total Non-SS Wealth to SS | | |
| 1969 | 1.45 | 1.03 | 1.22 | 0.78 |

[a]The column categories are defined by change in marital status between 1977 and 1979. The dollar entries are in 1979 dollars.

crude indicator of saving suggests that the early death of the husband was associated with considerably less saving out of earnings and that poverty of widows is partially explained by the failure to accumulate assets while the husband was living.[11]

Measures of health status indicate, in turn, that the lower saving rate may be associated with poor health. We have speculated about the role of the husband's health in the eventual poverty of the widow. In table 6.10 we offer direct evidence that poor widows tend to come from families in which the husband had bad health. The table records the average of a subjective health indicator: the higher the value the higher the respondent rates his own health. The health indicators are presented for the same marital transition categories as in table 6.9. The last response in the couple-to-widow column is that of the surviving spouse and is approximately equal to the response of continuing couples, typically that of the husband. We see, for example, that in 1969 the mean response of the husbands of continuing couples was 63, whereas the

Table 6.10          **Subjective Health Indicator of Respondent by 1975 → 1977 Marital Transition**[a]

| Year | Couple → Couple | Couple → Widow | Couple → Not Poor Widow | Couple → Poor Widow |
|------|------|------|------|------|
| 1969 | 63 | 49 | 50 | 48 |
| 1971 | 61 | 45 | 47 | 43 |
| 1973 | 59 | 40 | 42 | 38 |
| 1975 | 63 | 37 | 37 | 38 |
| 1977 | 61 | 55 | 56 | 54 |

[a]The column categories are defined by change in marital status between 1977 and 1979.

mean response in that year of the husbands of 1977 widows was 49. In later years the difference becomes much greater: by 1975 the figures are 63 and 37, respectively. In addition, just as poor widows came from families with lower levels of wealth than nonpoor widows, they also came from families in which the husband had worse health. The difference in health indicators between the poor and nonpoor widows is not very pronounced, however, whereas the comparable differences in wealth were very large. Data not shown indicate that poor widows also tend to rate their health worse than nonpoor widows do.

An obvious explanation for the change in bequeathable wealth at the husband's death is medical expenses. We do not have complete medical expenditure data, but we do have information on expenditures for doctor bills. Table 6.11 shows that they are small on average, and that they generally are larger for those surviving spouses who were not poor in 1979 than for those who were poor. If doctor bills are a good indicator of total medical expenditures, it does not appear that poor widows became poor because of unusually high medical expenditures.

### 6.3.5   Support from Children

Although intergenerational transfers are not the focus of this paper, we offer some evidence on how they might affect the poverty status

Table 6.11          **Mean Doctor Bills Paid by Prior Households of 1979 Surviving Spouses, by Poverty Status in 1979 and by Year**

| Year | Poor | Nonpoor |
|------|------|------|
| 1969 | 123 | 186 |
| 1971 | 142 | 154 |
| 1973 | 76 | 108 |
| 1975[a] | — | — |
| 1977 | 164 | 122 |

[a]Data were not collected in 1975.

of the elderly. The RHS does not have information on amounts transferred from children. As reported in Hurd and Shoven (1985), the amount transferred from relatives is very small: $12 per year in 1979; $23 per year for single females most of whom would be widows. For this project we collected data on the number of children who gave transfers. We report in table 6.12, by poverty status in 1979, the average number of living children and the average number from whom support is received. Again we see that the poor elderly have more children than the nonpoor. Only a small fraction of the elderly receive any support at all from their children, but the poor elderly are more likely than the nonpoor to receive support, no matter what their marital status. Poor widows are more than twice as likely as poor married couples to receive support. Although transfers may alleviate poverty somewhat, apparently the levels of support from children do not go far in alleviating the poverty of widows.

## 6.4  Summary and Conclusions

We verified that widows are much more likely than couples to be poor and that they make up a large proportion of the poor elderly; 80 percent are widows or other single individuals. We also verified that widows have substantially less wealth than couples; thus, the high frequency of poverty among widows when poverty is defined by income is also found when poverty is defined by wealth. There is an enormous amount of movement in and out of poverty when it is defined by income, however. The wealth definition provides a much better measure of permanent poverty; defined by wealth, there is much less movement from poor to nonpoor poverty status. Were one to include sources of income such as the value of housing services, the general conclusions about the incidence of poverty would be unchanged, although the

**Table 6.12**     **Number of Children and Support from Them, by Marital Status and Poverty Status, 1979[a]**

| Entry | Married | Widow | Single |
|-------|---------|-------|--------|
|  | | Poor | |
| Living Children | 4.15 | 3.32 | 1.80 |
| Receive Support from | 0.21 | 0.51 | 0.15 |
|  | | Not Poor | |
| Living Children | 2.63 | 2.24 | 0.78 |
| Receive Support from | 0.05 | 0.08 | 0.04 |

[a]The entries are number of children.

proportions classified as poor would be somewhat lower. Our rough valuation of Medicare/Medicaid transfers, however, reduced very substantially the fraction in poverty. It is clear that what is counted as income, together with assumptions about the cost of living for a single person versus a couple, can have an important effect on the proportion of the elderly classified as poor.

The death of the husband very often induces the poverty of the surviving spouse, even though the married couple was not poor. A large proportion of the wealth of the couple is lost when the husband dies. Poor widows had much less wealth when married than nonpoor widows had, and the loss in wealth at the death of the husband was greater for poor than for nonpoor widows. The prior private pension wealth of poor widows was almost totally lost when the husband died. The prior households of poor widows had accumulated very little housing or other bequeathable wealth. The value of life insurance was typically very small and, among subsequently poor widows, rarely enough to offset the loss in wealth when the husband died.

In addition, families of husbands who died during the period of the survey had accumulated less wealth than those who lived until the end of the survey; those in which the widow was poor had accumulated even less. The earnings of husbands who died were less, judging by Social Security wealth, than the earnings of those who lived throughout the survey; those who left poor widows earned the least. The crude evidence that we were able to use suggests also that the prior households of poor widows saved much less than the households of widows who were not poor. There is some evidence that the lower earnings of those who died, especially those who left poor widows, may have been associated with poor health. Indeed, the prior households of poor widows may have saved less than the prior households of nonpoor widows because of poor health as well. Poor health may have caused low earnings and low savings early in life, and then an early death later in life. In short: the prior households of poor widows earned and saved less, more of the smaller accumulated wealth was lost at the death of the husband, and the absence of survivorship benefits or life insurance ensured that the loss in wealth would leave the widow poor thereafter.

Several important issues have been addressed only tangentially in this paper but should be addressed in future research. An emphasized above, there is a need to develop a more robust measure of poverty that includes income transfers like medical insurance that were intended to help the elderly. The valuation method could produce wide swings in the fraction of the elderly that is thought to be poor.

The data that we reported suggests that saving differentials may have played an important role in the poverty of widows. The RHS data can be used to obtain accurate measures of lifetime earnings for each individual in the sample and these earnings can then be compared to individual lifetime wealth accumulation. This would yield a measure of saving out of earnings for each individual. The rate of saving can in turn be related to the likelihood that the death of the husband will leave a poor widow. The extent to which differential saving is due to differences in individual attributes, such as health status and number of children, should also be established.

Indeed, more formal analysis of change in wealth with change in marital status should in future research be based on the aggregation of individual changes over time rather than the comparison of medians of wealth and other measures by marital status. This work should be pursued in such a way that the effect of different definitions of poverty on the apparent well-being of the elderly can be formally analyzed.

Having estimated the loss in wealth when the husband dies, we are also now in a position to consider the amount and cost of survivorship insurance that would be necessary to prevent poverty among widows. We can also determine the effect on the income of widows of the recent legislation on survivorship arrangements that will be incorporated in firm pension plans in the future. This may have changed the importance of and need for other forms of life insurance.

Many original widows are in poverty in the earliest year of the RHS, and they remain in poverty over the ten years of the survey. Their Social Security benefits, which typically will be based on their deceased husbands' earnings, are lower than average. This is at least a partial explanation for original widows' poverty. For this group in particular, life insurance could have had an important effect on the financial fortunes of the widows. Yet we have little information on the life insurance coverage of their husbands. Future research can explore this issue by studying more carefully the life insurance coverage of the husbands who are still working in the RHS. In fact, the RHS has a special section in several of the survey years in which surviving spouse widows were asked specific questions on the estate left by the husband. In this way, one could learn more about the wealth value of life insurance and its potential effect on the poverty status of widows.

A final topic that we need to pursue further is the change in poverty levels as the RHS population ages. To the extent that widows maintain their financial position by drawing down bequeathable wealth, the prospect is for greater poverty in the future. We cannot explore this issue simply: what is needed is a utility-based model that will explain how consumption and wealth holdings vary with age. Such a model could be used to forecast future poverty levels. Initial work on this topic is represented by the companion paper to this one (Hurd, ch. 7, in this volume).

# Notes

1. See, for example, Hurd and Shoven (1983).
2. See, for example, Lillard and Willis (1978); Burkhauser, Holden, and Myers (1986); and Holden, Burkhauser, and Myers (1986).
3. See, for example, Burkhauser, Holden, and Feaster (1988) and Holden, Burkhauser, and Feaster (1987).
4. A similar treatment is followed by Hurd and Shoven (1983).
5. The precise definitions are found in the footnote to table 6.2.
6. Our measure (C) is a rough measure of the added income that could be obtained from selling the house and investing the equity in a bond that would both maintain its real value and return an additional 3 percent. Thus (C) is a slight understatement, but not a great understatement, of the income potential from converting housing equity to measured income flow.
7. Although these data based on the 1975–77 transition suggest that the prior poverty rate of households in which the husbands died were about the same as those in which they did not, the data for all possible comparisons made it clear that this is not the case. In ten of a possible fourteen comparisons, the continuing couple group had a lower rate of poverty than the couple-to-widow group. In the other four comparisons the rates were equal.
8. Errors in reporting will of course affect the proportion classified as poor and the change in the proportion from one survey period to the next. If a large fraction of those classified as poor are close to the poverty line, as the data above suggest, reporting errors will have a greater effect.
9. More detailed data show that new surviving spouse widows are the most likely to be poor. But original widows are more likely to be poor than surviving spouses who have been widows for a few years.
10. Because the sample averaged about 70 years old, very few of the children would be living in the couple's household.
11. This is not to say that ex ante these households made inappropriate saving decisions, or that they were based on incorrect knowledge or predictions about the future; they may have chosen to consume more earlier, running greater risk of limited financial circumstances later in life. According to this view, luck was against them when they became old.

# References

Burkhauser, R., K. Holden, and D. Feaster. 1988. Incidence, timing, and events associated with poverty: A dynamic view of poverty in retirement. *Journal of Gerontology* 43, no. 2 (March): S46–S52.
Burkhauser, R., K. Holden, and D. Myers. 1986. Marital disruption and poverty: The role of survey procedures in artificially creating poverty. *Demography* 23, no. 4 (November): 621–31.
Holden, K., R. Burkhauser, and D. Feaster. 1987. The timing of falls into poverty after retirement: An event-history approach. Vanderbilt University Working Paper 87–W18.
Holden, K., R. Burkhauser, and D. Myers. 1986. Income transitions at older stages of life: The dynamics of poverty. *The Gerontologist* 26 (3):292–97.

Hurd, Michael, and John Shoven. 1983. The economic status of the elderly. In *Financial aspects of the United States pension system,* ed. Z. Bodie and J. Shoven. Chicago: University of Chicago Press.

————. 1985. Inflation vulnerability, income, and wealth of the elderly, 1969–1979. In *Horizontal equity, uncertainty, and economic well-being,* ed. M. David and T. Smeeding. Chicago: University of Chicago Press.

Lillard, L., and R. Willis. 1978. Dynamic aspects of earning mobility. *Econometrica* 46, no. 5 (September): 985–1012.

# Comment     John B. Shoven

When considering poverty among the elderly, one has to take into account the fact that about 30 percent of single elderly are poor, while only 8 or 9 percent of married elderly are poor. This paper concentrates on the situation of widows and examines the wealth and income paths which frequently lead them into poverty. I think it assembles some very useful facts along the way and I like the paper very much. I take it to be my job, however, to qualify their result in the areas where I think qualification is needed.

The first comment I have concerns Hurd and Wise's four income measures of table 6.2. They show that the measures with increasing inclusiveness (adding sequentially the value of imputed car services and household debt service, imputed housing services, and the value of Medicaid and Medicare) lead to lower poverty rates. The most important inclusion is Medicaid and Medicare, which lowers the 1979 rate of poverty among single elderly from 33 + percent to 13.85 percent. The authors discuss the difficulty in assessing the true value of Medicaid and Medicare (they value the insurance at cost, which I feel is entirely reasonable). They do not, however, discuss the cutoff income level for poverty. It seems to me that there would be higher cutoff levels for more inclusive definitions of income. The official poverty level of income should be defined either as the amount of cash income one needs over and above the in-kind government medical insurance program, which I believe is the correct interpretation of current practice, or it should be defined as the sum of the cash and imputed income one needs to live at a certain level of decency. Keeping the critical level of income unchanged for four different definitions of income does not seem appropriate.

The figures in the paper indicate that the transition from couple to widow is accompanied by a sharp increase in poverty. There is even

John B. Shoven is Professor of Economics and Chairman of the Department of Economics at Stanford University and a Research Associate of the National Bureau of Economic Research.

a 37 percent incidence of poverty among widows of households which had not previously been classified as poor. I suspect that a large part of what is going on is due to the fairly arbitrary choice of equivalency scales in the definition of poverty. The official poverty line suggests a single needs 79 percent as much as a couple. However, with Hurd and Wise's calculation procedure, Medicaid and Medicare is only half as much for singles and Social Security retirement benefits are two-thirds as great for widows whose earnings histories do not qualify them for more than 50 percent of their husband's benefits. The widow's Social Security retirement benefits can fall by as much as half for those who use their own work history as a basis of computation rather than their husband's earnings record. It may be that the key to the finding that poverty sharply grows with widowhood is simply a reflection of these ratios and the importance of Social Security and Medicaid/Medicare in the resources available to the elderly. The authors could have shed more light on this if they had given some statistics reflecting the distribution of incomes near the poverty line. This would have allowed the readers to assess whether it is true that lots of households are moving from slightly over the poverty line to slightly under it, for example.

I take the author's evidence on wealth composition before and after widowhood to indicate that health expenses are not a major factor in the fall into poverty. The median amount of liquid (bequeathable) wealth is small both before and after widowhood. As the authors state, the big change in wealth occurs in the present value of Social Security retirement benefits and in annuities. This suggests the design of public and private pension systems is the major explanation.

One of the interesting findings of this paper is that the wealth accumulation of those who die in the sample is lower even several years before their death. This may indicate poorer long-term health or other factors. The interpretation of this finding, as well as others in this paper, is hampered by the lack of reporting of statistical significance and sample sizes.

I conclude that this is an interesting and important paper which opens as many questions as it closes. It suggests that further attention be paid to the definition of poverty income, to equivalency scales, and to the design of pension benefits. An interesting and important topic is the degree to which these facts have changed among the newly retired, when the default option for all private pensions has been a joint survivor annuity. Better new information could be assembled if we had a Retirement History Survey for a more recent cohort of retirees.

# 7  The Poverty of Widows: Future Prospects

Michael D. Hurd

## 7.1  Introduction

Although the economic well-being of the elderly has improved substantially over the past several decades, a high fraction of the elderly, especially of widows, is still in poverty. One might hope that as today's elderly population ages further this fraction will decline because the young elderly come from cohorts with substantially higher lifetime earnings than the cohorts of the old elderly. The purpose of this paper is to study the likelihood this will happen. The approach is to examine a number of the factors that will influence the fraction in poverty and to forecast how the fraction will change in the future.

One method to forecast the fraction of the elderly in poverty would be to study trends in income and apply the trends to the incomes of each age group. This would amount to forecasting the future economic status of today's young elderly from the economic status of today's old elderly and from trends in income. But this method is not likely to be reliable for a number of reasons. First, each cohort has had different lifetime earnings and rates of return on their savings; therefore, the current economic status of today's old elderly is probably not a useful guide to the current or future economic status of today's young elderly. Second, the elderly have had substantial changes in Social Security and Medicare/Medicaid whereas both of these programs will probably be stable in the future. Third, changes in mortality rates will mean that poverty rates of the young elderly will eventually be higher than a trend

Michael D. Hurd is a Professor of Economics at the State University of New York, Stony Brook, and a Research Associate of the National Bureau of Economic Research.

The author thanks Bryan Boudreau for research assistance. Financial support from the Commonwealth Fund is gratefully acknowledged.

analysis would indicate. Finally, a trend analysis can only answer a limited number of questions because it is not based on an economic model; for example, it cannot say how the poverty rate would change in response to a change in Social Security because it does not model how the individuals would respond to such a change.

In this paper I forecast the poverty rates of the elderly by using an economic model of consumption. The parameters of the model have been estimated from panel data. The model takes as initial conditions the resources of retirement-aged couples and individuals. Given those resources, the model predicts what consumption will be in each future time period. Thus one can trace out the future path of consumption, wealth, and income of each individual and couple. This method has a number of advantages. It is based on observed behavior, and it is founded on economic theory. Because it forecasts the consumption of individuals, it provides details on the distribution of consumption, income, and wealth, not just on the means. It can be used to study changes in poverty rates in response to changes in the environment. Finally, it can be used to define a consumption-based measure of poverty that, I believe, is more appropriate for the elderly than the usual income-based measure.

## 7.2   Forecasting the Economic Status of the Elderly

The future economic status of a cohort of the elderly depends on initial economic resources, the future economic environment, the choices the individuals make, and future random events. The problem is simplified considerably if one considers only people who have retired because their economic resources are known; forecasting the future economic status of workers is complicated because the resources of workers depend on future wage growth and labor force participation. Furthermore, many of the elderly have a rather stable economic environment because most of their assets (housing, Social Security, and Medicare/Medicaid) are indexed. Indeed, the elderly apparently were better protected against the fall in real income during the 1970s than the rest of the population (Hurd and Shoven 1983).

In this paper I concentrate on forecasting how the economic status of the elderly changes as a result of their consumption decisions. I take as initial conditions the distribution of resources, ages, and household structures in the 1979 Retirement History Survey (RHS). Using a utility-based model of consumption behavior that I have estimated over ten years of data from the RHS, I forecast the consumption and wealth trajectories of each household in the RHS. Each household will, with a probability that is based on the mortality tables, produce households of different composition in each future period. Thus the number of households defined by composition and assets grows each time period, but the weight attached to each type shrinks. From the forecasts, a future population of the elderly is generated. It is the elderly population that would be found in a steady-state economy in which each cohort reaches the age of the 1979 RHS population with the distribution of assets and household composition of the 1979 RHS. From this standing population, I study the distribution of assets, consumption, and poverty status at each age. Of course, an alternative statement is that the forecasts are of the 1979 RHS population at each future age.

The advantage of this paper's method is that it distinguishes how much poverty is due to initial conditions and how much is due to life-cycle behavior after retirement. It has the further advantage that a consumption-based measure of economic well-being comes naturally from the calculations. This is especially important for the elderly because income, the usual measure, is not a good measure of their economic position; life-cycle considerations indicate that at some age they will consume part of their capital. Although wealth is probably a better measure of economic position than income, it is not completely satisfactory either because of the importance of Social Security and other annuities. When they are exogenous it is not obvious how to aggregate them with bequethable wealth.

The model that is used to forecast consumption and wealth is based on utility maximization under uncertainty about the date of death. The utility-maximization problem can be solved for singles but not for couples because the utility function of couples changes depending on the future mortality realizations. Although the consumption model is appropriate for studying the future economic status of the 1979 widows in the RHS, by itself it cannot be used to forecast the poverty status of widows because the couples will generate new widows as they age; in order to project the economic status of the new widows, their initial conditions must be known. My ad hoc solution is to assume that couples consume their bequeathable wealth at the average rate that was observed over retired couples in the ten years of the RHS. This rate was 0.016 per year.

Because the forecasts depend on the quality of the model and the parameter estimates, I discuss in the appendix the specification and estimation of the economic model. (More details can be found in Hurd 1986.) Here I briefly outline the ideas behind the consumption model.

Suppose a retired individual wants to maximize lifetime utility when the date of death is uncertain. Utility depends on consumption each time period and on any bequests he might leave should he die. Economic resources are initial bequeathable wealth and annuities, which include Social Security, Medicare/Medicaid, and private pensions. It can be shown that the solution to this utility-maximization problem implies that desired consumption will depend on the parameters of the utility function, mortality rates, bequeathable wealth, the entire time path of annuities, and the strength of the bequest motive. I used the solution to the utility-maximization problem along with data from the ten years of the RHS to estimate the parameters of the utility function. Given the parameters, the economic resources, and the utility-based model, I can forecast the future consumption and wealth paths of each individual in the RHS.

## 7.3 Forecasting Consumption and Wealth

The consumption and wealth of each single person in the 1979 RHS can be projected given the estimated model and initial conditions by solving equations (5) of the appendix. The initial conditions are real annuities, which include Social Security benefits and Medicare/Medicaid, nominal annuities, which include pensions and bequeathable wealth, and the path of mortality rates which are defined by age, race, and sex. There are two types of solutions depending on which of the parameter estimates are used in the solution. As explained in the appendix, the different sets of parameter estimates come from different estimation methods. The first type of solution, which I call the nonlinear least squares (NLLS) solution, is illustrated in figure 7.1. The second type, which I call the nonlinear two-stage least squares (NL2SLS), is shown in figure 7.2. The NLLS path of consumption quickly falls so that bequeathable wealth is exhausted for most people at an early age.

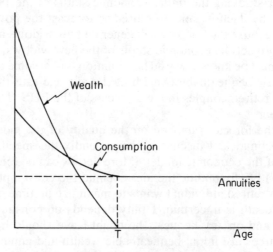

**Fig. 7.1**    Consumption and wealth trajectories based on the NLLS parameters

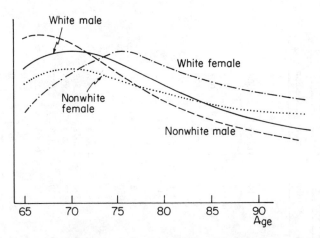

**Fig. 7.2**        Consumption paths based on the NL2SLS parameters

The NL2SLS path of consumption is much flatter, and wealth lasts to a greater age. Regardless of which estimates are used, the wealth and consumption paths of all the 1979 single people will, when weighted by the probabilities of living, give the expected distributions of wealth and consumption not only at each year but also across years.

Table 7.1 shows, for the 1979 RHS widows, the means and medians of consumption, wealth, and income every two years from 1979 through 1999.[1] Part A, based on the NLLS estimates, has consumption and wealth paths like those of figure 7.1. The widows are poor to begin with and rapidly become poorer. By 1989 median bequeathable wealth has fallen to zero, so that at least half of the surviving widows will live from their annuity income only. By 1999 mean bequeathable wealth is essentially zero; therefore, all observations will have exhausted their bequeathable wealth.

Regardless of what the definition of poverty is, it is obvious that, according to these projections, these surviving widows will be poor. It will be useful, however, to make an estimate of the fraction in poverty in each year. The U.S. Bureau of Labor Statistics (BLS) defines poverty according to observed income. For the elderly there are at least two weaknesses to this definition. First, if the rate of inflation is positive, using nominal income from capital implies real capital decumulation because the interest rate that is used to calculate the income is nominal. Thus, the welfare implications of nominal income are obscured. Second, according to the life-cycle hypothesis, income of the elderly is not a good welfare indicator because some wealth should be consumed at advanced ages. I use two measures to calculate the fraction below poverty. The first, an income-based measure, is the sum of annuities and real income from capital. I use a real rate of 0.03. The second is

**Table 7.1**　　Forecasts of the Economic Status of 1979 Widows, Summary Statistics (1979 dollars)

| | Median | Total | In Poverty | | | | Consumption | | Income | | Wealth | |
| | | | Cons | | Inc | | | | | | | |
| Year | Age | HH | # | % | # | % | Mean | Median | Mean | Median | Mean | Median |
|---|---|---|---|---|---|---|---|---|---|---|---|---|
| A. Based on the NLLS parameter estimates | | | | | | | | | | | | |
| Medicaid/Medicare Included in Wealth and Consumption | | | | | | | | | | | | |
| 1979 | 71.0 | 1,922 | 250 | 13 | 499 | 26 | 10,513 | 8,280 | 5,377 | 4,714 | 41,454 | 24,608 |
| 1981 | 73.0 | 1,830 | 294 | 16 | 524 | 29 | 9,143 | 7,147 | 4,986 | 4,476 | 29,072 | 15,562 |
| 1983 | 74.0 | 1,721 | 317 | 18 | 539 | 31 | 7,995 | 6,322 | 4,746 | 4,334 | 19,402 | 8,855 |
| 1985 | 76.0 | 1,595 | 346 | 22 | 540 | 34 | 6,092 | 5,512 | 4,527 | 4,177 | 12,123 | 4,087 |
| 1987 | 78.0 | 1,453 | 372 | 26 | 519 | 36 | 5,973 | 4,948 | 4,373 | 4,063 | 6,993 | 1,156 |
| 1989 | 80.0 | 1,299 | 379 | 29 | 476 | 37 | 5,238 | 4,498 | 4,274 | 3,998 | 3,677 | 0 |
| 1991 | 82.0 | 1,137 | 372 | 33 | 424 | 37 | 4,730 | 4,232 | 4,217 | 3,971 | 1,760 | 0 |
| 1993 | 84.0 | 968 | 341 | 35 | 366 | 38 | 4,434 | 4,084 | 4,190 | 3,941 | 773 | 0 |
| 1995 | 86.0 | 798 | 290 | 36 | 303 | 38 | 4,290 | 3,987 | 4,182 | 3,941 | 319 | 0 |
| 1997 | 88.0 | 630 | 234 | 37 | 239 | 38 | 4,231 | 3,971 | 4,184 | 3,942 | 119 | 0 |
| 1999 | 90.0 | 475 | 178 | 37 | 179 | 38 | 4,208 | 3,954 | 4,191 | 3,950 | 34 | 0 |
| Medicaid/Medicare Excluded from Wealth and Consumption | | | | | | | | | | | | |
| 1979 | 71.0 | 1,922 | 398 | 21 | 836 | 43 | 9,683 | 7,297 | 4,547 | 3,827 | 41,454 | 24,608 |
| 1981 | 73.0 | 1,830 | 465 | 25 | 872 | 48 | 8,313 | 6,275 | 4,156 | 3,594 | 29,072 | 15,562 |
| 1983 | 74.0 | 1,721 | 504 | 29 | 872 | 51 | 7,166 | 5,386 | 3,917 | 3,457 | 19,402 | 8,855 |
| 1985 | 76.0 | 1,595 | 555 | 35 | 854 | 54 | 6,074 | 4,532 | 3,699 | 3,309 | 12,123 | 4,087 |
| 1987 | 78.0 | 1,453 | 604 | 42 | 820 | 56 | 5,146 | 4,017 | 3,546 | 3,216 | 6,993 | 1,156 |
| 1989 | 80.0 | 1,299 | 618 | 48 | 751 | 58 | 4,413 | 3,614 | 3,449 | 3,154 | 3,677 | 0 |
| 1991 | 82.0 | 1,137 | 592 | 52 | 675 | 59 | 3,907 | 3,366 | 3,394 | 3,124 | 1,760 | 0 |
| 1993 | 84.0 | 968 | 543 | 56 | 580 | 60 | 3,614 | 3,193 | 3,369 | 3,097 | 773 | 0 |
| 1995 | 86.0 | 798 | 465 | 58 | 479 | 60 | 3,473 | 3,144 | 3,364 | 3,096 | 319 | 0 |
| 1997 | 88.0 | 630 | 373 | 59 | 378 | 60 | 3,418 | 3,122 | 3,371 | 3,102 | 119 | 0 |
| 1999 | 90.0 | 475 | 283 | 60 | 284 | 60 | 3,402 | 3,121 | 3,384 | 3,108 | 34 | 0 |

B. Based on the NL2SLS parameter estimates

Medicaid/Medicare Included in Wealth and Consumption

| | | | | | | | | | | | | |
|---|---|---|---|---|---|---|---|---|---|---|---|---|
| 1979 | 71.0 | 1,922 | 427 | 22 | 499 | 26 | 6,659 | 5,530 | 5,377 | 4,714 | 41,454 | 24,608 |
| 1981 | 73.0 | 1,830 | 387 | 21 | 487 | 27 | 6,712 | 5,608 | 5,202 | 4,637 | 36,257 | 21,162 |
| 1983 | 74.0 | 1,721 | 353 | 21 | 476 | 28 | 6,783 | 5,671 | 5,094 | 4,573 | 30,979 | 17,478 |
| 1985 | 76.0 | 1,595 | 326 | 20 | 464 | 29 | 6,726 | 5,630 | 4,936 | 4,477 | 25,731 | 14,123 |
| 1987 | 78.0 | 1,453 | 297 | 20 | 443 | 31 | 6,590 | 5,566 | 4,783 | 4,372 | 20,657 | 10,619 |
| 1989 | 80.0 | 1,299 | 279 | 21 | 417 | 32 | 6,370 | 5,372 | 4,641 | 4,278 | 15,894 | 7,467 |
| 1991 | 82.0 | 1,137 | 257 | 23 | 380 | 33 | 6,069 | 5,179 | 4,512 | 4,188 | 11,602 | 4,700 |
| 1993 | 84.0 | 968 | 241 | 25 | 335 | 35 | 5,709 | 4,923 | 4,405 | 4,112 | 7,958 | 2,377 |
| 1995 | 86.0 | 798 | 218 | 27 | 284 | 36 | 5,326 | 4,650 | 4,324 | 4,038 | 5,073 | 758 |
| 1997 | 88.0 | 630 | 188 | 30 | 227 | 36 | 4,964 | 4,424 | 4,270 | 3,988 | 2,984 | 0 |
| 1999 | 90.0 | 475 | 153 | 32 | 174 | 37 | 4,673 | 4,236 | 4,238 | 3,980 | 1,601 | 0 |

Medicaid/Medicare Excluded from Wealth and Consumption

| | | | | | | | | | | | | |
|---|---|---|---|---|---|---|---|---|---|---|---|---|
| 1979 | 71.0 | 1,922 | 662 | 34 | 836 | 43 | 5,828 | 4,539 | 4,547 | 3,827 | 41,454 | 24,608 |
| 1981 | 73.0 | 1,830 | 604 | 33 | 816 | 45 | 5,882 | 4,614 | 4,371 | 3,723 | 36,257 | 21,162 |
| 1983 | 74.0 | 1,721 | 562 | 33 | 787 | 46 | 5,954 | 4,704 | 4,264 | 3,672 | 30,979 | 17,478 |
| 1985 | 76.0 | 1,595 | 521 | 33 | 765 | 48 | 5,898 | 4,680 | 4,107 | 3,590 | 25,731 | 14,123 |
| 1987 | 78.0 | 1,453 | 485 | 33 | 722 | 50 | 5,763 | 4,647 | 3,956 | 3,501 | 20,657 | 10,619 |
| 1989 | 80.0 | 1,299 | 456 | 35 | 667 | 51 | 5,545 | 4,470 | 3,815 | 3,414 | 15,894 | 7,467 |
| 1991 | 82.0 | 1,137 | 425 | 37 | 605 | 53 | 5,246 | 4,245 | 3,689 | 3,342 | 11,602 | 4,700 |
| 1993 | 84.0 | 968 | 394 | 41 | 531 | 55 | 4,889 | 4,019 | 3,585 | 3,255 | 7,958 | 2,377 |
| 1995 | 86.0 | 798 | 356 | 45 | 452 | 57 | 4,508 | 3,774 | 3,507 | 3,207 | 5,073 | 758 |
| 1997 | 88.0 | 630 | 304 | 48 | 363 | 58 | 4,152 | 3,575 | 3,457 | 3,178 | 2,984 | 0 |
| 1999 | 90.0 | 475 | 244 | 51 | 276 | 58 | 3,866 | 3,419 | 3,431 | 3,156 | 1,601 | 0 |

consumption. For singles, consumption is estimated from the utility model. For couples, consumption is the sum of annuities, real income from capital, and the change in capital. Because of the ad hoc assumption about the trajectory of the capital stock of couples, the estimate of consumption for couples reduces to the sum of annuities and 4.6 percent of capital. I take the poverty levels to be those given by the BLS: $3,479 for one person over the age of 65, and $4,388 for two persons over the age of 65, both figures in 1979 dollars.

Any measure of the welfare of the elderly must address the problem of placing a value on Medicare/Medicaid. The program certainly is of some value. Were there no such program, the elderly would spend more of their own wealth on medical care. Rather then speculate about the value, I present two sets of consumption and income measures. The first follows Hurd and Shoven (1983). It includes a value roughly equal to the average transfer through the Medicare/Medicaid system to each eligible person. The idea is that the transfer is the value of a fair medical insurance policy which is given each year to those eligible. The second set of results excludes any valuation for Medicare/Medicaid.

According to the income-based measure of poverty that includes Medicare/Medicaid, the fraction of 1979 RHS widows in poverty begins at a high level and rises slowly as wealth is decumulated. It eventually reaches 38 percent. Because mean wealth is zero, the fraction in poverty will not change further: all the widows that are below the poverty line will remain in poverty and all above will remain out of poverty. The consumption-based measure shows the fraction in poverty starting at a modest level but eventually reaching the same point as the income-based level. This happens, of course, because when bequeathable wealth is exhausted, consumption equals annuity income.

If Medicare/Medicaid is excluded, the results change substantially. The fractions in poverty are much higher at the beginning, and they reach very high levels. Again, however, there are large differences in the early years between the consumption-based and income-based measures.

Part B of table 7.1 gives projections based on the NL2SLS parameter estimates. Typical consumption paths are shown in figure 7.2. The consumption paths are much flatter and more wealth is held than the paths based on the NLLS parameter estimates. This means that initially the consumption-based measure of poverty will show a higher fraction in poverty, but at more advanced ages the fraction in poverty will be smaller. The average fraction in poverty over all age groups is about the same.

The projections of the 1979 RHS widows do not give any idea of the economic status of a steady-state population of widows because the composition only changes by the mortality of the widows. In that couples are substantially more wealthy than widows, the mortality of husbands will add new widows that are more wealthy than the original widows. Because I do not have a utility-based model of the consumption decisions of couples, I take their wealth decumulation to be 1.6 percent per year, which is the average of all couples over the ten years of the RHS. Each time period each couple will generate three other households: a widow, a widower, and a couple, each with a probability that is calculated from the mortality tables. The new widows and widowers have initial conditions that are related to the wealth and annuities of the couple from which they came. The situation is shown in figure 7.3. For example, a couple in 1979 will generate four additional households by 1984, each of which will have a different wealth level because each is identified by the sex of the survivor and the date of creation.

I make some assumptions about changes in bequeathable wealth and annuities if the husband dies. All nominal annuities are lost. This is roughly confirmed in the RHS data; apparently most nominal annuities are pensions without survivors benefits (Hurd and Wise, ch. 6, in this volume). Human capital is lost as it is almost exclusively due to the husband's working. Social Security benefits become 0.67 of their former level, which assumes the family's benefit is based on the husband's earnings record. Medicare/Medicaid becomes half of its former level. I give two sets of results, each based on different assumptions about bequeathable wealth. In the first set I assume that bequeathable wealth decreases by 32 percent when the husband dies. This is the average

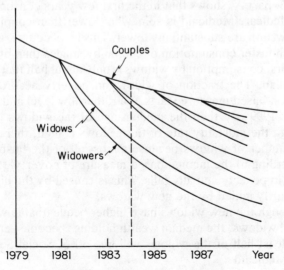

**Fig. 7.3**      Consumption trajectories of a couple and surviving widow and widower

figure over the ten years of the RHS (Hurd and Wise, ch. 6, in this volume). In the second set, bequeathable wealth does not change at the husband's death.

Table 7.2 gives medians and means of consumption, income, and wealth of couples from 1979 through 1999. Because these results are mostly used to generate initial conditions for the projections of the singles, and because they are so heavily dependent on the assumptions of the ad hoc model, I will only discuss them briefly. In the first panel, both consumption and income include an imputed flow from Medicare/Medicaid; in the second panel, the flow is excluded. Even for the very oldest couples, consumption and income including Medicare/Medicaid are substantial at both the mean and median, and the fraction in poverty is small. Excluding Medicare/Medicaid increases somewhat the fraction in poverty, but the general impression is that couples are reasonably well-off.

As shown in table 7.3, the results for widows when the composition is allowed to change due to the mortality of husbands are very different from the projections of the 1979 RHS widows: income, wealth, and consumption are much higher especially among older widows, and the fractions in poverty much lower. The reasons are that in each time period the widows who are added at the husband's death have much higher bequeathable wealth, even after the reduction for the wealth destruction at the husband's death, than the 1979 widows, and the new widows have substantially higher levels of Social Security benefits, even after reduction, than the 1979 widows.

Table 7.3, part A, shows that in the first few years consumption that includes Medicare/Medicaid is somewhat lower than couples, but income and wealth are substantially lower. This is, of course, a reflection of the much faster consumption of capital by singles than by couples.[2] In later years, consumption by widows is only about half that of couples at the median. The fraction of widows in poverty according to the consumption-based measure starts at a rather low level and rises to 20 percent by 1999. By then the median age of the widows is 89, and, even though the mortality rate of the widows is high, there are still a sizeable number of widows because almost all of the husbands have died. According to the income-based measure of poverty, the fraction of widows in poverty actually falls. This is caused by the high level of Social Security added by the new widows.

Even though the new widows have higher bequeathable wealth than the original widows, the median wealth holdings become zero by 1993, so that at least half of the widows will live off of Social Security and Medicare/Medicaid.

In the standing population of widows, the fraction in poverty is 17.6 percent based on the consumption measure and 24.6 percent based on

**Table 7.2   Forecasts of the Economic Status of 1979 Couples, Summary Statistics (1979 dollars)**

| | Median Age | | Total | In Poverty | | | | Consumption | | Income | | Wealth | |
|---|---|---|---|---|---|---|---|---|---|---|---|---|---|
| | | | | Cons | | Inc | | | | | | | |
| Year | M | F | HH | # | % | # | % | Mean | Median | Mean | Median | Mean | Median |
| | | | | | | | | Medicaid/Medicare Included in Wealth and Consumption | | | | | |
| 1979 | 71.0 | 69.0 | 2,418 | 45 | 2 | 60 | 2 | 13,594 | 11,830 | 11,871 | 10,651 | 93,714 | 58,300 |
| 1981 | 73.0 | 71.0 | 2,102 | 43 | 2 | 54 | 3 | 13,331 | 11,624 | 11,667 | 10,457 | 90,469 | 56,227 |
| 1983 | 75.0 | 72.0 | 1,777 | 35 | 2 | 45 | 3 | 13,356 | 11,697 | 11,750 | 10,614 | 87,369 | 54,276 |
| 1985 | 77.0 | 74.0 | 1,452 | 30 | 2 | 38 | 3 | 13,171 | 11,577 | 11,619 | 10,505 | 84,404 | 52,461 |
| 1987 | 79.0 | 76.0 | 1,139 | 24 | 2 | 31 | 3 | 12,989 | 11,452 | 11,489 | 10,368 | 81,545 | 50,586 |
| 1989 | 81.0 | 78.0 | 855 | 19 | 2 | 23 | 3 | 12,810 | 11,310 | 11,363 | 10,292 | 78,741 | 48,824 |
| 1991 | 83.0 | 80.0 | 611 | 13 | 2 | 17 | 3 | 12,630 | 11,156 | 11,234 | 10,175 | 75,916 | 47,061 |
| 1993 | 85.0 | 82.0 | 412 | 9 | 2 | 12 | 3 | 12,452 | 11,011 | 11,107 | 10,065 | 73,137 | 45,286 |
| 1995 | 86.0 | 84.0 | 260 | 6 | 2 | 8 | 3 | 12,274 | 10,881 | 10,979 | 9,983 | 70,417 | 43,629 |
| 1997 | 88.0 | 86.0 | 151 | 4 | 2 | 5 | 3 | 12,104 | 10,732 | 10,856 | 9,885 | 67,841 | 42,004 |
| 1999 | 90.0 | 87.0 | 80 | 2 | 3 | 3 | 3 | 11,940 | 10,584 | 10,737 | 9,806 | 65,388 | 40,488 |
| | | | | | | | | Medicaid/Medicare Excluded from Wealth and Consumption | | | | | |
| 1979 | 71.0 | 69.0 | 2,418 | 168 | 7 | 215 | 9 | 11,746 | 9,957 | 10,023 | 8,805 | 93,714 | 58,300 |
| 1981 | 73.0 | 71.0 | 2,102 | 149 | 7 | 191 | 9 | 11,484 | 9,732 | 9,820 | 8,625 | 90,469 | 56,227 |
| 1983 | 75.0 | 72.0 | 1,777 | 126 | 7 | 160 | 9 | 11,511 | 9,825 | 9,904 | 8,743 | 87,369 | 54,276 |
| 1985 | 77.0 | 74.0 | 1,452 | 104 | 7 | 132 | 9 | 11,327 | 9,707 | 9,775 | 8,624 | 84,404 | 52,461 |
| 1987 | 79.0 | 76.0 | 1,139 | 82 | 7 | 106 | 9 | 11,147 | 9,568 | 9,648 | 8,529 | 81,545 | 50,586 |
| 1989 | 81.0 | 78.0 | 855 | 61 | 7 | 81 | 9 | 10,972 | 9,431 | 9,524 | 8,447 | 78,741 | 48,824 |
| 1991 | 83.0 | 80.0 | 611 | 45 | 7 | 59 | 10 | 10,795 | 9,301 | 9,399 | 8,334 | 75,916 | 47,061 |
| 1993 | 85.0 | 82.0 | 412 | 31 | 8 | 40 | 10 | 10,620 | 9,166 | 9,275 | 8,242 | 73,137 | 45,286 |
| 1995 | 86.0 | 84.0 | 260 | 20 | 8 | 26 | 10 | 10,447 | 9,024 | 9,152 | 8,139 | 70,417 | 43,629 |
| 1997 | 88.0 | 86.0 | 151 | 12 | 8 | 15 | 10 | 10,283 | 8,901 | 9,035 | 8,046 | 67,841 | 42,004 |
| 1999 | 90.0 | 87.0 | 80 | 6 | 8 | 8 | 10 | 10,127 | 8,782 | 8,924 | 7,961 | 65,388 | 40,488 |

**Table 7.3**     Forecasts of the Economic Status of Widows in Steady-State: Decrease in Bequeathable Wealth at Husband's Death (1979 dollars)

| | | | In Poverty | | | | Consumption | | Income | | Wealth | |
|---|---|---|---|---|---|---|---|---|---|---|---|---|
| | | | Cons | | Inc | | | | | | | |
| Year | Median Age | Total HH | # | % | # | % | Mean | Median | Mean | Median | Mean | Median |
| A. Based on the NLLS parameter estimates | | | | | | | | | | | | |
| Medicaid/ Medicare Included in Wealth and Consumption | | | | | | | | | | | | |
| 1979 | 71.0 | 1,922 | 250 | 13 | 499 | 26 | 10,513 | 8,280 | 5,377 | 4,714 | 41,454 | 24,608 |
| 1981 | 72.0 | 2,047 | 298 | 15 | 534 | 26 | 10,000 | 7,843 | 5,295 | 4,694 | 33,739 | 18,014 |
| 1983 | 74.0 | 2,148 | 325 | 15 | 561 | 26 | 9,635 | 7,480 | 5,301 | 4,748 | 27,650 | 12,414 |
| 1985 | 76.0 | 2,214 | 359 | 16 | 576 | 26 | 9,234 | 6,999 | 4,277 | 4,787 | 22,756 | 8,058 |
| 1987 | 78.0 | 2,230 | 391 | 18 | 570 | 26 | 8,854 | 6,517 | 5,263 | 4,804 | 18,753 | 4,488 |
| 1989 | 80.0 | 2,186 | 406 | 19 | 539 | 25 | 8,467 | 6,016 | 5,249 | 4,832 | 15,367 | 1,976 |
| 1991 | 81.0 | 2,078 | 407 | 20 | 496 | 24 | 8,064 | 5,654 | 5,232 | 4,846 | 12,422 | 450 |
| 1993 | 83.0 | 1,906 | 384 | 20 | 443 | 23 | 7,667 | 5,438 | 5,213 | 4,866 | 9,859 | 0 |
| 1995 | 85.0 | 1,680 | 339 | 20 | 381 | 23 | 7,281 | 5,289 | 5,195 | 4,883 | 7,639 | 0 |
| 1997 | 87.0 | 1,414 | 285 | 20 | 313 | 22 | 6,900 | 5,196 | 5,179 | 4,884 | 5,741 | 0 |
| 1999 | 89.0 | 1,129 | 228 | 20 | 245 | 22 | 6,523 | 5,099 | 5,164 | 4,880 | 4,139 | 0 |
| Medicaid/Medicare Excluded from Wealth and Consumption | | | | | | | | | | | | |
| 1979 | 71.0 | 1,922 | 398 | 21 | 836 | 43 | 9,683 | 7,297 | 4,547 | 3,827 | 41,454 | 24,608 |
| 1981 | 72.0 | 2,047 | 472 | 23 | 903 | 44 | 9,127 | 6,862 | 4,423 | 3,802 | 33,739 | 18,014 |
| 1983 | 74.0 | 2,148 | 521 | 24 | 939 | 44 | 8,725 | 6,559 | 4,391 | 3,829 | 27,650 | 12,414 |
| 1985 | 76.0 | 2,214 | 586 | 26 | 963 | 43 | 8,293 | 5,995 | 4,336 | 3,810 | 22,756 | 8,058 |
| 1987 | 78.0 | 2,230 | 653 | 29 | 972 | 44 | 7,887 | 5,456 | 4,295 | 3,793 | 18,753 | 4,488 |
| 1989 | 80.0 | 2,186 | 690 | 32 | 942 | 43 | 7,478 | 5,017 | 4,260 | 3,793 | 15,367 | 1,976 |
| 1991 | 81.0 | 2,078 | 692 | 33 | 896 | 43 | 7,059 | 4,577 | 4,226 | 3,789 | 12,422 | 450 |
| 1993 | 83.0 | 1,906 | 670 | 35 | 819 | 43 | 6,648 | 4,327 | 4,194 | 3,777 | 9,859 | 0 |
| 1995 | 85.0 | 1,680 | 615 | 37 | 721 | 43 | 6,252 | 4,162 | 4,166 | 3,767 | 7,639 | 0 |
| 1997 | 87.0 | 1,414 | 533 | 38 | 605 | 43 | 5,863 | 4,056 | 4,142 | 3,763 | 5,741 | 0 |
| 1999 | 89.0 | 1,129 | 439 | 39 | 482 | 43 | 5,481 | 3,972 | 4,122 | 3,758 | 4,139 | 0 |

B. Based on the NL2SLS parameter estimates

Medicaid/Medicare Included in Wealth and Consumption

| 1979 | 71.0 | 1,922 | 427 | 22 | 499 | 26 | 6,659 | 5,530 | 5,377 | 4,714 | 41,454 | 24,608 |
|------|------|-------|-----|----|-----|----|-------|-------|-------|-------|--------|--------|
| 1981 | 72.0 | 2,047 | 394 | 19 | 497 | 24 | 7,128 | 5,886 | 5,488 | 4,877 | 40,160 | 23,403 |
| 1983 | 74.0 | 2,148 | 365 | 17 | 497 | 23 | 7,607 | 6,355 | 5,614 | 4,996 | 38,098 | 21,768 |
| 1985 | 76.0 | 2,214 | 342 | 15 | 496 | 22 | 7,963 | 6,621 | 5,656 | 5,135 | 35,385 | 19,544 |
| 1987 | 78.0 | 2,230 | 317 | 14 | 486 | 22 | 8,229 | 6,858 | 5,664 | 5,190 | 32,119 | 17,304 |
| 1989 | 80.0 | 2,186 | 302 | 14 | 469 | 21 | 8,383 | 6,999 | 5,639 | 5,184 | 28,380 | 14,174 |
| 1991 | 81.0 | 2,078 | 283 | 14 | 441 | 21 | 8,401 | 6,983 | 5,588 | 5,153 | 24,296 | 10,910 |
| 1993 | 83.0 | 1,906 | 269 | 14 | 400 | 21 | 8,284 | 6,807 | 5,520 | 5,127 | 20,091 | 7,625 |
| 1995 | 85.0 | 1,680 | 249 | 15 | 349 | 21 | 8,037 | 6,525 | 5,445 | 5,088 | 15,992 | 4,576 |
| 1997 | 87.0 | 1,414 | 220 | 16 | 291 | 21 | 7,678 | 6,131 | 5,373 | 5,044 | 12,203 | 2,264 |
| 1999 | 89.0 | 1,129 | 185 | 16 | 232 | 21 | 7,239 | 5,781 | 5,306 | 4,997 | 8,859 | 662 |

Medicaid/Medicare Excluded from Wealth and Consumption

| 1979 | 71.0 | 1,922 | 662 | 34 | 836 | 43 | 5,828 | 4,539 | 4,547 | 3,827 | 41,454 | 24,608 |
|------|------|-------|-----|----|-----|----|-------|-------|-------|-------|--------|--------|
| 1981 | 72.0 | 2,047 | 623 | 30 | 847 | 41 | 6,255 | 4,926 | 4,615 | 3,933 | 40,160 | 23,403 |
| 1983 | 74.0 | 2,148 | 596 | 28 | 851 | 40 | 6,697 | 5,342 | 4,705 | 4,052 | 38,098 | 21,768 |
| 1985 | 76.0 | 2,214 | 567 | 26 | 860 | 39 | 7,022 | 5,594 | 4,715 | 4,111 | 35,385 | 19,544 |
| 1987 | 78.0 | 2,230 | 540 | 24 | 848 | 38 | 7,262 | 5,887 | 4,696 | 4,132 | 32,119 | 17,304 |
| 1989 | 80.0 | 2,186 | 519 | 24 | 822 | 38 | 7,394 | 5,983 | 4,651 | 4,126 | 28,380 | 14,174 |
| 1991 | 81.0 | 2,078 | 494 | 24 | 784 | 38 | 7,396 | 5,940 | 4,582 | 4,099 | 24,296 | 10,910 |
| 1993 | 83.0 | 1,906 | 470 | 25 | 725 | 38 | 7,265 | 5,750 | 4,501 | 4,039 | 20,091 | 7,625 |
| 1995 | 85.0 | 1,680 | 440 | 26 | 650 | 39 | 7,008 | 5,451 | 4,416 | 3,983 | 15,992 | 4,576 |
| 1997 | 87.0 | 1,414 | 395 | 28 | 556 | 39 | 6,641 | 5,049 | 4,336 | 3,915 | 12,203 | 2,264 |
| 1999 | 89.0 | 1,129 | 339 | 30 | 452 | 40 | 6,197 | 4,649 | 4,264 | 3,863 | 8,859 | 662 |

the income measure. These fractions were found by taking a weighted average of the fractions in poverty in each year.

When Medicare/Medicaid is excluded from the income and consumption measures, the results change substantially; both income and consumption drop by about $1,000 as that is roughly the per person transfer amount imputed to the Medicare/Medicaid system. The fractions in poverty rise sharply, especially at older ages; both for the consumption-based and income-based measures, the fraction in poverty in 1999 almost doubles. In the standing population, the fraction in poverty increases to 30 percent by the consumption measure and to about 43 percent by the income measure.

Apparently a substantial number of widows have income and consumption near the poverty line, so that a fairly small change causes a large number to fall below the poverty line. This is illustrated in table 7.4, which gives the consumption distributions in 1983. Because the value of Medicare/Medicaid is large relative to the poverty line, many widows are shifted into poverty by excluding Medicare/Medicaid. Both the thickness of the distribution of widows near the poverty line and the shifting indicate the rather artificial nature of the official classification into poverty. In particular, if one wants to attach welfare significance to the poverty level, more research needs to be done on the valuation of Medicare/Medicaid.

Table 7.3, part B, has the projections based on the NL2SLS parameter estimates of the steady-state population of widows. As measured by consumption, the time path of the poverty rate is changed substantially. There is much more poverty at earlier ages and much less later. As measured by income, there is less poverty overall because more wealth is held. This points out again the weakness of an income-based definition of poverty; the population appears to be better-off even though they have consumed less. Although bequests at the death of the widow

Table 7.4    **Distribution of Consumption, by Number of Households (1979 dollars)**

| Consumption | Medicare/Medicaid Included | Medicare/Medicaid Excluded |
|---|---|---|
| < $1,000 | 63.5 | 72.6 |
| $1,000–2,000 | 47.9 | 106.8 |
| $2,000–5,000 | 544.4 | 666.0 |
| $5,000–10,000 | 748.0 | 665.8 |
| $10,000–20,000 | 571.9 | 486.4 |
| $20,000–50,000 | 155.8 | 134.5 |
| $50,000–100,000 | 15.5 | 15.0 |
| > $100,000 | 1.4 | 1.3 |
| Total households | 2,148.4 | 2,148.4 |

are not shown directly here, the results imply higher bequests simply because at each age more wealth is held. That is, even among poor widows the NL2SLS consumption paths imply that less wealth is consumed and more bequeathed.

Table 7.5 gives results similar to table 7.3 except I have assumed that no bequeathable wealth is lost at the husband's death. In that the differences between tables 7.3 and 7.5 are about the same for each estimation method, I will not discuss separately parts A and B. Of course, because bequeathable wealth is not lost at the husband's death, consumption, income, and wealth are higher. The largest changes are at mean levels because of the skewed distribution of bequeathable wealth. In fact, there is very little change in the poverty levels: those close to the poverty level have very little bequeathable wealth; thus, it matters little whether bequeathable wealth decreases by 32 percent at the husband's death or not.

Because the projections generate a complete distribution of couples and widows, a poverty rate over both groups is found by taking a weighted average. The rates based on the results of tables 7.2 and 7.3, part A, are:

| | Poverty Rates | |
| --- | --- | --- |
| Medicare/Medicaid | Income-based | Consumption-based |
| Included | 17% | 12% |
| Excluded | 31% | 22% |

This shows again the importance of Medicare/Medicaid. The difference between the consumption-based and income-based measures are not as large, but it should be remembered that the consumption of wealth by couples is not based on a utility model.

## 7.4   Conclusions

The widows in the 1979 RHS had little wealth and, according to my projections, they quickly became even poorer. Thus, the future prospects of the 1979 RHS widows are not bright. When the population of widows was allowed to change as husbands died, the extent of poverty was substantially less. The future prospects of the population of widows that would be generated in steady-state by the 1979 RHS sample of widows and couples are much better. A critical unresolved issue, however, is the measurement of poverty. I presented four measures, and they gave substantially different fractions in poverty. Over the steady-state population of couples and widows, the measures range from a low of 12 percent to a high of 31 percent. The welfare consequences are quite different at these extremes. For widows, the variation is even

**Table 7.5  Forecasts of the Economic Status of Widows in Steady-State: No Change in Bequeathable Wealth at the Husband's Death (1979 dollars)**

| Year | Median Age | Total HH | In Poverty | | | | Consumption | | Income | | Wealth | |
|---|---|---|---|---|---|---|---|---|---|---|---|---|
| | | | Cons | | Inc | | | | | | | |
| | | | # | % | # | % | Mean | Median | Mean | Median | Mean | Median |
| A. Based on the NLLS parameter estimates | | | | | | | | | | | | |
| | | | | | | Medicaid/Medicare Included in Wealth and Consumption | | | | | | |
| 1979 | 71.0 | 1,922 | 250 | 13 | 499 | 26 | 10,513 | 8,280 | 5,377 | 4,714 | 41,454 | 24,608 |
| 1981 | 72.0 | 2,047 | 297 | 15 | 534 | 26 | 10,178 | 7,865 | 5,339 | 4,699 | 35,179 | 18,247 |
| 1983 | 74.0 | 2,148 | 325 | 15 | 560 | 26 | 9,948 | 7,515 | 5,371 | 4,755 | 29,979 | 12,751 |
| 1985 | 76.0 | 2,214 | 358 | 16 | 575 | 26 | 9,650 | 7,067 | 5,361 | 4,825 | 25,556 | 8,393 |
| 1987 | 78.0 | 2,230 | 390 | 17 | 567 | 25 | 9,336 | 6,547 | 5,351 | 4,825 | 21,699 | 4,708 |
| 1989 | 80.0 | 2,186 | 404 | 18 | 536 | 25 | 8,978 | 6,089 | 5,334 | 4,856 | 18,214 | 2,154 |
| 1991 | 81.0 | 2,078 | 405 | 19 | 494 | 24 | 8,579 | 5,704 | 5,309 | 4,878 | 14,995 | 543 |
| 1993 | 83.0 | 1,906 | 382 | 20 | 441 | 23 | 8,158 | 5,496 | 5,279 | 4,897 | 12,056 | 0 |
| 1995 | 85.0 | 1,680 | 337 | 20 | 380 | 23 | 7,719 | 5,341 | 5,248 | 4,899 | 9,423 | 0 |
| 1997 | 87.0 | 1,414 | 284 | 20 | 312 | 22 | 7,270 | 5,231 | 5,220 | 4,897 | 7,125 | 0 |
| 1999 | 89.0 | 1,129 | 227 | 20 | 244 | 22 | 6,823 | 5,131 | 5,195 | 4,896 | 5,160 | 0 |
| | | | | | | Medicaid/Medicare Excluded in Wealth and Consumption | | | | | | |
| 1979 | 71.0 | 1,922 | 398 | 21 | 836 | 43 | 9,683 | 7,297 | 4,547 | 3,827 | 41,454 | 24,608 |
| 1981 | 72.0 | 2,047 | 472 | 23 | 901 | 44 | 9,305 | 6,875 | 4,466 | 3,803 | 35,179 | 18,247 |
| 1983 | 74.0 | 2,148 | 520 | 24 | 935 | 44 | 9,039 | 6,587 | 4,461 | 3,835 | 29,979 | 12,751 |
| 1985 | 76.0 | 2,214 | 584 | 26 | 957 | 43 | 8,709 | 6,052 | 4,420 | 3,821 | 25,556 | 8,393 |
| 1987 | 78.0 | 2,230 | 650 | 29 | 965 | 43 | 8,368 | 5,525 | 4,384 | 3,814 | 21,699 | 4,708 |
| 1989 | 80.0 | 2,186 | 685 | 31 | 933 | 43 | 7,989 | 5,098 | 4,346 | 3,821 | 18,214 | 2,154 |
| 1991 | 81.0 | 2,078 | 685 | 33 | 887 | 43 | 7,574 | 4,655 | 4,303 | 3,813 | 14,995 | 543 |
| 1993 | 83.0 | 1,906 | 663 | 35 | 811 | 43 | 7,139 | 4,370 | 4,260 | 3,802 | 12,056 | 0 |
| 1995 | 85.0 | 1,680 | 608 | 36 | 714 | 43 | 6,690 | 4,205 | 4,219 | 3,789 | 9,423 | 0 |
| 1997 | 87.0 | 1,414 | 527 | 37 | 601 | 42 | 6,233 | 4,098 | 4,183 | 3,772 | 7,125 | 0 |
| 1999 | 89.0 | 1,129 | 434 | 38 | 480 | 42 | 5,781 | 4,001 | 4,153 | 3,766 | 5,160 | 0 |

B. Based on the NL2SLS parameter estimates

Medicaid/ Medicare Included in Wealth and Consumption

| 1979 | 71.0 | 1,922 | 427 | 22 | 499 | 26 | 6,659 | 5,530 | 5,377 | 4,714 | 41,454 | 24,608 |
| 1981 | 72.0 | 2,047 | 393 | 19 | 496 | 24 | 7,219 | 5,901 | 5,531 | 4,880 | 41,601 | 23,674 |
| 1983 | 74.0 | 2,148 | 364 | 17 | 496 | 23 | 7,781 | 6,383 | 5,689 | 5,004 | 40,580 | 22,157 |
| 1985 | 76.0 | 2,214 | 341 | 15 | 494 | 22 | 8,211 | 6,681 | 5,752 | 5,151 | 38,566 | 20,045 |
| 1987 | 78.0 | 2,230 | 316 | 14 | 484 | 22 | 8,543 | 6,944 | 5,771 | 5,213 | 35,700 | 17,837 |
| 1989 | 80.0 | 2,186 | 301 | 14 | 467 | 21 | 8,748 | 7,092 | 5,751 | 5,213 | 32,095 | 14,917 |
| 1991 | 81.0 | 2,078 | 281 | 14 | 437 | 21 | 8,806 | 7,068 | 5,697 | 5,206 | 27,925 | 11,539 |
| 1993 | 83.0 | 1,906 | 268 | 14 | 398 | 21 | 8,711 | 6,914 | 5,621 | 5,168 | 23,459 | 8,104 |
| 1995 | 85.0 | 1,680 | 247 | 15 | 347 | 21 | 8,470 | 6,623 | 5,535 | 5,123 | 18,975 | 5,072 |
| 1997 | 87.0 | 1,414 | 218 | 15 | 289 | 20 | 8,097 | 6,258 | 5,448 | 5,070 | 14,724 | 2,627 |
| 1999 | 89.0 | 1,129 | 183 | 16 | 231 | 20 | 7,625 | 5,875 | 5,366 | 5,026 | 10,877 | 848 |

Medicaid/Medicare Excluded in Wealth and Consumption

| 1979 | 71.0 | 1,922 | 662 | 34 | 836 | 43 | 5,828 | 4,539 | 4,547 | 3,827 | 41,454 | 24,608 |
| 1981 | 72.0 | 2,047 | 622 | 30 | 845 | 41 | 6,347 | 4,938 | 4,658 | 3,938 | 41,601 | 23,674 |
| 1983 | 74.0 | 2,148 | 592 | 28 | 847 | 39 | 6,871 | 5,369 | 4,779 | 4,067 | 40,580 | 22,157 |
| 1985 | 76.0 | 2,214 | 563 | 25 | 856 | 39 | 7,270 | 5,654 | 4,811 | 4,132 | 38,566 | 20,045 |
| 1987 | 78.0 | 2,230 | 536 | 24 | 842 | 38 | 7,576 | 5,960 | 4,804 | 4,169 | 35,700 | 17,837 |
| 1989 | 80.0 | 2,186 | 515 | 24 | 814 | 37 | 7,759 | 6,056 | 4,762 | 4,159 | 32,095 | 14,917 |
| 1991 | 81.0 | 2,078 | 490 | 24 | 774 | 37 | 7,800 | 6,042 | 4,691 | 4,128 | 27,925 | 11,539 |
| 1993 | 83.0 | 1,906 | 464 | 24 | 717 | 38 | 7,692 | 5,858 | 4,602 | 4,082 | 23,459 | 8,104 |
| 1995 | 85.0 | 1,680 | 433 | 26 | 642 | 38 | 7,440 | 5,544 | 4,506 | 4,013 | 18,975 | 5,072 |
| 1997 | 87.0 | 1,414 | 388 | 27 | 549 | 39 | 7,060 | 5,153 | 4,411 | 3,953 | 14,724 | 2,627 |
| 1999 | 89.0 | 1,129 | 334 | 30 | 446 | 40 | 6,583 | 4,736 | 4,324 | 3,888 | 10,877 | 848 |

greater. The poverty rates of widows based on the results in table 7.3, part A, are:

| Medicare/Medicaid | Poverty Rates of Widows | |
| --- | --- | --- |
| | Income-based | Consumption-based |
| Included | 25% | 18% |
| Excluded | 43% | 30% |

Thus, the variation is from 18 percent in poverty to 43 percent depending on the definition. As between the income-based and consumption-based measures, I certainly prefer the consumption-based measure: the income-based measure gives no weight whatsoever to the stock of wealth that is consumed. As between the measures that include and exclude Medicare/Medicaid, the correct choice probably is, as usual, neither, but something in between.

# Appendix[3]

I assume that individuals maximize in the consumption path $(c_t)$ lifetime utility:

(1) $$\int U(c_t)e^{-\rho t}a_t dt + \int V(w_t)e^{-\rho t}m_t dt,$$

in which

$$U(c_t) = c_t^{1-\gamma}/(1 - \gamma), \text{ and}$$
$$a_t = 1 - \int_0^t m_s ds$$

is the probability that the individual is alive at $tw$ $m_t$ is the instantaneous mortality rate; $\rho$ is the subjective time rate of discount; $r$ is the real interest rate which is taken to be known and fixed; $V(.)$ is the utility from bequests. This formulation of utility maximization with bequests is from Yaari (1965). The resources available are bequeathable wealth, $w_t$, and annuities, including pensions, Social Security, and Medicare/Medicaid. Annuities are distinguished from bequeathable wealth in that they cannot be borrowed against and are not bequeathable. The conditions on the utility maximization are that initial wealth; $w_0$, is given, and that

(2) $$w_t = w_0 e^{rt} + \int_0^t (A_s - c_s)e^{(t-s)r}ds \geq 0 \text{ for all } t.$$

$A_s$ is the flow of annuities at time $s$. This formulation differs from the usual intertemporal utility-maximization problem in that the annuity stream cannot be summarized by its expected present value. It turns out, because many of the elderly have large annuities relative to their bequeathable wealth, that the corner solutions are important. I parameterize the bequest function by assuming that the marginal utility of bequests is constant. This assumption may be defended in several ways. First, from a practical point of view, without such an assumption the model cannot be solved; the estimation requires a model solution. Second, in other work I found that the strength of the bequest motive did not seem to depend on the wealth level (Hurd 1987). Third, variations in the level of wealth cause only small variations in the level of the wealth of the heirs; therefore, the marginal utility of wealth of the heirs will roughly be constant over variations in wealth of the older generation, and one would expect the marginal utility of bequests to be constant.

The Pontryagin necessary conditions associated with this problem are that

$$(3) \qquad\qquad c_t = A_t,$$

if $w_t = 0$, and that

$$(4) \qquad c_t^{-\gamma} a_t = c_{t+h}^{-\gamma} a_{t+h} e^{h(r-\rho)} + \alpha \int_t^{t+h} e^{(s-t)(r-\rho)} m_s ds,$$

over an interval $(t, t + h)$, in which $w_t > 0$; $\alpha$ is the constant marginal utility of bequests.

If $\rho > r$, these conditions generate consumption trajectories that slope downward, and, unless wealth is very large, wealth trajectories that also slope downward. A typical example is shown in figure 7.1: the consumption path follows equation (4) until bequeathable wealth is exhausted at $T$; then it follows equation (3). The present value of the area under the consumption path and above the annuity path equals initial bequeathable wealth. The solution is implicitly defined by:

$$(5.1) \qquad\qquad c_T = A_T,$$

$$(5.2) \qquad\qquad c_0^{-\gamma} = c_t^{-\gamma} a_t e^{t(r-\rho)} + \alpha \int_0^t e^{(r-\rho)s} m_s ds,$$

$$(5.3) \qquad\qquad w_T = w_0 e^{rT} + \int_0^T (A_s - c_s) e^{(T-s)r} ds,$$

$$(5.4) \qquad\qquad w_T = 0.$$

If initial wealth is very large, wealth will never go to zero, and the nature of the solution is different. Although these cases are taken care of in the estimation, I will not discuss them here because empirically they are not important.

## Data

The data are from the Longitudinal Retirement History Survey. About 11,000 households whose heads were born in 1906–11 were interviewed every two years from 1969 through 1979. Detailed questions were asked about all assets (except a meaningful question on life insurance), and the data were linked with official Social Security records so that one can calculate exactly Social Security benefits. There are some data on consumption, but they are not complete, so I estimate the parameters of the model over wealth data. Bequeathable wealth includes stocks and bonds, property, businesses, and savings accounts, all less debts. As suggested by King and Dicks-Mireaux (1982), I exclude housing wealth because the costs of adjusting housing consumption are substantial, so that people may not follow their desired housing consumption path. As long as the consumption of other goods follows its desired path, the parameters may be estimated over bequeathable wealth excluding housing wealth. Annuities include pensions, Social Security benefits, an estimated income value from Medicare/Medicaid, privately purchased annuities (which are very small), welfare transfers, and transfers from relatives. See Hurd and Shoven (1985) for a detailed description of the data.[4]

The estimation method is to use equations (5) to solve for the consumption path as a function of an initial choice of the parameter values. This requires numerical integration and a search for $T$. The solution will depend on initial wealth. Then, wealth in the next survey, $w_2$, is predicted from equation (2). That is, the necessary conditions and the boundary conditions, equations (5), implicitly define

$$w_2 = f(w_0, \{A\}, \theta),$$

in which $w_0$ is initial wealth, $(A)$ is the annuity stream, and $\theta$ is the parameter vector $(\gamma \ \varepsilon \ \alpha)'$. The parameter space is searched to minimize a function of $(w_2 - f)$.

Although $\alpha$ is, in principle, identified through nonlinearities in the functional form, the identification is very weak. Therefore, I specify that $\alpha$ is zero if a household has no living children.[5] The interpretation of $\alpha$ is the increase in the marginal utility of bequests across households according to whether they have living children or not. The first set of parameter estimates comes from solving

$$\min_{\theta} \sum \ [w_2 - f(w_0, \{A\}, \theta)]^2.$$

The estimated parameter values, which I refer to as the nonlinear least squares (NLLS) estimates, are

| $\gamma$ | $\rho$ | $\alpha$ |
|---|---|---|
| 0.729 | 0.0501 | $5.0 \times 10^{-7}$ |
| (0.004) | (0.091) | $(1 \times 10^{-4})$ |

Number of observations = 5,452

An analysis of the residuals was consistent with the hypothesis that wealth is observed with error. Therefore, I estimated the parameters by nonlinear two-stage least squares (NL2SLS), in which the parameter estimates come from solving

(15)     $$\min_{\theta} [w_2 - f(_{\theta})]' X(X'X)^{-1} X'[w_2 - f(\theta)].$$

$X$ is an $n \times 15$ matrix of observations on income from wealth; these data are not derived from the wealth data but come from separate questions in the RHS. Thus, they should not be correlated with the observation errors in $w_0$.

The results from the NL2SLS are

| $\gamma$ | $\rho$ | $\alpha$ |
|---|---|---|
| 1.12 | −0.011 | $6.0 \times 10^{-7}$ |
| (0.074) | (0.002) | $(32 \times 10^{-7})$ |

Number of observations = 5,452

The major difference between the two sets of results is in $r - \rho$, which, if the mortality rate were zero, would control the slope of the consumption trajectory. In the NLLS $r - \rho$ is approximately $-0.02$; even with a bequest motive, the consumption path will slope downward. In the NL2SLS estimates $r - \rho$ is about 0.04. Even without a bequest motive, the consumption slope will have a positive slope until the conditional mortality rate, $m_t/a_t$, exceeds 0.04. The NL2SLS consumption trajectories will be much flatter than the NLLS trajectories.

Both sets of estimates produce an estimate of $\gamma$ that is much smaller that what has typically been assumed in the literature. For example, Kotlikoff, Shoven, and Spivak (1983, 1984) use a value of 4 in their simulations. Hubbard [1987] uses values of 0.75, 2, and 4. Davies's (1981) "best guess" for his simulations is 4. Large values of $\gamma$ mean that the slope of the consumption trajectory is not sensitive to variations in mortality rates; my estimates imply that the consumption paths of the elderly will have substantial variation with mortality rates.

The marginal utility of bequests, $\alpha$, is estimated to be very small, which is consistent with other estimates I have made in a model that is almost free of functional form restrictions (Hurd 1987). The small estimate of $\alpha$ is caused by the fact that in the data there is no difference between the saving rates of households with children and households without children.

# Notes

1. I include housing wealth in these simulations because the simulations should give a good idea of the economic status of the elderly. A reasonable supposition is that housing wealth declines over long periods at the same rate as other bequeathable wealth. An alternative method would be to exclude housing wealth from the simulations and to impute a consumption value to the stock. The parameters used in the forecasts are those from the NLLS estimation.

2. Couples should decumulate wealth at a slower rate than singles because the life expectancy of the household is greater.

3. This section is drawn from Hurd (1986).

4. The estimation is over all singles observed in any two-year period. The real interest rate, $r$, is taken to be 0.03.

5. Although the RHS does not have information about the ages of the children, because of the ages of the RHS population the median age of the children would be about 30 in the first year of the survey. Thus, almost all the children will have their own households.

# References

Davies, J. 1981. Uncertain lifetime, consumption and dissaving in retirement. *Journal of Political Economy* 86 (June): 561–77.

Hubbard, R. G. 1987. Uncertain lifetimes, pensions, and individual saving. In *Issues in Pension Economics*, ed. Z. Bodie, J. Shoven, and D. Wise. Chicago: University of Chicago Press.

Hurd, M. 1986. Mortality risk and bequest. Typescript.

———. 1987. Savings of the elderly and desired bequests. *American Economic Review* 77 (June): 298–312.

Hurd, M., and J. Shoven. 1983. The economic status of the elderly. In *Financial aspects of the United States pension system*, ed. Z. Bodie and J. Shoven. Chicago: University of Chicago Press.

———. 1985. Inflation vulnerability, income, and wealth of the elderly, 1969–1979. In *Horizontal equity, uncertainty, and economic well-being*, ed. M. David and T. Smeeding. Chicago: University of Chicago Press.

King, M., and L-D. Dicks-Mireaux. 1982. Asset holdings and the lifecycle. *The Economic Journal* 92 (June):247–67.

Kotlikoff, L., J. Shoven, and A. Spivak. 1983. Annuity markets, saving, and the capital stock. NBER Working Paper no. 1250.

———. 1984. The impact of annuity insurance on savings and inequality. NBER Working Paper no. 1403.

Yaari, M. 1965. Uncertain lifetime, life insurance and the theory of the consumer. *Review of Economic Studies* 32 (April):137–50.

# Comment   David E. Bloom

Michael Hurd's paper is concerned with the future economic status of elderly widows. The paper's starting point is the observation that the incidence of poverty among elderly widows is substantial and that the availability of appropriate panel data makes it possible to research the dynamics of the process that led them into that state. By making certain assumptions about (1) the future economic environment, (2) the rate at which elderly widows are "born," (3) the magnitude of economic resources available to elderly widows when they are "born," and (4) the death rate of elderly widows, one can use estimates of a dynamic model of economic well-being among elderly women to project the size of the next generation of elderly widows as well as various aspects of their economic situation.

Two key exercises form the core of this paper. The first involves estimating a dynamic programming model of consumer choice by elderly widows using data contained in the Retirement History Survey (RHS). Since consumption expenditures are not directly observed, they are inferred from data on annuity income, asset income, and changes in assets. An intertemporal utility function is posited with consumption and bequests as its arguments. Individuals are assumed to make choices that maximize the value of this function subject to an intertemporal budget constraint. There are two ways in which individuals can become poor in this model: (1) their initial level of assets and annuity income may be too low to keep them out of poverty, or (2) they may decumulate their assets "too quickly," perhaps because they live longer than they expected. The empirical analysis is focused on the estimation of three key parameters: the marginal utility of bequests, a risk-aversion parameter in a constant risk-aversion utility function, and individuals' subjective rate of time discount. The parameters are estimated by nonlinear least squares and nonlinear two-stage least squares (to account for possible measurement error).

The second exercise reported in this paper involves the projection of consumption expenditures for elderly widows over the years 1979 to 1999. This projection involves the application of the parameters of Hurd's intertemporal consumption model to wealth and income data on (1) women who were elderly widows in 1979 and (2) women in the 1979 wave of the RHS who are at risk of becoming elderly widows by 1999. The data for both groups of women were adjusted for expected mortality using standard demographic life tables. Necessary data on initial economic resources (i.e., assets, asset income, and annuity

David E. Bloom is a Professor of Economics at Columbia University and a Research Associate of the National Bureau of Economic Research.

income) are directly available in the RHS for the first group of women. For the second group, these data are estimated under the (empirically justified) assumptions that couples decumulate their assets smoothly at the rate of 1.6 percent per year, and that there is roughly a one-third decline in the value of bequeathable assets at the point at which the husband dies and an elderly widow is "born."

The main result that emerges from Hurd's research is that the future incidence of poverty among elderly widows will be quite high. When the value of Medicare/Medicaid is included as part of an individual's resources, the rate of poverty is projected to lie between 16 percent and 22 percent, depending on whether one measures poverty in terms of income (i.e., annuity income plus asset income) or consumption (i.e., annuity income plus asset income plus changes in wealth) and whether one relies on the nonlinear least squares results or on the nonlinear two-stage least squares results. If one places zero value on Medicare/Medicaid benefits, the poverty rate projections increase to a range of 30 percent to 42 percent.

As the above summary should make clear, the ideas in Dr. Hurd's paper are fairly straightforward. In discussing it, I would like to focus on two issues: first, whether the paper addresses an interesting question, and second, the extent to which the paper answers the main question it sets for itself.

As noted above, the principal goal of this paper is to forecast the economic status of elderly widows, with special emphasis on the incidence of poverty among this group. Insofar as elderly widows are an easily identifiable group of individuals with an above-average rate of poverty (i.e., 19 percent according to the March 1986 Current Population Survey, as compared to about 14 percent in the overall population), it is hard to argue that this is not an interesting topic for research. Nonetheless, it is not clear that widows are either the most natural or the most interesting group of elderly women on which to focus such an analysis. The term widow is used to refer to women whose husbands died while they were still married. Although widows represent 85 percent of all elderly women who are not currently married (see table 7.6), it is not immediately apparent why they should be treated separately from never-married women and from women who divorced their last husband and never remarried. Both of these groups of women had even higher rates of poverty than elderly widows in 1986: 22 percent for elderly never-married women and 28 percent for elderly divorced or separated women. More importantly, because of the secular decline in the marriage rate and the increase in the divorce rate, the number of elderly women in these latter groups will probably grow at much faster rates over the remainder of this century than the number of elderly widows. Thus, while I think that Dr. Hurd's paper researches an in-

Table 7.6          Selected Characteristics of Women Aged 65 and Over,
                   by Marital Status

|  | All | Married | Widowed | Divorced or Separated | Never Married |
|---|---|---|---|---|---|
| Percent | 100.0 | 38.5 | 52.0 | 5.5 | 4.0 |
| Percent in income poverty | 14.1 | 4.6 | 19.0 | 28.4 | 21.7 |
| Percent not living with relatives | 42.0 | 1.3 | 69.3 | 69.4 | 41.4 |
| Percent in labor force | 7.0 | 6.7 | 6.0 | 14.0 | 12.5 |
| Percent with earnings in previous year | 9.4 | 9.3 | 8.1 | 15.0 | 19.9 |
| Average earnings in previous year for those who worked (in dollars) | 7,235 | 5,269 | 6,679 | 16,402 | 9,594 |

Source: Tabulations from the March 1986 Current Population Survey.

teresting question, I think it overlooks an even more interesting question that was well within its grasp. In other words, I would have preferred to comment on a paper entitled: "The Poverty of Elderly *Unmarried Women:* Future Prospects." It may sound a bit less sexy, but I think it would be somewhat more meaningful.

In terms of the question that Dr. Hurd does try to answer, I have some concerns about the appropriateness of his theoretical model. In particular, the model does not account for the two major responses that elderly women can make to evade poverty: (1) they can go to work, or (2) they can situate themselves within economically well-off households.

The labor supply of elderly widows has never been a major focus of empirical labor economics, undoubtedly because it is so low. Data contained in the March 1986 Current Population Survey indicate that the labor force participation rate of elderly widows is 6.0 percent, with a rate of 7.6 percent among elderly widows living alone and a rate of just 2.5 percent among elderly widows living with others (see table 7.7). In addition, 8.1 percent of the widows had positive earnings in 1985 and they earned an average of nearly $6,700. These labor force participation rates and average earnings levels are anything but large in magnitude, but they do make it clear that the imputation of consumption expenditure as the sum of annuity income plus asset income plus the change in assets introduces systematic error into Hurd's model.

Table 7.7          Selected Characteristics of Husbandless Women Aged 65 and Over,
                   by Marital Status and Living Arrangements

|  | Widowed | | Divorced or Separated | | Never Married | |
|---|---|---|---|---|---|---|
|  | Living with relatives | | Living with relatives | | Living with relatives | |
|  | No | Yes | No | Yes | No | Yes |
| Percent | 58.6 | 26.0 | 6.2 | 2.7 | 2.7 | 3.8 |
| Percent in income poverty | 24.6 | 6.2 | 34.7 | 14.1 | 31.5 | 14.7 |
| Percent in labor force | 7.6 | 2.5 | 12.4 | 17.6 | 12.9 | 12.2 |

Source: Tabulations from the March 1986 Current Population Survey.

The error introduced by the omission of reported earnings from the imputed value of consumption is likely to be further aggravated to the extent that the elderly are not reporting income earned as a result of labor supplied to the underground economy. Although it is obviously a complex problem requiring data that may be extremely difficult to generate, future research on the consumption of elderly individuals should not assume their labor supply to be exogenously fixed at zero.

The second problem with the theoretical model set out by Hurd is that it pays scant attention to the living arrangements of elderly widows. According to the March 1986 Current Population Survey, 30.7 percent of (noninstitutionalized) elderly widows live with relatives. The importance of living arrangements to the economic well-being of elderly widows is strongly suggested by the poverty rates reported in table 7.7. The poverty rate among elderly widows living with relatives is roughly one-fourth the poverty rate among elderly widows that do not live with relatives. For elderly women who are divorced, separated, or never married, poverty rates are also substantially lower for those living with relatives than for those not living with relatives. These data highlight the importance of accounting for living arrangements insofar as they may be correlated with intrahousehold transfers that can substantially affect individual well-being. Although somewhat less pronounced, comparisons for women in particular age groups exhibit similar relationships.

Another dimension of the relationship between living arrangements and economic well-being is illustrated by the fact that the dollar increase in the poverty line is only 26 percent when a household changes composition from one individual aged 65 and over to two such individuals. This less-than-proportional increase reflects economies of scale in the provision of household goods and further establishes the fact that "living arrangements" is likely to be a critical choice variable in whatever constrained utility-maximization process elderly widows go through. Ignoring the determinants and consequences of different living arrangements among elderly widows is potentially a gross oversight in Hurd's analysis.

Although it is disturbingly unclear in Hurd's paper, the future well-being of those women who are elderly widows in 1979 is not calculated in a way that accounts for their actual living arrangements in 1979. The RHS simply does not contain information on the income of all family/household members in which an elderly widow might reside. For this reason, the RHS is fundamentally inappropriate as a source of data for studying the economic well-being of the elderly, a point that seems to be frequently overlooked in the empirical literature on this subject.

It also appears that elderly widows who are "born" after 1979 are assumed by Hurd to live the remainder of their lives in single-person households. If this is so, the figures reported in table 7.7 clearly suggest that Hurd's poverty rate projections will be upward biased estimates of the true rates, since many elderly widows will undoubtedly become members of multi-person households in order to economize on their scarce resources.

One is not actually able to tell from the paper whether the parameters of the structural consumption model are estimated from a restricted sample that only includes elderly widows who are living alone or an unrestricted sample that includes all elderly widows but treats them as if they are living alone. If the sample is restricted to lone elderly widows, we clearly have a case in which sample selectivity is likely to be severe. We also have a set of projections that do not generalize to the entire population of elderly widows. In addition, biases introduced by having ignored the widows' labor supply are probably aggravated in such a sample, since the labor force participation rate of elderly widows living alone is more than three times that of elderly widows who do not live alone. On the other hand, if all elderly widows are treated as if they live alone, the poverty rate projections in Hurd's paper are likely to be biased upward, as explained above, perhaps by as much as 6 or 7 percentage points.

In addition to problems relating to the theoretical basis of Hurd's model, I feel quite apprehensive about several features of the empirical analysis. The paper offers no basis for careful assessment of the empirical results. Simple descriptive statistics are not even reported. In addition, although the overriding purpose of Hurd's analysis is prediction, the paper reports no evidence relating to the goodness-of-fit of the model to the data. The empirical model also ignores available data on a wide range of potentially useful control variables such as race, birth cohort, educational attainment, and geographic region. I am disconcerted by Hurd's inattention to variables that would almost certainly improve the predictive power of his predictive model substantially. It would also have been nice to see some details in the paper on the method used to impute the value of Medicare/Medicaid.

Doubts should also be expressed about the robustness and the plausibility of the parameter estimates. Estimates of the subjective rate of time discount vary between specifications from $-0.01$ to $0.05$, which translates into large differences in the (negative) slope of the intertemporal consumption profile. On the other hand, estimates of the risk-aversion parameter in the utility function vary less—between $0.73$ and $1.12$—but they are both in a range that implies much greater sensitivity of consumption to variations in mortality risk than would be considered sensible based on other literature in this general area. Finally, the marginal utility of bequests—assumed to be constant in wealth—is estimated to be close to zero. Although close in magnitude to estimates reported in previous work by Hurd, this parameter is identified largely off the functional form of the empirical model and by a somewhat arbitrary restriction. More analysis is required if we are to believe the parameter estimates presented in Hurd's paper.

My final comment simply involves stressing the fact that Dr. Hurd's paper focuses on only a small piece of the problem of forecasting the economic well-being of elderly widows—analyzing the evolution of their consumption over the last part of their life cycle. If one were truly interested in accurately projecting the future rate of poverty among elderly widows, a number of other factors would also deserve serious consideration. Included on a list of such factors would be increasing longevity, the emergence of alternative living arrangements among the elderly, the effect of changing generation sizes and a widening generation gap, increased geographic mobility among individuals of all ages, and increasing educational attainment, labor force participation, and "careerism" among women. The role of nursing homes and other residential institutions for the elderly deserves special research attention.

One factor that is likely to be of considerable importance to the future economic well-being of the elderly is the increasing tightness in the U.S. labor market. Over the past three decades, the American labor force has grown at an average annual rate of 2 percent, largely a consequence of the "baby boom" entering the labor market and of rapid growth in female labor force participation rates. During the remaining years of this century, the labor force will grow at perhaps 1.0 to 1.1 percent per year. Higher real wages are the most likely result of tighter labor markets, although I think we can also expect to see the expansion of employment opportunities that cater more closely to the needs and preferences of segments of the population that could potentially supply more labor, such as the elderly. For example, some employers in the service-producing industries have already begun to formulate and implement recruitment strategies that focus on elderly workers. As another example, the child-care industry is almost certain to undergo major growth in the next 10 to 15 years, and it is absolutely clear that many elderly widows have superb backgrounds and training for taking up jobs in that industry. Increases in hours worked by elderly widows, as well as in their earnings per hour, should certainly be accounted for in analyses of their future economic prospects.

Another factor that should be considered in assessing the future economic prospects of the elderly relates to their future political clout. There is little doubt that the United States will be a considerably nicer place for elderly persons to be at the turn of the century than it is today. Political favoritism of the elderly has already begun and will gain further momentum as the elderly become an increasingly powerful political constituency.

The bottom line of Dr. Hurd's paper is that elderly widows have a rather dim economic future. He reaches that conclusion by analyzing a narrow piece of the overall problem, using imperfect data to estimate a rather structured and restrictive economic model. Dr. Hurd's analysis notwithstanding, I am more optimistic about the future economic prospects of elderly widows on the basis of casual speculation about relevant social, economic, and political adjustments that have already begun and that will almost certainly continue to occur during the remainder of this century.

# 8  The Social Security Cost of Smoking

John B. Shoven, Jeffrey O. Sundberg, and
John P. Bunker

## 8.1  Introduction

Smoking in the United States is associated with enormous costs to society. The Congressional Office of Technology Assessment has estimated the annual cost of medical care for smoking-related illness at $15 to $30 billion, and that smoking-related illness is responsible for an additional $49 to $70 billion in lost productivity. There are also substantial costs to the individual who smokes in terms of lost wages over a lifetime, primarily affecting those who die of smoking-related disease while still active wage earners in the work force. Costs to the individual also include approximately $500 to $1,000 per annum for one-pack and two-pack-a-day smokers to purchase cigarettes. An additional cost to the individual is the loss of Social Security benefits as a result of smoking-induced loss of life expectancy. The data presented herein estimate the magnitude of this loss for single and married men and women born in 1920 and 1923, respectively.

While most of the previous literature on the costs of smoking and the benefits of quitting has overlooked the implications of smoking behavior on pension plans (see, for example, Oster, Colditz, and Kelly 1984), this is by no means universal. Gori, Richter, and Yu (1984) estimated that the savings realized by Ford Motor Company if the health of their employees improved (in terms of less expensive medical

John B. Shoven is a Professor of Economics and Chairman of the Department of Economics at Stanford University and a Research Associate of the National Bureau of Economic Research. Jeffrey O. Sundberg is a graduate student in economics at Stanford University. John P. Bunker is Director of the Division of Health Services Research in the Department of Health Research and Policy, Stanford University School of Medicine.

This work originated when John Shoven and John Bunker were Fellows at the Center for Advanced Study in the Behavioral Sciences in 1984–85.

insurance, disability insurance, and life insurance) would be much smaller than the additional pension costs due to their increased longevity. Atkinson and Townsend (1977) noted that the financial benefits the British National Health Service would enjoy if there was a 40 percent reduction in smoking in Britain would be more than offset by the increased cost of retirement pensions.

In this paper, we examine the Social Security consequences of smoking from the individual or household perspective. From that vantage point, Social Security can be thought of as a prepaid life annuity. Contributions or taxes are collected during one's work life which entitle one to an indexed life annuity beginning at age 65. The annuity can be commenced at age 62 with a roughly fair actuarial adjustment, or it can be started at an age beyond 65 with somewhat higher benefits reflecting the shorter expected remaining lifetime. In general, the system is not actuarially fair (favoring some cohorts relative to others, those with low incomes or short covered careers relative to others, and marrieds, especially one-earner couples, relative to singles).

Our point is that the system is unfair in a way very relevant to the decision of whether or not to smoke. Social Security does not have separate benefit structures for smokers and nonsmokers, even though smokers have a much lower chance of reaching retirement age and a shorter expected length of retirement conditional on reaching that age. The U.S. Office of Technology Assessment estimated that 273,000 people died in the United States in 1982 of smoking-related disease (Kronebusch 1985). Of those, 44 percent, or 121,000, died before they reached their 65th birthday. They may have never collected anything from Social Security. If they were married, their spouses may collect survivor's benefits, but it is clear that their premature deaths greatly reduce their return on their participation in Social Security.

Smoking also affects the Medicare portion of the Social Security system. While we concentrate on the old-age supplemental income (OASI) portion in this paper, it is probably worth noting that the health insurance (HI) component is similarly affected. Many estimates of the effect of smoking on the total demand for health care services in the country find that it is small in the long run. Smokers certainly experience more health problems per year of life, but this is offset by the fact that they live fewer years. With a lower incidence of smoking, there would be more elderly who require additional health care services. The reduced demand caused by the improved health status of the former smokers is offset by the extra care needed by the additional elderly. There might be some initial reduction in the demand for health care if smoking was reduced. The improvements in health status would presumably occur before the age structure was significantly altered. However, in the long run the two effects offset each other.

Despite the fact that total health care demand may be little affected by smoking, Medicare's finances are almost certainly affected. The reason is that it is a prepaid health insurance annuity for those over 65. Medicare does not bear the higher health costs of nonelderly smokers, but it benefits financially from the fewer numbers of elderly due to smoking. The other side of the coin is that smokers pay while they work for old-age health insurance, as with their retirement benefits, which they are less likely to collect or likely to collect for a shorter period than nonsmokers. Wright (1986) estimates that each person who quits smoking increases the deficit faced by the HI component of Social Security for just these reasons.

Our study is the OASI analog of Wright's (1986) HI research. We assemble separate life tables for smokers and nonsmokers and then estimate the Social Security taxes, benefits, and transfers for members of the 1920 birth cohort. We do this for those who earn median wages for their age and cohort and for those who earn 60 percent of the median, in each case beginning at age 20. The results can be previewed by saying that we find the expected loss in net Social Security benefits accompanying smoking to be very large relative to the other costs of smoking. The loss exceeds the lifetime costs of cigarettes, is large relative to the estimates of the medical costs and lost wages due to excess morbidity and mortality, and is perhaps 10 times greater than the corresponding Medicare figures of Wright.

Section 8.2 briefly reviews what is known about the effect of smoking on mortality. It discusses disease-specific effects and also our technique of using mortality ratios to yield approximate separate life tables for smokers and nonsmokers. Section 8.3 describes our simulation procedure for calculating the Social Security costs of smoking. It presents separate results for single individuals and for one-earner and two-earner couples because of their separate treatment by Social Security. We conclude the paper with an interpretation of what our findings imply about the private and social incentives to quit smoking.

## 8.2  Effect of Smoking on Mortality

There can be no statistical doubt that smoking is associated with increased mortality hazard rates. The overall finding of the 1979 Surgeon General's report on the subject was that the mortality of all male cigarette smokers is about 170 percent of that of male nonsmokers. For two-pack-a-day smokers, the average mortality ratio is 200 percent. For particular diseases the relative hazard is even greater. For example, two separate studies find smokers are between 9 and 15 times more likely than nonsmokers to die of lung cancer (Lubin et al. 1984; and Cowell and Hirst 1980). The risk of dying of arteriosclerotic and

degenerative heart disease and myocardial insufficiencies has been estimated at 2.7 times as great for smokers as nonsmokers (Cowell and
Hirst 1980). There is further evidence that there is a significant inter-
action between smoking and other environmental factors, such as exposure to asbestos. The finding is that while smoking is a major cause
of lung cancer, smoking combined with other assaults (such as industrial
exposure) greatly increases the mortality hazards (Scheiderman and
Levin 1977).

Our development of separate life tables for smokers and nonsmokers
utilizes the findings of E. C. Hammond (1966) regarding the effect of
smoking on mortality. Working for the American Cancer Society, he
conducted a comprehensive four-year study tracking a population of
over one million subjects. He determined the death rates and the prevalence of certain causes of death for smokers and nonsmokers of many
different characteristics. The technique was to examine death certificates for the cause of death and to request information from the at-
tending doctor whenever cancer was mentioned on the death certificate.
Hammond's results are a very detailed set of mortality ratios[1] for different types of smokers and for several different causes of death.

In 1959 and 1960, Hammond enrolled over one million volunteers
from twenty-five different states to provide data on mortality. Subjects
were classified by sex, age, type of tobacco smoked (cigarette, cigar,
pipe, or none), age at which subject began smoking, daily amount of
smoking, and degree of smoke inhalation. Each subject was contacted
annually for four years to track the number and timing of fatalities in
each group. Death certificates were received for over 97 percent of
reported deaths to provide better information as to causes of death.

Using the accumulated data, Hammond combined subjects with similar characteristics into five-year and ten-year age cohorts and divided
the number of deaths in each cohort during the study period by the
number of "person-years" experienced in each cohort. This provided
cohort death rates over the period for groups of similar age and sex
and varying smoking habits. This allowed Hammond to calculate mortality ratios for different groups. A sample of his findings is shown in
table 8.1

The separate mortality tables that we have produced are contained
in the appendix to this paper. The basic life tables used are the cohort
life tables for men and women born in 1920, as estimated by the Social
Security Administration. The mortality hazards are shown in column
(8) of the appendix table for men and women. If we let $Q_A^m(a)$ represent
the one-year death probability for males as a function of age (similarly
$Q_A^w(a)$ for females), let $f^m(a)$ represent the fraction of men who smoke
as a function of age, and $M^m(a)$ represent the mortality ratio of male
smoker to nonsmoker as a function of age, then

Table 8.1          Mortality Ratios for Smokers as Determined by E. C. Hammond

| Current Number Per Day | Age | | | | |
|---|---|---|---|---|---|
| | 35–44 | 45–54 | 55–64 | 65–74 | 75–84 |
| | Men with History of Only Cigarette Smoking | | | | |
| 1–9 | * | 1.84 | 1.53 | 1.50 | 1.36 |
| 10–19 | 1.36 | 2.26 | 1.92 | 1.65 | 1.55 |
| 20–39 | 1.91 | 2.41 | 2.05 | 1.71 | 1.26 |
| 40 + | 2.59 | 2.76 | 2.26 | 1.81 | * |
| | Women with History of Only Cigarette Smoking | | | | |
| 1–9 | 0.90 | 0.95 | 0.99 | 1.09 | 1.07 |
| 10–19 | 0.97 | 1.22 | 1.31 | 1.18 | 1.21 |
| 20–39 | 1.35 | 1.54 | 1.46 | 1.51 | * |
| 40 + | * | 1.96 | * | * | * |

Source: Hammond (1966), p. 133.
*Signifies a very low number of expected deaths (small sample or low death rate).

$$Q_{NS}^m(a) = \frac{Q_A^m(a)}{1 - f^m(a)[1 - M^m(a)]}$$

and

$$Q_S^m(a) = M^m(a) \times Q_{NS}^m(a),$$

where $Q_{NS}^m(a)$ is the annual death probability of male nonsmokers as a function of age and $Q_S^m(a)$ is the annual death probability for male smokers. The formulas for women are identical with all the superscripts changed to $w$'s.

The appendix tables display the assumptions for $M^m(a)$ and $M^w(a)$ derived from Hammond (1966), and for $f^m(a)$ and $f^w(a)$ for the 1920 cohort derived from Harris (1983). They also show the results for $Q_{NS}^m(a)$, $Q_S^m(a)$, $Q_{NS}^w(a)$, and $Q_S^w(a)$. Table 8.2 offers some summary statistics based on these derived life tables.

Our life tables for the 1920 birth cohort show that 85,758 males and 88,787 females out of 100,000 births live to age 20. It is well known that smoking affects the mortality of women less than men. That is partially due to the fact that women smokers smoke less, inhale less, and are more likely to smoke filter cigarettes. Again, out of 100,000 births, 53,051 male smokers (who began smoking at age 20) survive until age 65, whereas 67,465 male nonsmokers survive until that traditional retirement age. Conditional on living to age 20, almost 79 percent of nonsmokers make it to 65, whereas slightly less than 62 percent of smokers do so. At age 20, male smokers have a life expectancy 6.4 years shorter than male nonsmokers, and a median age of death 7 years younger. Conditional on surviving to 65, male smokers have a remaining

Table 8.2          Life Expectancy, Median Age at Death, And Surviving Population at
                   Ages 20 and 65 for 1920 Birth Cohort

|  | Survivors at Age 20 out of 100,000 Births | Survivors at Age 65 out of 100,000 Births | Life Expectancy Conditional on Age 20 | Life Expectancy Conditional on Age 65 | Median Age of Death Conditional on Age 20 | Median Age of Death Conditional on Age 65 |
|---|---|---|---|---|---|---|
| **Men** | | | | | | |
| Smokers | 85,758 | 53,051 | 68.7 | 78.8 | 70 | 77 |
| Nonsmokers | 85,758 | 67,465 | 75.1 | 81.5 | 77 | 81 |
| **Women** | | | | | | |
| Smokers | 88,787 | 69,303 | 77.2 | 84.6 | 79 | 84 |
| Nonsmokers | 88,787 | 74,461 | 80.5 | 86.6 | 84 | 86 |

life expectancy which is 2.7 years less than their nonsmoking cohort
members. The figures for women show that the life expectancy difference at age 20 is 3.3 years, while the difference at age 65 is 2 years.

Our life tables cannot sort out causality and correlation. It is certainly
true that smokers would not become identical to nonsmokers if they
stopped smoking. Smokers drink more alcohol than nonsmokers, have
a higher incidence of suicide, and, in general, may face higher mortality
risks than nonsmokers for reasons correlated with smoking but not
caused by smoking per se. We have not been able to separate these
effects, although it is our belief that most of the higher mortality risks
faced by smokers are due directly to the cigarette consumption. However, it should be kept in mind when interpreting our results that we
have attributed all of the mortality difference to the cigarette
consumption.

## 8.3 Simulation of the Social Security Costs of Smoking

We examine the Social Security consequences of smoking for 100,000
men born in 1920 and 100,000 women born in 1923. The three-year
difference approximates the average age gap in marriage for this cohort.
The 1920 cohort life tables compiled by Social Security are taken to
be applicable to the men and women in our study. We calculate the
Social Security outcomes separately for single men, single women, and
one-earner and two-earner couples. We assume that each person's
probability of death is given by the life tables and, therefore, is independent of the status of the spouse. The number of women who become
widowed in each year until the husbands retire is noted, and each
"widow cohort" is then tracked as a separate population. This is necessary because at retirement widows must choose between a benefit
based on their own work record and one based on that of their spouses.

In the case of the one-earner couples, we assume that the husband is employed until retirement or death. If the husband should die before retirement, the widow is assumed to work until retirement or death.

We have not been very sophisticated in developing our earnings profiles. The earnings series used are median earnings for men and women working full-time year-round, taken from the 1982 Census Bureau Current Population Report P-60, no. 142. Earnings before 1955 and 1982 are estimated using a related series from the Department of Labor's Employment, Hours, and Earnings Report. The earnings series are then adjusted to reflect a life-cycle pattern of lifetime earnings, using 1982 Census data on mean incomes for different age groups from Current Population Report P-60, no. 137. Our analysis for low-wage earners examines those who earn 60 percent of the median earnings profiles.

There are several factors which could be added to our earnings series. First, we do not take into account the effect of the increased morbidity of smokers on their earnings pattern. This is probably a relatively minor adjustment, but one which is conceptually desirable. Second, non-working wives entering the work force when widowed are assumed to immediately earn the median (or 60 percent of the median) amount for their age. This is certainly optimistic regarding their prospects. Finally, we do not take into account spells of unemployment, employment in the uncovered sector, or disability.

The surviving members of the cohort are assumed to retire at age 65 and begin to receive benefits based on the 1985 Social Security law. We assume that the initial benefit received is fully indexed for inflation for their remaining lives. The women in the simulations retire three years later, simply reflecting that they are three years younger than the men. Because the median earnings of men exceed those for women, the Social Security OASI benefit based on a man's earnings history exceeds the benefit based on a woman's work record. As a result, husbands and widowers will always elect to take their own benefit. Wives choose between their own benefit and one-half of their husband's, while widows may elect to receive their own benefit or the benefit which their husband would receive were he alive and had not worked since the year he actually died. In other words, a woman whose husband died in 1965 could take the benefit he would be receiving had he stopped working in 1965 and lived to receive his benefit, or she could take her own benefit. In the two-earner cohort, her benefit is based on her earnings from 1940 to her retirement in 1988, while in the one-earner cohort her benefit is based on a shorter work history, 1965–88, since we assume she only begins work upon her husband's death. This means that a widow's benefit may depend on when her husband died (and in the one-earner case must depend on it), necessitating our keeping track of the "widow cohorts" mentioned above.

Wives over the age of 65 whose husbands are still alive will always receive one-half of their husband's benefit in the one-earner family, since they have no earnings history of their own. In the two-earner family, since they have no earnings history of their own. In the two-earner case, wives will take their own benefit since their benefit exceeds half their husband's, given our earnings series. All benefits are calculated in real dollars, so comparison of 1985 and 1988 benefits is valid.

The results for singles are shown in table 8.3. All figures are stated in 1985 dollars, and the real discount rate used for cash flows occurring at other times is 3 percent. With those assumptions, the figures in the upper portion of the table for single men with median wage profiles in this cohort show that nonsmokers can expect to receive a net transfer from Social Security of $3,436, while the expected benefits received by smokers fall $17,782 short of the expected contributions. All of these figures are conditional on having survived to age 20. The Social Security cost of smoking for single men with median earnings patterns thus exceeds $21,000. The internal rate of return, which equates the expected value of payouts and payins, is 1.87 percent real for smokers and 3.17 percent for nonsmokers. If one only looked at those who survived until 65, the rates of return would naturally be higher. In that case, the real internal rate of return for median wage male smokers in this cohort is 3.18 percent, whereas the rate for nonsmokers is 3.78 percent. The dollar difference in the net transfer between male smokers and nonsmokers, conditional on surviving to 65, is still about $14,500.

Table 8.3 indicates that the Social Security cost of smoking is smaller for single women than for single men. In general single women get a higher rate of return from Social Security for two reasons. First, they have longer life expectancies, and, second, they have lower earnings and the system is progressive. Conditional on age 20, the difference in the net transfer to median wage women nonsmokers and smokers is slightly more than $9,000. The real internal rate of return for smoking women is 3.45 percent, while the figure is 3.87 percent for nonsmokers. Conditional on reaching age 65, the dollar difference between smoking and not is about $6500 for median wage single women.

The lower portion of table 8.3 shows the results for single individuals with earnings 60 percent of the median for their age and cohort. The loss due to smoking in the expected transfer from Social Security is almost $17,000 for men and $7,000 for women at this earnings level. We conclude that the Social Security cost of smoking is not terribly sensitive to earnings levels.

The corresponding results for one- and two-earner married couples with median earnings profiles are shown in table 8.4. One-earner couples receive larger transfers and a higher rate of return from Social Security because of the benefits received by the nonworking spouse.

**Table 8.3** Present Value of Social Security Benefits and Taxes (in 1985 dollars) and Internal Rate of Return to the Social Security Program for Members of the 1920 Birth Cohort, Single Men and Women

| | Expected Present Value of OASI Benefits | Expected Present Value of OASI Taxes | Net Expected Present Value | Net Present Value Conditional on Surviving until Age 65 | Real Internal Rate of Return | Real Internal Rate of Return Conditional on Surviving until Age 65 |
|---|---|---|---|---|---|---|
| | | | Median Earnings Profile | | | |
| Men | | | | | | |
| Smokers | 53,497 | 71,279 | −17,782 | 3,721 | 1.87 | 3.18 |
| Nonsmokers | 79,436 | 76,000 | 3,436 | 18,218 | 3.17 | 3.78 |
| Women | | | | | | |
| Smokers | 65,512 | 57,386 | 8,126 | 21,843 | 3.45 | 4.03 |
| Nonsmokers | 75,788 | 58,395 | 17,394 | 28,283 | 3.87 | 4.27 |
| | | | Low (60% Median) Earnings Profile | | | |
| Men | | | | | | |
| Smokers | 41,378 | 50,342 | 8,964 | 8,918 | 2.25 | 3.57 |
| Nonsmokers | 61,441 | 53,433 | 8,008 | 20,130 | 3.53 | 4.15 |
| Women | | | | | | |
| Smokers | 47,159 | 34,431 | 12,728 | 23,166 | 4.06 | 4.65 |
| Nonsmokers | 54,556 | 35,036 | 19,520 | 27,801 | 4.47 | 4.88 |

**Table 8.4** Present Value of Social Security Benefits and Taxes (in 1985 dollars) and Internal Rate of Return to the Social Security Program for Members of the 1920 Birth Cohort, Median Earnings Profile, One-Earner and Two-Earner Couples

| | Expected Present Value of OASI Benefits | Expected Present Value of OASI Taxes | Net Expected Present Value | Net Present Value Conditional on Surviving until Age 65 | Real Internal Rate of Return | Real Internal Rate of Return Conditional on Surviving until Age 65 |
|---|---|---|---|---|---|---|
| Married (one earner) | | | | | | |
| Both smoke | 118,223 | 79,466 | 38,757 | 81,270 | 4.40 | 5.41 |
| Nonsmokers | 149,229 | 81,004 | 68,225 | 95,872 | 5.14 | 5.63 |
| Male smoker, female nonsmoker | 128,748 | 79,722 | 49,026 | 95,123 | 4.67 | 5.67 |
| Female smoker, male nonsmoker | 139,353 | 80,860 | 58,493 | 87,010 | 4.93 | 5.43 |
| Married (two earners) | | | | | | |
| Both smoke | 126,687 | 128,664 | −1,977 | 38,639 | 2.95 | 3.87 |
| Nonsmokers | 162,985 | 134,395 | 28,590 | 56,371 | 3.68 | 4.18 |
| Male smoker, female nonsmoker | 138,313 | 129,673 | 8,640 | 48,103 | 3.22 | 4.04 |
| Female smoker, male nonsmoker | 151,494 | 133,386 | 18,108 | 48,402 | 3.46 | 4.05 |

*Note:* Figures are per household.

The Social Security expected cost of smoking is similar for couples in either circumstance. The net expected present value of participation in Social Security is $29,468 lower for one-earner couples who both smoke relative to one-earner couples where neither spouse smokes. If only the man smokes, the loss in the expected transfer from the system is $19,199, whereas if only the wife smokes the loss is $9,732, relative to a one-earner couple in which neither smokes. To put these figures in perspective, one might note that the median earnings of 64-year-old men in this cohort were $20,315. Thus, the Social Security loss for both smoking amounts to almost 1.5 years labor income. In fact, the loss is slightly greater than that given that Social Security benefits are taxed more favorably than labor income.

The numbers for two-earner couples are that their expected net Social Security transfer is $30,567 less if both spouses smoke than if neither does. The real internal rate of return for two-earner couples in which both smoke is 2.95 percent, whereas it is 3.68 percent if neither smokes. The cost of the husband only smoking is $19,950, and the cost of the wife only smoking is $10,482. For reference, the median annual earnings of women is about $12,500, so the loss if they both smoke is roughly equivalent to 2.4 years of the wife's earnings.

Table 8.5 contains the results for low-wage one- and two-earner couples. For one-earner couples, we find that the cost of both smoking is roughly $22,600. For two-earner couples, the cost of both smoking is $23,500. Once again, the cost is roughly twice as large for men as it is for women. The dollar costs to smoking are greater relative to earnings for low-wage households than for median earners.

The gain in Social Security benefits that accrue to the nonsmoker, or to the smoker who quits, represents an equal and opposite drain on Social Security funds. This drain is only partially offset by the increase in preretirement taxes paid by nonsmokers and ex-smokers in comparison with smokers, a substantially greater number of whom die prematurely. The potential cost to society, including the government, of a successful antismoking program has not gone unnoticed. In 1971, the British government, in response to a recommendation by the Royal College of Physicians to mount an antismoking campaign, estimated that such a campaign would save money in the short run. However, by the year 2000, they forecasted that a 40 percent reduction in cigarette smoking would result in a net loss to the government of 29 million pounds due to additional benefits received by surviving ex-smokers. The Congressional Office of Technology Assessment, in its recent report "Smoking-Related Death and Financial Costs" (Kronebusch 1985), indicated that, in the event of a reduction of smoking, "there will be some increase in revenues to the government and the Social Security and Medicare trust funds because people will be working more years.

**Table 8.5**    **Present Value of Social Security Benefits and Taxes (in 1985 dollars) and Internal Rate of Return to the Social Security Program for Members of the 1920 Birth Cohort, Low (60% Median) Earnings Profile, One-Earner and Two-Earner Couples**

| | Expected Present Value of OASI Benefits | Expected Present Value of OASI Taxes | Net Expected Present Value | Net Present Value Conditional on Surviving until Age 65 | Real Internal Rate of Return | Real Internal Rate of Return Conditional on Surviving until Age 65 |
|---|---|---|---|---|---|---|
| Married (one earner) | | | | | | |
| Both Smoke | 91,761 | 55,146 | 36,614 | 70,896 | 4.78 | 5.81 |
| Nonsmokers | 115,531 | 56,327 | 59,204 | 81,313 | 5.50 | 5.99 |
| Male smoker, female nonsmoker | 99,952 | 55,300 | 44,652 | 79,101 | 5.05 | 6.07 |
| Female smoker, male nonsmoker | 107,878 | 56,241 | 51,637 | 74,672 | 5.29 | 5.79 |
| Married (two earners) | | | | | | |
| Both Smoke | 96,843 | 84,772 | 12,071 | 45,609 | 3.47 | 4.43 |
| Nonsmokers | 124,085 | 88,469 | 35,616 | 58,131 | 4.18 | 4.70 |
| Male smoker, female nonsmoker | 105,689 | 85,378 | 20,311 | 52,959 | 3.74 | 4.61 |
| Female smoker, male nonsmoker | 115,429 | 87,864 | 27,566 | 52,003 | 3.97 | 4.56 |

*Note:* Figures are per household.

The increase in these revenues, however, may not equal the additional costs borne by these programs for the additional retirees" (p. 33). Limiting her attention to Medicare's hospital insurance fund, Wright (1986) has estimated that the individual 45-year-old male who quits smoking will cost the fund between $204 and $2,745.

We have emphasized the extent to which smoking reduces the expected value of Social Security payments below that of nonsmokers. We need to remember that because of the nature of the system, a drop in the number of smokers will provide a cost; every person who begins to smoke implicitly decreases the future liability of the system. The prevalence of smoking is an important factor in determining the financial viability of the system.

The percentage of U.S. adults who smoke has fallen drastically in the last 20 years. In 1965, 52 percent of men and 35 percent of women age 20 and older smoked; by 1983 the numbers fell to 35 percent and 30 percent, respectively (*Health United States* 1984). This should result in an increase in the average life span; since the majority of these people are below retirement age, we should expect retirees in the future to live longer on average than current retirees, who are already living longer than previous retirees due to the reduced use of cigarettes. A higher percentage of all workers will live to retirement; those who do will collect benefits for a longer period. This should be reflected in the demographic projections upon which Social Security taxes and benefits are based.

The trend toward fewer smokers has been a long one, especially among men. Unless that trend was adequately projected, we expect Social Security demographic projections to be too low. While the 1958 and 1966 Actuarial Studies by the Social Security Administration do a good job of predicting 1980 total population levels, they predict too high a number of young people and too low a number of retired persons. This implies offsetting errors, perhaps forecasting a longer "baby boom" than actually occurred and underestimating the additions to life expectancy, some of which can be attributed to lower smoking levels. This hurts the system twice; more retirees are currently drawing benefits than projected, and fewer workers will be paying taxes in the future than projected.

Our simulations suggest that each median-wage male smoker in the 1920 birth cohort roughly "saves" the Social Security system $20,000, and each median-wage female smoker saves $10,000. To get an approximate idea of the aggregate effect of smoking by members of this cohort on Social Security, we can multiply these saving figures by the number of smokers born in 1920. The result indicates that if no one had smoked in this cohort, the net transfer to this population from Social Security would have been $14.5 billion greater. As this reflects only the change for those born in one year, one can easily see that the total impact of smoking on the financial circumstances of Social Security amounts to hundreds of billions of dollars.

While we by no means claim that reduction in smoking is responsible for all the gains in life expectancy achieved in recent years, we have demonstrated the enormous potential impact on the system of reductions in smoking rates. Changes in the prevalence of smoking should be included in the system's attempts to model future populations.

## 8.4  Conclusion

The body of literature discussing the economic costs of smoking has largely ignored private and social costs with regard to Social Security. Our analysis is a first step in estimating these costs, both in terms of net benefits to smokers and reduced payments by the system. We find that the expected loss caused by smoking from participation in Social Security is a large one from the individual's perspective. The loss for a median-wage male smoker is about $20,000, or about 11 months of earnings. The loss for median-wage women is approximately $10,000 or about 10 months of earnings. These losses are quite significant even compared to the health cost consequences of smoking. We also found that these losses are not very different for workers with lower wages.

The aggregate implications of our results are that smokers "save" the Social Security system hundreds of billions of dollars. Certainly this does not mean that decreased smoking would not be socially beneficial. In fact, it is probably one of the most cost-effective ways of increasing average longevity. It does indicate, however, that if people alter their behavior in a manner which extends life expectancy, then this must be recognized by our national retirement program. Looked at in this way, it is not surprising that the large potential for increasing life spans that reduced smoking offers has sizeable consequences for Social Security.

# Appendix

**Life Tables, by Sex and Smoking Status, for the 1920 Birth Cohort**

| | Probability of Death within One Year | | | Survivors from 100,000 Births | | Fraction that Smoke | Mortality Ratio |
|---|---|---|---|---|---|---|---|
| Age (1) | Total Pop. (2) | Non-smokers (3) | Smokers (4) | Non-smokers (5) | Smokers (6) | (7) | (8) |
| A. Males | | | | | | | |
| 20 | .00244 | .00230 | .00253 | 85,758 | 85,758 | 0.60 | 1.10 |
| 21 | .00265 | .00250 | .00275 | 85,560 | 85,540 | 0.60 | 1.10 |
| 22 | .00287 | .00271 | .00298 | 85,346 | 85,305 | 0.60 | 1.10 |
| 23 | .00353 | .00333 | .00366 | 85,115 | 85,051 | 0.60 | 1.10 |
| 24 | .00369 | .00348 | .00383 | 84,832 | 84,739 | 0.60 | 1.10 |
| 25 | .00360 | .00340 | .00374 | 84,536 | 94,415 | 0.60 | 1.10 |
| 26 | .00231 | .00218 | .00240 | 84,249 | 84,100 | 0.60 | 1.10 |
| 27 | .00217 | .00205 | .00225 | 84,066 | 83,898 | 0.60 | 1.10 |
| 28 | .00210 | .00198 | .00218 | 83,894 | 83,709 | 0.60 | 1.10 |
| 29 | .00206 | .00194 | .00214 | 83,727 | 83,527 | 0.60 | 1.10 |
| 30 | .00213 | .00164 | .00246 | 83,565 | 83,348 | 0.60 | 1.50 |
| 31 | .00222 | .00171 | .00256 | 83,428 | 83,143 | 0.60 | 1.50 |
| 32 | .00227 | .00175 | .00262 | 83,285 | 82,930 | 0.60 | 1.50 |
| 33 | .00232 | .00178 | .00268 | 83,140 | 82,713 | 0.60 | 1.50 |
| 34 | .00230 | .00177 | .00265 | 82,991 | 82,492 | 0.60 | 1.50 |
| 35 | .00243 | .00157 | .00300 | 82,845 | 82,273 | 0.60 | 1.91 |
| 36 | .00256 | .00166 | .00316 | 82,714 | 82,026 | 0.60 | 1.91 |
| 37 | .00288 | .00186 | .00356 | 82,577 | 81,766 | 0.60 | 1.91 |
| 38 | .00311 | .00201 | .00384 | 82,424 | 81,475 | 0.60 | 1.91 |
| 39 | .00337 | .00218 | .00416 | 82,258 | 81,162 | 0.60 | 1.91 |
| 40 | .00375 | .00243 | .00463 | 82,078 | 80,824 | 0.60 | 1.91 |
| 41 | .00411 | .00266 | .00508 | 81,879 | 80,450 | 0.60 | 1.91 |
| 42 | .00451 | .00292 | .00557 | 81,662 | 80,041 | 0.60 | 1.91 |
| 43 | .00501 | .00324 | .00619 | 81,423 | 79,595 | 0.60 | 1.91 |
| 44 | .00557 | .00360 | .00688 | 81,160 | 79,103 | 0.60 | 1.91 |
| 45 | .00608 | .00329 | .00794 | 80,867 | 78,558 | 0.60 | 2.41 |
| 46 | .00681 | .00369 | .00889 | 80,601 | 77,935 | 0.60 | 2.41 |
| 47 | .00746 | .00404 | .00974 | 80,303 | 77,242 | 0.60 | 2.41 |
| 48 | .00842 | .00456 | .01099 | 79,979 | 76,490 | 0.60 | 2.41 |
| 49 | .00904 | .00490 | .01181 | 79,614 | 75,649 | 0.60 | 2.41 |
| 50 | .00972 | .00527 | .01269 | 79,224 | 74,756 | 0.60 | 2.41 |
| 51 | .01033 | .00568 | .01370 | 78,807 | 73,807 | 0.58 | 2.41 |
| 52 | .01125 | .00629 | .01515 | 78,359 | 72,797 | 0.56 | 2.41 |
| 53 | .01196 | .00679 | .01636 | 77,867 | 71,694 | 0.54 | 2.41 |
| 54 | .01272 | .00734 | .01769 | 77,338 | 70,521 | 0.52 | 2.41 |
| 55 | .01340 | .00879 | .01801 | 76,770 | 69,273 | 0.50 | 2.05 |
| 56 | .01422 | .00945 | .01938 | 76,096 | 68,025 | 0.48 | 2.05 |
| 57 | .01495 | .01008 | .02067 | 75,376 | 66,707 | 0.46 | 2.05 |
| 58 | .01598 | .01093 | .02241 | 74,616 | 65,328 | 0.44 | 2.05 |
| 59 | .01702 | .01181 | .02421 | 73,801 | 63,865 | 0.42 | 2.05 |
| 60 | .01845 | .01299 | .02664 | 72,929 | 62,318 | 0.40 | 2.05 |

*(continued)*

### Life Tables, by Sex and Smoking Status, for the 1920 Birth Cohort

| | Probability of Death within One Year | | | Survivors from 100,000 Births | | Fraction that Smoke (7) | Mortality Ratio (8) |
|---|---|---|---|---|---|---|---|
| Age (1) | Total Pop. (2) | Non-smokers (3) | Smokers (4) | Non-smokers (5) | Smokers (6) | | |
| A. Males | | | | | | | |
| 61 | .01967 | .01406 | .02882 | 71,982 | 60,658 | 0.38 | 2.05 |
| 62 | .02094 | .01520 | .03115 | 70,970 | 58,910 | 0.36 | 2.05 |
| 63 | .02280 | .01680 | .03444 | 69,891 | 57,075 | 0.34 | 2.05 |
| 64 | .02433 | .01821 | .03733 | 68,717 | 55,109 | 0.32 | 2.05 |
| 65 | .02605 | .02148 | .03672 | 67,465 | 53,051 | 0.30 | 1.71 |
| 66 | .02797 | .02333 | .03990 | 66,017 | 51,103 | 0.28 | 1.71 |
| 67 | .03007 | .02538 | .04341 | 64,476 | 49,064 | 0.26 | 1.71 |
| 68 | .03234 | .02763 | .04725 | 62,840 | 46,935 | 0.24 | 1.71 |
| 69 | .03476 | .03006 | .05141 | 61,103 | 44,717 | 0.22 | 1.71 |
| 70 | .03736 | .03272 | .05594 | 59,266 | 42,418 | 0.20 | 1.71 |
| 71 | .04017 | .03562 | .06091 | 57,327 | 40,045 | 0.18 | 1.71 |
| 72 | .04322 | .03881 | .06637 | 55,285 | 37,606 | 0.16 | 1.71 |
| 73 | .04653 | .04232 | .07237 | 53,140 | 35,110 | 0.14 | 1.71 |
| 74 | .05010 | .04617 | .07894 | 50,891 | 32,569 | 0.12 | 1.71 |
| 75 | .05404 | .05267 | .06636 | 48,541 | 29,998 | 0.10 | 1.26 |
| 76 | .05824 | .05705 | .07189 | 45,984 | 28,007 | 0.08 | 1.26 |
| 77 | .06249 | .06153 | .07753 | 43,361 | 25,994 | 0.06 | 1.26 |
| 78 | .06672 | .06603 | .08320 | 40,693 | 23,978 | 0.04 | 1.26 |
| 79 | .07108 | .07071 | .08910 | 38,006 | 21,983 | 0.02 | 1.26 |
| 80 | .07561 | .07561 | .07561 | 35,318 | 20,025 | 0.00 | 1.00 |
| 81 | .08066 | .08066 | .08066 | 32,648 | 18,511 | 0.00 | 1.00 |
| 82 | .08666 | .08666 | .08666 | 30,014 | 17,017 | 0.00 | 1.00 |
| 83 | .09380 | .09380 | .09380 | 27,413 | 15,543 | 0.00 | 1.00 |
| 84 | .10181 | .10181 | .10181 | 24,842 | 14,085 | 0.00 | 1.00 |
| 85 | .11024 | .11024 | .11024 | 22,313 | 12,651 | 0.00 | 1.00 |
| 86 | .11877 | .11877 | .11877 | 19,853 | 11,256 | 0.00 | 1.00 |
| 87 | .12708 | .12708 | .12708 | 17,495 | 9,919 | 0.00 | 1.00 |
| 88 | .13521 | .13521 | .13521 | 15,272 | 8,659 | 0.00 | 1.00 |
| 89 | .14322 | .14322 | .14322 | 13,207 | 7,488 | 0.00 | 1.00 |
| 90 | .15121 | .15121 | .15121 | 11,315 | 6,415 | 0.00 | 1.00 |
| 91 | .15934 | .15934 | .15934 | 9,604 | 5,445 | 0.00 | 1.00 |
| 92 | .16774 | .16774 | .16774 | 8,074 | 4,577 | 0.00 | 1.00 |
| 93 | .17654 | .17654 | .17654 | 6,719 | 3,810 | 0.00 | 1.00 |
| 94 | .18585 | .18585 | .18585 | 5,533 | 3,137 | 0.00 | 1.00 |
| 95 | .19499 | .19499 | .19499 | 4,505 | 2,554 | 0.00 | 1.00 |
| 96 | .20390 | .20390 | .20390 | 3,626 | 2,056 | 0.00 | 1.00 |
| 97 | .21250 | .21250 | .21250 | 2,887 | 1,636 | 0.00 | 1.00 |
| 98 | .22072 | .22072 | .22072 | 2,273 | 1,289 | 0.00 | 1.00 |
| 99 | .22850 | .22850 | .22850 | 1,771 | 1,004 | 0.00 | 1.00 |
| 100 | .23656 | .23656 | .23656 | 1,366 | 775 | 0.00 | 1.00 |
| 101 | .24490 | .24490 | .24490 | 1,043 | 591 | 0.00 | 1.00 |
| 102 | .25354 | .25354 | .25354 | 788 | 446 | 0.00 | 1.00 |

**Life Tables, by Sex and Smoking Status, for the 1920 Birth Cohort**

| | Probability of Death within One Year | | | Survivors from 100,000 Births | | Fraction that Smoke | Mortality Ratio |
|---|---|---|---|---|---|---|---|
| Age (1) | Total Pop. (2) | Non-smokers (3) | Smokers (4) | Non-smokers (5) | Smokers (6) | (7) | (8) |
| A. Males | | | | | | | |
| 103 | .26248 | .26248 | .26248 | 588 | 333 | 0.00 | 1.00 |
| 104 | .27174 | .27174 | .27174 | 433 | 245 | 0.00 | 1.00 |
| 105 | .28132 | .28132 | .28132 | 315 | 179 | 0.00 | 1.00 |
| 106 | .29125 | .29125 | .29125 | 227 | 128 | 0.00 | 1.00 |
| 107 | .30154 | .30154 | .30154 | 160 | 91 | 0.00 | 1.00 |
| 108 | .31218 | .31218 | .31218 | 112 | 63 | 0.00 | 1.00 |
| 109 | .32320 | .32320 | .32320 | 77 | 43 | 0.00 | 1.00 |
| 110 | .33461 | .33461 | .33461 | 52 | 29 | 0.00 | 1.00 |
| 111 | .34643 | .34643 | .34643 | 34 | 19 | 0.00 | 1.00 |
| 112 | .35867 | .35867 | .35867 | 22 | 12 | 0.00 | 1.00 |
| 113 | .37135 | .37135 | .37135 | 14 | 8 | 0.00 | 1.00 |
| 114 | .38448 | .38448 | .38448 | 9 | 5 | 0.00 | 1.00 |
| 115 | .39806 | .39806 | .39806 | 5 | 3 | 0.00 | 1.00 |
| 116 | .41213 | .41213 | .41213 | 3 | 1 | 0.00 | 1.00 |
| 117 | .42671 | .42671 | .42671 | 1 | 1 | 0.00 | 1.00 |
| 118 | .44180 | .44180 | .44180 | 1 | 0 | 0.00 | 1.00 |
| 119 | .45743 | .45743 | .45743 | 0 | 0 | 0.00 | 1.00 |
| 120 | .50000 | .50000 | .50000 | 0 | 0 | 0.00 | 1.00 |
| B. Females | | | | | | | |
| 17 | .00195 | .00191 | .00201 | 88,787 | 88,787 | 0.40 | 1.05 |
| 18 | .00191 | .00187 | .00197 | 88,617 | 88,608 | 0.40 | 1.05 |
| 19 | .00187 | .00183 | .00193 | 88,451 | 88,434 | 0.40 | 1.05 |
| 20 | .00191 | .00187 | .00197 | 88,289 | 88,264 | 0.40 | 1.05 |
| 21 | .00192 | .00188 | .00198 | 88,123 | 88,090 | 0.40 | 1.05 |
| 22 | .00190 | .00186 | .00196 | 87,957 | 87,916 | 0.40 | 1.05 |
| 23 | .00190 | .00186 | .00196 | 87,794 | 87,744 | 0.40 | 1.05 |
| 24 | .00182 | .00178 | .00187 | 87,630 | 87,573 | 0.40 | 1.05 |
| 25 | .00171 | .00168 | .00176 | 87,474 | 87,409 | 0.40 | 1.05 |
| 26 | .00163 | .00160 | .00168 | 87,327 | 87,255 | 0.40 | 1.05 |
| 27 | .00156 | .00153 | .00161 | 87,188 | 87,108 | 0.40 | 1.05 |
| 28 | .00145 | .00142 | .00149 | 87,054 | 86,968 | 0.40 | 1.05 |
| 29 | .00143 | .00140 | .00147 | 86,930 | 86,839 | 0.40 | 1.05 |
| 30 | .00143 | .00130 | .00163 | 86,809 | 86,711 | 0.40 | 1.25 |
| 31 | .00146 | .00133 | .00166 | 86,696 | 86,570 | 0.40 | 1.25 |
| 32 | .00148 | .00135 | .00168 | 86,581 | 86,426 | 0.40 | 1.25 |
| 33 | .00149 | .00135 | .00169 | 86,464 | 86,281 | 0.40 | 1.25 |
| 34 | .00149 | .00135 | .00169 | 86,347 | 86,135 | 0.40 | 1.25 |
| 35 | .00158 | .00139 | .00187 | 86,230 | 85,989 | 0.40 | 1.35 |
| 36 | .00166 | .00146 | .00197 | 86,111 | 85,828 | 0.40 | 1.35 |
| 37 | .00188 | .00165 | .00223 | 85,985 | 85,659 | 0.40 | 1.35 |
| 38 | .00196 | .00172 | .00232 | 85,843 | 85,469 | 0.40 | 1.35 |

(*continued*)

Life Tables, by Sex and Smoking Status, for the 1920 Birth Cohort

| | Probability of Death within One Year | | | Survivors from 100,000 Births | | Fraction that Smoke | Mortality Ratio |
|---|---|---|---|---|---|---|---|
| Age (1) | Total Pop. (2) | Non-smokers (3) | Smokers (4) | Non-smokers (5) | Smokers (6) | (7) | (8) |
| B. Females | | | | | | | |
| 39 | .00208 | .00182 | .00246 | 85,696 | 85,270 | 0.40 | 1.35 |
| 40 | .00235 | .00206 | .00278 | 85,539 | 85,060 | 0.40 | 1.35 |
| 41 | .00246 | .00216 | .00291 | 85,363 | 84,823 | 0.40 | 1.35 |
| 42 | .00273 | .00239 | .00323 | 85,179 | 84,576 | 0.40 | 1.35 |
| 43 | .00301 | .00264 | .00356 | 84,975 | 84,303 | 0.40 | 1.35 |
| 44 | .00324 | .00284 | .00384 | 84,750 | 84,002 | 0.40 | 1.35 |
| 45 | .00359 | .00295 | .00455 | 84,510 | 83,680 | 0.40 | 1.54 |
| 46 | .00393 | .00323 | .00498 | 84,260 | 83,300 | 0.40 | 1.54 |
| 47 | .00422 | .00347 | .00534 | 83,988 | 82,885 | 0.40 | 1.54 |
| 48 | .00467 | .00384 | .00591 | 83,696 | 82,442 | 0.40 | 1.54 |
| 49 | .00487 | .00400 | .00617 | 83,375 | 81,954 | 0.40 | 1.54 |
| 50 | .00528 | .00434 | .00669 | 83,041 | 81,449 | 0.40 | 1.54 |
| 51 | .00556 | .00459 | .00707 | 82,680 | 80,904 | 0.39 | 1.54 |
| 52 | .00577 | .00481 | .00741 | 82,301 | 80,332 | 0.37 | 1.54 |
| 53 | .00624 | .00522 | .00805 | 81,905 | 79,737 | 0.36 | 1.54 |
| 54 | .00652 | .00548 | .00844 | 81,477 | 79,096 | 0.35 | 1.54 |
| 55 | .00686 | .00596 | .00870 | 81,030 | 78,428 | 0.33 | 1.46 |
| 56 | .00726 | .00633 | .00924 | 80,548 | 77,746 | 0.32 | 1.46 |
| 57 | .00760 | .00665 | .00971 | 80,038 | 77,027 | 0.31 | 1.46 |
| 58 | .00813 | .00717 | .01047 | 79,505 | 76,279 | 0.29 | 1.46 |
| 59 | .00862 | .00764 | .01115 | 78,935 | 75,481 | 0.28 | 1.46 |
| 60 | .00954 | .00849 | .01239 | 78,332 | 74,639 | 0.27 | 1.46 |
| 61 | .01030 | .00924 | .01349 | 77,668 | 73,714 | 0.25 | 1.46 |
| 62 | .01099 | .00990 | .01445 | 76,950 | 72,720 | 0.24 | 1.46 |
| 63 | .01214 | .01098 | .01603 | 76,189 | 71,669 | 0.23 | 1.46 |
| 64 | .01297 | .01183 | .01727 | 75,352 | 70,520 | 0.21 | 1.46 |
| 65 | .01393 | .01264 | .01909 | 74,461 | 69,303 | 0.20 | 1.51 |
| 66 | .01499 | .01367 | .02064 | 73,520 | 67,980 | 0.19 | 1.51 |
| 67 | .01609 | .01481 | .02236 | 72,515 | 66,577 | 0.17 | 1.51 |
| 68 | .01719 | .01589 | .02400 | 71,441 | 65,089 | 0.16 | 1.51 |
| 69 | .01829 | .01699 | .02566 | 70,306 | 63,527 | 0.15 | 1.51 |
| 70 | .01948 | .01827 | .02759 | 69,111 | 61,897 | 0.13 | 1.51 |
| 71 | .02079 | .01959 | .02958 | 67,849 | 60,189 | 0.12 | 1.51 |
| 72 | .02219 | .02101 | .03173 | 66,519 | 58,409 | 0.11 | 1.51 |
| 73 | .02368 | .02264 | .03419 | 65,122 | 56,556 | 0.09 | 1.51 |
| 74 | .02532 | .02433 | .03673 | 63,647 | 54,622 | 0.08 | 1.51 |
| 75 | .02723 | .02676 | .03345 | 62,099 | 52,615 | 0.07 | 1.25 |
| 76 | .02938 | .02902 | .03627 | 60,437 | 50,855 | 0.05 | 1.25 |
| 77 | .03167 | .03136 | .03920 | 58,683 | 49,011 | 0.04 | 1.25 |
| 78 | .03407 | .03390 | .04238 | 56,843 | 47,090 | 0.02 | 1.25 |
| 79 | .03672 | .03663 | .04579 | 54,916 | 45,094 | 0.01 | 1.25 |
| 80 | .03969 | .03969 | .03969 | 52,905 | 43,030 | 0.00 | 1.00 |

**Life Tables, by Sex and Smoking Status, for the 1920 Birth Cohort**

| Age (1) | Probability of Death within One Year | | | Survivors from 100,000 Births | | Fraction that Smoke (7) | Mortality Ratio (8) |
|---|---|---|---|---|---|---|---|
| | Total Pop. (2) | Non-smokers (3) | Smokers (4) | Non-smokers (5) | Smokers (6)· | | |
| B. Females | | | | | | | |
| 81 | .04321 | .04321 | .04321 | 50,805 | 41,322 | 0.00 | 1.00 |
| 82 | .04750 | .04750 | .04750 | 48,610 | 39,536 | 0.00 | 1.00 |
| 83 | .05268 | .05268 | .05268 | 46,301 | 37,658 | 0.00 | 1.00 |
| 84 | .05866 | .05866 | .05866 | 43,861 | 35,674 | 0.00 | 1.00 |
| 85 | .06522 | .06522 | .06522 | 41,289 | 33,582 | 0.00 | 1.00 |
| 86 | .07222 | .07222 | .07222 | 38,596 | 31,391 | 0.00 | 1.00 |
| 87 | .07956 | .07956 | .07956 | 35,808 | 29,124 | 0.00 | 1.00 |
| 88 | .08723 | .08723 | .08723 | 32,959 | 26,807 | 0.00 | 1.00 |
| 89 | .09529 | .09529 | .09529 | 30,084 | 24,469 | 0.00 | 1.00 |
| 90 | .10380 | .10380 | .10380 | 27,217 | 22,137 | 0.00 | 1.00 |
| 91 | .11285 | .11285 | .11285 | 24,392 | 19,839 | 0.00 | 1.00 |
| 92 | .12251 | .12251 | .12251 | 21,640 | 17,600 | 0.00 | 1.00 |
| 93 | .13285 | .13285 | .13285 | 18,988 | 15,444 | 0.00 | 1.00 |
| 94 | .14392 | .14392 | .14392 | 16,466 | 13,392 | 0.00 | 1.00 |
| 95 | .15480 | .15480 | .15480 | 14,096 | 11,465 | 0.00 | 1.00 |
| 96 | .16527 | .16527 | .16527 | 11,914 | 9,690 | 0.00 | 1.00 |
| 97 | .17517 | .17517 | .17517 | 9,945 | 8,088 | 0.00 | 1.00 |
| 98 | .18429 | .18429 | .18429 | 8,203 | 6,671 | 0.00 | 1.00 |
| 99 | .19243 | .19243 | .19243 | 6,691 | 5,442 | 0.00 | 1.00 |
| 100 | .20095 | .20095 | .20095 | 5,403 | 4,395 | 0.00 | 1.00 |
| 101 | .20984 | .20984 | .20984 | 4,317 | 3,511 | 0.00 | 1.00 |
| 102 | .21912 | .21912 | .21912 | 3,411 | 2,774 | 0.00 | 1.00 |
| 103 | .22881 | .22881 | .22881 | 2,664 | 2,166 | 0.00 | 1.00 |
| 104 | .23893 | .23893 | .23893 | 2,054 | 1,671 | 0.00 | 1.00 |
| 105 | .24949 | .24949 | .24949 | 1,563 | 1,271 | 0.00 | 1.00 |
| 106 | .26054 | .26054 | .26054 | 1,173 | 954 | 0.00 | 1.00 |
| 107 | .27207 | .27207 | .27207 | 867 | 705 | 0.00 | 1.00 |
| 108 | .28411 | .28411 | .28411 | 631 | 513 | 0.00 | 1.00 |
| 109 | .29668 | .29668 | .29668 | 452 | 367 | 0.00 | 1.00 |
| 110 | .30981 | .30981 | .30981 | 318 | 258 | 0.00 | 1.00 |
| 111 | .32353 | .32353 | .32353 | 219 | 178 | 0.00 | 1.00 |
| 112 | .33785 | .33785 | .33785 | 148 | 120 | 0.00 | 1.00 |
| 113 | .35281 | .35281 | .35281 | 98 | 79 | 0.00 | 1.00 |
| 114 | .36842 | .36842 | .36842 | 63 | 51 | 0.00 | 1.00 |
| 115 | .38474 | .38474 | .38474 | 40 | 32 | 0.00 | 1.00 |
| 116 | .40178 | .40178 | .40178 | 24 | 20 | 0.00 | 1.00 |
| 117 | .41958 | .41958 | .41958 | 14 | 12 | 0.00 | 1.00 |
| 118 | .43816 | .43816 | .43816 | 8 | 6 | 0.00 | 1.00 |
| 119 | .45743 | .45743 | .45743 | 4 | 3 | 0.00 | 1.00 |
| 120 | .50000 | .50000 | .50000 | 2 | 2 | 0.00 | 1.00 |

# Note

1. A mortality ratio is the death rate of smokers divided by the death rate of nonsmokers of similar age and sex.

# References

Atkinson, A., and J. Townsend. 1977. Economic aspects of reduced smoking. *Lancet* (September 3) 492–95.

Cowell, M., and B. Hirst. 1980. Mortality differences between smokers and nonsmokers. *Society of Actuaries Transactions* 32:185–213.

Gori, G., and B. Richter. 1978. Macroeconomics of disease prevention in the United States. *Science* 200 (June 9): 1124–30.

Gori, G., B. Richter, and W. Yu. 1984. Economics and extended longevity— A case study. *Preventive Medicine* 13(4):396–410.

Hammond, E. C. 1966. Smoking in relation to the death rates of one million men and women. In *Epidemiological study of cancer and other chronic diseases,* 127–204. National Cancer Institute Monograph 19.

Harris, Jeffrey. 1983. Cigarette smoking among successive birth cohorts of men and women in the United States during 1900–80. *Journal of the National Cancer Institute* 71(3):473–79.

*Health United States.* 1984. National Center for Health Statistics, U.S. Department of Health and Human Services.

Kronebusch, Karl. 1985. *Smoking-related death and financial costs.* Preliminary Draft. Washington, D.C.: Congressional Office of Technology Assessment.

Lubin, J., W. Blot, F. Berrino, et al. 1984. Patterns of lung cancer risk according to type of cigarette smoked. *International Journal of Cancer* 33:569–76.

Oster, G., G. Colditz, and N. Kelly. 1984. *The economic costs of smoking and the benefits of quitting.* Lexington, Mass.: Lexington Books.

Rogot, Eugene. 1974. Smoking and mortality among U.S. veterans. *Journal of Chronic Disability* 27:189–203.

Scheiderman, M., and D. Levin. 1972. Trends in lung cancer. *Cancer* 30(5):1320–25.

Wright, Virginia. 1986. Will quitting smoking help Medicare solve its financial problems? *Inquiry* 23 (Spring): 76–82.

# Comment     Paul Taubman

Shoven, Sundberg, and Bunker have opened up a new area of study by examining the cost to smokers of being enrolled in the Social Security system. The cost arises because Social Security stops paying

Paul Taubman is a Professor of Economics at the University of Pennsylvania and a Research Associate of the National Bureau of Economic Research.

you when you die (though your spouse may still draw some of your benefits), and smokers die earlier. That smokers die earlier is well documented,[1] though it is an open question whether cigarette smoking *causes* the earlier death.

My comments will address the issue of how we might improve Shoven et al.'s estimates and also whether we should be "taxing" smokers. Their estimates essentially use previously collected information on (1) life tables of smokers and nonsmokers and (2) typical earnings of individuals to (3) calculate the expected Social Security benefits of smokers and nonsmokers. Both of the two pieces of information have some loose ends associated with them.

The life table for smokers and nonsmokers is based on Hammond's 1966 study which calculates death rates by age in the early 1960s. Let us accept the proposition that Hammond's results provide good estimates for the early 1960s. Since then age-specific death rates have declined markedly, and his relative death rates need not apply in the 1980s when the authors make their calculations. To illustrate this point, consider the effect of education on death rates among older males. Using death data matched to the 1960 Census, Kitagawa and Hauser (1973) found no difference among the variously educated groups. Using the 1973 CPS–Social Security Exact Match sample, which takes death information from Social Security records, Rosen and Taubman (1984) found the more educated had a 20–25 percent advantage over the least educated and that this differential persisted amoung those aged 78 and over, which is the remainder of the group studied by Kitagawa and Hauser. A more recent set of life tables based on smoking might yield different results than Hammond's, especially since work by Behrman, Sickles, and Taubman (1987) using time-series data for the period 1954–69 finds a life expectancy differential for smokers only about one-half as large as those found in Hammond, though Behrman, Sickles, and Taubman's work is based on a nonrandom sample.

The earnings data used may also be inappropriate given the structure of Social Security's benefit plan and the possibility that smoking affects labor market supply via morbidity. Some estimates that were based on actual earnings data of smokers and nonsmokers would be helpful. In any event, to sharpen the estimates by marital status which is related to labor supply, information on actual earnings histories or on benefits paid would be useful. Such information exists, though the smoking information may be suspect.

Next, let us turn to the question: Is it fair to tax cigarette smokers? Of course, a cigarette excise tax already exists which is often justified on the grounds of improving health, presumably a public policy based on the grounds that smokers are myopic. There are reasons to tax smokers. We, as taxpayers, help pay some of the medical bills of cigarette smokers if they are sicker than the rest of the population or if they are hospitalized at younger ages, both of which seem plausible. Finally, if passive smoking harms the nonsmoker, a still open question, then there is a market failure, which could be corrected by a "tax." Is the tax contained in the Social Security system optimal for this purpose? I don't know.

There is also a question of whether the Social Security system should be thought of as an annuity as the authors do in their analysis. There is no question that Social Security looks like an annuity, though the premium and benefit schedules are much different than the private one I invest in for retirement. Congress, however, now seems mostly concerned with using the Social Security system to provide a socially adequate standard of living to the elderly. Surely we can find a social welfare function consistent with this notion, and then the fact that smokers are penalized as annuitants doesn't matter as long as they receive a socially adequate income while alive. Perhaps this income level varies by smoking status, but I don't know if smoking costs are greater than substitutes such as candy used by nonsmokers.

Finally, one may ask whether the mandatory nature of Social Security is important or whether we could get to a voluntary first-best solution with private markets allowing for different life expectancies. Work by Rothschild and Stiglitz (1976) suggests a stable voluntary equilibrium may not be possible, though I hasten to add that some current life insurance policies take not smoking into account, and that insurance market seems to be functioning. But it may be that a voluntary annuity market with different life expectancies wouldn't work. We may need to have policies with one life expectancy used and force some people to make a bad buy.

## Note

1. See the references given by Shoven, Sundberg, and Bunker in this paper and those in Behrman, Sickles, and Taubman (1987).

## References

Behrman, J. R., R. Sickles, and P. Taubman. 1987. Age specific death rates. University of Pennsylvania. Mimeo.
Hammond, E. C. 1966. Smoking in relation to the death rates of one million men and women. In *Epidemiological study of cancer and other chronic diseases,* 127–204. National Cancer Institute Monograph 19.
Kitagawa, E., and P. Hauser. 1973. *Differential mortality in the United States of America: A study in socioeconomic epidemiology.* Cambridge, Mass.: Harvard University Press.

Rosen, S., and P. Taubman. 1984. Changes in the impact of education and income on mortality in the U.S. In *Statistical uses of administrative records with emphasis on mortality and disability research.* Washington, D.C.: U.S. Department of Health, Education and Welfare.

Rothschild, M., and J. E. Stiglitz. 1976. Equilibrium in competitive insurance markets: An essay on the economics of imperfect information. *Quarterly Journal of Economics* 90 (November): 630–49.

# 9    Long-Term Care, Wealth, and Health of the Disabled Elderly Living in the Community

Alan M. Garber

Providing and financing long-term care of the elderly are among the most pressing policy issues facing the aging American population. An expanding population at risk for chronic disability—the old and very old—promises to generate an unprecedented rise in the demand for long-term care. Advocates for the elderly, policymakers, and health care providers share a growing perception that the scope of services currently available to the elderly is inadequate, and that older Americans bear unacceptable financial risk as a consequence of chronic disability. Largely because most long-term care is uninsured, out-of-pocket expenses for health care of the elderly are greater today than they were before Medicare was instituted; in nominal terms, out-of-pocket health expenditures are estimated to have risen from $300 in 1964 to $1,575 in 1984 (U.S. Senate 1984). Secretary of Health and Human Services Otis Bowen's (1986) report on catastrophic health expenses drew attention to the financial disaster that can accompany chronic disability. Critics of Secretary Bowen's proposal, which did not recommend an expanded role for Medicare or other federally administered long-term care insurance, were quick to add that the costs of long-term care, not catastrophic hospital expenses, pose the greatest health-related financial risk confronting the elderly.

Long-term care consists of nursing home services and a variety of home health services, including visits by home health aides, nurses, physical therapists, and other nonphysician providers, as well as Meals on Wheels and other nonmedical services. Medicare's Prospective

Alan M. Garber is Assistant Professor of Medicine at Stanford University and a Research Associate of the National Bureau of Economic Research.

Acknowledgments are given to Ellen Jones for research assistance and to the National Bureau of Economic Research for support.

Payment System (PPS) for hospital services has increased both the number of days of nursing home care and its average resource intensity, since earlier hospital discharges have shifted some convalescent care from the hospital to homes and nursing homes.

Even before the PPS was put in place, nursing home expenditures had been rising (fig. 9.1). This trend is likely to continue in even more dramatic form as the American population becomes older. Changing demographics and changes in long-term care financing will accelerate this trend. Methods for predicting utilization will become especially important as the size of the long-term care sector grows.

This document presents the background and preliminary results of a study of the determinants of long-term care utilization by the disabled elderly. The larger study analyzes hospital, home health care, and nursing home utilization; this document describes primarily the first two aspects. The first two sections of this paper outline the background for the research. Section 9.1 describes the demographic changes that have lent

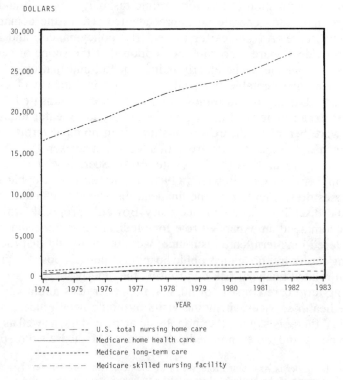

**Fig. 9.1**    U.S. nursing home expenditures (in 1982 dollars).
*Source:* Doty, Liu, and Wiener 1985.

urgency to the debate over long-term care. Section 9.2 reviews the current financing of long-term care, describing the roles of government and the private sector. Section 9.3 sketches some of the previous research on long-term care utilization which has concentrated on nursing homes. Selected characteristics of a sample of disabled elderly, part of the 1982 National Long-Term Care Survey, are presented in section 9.4. Results from an analysis of health care utilization in this population appear in section 9.5. The paper concludes with a discussion in section 9.6. The findings of this preliminary study underscore the differences between measures of health status that predict mortality and hospitalization, and the measures that correspond to chronic disability and the demand for personal care assistance. Here, as in other studies of long-term care, living arrangement and family supports appear to have large impacts on long-term care utilization.

### 9.1 The Changing Demography of Morbidity

The number of Americans aged 65 and over will double between 1980 and 2020; the boom is expected to continue until well into the next century. The aging of America is a consequence of three factors. First, perinatal mortality has fallen, raising life expectancy at birth to 71 years for men and 78 years for women. Second, the survival of adults has improved. Today 65-year-old men and women can expect to live about 15 and 19 more years, respectively. Third, by about 2010 aging baby-boomers will begin to swell the ranks of the elderly. A declining birth rate will further augment the fraction of the American population aged 65 and older. Fewer workers will be available to help fund their care; by the year 2020, there will be only three workers for every person 65 and over, as compared to five-to-one today (U.S. Senate 1986).

Future utilization of long-term care depends on trends in the functional status (disability level) of the elderly. Forecasts of these numbers require some speculation. Standardized measures of functional status were adopted too recently to assess time trends in overall levels of disability. Advances in prevention and medical care have prolonged survival, but many of the people whose lives have been extended are chronically ill and disabled.

Three views about recent changes in the "health," as distinct from the mortality, of the elderly have been espoused. The first, from Fries (1980) and Fuchs (1984), is that improvements in morbidity have accompanied improvements in survival. They expect the average morbidity of surviving elderly of a given age to fall as mortality continues to improve. The second view is that individuals who would have died in the past now survive to be chronically ill and disabled (Verbrugge

1984). Hence age-adjusted disability may increase with time. The third view, expressed by Poterba and Summers (1987), is that increases in the "frailty" of survivors approximately offset morbidity improvements due to medical and other progress, so that average disability changes little over time.

With the exception of Verbrugge, the above authors do little to distinguish long-term care from other forms of health care. The health characteristics that lead elderly patients to obtain long-term care are not the same as the predictors of hospitalization and physician utilization. First, the consumption of formal (paid) long-term care services may depend heavily on living arrangement. Disabled individuals who live with a spouse or other family member consume fewer formal services and are much less likely to enter a nursing home; the death of a spouse commonly precipitates nursing home admission. Second, many of the conditions that prompt the utilization of long-term care services are primarily diseases or disabilities of old age that may have only a weak direct association with mortality. People are admitted to nursing homes because of disability brought about by dementia, severe arthritis, and other such chronic ailments. But the leading cause of death among the elderly is heart disease. Falling death rates from heart disease have contributed to improved survival. Since heart disease does not usually cause the disabilities that lead to prolonged nursing home stays, declines in its morbidity and mortality would not be expected to reduce nursing home admission rates. Of course, reductions in the incidence or health effects of other illnesses that cause both chronic disability and death might lower nursing home admission rates while they reduced mortality; stroke is a prominent example. Nonfatal strokes frequently result in paralysis or speech impairments that make independent living impossible, so the declining incidence of strokes may have reduced long-term care utilization.

The disability of elderly survivors in the future thus depends on the particular conditions that are ameliorated by medical care. If effective prevention or treatment becomes available for illnesses that cause chronic disability, the elderly of the future may be less impaired than those of today. If the future instead brings diminution of the incidence or severity of fatal diseases that cause little disability, more of the elderly will survive to develop chronic degenerative conditions. Increasing life expectancy alone will increase the percentage of the elderly who are disabled, since disability becomes more common with advancing age. This results in greater utilization of long-term care; in 1980, only about 1.1 percent of Americans aged 65–69 were institutionalized, compared with 18.7 percent of the "oldest old"—the group aged 85 and over (U.S. Bureau of the Census 1984b). The number of oldest old is projected to quadruple over the next fifty years (U.S.

Bureau of the Census 1984a). Hence, even if age-specific disability does not change, the size of the population likely to use long-term care will expand.

## 9.2  Long-Term Care Financing

Out-of-pocket expenditures figure much more prominently in long-term care than in hospital and physician services. Medicare pays for nearly half of all expenditures for the health care of the elderly. The remainder is divided among the elderly and their families, who pay for 25 percent, Medicaid, which pays for 13 percent, and other sources, which pay for the remaining 13 percent. In contrast, Medicare paid for less than 1 percent of all skilled nursing facility expenditures in 1983 (Schieber et al. 1986). Its fraction of nursing home expenditures is even smaller when the denominator includes the categories of nursing homes that Medicare does not cover, such as intermediate and custodial care facilities. Medicare accounts for a larger fraction of the payments for formal (paid) home health care. In 1981, when nursing home expenditures were $24.2 billion, Medicare paid $404 million for care in skilled nursing facilities. Medicare home health care expenditures reached $939 million that year, while out-of-pocket and private insurance expenditures for home health care were estimated to total $2.3 billion (Doty, Liu, and Wiener 1985). By 1985, when nursing home expenditures reached $35.2 billion, Medicare paid for 1.7 percent of the total; its share of nursing home expenditures has fallen at least since 1970, when it paid 5.6 percent of the total (Lazenby, Levit, and Waldo 1986).

Medicare limits its nursing home expenditures by restricting coverage to a sharply circumscribed set of services and eligibility rules. According to 1986 rules, Medicare will pay for up to 100 days of nursing home care only if the following conditions are met: the institution is a skilled nursing facility (SNF); the beneficiary has been in a hospital for at least three days prior to transfer to a SNF; the condition treated in the hospital makes the SNF care necessary; admission to the SNF takes place within a month of hospital discharge; a doctor certifies that the enrollee needs daily skilled nursing or rehabilitation services; and the stay is not disallowed by a review committee. For days 21 through 100 of the nursing home stay, the patient is responsible for $61.50 of the daily charges. By limiting coverage to skilled nursing facilities and to 100 days of nursing home care, Medicare avoids paying for long nursing home stays (these stays are usually for custodial care, which does not require skilled nursing on a daily basis). Medicare's nursing home benefits cover convalescence from hospitalization, not care of the chronic conditions that may have catastrophic financial consequences for patients and their families.

"Medigap" policies, which help pay for Medicare deductibles and copayments, and sometimes extend the period of coverage for hospital care, are popular: about two thirds of the elderly purchase some form of this private supplemental coverage. However, nursing home coverage under these policies is largely limited to reducing copayments under the Medicare benefits.

Private long-term care insurance is not new, but availability has been limited and few of the policies have been attractive. Consequently, it has paid for less than 1 percent of nursing home expenditures (Doty, Liu, and Wiener 1985). This option for financing long-term care was given a boost by President Reagan's endorsement of the recommendations of Secretary of Health and Human Services Otis Bowen (1986), which included tax incentives and educational programs to promote the development of private long-term care insurance. Blue Cross and Blue Shield programs in several states are planning to offer long-term care benefit packages, the American Association of Retired Persons is planning to market a private long-term care insurance package with Prudential, and Congress may be asked to offer federal employees a long-term care insurance option. Almost seventy companies are offering long-term care insurance policies, double the number available two years ago (*American Medical News*, 6 March 1987).

Despite its growing availability, private long-term care insurance might not gain widespread acceptance by the elderly or by younger potential enrollees. Adverse selection and moral hazard are likely to be more severe problems for long-term care than for conventional health insurance. Patients at high risk of needing nursing home care might not be offered policies at attractive prices, unless they could enroll in a group plan. The remedies that private insurers have implemented to avoid adverse selection diminish its value as insurance. For example, several plans exclude dementia from coverage (Meiners 1984); yet "dementia is found in over 50 percent of nursing home residents and is the most common precipitating cause of institutionalization" (Rowe 1985). Additional exclusions for "preexisting conditions" further limit the range of conditions covered, so that the catastrophic nursing home costs of many subscribers would not be covered. The insurers may be prudent to refrain from offering generous benefits; already one major insurer, the United Equitable Insurance Company, has stopped offering long-term care insurance after experiencing losses that exceeded premiums by 40 percent ("Nursing Home Insurers Rise," *New York Times*, 17 March 1987).

Medicaid is the largest insurer of long-term care. The elderly account for a disproportionate share of Medicaid expenditures, and about 68 percent of Medicaid's expenditures for the elderly pay for nursing home care. An additional 17 percent is spent on hospital care. Medicaid's share amounts to about half of the total expenditures for nursing home care of the elderly, while the disabled elderly and their families pay most of the remainder directly. If Medicaid plays an important role in financing nursing home care, many of the elderly turn to it only after they exhaust other alternatives. In order to qualify for Medicaid, individuals who are not already destitute must have medical expenses sufficient to drain their financial resources—along with, in many states, the resources of their spouses—until they approach poverty levels. Nursing home care, which costs about $20,000 to $25,000 annually, is the most common cause of the "spend-down" to impoverishment. The resource and income limits for the states that have a "medically needy" category, by which the elderly might qualify for Medicaid, are stringent. As of 1984, in states that had medically needy programs, the average allowed assets were $2,021 for a single person and $2,950 for a couple, with protected income of $286 and $367, respectively. Several states allowed only $1,500 of protected assets for individuals and $2,250 for couples, with protected income of as little as $175 for the individual and $183 for a couple (Skellan and Yanek 1985). While many of the elderly have been able to protect assets by transferring them to relatives and by divorcing their spouses, stricter enforcement at the state and federal levels will make it harder to shield assets in the future. Hence the middle-class individual who develops a condition that requires extended nursing home care faces the prospect of destitution.

Unlike care for acute conditions, informal care—services provided by family and friends—is an important component of long-term care. The costs and quantity of these nonmarket services are not readily measured, but there is evidence that they are large. Muurinen (1986) found that informal caregivers reduced labor force participation by about one fourth in order to care for disabled persons; the caregivers who did not leave the labor force suffered reduced earnings because of increased absenteeism. Muurinen claimed that savings from a home-based intervention may have resulted from a shift of costs from formal to unreimbursed care.

Spouses are an important source of informal care, so that the loss of a spouse may result in either institutionalization or more extensive utilization of formal home services. When the elderly who live in the community become older, they are more likely to live alone or with a relative other than a spouse. In the community, 23 percent of the "oldest old"—those 85 and older—live with a spouse, as compared with 63 percent of 65 to 74 year olds. Although disability in the elderly living in the community becomes more common with advancing age, people who live alone are *less* likely to have a disability than those who live with a spouse or other relatives. For example, 9.6 percent of the oldest old who live alone have at least one activity limitation requiring personal care assistance, as compared with 18.8 percent of the oldest old who live with a spouse, and 25 percent of those who live with other family members (Feller 1983). Unless living with a spouse or other family member causes an activity limitation, these figures suggest that development of activity limitations signals an end to independent living for many of the elderly who live alone. Either they move in with relatives, or they are lost to the community because of death or institutionalization. If the future brings additional fragmentation of the family, or if a widening disparity between male and female mortality rates increases the number of single survivors, we can anticipate that more of the elderly will live alone and, if they become disabled, require either formal community services or institutionalization. Then the financing of long-term care will more closely resemble conventional health care, with increasing expenditures fueled by a reduction in the availability of unpaid help.

## 9.3    Determinants of Long-Term Care Utilization

As policymakers contemplate broadening insurance coverage to include long-term care, accurate prediction of long-term care expenditures and utilization has acquired new significance. Not only are such estimates needed in order to anticipate the potential financial risks faced by government programs, but they can help evaluate the risks faced by the elderly and by potential insurers. Studies of utilization might also help establish the most efficient means of providing services by assessing substitution between home care and institutional care, or between nursing homes and hospitals. Unfortunately, the literature on long-term care utilization does not provide the unequivocal answers we might desire.

Ambiguity in the literature on long-term care utilization arises from several important differences in the studies. First, the aims of the studies vary, as do their definitions of long-term care. Second, the risks of institutionalization, the socioeconomic characteristics, and the community settings differ substantially from one study to another. Finally, the methodologies also vary.

Many investigations of long-term care utilization assess the ability of community-based interventions to reduce institutionalization. The interventions usually include an array of home health services and a program or person to coordinate the services. In principle, such studies should elucidate the circumstances leading to institutionalization and utilization of community services. Most such studies collect longitudinal data on health and socioeconomic characteristics, with detailed health expenditures and utilization data as well as indicators of health and well-being. But since their goal is to determine whether the intervention is effective (and frequently the designers of the intervention are the evaluators), they usually employ case-control methods to compare the intervention group to a group of controls. This approach (used by Branch and Stuart 1984; Hughes, Cordray, and Spiker 1984; Yordi and Waldman 1985; and Gaumer et al. 1986, among others) may accurately evaluate the impact of the intervention, but the results are not usually reported in a form that enables one to infer, for example, the effect of age or disability levels on likelihood of institutionalization.

Differences among the interventions, the populations studied, as well as definitions thwart direct comparisons of these studies. Weissert (1985), reviewing eight community-based interventions, noted that institutionalization rates in the control groups varied tenfold. Some of the studies do not report the costs of home care (Branch and Stuart 1984; Nocks et al. 1986) or the amount of home care provided in the control and intervention groups (Nocks et al. 1986); few studies attempt to measure informal care.

Several other studies have sought to predict nursing home utilization. The dependent variable representing utilization varies from study to study. Several investigations estimate the lifetime risk of being admitted to a nursing home at least once. Others estimate the probability of nursing home admission during a fixed interval, such as a month, a year, or five years. Very few seek to predict the measure of utilization most appropriate for forecasting demand or expenditures—the probability distribution of nursing home days. Since nursing home stays fall into at least two groups—short stays and long stays—with very different implications for expenditures and for occupancy rates, predicting a lifetime risk of nursing home admission or admission rates in fixed intervals is less useful.

The studies that attempt to predict the lifetime risk of nursing home admission produce disparate estimates, ranging from about 25 percent to 50 percent (Palmore 1976; Vicente et al. 1979; McConnel 1984). Branch and Jette (1982), in a prospective study of 1,625 elderly Massachusetts individuals, used logistic regression to predict the likelihood of nursing home entry in a six-year period. Kane and Matthias (1984) used a similar method to predict likelihood of discharge to a nursing home for a sample of elderly hospitalized patients drawn from hospital cases reviewed by four Professional Standards Review Organizations (PSROs). Several other studies have used life-table methods or Markov models to predict likelihood of nursing home admission; some of these studies control for individual patient characteristics (Manton, Woodbury, and Liu 1984; Liu and Manton 1984), but most do not (Shapiro and Webster 1984; McConnel 1984; Lane et al. 1985; Cohen, Tell, and Wallack 1986).

Failure to control for individual characteristics severely impairs the ability to predict utilization from these studies. Those studies that predict the likelihood of institutionalization over a given interval, such as five years, are not suitable for estimating likelihoods of institutionalization during shorter intervals, unless a set of strict assumptions is valid. Furthermore, if they do not estimate duration and likelihood of institutionalization simultaneously, these studies may lead to erroneous forecasts of nursing home demand and occupancy rates. A researcher interested in assessing the effects of a change in age might use such studies to obtain the change in likelihood of institutionalization and multiply the result by either a mean or predicted length of stay (as suggested in Liu and Manton 1984). Unless certain conditions apply (e.g., the estimates are obtained in the same population), the result will be a biased and statistically inconsistent estimate of the expected change in nursing home days.

## 9.4   The Disabled Elderly Living in the Community

As the population at risk, the disabled elderly living in the community are the key to understanding several aspects of the future of long-term care and its financing. Health, disability, and living arrangement determine the utilization of formal long-term care services; financial status determines whether an older person can purchase private insurance, enroll in a continuing care facility, or participate in other privately funded forms of long-term care. Although long-term care insurance will be offered to nearly all of the elderly (as well as younger people), the disabled elderly are the most likely to collect benefits. Studies of long-term care utilization have concentrated on the high-risk elderly in order to obtain sufficient numbers of hospitalizations, deaths, and nursing home admissions. This section describes results from a national sample of disabled, noninstitutionalized Medicare enrollees, obtained from the 1982 National Long-Term Care Survey (NLTCS). Several aspects of the survey have been described by Macken (1986). The following discussion emphasizes disability in relation to socioeconomic characteristics and measures of hospital and long-term care utilization.

In 1982, the Health Care Financing Administration collected extensive data on a sample of Medicare enrollees who lived in the community and had an impairment in performing at least one "activity of daily living" (ADL) or "instrumental activity of daily living" (IADL). The ADLs were developed more than twenty years ago (Katz et al. 1963) and are widely used measures of functional impairment that have been found to help predict utilization and several aspects of outcomes. Besides obtaining information about the disabled elderly, the study also directed its attention to their caregivers—both paid helpers and the unpaid, informal caregivers who were usually spouses or other family members.

This data set gives important insights into the group of people most likely to receive long-term care. However, it has important limitations as a source of information. People who entered nursing homes for a prolonged time were likely to be censored from the sample, since the survey excluded institutionalized individuals. Hence the NLTCS does not illuminate one of the key issues confronting government and private insurers: whether home health care can prevent or delay long nursing home admissions.

Included in the NLTCS is extensive information about living arrangement, functional status, income, wealth, education, hospital utilization, and a host of other individual characteristics. The survey also included extensive information about paid and unpaid (informal) caregivers along with data on the sources of payment and insurance coverage.

The NLTCS data were constructed by screening 26,000 Medicare enrollees for activity limitations lasting at least three months. From the original sample, about 6,400 were found to have at least one limitation in an ADL or an IADL. This core group was interviewed in detail or, in those cases in which the study subject was unable to respond because of a mental or other limitation, interviews were conducted with proxies.

Tables 9.1 and 9.2 show sample means or proportions and ranges for key variables from the NLTCS. Respondents who did not complete the "reinterview" portion of the survey are deleted from these figures. Approximately 60 percent of the 1982 Medicare population was female.

**Table 9.1**      **Sample Characteristics**

| Name | Description | Mean or Proportion | Range |
|------|-------------|--------------------|-------|
| AGE | | 77 | 65–108 |
| EDUC | Highest grade completed | 8.5 | 0–18 |
| ALONE | Live alone | 32% | |
| MEDCAID1 | Have Medicaid card | 24% | |
| PRIHOSP | Have private hospital insurance | 57% | |
| PRIDOC | Private physician insurance | 53% | |
| HOSPDAYS | Days in hospital, past year | 5.4 | 0–115 |
| NHDAYS | Days in nursing home, past year | .3 | 0–90 |
| INC1 | Household income last 12 months | $11,711 | $2,000–$75,000 |
| LQ1 | Home owned by household member | 71% | |
| HOMEVAL | Value of home/property | $34,725 | 0–$200,000 |
| HOMEWLTH | Value of home minus amount owed | $31,974 | *–$200,000 |
| ADL | Number of ADL limitations | 1.9 | 0–9 |
| IADL | Number of IADL limitations | 4.0 | 0–9 |
| HELPCT | Number of helpers | 1.8 | 0–11 |
| HPAID | Number of paid helpers | .3 | 0–8 |
| DAYSCT | Days of help past week | 6.2 | 0–42 |
| DAYSPAID | Days of paid help | .7 | 0–21 |
| ICDAYS | Days of unpaid help | 5.5 | 0–42 |

*One respondent claimed to owe more than the value of the house; otherwise the minimum value of home wealth was 0.

Table 9.2          Percentage of Sample Respondents with Specific
                   Activity Limitations

| | | |
|---|---|---|
| ADL1 | Eating | 12% |
| ADL2 | Getting in/out of bed | 30 |
| ADL3 | Did not get out of bed at all | 1 |
| ADL4 | Getting around inside | 44 |
| ADL5 | Did not get around inside at all | 2 |
| ADL6 | Confined to wheelchair | 3 |
| ADL7 | Dressing | 24 |
| ADL8 | Bathing | 47 |
| ADL9 | Getting to/using toilet | 26 |
| IADL1 | Doing heavy work | 77 |
| IADL2 | Doing light work | 27 |
| IADL3 | Doing laundry | 47 |
| IADL4 | Preparing meals | 35 |
| IADL5 | Shopping for groceries | 61 |
| IADL6 | Getting around outside | 59 |
| IADL7 | Going outside/walking distance | 51 |
| IADL8 | Managing money | 30 |
| IADL9 | Making telephone calls | 18 |

Only 9.9 percent of the total Medicare population was aged 85 and over, as compared to 17.9 percent of the NLTCS population (Macken 1986). The sample analyzed here included 1,213 individuals less than 70 years old; 1,334 70–74 year olds; 1,301 75–79 year olds; 1,074 80–84 year olds; and 1,062 who were 85 and older. The picture that emerges from these statistics is of a population in which severe disability was relatively uncommon and in which a substantial minority lived alone. Although the less severe ADL impairments were relatively common, only 1 percent were unable to get out of bed at all, and 2 percent were unable to get around inside their living quarters at all. Difficulties in mobility and bathing were most common among the ADL impairments. Most sample respondents required assistance with some IADLs, such as heavy work, shopping for groceries, and getting about on the outside.

The medical conditions of the NLTCS population reflect the toll of chronic disease. Senility was identified as a problem afflicting 35 percent, and the questions were answered by a proxy about a third of the time. Nearly three quarters of the respondents complained of arthritis, about half complained of circulation trouble (peripheral vascular disease), about half had hypertension, and about a quarter complained of permanent numbness or stiffness. Only 7 percent noted a previous stroke, and about 7 percent had a prior heart attack. About 6 percent claimed to have cancer.

About 7 percent of the respondents had been in a nursing home before, mostly for brief stays. More than a third had been hospitalized during the preceding year.

Although the NLTCS did not collect detailed information about the financial assets of the participants, it queried them about home ownership, value of home, indebtedness, and income. About 71 percent of them owned, were buying, or lived with the owner of the housing they occupied. Only 14 percent of the sample still owed mortgage money. The variable HOMEWLTH was created to approximate the value of equity in the home; it is the difference between the respondent's estimate of the value of the home and the amount still owed. As figure 9.2 shows, not only did most of the respondents own their homes, but the value of equity averaged more than $30,000 for individuals with anywhere from 1 to 9 limitations in ADLs. The average annual income was about $12,000, and the family income per household member was about $7,150. Figure 9.3 demonstrates that above age 75, the difference between estimated home value and indebtedness increased with age, and there was no clear trend in income. These figures are approximate, since the NLTCS recorded only categorical information about income and home values. Despite these caveats, there is no evidence of a

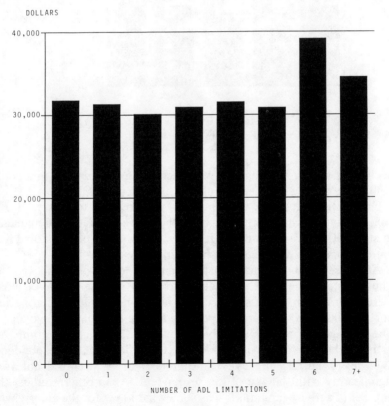

**Fig. 9.2.**        Home wealth by number of ADL limitations

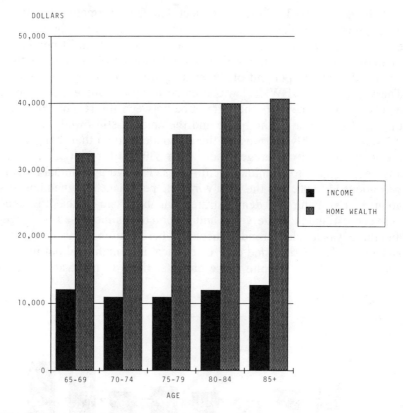

**Fig. 9.3.**          Financial status by age

decline in wealth with age or with increasing numbers of functional limitations among the disabled elderly in the community.

One might argue that the very old who are able to remain in the community are a hardier group, since they have survived and managed to stay out of nursing homes. However, the number of functional limitations increases with age, as shown in figure 9.4.

About a third lived alone; most of the remainder lived with a spouse. The income, home value, and age distribution of those who lived alone were very similar to those who were not alone. Children can be important additional supports, especially for the elderly who live alone. The average respondent who lived alone had 2.5 children, compared with 2.2 children for the others. Half of the children of the respondents lived less than an hour away. The number of children did not vary significantly with the age of the respondent. As in other studies, the number of activity limitations was somewhat lower for the elderly who lived alone; those who lived alone had 1.61 ADL impairments and 3.55

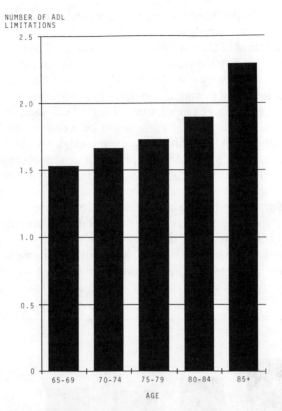

NUMBER OF ADL
LIMITATIONS

**Fig. 9.4.**        Number of ADL limitations by age

IADL impairments, on average, while those who did not live alone had
1.99 ADL impairments and 4.20 IADL impairments.

## 9.5   Health Service Utilization by the Disabled Elderly Living in the Community

Other studies have produced evidence that chronic disability is associated with increased hospital and long-term care utilization. Nursing
home patients are frequently admitted to hospitals; we might expect
to observe the same phenomenon in the disabled elderly who are in
the community. Although the NLTCS did not survey individuals who
were in nursing homes, by querying participants about prior nursing
home admissions it produced substantial information about short-term
nursing home admissions. These nursing home stays were almost always associated with hospital admission. Providers of home health care
were asked how many days they had visited the sample person during

the week prior to the interview. Paid helpers were also asked how much they were paid and who paid them.

About one third of the sample was hospitalized during the preceding year. As figure 9.5 demonstrates, the annual number of hospital days fell with age. If the very old who get severe acute illnesses are likelier to die, to be admitted to nursing homes, or to stay in institutions longer, they may have been censored from the NLTCS sample. Figure 9.6 illustrates the strong positive association between hospital utilization and the number of ADL limitations, even though the ADL limitations were not consistent predictors of number of unreimbursed care days. People without ADL limitations averaged less than four days of hospital care; those with five ADL limitations averaged about 11 days in the hospital. Not shown is the similar relation for nursing home days and ADL limitations; sample persons averaged only 0.3 nursing home days during the year prior to the interview.

Since most of the sample was not hospitalized, simple linear regressions are not appropriate for estimating the number of hospital days.

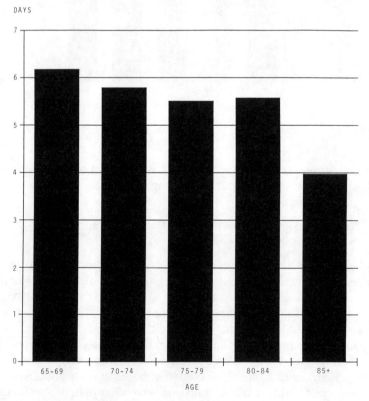

**Fig. 9.5.**    Hospital days (in preceding year) by age

DAYS

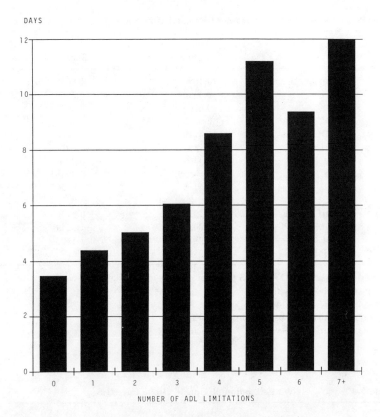

NUMBER OF ADL LIMITATIONS

**Fig. 9.6**          Hospital days by number of ADL limitations

Instead, Tobit regressions were performed to assess the correlates of various dimensions of utilization. A Tobit explaining hospital utilization, shown in table 9.3, confirms these univariate associations. Age has a highly significant negative association with hospital days, and the number of both ADL and IADL impairments are strong predictors of hospitalization. Increasing education has a positive effect on hospital days. The effects of variations in income, value of home, private supplemental insurance, and living arrangement are not statistically significant at conventional levels.

The number of days of informal care was strongly related to the number of children; days of formal home health care were higher for respondents who lived alone and who had more children. The number of children did not vary significantly with age of the respondent. These measures of utilization were also examined with Tobit regressions.

Table 9.4 reports estimates predicting days of unreimbursed home care. The actual number of days is the sum over all unpaid care providers

**Table 9.3**        **Tobit Estimation of Hospital Utilization**

|  | Parameter Estimate | t-Statistic |
|---|---|---|
| Constant | 10.169 | 1.8606 |
| AGE | −0.43604 | −6.2500 |
| SEX | 0.65650 | 0.64330 |
| ADL | 2.0015 | 6.9891 |
| IADL | 1.4799 | 6.1158 |
| MEDCAID1 | −2.1157 | −1.6971 |
| ALONE | −0.34007 | −0.29740 |
| PRIDOC | 0.64558 | 0.30685 |
| PRIHOSP | 1.4315 | 0.66567 |
| INC1 | −0.51890E−04 | −1.0678 |
| CHILDREN | 0.19112 | 0.91169 |
| HOMEWLTH | −0.20894E−04 | −1.4254 |
| EDUC | 0.28777 | 2.1302 |
| SIGMA | 24.051 | 43.669 |

Dependent variable: HOSPDAYS (number of days in hospital past year)
Log of likelihood function        = −6863.99
Number of observations          = 3688
Number of positive observations    = 1227
Percent positive observations      = 0.332701

**Table 9.4**        **Tobit Estimation of Unpaid Home Care Days**

|  | Parameter Estimate | t-Statistic |
|---|---|---|
| Constant | 5.2844 | 4.1480 |
| AGE | −0.21325E−01 | −1.3183 |
| SEX | 0.15167 | 0.63318 |
| ADL | −0.40240E−01 | −0.57851 |
| IADL | 0.10984E−01 | 0.19393 |
| MEDCAID1 | −0.50578 | −1.7445 |
| ALONE | 0.14044E−01 | 0.52615E−01 |
| PRIDOC | −0.99702 | −2.0042 |
| PRIHOSP | 0.63032 | 1.2406 |
| INC1 | −0.21385E−04 | −1.8473 |
| CHILDREN | 0.49610 | 9.9241 |
| HOMEWLTH | 0.45330E−05 | 1.3224 |
| EDUC | 0.21204E−01 | 0.66598 |
| SIGMA | 6.6807 | 70.335 |

Dependent variable: ICDAYS (days of informal care past week)
Log of likelihood function        = −10071.4
Number of observations          = 3688
Number of positive observations    = 2776
Percent positive observations      = 0.752711

of the number of days that they saw the respondent during the preceding week; hence, the total can exceed seven. The individuals who had supplementary insurance that paid for physician care received fewer days of informal care; the number of children, which may reflect the availability of informal caregivers, had a dramatic positive impact on the number of days of informal care. Living arrangement, however, had little effect on reported days of informal care.

Table 9.5, which presents the results for a Tobit estimation of days of paid home care, shows that respondents who lived alone received more paid care; respondents who had more children were also likely to receive more paid care. In contrast to the results for informal care, the number of days of paid care rose with the number of ADL limitations (but not with IADL limitations). The value of home equity had a positive association with days of paid care. The purchase of private insurance for hospital care or physician care had statistically insignificant effects on the utilization of formal home care, a result that might have been anticipated since few supplemental insurance plans would have provided substantial benefits for home health care. Medicaid enrollment was associated with fewer reported days of both paid home care and informal care. Several hypotheses are consistent with this observation. Perhaps children and relatives felt less willing to provide free long-term care when the respondent was eligible for nursing home care that would be paid by Medicaid; perhaps the individuals on Medicaid

**Table 9.5     Tobit Estimation of Days of Formal Home Health Care**

|  | Parameter Estimate | $t$-Statistic |
|---|---|---|
| Constant | −4.4526 | −2.3900 |
| AGE | −0.29884E−01 | −1.2655 |
| SEX | −0.31956 | −0.92219 |
| ADL | 0.19969 | 2.0154 |
| IADL | −0.49798E−01 | −0.60410 |
| MEDCAID1 | −0.65376 | −1.5390 |
| ALONE | 1.0629 | 2.8051 |
| PRIDOC | −0.38879 | −0.54029 |
| PRIHOSP | −0.56444 | −0.77056 |
| INC1 | 0.56184E−07 | 0.33083E−02 |
| CHILDREN | 0.23018 | 3.2367 |
| HOMEWLTH | 0.98799E−05 | 2.0252 |
| EDUC | −0.70257E−01 | −1.5237 |
| SIGMA | 6.8054 | 28.127 |

Dependent variable: DAYSPAID
Log of likelihood function          =   −2,887.50
Number of observations              =     3,688
Number of positive observations     =       576
Percent positive observations       =        0.156182

who became disabled were more likely to enter nursing homes because they bore none of the cost of their stay.

The Tobits predicting these measures of home health care utilization show a trend toward decreasing utilization with age; although the age coefficient does not achieve statistical significance, the pattern is consistent across all the measures of utilization that were examined.

## 9.6  Discussion

Although the NLTCS provides a detailed look at the disabled elderly who live in the community, it has important limitations as a source of data on long-term care utilization. The failure to track individuals into nursing homes is its most obvious shortcoming. The censoring of the elderly who went into nursing homes may also complicate the interpretation of some of the results. The very old in this sample spent fewer days in the hospital than did the younger old, and they tended to receive fewer days of home health care. But we would expect hospital utilization to increase with age. One explanation for this phenomenon is that the very old who had long hospital stays or frequent admissions were likely to be removed from the sample—either by death or institutionalization. If long-term care is a continuum that ranges from less intensive informal and formal home care to nursing home care, censoring due to institutionalization means that the "oldest old" in the community are very different from the 25 percent in nursing homes.

It is noteworthy that many of the personal characteristics that are widely considered to be predictive of health status generally—such as education, wealth, and income—were not nearly as predictive of home health service use, activity limitations, or hospitalization in this data set. The activity limitations are self-reported, highly subjective appraisals, so their reproducibility and validity as measures of underlying chronic disability are debatable (see Feinstein, Josephy, and Wells 1986 for a detailed critique of indexes of functional status). However, many of the health characteristics that lead to institutionalization and the need for personal care assistance are degenerative conditions for which no effective preventions are known. For example, most dementia in the elderly is due to senile dementia of the Alzheimer's type (SDAT); as of this writing, its cause is unknown, and there is no effective prevention, treatment, or cure. In contrast, it has been known for several years that elevated cholesterol, smoking, and hypertension increase the risk of heart disease. Individuals can modify these risk factors, and there are effective treatments for some of the associated morbidities; there is no analogous opportunity for the prevention of most cases of dementia, incontinence, or joint disorders. Hence the beneficial effects of schooling (see Grossman 1975), income, and wealth on health, which depend in part on individual choices to improve health, might not be observed here.

These data are insufficient to predict the expected costs of nursing home care faced by this population. Another study conducted in the early 1980s suggests that the expected costs are manageable. The National Long-Term Care Channeling Demonstration, a large, multiple-site randomized trial of an intervention designed to reduce institutionalization, enrolled individuals who were thought to be at very high risk of institutionalization; they were older and had more severe disabilities than the NLTCS sample. Adjusted for age, the Channeling population had somewhat higher nursing home admission rates than did other Medicare recipients. Even in the Channeling demonstration, mean nursing home expenditures for the participants in the control group were less than $900 during the twelve months following enrollment (Wooldridge and Schore 1986, pp. D.10, D.11). The NLTCS population had substantial assets, and within this sample there was no clear association between disability and wealth. Severe disability resulting in institutionalization and depletion of assets may be responsible for the negative association between disability and wealth that has been observed elsewhere, rather than lower wealth causing increased disability. If so, the disabled elderly in the community might have sufficient assets to purchase long-term care insurance, at least at actuarially fair prices. If moral hazard and adverse selection are sufficiently severe, and administrative costs sufficiently high, it may not be feasible to offer private long-term care insurance plans at prices low enough to attract widespread participation.

Although the 1982 NLTCS provides a great deal of information about the characteristics of the disabled elderly in the community, censoring by death and institutionalization limits its usefulness for predicting either hospital or nursing home utilization. These drawbacks will be rectified by the 1984 follow-up to the NLTCS, which determined institutionalization rates and mortality for the 1982 sample. Analysis of this data set should resolve many of the censoring problems and enable us to trace the changes in health status, wealth, mortality, and health service utilization that occur with aging.

# References

Bowen, O. R. 1986. Catastrophic illness expense: Report to the president. Washington, D.C.: Department of Health and Human Services.

Branch, L. G., and A. M. Jette. 1982. A prospective study of long-term care institutionalization among the aged. *American Journal of Public Health* 72:1373–79.

Branch, L. G., and N. E. Stuart. 1984. A five-year history of targeting home care services to prevent institutionalization. *Gerontologist* 24:387–91.

Cohen, M. A., E. J. Tell, and S. S. Wallack. 1986. The lifetime risks and costs of nursing home use among the elderly. *Medical Care* 24:1161–72.

Doty, P., K. Liu, and J. Wiener. 1985. An overview of long-term care. *Health Care Financing Review* 6:69–78.

Feinstein, A. R., B. R. Josephy, and C. K. Wells. 1986. Scientific and clinical problems in indexes of functional disability. *Annals of Internal Medicine* 105:413–20.

Feller, B. A. 1983. Need for care among the noninstitutionalized elderly. In *Health, United States, 1983,* National Center for Health Statistics, DHHS Pub. no. (PHS) 84–1232 (Public Health Service). Washington, D.C.: GPO.

Fries, J. F. 1980. Aging, natural death, and the compression of morbidity. *New England Journal of Medicine* 303:130–35.

Fuchs, V. R. 1984. "Though much is taken": Reflections on aging, health, and medical care. *Milbank Memorial Fund Quarterly* 62:143–66.

Gaumer, G. L., H. Birnbaum, F. Pratter et al. 1986. Impact of the New York long-term home health care program. *Medical Care* 24:641–53.

Grossman, M. 1975. The correlation between health and schooling. In *Household production and consumption,* ed. N. E. Terleckyj. New York: Columbia University Press.

Hughes, S. L., D. S. Cordray, and V. A. Spiker. 1984. Evaluation of a long-term home care program. *Medical Care* 22:460–75.

Kane, R. L., and R. Matthias. 1984. From hospital to nursing home: The long-term care connection. *Gerontologist* 24:604–9.

Katz, S., A. B. Ford, R. W. Moskowitz, et al. 1963. Studies of illness in the aged. *Journal of the American Medical Association* 185:914–19.

Lane, D., D. Uyeno, A. Stark, E. Kliewer, and G. Gutman. 1985. Forecasting demand for long-term care services. *Health Services Research* 20:435–60.

Lazenby, H., K. R. Levit, and D. R. Waldo. 1986. National health expenditures, 1985. *Health Care Financing Notes.* HCFA Pub. no. 03232. Office of the Actuary, Health Care Financing Administration. Washington, D.C.: GPO.

Liu, K., and K. G. Manton. 1984. The characteristics and utilization pattern of an admission cohort of nursing home patients (II). *Gerontologist* 24:70–76.

Macken, C. L. 1986. A profile of functionally impaired elderly patients living in the community. *Health Care Financing Review* 7:33–49.

Manton, K. G., M. A. Woodbury, and K. Liu. 1984. Life table methods for assessing the dynamics of U.S. nursing home utilization: 1976–1977. *Journal of Gerontology* 39:79–87.

McConnel, C. E. 1984. A note on the lifetime risk of nursing home residency. *Gerontologist* 24:193–98.

Meiners, M. R. 1984. The state of the art in long-term care insurance. National Center for Health Services Research. Typescript.

Muurinen, J-M. 1986. The economics of informal care: Labor market effects in the National Hospice Study. *Medical Care* 24:1007–17.

Nocks, B. C., R. M. Learner, D. Blackman, and T. E. Brown. 1986. The effects of a community-based long-term care project on nursing home utilization. *Gerontologist* 26:150–57.

Palmore, E. 1976. Total chance of institutionalization among the aged. *Gerontologist* 16:504–7.

Poterba, J. M., and L. H. Summers. 1987. Public policy implications of declining old-age mortality. In *Work, health, and income among the elderly,* ed. G. Burtless. Washington, D.C.: The Brookings Institution.

Rowe, J. W. 1985. Health care of the elderly. *New England Journal of Medicine* 312:827–35.

Schieber, G., J. Wiener, K. Liu, and P. Doty. 1986. Prospective payment for Medicare skilled nursing facilities: Background and issues. *Health Care Financing Review* 8:79–85.

Shapiro, E., and L. M. Webster. 1984. Nursing home utilization patterns for all Manitoba admissions, 1974–1981. *Gerontologist* 24:610–15.

Skellan, D., and J. Yanek. 1985. *Health care financing program statistics: Analysis of state Medicaid program characteristics, 1984.* Office of the Actuary, Health Care Financing Administration. Baltimore, Md.: U.S. Department of Health and Human Services.

U.S. Bureau of the Census. 1984a. *Projections of the population of the U.S. by age, sex, and race: 1983 to 2080.* Current Population Reports, Series P-25, no. 952. Washington, D.C.: GPO.

U.S. Bureau of the Census. 1984b. 1980 Census of population, persons in institutions and other group quarters. Vol. 2, *Subject reports,* PC-80-2-4D. Washington, D.C.: GPO.

U.S. Senate, Special Committee on Aging. 1984. *Medicare and the health costs of older Americans: The extent and costs of cost sharing.* Washington, D.C.: U.S. Senate.

U.S. Senate, Special Committee on Aging. 1986. *Aging America: Trends and projections.* Washington, D.C.: U.S. Department of Health and Human Services.

Verbrugge, L. M. 1984. Longer life but worsening health? Trends in health and mortality of middle-aged and older persons. *Milbank Memorial Fund Quarterly* 62:475–519.

Vicente, L., J. A. Wiley, and R. A. Carrington. 1979. The risk of institutionalization before death. *Gerontologist* 19:361–67.

Weissert, W. G. 1985. Seven reasons why it is so difficult to make community-based long-term care cost-effective. *Health Services Research* 20:423–33.

Wooldridge, J., and J. Schore. 1986. *Evaluation of the National Long-Term Care Demonstration: Channeling effects on hospital, nursing home, and other medical services.* Princeton, N.J.: Mathematica Policy Research, Inc.

Yordi, C. L., and J. Waldman. 1985. A consolidated model of long-term care: Service utilization and cost impacts. *Gerontologist* 25:389–97.

# 10 Employee Retirement and a Firm's Pension Plan

Laurence J. Kotlikoff and David A. Wise

In previous work we analyzed the incentive effects of the provisions of private pension plans.[1] The incentive effects were described by the accrual of pension wealth resulting from an additional year of work, treating the addition to pension wealth as a form of compensation in units comparable to the wage. We found that the provisions of almost all plans implied a large loss in pension wealth for work past the age of 65. Often this loss was more than 40 percent of the wage that would be earned for the additional work. In some plans wage earnings after 65 would be entirely offset by the concomitant loss in pension wealth. The typical plan also provided a substantial incentive to retire at the age of early retirement provided in the plan. This was often as young as 55. In addition, the typical plan provides a strong incentive not to retire before the early retirement age. Although this work documented the incentive effects inherent in the timing of the accrual of pension benefits, no attempt was made to estimate the actual effects of these incentives on retirement. That is, we considered the effect of pension benefit accrual on compensation by age, but not the effect of compensation on continued labor force participation. Indeed, based on the data used for that analysis there was no way to relate the plan provisions to retirement or to departure rates from the firm.

Laurence J. Kotlikoff is a Professor of Economics and Chairman of the Department of Economics at Boston University and a Research Associate of the National Bureau of Economic Research. David A. Wise is John F. Stambaugh Professor of Political Economy at the John F. Kennedy School of Government, Harvard University, and a Research Associate of the National Bureau of Economic Research.

The research reported here was supported by grant no. 3 PO1 AG05842-01 from the National Institute on Aging and by the W. E. Upjohn Institute for Employment Research. The research is part of the National Bureau of Economic Research project on the economics of aging. Any opinions expressed in this paper are those of the authors and not of the NBER or the sponsoring organizations.

In this paper, the relationship between pension accrual and retirement is analyzed based on the experience in a large Fortune 500 firm engaged in sales. Its name may not be disclosed. The data are the employment and earnings histories between 1969 and 1984 of all workers who were employed by the firm in any of the years between 1980 and 1984. The provisions of the firm pension plan are such that persons of the same age face very different pension accrual profiles and thus pension compensation at a given age. Hence, different individuals face very different incentives for continued work versus retirement.

The paper begins with a detailed description of the pension plan and the incentive effects inherent in its provisions. The incentive effects of the provisions are described in terms of their effects on the budget constraints facing employees over their working lives. For completeness, the accrual of Social Security benefits is described together with pension benefit accrual.

The evaluation of the incentive effects of plan provisions requires the estimation of wage earnings. The procedure used to estimate these profiles is described in section 10.2.

We then show the relationship between wage earnings, pension wealth accrual, and Social Security accrual, on the one hand, and departure rates from the firm, on the other. It is apparent from this relationship that the effect of the pension plan provisions on departure rates is very substantial. In subsequent analysis we will develop a model that will allow us to predict the effect of changes in the provisions on departure rates. That is not possible based only on the relationships presented here. But the detail shown here provides information that is often lost in formal statistical models.

The analysis makes clear that an estimation of the effects of pension plans on labor force participation of older workers can only be done by taking account of the precise provisions of individual plans. Simply knowing that an employee has a private pension plan tells nothing about the labor force incentive effects of the plan's provisions. While a great deal of effort has been directed to estimating the effects of Social Security provisions on labor force participation, much less attention has been given to the effects of private pension plans. The data presented here suggest that pension plans are likely to have a much greater effect than, for example, the recent changes in Social Security benefits.

## 10.1 The Firm Pension Plan

### 10.1.1 The Plan's Provisions

The firm has a defined benefit pension plan with earnings-related benefits and a Social Security offset. The plan's early and normal retirement ages are 55 and 65, respectively, with vesting after ten years. Actuarially reduced benefits are available starting at age 55 for *vested terminators*—vested workers who leave the firm prior to age 55. *Early retirees*—workers who retire between ages 55 and 65— are eligible to receive less than actuarially-reduced benefits. For workers who retire after age 65 there is no special actuarial benefit increase.

In addition to the more favorable benefit reduction afforded to early retirees, they also receive a supplemental benefit equal to their Social Security offset between the time they retire and the time they reach age 65. Hence, in comparison to a vested terminator who leaves the firm at age 54 and starts collecting benefits at age 55, an early retiree who leaves at age 55 enjoys a smaller benefit reduction and also receives a supplemental benefit until age 65. Not surprisingly, the profile of vested accrued benefits by age jumps sharply for most workers at age 55. Thus there is a large bonus for remaining with the firm until age 55.

The formula for the basic benefit before reduction for early retirement and before any applicable Social Security offset is the average earnings base times $x$ percent times the first $N$ years of continuous service, plus $y$ percent times the rest of continuous service:

(1)     Benefits = (Earnings Base) $[(x)(\text{Service})]$,
        if Service is less than $N$ years.
        Benefits = (Earnings Base) $[(x)(\text{Service}) + (y)(\text{Service} - N)]$,
        if Service is greater than $N$ years.

The parameters $x$ and $y$ are both less than 0.05, and $y$ is less than $x$. $N$ lies between 15 and 30. The average earnings base is calculated based on earnings between the start year and the year of either vested termination or retirement. The start year has traditionally been increased by two years every other year, varying from $k$ to $k + 1$ years before the current year, where $k$ is between 5 and 10. In our accrual calculations, we assume a one- or two-year increase in the start year every two years. Excluding the two lowest years of earnings (except that the number of earnings years used cannot be reduced below 5), the earnings base is calculated as the average annual earnings from the start year to the year of vested termination or retirement.

The Social Security adjustment (SSADJ) is $p$ ($p$ lies between 0.5 and 1) of the Social Security benefit (SSB) calculated by the firm times the ratio of completed service to the amount of service the worker would have if he or she stayed until age 65, less $Z$ ($Z$ lies between $1,000 and $5,000) times the ratio of continuous service as of 1 January 1976 to the continuous service the worker would have if he or she stayed until age 65:

$$
(2) \qquad \text{SSADJ} = p\text{SSB}\frac{S}{S + (65-A)} - Z\frac{S(76)}{S + (65-A)} .
$$

Here, $S$ is years of service, $S(76)$ is the years of service the worker had in 1976, and $A$ is the worker's current age. The first term is smaller the younger the age of retirement, which reduces the adjustment. But if the worker has pre-1976 service, the second term is also smaller the younger the retirement age, and this increases the adjustment.

SSB, the firm's calculation of the worker's age 65 Social Security benefit, is based on the worker's earnings to date with the firm. In the SSB formula, earnings last year are extrapolated forward, assuming no growth factor, until the worker reaches age 65. The average of past earnings with the firm as well as extrapolated future earnings is then entered into a three-bracket progressive benefit formula to determine SSB.

For early retirees the factor by which benefits are reduced depends on age and service. For example, if the worker retires at age 55 with 20 years of service the reduction is 50 percent; it would be only 33 percent if the worker had 26 or more years of service. For workers with 30 or more years of service, the reduction drops to zero at retirement ages between 60 and 64.

The pension accrual can vary widely for workers of the same age but with different service and for workers with the same service but of different ages. These accrual differences reflect the fact that many of the features of the benefit and Social Security formulas involve either age or service or both. Indeed, it is fair to say that the firm's benefit formula could hardly be better designed from the perspective of maximizing service and age-related differences in accruals. This variation comes at the cost of a fairly complicated set of provisions that may not be fully understood by individual workers.

### 10.1.2   Pension Accrual

To describe the effect of the provisions on pension wealth, the accrual profiles for persons born in different years and hired by the firm in several different years have been calculated for the calendar period beginning in 1980. For each employee group defined by year of birth and year of hire, accruals are calculated through age 70; the number of years of accruals presented thus depends on the age of the employee in 1980. One profile is graphed in figure 10.1a to illustrate the derivation of such profiles. Profiles for different employee and age groups are compared in subsection 10.1.4.

Figure 10.1a shows the pension accrual profile for male managers born in 1930 and hired by the firm in 1960. By 1980, they were 50 and had 20 years of service with the firm. (To calculate pension accrual,

DPW 3060

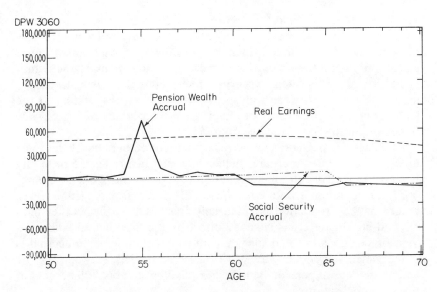

**Fig. 10.1a**     Pension wealth accrual, SS accrual, and wage earnings for male managers born in 1930 and hired in 1960, in real 1985 dollars

we have used the convention that a person hired in a given year has one year of experience in that year. Thus in some of the tables shown below, the person used in this example would be assumed to have 21 years of experience in 1980.) The accrual is the change in the discounted value of future pension benefit entitlements for an additional year of employment. The accrual of Social Security benefits is shown on the same graph. Predicted wage earnings for each year are also shown. These predictions are based on actual average earnings of firm employees, by age and years of service. The prediction method is described and the results are discussed in detail in section 10.2. All of the numbers presented in this section are in real 1985 dollars.

At age 50, in 1980, the typical male manager has wage earnings of about $48,446 per year. Compensation in the form of pension accrual is $2,646, or about 5.5 percent of wage earnings. If the manager were to retire at this age, he would be entitled to benefits at age 65, based on his earnings in the 7 or 8 preceding years. The benefits would not be available until age 65 and thus would have a relatively low present value at age 50.

As described above, normal retirement benefits could be taken earlier, as early as age 55, but they would be reduced actuarially so that the present discounted value of the benefits remains unchanged. The reduction in the benefit would be just enough to offset the fact that benefits would be received for more years. If the person remains in the firm until age 55 and then retires, however, benefits are available immediately and the reduction in benefits for early retirement is less than the actuarial reduction. In addition, the worker who remains until age 55 and then retires is eligible to receive a supplemental benefit until age 65 equal to his Social Security offset. Thus there is a very large increase in pension wealth at age 55, $72,527, corresponding to the large spike in figure 10.1a. In effect, there is a bonus of $72,527 for remaining in the firm from age 54 to 55.

After age 55, pension accrual falls, to about 10 percent of the wage at age 60 (in 1990). Accrual is higher than just before age 55 primarily because the early retirement reduction factor if the worker remains until 55 is less than it would be if he left the firm before 55. (If he leaves before 55, the reduction is actuarially fair.) But as the worker ages beyond 56, this effect is partially offset by the fact that an additional year of service adds a smaller percent to benefits. Pension accrual is in fact negative beginning at age 61 (in 1991). Indeed, between ages 61 and 65 the loss in pension benefits is equivalent to about 20 percent of wage compensation.

The loss in compensation between ages 60 and 61 is equivalent to a wage cut of about 14 percent. The worker has 30 years of service at that age and, because of the plan's early retirement reduction factors, is already eligible for full retirement benefits. Thus no increase in benefits will result for working another year from the application of one fewer year of early retirement reduction, as was the case before 30 years of service. In addition, for each year that benefits are not taken between ages 55 and 65, the receipt of benefits for a year without the Social Security adjustment (reduction) is foregone. This advantage is lost at age 65 (in 1995). Thereafter, the loss in benefits from working an additional year is smaller because this foregone opportunity is no longer available. In addition, the accruals depend on the Social Security adjustment and to a small extent on the updating of the years used in the calculation of the earnings base.

Social Security accruals for the male managers considered in figure 10.1a range from about $1,000 to $8,000 between ages 50 and 65. After 65, Social Security accrual becomes negative, about − $8,500 at age 66.

In summary, the typical manager in the firm, marking about $48,000 per year in wage earnings at age 60, would lose about $42,000 in pension wealth were he to continue working until age 65. Thus, in addition to the expected concentration of retirement at age 55, we would expect a large proportion of this group to retire before 65. After age 65, Social Security benefit accrual also becomes negative. At 66, the loss in private pension benefits and Social Security benefits together amounts to about 32 percent of wage earnings at that age. This suggests a concentration of retirement at 65 as well.

The data in figure 10.1a are shown in the standard budget constraint form in figure 10.1b. Total compensation, including wage earnings, Social Security wealth, and pension wealth, is graphed against age, beginning in 1980. The vertical axis shows the total resources that the person would acquire from employment with this firm. Accumulated earnings before 1980 are ignored in the graph.

There is a discontinuous jump in the graph at age 55. For reasonable preferences for income (that can be used for consumption) versus retirement leisure, one would expect to see a large proportion of workers facing this constraint retiring at age 55 and most retiring prior to age 65.

Additional graphs showing wage earnings, pension accrual, and Social Security accrual over the working span are shown in figures 10.2a and 10.2b; again, the first shows accruals by year, and the second shows cumulated amounts in the standard budget constraint form. These graphs pertain to a male manager who is hired in 1980 at age 20, and who continues working with the firm until age 70. For such workers, the pension accrual at age 55 is $168,000, equivalent to 164 percent of the wage at that age. Wage earnings for this group reach a maximum at age 59. Pension benefit accrual becomes negative at age 61, and Social Security benefit accrual becomes negative at age 65. In the first year of work after age 65, the loss in pension benefits and Social Security benefits together amounts to $40,000, about 45 percent of wage earnings at that age. Thus the lifetime budget constraint shows an upward discontinuity at age 55 and a decline in the rate of wage increase around

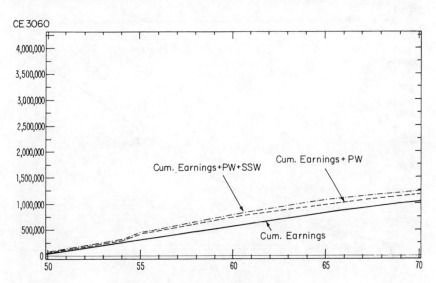

**Fig. 10.1b**     Cumulated total income from employment versus year of retirement, male managers born in 1930 and hired in 1960

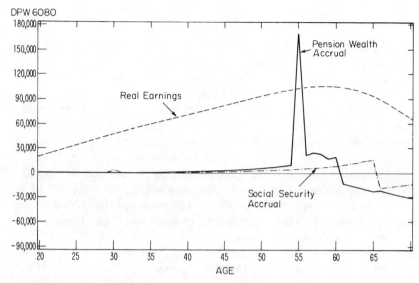

**Fig. 10.2a**    Pension wealth accrual, SS accrual, and wage earnings for male managers born in 1960 and hired in 1980, in real 1985 dollars

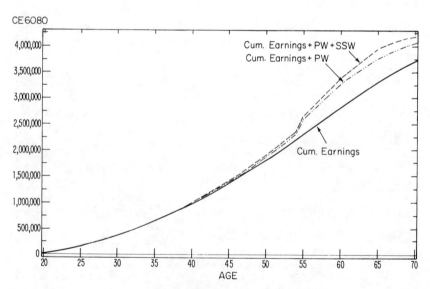

**Fig. 10.2b**    Cumulated total income from employment versus year of retirement, male managers born in 1960 and hired in 1980

age 60. The decline is especially abrupt after age 65.[2] Retirement at age 55, between 55 and 65, and possibly at 65 would seem to be quite likely for workers facing budget constraints like this one.

### 10.1.3    Decomposition of Pension Accrual

The calculations underlying the pension accrual in figures 10.1a and 10.1b are explained in this section. The wage earnings and other dollar values in this section are in current dollars, however, while the graphs are in constant 1985 dollars. The nominal interest rate assumed throughout this analysis is 0.09, and the real interest is assumed to equal 0.03.

The calculations are shown in table 10.1 for male managers who were born in 1930 and hired by the firm in 1960, the same group whose accrual profile is illustrated in figures 10.1a and 10.1b. Columns (1) through (4) are self-explanatory. Column (5) is the average earnings base used to calculate pension benefits. The normal retirement benefit is shown in column (6). It is calculated using the formula in equation (1) above. The Social Security benefit in column (7) is calculated by the firm based on earnings projected forward to age 65. Column (8) is the Social Security adjustment shown in equation (2). Column (9) is column (7) minus column (8). Column (10) is 1 minus the early retirement adjustment, the proportion of the benefit that remains after the adjustment. Once the person has worked for 30 years there is, according to the firm's early retirement reduction provisions, no reduction even though the person is only 60 years old at that time.

Column (11) is column (10) times column (6). It is the benefit that a person who retired early would receive between the early retirement age and age 65. After age 65, benefits are based on the adjusted retirement benefits, reduced by the early retirement reduction factor. These benefits are shown in column (12), which is column (10) times column (9).

The annuity value of a dollar received each year from 65 until death is shown in column (13). It accounts for the probability that a person will be alive at each year in the future. The probability that a person will live from the current age until 65 is shown in column (14). The current value of a dollar that will be received at age 65 is shown in column (15). At the current age, the present value of the pension benefits that the manager can receive at age 65 is shown in column (16), and is given by column (12) × column (13) × column (14) × column (15).

If the manager retires at age 55 or later, he will receive benefits until age 65 that are not reduced by the Social Security adjustment. He receives the normal retirement benefits in column (6) reduced only by the early retirement reduction factor, column (10), and shown in column (11). The present value of these benefits from the year of first collection until age 65 is shown in column (17). These benefits plus those that

**Table 10.1    Calculation of Pension Benefits and Wealth Accrual**

| Year (1) | Age (2) | Yrs. Svc. (3) | Wage (4) | Avg. Earn. Base (5) | Normal Ret. Ben. (6) | SS Ben. (7) | SS Adjmt. (8) | Adj. Ret. Ben. Factor (9) | Early Ret. Reduct. Ben. (10) | Reduced Normal Ret. Ben. (11) | Reduced Adj. Ret. Ben. (12) | Annuity Value (13) | Prob. Survive to 65 (14) | Discount 65 to Current Age (15) | Present Value Ret. Ben. from 65 (16) | Present Value Ret. Ben. to 65 (17) | Pension Wealth (18) | Pension Accrual (19) | Pension Accrual Wage (20) |
|---|---|---|---|---|---|---|---|---|---|---|---|---|---|---|---|---|---|---|---|
| 1979 | 49 | 20 | 32,393 | 24,788 | 9,915 | 10,227 | 3,846 | 6,069 | 1.00 | 9,915 | 6,069 | 7.999 | 0.8196 | 0.2519 | 10,023 | 0 | 10,023 | 0 | 0.0 |
| 1980 | 50 | 21 | 37,109 | 27,501 | 11,550 | 10,626 | 4,276 | 7,274 | 1.00 | 11,550 | 7,274 | 7.999 | 0.8243 | 0.2745 | 13,167 | 0 | 13,167 | 2,057 | 6.4 |
| 1981 | 51 | 22 | 41,266 | 29,221 | 12,857 | 10,921 | 4,673 | 8,185 | 1.00 | 12,857 | 8,185 | 7.999 | 0.8294 | 0.2993 | 16,250 | 0 | 16,250 | 1,741 | 4.7 |
| 1982 | 52 | 23 | 44,055 | 32,165 | 14,796 | 11,060 | 5,000 | 9,796 | 1.00 | 14,796 | 9,796 | 7.999 | 0.8351 | 0.3262 | 21,346 | 0 | 21,346 | 3,334 | 8.1 |
| 1983 | 53 | 24 | 45,661 | 33,664 | 16,159 | 11,128 | 5,293 | 10,866 | 1.00 | 16,159 | 10,866 | 7.999 | 0.8415 | 0.3555 | 26,004 | 0 | 26,004 | 2,510 | 5.7 |
| 1984 | 54 | 25 | 48,426 | 38,018 | 19,009 | 11,248 | 5,620 | 13,388 | 1.00 | 19,009 | 13,388 | 7.999 | 0.8485 | 0.3875 | 35,216 | 0 | 35,216 | 6,205 | 13.8 |
| 1985 | 55 | 26 | 50,919 | 39,451 | 20,120 | 11,341 | 5,937 | 14,183 | 0.67 | 13,480 | 9,503 | 7.999 | 0.8562 | 0.4224 | 27,494 | 89,947 | 117,441 | 72,527 | 149.8 |
| 1986 | 56 | 27 | 54,674 | 44,313 | 23,043 | 11,528 | 6,316 | 16,727 | 0.73 | 16,821 | 12,210 | 7.999 | 0.8648 | 0.4604 | 38,891 | 105,041 | 143,932 | 14,607 | 28.7 |
| 1987 | 57 | 28 | 58,564 | 45,896 | 24,325 | 11,719 | 6,707 | 17,618 | 0.80 | 19,460 | 14,095 | 7.999 | 0.8742 | 0.5019 | 49,468 | 112,461 | 161,930 | 4,627 | 8.5 |
| 1988 | 58 | 29 | 62,556 | 49,248 | 26,594 | 11,911 | 7,107 | 19,487 | 0.87 | 23,137 | 16,954 | 7.999 | 0.8847 | 0.5470 | 65,637 | 121,970 | 187,606 | 10,187 | 17.4 |
| 1989 | 59 | 30 | 66,616 | 52,526 | 28,890 | 12,099 | 7,513 | 21,377 | 0.93 | 26,867 | 19,880 | 7.999 | 0.8963 | 0.5963 | 84,994 | 126,740 | 211,734 | 6,645 | 10.6 |
| 1990 | 60 | 31 | 70,697 | 55,797 | 31,246 | 12,289 | 7,929 | 23,317 | 1.00 | 31,246 | 23,317 | 7.999 | 0.9092 | 0.6499 | 110,219 | 128,422 | 238,640 | 7,202 | 10.8 |
| 1991 | 61 | 32 | 74,741 | 59,206 | 33,747 | 12,475 | 8,352 | 25,395 | 1.00 | 33,747 | 25,395 | 7.999 | 0.9235 | 0.7084 | 132,909 | 116,203 | 249,112 | -10,097 | -14.3 |
| 1992 | 62 | 33 | 78,682 | 62,875 | 36,468 | 12,658 | 8,781 | 27,687 | 1.00 | 36,468 | 27,687 | 7.999 | 0.9395 | 0.7722 | 160,676 | 98,801 | 259,477 | -11,060 | -14.8 |
| 1993 | 63 | 34 | 82,443 | 66,655 | 39,326 | 12,848 | 9,223 | 30,103 | 1.00 | 39,326 | 30,103 | 7.999 | 0.9574 | 0.8417 | 194,046 | 74,665 | 268,711 | -12,953 | -16.5 |
| 1994 | 64 | 35 | 85,930 | 70,545 | 42,327 | 13,047 | 9,682 | 32,645 | 1.00 | 42,327 | 32,645 | 7.999 | 0.9774 | 0.9174 | 234,174 | 42,327 | 276,501 | -15,040 | -18.2 |
| 1995 | 65 | 36 | 89,053 | 74,365 | 45,362 | 13,264 | 10,164 | 35,198 | 1.00 | 45,362 | 35,198 | 7.999 | 1.0000 | 1.0000 | 281,568 | 0 | 281,568 | -18,181 | -21.2 |
| 1996 | 66 | 37 | 91,700 | 78,046 | 48,389 | 13,757 | 10,575 | 37,814 | 1.00 | 48,389 | 37,814 | 7.824 | 1.0000 | 1.0000 | 295,848 | 0 | 295,848 | -10,148 | -11.4 |
| 1997 | 67 | 38 | 93,772 | 81,515 | 51,354 | 14,273 | 11,005 | 40,349 | 1.00 | 51,354 | 40,349 | 7.646 | 1.0000 | 1.0000 | 308,518 | 0 | 308,518 | -12,804 | -14.0 |
| 1998 | 68 | 39 | 95,164 | 84,687 | 54,200 | 14,813 | 11,455 | 42,745 | 1.00 | 54,200 | 42,745 | 7.466 | 1.0000 | 1.0000 | 319,112 | 0 | 319,112 | -15,754 | -16.8 |
| 1999 | 69 | 40 | 95,769 | 87,473 | 56,857 | 15,377 | 11,926 | 44,932 | 1.00 | 56,857 | 44,932 | 7.281 | 1.0000 | 1.0000 | 327,147 | 0 | 327,147 | -18,978 | -19.9 |
| 2000 | 70 | 41 | 95,509 | 89,780 | 59,255 | 15,972 | 12,421 | 46,834 | 1.00 | 59,255 | 46,834 | 7.093 | 1.0000 | 1.0000 | 332,181 | 0 | 332,181 | -22,394 | -23.4 |

will be received after age 65 and the present value of his pension wealth and are shown in column (18) (column [16] plus column [17]).

The change in pension wealth from one year to the next, $I(a)$, the pension accrual, is shown in column (19). The accrual at age $a$ is given by

(3) $$I(a) = Pw(a + 1) - Pw(a)(1 + r)$$

where $Pw$ is pension wealth and $r$ is the nominal interest rate (0.09). Again, these pension accruals, together with Social Security accruals and the wage, are graphed in figure 10.1a, but in 1985 dollars. The accrual as a percentage of wage earnings is shown in column (20).[3]

### 10.1.4   Variation in Accrual Profiles by Age and Year of Hire

The two accrual profiles discussed above pertain to persons who were born in a given year and who were hired by the firm in a given year. The profile in the calendar period beginning in 1980 may be quite different for persons of different ages and with different years of service. Thus, profiles have been calculated for several additional groups, fifteen in all, defined by year of birth and year of hire, as shown in table 10.2. Pension accruals for managers with these birth and hire years are shown in table 10.3. Those born in 1940 reach age 55 in 1995, and for each of these groups there is a discontinuous increase in pension wealth in that year. It is $29,639 for those with 15 years of service in that year and $82,953 for those with 25 years of service. Comparable jumps occur in 1985 for those born in 1930. Accruals are often negative for persons over 60.

Pension accruals provide a large incentive for some groups to stay in the firm for another year and a strong incentive for others to leave. For example, staying with the firm in 1985 brings pension accrual of $72,527 for 55-year-old managers with 25 years of service (born in 1930 and hired in 1960), but a loss of $14,936 for 65 year olds with 35 years of experience (born in 1920 and hired in 1950). Thus there is enormous variation in the effective compensation for continued service. One might expect, therefore, that some groups would be much more likely than others to retire in a given year.

**Table 10.2**      **Accrual Profile Groups**

| Year of Birth | Year of Hire | | | | |
|---|---|---|---|---|---|
| 1960 | 1980 | | | | |
| 1950 | 1980 | 1975 | | | |
| 1940 | 1980 | 1975 | 1970 | | |
| 1930 | 1980 | 1975 | 1970 | 1960 | |
| 1920 | 1980 | 1975 | 1970 | 1960 | 1950 |

**Table 10.3**     Accrual in Pension Wealth by Year of Birth and Year of Hire for Managers

| Year Born | 1960 | 1950 | | 1940 | | | 1930 | | | | 1920 | | | |
|---|---|---|---|---|---|---|---|---|---|---|---|---|---|---|
| Hired | 1980 | 1980 | 1975 | 1980 | 1975 | 1970 | 1980 | 1975 | 1970 | 1960 | 1975 | 1970 | 1960 | 1950 |
| 1980 | 0 | 0 | 0 | 0 | 0 | 508 | 0 | 0 | 835 | 2,686 | 0 | 1,178 | 5,146 | 442 |
| 1981 | 0 | 0 | 0 | 0 | 0 | 380 | 0 | 0 | 562 | 2,059 | 0 | −616 | −105 | −9,132 |
| 1982 | 0 | 0 | 0 | 0 | 0 | 770 | 0 | 0 | 1,413 | 3,716 | 0 | 451 | 2,175 | −5,043 |
| 1983 | 0 | 0 | 0 | 0 | 0 | 582 | 0 | 0 | 1,079 | 2,710 | 0 | −2,739 | −2,721 | −13,235 |
| 1984 | 0 | 0 | 1,278 | 0 | 2,470 | 1,494 | 0 | 2,968 | 3,053 | 6,530 | 5,090 | 658 | 3,575 | −2,995 |
| 1985 | 0 | 0 | 251 | 0 | 475 | 767 | 0 | 18,226 | 2,6481 | 72,527 | −5,357 | −5,328 | −8,152 | −14,936 |
| 1986 | 0 | 0 | 663 | 0 | 1,335 | 2,090 | 0 | 5,616 | 8,227 | 13,781 | 0 | 8,151 | 3,728 | 831 |
| 1987 | 0 | 0 | 353 | 0 | 651 | 994 | 0 | 2,593 | 3,691 | 4,118 | 0 | 2,108 | −4,957 | −10,017 |
| 1988 | 0 | 0 | 663 | 0 | 1,289 | 1,978 | 0 | 4,105 | 5,874 | 8,553 | 4,176 | 3,987 | −1,882 | −6,347 |
| 1989 | 1,008 | 2,158 | 767 | 4,037 | 1,479 | 2,323 | 22,194 | 3,745 | 5,342 | 5,263 | 5,038 | 2,968 | −3,049 | −7,920 |
| 1990 | 194 | 388 | 890 | 688 | 1,709 | 2,676 | 831 | 3,280 | 4,726 | 5,382 | 4,265 | 2,109 | −3,889 | −8,984 |
| 1991 | 341 | 690 | 1,051 | 1,297 | 2,174 | 3,168 | 1,060 | 1,685 | 2,376 | −7,118 | 0 | 0 | 0 | 0 |
| 1992 | 418 | 845 | 1,260 | 1,601 | 2,675 | 3,820 | 609 | 1,389 | 2,029 | −7,356 | 0 | 0 | 0 | 0 |
| 1993 | 504 | 1,016 | 1,485 | 2,021 | 3,202 | 4,515 | −89 | 683 | 1,312 | −8,127 | 0 | 0 | 0 | 0 |
| 1994 | 606 | 1,220 | 1,756 | 2,603 | 3,851 | 5,351 | −908 | −155 | 419 | −8,902 | 0 | 0 | 0 | 0 |
| 1995 | 716 | 1,441 | 2,043 | 29,639 | 40,727 | 82,953 | −2,067 | −1,384 | −3,515 | −10,152 | 0 | 0 | 0 | 0 |
| 1996 | 843 | 1,695 | 2,555 | 7,130 | 9,538 | 9,898 | 5,217 | 3,628 | −939 | −5,346 | 0 | 0 | 0 | 0 |
| 1997 | 987 | 1,986 | 2,992 | 7,349 | 9,672 | 11,334 | 4,579 | 2,855 | −1,652 | −6,363 | 0 | 0 | 0 | 0 |
| 1998 | 1,153 | 2,422 | 3,499 | 7,437 | 9,641 | 10,665 | 3,902 | 2,041 | −2,384 | −7,386 | 0 | 0 | 0 | 0 |
| 1999 | 1,342 | 2,969 | 4,085 | 7,377 | 9,426 | 7,844 | 3,186 | 1,187 | −3,129 | −8,394 | 0 | 0 | 0 | 0 |
| 2000 | 1,558 | 3,492 | 3,900 | 7,140 | 6,196 | 8,643 | 2,423 | −1,882 | −3,874 | −9,344 | 0 | 0 | 0 | 0 |
| 2001 | 1,807 | 4,095 | 4,481 | 4,432 | 2,198 | −6,178 | 0 | 0 | 0 | 0 | 0 | 0 | 0 | 0 |
| 2002 | 2,093 | 4,790 | 5,149 | 3,750 | 1,206 | −7,237 | 0 | 0 | 0 | 0 | 0 | 0 | 0 | 0 |

| 2003 | 2,517 | 5,587 | 5,904 | 2,870 | −15 | −8,380 | 0 | 0 | 0 | 0 | 0 | 0 | 0 |
| 2004 | 3,037 | 6,502 | 6,763 | 1,791 | 4,378 | −9,658 | 0 | 0 | 0 | 0 | 0 | 0 | 0 |
| 2005 | 2,918 | 95,433 | 117,775 | −2,553 | −8,981 | −11,004 | 0 | 0 | 0 | 0 | 0 | 0 | 0 |
| 2006 | 3,361 | 11,955 | 14,674 | −1,993 | −4,042 | −6,843 | 0 | 0 | 0 | 0 | 0 | 0 | 0 |
| 2007 | 3,872 | 13,705 | 16,840 | −2,784 | −4,988 | −7,994 | 0 | 0 | 0 | 0 | 0 | 0 | 0 |
| 2008 | 4,461 | 13,022 | 15,944 | −3,601 | −4,988 | −9,155 | 0 | 0 | 0 | 0 | 0 | 0 | 0 |
| 2009 | 5,139 | 9,809 | 11,879 | −4,436 | −5,955 | −10,299 | 0 | 0 | 0 | 0 | 0 | 0 | 0 |
| 2010 | 5,910 | 10,923 | 13,211 | −5,265 | −6,930 | −11,375 | 0 | 0 | 0 | 0 | 0 | 0 | 0 |
| 2011 | 6,792 | −6,583 | −8,668 | 0 | −7,875 | 0 | 0 | 0 | 0 | 0 | 0 | 0 | 0 |
| 2012 | 7,801 | −7,785 | −10,184 | 0 | 0 | 0 | 0 | 0 | 0 | 0 | 0 | 0 | 0 |
| 2013 | 8,940 | −9,069 | −11,809 | 0 | 0 | 0 | 0 | 0 | 0 | 0 | 0 | 0 | 0 |
| 2014 | 10,223 | −10,418 | −13,531 | 0 | 0 | 0 | 0 | 0 | 0 | 0 | 0 | 0 | 0 |
| 2015 | 168,439 | −11,848 | −15,345 | 0 | 0 | 0 | 0 | 0 | 0 | 0 | 0 | 0 | 0 |
| 2016 | 21,859 | −8,684 | −12,662 | 0 | 0 | 0 | 0 | 0 | 0 | 0 | 0 | 0 | 0 |
| 2017 | 25,137 | −9,994 | −14,317 | 0 | 0 | 0 | 0 | 0 | 0 | 0 | 0 | 0 | 0 |
| 2018 | 23,904 | −11,319 | −15,955 | 0 | 0 | 0 | 0 | 0 | 0 | 0 | 0 | 0 | 0 |
| 2019 | 17,968 | −12,627 | −17,524 | 0 | 0 | 0 | 0 | 0 | 0 | 0 | 0 | 0 | 0 |
| 2020 | 19,964 | −13,849 | −18,933 | 0 | 0 | 0 | 0 | 0 | 0 | 0 | 0 | 0 | 0 |
| 2021 | −12,355 | 0 | 0 | 0 | 0 | 0 | 0 | 0 | 0 | 0 | 0 | 0 | 0 |
| 2022 | −14,649 | 0 | 0 | 0 | 0 | 0 | 0 | 0 | 0 | 0 | 0 | 0 | 0 |
| 2023 | −1.7087 | 0 | 0 | 0 | 0 | 0 | 0 | 0 | 0 | 0 | 0 | 0 | 0 |
| 2024 | −19,659 | 0 | 0 | 0 | 0 | 0 | 0 | 0 | 0 | 0 | 0 | 0 | 0 |
| 2025 | −22,287 | 0 | 0 | 0 | 0 | 0 | 0 | 0 | 0 | 0 | 0 | 0 | 0 |
| 2026 | −21,570 | 0 | 0 | 0 | 0 | 0 | 0 | 0 | 0 | 0 | 0 | 0 | 0 |
| 2027 | −24,026 | 0 | 0 | 0 | 0 | 0 | 0 | 0 | 0 | 0 | 0 | 0 | 0 |
| 2028 | −26,391 | 0 | 0 | 0 | 0 | 0 | 0 | 0 | 0 | 0 | 0 | 0 | 0 |
| 2029 | −2,8576 | 0 | 0 | 0 | 0 | 0 | 0 | 0 | 0 | 0 | 0 | 0 | 0 |
| 2030 | −30,436 | 0 | 0 | 0 | 0 | 0 | 0 | 0 | 0 | 0 | 0 | 0 | 0 |

Table 10.4     Pension Wealth by Year of Birth and Year of Hire for Managers

| Year Born | 1960 | 1950 | | 1940 | | | 1930 | | | | 1920 | | | | |
| --- | --- | --- | --- | --- | --- | --- | --- | --- | --- | --- | --- | --- | --- | --- | --- |
| Hired | 1980 | 1980 | 1975 | 1980 | 1975 | 1970 | 1980 | 1975 | 1970 | 1960 | 1980 | 1975 | 1970 | 1960 | 1950 |
| 1980 | 0 | 0 | 0 | 0 | 0 | 2,356 | 0 | 0 | 3,747 | 17,190 | 0 | 0 | 20,270 | 69,954 | 157,647 |
| 1981 | 0 | 0 | 0 | 0 | 0 | 2,741 | 0 | 0 | 4,313 | 19,221 | 0 | 0 | 19,347 | 68,974 | 145,742 |
| 1982 | 0 | 0 | 0 | 0 | 0 | 3,654 | 0 | 0 | 5,969 | 23,790 | 0 | 0 | 20,361 | 73,204 | 144,173 |
| 1983 | 0 | 0 | 0 | 0 | 0 | 4,493 | 0 | 0 | 7,480 | 28,076 | 0 | 0 | 18,515 | 74,336 | 137,819 |
| 1984 | 0 | 0 | 1,393 | 0 | 2,692 | 6,327 | 0 | 3,235 | 11,149 | 36,475 | 0 | 5,549 | 20,077 | 81,625 | 140,844 |
| 1985 | 0 | 0 | 1,740 | 0 | 3,350 | 7,494 | 0 | 23,271 | 40,597 | 117,141 | 0 | 0 | 15,322 | 77,017 | 131,943 |
| 1986 | 0 | 0 | 2,513 | 0 | 4,901 | 9,985 | 0 | 30,051 | 50,713 | 135,785 | 0 | 0 | 24,639 | 83,260 | 136,584 |
| 1987 | 0 | 0 | 2,969 | 0 | 5,750 | 11,351 | 0 | 33,728 | 56,172 | 144,117 | 0 | 0 | 27,634 | 80,214 | 129,531 |
| 1988 | 0 | 0 | 3,775 | 0 | 7,317 | 13,828 | 0 | 39,157 | 64,165 | 157,520 | 0 | 4,552 | 32,763 | 80,434 | 126,280 |
| 1989 | 1,098 | 2,352 | 4,718 | 4,400 | 9,136 | 16,751 | 24,192 | 44,347 | 71,802 | 167,710 | 0 | 10,173 | 36,925 | 79,385 | 121,217 |
| 1990 | 1,341 | 2,842 | 5,821 | 5,274 | 11,257 | 20,142 | 25,781 | 49,175 | 78,983 | 178,316 | 0 | 15,109 | 40,267 | 77,390 | 114,850 |
| 1991 | 1,750 | 3,675 | 7,132 | 6,837 | 13,946 | 24,166 | 27,668 | 52,407 | 83,814 | 175,617 | 0 | 0 | 0 | 0 | 0 |
| 1992 | 2,256 | 4,700 | 8,707 | 8,776 | 17,257 | 29,015 | 29,115 | 55,404 | 88,399 | 172,570 | 0 | 0 | 0 | 0 | 0 |
| 1993 | 2,869 | 5,940 | 10,572 | 11,227 | 21,234 | 34,755 | 29,840 | 57,713 | 92,326 | 168,587 | 0 | 0 | 0 | 0 | 0 |
| 1994 | 3,610 | 7,439 | 12,785 | 14,382 | 26,033 | 41,572 | 29,695 | 59,178 | 95,397 | 163,658 | 0 | 0 | 0 | 0 | 0 |
| 1995 | 4,493 | 9,220 | 15,373 | 47,095 | 71,162 | 133,166 | 28,282 | 59,343 | 94,264 | 157,222 | 0 | 0 | 0 | 0 | 0 |
| 1996 | 5,539 | 11,329 | 18,594 | 56,201 | 83,574 | 147,728 | 34,770 | 64,980 | 95,910 | 155,849 | 0 | 0 | 0 | 0 | 0 |
| 1997 | 6,772 | 13,814 | 22,381 | 65,802 | 96,481 | 164,262 | 40,746 | 69,931 | 96,824 | 153,324 | 0 | 0 | 0 | 0 | 0 |
| 1998 | 8,220 | 16,844 | 26,827 | 75,768 | 109,717 | 180,531 | 46,151 | 74,133 | 96,962 | 149,607 | 0 | 0 | 0 | 0 | 0 |
| 1999 | 9,915 | 20,558 | 32,040 | 85,956 | 123,101 | 194,197 | 50,931 | 77,527 | 96,299 | 144,698 | 0 | 0 | 0 | 0 | 0 |
| 2000 | 11,894 | 24,946 | 37,197 | 96,169 | 133,336 | 209,110 | 55,012 | 77,669 | 94,800 | 138,605 | 0 | 0 | 0 | 0 | 0 |
| 2001 | 14,201 | 30,116 | 43,135 | 103,721 | 139,506 | 208,294 | 0 | 0 | 0 | 0 | 0 | 0 | 0 | 0 | 0 |
| 2002 | 16,884 | 36,190 | 49,968 | 110,745 | 144,770 | 206,303 | 0 | 0 | 0 | 0 | 0 | 0 | 0 | 0 | 0 |

| Year | | | | | | | | | | | | | | | | | | | | | | | | | | | |
|---|---|---|---|---|---|---|---|---|---|---|---|---|---|---|---|---|---|---|---|---|---|---|---|---|---|---|---|
| 2003 | 20,105 | 43,304 | 57,817 | 117,006 | 148,850 | 203,005 | 0 | 0 | 0 | 0 | 0 | 0 | 0 | 0 | 0 | 0 | 0 | 0 | 0 | 0 | 0 | 0 | 0 | 0 | 0 | 0 | 0 |
| 2004 | 23,984 | 51,616 | 66,824 | 122,269 | 157,833 | 198,220 | 0 | 0 | 0 | 0 | 0 | 0 | 0 | 0 | 0 | 0 | 0 | 0 | 0 | 0 | 0 | 0 | 0 | 0 | 0 | 0 | 0 |
| 2005 | 27,844 | 157,100 | 197,093 | 122,952 | 152,517 | 191,845 | 0 | 0 | 0 | 0 | 0 | 0 | 0 | 0 | 0 | 0 | 0 | 0 | 0 | 0 | 0 | 0 | 0 | 0 | 0 | 0 | 0 |
| 2006 | 32,295 | 174,574 | 218,662 | 124,257 | 152,424 | 189,811 | 0 | 0 | 0 | 0 | 0 | 0 | 0 | 0 | 0 | 0 | 0 | 0 | 0 | 0 | 0 | 0 | 0 | 0 | 0 | 0 | 0 |
| 2007 | 37,429 | 194,452 | 243,204 | 124,738 | 151,301 | 186,468 | 0 | 0 | 0 | 0 | 0 | 0 | 0 | 0 | 0 | 0 | 0 | 0 | 0 | 0 | 0 | 0 | 0 | 0 | 0 | 0 | 0 |
| 2008 | 43,351 | 214,150 | 267,468 | 124,345 | 149,092 | 181,767 | 0 | 0 | 0 | 0 | 0 | 0 | 0 | 0 | 0 | 0 | 0 | 0 | 0 | 0 | 0 | 0 | 0 | 0 | 0 | 0 | 0 |
| 2009 | 50,180 | 230,907 | 287,992 | 123,032 | 145,761 | 175,690 | 0 | 0 | 0 | 0 | 0 | 0 | 0 | 0 | 0 | 0 | 0 | 0 | 0 | 0 | 0 | 0 | 0 | 0 | 0 | 0 | 0 |
| 2010 | 58,041 | 249,344 | 310,538 | 120,773 | 141,301 | 168,260 | 0 | 0 | 0 | 0 | 0 | 0 | 0 | 0 | 0 | 0 | 0 | 0 | 0 | 0 | 0 | 0 | 0 | 0 | 0 | 0 | 0 |
| 2011 | 67,087 | 249,226 | 309,879 | 0 | 0 | 0 | 0 | 0 | 0 | 0 | 0 | 0 | 0 | 0 | 0 | 0 | 0 | 0 | 0 | 0 | 0 | 0 | 0 | 0 | 0 | 0 | 0 |
| 2012 | 77,489 | 247,793 | 307,546 | 0 | 0 | 0 | 0 | 0 | 0 | 0 | 0 | 0 | 0 | 0 | 0 | 0 | 0 | 0 | 0 | 0 | 0 | 0 | 0 | 0 | 0 | 0 | 0 |
| 2013 | 89,425 | 244,918 | 303,375 | 0 | 0 | 0 | 0 | 0 | 0 | 0 | 0 | 0 | 0 | 0 | 0 | 0 | 0 | 0 | 0 | 0 | 0 | 0 | 0 | 0 | 0 | 0 | 0 |
| 2014 | 103,100 | 240,494 | 297,212 | 0 | 0 | 0 | 0 | 0 | 0 | 0 | 0 | 0 | 0 | 0 | 0 | 0 | 0 | 0 | 0 | 0 | 0 | 0 | 0 | 0 | 0 | 0 | 0 |
| 2015 | 289,618 | 234,391 | 288,904 | 0 | 0 | 0 | 0 | 0 | 0 | 0 | 0 | 0 | 0 | 0 | 0 | 0 | 0 | 0 | 0 | 0 | 0 | 0 | 0 | 0 | 0 | 0 | 0 |
| 2016 | 321,636 | 231,555 | 283,275 | 0 | 0 | 0 | 0 | 0 | 0 | 0 | 0 | 0 | 0 | 0 | 0 | 0 | 0 | 0 | 0 | 0 | 0 | 0 | 0 | 0 | 0 | 0 | 0 |
| 2017 | 358,138 | 227,214 | 275,686 | 0 | 0 | 0 | 0 | 0 | 0 | 0 | 0 | 0 | 0 | 0 | 0 | 0 | 0 | 0 | 0 | 0 | 0 | 0 | 0 | 0 | 0 | 0 | 0 |
| 2018 | 394,330 | 221,307 | 266,097 | 0 | 0 | 0 | 0 | 0 | 0 | 0 | 0 | 0 | 0 | 0 | 0 | 0 | 0 | 0 | 0 | 0 | 0 | 0 | 0 | 0 | 0 | 0 | 0 |
| 2019 | 425,077 | 213,809 | 254,529 | 0 | 0 | 0 | 0 | 0 | 0 | 0 | 0 | 0 | 0 | 0 | 0 | 0 | 0 | 0 | 0 | 0 | 0 | 0 | 0 | 0 | 0 | 0 | 0 |
| 2020 | 458,866 | 204,763 | 241,094 | 0 | 0 | 0 | 0 | 0 | 0 | 0 | 0 | 0 | 0 | 0 | 0 | 0 | 0 | 0 | 0 | 0 | 0 | 0 | 0 | 0 | 0 | 0 | 0 |
| 2021 | 458,390 | 0 | 0 | 0 | 0 | 0 | 0 | 0 | 0 | 0 | 0 | 0 | 0 | 0 | 0 | 0 | 0 | 0 | 0 | 0 | 0 | 0 | 0 | 0 | 0 | 0 | 0 |
| 2022 | 455,392 | 0 | 0 | 0 | 0 | 0 | 0 | 0 | 0 | 0 | 0 | 0 | 0 | 0 | 0 | 0 | 0 | 0 | 0 | 0 | 0 | 0 | 0 | 0 | 0 | 0 | 0 |
| 2023 | 449,660 | 0 | 0 | 0 | 0 | 0 | 0 | 0 | 0 | 0 | 0 | 0 | 0 | 0 | 0 | 0 | 0 | 0 | 0 | 0 | 0 | 0 | 0 | 0 | 0 | 0 | 0 |
| 2024 | 440,956 | 0 | 0 | 0 | 0 | 0 | 0 | 0 | 0 | 0 | 0 | 0 | 0 | 0 | 0 | 0 | 0 | 0 | 0 | 0 | 0 | 0 | 0 | 0 | 0 | 0 | 0 |
| 2025 | 429,144 | 0 | 0 | 0 | 0 | 0 | 0 | 0 | 0 | 0 | 0 | 0 | 0 | 0 | 0 | 0 | 0 | 0 | 0 | 0 | 0 | 0 | 0 | 0 | 0 | 0 | 0 |
| 2026 | 417,780 | 0 | 0 | 0 | 0 | 0 | 0 | 0 | 0 | 0 | 0 | 0 | 0 | 0 | 0 | 0 | 0 | 0 | 0 | 0 | 0 | 0 | 0 | 0 | 0 | 0 | 0 |
| 2027 | 403,414 | 0 | 0 | 0 | 0 | 0 | 0 | 0 | 0 | 0 | 0 | 0 | 0 | 0 | 0 | 0 | 0 | 0 | 0 | 0 | 0 | 0 | 0 | 0 | 0 | 0 | 0 |
| 2028 | 386,063 | 0 | 0 | 0 | 0 | 0 | 0 | 0 | 0 | 0 | 0 | 0 | 0 | 0 | 0 | 0 | 0 | 0 | 0 | 0 | 0 | 0 | 0 | 0 | 0 | 0 | 0 |
| 2029 | 365,842 | 0 | 0 | 0 | 0 | 0 | 0 | 0 | 0 | 0 | 0 | 0 | 0 | 0 | 0 | 0 | 0 | 0 | 0 | 0 | 0 | 0 | 0 | 0 | 0 | 0 | 0 |
| 2030 | 343,022 | 0 | 0 | 0 | 0 | 0 | 0 | 0 | 0 | 0 | 0 | 0 | 0 | 0 | 0 | 0 | 0 | 0 | 0 | 0 | 0 | 0 | 0 | 0 | 0 | 0 | 0 |

**Table 10.5    Social Security Accrual by Year of Birth and Year of Hire for Managers**

| Year Born Hired | 1960 | 1950 | 1950 | 1940 | 1940 | 1940 | 1930 | 1930 | 1930 | 1930 | 1920 | 1920 | 1920 | 1920 | 1920 |
|---|---|---|---|---|---|---|---|---|---|---|---|---|---|---|---|
|  | 1980 | 1980 | 1975 | 1980 | 1975 | 1970 | 1980 | 1975 | 1970 | 1960 | 1980 | 1975 | 1970 | 1960 | 1950 |
| 1980 | 0 | 1,696 | 2,286 | 398 | 455 | 467 | 936 | 982 | 1,022 | 1,071 | 2,936 | 3,000 | 3,057 | 3,125 | 1,263 |
| 1981 | 0 | 235 | 338 | 474 | 567 | 635 | 1,121 | 1,240 | 1,291 | 1,356 | 3,726 | 3,808 | 3,880 | 2,013 | 4,053 |
| 1982 | 0 | 289 | 421 | 571 | 676 | 742 | 1,346 | 1,462 | 1,524 | 802 | 4,460 | 4,557 | 4,644 | 4,843 | 4,878 |
| 1983 | 0 | 364 | 522 | 730 | 863 | 954 | 1,730 | 1,893 | 1,978 | 2,137 | 5,850 | 5,982 | 3,317 | 6,383 | 6,431 |
| 1984 | 0 | 293 | 390 | 588 | 273 | 734 | 1,394 | 1,489 | 1,525 | 1,673 | 4,893 | 4,974 | 5,206 | 5,332 | 5,361 |
| 1985 | 0 | 129 | 382 | 612 | 767 | 760 | 1,471 | 1,578 | 1,611 | 1,777 | 5,023 | 1,436 | 5,307 | 5,483 | 5,510 |
| 1986 | 0 | 419 | 440 | 751 | 910 | 919 | 1,822 | 1,949 | 2,003 | 2,200 | −5,991 | −5,837 | −6,118 | −6,463 | −6,540 |
| 1987 | 0 | 520 | 560 | 971 | 1,165 | 1,199 | 2,385 | 2,577 | 1,232 | 2,914 | −5,587 | −5,443 | −5,706 | −6,028 | −6,100 |
| 1988 | 0 | 588 | 608 | 1,098 | 1,294 | 1,334 | 2,725 | 2,930 | 3,129 | 3,313 | −5,208 | −5,074 | −5,319 | −5,618 | −5,686 |
| 1989 | 0 | 664 | 664 | 1,242 | 1,441 | 1,488 | 3,117 | 3,338 | 3,566 | 3,774 | −4,856 | −4,731 | −4,959 | −5,238 | −5,301 |
| 1990 | 3,965 | 737 | 729 | 1,404 | 1,609 | 1,663 | 3,568 | 3,810 | 4,072 | 4,308 | −4,530 | −4,413 | −4,627 | −4,887 | −4,945 |
| 1991 | 358 | 801 | 804 | 690 | 1,801 | 1,863 | 4,090 | 2,095 | 4,661 | 4,929 | 0 | 0 | 0 | 0 | 0 |
| 1992 | 382 | 875 | 889 | 1,865 | 2,022 | 2,092 | 4,696 | 5,103 | 5,349 | 5,653 | 0 | 0 | 0 | 0 | 0 |
| 1993 | 416 | 961 | 985 | 2,096 | 2,273 | 2,353 | 5,402 | 5,878 | 6,158 | 6,504 | 0 | 0 | 0 | 0 | 0 |
| 1994 | 456 | 1,060 | 1,093 | 2,361 | 2,562 | 2,653 | 6,330 | 6,815 | 7,169 | 7,589 | 0 | 0 | 0 | 0 | 0 |
| 1995 | 503 | 1,173 | 1,216 | 2,665 | 2,892 | 2,994 | 6,924 | 7,376 | 7,801 | 8,257 | 0 | 0 | 0 | 0 | 0 |
| 1996 | 556 | 1,301 | 1,355 | 3,015 | 3,271 | 3,387 | −6,909 | −7,275 | −7,825 | −8,497 | 0 | 0 | 0 | 0 | 0 |
| 1997 | 616 | 1,448 | 1,512 | 3,418 | 3,709 | 3,839 | −6,444 | −6,784 | −7,298 | −7,925 | 0 | 0 | 0 | 0 | 0 |
| 1998 | 683 | 1,614 | 1,689 | 3,885 | 4,213 | 4,361 | −6,006 | −6,324 | −6,802 | −7,387 | 0 | 0 | 0 | 0 | 0 |
| 1999 | 758 | 1,803 | 1,891 | 4,426 | 4,797 | 4,965 | −5,600 | −5,896 | −6,343 | −6,888 | 0 | 0 | 0 | 0 | 0 |
| 2000 | 841 | 2,018 | 2,119 | 5,052 | 5,472 | 5,662 | −5,224 | −5,501 | −5,917 | −6,425 | 0 | 0 | 0 | 0 | 0 |
| 2001 | 935 | 2,263 | 2,378 | 5,779 | 6,256 | 6,471 | 0 | 0 | 0 | 0 | 0 | 0 | 0 | 0 | 0 |

| Year | | | | | | | | | | | | | | |
|---|---|---|---|---|---|---|---|---|---|---|---|---|---|---|
| 2002 | 1,040 | 2,542 | 2,674 | 6,628 | 7,169 | 7,413 | 0 | 0 | 0 | 0 | 0 | 0 | 0 | 0 |
| 2003 | 1,158 | 2,861 | 3,010 | 7,624 | 8,241 | 8,518 | 0 | 0 | 0 | 0 | 0 | 0 | 0 | 0 |
| 2004 | 1,291 | 3,225 | 3,394 | 8,900 | 9,648 | 9,986 | 0 | 0 | 0 | 0 | 0 | 0 | 0 | 0 |
| 2005 | 1,440 | 3,641 | 3,832 | 9,684 | 10,496 | 10,863 | 0 | 0 | 0 | 0 | 0 | 0 | 0 | 0 |
| 2006 | 1,607 | 4,119 | 4,334 | −10,010 | −11,207 | −11,747 | 0 | 0 | 0 | 0 | 0 | 0 | 0 | 0 |
| 2007 | 1,796 | 4,668 | 4,912 | −9,335 | −10,452 | −10,956 | 0 | 0 | 0 | 0 | 0 | 0 | 0 | 0 |
| 2008 | 2,009 | 5,302 | 5,578 | −8,702 | −9,743 | −10,212 | 0 | 0 | 0 | 0 | 0 | 0 | 0 | 0 |
| 2009 | 2,251 | 6,034 | 6,346 | −8,114 | −9,085 | −9,522 | 0 | 0 | 0 | 0 | 0 | 0 | 0 | 0 |
| 2010 | 2,524 | 6,878 | 7,232 | −7,569 | −8,475 | −8,883 | 0 | 0 | 0 | 0 | 0 | 0 | 0 | 0 |
| 2011 | 2,834 | 7,858 | 8,259 | 0 | 0 | 0 | 0 | 0 | 0 | 0 | 0 | 0 | 0 | 0 |
| 2012 | 3,188 | 8,999 | 9,454 | 0 | 0 | 0 | 0 | 0 | 0 | 0 | 0 | 0 | 0 | 0 |
| 2013 | 3,590 | 10,337 | 10,855 | 0 | 0 | 0 | 0 | 0 | 0 | 0 | 0 | 0 | 0 | 0 |
| 2014 | 4,049 | 12,137 | 12,766 | 0 | 0 | 0 | 0 | 0 | 0 | 0 | 0 | 0 | 0 | 0 |
| 2015 | 4,571 | 13,201 | 13,885 | 0 | 0 | 0 | 0 | 0 | 0 | 0 | 0 | 0 | 0 | 0 |
| 2016 | 5,169 | −14,510 | −15,516 | 0 | 0 | 0 | 0 | 0 | 0 | 0 | 0 | 0 | 0 | 0 |
| 2017 | 5,858 | −13,532 | −14,471 | 0 | 0 | 0 | 0 | 0 | 0 | 0 | 0 | 0 | 0 | 0 |
| 2018 | 6,651 | −12,614 | −13,489 | 0 | 0 | 0 | 0 | 0 | 0 | 0 | 0 | 0 | 0 | 0 |
| 2019 | 7,566 | −11,761 | −12,577 | 0 | 0 | 0 | 0 | 0 | 0 | 0 | 0 | 0 | 0 | 0 |
| 2020 | 8,622 | −10,972 | −11,733 | 0 | 0 | 0 | 0 | 0 | 0 | 0 | 0 | 0 | 0 | 0 |
| 2021 | 9,844 | 0 | 0 | 0 | 0 | 0 | 0 | 0 | 0 | 0 | 0 | 0 | 0 | 0 |
| 2022 | 11,265 | 0 | 0 | 0 | 0 | 0 | 0 | 0 | 0 | 0 | 0 | 0 | 0 | 0 |
| 2023 | 12,933 | 0 | 0 | 0 | 0 | 0 | 0 | 0 | 0 | 0 | 0 | 0 | 0 | 0 |
| 2024 | 15,222 | 0 | 0 | 0 | 0 | 0 | 0 | 0 | 0 | 0 | 0 | 0 | 0 | 0 |
| 2025 | 16,557 | 0 | 0 | 0 | 0 | 0 | 0 | 0 | 0 | 0 | 0 | 0 | 0 | 0 |
| 2026 | −18,659 | 0 | 0 | 0 | 0 | 0 | 0 | 0 | 0 | 0 | 0 | 0 | 0 | 0 |
| 2027 | −17,401 | 0 | 0 | 0 | 0 | 0 | 0 | 0 | 0 | 0 | 0 | 0 | 0 | 0 |
| 2028 | −16,220 | 0 | 0 | 0 | 0 | 0 | 0 | 0 | 0 | 0 | 0 | 0 | 0 | 0 |
| 2029 | −15,124 | 0 | 0 | 0 | 0 | 0 | 0 | 0 | 0 | 0 | 0 | 0 | 0 | 0 |
| 2030 | −14,109 | 0 | 0 | 0 | 0 | 0 | 0 | 0 | 0 | 0 | 0 | 0 | 0 | 0 |

Table 10.6    Social Security Wealth by Year of Birth and Year of Hire for Managers

| Year Born Hired | 1960 | 1950 | | 1940 | | | 1930 | | | | 1920 | | | | |
|---|---|---|---|---|---|---|---|---|---|---|---|---|---|---|---|
| | 1980 | 1980 | 1975 | 1980 | 1975 | 1970 | 1980 | 1975 | 1970 | 1960 | 1980 | 1975 | 1970 | 1960 | 1950 |
| 1980 | 0 | 1,849 | 2,491 | 3,818 | 4,854 | 5,277 | 9,217 | 10,544 | 11,703 | 13,137 | 30,795 | 32,286 | 33,612 | 35,218 | 33,536 |
| 1981 | 0 | 2,082 | 2,828 | 4,287 | 5,412 | 5,905 | 10,325 | 11,765 | 12,966 | 14,452 | 34,476 | 36,037 | 37,425 | 36,976 | 37,540 |
| 1982 | 0 | 2,453 | 3,364 | 5,025 | 6,295 | 6,873 | 12,070 | 13,676 | 14,977 | 15,716 | 40,267 | 41,976 | 43,496 | 43,251 | 43,869 |
| 1983 | 0 | 2,988 | 4,121 | 6,102 | 7,588 | 8,297 | 14,633 | 16,505 | 17,971 | 18,925 | 48,898 | 50,847 | 49,546 | 52,631 | 53,335 |
| 1984 | 0 | 3,444 | 4,734 | 7,021 | 8,232 | 9,476 | 16,820 | 18,881 | 20,454 | 21,613 | 56,463 | 58,589 | 57,482 | 60,844 | 61,612 |
| 1985 | 0 | 3,765 | 5,398 | 8,055 | 9,499 | 10,801 | 19,305 | 21,590 | 23,281 | 24,682 | 64,896 | 63,223 | 66,278 | 70,009 | 70,846 |
| 1986 | 0 | 4,328 | 6,031 | 9,101 | 10,760 | 12,109 | 21,837 | 24,326 | 26,123 | 27,779 | 60,203 | 58,651 | 61,485 | 64,946 | 65,722 |
| 1987 | 0 | 5,017 | 6,811 | 10,417 | 12,334 | 13,759 | 25,054 | 27,823 | 28,206 | 31,742 | 55,816 | 54,377 | 57,005 | 60,214 | 60,934 |
| 1988 | 0 | 5,800 | 7,667 | 11,909 | 14,094 | 15,603 | 28,734 | 31,804 | 32,415 | 36,252 | 51,720 | 50,387 | 52,821 | 55,795 | 56,462 |
| 1989 | 0 | 6,689 | 8,607 | 13,599 | 16,062 | 17,666 | 32,944 | 36,342 | 37,218 | 41,390 | 47,889 | 46,654 | 48,909 | 51,662 | 52,280 |
| 1990 | 4,321 | 7,681 | 9,645 | 15,514 | 18,270 | 19,978 | 37,764 | 41,522 | 42,708 | 47,255 | 44,305 | 43,162 | 45,248 | 47,796. | 48,367 |
| 1991 | 4,834 | 8,771 | 10,795 | 16,706 | 20,752 | 22,576 | 43,294 | 44,984 | 49,000 | 53,969 | 0 | 0 | 0 | 0 | 0 |
| 1992 | 5,387 | 9,973 | 12,069 | 19,213 | 23,543 | 25,495 | 49,638 | 51,820 | 56,218 | 61,658 | 0 | 0 | 0 | 0 | 0 |
| 1993 | 5,992 | 11,303 | 13,484 | 22,040 | 26,686 | 28,780 | 56,928 | 59,691 | 64,518 | 70,489 | 0 | 0 | 0 | 0 | 0 |
| 1994 | 6,659 | 12,778 | 15,058 | 25,238 | 30,235 | 32,487 | 65,441 | 68,810 | 74,160 | 80,757 | 0 | 0 | 0 | 0 | 0 |
| 1995 | 7,396 | 14,418 | 16,809 | 28,856 | 34,242 | 36,670 | 74,839 | 78,796 | 84,760 | 92,041 | 0 | 0 | 0 | 0 | 0 |
| 1996 | 8,212 | 16,245 | 18,762 | 32,960 | 38,778 | 41,400 | 69,429 | 73,099 | 78,632 | 85,387 | 0 | 0 | 0 | 0 | 0 |
| 1997 | 9,115 | 18,283 | 20,941 | 37,618 | 43,918 | 46,757 | 64,370 | 67,773 | 72,903 | 79,166 | 0 | 0 | 0 | 0 | 0 |
| 1998 | 10,117 | 20,559 | 23,375 | 42,917 | 49,752 | 52,832 | 59,643 | 62,796 | 67,549 | 73,352 | 0 | 0 | 0 | 0 | 0 |
| 1999 | 11,230 | 23,107 | 26,098 | 48,957 | 56,391 | 59,741 | 55,229 | 58,149 | 62,550 | 67,923 | 0 | 0 | 0 | 0 | 0 |
| 2000 | 12,464 | 25,960 | 29,145 | 55,848 | 63,950 | 67,602 | 51,096 | 53,798 | 57,869 | 62,841 | 0 | 0 | 0 | 0 | 0 |
| 2001 | 13,836 | 29,161 | 32,562 | 63,728 | 72,579 | 76,568 | 0 | 0 | 0 | 0 | 0 | 0 | 0 | 0 | 0 |

| Year | | | | | | | | | | | | | | |
|------|---|---|---|---|---|---|---|---|---|---|---|---|---|---|
| 2002 | 15,362 | 32,758 | 36,398 | 72,757 | 82,448 | 86,815 | 0 | 0 | 0 | 0 | 0 | 0 | 0 | 0 |
| 2003 | 17,059 | 36,803 | 40,709 | 83,126 | 93,763 | 98,557 | 0 | 0 | 0 | 0 | 0 | 0 | 0 | 0 |
| 2004 | 18,948 | 41,360 | 45,561 | 95,178 | 106,932 | 112,229 | 0 | 0 | 0 | 0 | 0 | 0 | 0 | 0 |
| 2005 | 21,054 | 46,502 | 51,030 | 108,431 | 121,404 | 127,251 | 0 | 0 | 0 | 0 | 0 | 0 | 0 | 0 |
| 2006 | 23,402 | 52,306 | 57,197 | 100,587 | 112,621 | 118,045 | 0 | 0 | 0 | 0 | 0 | 0 | 0 | 0 |
| 2007 | 26,021 | 58,874 | 64,169 | 93,258 | 104,415 | 109,444 | 0 | 0 | 0 | 0 | 0 | 0 | 0 | 0 |
| 2008 | 28,948 | 66,320 | 72,065 | 86,413 | 96,751 | 101,410 | 0 | 0 | 0 | 0 | 0 | 0 | 0 | 0 |
| 2009 | 32,222 | 74,775 | 81,023 | 80,016 | 89,589 | 93,904 | 0 | 0 | 0 | 0 | 0 | 0 | 0 | 0 |
| 2010 | 35,884 | 84,387 | 91,198 | 74,029 | 82,886 | 86,877 | 0 | 0 | 0 | 0 | 0 | 0 | 0 | 0 |
| 2011 | 39,989 | 95,342 | 102,782 | 0 | 0 | 0 | 0 | 0 | 0 | 0 | 0 | 0 | 0 | 0 |
| 2012 | 44,595 | 107,848 | 115,995 | 0 | 0 | 0 | 0 | 0 | 0 | 0 | 0 | 0 | 0 | 0 |
| 2013 | 49,770 | 122,167 | 131,108 | 0 | 0 | 0 | 0 | 0 | 0 | 0 | 0 | 0 | 0 | 0 |
| 2014 | 55,592 | 138,854 | 148,734 | 0 | 0 | 0 | 0 | 0 | 0 | 0 | 0 | 0 | 0 | 0 |
| 2015 | 62,149 | 157,176 | 168,081 | 0 | 0 | 0 | 0 | 0 | 0 | 0 | 0 | 0 | 0 | 0 |
| 2016 | 69,541 | 145,806 | 155,922 | 0 | 0 | 0 | 0 | 0 | 0 | 0 | 0 | 0 | 0 | 0 |
| 2017 | 77,894 | 135,183 | 144,562 | 0 | 0 | 0 | 0 | 0 | 0 | 0 | 0 | 0 | 0 | 0 |
| 2018 | 87,349 | 125,260 | 133,950 | 0 | 0 | 0 | 0 | 0 | 0 | 0 | 0 | 0 | 0 | 0 |
| 2019 | 98,068 | 115,986 | 124,033 | 0 | 0 | 0 | 0 | 0 | 0 | 0 | 0 | 0 | 0 | 0 |
| 2020 | 110,241 | 107,308 | 114,753 | 0 | 0 | 0 | 0 | 0 | 0 | 0 | 0 | 0 | 0 | 0 |
| 2021 | 124,092 | 0 | 0 | 0 | 0 | 0 | 0 | 0 | 0 | 0 | 0 | 0 | 0 | 0 |
| 2022 | 139,882 | 0 | 0 | 0 | 0 | 0 | 0 | 0 | 0 | 0 | 0 | 0 | 0 | 0 |
| 2023 | 157,939 | 0 | 0 | 0 | 0 | 0 | 0 | 0 | 0 | 0 | 0 | 0 | 0 | 0 |
| 2024 | 179,001 | 0 | 0 | 0 | 0 | 0 | 0 | 0 | 0 | 0 | 0 | 0 | 0 | 0 |
| 2025 | 202,114 | 0 | 0 | 0 | 0 | 0 | 0 | 0 | 0 | 0 | 0 | 0 | 0 | 0 |
| 2026 | 187,497 | 0 | 0 | 0 | 0 | 0 | 0 | 0 | 0 | 0 | 0 | 0 | 0 | 0 |
| 2027 | 173,836 | 0 | 0 | 0 | 0 | 0 | 0 | 0 | 0 | 0 | 0 | 0 | 0 | 0 |
| 2028 | 161,075 | 0 | 0 | 0 | 0 | 0 | 0 | 0 | 0 | 0 | 0 | 0 | 0 | 0 |
| 2029 | 149,149 | 0 | 0 | 0 | 0 | 0 | 0 | 0 | 0 | 0 | 0 | 0 | 0 | 0 |
| 2030 | 137,991 | 0 | 0 | 0 | 0 | 0 | 0 | 0 | 0 | 0 | 0 | 0 | 0 | 0 |

**Table 10.7**    Wage Earnings by Year of Birth and Year of Hire for Managers

| Year Born | 1920 | | | | | 1930 | | | | 1940 | | | 1950 | | 1960 |
|---|---|---|---|---|---|---|---|---|---|---|---|---|---|---|---|
| Hired | 1950 | 1960 | 1970 | 1975 | 1980 | 1960 | 1970 | 1975 | 1980 | 1970 | 1975 | 1980 | 1975 | 1980 | 1980 |
| 1980 | 47,598 | 40,186 | 36,519 | 35,788 | 35,723 | 48,446 | 38,666 | 34,945 | 31,825 | 40,712 | 34,020 | 27,894 | 33,021 | 24,053 | 20,405 |
| 1981 | 46,774 | 39,794 | 36,470 | 35,902 | 36,006 | 48,813 | 39,226 | 35,666 | 32,739 | 41,853 | 35,354 | 29,403 | 34,967 | 26,082 | 22,852 |
| 1982 | 45,765 | 39,280 | 36,323 | 35,919 | 36,188 | 49,098 | 39,693 | 36,289 | 33,548 | 42,898 | 36,586 | 30,819 | 36,807 | 28,057 | 25,312 |
| 1983 | 44,568 | 38,642 | 36,080 | 35,845 | 36,276 | 49,300 | 40,074 | 36,819 | 34,256 | 43,858 | 37,720 | 32,141 | 38,542 | 29,965 | 27,757 |
| 1984 | 43,828 | 38,446 | 36,277 | 36,215 | 36,819 | 50,156 | 40,977 | 37,818 | 35,390 | 45,410 | 39,342 | 33,869 | 40,774 | 32,271 | 30,615 |
| 1985 | 42,847 | 38,092 | 36,362 | 36,488 | 37,271 | 50,919 | 41,803 | 38,741 | 36,447 | 46,913 | 40,904 | 35,535 | 42,948 | 34,543 | 34,479 |
| 1986 | 41,624 | 37,574 | 36,333 | 36,660 | 37,632 | 51,579 | 42,551 | 39,588 | 37,427 | 48,374 | 42,409 | 37,140 | 45,069 | 36,774 | 36,331 |
| 1987 | 40,157 | 36,885 | 36,181 | 36,728 | 37,900 | 52,122 | 43,216 | 40,358 | 38,331 | 49,794 | 43,859 | 38,685 | 47,139 | 38,960 | 39,155 |
| 1988 | 38,445 | 36,014 | 35,895 | 36,679 | 38,066 | 52,524 | 43,785 | 41,042 | 39,152 | 51,168 | 45,250 | 40,163 | 49,158 | 41,092 | 41,933 |
| 1989 | 36,499 | 34,956 | 35,467 | 36,507 | 38,124 | 52,765 | 44,249 | 41,633 | 39,886 | 52,493 | 46,580 | 41,572 | 51,128 | 43,166 | 44,653 |
| 1990 | 34,339 | 33,713 | 34,891 | 36,205 | 38,067 | 52,826 | 44,599 | 42,127 | 40,530 | 53,766 | 47,850 | 42,913 | 53,056 | 45,183 | 47,309 |
| 1991 | 0 | 0 | 0 | 0 | 0 | 52,690 | 44,827 | 42,517 | 41,083 | 54,987 | 49,059 | 44,187 | 54,951 | 47,147 | 49,904 |
| 1992 | 0 | 0 | 0 | 0 | 0 | 52,329 | 44,914 | 42,790 | 41,533 | 56,140 | 50,198 | 45,387 | 56,809 | 49,052 | 52,429 |
| 1993 | 0 | 0 | 0 | 0 | 0 | 51,724 | 44,847 | 42,935 | 41,873 | 57,216 | 51,262 | 46,509 | 58,636 | 50,900 | 54,889 |
| 1994 | 0 | 0 | 0 | 0 | 0 | 50,861 | 44,616 | 42,946 | 42,099 | 58,206 | 52,247 | 47,553 | 60,438 | 52,698 | 57,292 |
| 1995 | 0 | 0 | 0 | 0 | 0 | 49,725 | 44,207 | 42,809 | 42,200 | 59,093 | 53,142 | 48,514 | 62,216 | 54,444 | 59,645 |
| 1996 | 0 | 0 | 0 | 0 | 0 | 48,307 | 43,607 | 42,513 | 42,166 | 59,860 | 53,935 | 49,382 | 63,969 | 56,140 | 61,954 |
| 1997 | 0 | 0 | 0 | 0 | 0 | 46,602 | 42,805 | 42,048 | 41,988 | 60,487 | 54,615 | 50,151 | 65,695 | 57,786 | 64,230 |
| 1998 | 0 | 0 | 0 | 0 | 0 | 44,615 | 41,794 | 41,403 | 41,656 | 60,954 | 55,166 | 50,812 | 67,389 | 59,380 | 66,481 |
| 1999 | 0 | 0 | 0 | 0 | 0 | 42,359 | 40,568 | 40,570 | 41,161 | 61,236 | 55,573 | 51,353 | 69,047 | 60,920 | 68,717 |
| 2000 | 0 | 0 | 0 | 0 | 0 | 39,852 | 39,125 | 39,542 | 40,493 | 61,307 | 55,816 | 51,760 | 70,655 | 62,398 | 70,946 |
| 2001 | 0 | 0 | 0 | 0 | 0 | 0 | 0 | 0 | 0 | 61,148 | 55,879 | 52,023 | 72,206 | 63,814 | 73,178 |
| 2002 | 0 | 0 | 0 | 0 | 0 | 0 | 0 | 0 | 0 | 60,728 | 55,739 | 52,123 | 73,676 | 65,151 | 75,415 |

| Year | | | | | | | | | | | | | | |
|---|---|---|---|---|---|---|---|---|---|---|---|---|---|---|
| 2003 | 77,667 | 66,402 | 75,052 | 52,047 | 55,381 | 60,028 | 0 | 0 | 0 | 0 | 0 | 0 | 0 | 0 |
| 2004 | 79,931 | 67,550 | 76,307 | 51,779 | 54,783 | 59,027 | 0 | 0 | 0 | 0 | 0 | 0 | 0 | 0 |
| 2005 | 82,213 | 68,581 | 77,417 | 51,305 | 53,931 | 57,709 | 0 | 0 | 0 | 0 | 0 | 0 | 0 | 0 |
| 2006 | 84,502 | 69,471 | 78,349 | 50,609 | 52,810 | 56,063 | 0 | 0 | 0 | 0 | 0 | 0 | 0 | 0 |
| 2007 | 86,796 | 70,199 | 79,069 | 49,678 | 51,410 | 54,084 | 0 | 0 | 0 | 0 | 0 | 0 | 0 | 0 |
| 2008 | 89,081 | 70,739 | 79,543 | 48,503 | 49,727 | 51,778 | 0 | 0 | 0 | 0 | 0 | 0 | 0 | 0 |
| 2009 | 91,347 | 71,067 | 79,735 | 47,081 | 47,764 | 49,160 | 0 | 0 | 0 | 0 | 0 | 0 | 0 | 0 |
| 2010 | 93,567 | 71,151 | 79,604 | 45,408 | 45,526 | 46,251 | 0 | 0 | 0 | 0 | 0 | 0 | 0 | 0 |
| 2011 | 95,721 | 70,965 | 79,114 | 0 | 0 | 0 | 0 | 0 | 0 | 0 | 0 | 0 | 0 | 0 |
| 2012 | 97,774 | 70,478 | 78,230 | 0 | 0 | 0 | 0 | 0 | 0 | 0 | 0 | 0 | 0 | 0 |
| 2013 | 99,694 | 69,665 | 76,922 | 0 | 0 | 0 | 0 | 0 | 0 | 0 | 0 | 0 | 0 | 0 |
| 2014 | 101,438 | 68,503 | 75,168 | 0 | 0 | 0 | 0 | 0 | 0 | 0 | 0 | 0 | 0 | 0 |
| 2015 | 102,959 | 66,974 | 72,952 | 0 | 0 | 0 | 0 | 0 | 0 | 0 | 0 | 0 | 0 | 0 |
| 2016 | 104,202 | 65,062 | 70,267 | 0 | 0 | 0 | 0 | 0 | 0 | 0 | 0 | 0 | 0 | 0 |
| 2017 | 105,115 | 62,766 | 67,124 | 0 | 0 | 0 | 0 | 0 | 0 | 0 | 0 | 0 | 0 | 0 |
| 2018 | 105,638 | 60,090 | 63,546 | 0 | 0 | 0 | 0 | 0 | 0 | 0 | 0 | 0 | 0 | 0 |
| 2019 | 105,712 | 57,051 | 59,572 | 0 | 0 | 0 | 0 | 0 | 0 | 0 | 0 | 0 | 0 | 0 |
| 2020 | 105,277 | 53,675 | 55,254 | 0 | 0 | 0 | 0 | 0 | 0 | 0 | 0 | 0 | 0 | 0 |
| 2021 | 104,279 | 0 | 0 | 0 | 0 | 0 | 0 | 0 | 0 | 0 | 0 | 0 | 0 | 0 |
| 2022 | 102,671 | 0 | 0 | 0 | 0 | 0 | 0 | 0 | 0 | 0 | 0 | 0 | 0 | 0 |
| 2023 | 100,415 | 0 | 0 | 0 | 0 | 0 | 0 | 0 | 0 | 0 | 0 | 0 | 0 | 0 |
| 2024 | 97,484 | 0 | 0 | 0 | 0 | 0 | 0 | 0 | 0 | 0 | 0 | 0 | 0 | 0 |
| 2025 | 93,875 | 0 | 0 | 0 | 0 | 0 | 0 | 0 | 0 | 0 | 0 | 0 | 0 | 0 |
| 2026 | 89,598 | 0 | 0 | 0 | 0 | 0 | 0 | 0 | 0 | 0 | 0 | 0 | 0 | 0 |
| 2027 | 84,690 | 0 | 0 | 0 | 0 | 0 | 0 | 0 | 0 | 0 | 0 | 0 | 0 | 0 |
| 2028 | 79,209 | 0 | 0 | 0 | 0 | 0 | 0 | 0 | 0 | 0 | 0 | 0 | 0 | 0 |
| 2029 | 73,239 | 0 | 0 | 0 | 0 | 0 | 0 | 0 | 0 | 0 | 0 | 0 | 0 | 0 |
| 2030 | 66,886 | 0 | 0 | 0 | 0 | 0 | 0 | 0 | 0 | 0 | 0 | 0 | 0 | 0 |

**Table 10.8**    Cumulated Earnings by Year of Birth and Year of Hire for Managers

| Year Born | 1960 | 1950 | | 1940 | | | 1930 | | | | 1920 | | | | |
|---|---|---|---|---|---|---|---|---|---|---|---|---|---|---|---|
| Hired | 1980 | 1980 | 1975 | 1980 | 1975 | 1970 | 1980 | 1975 | 1970 | 1960 | 1980 | 1975 | 1970 | 1960 | 1950 |
| 1980 | 20,405 | 24,053 | 33,021 | 27,894 | 34,020 | 40,712 | 31,825 | 34,945 | 38,666 | 48,446 | 35,723 | 35,788 | 36,519 | 40,186 | 47,598 |
| 1981 | 43,257 | 50,135 | 67,987 | 57,297 | 69,374 | 82,565 | 64,564 | 70,611 | 77,892 | 97,258 | 71,728 | 71,690 | 72,990 | 79,980 | 94,372 |
| 1982 | 68,569 | 78,192 | 104,795 | 88,116 | 105,960 | 125,463 | 98,112 | 106,900 | 117,585 | 146,356 | 107,916 | 107,609 | 109,312 | 119,259 | 140,137 |
| 1983 | 96,326 | 108,157 | 143,337 | 120,257 | 143,679 | 169,320 | 132,368 | 143,719 | 157,659 | 195,656 | 144,193 | 143,453 | 145,392 | 157,901 | 184,704 |
| 1984 | 126,941 | 140,428 | 184,111 | 154,126 | 183,022 | 214,730 | 167,758 | 181,537 | 198,636 | 245,812 | 181,012 | 179,669 | 181,669 | 196,348 | 228,532 |
| 1985 | 160,419 | 174,970 | 227,059 | 189,661 | 223,926 | 261,644 | 204,205 | 220,277 | 240,439 | 296,731 | 218,283 | 216,157 | 218,031 | 234,440 | 271,379 |
| 1986 | 196,750 | 211,745 | 272,127 | 226,801 | 266,335 | 310,017 | 241,631 | 259,865 | 282,989 | 348,310 | 255,915 | 252,817 | 254,364 | 272,014 | 313,003 |
| 1987 | 235,905 | 250,750 | 319,267 | 265,486 | 310,194 | 359,811 | 279,962 | 300,224 | 326,205 | 400,432 | 293,815 | 289,545 | 290,545 | 308,900 | 353,159 |
| 1988 | 277,838 | 291,797 | 368,425 | 305,649 | 355,444 | 410,979 | 319,114 | 341,266 | 369,990 | 452,956 | 331,881 | 326,224 | 326,440 | 344,913 | 391,604 |
| 1989 | 322,490 | 334,963 | 419,553 | 347,221 | 402,025 | 463,472 | 359,000 | 382,899 | 414,239 | 505,721 | 370,005 | 362,731 | 361,907 | 379,870 | 428,104 |
| 1990 | 369,799 | 380,146 | 472,609 | 390,134 | 449,874 | 517,238 | 399,530 | 425,026 | 458,838 | 558,547 | 408,072 | 398,936 | 396,799 | 413,582 | 462,442 |
| 1991 | 419,703 | 427,293 | 527,560 | 434,321 | 498,933 | 572,225 | 440,613 | 467,543 | 503,665 | 611,237 | 0 | 0 | 0 | 0 | 0 |
| 1992 | 472,132 | 476,345 | 584,369 | 479,708 | 549,132 | 628,365 | 482,147 | 510,333 | 548,579 | 663,567 | 0 | 0 | 0 | 0 | 0 |
| 1993 | 527,021 | 527,245 | 643,004 | 526,216 | 600,394 | 685,581 | 524,020 | 553,268 | 593,426 | 715,290 | 0 | 0 | 0 | 0 | 0 |
| 1994 | 584,313 | 579,942 | 703,442 | 573,770 | 652,640 | 743,787 | 566,118 | 596,214 | 638,043 | 766,151 | 0 | 0 | 0 | 0 | 0 |
| 1995 | 643,958 | 634,387 | 765,658 | 622,283 | 705,782 | 802,880 | 608,318 | 639,024 | 682,250 | 815,877 | 0 | 0 | 0 | 0 | 0 |
| 1996 | 705,913 | 690,527 | 829,626 | 671,666 | 759,717 | 862,740 | 650,484 | 681,537 | 725,857 | 864,183 | 0 | 0 | 0 | 0 | 0 |
| 1997 | 770,143 | 748,313 | 895,321 | 721,817 | 814,332 | 923,228 | 692,472 | 723,585 | 768,662 | 910,785 | 0 | 0 | 0 | 0 | 0 |
| 1998 | 836,623 | 807,692 | 962,710 | 772,629 | 869,498 | 984,181 | 734,128 | 764,987 | 810,456 | 955,400 | 0 | 0 | 0 | 0 | 0 |
| 1999 | 905,341 | 868,612 | 1,031,757 | 823,981 | 925,071 | 1,045,417 | 775,289 | 805,557 | 851,024 | 997,759 | 0 | 0 | 0 | 0 | 0 |
| 2000 | 976,286 | 931,010 | 1,102,412 | 875,741 | 980,887 | 1,106,724 | 815,782 | 845,099 | 890,149 | 1,037,610 | 0 | 0 | 0 | 0 | 0 |
| 2001 | 1,049,464 | 994,824 | 1,174,617 | 927,764 | 1,036,766 | 1,167,871 | 0 | 0 | 0 | 0 | 0 | 0 | 0 | 0 | 0 |
| 2002 | 1,124,879 | 1,059,974 | 1,248,293 | 979,886 | 1,092,505 | 1,228,598 | 0 | 0 | 0 | 0 | 0 | 0 | 0 | 0 | 0 |

| Year | | | | | | | | | | | | | | |
|------|---|---|---|---|---|---|---|---|---|---|---|---|---|---|
| 2003 | 1,202,545 | 1,126,376 | 1,323,345 | 1,031,934 | 1,147,885 | 1,288,626 | 0 | 0 | 0 | 0 | 0 | 0 | 0 | 0 |
| 2004 | 1,282,476 | 1,193,926 | 1,399,652 | 1,083,712 | 1,202,667 | 1,347,652 | 0 | 0 | 0 | 0 | 0 | 0 | 0 | 0 |
| 2005 | 1,364,688 | 1,262,507 | 1,477,069 | 1,135,017 | 1,256,598 | 1,405,361 | 0 | 0 | 0 | 0 | 0 | 0 | 0 | 0 |
| 2006 | 1,449,190 | 1,331,987 | 1,555,417 | 1,185,625 | 1,309,408 | 1,461,423 | 0 | 0 | 0 | 0 | 0 | 0 | 0 | 0 |
| 2007 | 1,535,985 | 1,402,176 | 1,634,486 | 1,235,302 | 1,360,818 | 1,515,506 | 0 | 0 | 0 | 0 | 0 | 0 | 0 | 0 |
| 2008 | 1,625,066 | 1,472,915 | 1,714,028 | 1,283,805 | 1,410,544 | 1,567,283 | 0 | 0 | 0 | 0 | 0 | 0 | 0 | 0 |
| 2009 | 1,716,412 | 1,543,982 | 1,793,763 | 1,330,886 | 1,458,307 | 1,616,442 | 0 | 0 | 0 | 0 | 0 | 0 | 0 | 0 |
| 2010 | 1,809,979 | 1,615,133 | 1,873,366 | 1,376,293 | 1,503,833 | 1,662,692 | 0 | 0 | 0 | 0 | 0 | 0 | 0 | 0 |
| 2011 | 1,905,700 | 1,686,097 | 1,952,480 | 0 | 0 | 0 | 0 | 0 | 0 | 0 | 0 | 0 | 0 | 0 |
| 2012 | 2,003,474 | 1,756,574 | 2,030,709 | 0 | 0 | 0 | 0 | 0 | 0 | 0 | 0 | 0 | 0 | 0 |
| 2013 | 2,013,168 | 1,826,239 | 2,107,631 | 0 | 0 | 0 | 0 | 0 | 0 | 0 | 0 | 0 | 0 | 0 |
| 2014 | 2,204,605 | 1,894,742 | 2,182,799 | 0 | 0 | 0 | 0 | 0 | 0 | 0 | 0 | 0 | 0 | 0 |
| 2015 | 2,307,564 | 1,961,716 | 2,255,750 | 0 | 0 | 0 | 0 | 0 | 0 | 0 | 0 | 0 | 0 | 0 |
| 2016 | 2,411,765 | 2,026,778 | 2,326,016 | 0 | 0 | 0 | 0 | 0 | 0 | 0 | 0 | 0 | 0 | 0 |
| 2017 | 2,516,879 | 2,089,544 | 2,393,140 | 0 | 0 | 0 | 0 | 0 | 0 | 0 | 0 | 0 | 0 | 0 |
| 2018 | 2,622,516 | 2,149,634 | 2,456,686 | 0 | 0 | 0 | 0 | 0 | 0 | 0 | 0 | 0 | 0 | 0 |
| 2019 | 2,728,227 | 2,206,684 | 2,516,257 | 0 | 0 | 0 | 0 | 0 | 0 | 0 | 0 | 0 | 0 | 0 |
| 2020 | 2,833,503 | 2,260,359 | 2,571,510 | 0 | 0 | 0 | 0 | 0 | 0 | 0 | 0 | 0 | 0 | 0 |
| 2021 | 2,937,782 | 0 | 0 | 0 | 0 | 0 | 0 | 0 | 0 | 0 | 0 | 0 | 0 | 0 |
| 2022 | 3,040,452 | 0 | 0 | 0 | 0 | 0 | 0 | 0 | 0 | 0 | 0 | 0 | 0 | 0 |
| 2023 | 3,140,866 | 0 | 0 | 0 | 0 | 0 | 0 | 0 | 0 | 0 | 0 | 0 | 0 | 0 |
| 2024 | 3,238,350 | 0 | 0 | 0 | 0 | 0 | 0 | 0 | 0 | 0 | 0 | 0 | 0 | 0 |
| 2025 | 3,332,224 | 0 | 0 | 0 | 0 | 0 | 0 | 0 | 0 | 0 | 0 | 0 | 0 | 0 |
| 2026 | 3,421,822 | 0 | 0 | 0 | 0 | 0 | 0 | 0 | 0 | 0 | 0 | 0 | 0 | 0 |
| 2027 | 3,506,511 | 0 | 0 | 0 | 0 | 0 | 0 | 0 | 0 | 0 | 0 | 0 | 0 | 0 |
| 2028 | 3,585,719 | 0 | 0 | 0 | 0 | 0 | 0 | 0 | 0 | 0 | 0 | 0 | 0 | 0 |
| 2029 | 3,658,958 | 0 | 0 | 0 | 0 | 0 | 0 | 0 | 0 | 0 | 0 | 0 | 0 | 0 |
| 2030 | 3,725,843 | 0 | 0 | 0 | 0 | 0 | 0 | 0 | 0 | 0 | 0 | 0 | 0 | 0 |

In some instances there are erratic fluctuations from one year to the next, from negative to positive to negative, for example. This typically occurs if an increase in benefits in one year is not followed by a comparable increase in the next. For example, suppose that the normal retirement benefit is higher in year $a$ than in either year $a - 1$ or in year $a + 1$. Then the accrual from $a - 1$ to $a$ will tend to be positive, but the accrual from $a$ to $a + 1$ will tend to be negative. Dropping a low earnings year and adding a higher one in the calculation of the earnings base may create this effect. Other provisions in the pension calculation formula may do so as well. For convenience, total cumulated pension wealth is shown in table 10.4 for the same groups. Social Security accruals and cumulated Social Security wealth are shown in tables 10.5 and 10.6, respectively. Annual wage earnings and cumulated earnings are shown in tables 10.7 and 10.8.

Two of the profiles were shown in figures 10.1 and 10.2 above; several others are shown below. Young new hires will have rapid wage growth in the subsequent 20 years, but very little accrual of pension wealth. This is shown in figure 10.2 for persons born in 1960, 20 years old at the time of hire in 1980. Their incomes will rise from about $20,000 in 1980 to over $70,000 in the year 2000, when they are 40 years old. But even in 2000 their pension accrual will be only $1,558. Their total accrued pension wealth at age 40 will be only $11,894, a very small fraction (1.2 percent) of their total earnings over the period.

A manager hired in 1980, but born in 1940, will have much lower wage growth over the next 20 years, from about $28,000 in 1980 to under $52,000 at age 60 in 2000 (see figs. 10.3a and 10.3b). This person will also have little pension wealth accrual through age 54, when his total pension wealth will be less than $13,000. In 1995, however, when the person is 55 and eligible for early retirement, it will increase by almost $30,000 to a total of over $47,000. In the next few years accrual is less than $7,000 per year. The age 55 spike in accrual suggests a potential concentration of retirement among this group at age 55 (in 1995). But the actual pension that would be received is still very small, only about 12 percent of salary (from tables not shown). Thus retirement may be unlikely.

Managers of the same age, but hired 10 years earlier may be much more likely to retire in that year (see figs. 10.4a and 10.4b). They experience a much sharper increase in pension wealth in 1985, from just under $42,000 to over $133,000. The pension benefit to wage replacement rate at 55 for this group is about 26 percent. But accrual after 55 remains positive for this group; pension wealth increases to almost $209,000 by age 60. Thus pension wealth accrual may still provide a substantial incentive to remain with the firm.

In contrast, persons born in 1920 and hired by the firm at age 40 (in 1960) will have essentially no pension accrual in 1985, and, indeed, it

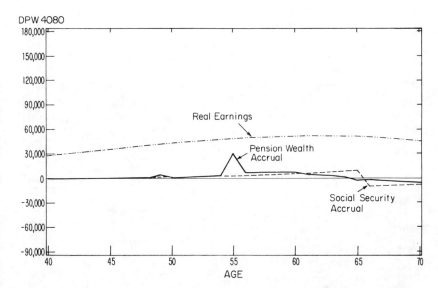

**Fig. 10.3a**    Pension wealth accrual, SS accrual, and wage earnings for male managers born in 1940 and hired in 1980, in real 1985 dollars

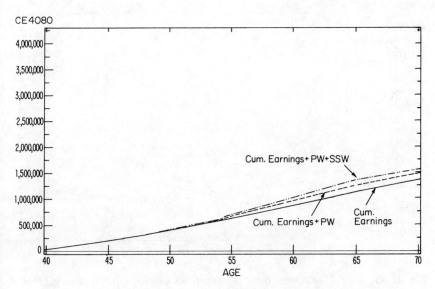

**Fig. 10.3b**    Cumulated total income from employment versus year of retirement, male manager born in 1940 and hired in 1980

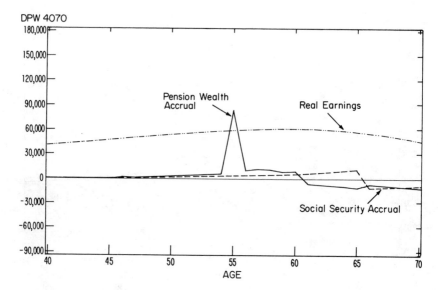

**Fig. 10.4a**      Pension wealth accrual, SS accrual, and wage earnings for male managers born in 1940 and hired in 1970, in real 1985 dollars

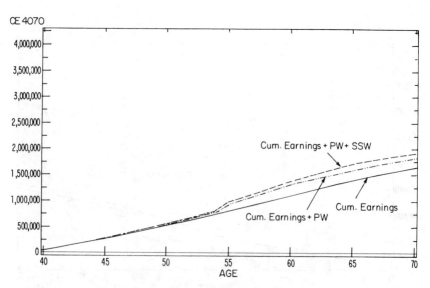

**Fig. 10.4b**      Cumulated total income from employment versus year of retirement, male managers born in 1940 and hired in 1970

will become negative in a few years (see figs. 10.5a and 10.5b). Earnings for this group are declining as well. One might think that persons who are in this group and are still working would be likely to retire. But, if still working, they chose not to retire earlier, when compensation from continued work began to decline. They would have been eligible for early retirement at age 55 (in 1975), when they had been employed for 15 years.

At that time they would have faced earnings and pension accrual profiles like those shown in figures 10.6a and 10.6b. The group described in these graphs was born and hired 10 years later (in 1930 and 1970, respectively) and thus had 15 years of service at age 55 (in 1985), when pension accrual was at a maximum. Thereafter, accrual declines and becomes negative around age 65, after 25 years of service. That the group pictured in figure 10.5 did not retire earlier may suggest that their preferences are such that they are also not likely to retire in a given subsequent year either. They may want to work more than others and that may be why they did not retire when pension accrual and earnings started to decline. In addition, however, the group had not accumulated substantial pension wealth at any time, even before it began to decline, and thus they may always have been in a poor position to leave the labor force.

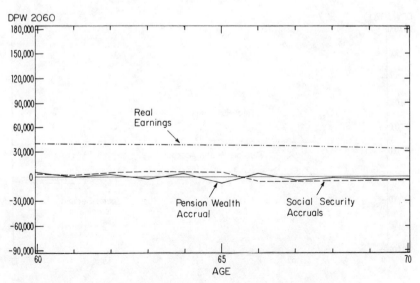

**Fig. 10.5a**     Pension wealth accrual, SS accrual, and wage earnings for male managers born in 1920 and hired in 1960, in real 1985 dollars

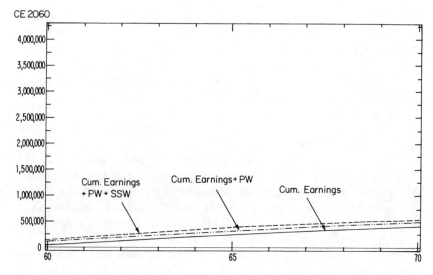

**Fig. 10.5b**    Cumulated total income from employment versus year of retirement, male managers born in 1920 and hired in 1960

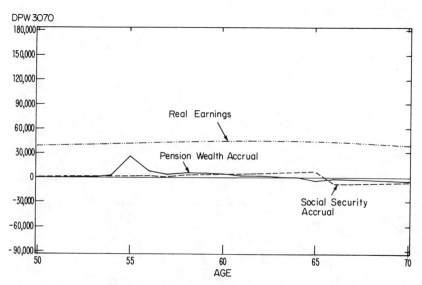

**Fig. 10.6a**    Pension wealth accrual, SS accrual, and wage earnings for male managers born in 1930 and hired in 1970, in real 1985 dollars

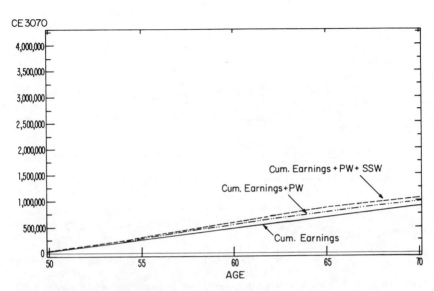

**Fig. 10.6b**    Cumulated total income from employment versus year of retirement, male managers born in 1930 and hired in 1970

### 10.1.5    Variation by Employee Type

The pension accrual profiles for other employee groups look very much like those described above. Accrual is minimal during the first years of service. There is typically a discontinuous increase in pension wealth at age 55. And accrual typically becomes negative after 30 years of service, sometimes before that. Social Security accrual becomes negative after 65. The major differences among the groups stem from different age-earnings profiles. An illustration of the similarity and difference is provided by graphs like that in figure 10.2, but for different employee groups. These are shown in figures 10.7 through 10.11 for male managers, salesmen, saleswomen, male office workers, and female office workers, respectively. (The graphs for male managers are reproduced here for ease of comparison.) In each case the data pertain to persons born in 1960 and hired in 1980. Thus they all pertain to compensation over the life cycle for persons who remain in the firm. As is clear from the graphs, the accrual profiles are qualitatively similar; but there are some important differences.

First, managers earn more than the other employee groups. The wage earnings profiles also differ in shape. The peak earnings for managers occur at age 59. At age 66, if they still are in the labor force, 45 percent of their wage earnings are offset by negative pension and Social Security accrual. The earnings of salesmen peak much earlier, at age 50. At age 66, almost 95 percent of their wage earnings are offset by loss

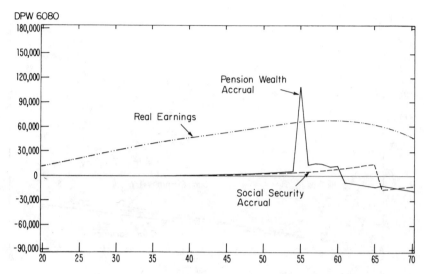

**Fig. 10.7a**    Pension wealth accrual, SS accrual, and wage earnings for
male managers born in 1960 and hired in 1980, in real 1985
dollars

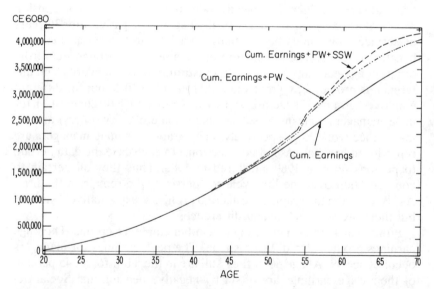

**Fig. 10.7b**    Cumulated total income from employment versus year of
retirement, male managers born in 1960 and hired in 1980

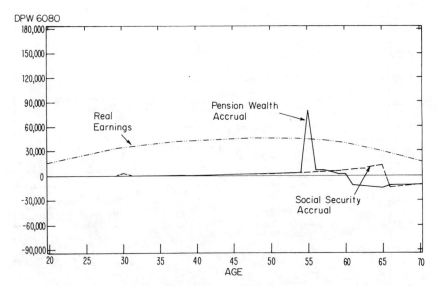

**Fig. 10.8a**  Pension wealth accrual, SS accrual, and wage earnings for salesmen born in 1960 and hired in 1980, in real 1985 dollars

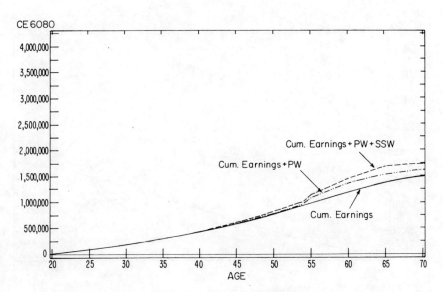

**Fig. 10.8b**  Cumulated total income from employment versus year of retirement, salesmen born in 1960 and hired in 1980

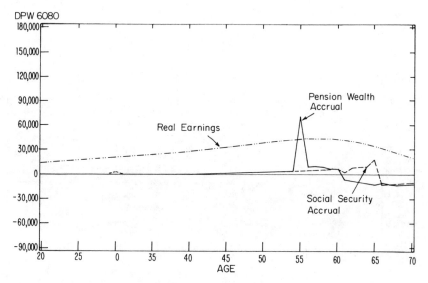

**Fig. 10.9a**      Pension wealth accrual, SS accrual, and wage earnings for saleswomen born in 1960 and hired in 1980, in real 1985 dollars

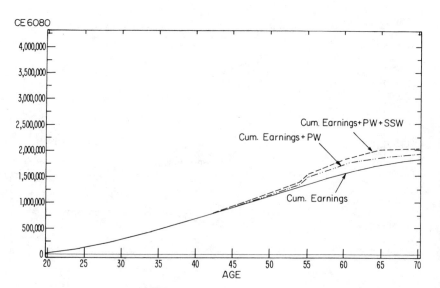

**Fig. 10.9b**      Cumulated total income from employment versus year of retirement, saleswomen born in 1960 and hired in 1980

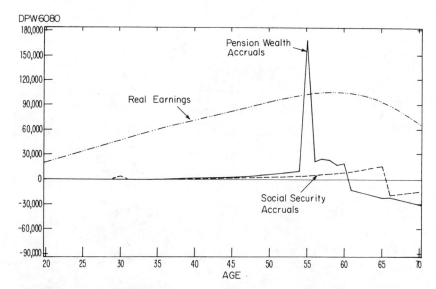

**Fig. 10.10a**    Pension wealth accrual, SS accrual, and wage earnings for male office workers born in 1960 and hired in 1980, in real 1985 dollars

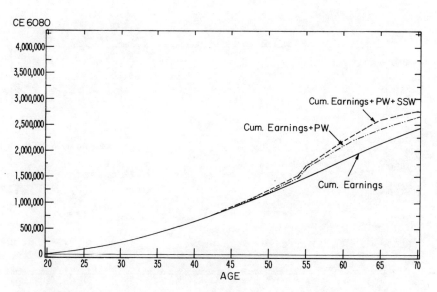

**Fig. 10.10b**    Cumulated total income from employment versus year of retirement, male office workers born in 1960 and hired in 1980

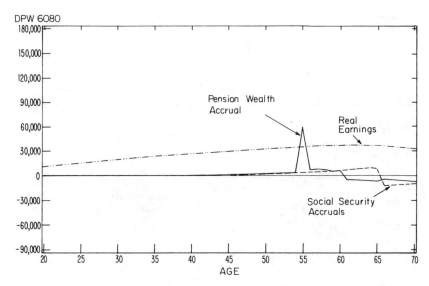

**Fig. 10.11a**      Pension wealth accrual, SS accrual, and wage earnings for female office workers born in 1960 and hired in 1980, in real 1985 dollars

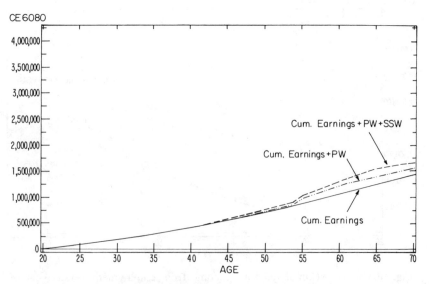

**Fig. 10.11b**      Cumulated total income from employment versus retirement, female office workers born in 1960 and hired in 1980

in pension and Social Security wealth. Thus this effect creates a greater incentive for the salesmen than for the managers to retire after age 65.[4] The peak wage earnings for saleswomen occur at age 57; at 66 almost 75 percent of their wage earnings are offset by pension and Social Security wealth losses. The peak earnings for male and female office workers occur at ages 59 and 62, respectively. At age 66, 48 and 46 percent, respectively, of their earnings would be offset by loss in pension and Social Security wealth.[5]

The budget constraints for all groups show a discontinuous jump at age 55, but it seems most pronounced for managers. The budget constraint for salesmen is essentially flat after 65; their net compensation after 65 is virtually zero. The same is true for saleswomen. The net compensation of managers and male office workers is positive, but declining rapidly at age 65, and the budget constraints for these two groups become flatter after 65. The budget constraint nonlinearities seem to be the least pronounced for female office workers.

## 10.2   The Prediction of Earnings of the Firm's Workers

Data are available for each worker employed in the firm from the beginning of 1980 through the end of 1984. Most were in the firm in more than one year and many for all years. These years define the sample. Earnings for anyone in the sample are available beginning in 1969 if the person was employed then or beginning in the year that the person joined the firm if it was after 1969. Thus it is possible to follow the same person for up to 17 years. In particular, it is possible to estimate individual-specific earnings effects. By combining data for workers of different ages and with different years of service in the firm, it is possible to predict earnings. We use these predicted earnings in considering whether a person leaves the firm in a given sample year, like 1980. The probability of departure in a given year is related to how much the person would have earned during that year and on pension and Social Security accrual during that year. In future estimations, we will consider not only next year's earnings and pension and Social Security accrual, but also the effects of future earnings and pension and Social Security accrual.

Because earnings in the first and last years in the firm are likely to represent pay for only part of the year, they are excluded in the estimation of earnings. To be included, a person must have earnings data for at least three years. Workers with three years of data would have only one usable earnings observation. This group must be distinguished in the estimation procedure. Although persons with fewer than three years of earnings are not used in the estimation of earnings equations, they are included in the analysis of retirement discussed in section 10.3.

In this section the earnings estimation procedure is discussed first, then the results are presented. In addition to their use in the subsequent prediction of retirement, the earnings results are of considerable interest in their own right. It is rare to have access to earnings data for the same persons over such a long period. It is often claimed, for example, that real wage earnings decline late in a person's working life. We are able to determine with relative certainty whether this is true for this firm.

### 10.2.1   The Method

Earnings histories from 1969 are available for workers employed during the period 1980 through 1984. To explain the main features of the estimation procedure, figure 10.12 describes the earnings of two persons who are in the data set for seven years. The first person is age 40 to 46 over these seven years, and the second is age 45 to 51. (They could also have different years of service, but that is ignored in this example.) Earnings by age for the typical person in the firm are represented by the solid line in the middle of the graph. The first person has higher earnings than the average employee. His earnings exceed those of the typical person by an amount $u_1$, the individual-specific earnings effect for person 1. It may arise, for example, because this person works harder than the typical employee or because he has greater ability or more training. Earnings for person 1 fluctuate from year to year, however. The deviations with age from the central tendency of his earnings, indicated by the person 1 average, are indicated by $n_{1t}$, where $t$ indicates the deviation in year $t$. Future earnings for person 1 must be estimated for our analysis. They are indicated by the dashed part of the line. They depend on $u_1$ and on the estimated re-

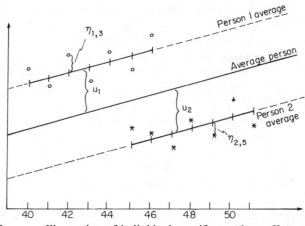

**Fig. 10.12**          Illustration of individual-specific earnings effects

lationship between age and earnings, which, aside from the individual-specific term, is assumed to be the same for individuals within a sex-occupation group. The earnings model is presented more formally in the following subsections.

### Earnings Equation Specification

To simplify the presentation, we include only one right-hand variable, age. In practice, estimation is based on age and years of service. The exact specification is presented below. An earnings equation that captures the ideas discussed above is:

(4)     $\ln E_{it} = \beta_0 + \beta_1 A_{it} + \beta_2 A_{it}^2 + \varepsilon_{it}$

$$= \mu_{it} + \varepsilon_{it}.$$

$$\varepsilon_{it} = u_i + \eta_{it}.$$

$$\text{Var}(\varepsilon) = \text{Var}(u) + \text{Var}(\eta) = \sigma_\varepsilon^2, \text{Var}(u) = \sigma_u^2, \text{Var}(\eta) = \sigma_\eta^2.$$

$$\text{Cov}(u_i, \eta_{it}) = \text{Cov}(\eta_{it}, \eta_{it}) = 0.$$

$$E \equiv \text{Annual earnings},$$

$$A \equiv \text{Age},$$

$$i \equiv \text{Indexes individuals},$$

$$t \equiv \text{Indexes year (e.g., 1978, \ldots , 1983)},$$

$$u_i \equiv \text{Individual-specific earnings effect}.$$

$$E_{it} = e^{\mu_{it}} e^{\varepsilon_{it}} = e^{\mu_{it}} e^{u_i} e^{\eta_{it}}.$$

$$E(E_{it} | \mu_{it}, u_i) = e^{\mu_{it}} e^{u_i} E(e^{\eta_{it}}) \doteq e^{\mu_{it}} e^{u_i} \left( 1 + \frac{\sigma_\eta^2}{2} \right).$$

The last approximation is a reminder that because of the nonlinear relationship between earnings and age, the expected value of $\exp(\eta_{it})$ is not equal to 1, even though the expected value of $\eta_{it}$ is 0.

In addition to the parameters $\beta$, the variances of $u$ and $\eta$ are also of interest. The first indicates the systematic earnings variation across individuals due to individual-specific effects. The second is a measure of the extent of nonsystematic variation. The method of estimation used here does not allow for the possibility that the individual-specific terms $u$ may be correlated with age. For example, it may be that persons whose earnings are higher, because of the attributes $u$, are more likely to continue working at older ages. We did obtain such estimates using a differencing procedure. But for our purposes the procedure has two important shortcomings: First, it means that certain age and service parameters are not identified. Second, it imposes the rate of salary increase by age that existed over the period of the data, because this relationship depends only on changes in earnings over the period of the data. (The method we use allows the effect of age to be determined in part by comparison of the earnings of workers with very different ages.) This increase is apparently low relative to longer term increases and, hence, may imply expected future increases with age and service that are too low. We also discovered that individual-specific terms based on the method that we have used are not correlated with firm departure rates.

*Estimation Method*

Estimation of equation (4) yields residuals

$$
(5) \qquad e_{it} = \ln E_{it} - \hat{\beta}_0 - \hat{\beta}_1 A_{it} - \hat{\beta}_2 A_{it}^2.
$$

The estimated variance of $e$ is given by

$$
(6) \qquad \hat{\sigma}_\varepsilon^2 = \frac{\sum\limits_{i,t} e_{it}^2}{\sum\limits_{i} n_i - k},
$$

where $n_i$ is the number of observations for person $i$, and $k$ is the number of parameters (three in this example). To obtain estimates of additional parameters of interest we need to distinguish persons with more than one observation from those with only one.

*Using Persons with $n_i > 1$.* From the residuals for person $i$, the individual-specific effect for $i$ is calculated by

$$
(7) \qquad \hat{u}_i = \frac{\sum\limits_{t} e_{it}}{n_i}.
$$

The variances of $\eta$ and $u$ are then given, respectively, by

$$
(8) \qquad \hat{\sigma}_\eta^2 = \frac{\sum\limits_{i,t} (e_{it} - \hat{u}_i)^2}{\sum\limits_{i} n_i - k - I}, \text{ and}
$$

$$
(9) \qquad \text{Var}(u) = \text{Var}(e) - \text{Var}(n),
$$

where $I$ is the number of persons in the sample (in this instance those with $n_i \geq 2$), and

$$
(10) \qquad \hat{\eta}_{it} = e_{it} - \hat{u}_i.
$$

*For Persons with $n_i = 1$.* If a person has only one observation, we cannot distinguish $\eta_{it}$ from $u_i$, since we do not observe any variation around an average. First note that if $u$ and $\eta$ are normally distributed, and thus $\varepsilon$ is also, then

$$E(u|E) = E(u) + \rho_{u,\varepsilon}\frac{\sigma_u}{\sigma^\varepsilon}[\varepsilon - E(\varepsilon)]$$

$$= 0 + \rho_{u,\varepsilon}\frac{\sigma_u}{\sigma_\varepsilon}(\varepsilon - 0)$$

$$= \rho_{u,\varepsilon}\frac{\sigma_u}{\sigma_\varepsilon},$$

$$\text{Cov}(u,\varepsilon) = E[u(u + \eta)] = \sigma_u^2,$$

$$\rho_{u,\varepsilon} = \frac{\text{Cov}(u,\varepsilon)}{\sqrt{\text{Var}(u)}\cdot\sqrt{\text{Var}(\varepsilon)}} = \frac{\sigma_u^2}{\sigma_u\sqrt{\sigma_u^2 + \sigma_\eta^2}} = \frac{\sigma_u}{\sigma_\varepsilon},$$

$$\rho_{u,\varepsilon}\cdot\frac{\sigma_u}{\sigma_\varepsilon} = \frac{\sigma_u^2}{\sigma_\varepsilon^2},$$

where $\rho$ is a correlation coefficient. Thus,

$$E(u_i|\varepsilon_{it}) = \frac{\sigma_u^2}{\sigma_\varepsilon^2}\varepsilon_{it} = \frac{\sigma_\varepsilon^2 - \sigma_\eta^2}{\sigma_\varepsilon^2}\cdot\varepsilon_{it}.$$

If $\sigma_\eta^2$ were 0 and we observed $\varepsilon_{it}$, we would assume it represented entirely an individual-specific effect $u_i$. If $\sigma_u^2$ were 0, we would assume the $\varepsilon_{it}$ were equal to the random term $\eta_{it}$, and that there was no individual effect $u_i$. Letting $e_{it}$ be the sample analog of $\varepsilon_{it}$ and using the estimates in equations (2) and (4) for $\sigma_\varepsilon^2$ and $\sigma_\eta^2$, respectively, $u_i$ for persons with only one observation is estimated by

$$(11) \qquad \hat{u}_i = \frac{\hat{\sigma}_\varepsilon^2 - \hat{\sigma}_\eta^2}{\hat{\sigma}_\varepsilon^2}e_{it},$$

and $\eta_{it}$ by

$$\hat{\eta}_{it} = e_{it} - \hat{u}_i.$$

*Predicted Earnings.* For an estimation of the likelihood that a person will retire in the next year, we need to use predicted earnings in that year. For future analysis we will need to predict earnings in subsequent years as well. The predictions are given by:

$$(12) \quad \hat{E}_{it} = e^{\hat{\mu}_{it}}e^{\hat{u}_i}E(e^{\eta_{it}}) = e^{\hat{\mu}_{it}+\hat{u}_i}(1 + \hat{\sigma}_\eta^2/2), \qquad \text{for } n_i \geq 2.$$

$$\hat{E}_{it} = e^{\hat{\mu}_{it}}e^{\hat{u}_i}E(e^{\eta_{it}}) = e^{\hat{\mu}_{it}+\hat{u}_i}(1 + \hat{\sigma}_\eta^2/2), \qquad \text{for } n_i \geq 1.$$

For out-of-sample estimates, $\hat{\mu}_{it}$ would be predicted from future age, for example.[6]

*The Estimated Components of Earnings.* To consider how much earnings deviate from what might be predicted for that person, or from what that person himself might predict, it is useful to divide earnings into expected and unexpected components. We do that by defining

(13)      $\ln E_{it} \equiv \hat{\mu}_{it} + \hat{u}_i + \hat{\eta}_{it}$ .

$\hat{\mu}_{it} + \hat{u}_i \equiv$ "permanent" or "expected" component.

$\hat{\eta}_{it} \equiv$ "transitory" or "unexpected" component.

These definitions do not necessarily correspond to usual definitions of permanent versus transitory income, so the expected versus unexpected terminology may be better. In levels, the two components are given by

(14)      $E_{it} \equiv e^{\hat{\mu}_{it} + \hat{u}_i} \cdot e^{\hat{\eta}_{it}}$

$= e^{\hat{\mu}_{it} + \hat{u}_i} + e^{\hat{\mu}_{it} + u_i} (e^{\hat{\eta}_{it}} - 1)$

$= \dfrac{\text{permanent}}{\text{component}} + \dfrac{\text{transitory}}{\text{component}}.$

### A More Detailed Specification of the Earnings Function

Earnings were predicted using the following variables:

Age
Age Squared
Age Squared times Service
Service
Service Squared
Service Squared times Age
Age times Service
Age Squared times Service Squared
Calendar Year Variables for 1969, . . . , 1979 and 1981, . . . , 1983.

The calendar year variables pick up changes in real earnings over time. Each of the year estimates is relative to the 1980 base.

### Earnings Function Estimates

The estimated earnings function parameters are shown in table 10.9. The implications of the estimates are shown in figures 10.13a through 10.13e, distinguished by employee group. Figure 10.13a, for example, shows earnings profiles for managers by age of hire in 1980, where the nine profiles on the graph pertain to persons hired at successively older ages—from 20 to 60 in five-year intervals. Earnings are calculated through age 70 for each cohort. First, it is clear that, for any age, earnings increase substantially with years of service. Earnings at the

**Table 10.9**     **Earnings Parameter Estimates by Employee Group (1980 $)[a]**

| Variable | Managers | Salesmen | Saleswomen | Male Office Workers | Female Office Workers |
|---|---|---|---|---|---|
| Constant | 9.28 | 8.87 | 8.65 | 6.80 | 8.39 |
| | (122.2) | (303.6) | (77.0) | (210.9) | (826.6) |
| $A$ | 0.021 | 0.037 | 0.042 | 0.16 | 0.45 |
| | (4.8) | (23.5) | (7.0) | (83.3) | (71.6) |
| $A^2$ | −.000082 | −0.00041 | −0.00051 | −0.0019 | −0.00057 |
| | (−1.4) | (−20.7) | (−6.5) | (−77.2) | (−66.3) |
| $A^2 \cdot S$ | 0.000021 | 0.000064 | −0.000047 | 0.000044 | 0.000029 |
| | (3.0) | (19.7) | (−2.0) | (12.9) | (20.1) |
| $S$ | 0.18 | 0.20 | −0.036 | 0.10 | 0.10 |
| | (14.0) | (31.5) | (−0.9) | (17.5) | (48.7) |
| $S^2$ | −0.01 | −0.0044 | −0.0086 | −0.0060 | −0.0031 |
| | (−7.8) | (−11.5) | (−2.9) | (−19.8) | (−24.4) |
| $S^2 \cdot A$ | 0.00020 | 0.00017 | 0.00023 | 0.00018 | 0.00010 |
| | (7.5) | (11.9) | (1.8) | (16.7) | (21.5) |
| $A \cdot S$ | −0.0043 | −0.0068 | 0.0040 | −0.0033 | −0.0030 |
| | (−7.1) | (−23.8) | (2.0) | (−11.5) | (−26.3) |
| $A^2 \cdot S^2$ | −0.0000016 | −0.0000017 | −0.0000016 | −0.0000016 | −9.035 |
| | (−6.5) | (−12.7) | (−1.2) | (−15.7) | (−19.5) |
| 1969 | 0.11 | 0.15 | −0.027 | 0.031 | 0.039 |
| | (9.4) | (31.4) | (−0.6) | (3.8) | (11.2) |
| 1970 | 0.16 | 0.19 | −0.014 | 0.063 | 0.058 |
| | (14.1) | (38.8) | (−0.3) | (7.8) | (17.5) |
| 1971 | 0.19 | 0.19 | 0.0036 | 0.062 | 0.036 |
| | (17.2) | (39.6) | (0.1) | (8.0) | (11.5) |
| 1972 | 0.21 | 0.21 | −0.012 | 0.088 | 0.065 |
| | (19.1) | (45.6) | (−0.3) | (11.6) | (21.3) |
| 1973 | 0.21 | 0.21 | 0.0027 | 0.094 | 0.076 |
| | (19.3) | (46.3) | (0.1) | (12.8) | (25.7) |
| 1974 | 0.16 | 0.20 | −0.0074 | 0.079 | 0.069 |
| | (15.2) | (44.3) | (−0.2) | (11.0) | (24.6) |
| 1975 | 0.10 | 0.14 | −0.012 | 0.071 | 0.049 |
| | (9.7) | (31.6) | (−0.4) | (10.2) | (18.0) |
| 1976 | 0.15 | 0.16 | 0.042 | 0.12 | 0.11 |
| | (14.2) | (36.0) | (1.6) | (17.5) | (41.1) |
| 1977 | 0.14 | 0.16 | 0.094 | 0.10 | 0.084 |
| | (13.6) | (36.1) | (4.2) | (15.4) | (33.6) |
| 1978 | 0.18 | 0.18 | 0.13 | 0.09 | 0.078 |
| | (17.7) | (41.9) | (6.7) | (14.3) | (32.3) |
| 1979 | 0.13 | 0.10 | 0.064 | 0.058 | 0.044 |
| | (13.5) | (24.6) | (3.7) | (9.0) | (18.8) |
| 1980 | — | — | — | — | — |
| 1981 | 0.03 | 0.0091 | 0.025 | 0.021 | 0.013 |
| | (3.0) | (2.1) | (1.5) | (3.3) | (5.6) |
| 1982 | −0.0086 | −0.077 | −0.033 | 0.033 | 0.012 |
| | (−0.9) | (−18.0) | (−2.1) | (5.1) | (5.1) |

*(continued)*

**Table 10.9** (continued)

| Variable | Managers | Salesmen | Saleswomen | Male Office Workers | Female Office Workers |
|---|---|---|---|---|---|
| 1983 | 0.0028 | −0.099 | −0.041 | 0.073 | 0.066 |
| | (−0.3) | (−23.0) | (−2.6) | (11.3) | (28.4) |
| 1984 | 0.068 | −0.11 | −0.050 | 0.0078 | 0.032 |
| | (7.0) | (−25.2) | (−3.3) | (1.2) | (13.8) |
| $\sigma_\epsilon^2$ | 0.135 | 0.155 | 0.163 | 0.168 | 0.065 |
| $\sigma_u^2$ | 0.083 | 0.140 | 0.110 | 0.150 | 0.06 |
| $\sigma_n^2$ | 0.52 | 0.015 | 0.053 | 0.018 | 0.005 |

[a]$t$-statistics are in parentheses.

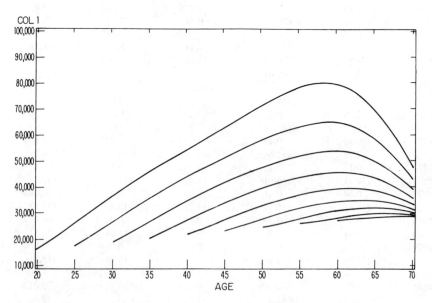

**Fig. 10.13a**     Age-earnings profiles for persons hired in 1980, by age when hired, male managers

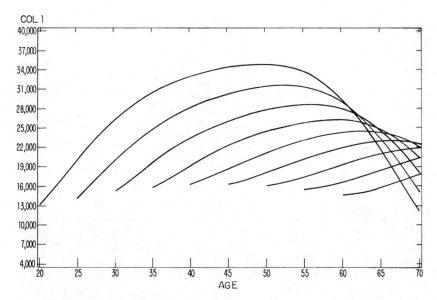

**Fig. 10.13b**      Age-earnings profiles for persons hired in 1980, by age when hired, salesmen

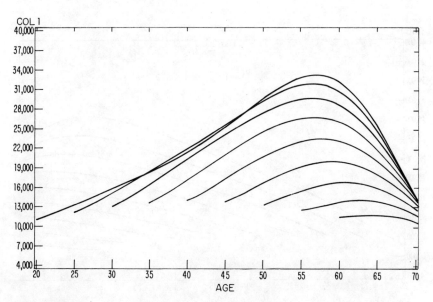

**Fig. 10.13c**      Age-earnings profiles for persons hired in 1980, by age when hired, saleswomen

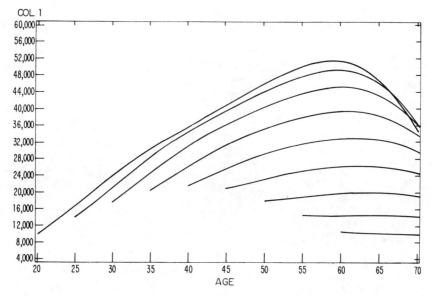

**Fig. 10.13d**     Age-earnings profiles for persons hired in 1980, by age when hired, male office workers

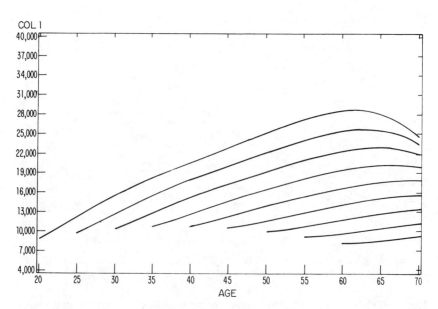

**Fig. 10.13e**     Age-earnings profiles for persons hired in 1980, by age when hired, female office workers

time of hire increase with age, but the bulk of the difference in earnings is accounted for by years of service in the firm. For example, persons who are 55 and just hired earn much less than those who are 55, but have been working for the firm since age 20. Finally, the decline in earnings for older workers is much greater for long-term employees than for those who have been hired recently.

Similar patterns apply to other employee groups, but with some significant variations. The earnings of male office workers at the time of hire vary greatly by age, increasing and then declining rapidly (fig. 10.13d). The importance of these profiles for our work is that future expected earnings depend in an important way on the age and years of service of an employee, and on the employee group.

In our prediction of earnings beyond 1984, we use the 1984 year dummy and add a 1.5 percent real wage growth factor; that is, the predicted earnings for year $t$ is the predicted earnings for 1984 times $(1.5)(t - 1984)$.

## 10.3  The Relationship between Retirement, Age, and Years of Service

In this section, the relationship of retirement to age and years of service is described. The intention is to consider the extent to which retirement behavior is consistent, by economic reasoning, with the budget constraints described in section 10.2. To do this, we consider in detail empirical hazard rates by age and years of service. These results will serve as a guide to future development and estimation of more formal models of retirement. They are the empirical regularities with which the models must be consistent. This extensive descriptive analysis supports several initial conclusions:

- The favorable early retirement benefits have a very strong effect on departures from the firm, increasing departure rates between ages 55 and 60 by possibly as much as 30 percentage points (e.g., from 14 to 44 percent).
- The loss in compensation due to negative pension accrual for many employees after age 60 and negative Social Security accrual after age 65 apparently also induces departure; only 58 percent of those employed at age 54 remain through age 59, and only 21 percent of those employed at 59 remain through 64. About half of the few remaining at 65 retire at that age.
- The special early retirement incentive offered in one year increased departure rates very substantially.

### 10.3.1  Empirical Hazard Rates

Hazard rates by age and years of service are shown for all employees combined in table 10.10. The yearly hazard rate is the proportion of

**Table 10.10**  Empirical Hazard Rates, by Age and Years of Service, All Employee Groups (percent)

| Age | ≤5 | 6–9 | 10 | 11–15 | 16–20 | 21–23 | 24 | 25 | 26 | 27 | 28 | 29 | 30 | 31+ |
|---|---|---|---|---|---|---|---|---|---|---|---|---|---|---|
| 40 | 15 | 8 | 5 | 7 | 4 | 3 | 0 | | | | | | | |
| 41 | 14 | 9 | 5 | 7 | 5 | 5 | 3 | 5 | | | | | | |
| 42 | 14 | 10 | 8 | 8 | 4 | 2 | 2 | 2 | 0 | 0 | | | | |
| 43 | 15 | 7 | 6 | 5 | 4 | 4 | 4 | 3 | 2 | 0 | 0 | 0 | | 0.5 |
| 44 | 13 | 8 | 5 | 7 | 3 | 2 | 3 | 1 | 1 | 1 | 0 | 0 | 0 | 0 |
| 45 | 11 | 7 | 5 | 6 | 6 | 4 | 3 | 1 | 4 | 2 | 3 | 5 | 0 | 0 |
| 46 | 12 | 9 | 3 | 5 | 3 | 4 | 4 | 1 | 0 | 5 | 2 | 2 | 0 | 0 |
| 47 | 14 | 8 | 8 | 5 | 4 | 3 | 3 | 4 | 4 | 4 | 0 | 4 | 2 | 2 |
| 48 | 12 | 7 | 5 | 6 | 4 | 4 | 2 | 5 | 1 | 2 | 4 | 2 | 3 | 0 |
| 49 | 14 | 9 | 4 | 7 | 4 | 3 | 5 | 1 | 1 | 1 | 1 | 2 | 0 | 0 |
| 50 | 14 | 8 | 4 | 6 | 4 | 3 | 3 | 2 | 2 | 1 | 1 | 3 | 2 | 3 |
| 51 | 14 | 9 | 3 | 5 | 3 | 3 | 5 | 2 | 3 | 4 | 2 | 2 | 2 | 3 |
| 52 | 11 | 7 | 5 | 6 | 4 | 4 | 4 | 4 | 2 | 4 | 1 | 3 | 6 | 5 |
| 53 | 12 | 7 | 4 | 7 | 4 | 3 | 3 | 3 | 3 | 2 | 3 | 3 | 3 | 6 |
| 54 | 11 | 7 | 4 | 6 | 4 | 2 | 4 | 2 | 2 | 3 | 1 | 0 | 1 | 3 |
| 55 | 9 | 5 | 4 | 11 | 9 | 11 | 13 | 10 | 13 | 11 | 12 | 7 | 9 | 9 |
| 56 | 11 | 6 | 6 | 12 | 11 | 12 | 7 | 8 | 11 | 11 | 12 | 16 | 14 | 12 |
| 57 | 12 | 10 | 1 | 11 | 8 | 9 | 10 | 8 | 9 | 9 | 3 | 14 | 11 | 11 |
| 58 | 13 | 10 | 2 | 8 | 8 | 12 | 13 | 11 | 15 | 15 | 9 | 10 | 13 | 12 |
| 59 | 7 | 10 | 2 | 17 | 8 | 11 | 17 | 14 | 14 | 14 | 9 | 10 | 12 | 15 |
| 60 | 9 | 9 | 3 | 15 | 12 | 19 | 16 | 17 | 20 | 16 | 20 | 15 | 19 | 26 |
| 61 | 9 | 7 | 2 | 16 | 17 | 15 | 19 | 12 | 25 | 16 | 23 | 21 | 24 | 30 |
| 62 | 11 | 15 | 7 | 27 | 34 | 37 | 34 | 33 | 38 | 40 | 42 | 34 | 30 | 41 |
| 63 | 14 | 18 | 4 | 33 | 35 | 37 | 43 | 35 | 43 | 41 | 62 | 33 | 47 | 40 |
| 64 | 5 | 8 | 3 | 36 | 33 | 34 | 18 | 32 | 26 | 27 | 42 | 53 | 41 | 34 |
| 65 | 12 | 35 | 45 | 57 | 52 | 54 | 44 | 55 | 57 | 70 | 50 | 54 | 69 | 59 |
| 66 | 26 | 17 | 25 | 16 | 16 | 43 | 50 | 16 | 20 | 25 | 38 | 33 | 9 | 24 |
| 67 | 13 | 28 | 18 | 32 | 17 | 29 | 0 | 14 | 21 | 0 | 13 | 33 | 50 | 21 |
| 68 | 13 | 50 | 50 | 15 | 25 | 11 | 0 | 50 | 0 | 29 | 0 | 0 | 0 | 12 |

Years of Service

those employed at the beginning of the year that retires—strictly speaking, leaves the firm—during the forthcoming year. Several aspects of the data stand out. There is substantial turnover in the first 9 years of employment, especially during the first 5 years. On average, about 15 percent of those employed 5 years or less leave in a given year. The table shows rates only for employees 40 and older. The departure rates are somewhat higher for younger workers, 16 or 17 percent for those employed 5 years or less and 10 to 12 percent for those employed 6 to 9 years. There is a sharp decline in departure rates at 10 years of service, when employees are about to become vested in the pension plan. Before the early retirement age, 55, the typical decline is from 8 or 9 to 4 or 5 percent. After 55, when vesting carries with it eligibility for early retirement, it is much sharper, often from 10 percent or more to 3 percent or less.

The availability of early retirement benefits at 55 apparently has a substantial effect on retirement. Before 55 departure rates are typically around 2 percent. At 55, they jump to 10 percent or more. It is important to notice that the departure rates stay at that level until age 60, when there is another jump in the rate of departure. The jump at 60 corresponds to the age at which pension accrual becomes negative for many employees. (For those with 25 or more years of service, benefits increase at a smaller percent per year. After age 60 with 30 years of service, there is no early retirement reduction; full retirement benefits are available.)

To understand the potential importance of the early retirement benefits, suppose that if it were not for this inducement, the departure rates would remain at 3 percent until age 60 instead of the 10 or 12 percent rates that are observed. (Notice that the departure rates for employees aged 55 to 61 who are in their tenth year of service—not yet vested and hence not eligible for early retirement benefits—are also 2 or 3 percent on average.) Departure at 3 percent per year would mean that 14 percent of those who were employed at 55 would have left before age 60. At a departure rate of 11 percent per year, 44 percent would leave between 55 and 59. Such a difference, even if only for a small proportion of all firms, can have a very substantial effect on aggregate labor force participation rates. It is in part the dramatic fall in labor force participation rates for the older population that has motivated research such as ours.

The jump in departure rates at 60, especially noticeable for persons with 25 or more years of service, has just been mentioned above. There is another sharp increase in departure rates at 62 when Social Security benefits are first available. (There is no sharp kink in the budget constraint at this age because of the actuarially fair increase in Social Security benefits if their receipt is postponed until age 65.) The increase at 62 is also noticeable for employees with less than 10 years of service and not yet vested in the firm pension plan. They can take Social Security benefits, of course.

Finally, there is a very sharp increase in the departure rate at age 65. At this age the loss in Social Security benefits with continued work induces a kink in the budget constraint. As described above, the budget constraint for many workers becomes essentially flat at this age, due to negative pension accruals and falling wage earnings, as well as the loss in Social Security wealth. The fall in wage earnings and pension wealth typically begins at an earlier age, as emphasized above. It is important to keep in mind that the large departure rates before 65 mean that most employees have left well before that age. Thus high departure rates at 65 indicate only that a large proportion of the few that continue work until 65 retire then. The cumulative hazard rates below highlight this point.

A more compact version of table 10.10 is shown in table 10.11 for salesmen. About 40.7 percent of employees are salesmen and women, about 56.2 percent are office workers, and only 3.1 percent are managers. Thus, for purposes of comparison, it is best to have in mind the accrual and budget constraint graphs for sales and office workers. These results confirm the findings for all employees discussed above. They may be summarized briefly:

**Table 10.11      Hazard Rates for Salesmen by Age and Years of Service**

| Age | <10 | 11–15 | 16–20 | 21–25 | 26–30 | — | — |
|-----|-----|-------|-------|-------|-------|---|---|
| | | | | Years of Service | | | |
| <50 | 19 | 9 | 5 | 4 | 3 | — | — |
| 50–54 | 14 | 7 | 4 | 3 | 3 | 2 | 0 |
| | | | | | | | |
| 55 | 11 | 14 | 9 | 11 | 12 | 15 | — |
| 56–59 | 14 | 13 | 9 | 11 | 11 | 14 | — |
| | | | | | | | |
| 60 | 11 | 12 | 14 | 19 | 14 | 29 | 35 |
| 61 | 13 | 12 | 13 | 13 | 19 | 32 | 28 |
| | | | | | | | |
| 62 | 12 | 27 | 32 | 38 | 36 | 52 | 35 |
| 63 | 20 | 28 | 33 | 36 | 47 | 48 | 56 |
| 64 | 0 | 37 | 36 | 30 | 36 | 38 | 28 |
| | | | | | | | |
| 65 | 34 | 56 | 51 | 50 | 49 | 47 | 43 |
| | | | | | | | |
| 66 | 17 | 28 | 10 | 34 | 18 | 16 | 12 |
| 67 | 20 | 16 | 25 | 21 | 8 | 5 | 18 |

- There is a large increase in the departure rates at the early retirement age of 55, but only for vested employees, those with at least 10 years of service. For employees with 16 or more years of service, the jump in departure rates increases very noticeably with age.
- The departure rates remain at these higher rates through age 59.
- At age 60, the departure rates increase very precipitously for persons with 30 or more years of service, for whom full benefits are available; there is no longer an early retirement reduction and subsequent pension accrual is negative.
- When Social Security benefits become available at 62, the departure rates increase very sharply, but apparently only for those who are vested in the firm plan, contrary to the results for all employees taken together.
- Finally, there is a large increase in departure rates at 65, after which Social Security accrual rates become strongly negative.

Cumulative hazard rates for all employees are shown in table 10.12 for three years, together with the rates by age. The cumulative rates are actually one minus the percent who have departed. These departure rates were obtained by calculating hazard rates over the next four years separately for persons who were age 50 in 1980, age 51 in 1980, . . . , and age 63 in 1980. Those who were age 50 in 1980 were 51 in 1981, 52 in 1983, etc. Thus these calculations yield hazard rates in different years for employees of the same age. In particular, given employment at age 50, the cumulative rates show the percent still employed at older ages. (The cumulative rates for those aged 50 are all based on the 1980 departure rate of 0.031. The rates for those aged 51 are all based on the 1981 rate of 0.033. The 1983 rate for those aged 52 is based on the 1982 rate. The rate for those who were 65 in 1981 is based on the 1983 rate.)

Note first that departure rates of employees who have been in the firm for only 8 to 10 years, and are not yet vested, are very low at every age, as emphasized above. And again, the increase in the departure rates at 55, 60, 62, and 65 stands out. Based on the 1981 and 1982 departure rates, only 48 percent of those employed at 50 would still be employed at 60, and then 17 percent of these would leave. Only 10 percent would remain until age 65 and then about 50 percent of these would leave.

The data also show the effect of a special early retirement incentive that was in effect in 1982 only. The incentive program provided a bonus to employees who were eligible for early retirement in 1982; that is, those who were vested and were 55 years old or older. The bonus was equivalent to three months salary for 55-year-old employees and increased to 12 months salary for 60 year olds. At age 65, the bonus was

**Table 10.12**      **Cumulative and Yearly Hazard Rates by Calendar Year, Years of Service (YOS), and Age**

| | Yearly Hazards | | | | | | |
|---|---|---|---|---|---|---|---|
| | 8–10 YOS | 11+ YOS | | | 11+YOS | | |
| Age | 1980 | 1981 | 1982 | 1983 | 1981 | 1982 | 1983 |
| 50 | 7 | 3 | | | 97 | 97 | 97 |
| 51 | 9 | 3 | | | 94 | 94 | 94 |
| 52 | 3 | 5 | 5 | 5 | 89 | 89 | 89 |
| 53 | 0 | 4 | 4 | 4 | 85 | 86 | 86 |
| 54 | 4 | 3 | 4 | 2 | 83 | 83 | 84 |
| | — | — | — | | — | — | — |
| 55 | 5 | 11 | 12 | 10 | 74 | 73 | 75 |
| 56 | 4 | 12 | 14 | 10 | 66 | 63 | 68 |
| 57 | 2 | 9 | 12 | 11 | 60 | 56 | 61 |
| 58 | 5 | 10 | 14 | 12 | 54 | 48 | 54 |
| 59 | 2 | 11 | 20 | 10 | 48 | 38 | 48 |
| | — | — | — | — | — | — | |
| 60 | 4 | 17 | 29 | 17 | 40 | 27 | 40 |
| 61 | 0 | 17 | 32 | 18 | 33 | 18 | 33 |
| | — | — | — | — | — | — | — |
| 62 | 8 | 36 | 48 | 31 | 21 | 10 | 23 |
| 63 | 14 | 37 | 54 | 37 | 13 | 5 | 14 |
| 64 | 11 | 29 | 49 | 26 | 10 | 2 | 11 |
| | — | — | — | — | — | — | — |
| 65 | 25 | 53 | 58 | 45 | 5 | 1 | 6 |

12 months salary for employees with 20 or fewer years of service and declined to 6 months salary for those with 30 to 39 years of service.

It is clear that the effect of the incentive was large. The departure rates for 1981 and for 1983 are virtually identical. But the rates were much higher in 1982. For example, the departure rate for 60 year olds was 17 percent in 1981 and in 1983, but 29 percent in 1982. For those age 63, the departure rate was 37 percent in 1981 and in 1983, but 54 percent in 1982. Of those employed at age 50, 40 percent would still have been employed after age 60 based on the 1981 and 1983 departure rates. Only 27 percent would remain after age 60 based on the 1982 rates.[7]

Even under the normal plan, only 10 percent of those employed at age 50 would still be employed at 65. Only 1 percent would remain until 65 with the special incentive.

## 10.4   Summary and Conclusions

The provisions of the pension plan in a large corporation have been described in detail. The implications of the provisions are described by pension accrual profiles. The pension accrual profiles are set forth together with standard age-earnings profiles and Social Security accrual profiles in the form of lifetime budget constraints. The plan provides very strong incentives to retire beginning at age 55. After age 65, negative pension accruals and negative Social Security accruals effectively impose almost a 100 percent tax rate on wage earnings for many employees of the firm.

Departure rates from the firm have been compared with economic incentives inherent in the plan provisions. It is clear from this descriptive analysis that the inducements in the plan provisions to retire early have had a very substantial effect on departure rates from the firm. Indeed over 50 percent of those employed by the firm at age 50 leave before 60 and 90 percent before age 65. The jumps in departure rates at specific ages coincide precisely with the discontinuities and kink points in the worker compensation profiles that result from the pension plan provisions together with wage earnings profiles and Social Security accrual.

A great deal of effort has been devoted to estimating the effect of Social Security provisions on labor force participation. In particular, Hausman and Wise (1985), Burtless (1986), and Hurd and Boskin (1984) have attempted to estimate the effect on labor force participation of the increases in Social Security benefits during the early 1970s. It would appear from the results here that the effects of these across-the-board increases in Social Security benefits are likely to be small relative to the effects of the private pension provisions. For example, it seems clear that shifting the age of early retirement from 55 to 60 would have a very dramatic effect on departure rates. Leaving the early retirement age at 55 but eliminating negative pension and Social Security accruals thereafter would apparently also have a substantial effect on retirement rates. Precise estimates of the effects of such changes will be made in future work.

# Notes

1. See Kotlikoff and Wise (1985, 1987).
2. The decline in this firm at age 65 is likely to be mild compared to that in many other firms in which the fall in pension accrual at age 65 is much greater than it is here. See Kotlikoff and Wise (1985, 1987).
3. For more algebraic detail on the calculation of pension wealth, see Kotlikoff and Wise (1985).
4. Managerial compensation is primarily in the form of salary, whereas the compensation of salespeople is in the form of commissions to a large extent. They may be more like self-employed or piece-rate workers. In particular, their earnings may be determined to a large extent by the number of hours that they

choose to work. This may also affect the relationship between compensation and retirement. Firm officials inform us, however, that most salespeople work only for the firm. To the extent that the number of hours that they work do not decline substantially with the wage, these graphs may reflect age-productivity profiles.

5. There should be no presumption that men and women classified by us as office workers are performing the same jobs. The classification does not assure that.

6. Simulated actual future earnings could be obtained by taking a random draw $\tilde{\eta}_{it}$ from the estimate distribution of $\eta$, $N(O, \hat{\sigma}_{\tilde{\eta}}^2)$, for each future year and using $E_{it} = e^{\hat{\mu}_{it} + \hat{a}_i} e^{\tilde{\eta}_{it}}$. If $E_{it}$ were used in equation (4) instead of $\ln E_{it}$, there is no need to use the nonlinearity correction.

7. This comparison may not be precise because the special incentive, were it to be prolonged, would alter the retirement rates prior to each of the ages considered in 1982.

# References

Burtless, Gary. 1986. Social Security, unanticipated benefit increases, and the timing of retirement. *Review of Economic Studies* 53 (October):781–805.

Hausman, Jerry, and David Wise. 1985. Social Security, health status, and retirement. In *Pensions, labor, and individual choice,* ed. D. Wise. Chicago: University of Chicago Press.

Hurd, Michael, and Michael Boskin. 1984. The effect of Social Security on retirement in the early 1970s. *Quarterly Journal of Economics* (November):767–90.

Kotlikoff, Laurence, and David Wise. 1985. Labor compensation and the structure of private pension plans: Evidence for contractual versus spot labor markets. In *Pensions, labor, and individual choice,* ed. D. Wise. Chicago: University of Chicago Press.

———. 1987. The incentive effects of private pension plans. In *Issues in pension economics,* ed. Z. Bodie, J. Shoven, and D. Wise. Chicago: University of Chicago Press.

# Comment    Ariel Pakes

Larry and David have demonstrated, I think convincingly, that pension plan provisions can influence retirement behavior. Indeed, the empirical results in this paper make it clear that, at least in the firm studied here, retirement is responsive to jumps in pension accruals, and that the extent of the response depends positively on the magnitude of the jump. On the other hand, it is not clear whether they (or anybody else) can

Ariel Pakes is an Associate Professor of Economics at the University of Wisconsin-Madison and a Research Associate of the National Bureau of Economic Research.

do as convincing a job on the second stage of the analysis, that is on obtaining interpretable estimates of the response coefficients of interest. To obtain such estimates will require a more detailed model. Since I have little to add to their descriptive work, I shall focus my comments on the modeling problems that are likely to arise in obtaining these estimates (even though many of these problems were noted in the presentation).

Models for stopping full-time employment, like all stopping models, should work off the differences between the perceived distributions of the stream of benefits from full-time employment and the benefits from the relevant alternatives. As other papers in this conference have illustrated, the relevant alternatives include both partial retirement and full-time leisure. There is, however, no information in this data on whether an individual who left full-time employment did so for partial retirement or for full-time leisure. Further, there is very little information available on individual characteristics. It would, therefore, be difficult to build a model which would allow us to determine the motivation for, and the benefits from, partial retirement from data and estimated parameters. Models which do not allow for partial retirement estimate the impact of pensions (and for that matter of Social Security) on retirement by comparing the benefits from full-time leisure to the benefits from full-time work. If partial retirement is an effective alternative, then the income differences the model attributes to "retiring" will be overstated, and responses to monetary incentives (such as to changes in pension accruals) will be inconsistently estimated. Moreover, when we consider the impact of pension schemes on labor force participation rates, the problems generated by this inconsistency will be compounded by the fact that many of the people we are counting as retired will in fact be employed—albeit only part of the time.

The age-earnings profiles estimated in this paper illustrate the confounding effects of retirement behavior on the interpretation of the parameters of interest. A stopping model of retirement behavior would predict that the people who are working at later ages are those whose returns from work (wages) are abnormally high (for those ages), while those who retire should have low returns. In the years where there is a lot of retirement we ought to find that this selection process increases the average wage of those continuing to work—even though every individual's wage profile may well be declining. Figure 10.1 illustrates this point. At age 55 there is a jump in pension accruals and a consequent sharp increase in the hazard for retiring. At age 62 there is a fall in pension accruals and a consequent prior increase in the retirement hazard. At both these ages Larry and David estimate an increase in the earnings-age profile. These increases may have little to do with the earnings-age profile of any individual in the sample. It is just that the retirees should be precisely those individuals whose earnings are low and falling. If we were to estimate an age-earnings profile in conjunction with a stopping model of retirement behavior, the model itself would account for the selection induced by the endogenous retirement decision, and we might well find a falling profile. Clearly, without such a model we should be very careful how we interpret the profile's estimated parameters.

A comment on the process assumed to generate earnings is also in order. The assumption made here is that the unobservable, or disturbance, component of (log) earnings consists of a time-invariant individual-specific "random" effect, $\mu_i$, plus an independent and identically distributed, $\eta_{i,t}$. Though this process has been used frequently in the past, I think it is inappropriate in the current context. It states that the unobservable component of earnings at age 60 has the same correlation with the unobserved component of earnings at age 59 as it does with the unobserved component of earnings at any other age (say 30). Though this may well be a good approximation for labor force participants in the prime of their working life, it is unlikely to be adequate in later ages when health and family status considerations are likely to play a dominant role in determining the value of these unobserved determinants of retirement behavior.

Use of the random-effect model will also create econometric problems. If $\tau_{R,i}$ is the random retirement time of individual $i$, and $P\{\tau_{R,i} = t\}$ designates the probability that $\tau_{R,i} = t$, then whatever model is eventually used will have an equation of the form:

$$P\{\tau_{R,i} = t\} = f(E_{it}, \tilde{E}_{it+\tau}, \ldots, \mathrm{PW}_{it}, \mathrm{PW}_{it+1}, \ldots; \beta),$$

where $E_{it}$ is earnings in year $t$, $\tilde{E}_{it+\tau}$ signifies parameters of the distribution of earnings in year $t + \tau$ given the information of year $t$, PW denotes pension wealth, and $\beta$ is a vector of parameters to be estimated. A crucial parameter of $\tilde{E}_{it+\tau}$ will be $\mu_i$. However, $\mu_i$ will only be consistently estimated as the number of observed time-periods per individual grows large (the usual asymptotics for panel data problems is in dimension $N$, the number of individuals). In short panels, $\mu_i$ will be estimated with error. This creates an errors in variables problem. Moreover, since $P\{\tau_{R,i} = t\}$ is a probability statement, $f(\cdot)$ must be nonlinear, so the error must be inside a nonlinear function. To consistently estimate the parameters of a nonlinear errors in variables problem we need to know the entire distribution of the error and then integrate out with respect to it. Though this may be feasible, it seems unduly difficult, especially when the specification causing the problem is so much in doubt. The authors may well be better off making a more conventional Markov assumption on the disturbance in log-earnings.

One final suggestion. The authors correctly stress that there is a great deal of variation in the provisions of pension plans. One question that arises and that these data seem, therefore, particularly well suited to analyze is: What forces underlie the structure of the pension plan? Indeed, when we do finally obtain adequate estimates of the effect of pension provisions on retirement and then experiment with the effects of alternative pension schemes, we will also want to ask ourselves what effects will changes in the pension scheme have on alternative aspects of individual behavior. The other aspects of behavior that pensions have marked effects on are likely to be precisely the same aspects that generated the shape of the current pension provisions.

# 11    The Timing of Retirement: A Comparison of Expectations and Realizations

B. Douglas Bernheim

## 11.1  Introduction

Modern life-cycle theory is based upon the premise that consumers think seriously and coherently about the relatively distant and uncertain future. While the empirical validity of this premise is controversial, existing evidence is either highly indirect or anecdotal. To resolve this controversy, it is necessary to conduct direct comparisons of consumers' plans and expectations with eventual realizations.

Previous empirical work on household expectations has focused primarily on short-run inflation (see Huizinga 1980, Curtin 1982, Gramlich 1983, and Papadia 1982; Aiginger 1979 considers a somewhat broader range of variables). Accordingly, these studies shed very little light on the issue of whether consumers form accurate expectations and successful economic plans over relatively long time horizons.

In a separate paper (Bernheim 1988), I have studied the accuracy of pre-retirement expectations concerning Social Security benefits. I found that while survey responses to questions about expected benefits contain a relatively high level of noise, there is nevertheless strong evidence that consumers do think seriously about future events. While consumers do not form expectations on the basis of all available information, they do appear to be reasonably competent at making relatively accurate forecasts conditional upon the information that they do use. Indeed, the data broadly suggest that consumers correctly

B. Douglas Bernheim is the Harold J. Hines Professor of Risk Management at the J. L. Kellogg graduate School of Management, Northwestern University, and a Research Associate of the National Bureau of Economic Research.

The author would like to thank the National Institute on Aging for financial support. Laurence Levin provided invaluable research assistance. The opinions expressed here are those of the author and should not be attributed to any other individual or organization.

anticipated the general effects of legislative action during the early 1970s, contrary to the supposition of most previous authors (see, e.g., Hurd and Boskin 1981; Anderson, Burkhauser, and Quinn 1986; and Burtless 1986).

In the current paper, I employ data drawn from the Social Security Administration's Retirement History Survey (RHS) to study the accuracy of expectations concerning the timing of retirement. This is an important complement to my earlier work, in that Social Security benefits are largely determined by exogenous events, while retirement is a fundamental decision variable. Accordingly, the emphasis here is on the accuracy of economic *plans,* rather than pure expectations. While many authors have previously studied determinants of the retirement decision (see the surveys by Hurd 1983, and Mitchell and Fields 1982), all have simply assumed that workers make systematic and viable retirement plans. There is no previous test of this proposition.

The major findings of this study are as follows.

1. Survey responses to questions about expected dates of retirement reflect modes, rather than means. That is, consumers report the most likely date of retirement, rather than the mean date, given subjective probabilities. This distinction is extremely important, since the distribution of actual retirement dates for a fixed expectation is highly skewed. Unlike the case of Social Security benefits, the evidence does not support the view that consumers report noisy measures of expectations.

2. Most individuals are reasonably competent at forming relatively accurate expectations about the timing of retirement. Alternatively, consumers apparently form serious economic plans and ordinarily stick to them. Perhaps surprisingly, there is once again very little evidence to support the view that expectations were abnormally inaccurate during periods in which Social Security benefits enjoyed significant statutory increases.

3. The accuracy of expectations differs systematically by population subgroup. In contrast to my findings for Social Security benefits, I find that men form more accurate retirement expectations than women, although single women do appear to gain relative accuracy as retirement approaches. Married women are particularly prone to discover that they must work longer than expected. Comparatively wealthy individuals tend to make somewhat more accurate forecasts, but education does not improve predictive skill. Some evidence also suggests that workers with mandatory retirement dates typically retire much sooner than expected, perhaps because they suppose erroneously that alternative employment will be easy to find.

Work by Anderson, Burkhauser, and Quinn (1986) has also employed the RHS data on retirement expectations. Their object was to use this data in an analysis of behavior rather than to identify properties of reported expectations, as in the current paper. My findings are at odds with the implicit assumptions upon which these authors based their behavioral analysis, and therefore they call their results into question. Hall and Johnson (1980) have also studied retirement expectations, but their object was to model the formation of plans rather than to compare these plans with later realizations.

This paper is organized as follows. Section 11.2 discusses some alternative hypotheses about the nature of reported expectations concerning the timing of retirement. I describe the data in section 11.3. Section 11.4 tests the view that individuals report mean realizations given probabilistic beliefs. In section 11.5, I consider the hypothesis that respondents report modal beliefs, i.e., most likely dates of retirement. Finding the evidence favorable, I proceed to a comparison of various population subgroups in different survey years.

## 11.2  The Alternative Hypotheses

When an individual is asked to report his expected date of retirement, what does his answer represent? Survey questions about expectations are unfortunately ambiguous and admit several possible interpretations. Yet if we are to make valid use of these data in any behavioral context, it is essential to resolve this issue.

One possibility is that the typical individual reports the mean of some subjective probability distribution. It is useful to set up this hypothesis formally. Let $R$ be the individual's actual date of retirement. At some time $t$, he has access to information, $I(t)$, which he uses to form subjective beliefs about the timing of retirement. Let $p[r|I(t)]$ denote the subjective probability that the individual will retire at date $r$, given available information at time $t$, and let $ER(t)$ denote his reported expectation at time $t$. The first hypothesis is that

$$(1) \qquad ER(t) = E[R \mid I(t)],$$

where $E[.]$ indicates a mathematical expectation based on the probability distribution $p[.]$.

Unless we place some additional restriction on the subjective probability distribution, this proposition is not testable. My strategy is to test it jointly with the hypothesis of rational expectations. Specifically, if one assumes that the subjective probability distribution $p[.]$ coincides with the objective distribution, then equation (1) suggests a regression of $R$ on an intercept, $ER(t)$, and $I(t)$. Under the joint hypotheses, the intercept and coefficients of $I(t)$ should be 0, while the coefficient of $ER(t)$ should be 1. It is, of course, essential that one only include informational variables that the individual actually used in forming his expectations. Since this is difficult to establish a priori, it is advisable to conduct a weak form of this test by omitting the $I(t)$ entirely.

My study of expected Social Security benefits provided strong support for the analog of this first hypothesis, and one might therefore expect to find the data supportive here as well. Yet it is essential to understand that retirement is a very different kind of event than the realization of Social Security benefits. Many workers form extremely specific retirement plans, which they intend to follow barring unforeseen circumstances. In contrast, workers may have only "ballpark" notions about their Social Security benefits. Accordingly, it is easily conceivable that, when asked about their expectations, individuals report means for Social Security benefits but report the most likely outcome for date of retirement.

This discussion leads naturally to the second hypothesis, which is that measured expected dates of retirement reflect modes of subjective distributions. Formally,

$$(2) \qquad ER(t) = \text{argmax}_r \ p[r \mid I(t)].$$

Once again, this proposition is not testable in the absence of further restrictions on the subjective distribution. As before, my strategy is to test it jointly with the hypothesis of rational expectations. Assuming that $p[.]$ coincides with the true objective distribution, one can compare measured expectations with modal realizations.

While these two hypotheses certainly do not exhaust all conceivable alternatives (e.g., perhaps individuals report medians, or pure noise),[1] I take them to be the most interesting possibilities.

## 11.3  Data

The data for this study are drawn from the Social Security Administration's Retirement History Survey (RHS), which followed a sample of retirement-aged households (58 to 63 years old in 1969) for a period of 10 years, beginning in 1969. Each household was surveyed once every two years (1969, 1971, 1973, 1975, and 1979). Although the initial wave included more than 11,000 households, there was substantial attrition over successive waves.

Each working respondent reported his or her expected age of retirement in every survey year, with the exception of married women, who were not asked this question in 1973. Using the respondent's age, I transformed this variable into ERET, the expected date of retirement. Survey responses to questions about expected retirement were extremely sparse in 1977 and 1979 (primarily because most of the sample had already retired by 1977); I therefore focus on expectations reported in the first four survey waves.

The primary advantage of the RHS is that it allows the analyst to identify realizations by employing data from subsequent survey waves. While the identification of a date of retirement is usually problematic, here it poses few difficulties. In the current context, it is not necessary or even desirable to obtain a conceptually "correct" measure of retirement. When an individual reports an expected date of retirement, he may well have in mind some idiosyncratic notion of what retirement means. However, unless he changes his notion over time, one can assume that self-reported retirement refers to the same potentially idiosyncratic event. Accordingly, I use self-reported retirement to construct RET, my measure of the eventual realization.

Unfortunately, data on self-reported retirement are somewhat incomplete. Although individuals do report whether or not they consider themselves retired in each survey year, they are not asked to indicate exactly when retirement took place. This creates a problem in that surveys were administered in alternate years. In practice, I calculate RET as follows. First, I identify the first survey year in which the respondent reported himself to be retired. Second, for this same survey year, I determine the date at which the respondent left his last job. If this falls within the previous two years, I take it to be his date of retirement. If it does not (typically because of missing information), I determine the date at which the respondent began to receive Social Security benefits. If this falls within the previous two years, I take it to be his date of retirement. If it does not, I simply assume that he retired midway between the surveys.

In conjunction with testing the first set of joint hypotheses, I relate forecast errors to available information in order to identify the kinds of information that individuals either ignore or process incorrectly. I consider a large number of informational variables, which I group into three categories.

The first category contains variables which measure other reported expectations. The inclusion of these variables allows me to determine whether or not individuals have internally consistent expectations, in the sense that they base all expectations on the same set of information. Definitions of specific variables follow:

ESS: expected Social Security benefits
EOI: expected retirement income, other than Social Security

Data on expectations are, of course, incomplete—many individuals who report an expected date of retirement do not, for example, report expected Social Security benefits. Accordingly, I also use dummy variables, which equal 1 if the individual reports the associated expectation, and 0 otherwise. I refer to the dummies corresponding to the two variables listed above as DSS and DOI.

The second category includes a single variable, which is the individual's current Social Security entitlement, CSS, defined as the level of benefits he would receive under current law if he retired immediately. CSS is, theoretically, part of each individual's information set, in that it depends only upon his own past earnings history and upon current law (which is public information). My previous study of Social Security benefits suggested that individuals fail to use much of the information contained in CSS; since it is natural to suppose that workers adjust retirement plans upon learning more about Social Security entitlements, this information could be correlated with the forecast error for date of retirement as well.

The third and final category includes various demographic variables and other household characteristics which might be useful in predicting retirement. The list of variables includes:

MAR:       a dummy variable, indicating whether or not the respondent is married (1 = married, 0 = other)
DIV:        a dummy variable, indicating whether or not the respondent is divorced (1 = divorced, 0 = other)
WID:        a dummy variable, indicating whether or not the respondent is a widow or widower (1 = widow or widower, 0 = other)
AGE:        the respondent's age
SAGE:      the respondent's spouse's age
ED:         the respondent's level of educational attainment (measured in number of years)
SED:        the respondent's spouse's level of educational attainment
W:          the household's net wealth (including financial assets, businesses, and real property)
GH:         a dummy variable, indicating whether or not the respondent reports his health as being better than average for his age (1 = better, 0 = other)
BH:         a dummy variable, indicating whether or not the respondent reports his health as being worse than average for his age (1 = worse, 0 = other)
KIDS:       number of children
COMPRET:   a dummy variable, indicating whether or not the respondent's employer maintains a compulsory retirement age (1 = yes, 0 = no)
MOVE:       a dummy variable, indicating whether or not the respondent has moved within the past two years.

Before passing on to analysis of the data, it is important to discuss two potential problems. The first concerns sample selection biases. I drop observations from the analysis for three reasons: 1) the respondent fails to report an expected date of retirement, 2) the reported date is obviously nonsensical (e.g., it precedes the date at which it was reported), or 3) the household disappeared from the RHS prior to retirement. Note that the first two items both reflect household characteristics that are known when the respondent makes his forecast. Since the forecasts are then presumably conditioned on this information, no sample selection biases arise. The third item (subsequent attrition) is potentially problematic. I return to this issue in section 11.4, where I propose and implement a statistical correction.

The second problem concerns the non-independence of realizations. In a short panel such as the RHS, forecast errors are probably correlated across observations due to "macro" events. Since the 1970s witnessed several large and potentially unexpected real increases in Social Security benefits, this problem is potentially severe. In particular, real Social Security benefits increased by 4.2 percent in January 1970, 4.8 percent in January 1971, and 14.1 percent in September 1972. In addition, benefits were "double indexed" for inflation from 1975 to 1977. If, as suggested by many analysts, unanticipated increases in Social Security benefits caused many workers to retire unexpectedly early, then we might well find that expectations were systematically off during this period. On the other hand, the major benefit increases were primarily concentrated in a few years (especially 1972). It should be possible to shed some light on the question of whether these changes were indeed unanticipated by looking for evidence of systematic forecast errors at those points in time.

### 11.4  The Mean Value Hypothesis

I begin formal analysis of the data by comparing expectations to mean realization in order to test the first hypothesis discussed in section 11.2. Table 11.1 contains some highly revealing summary statistics for married men. For each survey year, I have grouped observations by common values of ERET. For each group, I report four things: the difference between the average date of actual retirement and ERET, the standard deviation of the retirement date, the mean squared forecast error, and the number of observations.

The most striking feature of table 11.1 is that there is very little relationship between ERET and the average date of retirement. To be sure, those with higher values of ERET tend to retire later, on average. However, the mean date of retirement coincides with ERET in few if any cells. Indeed, in 19 out of 20 cells one can reject the hypothesis

**Table 11.1**          **Expectations and Mean Realizations for Married Men**

| ERET | Survey Year | | | |
|------|------|------|------|------|
|      | 1969 | 1971 | 1973 | 1975 |
| 1969 | 1.9 | — | — | — |
|      | 2.0 | | | |
|      | 7.6 | | | |
|      | 157 | | | |
| 1970 | 1.3 | — | — | — |
|      | 1.9 | | | |
|      | 5.3 | | | |
|      | 311 | | | |
| 1971 | 0.9 | 1.2 | | |
|      | 1.9 | 1.6 | | |
|      | 4.5 | 4.1 | | |
|      | 411 | 281 | | |
| 1972 | 0.7 | 0.9 | | |
|      | 2.1 | 1.6 | | |
|      | 5.0 | 3.5 | | |
|      | 375 | 367 | | |
| 1973 | −0.1 | 0.2 | 1.0 | — |
|      | 2.0 | 1.5 | 1.3 | |
|      | 4.0 | 2.4 | 2.6 | |
|      | 290 | 309 | 198 | |
| 1974 | −0.5 | −0.2 | 0.6 | |
|      | 2.1 | 1.6 | 1.4 | |
|      | 4.9 | 2.8 | 2.2 | |
|      | 240 | 241 | 225 | |
| 1975 | −1.1 | −0.5 | 0.3 | 0.7 |
|      | 2.1 | 1.8 | 1.4 | 0.9 |
|      | 5.7 | 3.3 | 1.9 | 1.3 |
|      | 263 | 255 | 253 | 135 |
| 1976 | −2.0 | −1.7 | −0.3 | 0.3 |
|      | 2.3 | 1.8 | 1.3 | 0.9 |
|      | 9.4 | 5.9 | 1.7 | 0.9 |
|      | 112 | 93 | 78 | 76 |

that the mean date equals ERET with at least 95 percent confidence.[2] Roughly speaking, it appears that a one-year change in the expected date is associated with slightly less than a one-half year change in the average realized date. The implications of equation (1) are strongly contradicted.

Other aspects of table 11.1 are also puzzling. The standard deviation of RET does not appear to be higher for groups that intend to retire in the more distant future, despite the fact that information should improve as retirement grows more imminent. Similarly, mean squared forecast errors do not rise monotonically with ERET. Yet standard errors and mean squared forecast errors both fall monotonically between successive survey years. The mean value hypothesis provides no clue as to the source of this trend.

As remarked in section 11.3, these calculations suffer from potential sample selection biases. Specifically, I have dropped from my sample all individuals who leave the survey before retiring. Unless attrition is associated with earlier-than-normal retirement, the (objective) expected date of retirement for such individuals, conditional upon ERET and observed behavior, exceeds the expectation based upon ERET alone. Accordingly, the omission of these observations probably biases the estimated mean retirement date downward.

To correct for this problem, one must know something about the retirement behavior of individuals after they leave the sample. By definition, this is unobservable. Consequently, it is necessary to maintain an ancillary hypothesis. In order to make some illustrative calculations, I assume that attrition is not systematically related to subsequent retirement.[3] This assumption allows me to correct for sample selection as follows. For each subsample (characterized by survey year and ERET), I calculate hazard rates for retirement in each year, i.e., the number of individuals retiring in that year divided by the total number of individuals remaining from the original subsample (including those who subsequently left the sample before retiring). Under my maintained hypothesis, this yields a consistent estimate of the true population hazard rate. From these rates, one can then reconstruct the true distribution of retirement dates.

In practice, relatively few individuals who met my other selection criteria actually left the sample before retiring. As a result, the impact of this correction was extremely small. For most cells, the mean of the corrected distribution exceeded the uncorrected mean by 0.1 year; in a few cases the difference was 0.2 years, and in a few others it was virtually zero. The corrected distributions strongly resembled the uncorrected distributions, and indeed the modes did not differ in any cell. Thus, I conclude that the sample selection bias is of little consequence. Furthermore, I suspect that the correction used here overstates the bias, in that attrition is probably correlated with earlier-than-normal retirement.

In light of the results in table 11.1, it should hardly be surprising that a regression of RET on ERET produces extremely negative results. Coefficient estimates appear in equation 1 of table 11.2. These results are based on expectations reported in 1971 but are representative of other years as well. I have chosen to report results for 1971 only because the data for that year are somewhat superior (in 1969, the ESS variable, used below, is flawed; in 1973, ERET is not available for married women; in 1975, the total data sample is much smaller). Note that the intercept is non-zero and dwarfs its standard error. The coefficient of ERET is

Table 11.2    Regression Results for 1971

| | Equation Number | | | |
| | 1 | 2 | 3 | 4 |
|---|---|---|---|---|
| Technique | OLS | IV | IV | IV |
| Instruments | None | Set #1 | Set #2 | Set #3 |
| Intercept | 56.5 | 45.2 | 20.7 | 37.1 |
| | (1.3) | (13.1) | (6.22) | (3.44) |
| ERET | 0.234 | 0.374 | 0.722 | 0.499 |
| | (0.018) | (0.179) | (0.085) | (0.047) |
| $R^2$ | 0.080 | 0.002 | 0.036 | 0.055 |

far below unity and is estimated very precisely. Formally, this signals a resounding rejection of the null hypothesis.

Yet one should not be too hasty in discarding the mean value hypothesis. I obtained similar negative findings in my analysis of expectations concerning Social Security benefits, but noted that these could be attributable to "noisy" measurement of the expectations variable. Formal analysis bore this conjecture out. It is therefore advisable to investigate the same possibility in the current context.

The classical remedy for measurement error is instrumental variables. In the current context, a variable is a valid instrument if it belongs to the information set on which the individual based his expectation. Unfortunately, the identity of this set is known only to the individual. Accordingly, one must maintain the hypothesis that individuals do use certain kinds of information in order to conduct the test.

The evidence in my previous study supported the view that individuals use the same information to form all of their expectations. This suggests that other expectations (ESS, EOI) are valid instruments. Of course, these variables may also be measured with error, but this is of no consequence as long as the measurement errors are uncorrelated. Equation 2 in table 11.2 provides estimated coefficients, where the expectational variables have been used as instruments. While the estimates are somewhat less precise than those obtained through OLS, the overall picture is unchanged.

For completeness, I have included two additional regressions, using the other two sets of informational variables as instruments. One can think of these regressions as reflecting alternative hypotheses about the kinds of information that workers actually use when constructing their forecasts. The results are uniformly negative. I obtain the most favorable estimates by using CSS as an instrument (equation 3). However, my previous study clearly established that individuals do not make use of all the information contained in CSS; it is therefore an unsuitable instrument.

These results contrast with my findings for expectations about Social Security benefits. The statistical failure of the mean value hypothesis cannot in this case be traced to the presence of measurement error. Upon reflection, this is hardly surprising. Since individuals probably do not have very precise notions about their future Social Security benefits, it stands to reason that they will report "ballpark" figures. However, it seems likely that most workers form very specific plans about the timing of retirement, particularly as it becomes more imminent. It is difficult to understand why an individual would report that he intends to retire at age 63, if in fact he plans to do so at age 65.

It is, of course, possible that the negative results in table 11.2 all stem from a failure to identify appropriate instruments. I therefore present one final set of estimates in table 11.3. Here, I have regressed the forecast error (RET − ERET) on the full complement of informational variables. This procedure yields consistent estimates even if ERET is measured with error (unfortunately, it precludes us from testing the theory by examining the coefficient of ERET). If the mean value hypothesis is correct, then one can determine the kinds of information that individuals either ignore or use improperly by examining the coefficient estimates. Note first that the coefficients of the expectational variables are not significantly different from zero. This finding validates

**Table 11.3     Forecast Error Regression, 1971**

| Variable | Coefficient | Variable | Coefficient |
|---|---|---|---|
| Intercept | −11.3 | $ED/10^3$ | −0.59 |
|  | (2.7) |  | (7.02) |
| $ESS/10^5$ | 6.02 | $SPED/10^3$ | −5.37 |
|  | (8.70) |  | (8.47) |
| DSS | −0.197 | $W/10^7$ | 9.06 |
|  | (0.215) |  | (7.39) |
| $EOI/10^5$ | 1.60 | GH | −0.219 |
|  | (6.59) |  | (0.112) |
| DOI | −0.121 | PH | 0.082 |
|  | (0.149) |  | (0.174) |
| $CSS/10^5$ | −1.60 | $KIDS/10^2$ | 0.06 |
|  | (6.59) |  | (2.65) |
| AGE | 0.195 | COMPRET | −0.847 |
|  | (0.044) |  | (0.125) |
| $SPAGE/10^3$ | −6.04 | MOVE | 0.301 |
|  | (7.62) |  | (0.182) |
| MAR | 0.653 | $R^2$ | 0.051 |
|  | (0.484) |  |  |
| DIV | −0.147 | Observations | 1919 |
|  | (0.303) |  |  |
| WID | 0.306 |  |  |
|  | (0.242) |  |  |

the use of these variables as instruments, and strengthens the conclusion that my negative results are not attributable to measurement error. Variables appearing with statistically significant coefficients include AGE, GH, and COMPRET. The last of these is particularly interesting, since it suggests that workers at jobs with mandatory retirement ages tend to believe that they will be able to continue working longer than they actually can. However, I caution that this conclusion is based upon a suspect empirical specification, in that my findings are generally unfavorable to the mean value hypothesis.

## 11.5    The Modal Value Hypothesis

I now turn to the possibility that respondents report their most likely dates of retirement, rather than mean dates. To investigate this hypothesis, I group observations by common values of ERET for each survey year and compute the modal realization for each group. Table 11.4 presents results for married men. This table contains 20 cells, identified by the survey year and value of ERET. In each cell, I report (in order) the modal value of RET minus ERET, the fraction of the group for which RET and ERET coincide, the fraction of the group for which RET is within one year of ERET, and the total number of observations.

The most striking aspect of table 11.4 is that the modal realization coincides with ERET in 16 out of 20 cells. In the four remaining cases, the mode differs from ERET by only a single year, and ERET is the second most common outcome, lagging the mode by a relatively small margin. Since ERET exceeds the mode in exactly half (two) of these cases, there is no indication of systematic bias.

One can also obtain some feeling for the accuracy of reported expectations by examining the second and third entries in each cell. I caution against placing too much emphasis on the fraction of respondents for whom RET and ERET coincide exactly. An individual who is 62 years old in 1969 and who reports that he intends to retire when 65 could plan to leave his job in either 1971, 1972, or 1973, depending upon his exact date of birth. Since it is impossible to identify the month during which an individual retires, I cannot adjust for this ambiguity. Accordingly, it is more appropriate to examine the fraction of individuals for which RET differs from ERET by at most one year. Note that as long as individuals do not intend to retire too far in the future, expectations are highly accurate; in all 16 cells for which ERET exceeds the survey year by four years or less, more than 60 percent of the respondents retired within one year of ERET.

As an individual approaches retirement, he presumably forms his expectation on the basis of more complete information. We would

**Table 11.4        Expectations and Model Realizations for Married Men**

| ERET | Survey Year | | | |
|---|---|---|---|---|
|  | 1969 | 1971 | 1973 | 1975 |
| 1969 | 1 | — | — | — |
|  | 0.26 |  |  |  |
|  | 0.61 |  |  |  |
|  | 157 |  |  |  |
| 1970 | 0 | — | — | — |
|  | 0.39 |  |  |  |
|  | 0.65 |  |  |  |
|  | 311 |  |  |  |
| 1971 | 0 | 0 | — | — |
|  | 0.28 | 0.43 |  |  |
|  | 0.67 | 0.75 |  |  |
|  | 411 | 281 |  |  |
| 1972 | 0 | 0 | — | — |
|  | 0.29 | 0.44 |  |  |
|  | 0.57 | 0.74 |  |  |
|  | 375 | 367 |  |  |
| 1973 | −1 | 0 | 0 | — |
|  | 0.22 | 0.32 | 0.44 |  |
|  | 0.60 | 0.79 | 0.79 |  |
|  | 290 | 309 | 198 |  |
| 1974 | 0 | 0 | 0 | — |
|  | 0.26 | 0.32 | 0.47 |  |
|  | 0.50 | 0.60 | 0.80 |  |
|  | 240 | 241 | 225 |  |
| 1975 | 1 | 0 | −1 | 0 |
|  | 0.18 | 0.24 | 0.29 | 0.47 |
|  | 0.53 | 0.64 | 0.80 | 0.85 |
|  | 263 | 255 | 253 | 135 |
| 1976 | 0 | 0 | 0 | 0 |
|  | 0.22 | 0.23 | 0.39 | 0.62 |
|  | 0.38 | 0.42 | 0.66 | 0.84 |
|  | 112 | 93 | 78 | 76 |

therefore expect the accuracy of his forecast to improve. It is possible to examine this prediction in two different ways. First, one can investigate the relationship between ERET and accuracy during any survey year by reading down columns. While accuracy does not decline monotonically with the expected date of retirement, there is a general tendency for it to fall. Second, one can examine the relationship between accuracy and the survey date for any given value of ERET by reading across rows. Note that in 23 of 24 possible pairwise comparisons (12 for fractions with RET = ERET, 12 for fractions with RET within one year of ERET), accuracy improves when the question is posed at a later date. In the one remaining case, it is simply unchanged. This finding provides striking confirmation for the view that information improves as individuals approach retirement.

An additional feature of table 11.4 merits comment. Let $T$ denote the survey year. Fix $t$, and consider individuals who expect to retire in year $T + t$. There is a strong tendency for the accuracy of expectations to rise with $T$ (to see this, read table 11.4 diagonally). The reason for this phenomenon is not immediately obvious. At first, one might suppose that, given $t$ (expected length of time until the event of interest), the date of reporting should not affect accuracy. However, one must bear in mind that average age is greater in later survey years. This causes significant compression of the retirement distribution, which leads in turn to greater accuracy. This observation underscores an important point: one should not assume that the shape of the conditional distribution is invariant with respect to either ERET or age. I will return to this point shortly.

Table 11.4 also sheds some light on the question of whether unanticipated changes in Social Security benefits during the early 1970s caused many workers to retire earlier than expected. Recall that by far the largest real benefit increase took place in 1972. If this change induced substantial early retirement, we would expect to see abnormal deviations from retirement plans during this period. There is little evidence of this in table 11.4. A substantial number of respondents in both 1969 and 1971 reported that they expected to retire after 1972. In 6 of the 8 relevant cells, the modal expectation still coincides with ERET. For those reporting ERET = 1975 in 1969, the modal realization was actually *after* 1975, not before. Only for those reporting ERET = 1973 in 1969 was the modal realization less than ERET, and indeed in this case 1972 was the most frequent date of retirement. Note, however, that 1969 forecasts for those with ERET = 1973 are only slightly less accurate than 1971 forecasts for those with ERET = 1975 (also 4 years in the future). Note also that 1971 forecasts for those with ERET = 1973 are actually more accurate than either 1973 forecasts for those with ERET = 1975, or 1969 forecasts for those with ERET = 1971 (both also 2 years in the future). Together, these observations suggest that changes in benefit levels did not induce substantial early retirement for individuals who had expected to stop working in 1973.

The substantial divergence of means and modes (tables 11.1 and 11.4) suggests that the conditional distributions of retirement dates may be highly skewed. This supposition is in fact correct. Figures 11.1 and 11.2 illustrate the distribution of retirement dates by ERET for 1969. One can see that when ERET is low, the conditional distribution is skewed to the right; as ERET rises, the skew shifts to the left. If reported expectations represent modes rather than means, this pattern is natural. Those expecting to retire very soon will, if surprised, generally retire later, and those expecting to retire late will, if surprised, generally retire sooner. This explains why the mean moves so much less than the mode, as noted in tables 11.1 and 11.4.

Failure to recognize this pattern can easily lead to misinterpretation of the data. Consider for example the study by Anderson, Burkhauser, and Quinn (1986). These authors examined the relationship between unexpected deviations from retirement plans and unexpected changes in Social Security benefits. They calculated the latter variable by comparing actual benefits available in the year of expected retirement to the level of benefits that would have been available had the 1969 statutes been adjusted for cost of living only. Through multinomial logit analysis, they found that respondents who experienced larger unexpected increases in Social Security benefits were much more prone to retire earlier than planned. Yet it now seems likely that this finding is merely an artifact of the data. Note that the authors' measure of unexpected benefit increases is primarily determined by ERET; the later the respondent expects to retire, the more the 1969 legislation will understate benefits available in the year of expected retirement. Furthermore, the pattern of skewness implies that higher values of ERET are associated with a greater frequency of unexpected early retirement. Combining these two observations leads one to expect a strong positive association between unexpected benefits and early retirement, even in the absence of a behavioral response. It is therefore conceivable that the finding is entirely spurious.

In fact, figures 11.1 and 11.2 provide only a very slight indication that the 1972 benefit changes may have induced some early retirement. In particular, the distributions for ERET = 1969, 1973, and 1975 exhibit somewhat higher frequencies for 1972 than one might ordinarily expect. However, the pattern is certainly far from overwhelming.

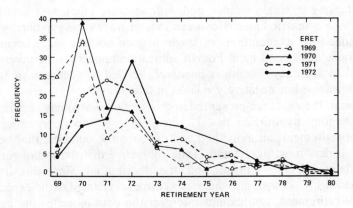

**Fig. 11.1**    Distribution of RET by ERET, 1969, part 1

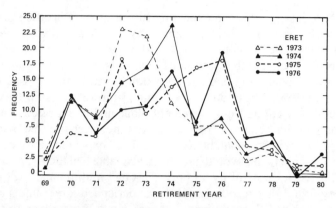

**Fig. 11.2**     Distribution of RET by ERET, 1969, part 2

As a final step, I provide a comparison of expectations and realizations for various population subgroups, including married men, married women, single men, single women, widowers, widows, married men with high wealth, married men with low wealth, married men with high levels of educational attainment, and married men with low levels of educational attainment. I present results in tables 11.5 through 11.8, which correspond to each of four different survey years (1969 through 1975). Several consistent patterns emerge. First, married women form the least accurate expectations and are most likely to work longer than planned. Lower accuracy results in part from the fact that women tend to be younger and therefore further from retirement than their husbands. However, even if one compensates for this by, for example, comparing married men in 1969 to married women in 1975, the pattern is still evident. Second, there is a general tendency for single individuals, widows, and widowers to retire earlier than expected more frequently than married individuals. Third, in early survey waves the expectations of single women and widows were much less accurate than those of married men. However, in later waves this gap narrowed, and indeed the expectations of single women became more accurate than those of married men. Fourth, education appears to be inversely related to accuracy. Wealth is positively related to accuracy in early survey waves, but negatively related in later waves.

Overall, the evidence presented in this section is strongly consistent with the joint hypotheses that 1) when asked to report an expected date of retirement, an individual will describe the outcome that he or she considers most likely, and 2) the subjective distribution of retirement dates coincides with the objective distribution. Since this distribution is highly skewed, and since the skewness is related to the expected date of retirement, one cannot interpret the data as reflecting mean retirement dates. Finally, there is little or no evidence to support the

**Table 11.5 Expectations and Realizations by Subgroup, 1969**

| Subgroup | Number of Observations | Mean of ERET | Fraction with RET = ERET | Fraction with RET = ERET ± 1 | Fraction with RET < ERET − 1 | Fraction with RET > ERET + 1 |
|---|---|---|---|---|---|---|
| Married men | 2,240 | 72.5 | 0.259 | 0.570 | 0.232 | 0.198 |
| Married women | 482 | 74.8 | 0.154 | 0.361 | 0.247 | 0.392 |
| Single men | 73 | 71.7 | 0.301 | 0.562 | 0.315 | 0.123 |
| Single women | 114 | 72.0 | 0.246 | 0.526 | 0.281 | 0.193 |
| Widowers | 77 | 72.2 | 0.234 | 0.610 | 0.182 | 0.208 |
| Widows | 272 | 72.1 | 0.250 | 0.533 | 0.261 | 0.206 |
| High wealth: married men | 1,383 | 72.4 | 0.267 | 0.587 | 0.244 | 0.168 |
| Low wealth: married men | 857 | 72.7 | 0.247 | 0.543 | 0.212 | 0.245 |
| High education: married men | 1,002 | 72.7 | 0.237 | 0.566 | 0.235 | 0.200 |
| Low education: married men | 1,238 | 72.3 | 0.278 | 0.574 | 0.230 | 0.196 |

**Table 11.6    Expectations and Realizations by Subgroup, 1971**

| Subgroup | Number of Observations | Mean of ERET | Fraction with RET = ERET | Fraction with RET = ERET ± 1 | Fraction with RET < ERET − 1 | Fraction with RET > ERET + 1 |
|---|---|---|---|---|---|---|
| Married men | 1,619 | 73.3 | 0.334 | 0.672 | 0.170 | 0.158 |
| Married women | 639 | 75.4 | 0.178 | 0.426 | 0.224 | 0.351 |
| Single men | 55 | 73.1 | 0.400 | 0.673 | 0.218 | 0.109 |
| Single women | 91 | 73.5 | 0.396 | 0.747 | 0.121 | 0.132 |
| Widowers | 86 | 73.1 | 0.256 | 0.640 | 0.209 | 0.151 |
| Widows | 230 | 73.3 | 0.291 | 0.604 | 0.222 | 0.174 |
| High wealth: married men | 1,071 | 73.3 | 0.347 | 0.676 | 0.169 | 0.155 |
| Low wealth: married men | 548 | 73.4 | 0.307 | 0.664 | 0.173 | 0.162 |
| High education: married men | 773 | 73.5 | 0.339 | 0.656 | 0.172 | 0.172 |
| Low education: married men | 846 | 73.1 | 0.329 | 0.687 | 0.169 | 0.144 |

**Table 11.7**     **Expectations and Realizations by Subgroup, 1973**

| Subgroup | Number of Observations | Mean of ERET | Fraction with RET = ERET | Fraction with RET = ERET ± 1 | Fraction with RET < ERET − 1 | Fraction with RET > ERET + 1 |
|---|---|---|---|---|---|---|
| Married men | 853 | 74.8 | 0.353 | 0.720 | 0.158 | 0.122 |
| Married women | NA | NA | NA | NA | NA | NA |
| Single men | 32 | 75.1 | 0.344 | 0.719 | 0.156 | 0.125 |
| Single women | 51 | 74.5 | 0.431 | 0.804 | 0.176 | 0.020 |
| Widowers | 48 | 74.3 | 0.375 | 0.688 | 0.188 | 0.125 |
| Widows | 140 | 74.5 | 0.386 | 0.707 | 0.179 | 0.114 |
| High wealth: married men | 574 | 74.9 | 0.357 | 0.711 | 0.171 | 0.118 |
| Low wealth: married men | 279 | 74.7 | 0.344 | 0.738 | 0.133 | 0.129 |
| High education: married men | 423 | 75.1 | 0.336 | 0.671 | 0.184 | 0.144 |
| Low education: married men | 430 | 74.6 | 0.370 | 0.768 | 0.133 | 0.100 |

**Table 11.8   Expectations and Realizations by Subgroup, 1975**

| Subgroup | Number of Observations | Mean of ERET | Fraction with RET = ERET | Fraction with RET = ERET ± 1 | Fraction with RET < ERET − 1 | Fraction with RET > ERET + 1 |
|---|---|---|---|---|---|---|
| Married men | 297 | 76.3 | 41.4 | 76.8 | 10.8 | 12.5 |
| Married women | 478 | 78.6 | 19.7 | 48.1 | 20.1 | 31.8 |
| Single men | 6 | 77.2 | 16.7 | 50.0 | 16.7 | 33.3 |
| Single women | 16 | 76.0 | 50.0 | 87.5 | 12.5 | 0.0 |
| Widowers | 21 | 75.5 | 38.1 | 66.7 | 33.3 | 0.0 |
| Widows | 50 | 76.3 | 40.0 | 78.0 | 18.0 | 4.0 |
| High wealth: married men | 198 | 76.3 | 40.9 | 75.8 | 11.6 | 12.6 |
| Low wealth: married men | 99 | 76.2 | 42.4 | 78.8 | 9.1 | 12.1 |
| High education: married men | 168 | 76.5 | 38.1 | 72.0 | 13.1 | 14.9 |
| Low education: married men | 129 | 75.9 | 45.7 | 82.9 | 7.8 | 9.3 |

view that unanticipated benefit increases led many workers to retire unexpectedly during the early 1970s.

## Notes

1. It is worth noting that the data do not appear to be consistent with the hypothesis that individuals report the medians of objective distributions. In fact, the pattern of medians is quite similar to the pattern of means.

2. It is possible to obtain the standard deviation of the mean retirement date in each cell from the standard deviation of the retirement date and the number of observations.

3. This assumption may seem peculiar when attrition is due to death. If, however, one believes (as seems natural) that individuals report expected dates of retirement conditional upon surviving until retirement, then the assumption is appropriate, since one wishes to know what each individual would have done had he survived.

## References

Aiginger, Karl. 1979. Empirische Information zur Bildung von Erwartungen. *Ifo-Studien* 25:83–135.

Anderson, Kathryn H., Richard V. Burkhauser, and Joseph F. Quinn. 1986. Do retirement dreams come true? The effect of unanticipated events on retirement plans. *Industrial and Labor Relations Review* 39:518–26.

Bernheim, B. Douglas. 1988. Social Security benefits: An empirical study of expectations and realizations. In *Issues in contemporary retirement,* ed. E. Lazear and R. Ricardo-Campbell. Stanford, Calif.: Hoover Institution. Pp. 312–48.

Burtless, Gary. 1986. Social security, unanticipated benefit increases, and the timing of retirement. *Review of Economic Studies* 53 (October): 781–805.

Curtin, Richard T. 1982. Determinants of price expectations: Evidence from a panel study. In *International research on business cycle surveys,* ed. M. Laumer and M. Ziegler. Aldershot: Gower.

Gramlich, Edward M. 1983. Models of inflation expectations formation: A comparison of household and economist forecasts. *Journal of Money, Credit, and Banking* 11:155–73.

Hall, Arden, and Terry Johnson. 1980. The determinants of planned retirement age. *Industrial and Labor Relations Review* 33:240–55.

Huizinga, John. 1980. *Real wages, employment, and expectations.* Ph.D. diss., Massachusetts Institute of Technology.

Hurd, Michael. 1983. The effects of Social Security on retirement: Results and issues. State University of New York, Stony Brook. Mimeo.

Hurd, Michael, and Michael Boskin. 1981. The effect of Social Security on retirement in the early 1970s. National Bureau of Economic Research Working Paper no. 659.

Mitchell, Olivia S., and Gary S. Fields. 1982. The effects of pensions and earnings on retirement: A review essay. In *Research in labor economics,* ed. Ronald E. Ehrenberg. Greenwich, Conn.: JAI Press.

Papadia, Francesco. 1982. Rationality of inflationary expectations in the European Community's countries. European Economic Community Working Paper, Brussels.

# Comment    Edward P. Lazear

I am a fan of Bernheim's work, and this paper has done nothing to change my view. It is a careful analysis of the relation of expected retirement age to actual retirement age. The main question that I want to raise is, "Why is this interesting?" Or, put otherwise, "What else would we like to know?" Bernheim motivates the analysis by stating that life-cycle theory is based on the premise that consumers think seriously and coherently about the distant future. But for most of life-cycle theory, what is relevant is opportunities rather than outcomes. Retirement is an outcome, a point chosen on an opportunity locus, and it is not clear what it means or why it is relevant. Bernheim did some work on Social Security that spoke directly to this issue.

To make the point, consider the work-leisure diagram in figure 11.3.

Point A is the expected outcome, and points B and C are actual outcomes under two different scenarios. Both B and C correspond to lower retirement ages than A since more years of retirement leisure are taken. The retirement age could be lower than the expected retirement age for one of two reasons. First, as illustrated by point B, opportunities get worse and wage offers fall. The substitution effect induces the worker to take more leisure, but he is worse off than he was at A. Second, income from nonlabor sources may rise, as illustrated by point C. The income effect induces the worker to take more leisure, and he is better off than he was at A. Bernheim looks at Social Security payments, so he goes part of the way there. But pension buyouts are important, as Laurence Kotlikoff and David Wise have found in their data (ch. 10, in this volume). Additionally, spousal income may be a factor. Although both cases show up as an actual retirement date that is earlier than the expected one, and although both have implications for life-cycle models, the implications are very different. In one case, early retirement implies an unanticipated fall in standard of living. In the other, it implies a rise.

The following extensions are the most important:

First, forecasts of variables that are the determinants, rather than the outcome, of retirement are more interesting. Data are lacking, except perhaps for health status.

Second, it would be useful to find out what happens to those who fail to predict their ages of retirement correctly. Specifically, what happens to income, assets, housing, and food consumption? Hausman and

Edward P. Lazear is a Professor of Industrial Relations at the Graduate School of Business, University of Chicago, a Senior Fellow, Hoover Institution, and a Research Associate of the National Bureau of Economic Research.

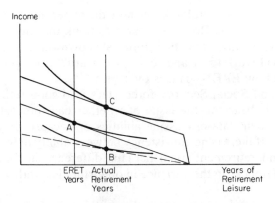

**Fig. 11.3** Work-leisure diagram

Paquette (1987) find that food consumption falls for those who suffer early retirement.

Third, the distinction between anticipated and unanticipated and between voluntary and compulsory retirement is significant. Voluntary might be defined as an improvement in one's leisure or alternative work opportunities. Compulsory might be defined as the current job situation getting worse. Is the group of those who retire earlier than anticipated dominated by compulsory or voluntary retirements? The answer has important implications for welfare.

Fourth, and related, married women forecast badly. They seem to work longer than expected. Are they widows who forecast their husband's life expectancy badly, or are they pleasantly surprised by the wonderful job offer that McDonald's made them to make french fries?

Fifth, and a more general way to put the point: When workers are wrong, does it matter? Is the change in rent associated with the unanticipated event large or small? For example, it could be that expected retirement deviates by a large amount from actual retirement because wages are close to alternatives so that a small change in either induces a large change in retirement ages. Under these circumstances, little consumer surplus is lost even when there are big differences between expected and actual retirement.

Sixth, are bad forecasters bad because they experience more unanticipated events than others or are they poorer at data processing? It is one thing to say that women forecast badly because they are faced with more uncertainty. It is another to say that they are worse at making decisions, given the same amount of uncertainty.

Here are some other minor points:

1. The analysis does not exploit the panel fully. Although it does look at whether predictions get better as the individual nears the

retirement age, it is useful to know how the expected age of retirement changes as one ages. Do all 55 year olds think that they will work to 70 and subsequently revise their forecasts downward, or do they think that they will work to 57 and revise it upward? More generally, what determines how ERET changes over time?

2. Are good Social Security forecasters also good retirement forecasters? This bears on the issue of whether bad forecasters are bad because of their data-processing abilities or because they face more uncertainty. If there is no consistency between ability to forecast Social Security and retirement, then perhaps difference in forecast ability reflects differences in the variance in opportunities, rather than in data processing.

This was a good paper. I learned something from it, and the results are credible. At worst, it does not go far enough.

### Reference

Hausman, Jerry A., and Lynn Paquette. 1987. Involuntary early retirement and consumption. In *Work, health and income among the elderly,* ed. Gary Burtless. Washington, D.C.: The Brookings Institution.

# 12 A Dynamic Programming Model of Retirement Behavior

John Rust

## 12.1 Introduction

This paper derives a model of the retirement behavior of older male workers from the solution to a stochastic dynamic programming problem. The worker's objective is to maximize expected discounted utility over his remaining lifetime. At each time period $t$ the worker chooses control variables $(c_t, d_t)$ where $c_t$ denotes the level of consumption expenditures and $d_t$ denotes the decision whether to work full-time, part-time, or to exit the labor force. The model accounts for the sequential nature of the retirement decision problem and the role of expectations of the uncertain future values of state variables $(x_t)$ such as the worker's future lifespan, health status, marital or family status, employment status, and earnings from employment, assets, Social Security retirement, disability, and Medicare payments. Given specific assumptions about workers' preferences and expectations, the model generates a predicted stochastic process for the variables $\{c_t, d_t, x_t\}$. This paper, however, focuses on the inverse or "revealed preference" problem: given data on $\{c_t, d_t, x_t\}$, how can one go backward and "uncover" the worker's underlying preferences and expectations?

One can formalize the revealed preference problem as a problem of statistical inference. The null hypothesis is that the data $\{c_t, d_t, x_t\}$ are

John P. Rust is an Associate Professor of Economics at the University of Wisconsin-Madison and a Faculty Research Fellow of the National Bureau of Economic Research.

This research is part of a project on the economics of aging funded by National Institute for Aging grant 3-PO1-AG05842-01. CPU time on the Cray-2 supercomputer was provided under grant SES-8419570 of the National Science Foundation.

realizations of a controlled stochastic process generated from the solution to a stochastic dynamic programming problem with utility function $u$ and a stochastic law of motion $\pi$ that depend on a vector of unknown parameters $\theta$. The underlying preferences $u$ and expectations $\pi$ are "uncovered" by finding the parameter vector $\hat{\theta}$ that maximizes the likelihood function for the sample of data. Standard likelihood ratio, Lagrange multiplier, and chi-square goodness-of-fit statistics allow one to test whether or not workers are rational in the sense of acting "as if" they were solving the specified dynamic programming problem. If the data appear to be consistent with the dynamic programming model, the estimated model can be used to forecast the effect of policy changes such as reductions in Social Security retirement or disability benefits. Policy forecasts require a "structural" approach that attempts to uncover the underlying preferences $u$ rather than the traditional "reduced-form" approach which can be viewed as uncovering the historical stochastic process for $\{c_t, d_t, x_t\}$. The problem with reduced-form methods, noted by Marschak (1953) and later by Lucas (1976), is that policy changes cause workers to reoptimize, yielding a new controlled stochastic process for $\{c_t, d_t, x_t\}$ that is generally different from the historical process of the previous policy regime. The structural approach allows one to solve the dynamic programming problem under the new policy regime and to derive a predicted stochastic process for $\{c_t, d_t, x_t\}$. Recovering the underlying utility function is also useful for quantifying the extent to which workers are hurt by various policy changes.

Unfortunately, stochastic dynamic programming problems generally have no tractable analytic solutions and are typically only described recursively via Bellman's "principal of optimality". Without such a solution it appears impossible to write down a simple, analytic likelihood function for the data. This problem may have deterred previous researchers from estimating structural models of retirement behavior that capture both uncertainty and the sequential nature of the decision process.[1] Recently, the advent of new estimation algorithms and powerful supercomputers has begun to make estimation of more realistic stochastic dynamic programming models feasible, even though such models have no analytic solution. The basic idea is very simple: the dynamic programming problem and associated likelihood function can be numerically computed in a subroutine of a standard nonlinear maximum likelihood algorithm. Rust (1988) developed a nested fixed point (NFXP) algorithm that computes maximum likelihood estimates of structural parameters of discrete control processes, a class of Markovian decision processes for which the control is restricted to a finite set of alternatives. As its name implies, the NFXP algorithm works by converting the dynamic programming problem into the problem of computing a fixed point to a certain contraction mapping. A measure of the inherent difficulty or computational complexity of the dynamic programming problem is the dimension of the associated fixed point problem. The NFXP algorithm has been successfully programmed on an IBM-PC and applied to estimate a model of bus engine replacement where the fixed point dimension was at most 180 (Rust 1987). By comparison, the fixed point dimension for the retirement problem can be as large as several million.

This paper shows how to apply the NFXP algorithm to the retirement problem and demonstrates how to exploit the algebraic structure of the fixed point problem in order to rapidly compute high-dimensional fixed points on parallel vector processors like the Cray-2. With this technology one can formulate more realistic models of retirement behavior. Section 12.2 reviews some of the empirical issues that motivated the construction of the model. Section 12.3 develops the model, formulating the retirement decision process as a discrete control process. Section 12.4 presents computational results which show that fixed points as large as several million dimensions can be rapidly and accurately calculated on the Cray-2. Future work (see Rust 1989) will use the NFXP algorithm and data from the longitudinal Retirement History Survey (RHS) to actually estimate the unknown parameters of the model.

## 12.2 Empirical Motivation for the Dynamic Programming Model

The a priori structure of the dynamic programming model has been heavily influenced by my interpretation of the extensive empirical literature on retirement and consumption/savings behavior that has appeared over the last twenty years. This section summarizes some of the basic empirical and policy issues of the retirement process that I wanted the model to capture.

### 12.2.1 Accounting for Unplanned Events and the Sequential Nature of Decision-Making

Several existing models, such as Anderson, Burkhauser, and Quinn (1984) and Burtless and Moffitt (1984), studied retirement behavior in the context of a two-period model that divided time into a preretirement and postretirement phase. At some initial planning date before retirement, the worker is assumed to choose a fixed optimal retirement date and fixed preretirement and postretirement consumption levels. Anderson, Burkhauser, and Quinn used data from the RHS survey to find out how closely workers followed their initial retirement plans. In the initial 1969 wave of the survey, nonretired workers reported their planned retirement age. By tracing workers over the subsequent ten years they were able to compare the actual and planned retirement dates, and found that over 40 percent of the initial sample deviated from their initial retirement plans by over one year.

Clearly workers do not make single, once-and-for-all plans about consumption levels and retirement date. Rather, workers are constantly modifying their plans in light of new information. Anderson, Burkhauser, and Quinn found that unexpected changes in health, labor market conditions, and government policy (Social Security regulations, in particular) were the most important factors leading to revised retirement plans. This suggests a stochastic dynamic programming formulation where the solution takes the form of an optimal decision rule that specifies workers' optimal consumption and labor supply decisions as a function of their current information.

### 12.2.2  Accounting for Bequests

Many of the early studies of the impact of Social Security on private saving were based on the life-cycle consumption hypothesis of Modigliani and Brumberg (1954). Under the simple life-cycle model with no bequests: (1) consumption is predicted to remain constant or increase with age (depending on whether the interest rate is greater than or equal to the subjective discount rate), (2) workers are predicted to run down their accumulated wealth to zero by their (certain) date of death, and (3) intergenerational transfers like Social Security displace an equal amount of private savings (a greater amount if there is a net wealth transfer, due to the wealth effect on consumption). Initial work using cross-sectional data (Mirer 1979, Danziger et al. 1982, Kurz 1984, and Menchik and David 1983) provided evidence that contrary to the simple life-cycle model, age-wealth profiles are constant (or possibly increase) with age, and "the elderly not only do not dissave to finance their consumption during retirement, they spend less on consumption goods and services (save significantly more) than the nonelderly at all levels of income" (Danziger et. al. 1982, p. 224). A study of consumption profiles using the RHS data by Hamermesh (1984) found that on average consumption exceeds earnings by 14 percent early in retirement, but that workers respond "by reducing consumption at a rate sufficient to generate positive changes in net financial worth within a few years after retirement" (p. 1). A study of estimated earnings and consumption paths by Kotlikoff and Summers (1981) indicated that intergenerational transfers account for the vast majority of the capital stock in the United States, with only a negligible fraction attributable to life-cycle savings. Direct observations of bequests from probate records (Menchik and David 1985) showed that bequests are a substantial fraction of lifetime earnings. Their results also demonstrated that bequests are a luxury good, with a "marginal propensity to bequeath" that is about six times higher in the top wealth quintile than in the lower four quintiles. As a whole, these studies provide a strong case for including bequests in a properly specified empirical model.

The policy implications of bequests were first pointed out by Barro (1974). Barro's "equivalence result" shows that under general conditions consumers can offset the effects of government tax policy (such as Social Security) by corresponding changes in private intergenerational transfers. In particular, the net wealth transfers to Social Security beneficiaries during the 1970s are predicted to be completely offset by increases in private saving for bequests.

Recent theoretical and empirical research, however, has questioned the importance of bequests as a determinant of consumption behavior during retirement. Davies (1981) showed that in a model with imperfect annuities markets and uncertain lifetimes, risk averse consumers can continue to accumulate wealth during retirement through a precautionary savings motive even though there is no bequest motive. Given that lifetimes are not certain, this creates the empirical problem of distinguishing between intended and accidental bequests. Recent panel data studies by Diamond and Hausman (1984b), Bernheim (1984), and Hurd (1986) found that the elderly do dissave after retirement. Hurd found that average real wealth in the RHS decreased by 27 percent over the ten-year period of the survey and concluded that "there is no bequest motive in the RHS, and, by extension, in the elderly population with the possible exception of the very wealthy. Bequests seem to be simply the result of mortality risk combined with a very weak market for private annuities" (p. 35). Menchik and David's (1985) study also casts doubt on the empirical relevance of Barro's equivalence result. Their regressions of bequests on gross Social Security wealth and the lifetime wealth increment, LWI (the difference between the discounted value of Social Security receipts and Social Security taxes), produced no evidence that bequests increase to offset increases in LWI; in fact, those in the top wealth quintile appeared to decrease bequests in response to an increase in LWI. However, their results also cast doubt on the Davies variant of the life-cycle model. To the extent that Social Security is a replacement for an incomplete annuities market, one would expect that gross Social Security benefits would decrease accumulated private wealth and unanticipated bequests. Menchik and David found a positive (albeit statistically insignificant) coefficient on gross Social Security benefits, and concluded that the "results indicate no significant effect of Social Security wealth on the age-wealth profile, a finding at odds with the life-cycle hypothesis. We find that Social Security does not depress or displace private saving and that people do not deplete their private assets in old age as is commonly assumed" (p. 432).

These conflicting theoretical and empirical results suggest the need to build a model that allows for both uncertain lifetimes and a bequest motive. A unified treatment may help to sort out their separate effects on the path of consumption during retirement. However, the fact that bequests are not needed to explain the slow rate of wealth decumulation suggests that it will be very difficult to separately identify workers' subjective discount factors, the parameters of their bequest functions, and their subjective mortality probability distributions.

### 12.2.3    Accounting for the Joint Endogeneity of Labor Supply and Savings Decisions

The decline in the labor force participation rate of older males over the past thirty years is a well-known phenomenon; the participation rate for workers aged 55–64 declined from 86.8 percent in 1960 to 72.3 percent in 1980, and the rate for workers aged 65+ declined from 33.1 percent to 19.1 percent over the same period. Many people have blamed this decline on the historical increase in Social Security retirement benefits, which increased in real terms by more than 50 percent from 1968 to 1979, the decade of the RHS survey. Savings rates have also declined in the postwar era, from an average of 8.8 percent in the 1950s, 8.7 percent in the 1960s, 7.7 percent in the 1970s, to only 5.1 percent since 1980. Some researchers, including Feldstein, have claimed that Social Security "depresses personal saving by 30–50 percent" (Feldstein 1974, p. 905). However, according to economic theory an actuarially fair Social Security program should have no effect on aggregate savings or labor supply decisions; instead, simply inducing a 1-for-1 displacement of private savings by public savings (Crawford and Lilien 1982). It is well known, however, that the Social Security benefit formulas are not actuarially fair, but rather have strong incentives for early retirement (especially beyond age 65, see Burtless and Moffitt 1984). However, if workers increase their savings to prepare for earlier retirement, then the theoretical impact of Social Security on aggregate savings is ambiguous: the decreased savings due to the tax and wealth transfer effects may be offset by the increased savings due to the early retirement effect.

Empirical work designed to resolve these questions has failed to provide clear conclusions about Social Security's impact on labor supply and savings behavior. While analyses of labor supply decisions generally agree that Social Security does induce earlier retirement, there is substantial disagreement over the magnitude of the effect. Some studies such as Boskin and Hurd (1974) find a substantial impact, while others such as Sueyoshi (1986) find a moderate impact, and still others such as Burtless and Moffitt (1984) and Fields and Mitchell (1985) find a very small impact. In fact, the latter study found that a 10 percent decrease in benefits would increase the average retirement age by at most 1.7 months. Studies of Social Security's impact on aggregate savings are in disagreement about even the sign of the effect. For example, Barro (1978) used the same time series data as Feldstein (1974) and an alternative measure of Social Security wealth, and found that increases in Social Security increased aggregate savings. He concluded that "the time-series evidence for the United States does not support the hypothesis that Social Security depresses private saving" (p. 1). Studies using longitudinal data such as Kotlikoff (1979) have generally found that Social Security reduces private saving, but have not found the 1-for-1 displacement of private savings that the simple life-cycle model predicts. Kotlikoff's results show a partial offset ranging from 40 to 60 cents for every additional dollar of Social Security benefits; the increased savings due to early retirement did not turn out to be large enough to offset Social Security's negative tax and wealth transfer effects.

A careful analysis of the impact of changes in Social Security benefits requires a model that treats labor supply and consumption as jointly endogenous decisions. Although a model that focuses on the last stage of the life-cycle probably will not be able to shed much light on Social Security's impact on aggregate savings, it should address the historical decline in labor force participation of older men. The discrepancies in previous empirical results emphasize the need to carefully model the actuarial and benefit structure of the Social Security system, and if possible, to model workers' expectations and uncertainties about changes in future benefits.

### 12.2.4  Accounting for Health and the Impact of Social Security Disability Insurance

Health problems are a major source of uncertainty in retirement planning, especially in terms of lost earning potential and unanticipated health care costs. Data from the NLS and RHS surveys indicate that poor health is a major factor in retirement decisions, especially among early retirees. Of the people retired in the 1969 wave of the RHS survey, 65 percent reported they were retired due to poor health; for those who had been out of the labor force for more than six years (the early retirees) the figure was 82 percent. Health problems are prevalent even among those who work; 39 percent of the 1969 RHS sample reported a health problem that limited their ability to work or get around, even though 63 percent of this group continued to work at a full- or part-time job. However, the inherent subjectivity of self-reported health measures and the financial incentives for claiming poor health in order to receive disability payments have led some to question the accuracy of health variables and the importance of poor health as a cause of retirement (Parsons 1982). In fact, some researchers (Bound 1986) have presented evidence (see figure 12.1) that suggests that much of the decline in the labor force participation rates of older males over the last thirty years can be ascribed to increases in disability claims allowed

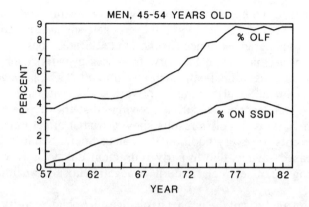

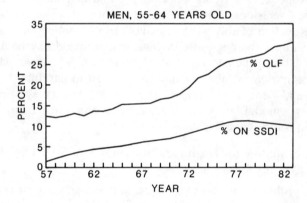

**Figure 12.1**

under the Social Security disability insurance program instituted in the late 1950s and substantially liberalized during the 1970s. Other researchers, such as Kotlikoff (1986), suggest that disability insurance may also be partly responsible for the decline in saving rates since it eliminates the need for precautionary saving to insure against unexpected illness or disability.

To the extent that qualification for disability insurance requires medical examination, the classification "disabled" is relatively more objective than self-reported measures of poor health. However, other approaches that use more "objective" measures of health status such as impairment indices (Chirikos and Nestel 1981), or ex post mortality (Parsons 1982, Mott and Haurin 1981), generally obtain results that are in broad agreement with studies that use self-reported measures of health status (although there are certain questions for which the alternative measures lead to important differences, see Chirikos and Nestel

1981, p. 113). Regardless of how it is measured, health status clearly has a significant impact on the labor force participation decision and appears to be one of the most important variables driving the dynamics of the retirement process. It is important, however, to find a measure of health status that does not rely heavily on subjective self-assessments, for example, classifying as disabled only those who have had doctor certification of disability (as is required in order to obtain disability benefits). The model must also incorporate the regulations and uncertainties governing the receipt of Social Security disability insurance; only by doing so can we hope to sort out the relative impact of liberalized disability vs. retirement benefits on the declining labor force participation rate of older males.

### 12.2.5   Accounting for "Partial Retirement" and Multiple Labor Force Transitions

Many models treat retirement as a dichotomous choice between full-time work and zero hours of work. However, economic theory suggests that workers might be better off if they could make a gradual transition from full-time work into retirement. Thus, at the other extreme are the labor supply models of Gordon and Blinder (1980) and MaCurdy (1983) that treat hours of work as a continuous choice variable. Gustman and Steinmeier (1983, 1984) have shown that a majority of non-self-employed workers face implicit or explicit minimum hours constraints that prevent them from gradually phasing out of their full-time jobs. Their analysis of the RHS data showed that approximately one third of all workers attempt to circumvent the minimum hours constraint through a spell of "partial retirement" in a part-time job. This suggests that a trichotomous choice model with the alternatives of full-time work, part-time work, and retirement, may be a better approximation to the actual choice sets facing workers than either the binary or continuous-choice formulations.

The RHS data show substantial variation in the paths workers follow into retirement. Table 12.1 presents the sequence of self-reported labor market states in the first four waves of the RHS. The table indicates that one needs at least a three-alternative choice set to adequately explain the variety of labor force transitions that occur along the path to retirement. It also indicates that the transition into retirement seems to be nearly an absorbing state; very few people "unretire" by re-entering a full-time job once fully or partially retired (or part-time job once fully retired). These numbers differ significantly from labor market re-entry rates presented by Diamond and Hausman (1984b) using NLS data. Table 12.2 reproduces their estimates of the fraction of men in the NLS survey that re-enter full-time work from the state of retirement or partial retirement. A possible explanation for the discrepancy is that

**Table 12.1    Distributions of Retirement Sequences**

| Sequence | Frequency | Sequence | Frequency |
|----------|-----------|----------|-----------|
| ffrr | 16.2% | frxx | 1.6% |
| ffff | 14.4 | rrrx | 1.5 |
| fffr | 11.2 | fppp | 1.4 |
| rrrr | 8.6 | frrx | 1.1 |
| frrr | 7.3 | prrr | 1.1 |
| ffxx | 5.4 | ffrp | 1.1 |
| fffp | 4.8 | ffpx | 0.7 |
| ffpp | 2.8 | ffpf | 0.6 |
| ffpr | 2.8 | fppr | 0.5 |
| ffrx | 2.5 | pqrr | 0.5 |
| rrxx | 2.2 | others | 9.8 |
| fprr | 2.1 |  |  |

*Source:* Gustman and Steinmeier (1986, p. 566). The first letter in the retirement sequence is the individual's status in 1969, the first year of the RHS. The second, third, and fourth letters indicate their status in 1971, 1973, and 1975, respectively. The notation of the letters is: f = working full-time, p = working part-time, r = fully retired, x = status indeterminant. Sequences with a frequency less than 0.5 percent were grouped in the category "others".

**Table 12.2    Labor Market Re-entry Rates**

| | One-Year Re-entry Rates | | Two-Year Re-entry Rates | |
|-----|-----|-----|-----|-----|
| Age | Self-described Retired or Unable to Work | Not Full-time Worker | Self-described Retired or Unable to Work | Not Full-time Worker |
| 45–59 | 18.54 | 52.55 | 4.00 | 53.76 |
| 50–54 | 16.23 | 46.93 | 17.68 | 41.03 |
| 55–59 | 15.94 | 31.85 | 10.31 | 25.23 |
| 60–64 | 13.37 | 15.45 | 9.57 | 7.15 |
| 65–69 | 11.74 | 5.02 | 9.04 | 2.94 |
| Total | 14.53 | 29.48 | 10.13 | 16.72 |

Gustman and Steinmeier used a self-reported measure of labor force status to construct table 12.1.[2] The concept of retirement is ambiguous: Is someone who quits their full-time career job and takes a part-time job retired? Workers may interpret the concept differently and respond differently even though they are in identical labor force states. This suggests the use of objective measures of labor force status based on reported hours of work. Furthermore, from a modelling standpoint it seems undesirable to impose a priori constraints such as making retirement an absorbing state or prohibiting various transitions to and from different labor market states. The model should have the flexibility to allow the data and the estimated parameter values "explain" what types of transitions actually occur.

Developing a tractable empirical model that incorporates all of these features is a challenging undertaking. Certainly a unified model will lack some of the fine detail of previous models that focused on specific aspects of the retirement process. However, the most important cost is the computer time required to solve and estimate the model. To my knowledge there is no simple analytic solution to the model I present in the next section: it seems to require numerical solution, a substantial computational task. Before presenting the model, I should answer a natural question: Isn't there a better way to estimate the model than by "brute force" numerical solution of the dynamic programming problem? In particular, MaCurdy (1983) developed a relatively simple scheme for estimating an intertemporal model of labor supply and consumption in the presence of taxes and uncertainty. Why not use MaCurdy's method? MaCurdy's approach is not well-suited to the retirement problem due to his assumption that consumption and hours of work are continuous choice variables. This allows MaCurdy to derive first-order conditions for the stochastic dynamic programming problem that equate the marginal rate of substitution between consumption and leisure to the real wage rate. This provides a computationally convenient orthogonality condition to estimate the identified parameters of the model. Unfortunately, the method depends critically on the assumption that workers do not face minimum hours constraints in their full-time jobs, and that one always has an interior solution with positive values for consumption and hours of work. MaCurdy recognizes this: "Because the procedure ignores statistical problems relating to the endogeneity of labor decisions, [it is] of limited use in estimating period-specific utilities associated with households in which corner solutions for hours of work are not a certainty . . . such as households with wives and older households where retirement may occur" (MaCurdy 1983, p. 277). The next section presents a model and estimation algorithm that can accommodate minimum hours constraints and corner solutions, but at the cost of repeated numerical solution of the dynamic programming problem over the course of the maximum likelihood estimation procedure.

## 12.3   Formulation of the Dynamic Programming Model

This section presents a theoretical model of retirement behavior that attempts to account for some of the empirical issues raised in section 12.2. The ultimate goal is to estimate and test the model using the RHS panel data. The primary factors limiting the realism of the model are computational feasibility and the availability of good data. The construction of the theoretical model reflects these practical constraints. In particular, the RHS has limited data on private pension plans, so I restrict the model to male heads of household with no private pensions. Given the negligible use of private annuities and health plans among RHS respondents, it follows that Social Security is the predominant source of both retirement and health insurance benefits for this subsample.

### 12.3.1 State and Control Variables

In order to capture the fundamental dynamics of retirement behavior the model should include the following state variables which directly or indirectly affect workers' realized utility levels:

$w_t$:   accumulated financial and nonfinancial wealth
$y_t$:   total income from earnings and assets
$aw_t$:   the Social Security average monthly wage
$h_t$:   health status of worker (good health/poor health/disabled/dead)
$a_t$:   age of worker
$e_t$:   employment status (full-time/part-time/not employed)
$ms_t$:   marital status (married/single)

The state variables represent a subset of workers' current information that affects their expectations about their remaining lifespan, future earnings and retirement benefits, and their future health and family status. Since Social Security retirement and disability benefits are determined from the worker's primary insurance amount (a function of $aw_t$, which is in turn a complicated weighted average of past earnings), the variable $aw_t$ summarizes the worker's expectations of future benefits accruing to him in retirement or disability, assuming fixed Social Security rules governing timing and eligibility for benefits. Since it is very difficult to formulate a low-dimensional state variable representing how the Social Security benefit structure changes over time, I assume that workers had "semi-rational" expectations of the benefit structure, equal to the regulations in force as of 1973. Although real benefits increased 51.2 percent between 1968 and 1979, the majority of the increase, 46.7 percent, was in effect by 1973 (see Anderson, Burkhauser, and Quinn 1984). The 1973 Social Security Act also changed the "earnings test" to reduce the 100 percent tax on earnings beyond the previous earnings limit to a 50 percent tax on all earnings over $2,100. I describe the expectations assumption as semi-rational because I assume that workers correctly anticipated the cumulative changes in Social Security that came into effect over the period 1969–73, but maintained static expectations that no further changes would occur thereafter.

Given their expectations, at each time $t$ workers must choose values of the following control variables:

$d_t$: the employment decision (full-time/part-time/exit labor force)
$c_t$: the level of planned consumption expenditures

The workers' sequential decision problem is to choose at each time $t$ values for the control variables $i_t \equiv (c_t, d_t)$ that maximize the expected discounted value of utility over their remaining lifetime, where expectations are conditioned by the current values of the state variables $x_t \equiv (w_t, h_t, a_t, ms_t, e_t, y_t, aw_t)$. The goal is to specify a model that is parsimonious, yet rich enough to allow for certain kinds of heterogeneity. Perhaps the most important source of heterogeneity is differences in workers' attitudes toward retirement. Some workers may be "workaholics" who prefer working to the idle leisure of retirement, whereas others are "leisure lovers" who would jump at the chance to quit their jobs.

Notice that the formulation distinguishes between the worker's employment state and his employment decision. This feature allows the model to account for various labor force transitions, including "unretirement" and job search behavior, summarized in table 12.3.

### 12.3.2 Formulating Retirement Behavior as a Discrete Control Process

I model retirement behavior as a *discrete control process*, a discrete-time Markovian decision problem where the control variable is restricted to a finite set of alternatives. This framework represents workers' preferences as a discounted sum of a state-dependent utility function $u(x_t, i_t)$, and their expectations as a Markov transition probability $\pi(x_{t+1} | x_t, i_t)$. Blackwell's Theorem (Blackwell 1965, theorem 6) establishes that under very general conditions, the solution to a Markovian decision problem takes the form of a decision rule $i_t = f_t(x_t)$ that specifies the agent's optimal action $i_t$ in state $x_t$. Note, however, that if the econometrician is assumed to observe the complete state vector $x_t$, this framework implies that knowledge of the true utility function $u$ would enable him to solve for $f$ and perfectly predict the agent's choice in each state $x$, producing a degenerate statistical model.[3] A possible solution is to add an error term in order to obtain a nondegenerate statistical model of the form $i_t = f_t(x_t) + \eta_t$. Unfortunately, such ad hoc solutions are internally inconsistent: the economic model assumes that the agent behaves optimally, yet the statistical implementation of the model assumes that the agent randomly departs from optimal behavior. One wants a framework that can account for the fact that the agent has information $\varepsilon_t$ that the econometrician does not observe. By

**Table 12.3**     **Accounting for Labor Force Transitions in the Dynamic Programming Model**

| Employment state, $e_t$ | Employment decision, $d_t$ | Interpretation |
| --- | --- | --- |
| ft | ft | Continue working at current full-time job |
| ft | pt | Quit current full-time job, search for a new part-time job |
| ft | ne | If $a_t \geq 62$, retire; if $a_t < 62$ and disabled, receive disability insurance; otherwise exit labor force |
| pt | ft | Quit current part-time job and search for a full-time job |
| pt | pt | Continue working at current part-time job |
| pt | ne | If $a_t \geq 62$, retire; if $a_t < 62$ and disabled, collect disability insurance; otherwise exit labor force |
| ne | ft | Unemployed, disabled, or retired worker searching for full-time job |
| ne | pt | Unemployed, disabled, or retired worker searching for part-time job |
| ne | ne | If $a_t \geq 62$, remain retired; if $a_t < 62$ and disabled, collect disability insurance; otherwise remain out of labor force |

incorporating such unobserved state variables one obtains a nondegenerate, internally consistent statistical model generated by optimal decision rules of the form $i_t = f_t(x_t, \varepsilon_t)$. Rust (1988) developed a formal statistical framework for structural estimation of discrete Markovian decision problems with unobserved state variables. Table 12.4 summarizes the basic structure of the problem.

The solution to the decision problem consists of a sequence of decision rules or *controls* $f_t(x_t, \varepsilon_t)$ that maximize expected discounted utility over an infinite horizon. Define the value function $V$ by

$$(1) \qquad V(x_t, \varepsilon_t) = \sup_\Pi E\left\{ \sum_{j=t}^{\infty} \beta^{(j-t)} [u(x_j, f_j) + \varepsilon_j(f_j)] \big| x_t, \varepsilon_t \right\},$$

where $\Pi = \{f_t, f_{t+1}, f_{t+2}, \ldots\}$, $f_t(x_t, \varepsilon_t) \in C(x_t)$ for all $t$, $x_t$, and $\varepsilon_t$, and where the expectation is taken with respect to the transition density for the controlled stochastic process $\{x_t, \varepsilon_t\}$ determined from $\Pi$ and the transition density $p(x_{t+1}, \varepsilon_{t+1} | x_t, \varepsilon_t, i)$. Under general conditions the value function $V$ will be the unique solution to Bellman's equation

**Table 12.4**          **Summary of Notation for Discrete Control Problem**

| Symbol | Interpretation |
|---|---|
| $C(x_t)$ | Choice set: a finite set of feasible values for the control variable $i_t$ when the observed state variable is $x_t$ |
| $\varepsilon_t = \{\varepsilon_t(i) \mid i \in C(x_t)\}$ | A $\#C(x_t)$-dimensional vector of state variables observed by the agent but not by the econometrician; $\varepsilon_t(i)$ is interpreted as an unobserved component of utility of alternative $i$ in time period $t$ |
| $x_t = \{x_t(1), \ldots, x_t(M)\}$ | An $M$-dimensional vector of state variables observed by the agent and econometrician |
| $u(x_t, i) + \varepsilon_t(i)$ | Realized single period utility obtained in state $(x_t, \varepsilon_t)$ when alternative $i$ is chosen |
| $p(x_{t+1}, \varepsilon_{t+1} \mid x_t, \varepsilon_t, i)$ | Markov transition density for next period state variable when alternative $i$ is chosen and when the current state is $(x_t, \varepsilon_t)$ |

$$(2) \qquad V(x, \varepsilon) = \max_{i \in C(x)} [u(x, i) + \varepsilon(i) + \beta EV(x, \varepsilon, i)],$$

where the function $EV(x, \varepsilon, i)$ is defined by

$$(3) \qquad EV(x, \varepsilon, i) \equiv \int_y \int_\eta V(y, \eta) p(dy, d\eta \mid x, \varepsilon, i).$$

Blackwell's Theorem implies that the solution $\Pi$ is stationary, $\Pi = \{f, f, f, \ldots\}$, and Markovian so the agent's optimal decision rule $i = f(x, \varepsilon)$ depends only on the current values of the state variables determined by finding the alternative $i$ that attains the maximum in Bellman's equation

$$(4) \qquad f(x, \varepsilon) = \underset{i \in C(x)}{\operatorname{argmax}} [u(x, i) + \varepsilon(i) + \beta EV(x, \varepsilon, i)].$$

The sample likelihood function is derived from the conditional choice probabilities $P(i \mid x)$, which are obtained from the agent's optimal decision rule $i = f(x, \varepsilon)$ by integrating out over the unobserved state variable $\varepsilon$ using the conditional density of $\varepsilon$ given $x$. From equation (4) one can see that the unobservables enter nonlinearly in the conditional expectation of the value function, $EV(x, \varepsilon, i)$. Under standard distributional assumptions for the unobservables, $\varepsilon_t$ will be continuously distributed on $R^N$, where $N = \#C(x_t)$. This raises serious computational difficulties, since calculation of $P(i \mid x)$ will ordinarily require $N$-dimensional numerical integration over $\varepsilon$ in the optimal decision rule defined by (4). However, the expected value function $EV(x, \varepsilon, i)$ entering (4) will almost never have a convenient analytic formula, but must be computed by numerically integrating the value function $V$ in (3). The value function must in turn be numerically computed by solving $V$ as a functional fixed point to Bellman's equation (2). Since $\varepsilon$ is a vector

of continuous state variables, it must be discretized in order to compute
$V$ on a digital computer. The discretization procedure approximates
the true function $V$, an element of an infinite-dimensional Banach space
$B$, by a suitable vector in a high-dimensional Euclidean space. Even
with a very coarse grid approximation to the true continuous distribution of $\varepsilon_t$, the dimensionality of the resulting discrete approximation
will generally be too large to be computationally tractable. These computational problems motivate the following assumption on the joint
transition density for $\{x_t, \varepsilon_t\}$:

*Conditional Independence Assumption:* The Markov transition density
factors as

$$(5) \qquad p(x_{t+1}, \varepsilon_{t+1}|x_t,\varepsilon_t,i) = q(\varepsilon_{t+1}|x_{t+1}) \, \pi(x_{t+1}|x_t,i), \qquad i \in C(x_t).$$

This assumption involves two restrictions. First, $x_{t+1}$ is a sufficient
statistic for $\varepsilon_{t+1}$, which implies that any statistical dependence between
$\varepsilon_t$ and $\varepsilon_{t+1}$ is transmitted entirely through the vector $x_{t+1}$. Second, the
probability density for $x_{t+1}$ depends only on $x_t$ and $i$, and not on $\varepsilon_t$.
Although (5) is a strong assumption, Rust (1988) developed a simple
Lagrange multiplier statistic to test its validity. The payoff to assumption (5) is given by the following theorems of Rust (1988).

   *Theorem 1:* Let $G(v(x)|x)$ denote the Social Surplus function, defined
by

$$(6) \qquad G(v(x)|x) \equiv \int \max_{i \in C(x)} [v(x,i) + \varepsilon(i)] q(d\varepsilon|x) \, ,$$

and let $G_i(v(x)|x)$ denote the partial derivative of $G(v(x)|x)$ with respect
to $v(x,i)$. Then under the Conditional Independence assumption the
conditional choice probability $P(i|x)$ is given by

$$(7) \qquad P(i|x) = G_i(v(x)|x) \qquad i \in C(x),$$

where the function $v$ is the unique fixed point to the contraction mapping
$v = T(v)$ defined by

$$(8) \qquad T(v)(x,i) = u(x,i) + \beta \int_y G(v(y)|y) \, \pi(dy|x,i) \qquad i \in C(x).$$

The function $v$ is related to the value function $V$ defined in (1) and (2)
by

$$(9) \qquad V(x,\varepsilon) = \max_{i \in C(x)} [v(x,i) + \varepsilon(i)].$$

   *Theorem 2:* Under assumption (5) the controlled stochastic process
$\{i_t, x_t\}$ is Markovian with transition density given by

$$(10) \qquad \Pr\{i_{t+1}, x_{t+1}|i_t, x_t\} = P(i_{t+1}|x_{t+1})\pi(x_{t+1}|x_t,i_t).$$

Products of the transition density given in (10) form the likelihood
function for the process $\{i_t, x_t\}$. This function is difficult to evaluate

primarily because the conditional choice probability $P(i|x)$ requires calculation of the value function $v$ as a fixed point of the contraction mapping (8). Theorem 1 shows that from the standpoint of evaluating (10), there are two major payoffs to assumption (5). First, it implies that $\varepsilon$ does not enter the expected value function $EV(x,\varepsilon,i)$, so that $\varepsilon$ enters $V$ only additively as shown in (9). This implies that the conditional choice probabilities $P(i|x)$ for the dynamic discrete choice model are given by exactly the same formulas as for static discrete choice models, except that the relevant utility function is not the static utility function $u$, but the fixed point $v$ of the contraction mapping (8). Second, assumption (5) implies that the dynamic programming problem can be solved by computing the fixed point $v = T(v)$ over the space $\Gamma = \{(x,i)|x\in R^M, i\in C(x)\}$. This is a much easier task than computing the fixed point $V(x,\varepsilon)$ over the direct state space $V = \{(x,\varepsilon)|x\in R^M, \varepsilon\in R^N\}$ since $\varepsilon$ is a continuous-valued $N$-dimensional vector which must be discretized into $K^N$ values (where $K$ is the diameter of the grid for $\varepsilon$), whereas the argument $i$ entering $v(x,i)$ is already discrete and assumes at most $N$ values.

Given a parametric specification for the unknown objects $u$, $q$ and $\pi$, one can "recover" the agent's underlying preferences $(\beta,u)$ and expectations $(\pi,q)$ by finding parameter values that maximize the likelihood function. This suggests the following *nested fixed point algorithm*: an "outer" nonlinear optimization algorithm searches for the parameter vector $\theta$ that maximizes the likelihood function, and an "inner" fixed point algorithm recalculates the fixed point $v_v$ of (8) each time the outer optimization algorithm updates its estimate of $\theta$. Rust (1988) showed that under certain regularity conditions, the NFXP algorithm produces consistent and asymptotically normally distributed parameter estimates.

Before presenting parametric specifications for $u$, $q$ and $\pi$, I should mention some drawbacks of the discrete control formulation. Although I have argued that there are good reasons for treating the employment decision $d_t$ as discrete, both time $t$ and the consumption decision $c_t$ appear to be better approximated by continuous variables. My response is that the discrete formulation seems to be the best available approximation given the computational and data limitations I face. The computational limitation is that, to my knowledge, there are no estimation algorithms available for continuous-time stochastic control problems, or for dynamic programming models where the decision variable is mixed discrete/continuous.[4] The data limitation is that individuals in the RHS are sampled at two-year intervals with only limited retrospective information on their states and decisions between survey dates. In theory, one could formulate a very fine grain, discrete-time model (regarded as a close approximation to the actual continuous-time decision process) and "integrate out" the dates for which no data are available, but the computational burden required to solve the model and perform the integrations appears to be prohibitive. Therefore I interpret the decisions $i_t = (d_t, c_t)$ as "plans", as of date $t$, that are revised at the same two-year time intervals as the survey dates. Thus, the state variables $x_t$ refer to the worker's state in the previous two years, and the decisions $i_t = (d_t, c_t)$ refer to the worker's plans regarding consumption and labor force participation over the next two years. The plans need not be fulfilled, hence there will be a conditional probability distribution for the state $x_{t+1}$ at time $t+1$ conditional on the current state $x_t$, and plan $i_t = (d_t, c_t)$ chosen at time $t$. Under this interpretation it is much more natural to regard the choice of a consumption plan $c_t$ as an interval rather than a specific number since there will be unforeseen future events that cause actual consumption to deviate from the plan. The use of consumption intervals may also help mitigate the effects of the inevitable errors in variables in the constructed consumption data.[5] Since I do not actually observe the consumption plan chosen by the worker in the RHS, in the empirical implementation of the model I will assume that the ex post realized consumption interval coincides with the ex ante plan.

### 12.3.3    Specification of Workers' Preferences

Table 12.5 summarizes the formulation of the retirement problem as a discrete control process. Death, quite naturally, is treated as an absorbing state and the bequest function specifies the utility of entering this state. The dynamic programming problem proceeds by backward induction from the (uncertain) age of death over two-year intervals back to an initial age, 58, the age of the youngest respondent in the first wave of the RHS.

It remains to specify the functional forms for $b$, $u$, $\pi$, and $q$.[6] The NFXP algorithm places no restrictions on the functional forms for $b$, $u$, and $\pi$, but computational tractability appears to require that the distribution of unobservables $q$ be a member of McFadden's (1981)

**Table 12.5    Summary of the Retirement Decision Problem**

| Item | Notation |
|---|---|
| Choice set | $C(x) = \{1,2,3\} \otimes \{c^1, \ldots, c^J\}$,   $1 = $ ft, $2 = $ pt, $3 = $ ne |
| Control vector | $i_t = (d_t, c_t)$; $d_t \in \{1,2,3\}$,   $c_t \in \{c^1, \ldots, c^J\}$ |
| State vector (observed) | $x_t = (w_t, h_t, a_t, ms_t, cs_t, e_t, y_t, aw_t)$ |
| State vector (unobserved) | $\varepsilon_t \equiv \{\varepsilon_t(i) | i \in C(x_t)\}$,   $\varepsilon_t(i) = \varepsilon_t(d,c)$ |
| Bequest function | $b(w_t, ms_t, cs_t, \theta_1)$ |
| Utility function | $u(d_t, c_t, e_t, h_t, a_t, ms_t, \theta_2)$ |
| Transition density ($x_t$) | $\pi(x_{t+1} | x_t, i_t, \theta_3)$ |
| Transition density ($\varepsilon_t$) | $q(\varepsilon_t | x_t, \theta_4) \sim \text{GEV}(C(x_t), \theta_4)$,   see (11) |
| Parameter vector | $\theta = (\beta, \theta_1, \theta_2, \theta_3, \theta_4)$,   $1 \times (1 + K_1 + K_2 + K_3 + K_4)$ |

generalized extreme value (GEV) family.[7] The GEV family is closed under the operation of maximization, leading to convenient closed-form expressions for the social surplus function (6) and its derivatives, the choice probabilities (7). This feature greatly simplifies the NFXP algorithm, avoiding the numerical integrations that are normally required for other multivariate distributions. I chose a particular member of this family whose cumulative distribution function $Q(\varepsilon,\theta_4)$ is given below.

$$(11) \qquad Q(\varepsilon,\theta_4) = \exp\left\{ -\sum_{\delta=1}^{3}\left[\sum_{j=1}^{J} \exp\{\varepsilon(\delta,j)/\theta_{4\delta}\}\right]^{\theta_{4\delta}}\right\},$$
$$0 \le \theta_{4\delta} \le 0, \quad \delta = 1,2,3.$$

Since the corresponding density $q$ does not depend on $x$, it follows that the unobserved state variables are serially independent in this specification. Formula (11) includes the standard multivariate extreme value distribution as a special case when $\theta_{4\delta} = 1$, $\delta = 1,2,3$. The latter distribution satisfies the well-known IIA property: the components $\varepsilon(\delta,j)$ and $\varepsilon(d,c)$ are contemporaneously independent when $(d,c) \ne (\delta,j)$. When $\theta_{4\delta}$ are not all equal to 1 one obtains a pattern of contemporaneous correlation in the components of $\varepsilon_t$ represented by the choice tree shown in figure 12.2.

Thus, (11) allows correlation in the unobserved state variables affecting the consumption decision $c_t$ given the labor supply decision $d_t$, but assumes independence in unobserved state variables corresponding to different labor supply choices. Formula (11) yields the following nested logit formulas for the conditional choice probabilities:

$$(12) \qquad\qquad P(d,c|x,\theta) = P(c|x,d,\theta)P(d|x,\theta),$$

where $P(c|x,d,\theta)$ and $P(d|x,\theta)$ are given by

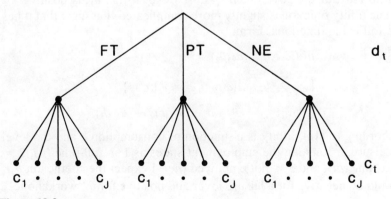

Figure 12.2

$$(13) \qquad P(c|x,d,\theta) = \frac{\exp\{v_\theta(x,c,d)/\theta_{4d}\}}{\sum\limits_{j=1}^{J} \exp\{v_\theta(x,j,d)/\theta_{4d}\}},$$

$$(14) \qquad P(d|x,\theta) = \frac{\exp\{I(d)\theta_{4d}\}}{\sum\limits_{\delta=1}^{3} \exp\{I(\delta)\theta_{4\delta}\}},$$

where the *Inclusive Value*, $I(d)$, is defined by

$$(15) \qquad I(d) = \ln\left[\sum_{j=1}^{J} \exp\{v_\theta(x,d,j)/\theta_{4d}\}\right] \qquad d = 1,2,3.$$

Finally (11) yields an explicit formula for the fixed point condition (8)

$$(16) \qquad v_\theta(x,d,c) = u(x,d,c,\theta_2) +$$

$$\beta\int_y \ln\left[\sum_{\delta=1}^{3}[\sum_{j=1}^{J}\exp\{v_\theta(y,\delta,j)/\theta_{4\delta}\}]^{\theta_{4\delta}}\right]\pi(dy|x,d,c,\theta_3),$$

with the implicit "terminal condition" that $v_\theta(x,d,c) = b(w,ms,\theta_1)$ if $h = $ "dead".

It remains to specify the functional forms for the bequest and utility functions, $b$ and $u$. I assume that the bequest function has the following functional form

$$(17) \qquad b(w,ms,\theta_1) = w^{\theta_{11}}(\theta_{12} + \theta_{13}ms).$$

The coefficient $\theta_{11}$ will reflect a diminishing or increasing marginal utility of bequests depending on whether $\theta_{11}$ is greater or less than 1. The Menchik and David study discussed in section 12.2.2 suggests that possibly $\theta_{11} > 1$. Presumably a married worker obtains greater utility from bequests to the remaining spouse than from bequests to friends, institutions, or the government. Thus, I expect that $\theta_{13}$ is positive.

The utility function is slightly more complicated. I assume that it has the following functional form:

$$(18) \qquad u(d,c,e,h,a,ms,\theta_2) =$$

$$[\sum_{i=1}^{3}\sum_{j=1}^{3}\theta_{2,i*j}\,I\{d = i,e = j\}][c^{\theta_{210}}]$$

$$[e^{\theta_{211}}][\theta_{212} + \theta_{213}\,a + \theta_{214}ms + \theta_{215}h].$$

According to (18), utility is a function of consumption $c$ and the level of leisure $e$. Ranking the employment states as $1 = $ full-time (*ft*), $2 = $ part-time (*pt*), and $3 = $ not employed (*ne*), I expect the coefficient $\theta_{211}$ should be negative for a leisure lover and positive for a "workaholic".

The coefficient $\theta_{210}$ should be positive and less than 1 if there is diminishing marginal utility of consumption. The basic utility obtained from consumption and leisure is modified by the last factor in (18) which accounts for health status, age, marital status, and the presence of children. Ranking the health states as 1 = good health, 2 = fair health, 3 = disabled, I expect that the coefficient $\theta_{215}$ should be negative; being in worse health diminishes the utility obtained from consumption or leisure (or work, if he is a work-lover). It is not clear what sign to expect for the coefficient $\theta_{213}$ on the age variable. Perhaps as one gets older, one's remaining lifetime becomes more precious, suggesting a positive coefficient. However, aging might also result in general mental and physical deterioration independent of that captured by the health variable, suggesting a negative sign. One would ordinarily expect the presence of a spouse to increase the worker's utility, suggesting a positive value for $\theta_{214}$.

The final term in (18) is the double summation term that reflects the monetary and psychic search costs of changing employment states. Perhaps the hardest transition to make is from the retired state to finding a new full-time job. This suggests the coefficient on $I\{d=1, e=3\}$ should be a large negative number, reflecting the data in table 12.1 that very few retired workers ever "unretire" and return to work at a full-time job. On the other hand, it should be relatively easy to make the reverse transition and retire from either a full- or part-time job: $I\{d=3, e=1\}$ or $I\{d=3, e=2\}$. Thus, the coefficients on these terms should be positive, possibly reflecting the utility value of any retirement bonuses or incentives. I would also expect that it is relatively easier to move into a part-time job from a full-time job, than vice versa, so I expect the coefficient on $I\{d=2, e=1\}$ to exceed the coefficient for $I\{d=1, e=2\}$. To the extent that workers desire to make a gradual transition from work to retirement, the coefficient on $I\{d=2, e=1\}$ should be positive, reflecting the prevalence of partial retirement discussed in section 12.2.5. The remaining coefficients reflect the utility costs of decisions to remain in the current employment state: $I\{d=3, e=3\}$, $I\{d=2, e=2\}$, and $I\{d=1, e=1\}$. For leisure lovers, there should be disutility associated with the decision to continue working, hence I expect the coefficient on $I\{d=1, e=1\}$ to be negative, but substantially less than coefficients for $I\{d=1, e=2\}$ or $I\{d=1, e=3\}$. The workers who partially retire might enjoy the experience, so it is possible that the coefficient for $I\{d=2, e=2\}$ is positive. In any case, it should be easier to remain on a current part-time job than to find a new one, so the coefficient for $I\{d=2, e=2\}$ should exceed the coefficients for $I\{d=2, e=1\}$ or $I\{d=2, e=3\}$. Of all the decisions, it is perhaps easiest to remain retired; thus, at least for leisure lovers, I expect that the coefficient for $I\{d=3, e=3\}$ to be positive.

The primary source of population heterogeneity that I wish to account for is the distinction between work lovers and leisure lovers. Rather than treat this as unobserved heterogeneity, one can use the responses from attitudinal questions in the RHS to classify each worker as a work lover or leisure lover, interacting this taste variable with the coefficients of $u$ that can be expected to differ between work lovers and leisure lovers. One can account for additional heterogeneity by making certain parameters functions of time-invariant sociodemographic variables, the most important of which are race and the worker's main career occupation and industry.

### 12.3.4 Specification of Workers' Expectations[8]

Having specified the general form of the worker's per period objective function, it remains to specify the law of motion for the state variables. I assume that the observed state vector $x_t = (w_t, h_t, a_t, ms_t, e_t, y_t, aw_t)$ evolves according to a parametric Markov transition density $\pi(x_{t+1}|x_t, i_t, \theta_3)$ that depends on the worker's consumption and labor supply decision $i_t = (d_t, c_t)$. The transition density embodies the worker's expectations about his future health, his lifespan, and the future levels of his income and stock of wealth. More precisely, I assume that workers' individual expectations about future values of the state variables coincide with the population behavior of these variables (as represented by the estimated transition density $\pi$) within each sociodemographic stratum.

Since the transition probability $\pi$ only depends on observable variables $\{i_t, x_t\}$, one could in principle use nonparametric methods to estimate it. With a discrete state space, the nonparametric estimate of $\pi(x_{t+1}|x_t, i_t)$ is simply the number of transitions $(x_{t+1}, x_t, i_t)$ divided by the total number of transitions of the form $(y, x_t, i_t)$ summed over all states $y$. However, with a large number of discrete cells and a limited amount of data, the nonparametric estimate of $\pi$ will be identically zero for many transitions $(x_{t+1}, x_t, i_t)$, even though it is clear that such transitions can actually occur with positive probability. Therefore it is preferable to use parametric functional forms for $\pi$ that "smooth out" the data on state transitions to yield positive estimates for all transition probabilities that are logically possible. It is also desirable to use flexible functional forms that do not impose arbitrary a priori restrictions on possible transitions. The conditional logit model (with full sets of alternative-specific dummies and sufficient terms for interactions of different explanatory variables) is an ideal candidate. However, given the very large number of possible states for $x_{t+1}$, a single joint estimation of $\pi$ is out of the question. It is much simpler to decompose $\pi$ as a product of conditional probabilities for each component $x_t(m)$, resulting in a series of tractable conditional logit estimations where the number of alternatives equals the (relatively small) number of values that each component $x_t(m)$ can assume. Since a multivariate probability density can always be decomposed as a product of the conditional and marginal densities of its components, there is no loss in generality in this approach.

The state variable $a_t$ representing the worker's age has the simplest law of motion: $a_{t+1} = a_t + 2$. To keep $a_t$ in a finite number of cells, I will assume that there is a maximum age of, say, 98 years which is treated as an absorbing state. This does not necessarily imply that all people die with probability 1 at age 98, rather the model simply does not account for further increases in the mortality hazard beyond age 98. For all practical purposes, however, the mortality rate for men over age 90 is so high that there is no effective loss in generality from assuming that all workers die with probability 1 at age 98, an assumption that leads to substantial computational simplifications, as I show in section 12.4. Therefore I assume that life ends with probability 1 at age 98 or before, implying that $a_t$ takes on twenty values in increments of two from a starting age of 58.

The state variable $h_t$ representing health takes on one of four values, $\{1,2,3,4\}$, where 1 denotes good health, 2 denotes a health condition which the respondent reports limits his ability to get around or to work (yet which is not so severe that the worker is actually disabled), 3 denotes that the worker has been certified by a doctor to be disabled (and hence is not working and is eligible for Social Security disability benefits), and 4 denotes the absorbing state of death. States 1 and 2 are obviously somewhat subjective in nature. State 3, on the other hand, is much less subjective since Social Security has fairly strict rules regarding doctor certification of disability in order for a worker to receive disability benefits. According to Social Security rules, any person receiving disability benefits cannot work (except for a brief "trial employment" period lasting at most twelve months), so the employment state for a person with $h_t = 3$ should be the singleton $e_t = \{ne\}$. It is possible, however, for a disabled person to try to search for a job at the risk of losing his disability benefits. Thus, even though a person is disabled I allow the worker the full set of employment decisions, $d_t = \{ft,pt,ne\}$. This allows me (in at least a crude way) to study the effect of disability insurance on workers' incentives to re-enter the labor force.

Transitions between health states 1, 2, and 3 obey a parametric transition probability of the form

(19) $$\pi_1(h_{t+1}|\ h_t,a_t,ms_t,e_t,w_t,c_t,d_t;\theta_{31}),$$

which gives the probability of health next period as a function of health this period together with age, marital status, employment status, wealth, and the labor supply and consumption decisions. The function $\pi$ can be taken to have a trinomial logit form, with separate coefficients for each of the independent variables and their interactions. The estimated health transition probability can be interpreted as accounting for workers' perceptions of the "leniency" of admission to the disability program. For example, the conditional probability that $h_{t+1} = 3$ given $h_t = 2$ equals the worker's chances of getting onto the disability roles given that he is not in good health at time $t$. A separate binomial logit probability function captures workers' mortality assessments as a function of their age and other state variables $x_t$.

A binomial logit probability function will also be used to capture the stochastic process for worker marital status, $ms_t$, as a function of the state variables $x_t$ and decision variables $(c_t, d_t)$. Marital status takes on two states, married or single. A married man may lose his wife through death or divorce, but once single, is allowed to remarry.

The state variable $e_t$ representing the worker's employment status takes on three values $\{1, 2, 3\}$, corresponding to full-time work, part-time work, and not in the labor force, respectively. The conditional probability density for $e_{t+1}$ has a trinomial logit form

(20)  $$\pi_2(e_{t+1}|\ e_t, a_t, ms_t, w_t, h_t, y_t, d_t; \theta_{32}).$$

It is particularly important to allow for the effects of age and health on re-employment probabilities. Wealth and income are included as proxies for unobserved job skills which may make the worker more employable; presumably wealthier, higher income workers have better job skills and are thus more employable. I include last period employment status $e_t$ to control for any structural state dependence due to past lapses into unemployment or retirement. Presumably there is more stigma to being unemployed rather than retired, so an unemployed worker might face lower probabilities of re-employment than a retired person. Thus, the model might be able to provide some insight into the "discouraged worker effect" wherein a worker decides to retire rather than face the frustration of trying to search for a new job. I expect that a worker's chance of being fired from his current job increases with age and poor health, and decreases with "experience" as proxied by his current income and wealth, $y_t$ and $w_t$. I also expect that full-time jobs are more secure than part-time jobs. Mandatory retirement beyond a certain age can be incorporated as a probability 1 chance of being fired when $a_t$ exceeds the mandatory retirement age.

It remains to describe the transition probability function for wealth, $w_t$. The standard budget equation is that wealth next period equals wealth this period plus earnings and income from investments, less consumption expenditures:

(21)  $$w_{t+1} = w_t + y_t - c_t.$$

Thus, predicting next period's wealth reduces to predicting next period's earnings conditional on a specific choice of consumption interval

$c_t$. This requires estimating a transition density for total income $y_t$ of the form

(22)     $\pi_3(y_{t+1}| y_t, w_t, aw_t, h_t, a_t, e_t, ms_t, d_t; \theta_{33})$.

Here the function $\pi_3$ can be thought of as an earnings function which predicts the worker's earnings and investment income over the next two years as a function of his observed state $x_t$ (including his last period income $y_t$) and employment decision $d_t$. The earnings function captures workers' expectations about their future earnings streams and the retirement or disability benefits due to them under Social Security. For example, if the worker is currently employed full-time ($e_t = 1$), then $\pi_3$ will predict his next period earnings on his job. These earnings will be a function of his age, health, and level of job experience. Wealth $w_t$ and income $y_t$ are included as proxies for job skills, since presumably wealth, job earnings, and ability/experience are highly correlated. $\pi_3$ also includes investment income on existing wealth, $\bar{r}w_t$, where $\bar{r}$ is a random rate of return on the worker's investment portfolio. Wealth will be measured to include both real and financial wealth, including real estate, the cash value of insurance policies, and other personal property such as automobiles and furniture, etc. If the worker is currently unemployed and searching for work, ($d_t = 2$ or $d_t = 1$, and $e_t = 3$), then the earnings function predicts the worker's unemployment insurance benefits. If the worker is retired, ($e_t = 3$ and $a_t \geq 62$), then $\pi_3$ predicts the worker's Social Security benefits. These benefits are a function of the worker's average monthly wage, $aw_t$ (which determines his primary insurance amount and benefits), and his marital status, $ms_t$. $\pi_3$ also predicts payments from Social Security disability insurance and Medicare in the event the worker is disabled or in bad health, and the death benefit in the event the worker dies. Thus, the earnings function $\pi_3$ completely embodies the worker's expectations of his future earnings streams under all eventualities—retirement, employment, or unemployment—and includes contingent payments for health and life insurance. Changes in Social Security policy, such as changes in benefit levels or retirement ages, can be represented through appropriate changes in the earnings function. One can simulate the effects of changes in Social Security policy by appropriately altering the earnings function $\pi_3$ and recomputing the new optimal retirement strategy. This allows one to quantify how much workers are "hurt" by a policy change by measuring the lump-sum fee workers would be willing to pay in order to keep the existing Social Security rules intact. One can also measure how the policy change alters the probability of retirement for each configuration of the state variables.

The final state variable is the average monthly wage, $aw_t$. As an average of lifetime earnings, $aw_t$ will be fairly insensitive to earnings levels and labor supply choices at the end of the worker's career, especially once it is discretized. Thus, there are no real dynamics for $aw_t$; it is simply an indicator of the level of benefits coming due to the worker. There is some question as to whether the average wage need even be included in the model since it should be very highly correlated with the earnings $y_t$ on the worker's full-time job and wealth $w_t$. This is an empirical issue. If $aw_t$ can be adequately proxied by $y_t$ and $w_t$, I would eliminate it as a state variable to conserve on the dimensionality of the fixed point problem.

## 12.4  Numerical Computation of the Dynamic Programming Model

As described in section 12.3, the revealed preference problem reduces to estimation of the unknown parameter vector $\theta = (\beta,\theta_1,\theta_2, \theta_3,\theta_4)$, where $0<\beta<1$ is the worker's intertemporal discount factor, $\theta_1$ are the parameters entering the bequest function, $b$, $\theta_2$ are the parameters entering the utility function $u$, $\theta_3$ are the parameters of the transition probability for the observed state variables $\pi$, and $\theta_4$ are the parameters of the transition probability for the unobserved state variables $q$. The unknown parameters can be estimated by maximum likelihood method using the following three-step procedure.

*Step 1.* Estimate the vector $\theta_3$, entering the transition density $\pi(x_{t+1}|x_t,i_t,\theta_3)$ using the partial likelihood function $L_1(\theta_3)$ defined by

$$(23) \qquad L_1(\theta_3) \equiv \prod_{k=1}^{K} \prod_{t=1}^{5} \pi(x_{t+1,k}|x_{t,k},i_{t,k},\theta_3),$$

where $k$ indexes individuals in the RHS sample.

*Step 2.* Using the initial consistent estimate of $\hat{\theta}_3$ from step 1, estimate $(\beta,\theta_1,\theta_2,\theta_4)$ using the partial likelihood function $L_2(\beta,\theta_1, \theta_2,\hat{\theta}_3,\theta_4)$ defined by

$$(24) \qquad L_2(\beta,\theta_1,\theta_2,\hat{\theta}_3,\theta_4) \equiv \prod_{k=1}^{K} \prod_{t=1}^{5} P(i_{t,k}|x_{t,k},(\beta,\theta_1,\theta_2,\hat{\theta}_3,\theta_4)),$$

where $P$ is defined by (12) through (15) and the fixed point condition (16).

*Step 3.* To get correct estimated standard errors and asymptotically efficient parameter estimates for $\hat{\theta}$, compute one Newton-step from the initial consistent estimate $\hat{\theta}$ using the full likelihood function $L_f(\theta)$ defined by

$$(25) \qquad L_f(\theta) \equiv \prod_{k=1}^{K} \prod_{t=1}^{5} P(i_{t+1,k}|x_{t+1,k},\theta)\pi(x_{t+1,k}|x_{t,k},i_{t,k},\theta_3).$$

The nested fixed point algorithm is required only in steps 2 and 3 in order to compute the value function $v_\theta$ entering the conditional choice probabilities $P$. This requires recomputing the fixed point $v_\theta$ of the contraction mapping (16) each time the outer nonlinear maximization algorithm computes new values for $\theta$. As discussed in section 12.3, if there are continuous state variables, then the fixed point $v_\theta$ is an element of an infinite-dimensional Banach space $B$. The computational strategy is to discretize the continuous state variables, and in effect, approximate the infinite-dimensional space $B$ by a high-dimensional Euclidean space $R^N$. The dimension of the fixed point problem $N$ is equal to the number of possible values of $i$ and the discretized values that $x$ can assume. Suppose that $w_t$ is discretized into 100 cells, $y_t$ into 5 cells, and $c_t$ into 5 cells. Assuming that $aw_t$ can be proxied by $w_t$ and $y_t$, the remaining state variables assume the following number of values: $h_t$:4, $a_t$:20, $e_t$:3, $ms_t$:2, $d_t$:3. The implied fixed point dimension is $N = 3{,}600{,}000 = 100*5*5*4*20*3*2*3$. Thus, a 3.6 million dimensional fixed point must be repeatedly recalculated in the fixed point subroutine of the nested fixed point algorithm during the course of the parameter search. It is therefore necessary to find algorithms to compute high-dimensional fixed points as rapidly as possible, say, in less than thirty seconds on a supercomputer such as the Cray-2.

By theorem 1 the fixed point problem can be written as $v = T(v)$, where the contraction operator $T$ is defined in formula (16). There are two principal algorithms for computing contraction fixed points: contraction iterations and Newton-Kantorovich iterations. Contraction iterations involve repeated evaluations of the contraction mapping $T$ starting from an arbitrary initial estimate $v_0$:

$$(26) \qquad v_{k+1} = T(v_k)$$

The Newton-Kantorovich method converts the fixed point problem into the problem of finding a zero of a nonlinear operator, $(I - T)(v) = 0$, where $I$ is the identity operator on $B$ and 0 is the zero element of $B$. This nonlinear equation is then solved for $v$ using Newton's method:

$$(27) \qquad v_{k+1} = v_k - [I - T'(v_k)]^{-1}[I - T](v_k)$$

where $T'(v_k)$ is the Frêchet derivative of $T$ with respect to $v$ evaluated at the point $v_k$. The method of successive approximations is guaranteed to converge for contraction mappings, however, the convergence is very slow (especially when $\beta$ is close to 1). Newton's method has a very rapid quadratic rate of convergence, however the method is only guaranteed to work in a "domain of attraction" of points sufficiently close to the true fixed point $v$. The other disadvantage of Newton's method is that one must solve an $N \times N$ linear system involving the matrix $[I - T'(v_k)]$. For large $N$ the time and storage required to solve the linear system becomes prohibitive.

Although the fixed point problem looks formidable at first glance, the retirement problem has a special structure that can be exploited in order to dramatically reduce the computational burden. There are two principal features of the retirement problem that can be effectively exploited: (1) using the absorbing state of death to induce a backward recursion for the value function, and (2) exploiting the sparsity structure of the transition probability matrix representation of $\pi$, in particular exploiting the deterministic transitions for $a_t$ and the banded structure of the wealth transition probabilities. The first feature is based on the observation that in the absorbing state of death the value function has an a priori known functional form, $v_\theta = b$. Therefore $v_\theta$ need only be calculated for the three remaining health states, reducing the effective dimension of the problem from $N = 3.6$ million to $N = 2.7$ million. Under the additional assumption that workers die with probability 1 beyond some fixed age, say 98, one can compute the fixed point $v_\theta$ in a single contraction iteration, essentially by backwards induction from the last year of life (in this case, age 98). From an economic perspective, this is a relatively innocuous assumption since extremely few males live beyond age 98. However, without this assumption one is faced with an infinite-horizon problem since the model places no upper bound on the lifespan of the worker. In this case a combination of contraction and Newton-Kantorovich iterations are required in order to compute $v_\theta$, increasing the required computer time by several orders of magnitude. Since the assumption of fixed lifespan is basically harmless and leads to substantial computational simplifications, I will adopt it in my empirical work. The second feature, exploiting the sparsity structure, allows one to economize on the number of storage locations required to hold the matrix representation of $\pi$, and to significantly reduce the number of operations needed to evaluate the contraction mapping $T$ (16) or solve the $N \times N$ linear system in the Newton-Kantorovich iteration (27).

To understand the latter point, consider the work involved in computing a single evaluation of the contraction mapping $T$. Once the state vector $x$ is discretized, the majority of the work is the required integration with respect to the transition probability $\pi$. This is equivalent to left matrix multiplication of the "vectorized" integrand by the matrix representation of $\pi$. Matrix multiplication is a very simple operation that is easily vectorized for maximum efficiency on a vector processor like the Cray-2. However, such matrix-vector multiplications require order $N^2$ multiplications and additions, where $N$ is the number of discrete cells that $x_t$ can assume. Even a machine that can multiply at 400 megaflops (400 million floating point operations per second) can get quickly bogged down when $N$ exceeds several hundred thousand. It is therefore essential to reduce the total number of multiplications by exploiting the sparsity of the matrix representation of $\pi$. Unfortunately, standard algebraic techniques for sparse matrices typically do not perform well on vector processors owing to the irregular memory reference patterns for their elements, creating "bank conflicts" that prevent the processors from running at maximum efficiency with continuously full vector pipelines. For example, even after extensive modification and optimization of standard sparse linear equation solvers, the resulting code typically runs slower than 12 megaflops on the Cray-1 (Duff 1984). This is significantly slower than the Cray-1's peak rates of 160 megaflops on dense linear algebra problems. The trick, then, is to exploit the sparsity structure of the transition matrix to reduce the total number of operations while at the same time attempting to keep the nonzero elements in a "locally dense" configuration so they can be fed to the vector registers in a continuous stream, allowing the processors to run uninterrupted at nearly peak speed.

Figures 12.3 through 12.8 depict different sparsity patterns for the matrix representation of $\pi$ depending on the ordering of the component state variables in $x_t$. $\pi$ can be regarded as a direct product of three types of transition matrices: (1) a circulant matrix for $a_t$, (2) a banded matrix for $w_t$, and (3) a dense matrix representing the joint transition matrix for the remaining state variables. These component matrices are depicted in figure 12.3. By varying the order of these component matrices in the construction of the direct product, one obtains different sparsity patterns for $\pi$. Figures 12.4, 12.5, and 12.6 depict the sparsity patterns for the orderings $(d,w,a)$, $(w,a,d)$, and $(a,d,w)$, respectively. None of these orderings is particularly desirable, for they all lead to fairly irregular and dispersed memory reference patterns. Figure 12.7 depicts the "optimal" sparsity pattern, $(a,w,d)$, which produces the maximum amount of local density in the storage pattern for the matrix elements. The matrix-vector multiplication under this structure occurs in an outer do-loop over age values 1 to 20, calling a block-banded matrix multiplication subroutine specially designed to keep the vector pipelines continuously full. Figure 12.8 shows the packed storage arrangement for the block-banded matrices that form the off-diagonal sectors of $\pi$. This arrangement allows one to fully exploit the sparsity of $\pi$ while keeping the vector processor running at nearly maximum efficiency.

Exploitation of sparsity patterns is particularly important in the infinite horizon case. For sufficiently high discount factors, $\beta$, it will be optimal to use Newton-Kantorovich iterations rather than contraction iterations alone, but the former requires the solution of the linear system involving the matrix $[I - T'(v)]$. However it is easy to see that $T'(v)$ is simply $\beta$ times the transition probability matrix for the controlled process $\{i_t, x_t\}$ which is isomorphic to the basic transition matrix

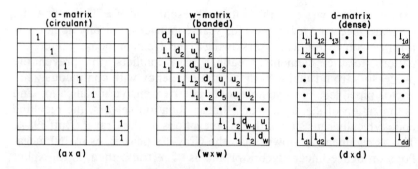

**Figure 12.3**     State transition matrices

**Figure 12.4**     Sparsity pattern: $(d, w, a)$

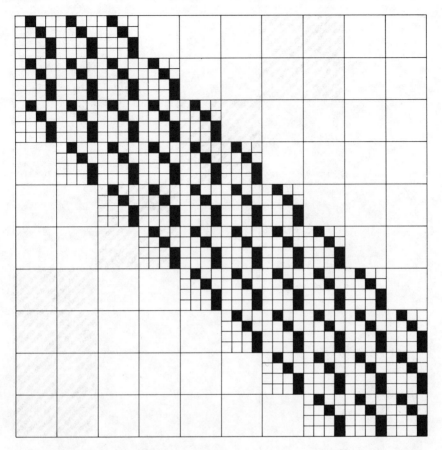

**Figure 12.5**     Sparsity pattern: $(w,a,d)$

for $\pi$. Thus, for each ordering of the underlying state variables, the matrix $[I - T'(v)]$ will have the same sparsity pattern as the matrix representation of $\pi$ in figures 12.4 through 12.7 except for the 1's along the diagonal. Under the "optimal" ordering $(a,w,d)$, one can see from figure 12.8 that except for the lower $(a,a)$ block, this matrix $[I - T'(v)]$ is already in upper triangular form. Thus, solving the linear system only requires an LU factorization of the lower $(a,a)$ block followed by recursive back-substitution to compute the solution for age groups $a - 1$ to 1. Since LU factorization is an order $N^3$ operation, the time saved under the optimal ordering is proportional to $a^3$, which amounts to a speedup of 8,000 times when $a = 20$. Further speedups can be obtained by accounting for the block-banded structure of the $(a,a)$

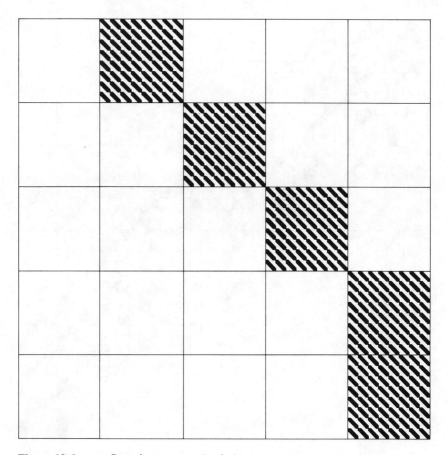

**Figure 12.6**        Sparsity pattern: $(a,d,w)$

block of $[I - T'(v)]$. I have designed a block elimination algorithm which LU factors the $(a,a)$ block of $[I - T'(v)]$ using a banded-Crout decomposition, with elimination operations that are performed on $d \times d$ blocks instead of individual matrix elements. The matrix $[I - T'(v)]$ has sufficient diagonal dominance that the block elimination algorithm is numerically stable even though pivot operations only occur within the elementary $d \times d$ block operations of the block elimination procedure.[9] Thus, by determining the optimal ordering of state variables one can design a special linear equation algorithm that fully exploits the sparsity structure of the $[I - T'(v)]$ matrix while keeping the vector processors running continuously at nearly peak efficiency. This fortuitous situation allows one to solve linear systems that are orders of

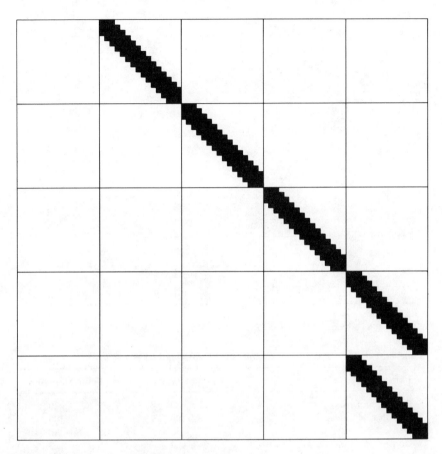

**Figure 12.7**    Sparsity pattern: $(a,w,d)$

magnitude larger than the largest systems solvable using standard sparse matrix software.

I conclude with table 12.6 which presents timings of the fixed point algorithm on the Cray-2. As one can see, the "finite horizon" assumption that workers die with probability 1 after age 98 allows one to expand the dimension of the problem by an order of magnitude. The average performance rate of 220 megaflops is good performance for a single processor bank of the Cray-2.[10] Overall, table 12.6 demonstrates that one can exploit the power of the supercomputer and the special structure of the fixed-point problem to permit estimation of a fairly realistic model of retirement behavior. In future work I plan to use this technology to actually estimate the unknown parameters of the model.[11]

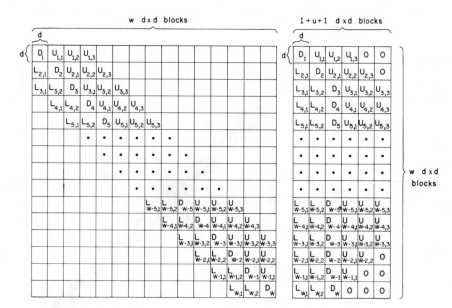

**Figure 12.8**    Packed storage form for block-banded matrix

**Table 12.6**    **Fixed Point Computation Times on the Cray-2**

| Item | Infinite Horizon | Finite Horizon |
|---|---|---|
| Age categories, $a$ | 20 | 20 |
| Wealth categories, $w$ | 100 | 100 |
| Dense block size, $d$ | 50 | 90 |
| Consumption levels, $\#c$ | 0 | 5 |
| Labor decisions, $\#d$ | 3 | 3 |
| Maximum bandwidth (blocks) | 10 | 10 |
| Fixed point dimension, $N$ | 300,000 | 2,700,000 |
| CPU time (seconds) | 14.3 | 6.9 |
| Average rate (megaflops) | 198 | 220 |

*Note:* Times are for one processor on the University of Minnesota four-processor Cray-2 with 256 million word common memory.

# Notes

1. Burtless and Moffitt (1984) and Gustman and Steinmeier (1986) provided two of the most recent structural analyses of retirement behavior. Burtless and Moffitt allowed state-dependent preferences, but simplified the sequential decision problem by assuming that pre- and post-retirement consumption levels are fixed, leading to a two-stage approximation to the sequential labor supply-consumption decision. Gustman and Steinmeier estimated a fully sequential continuous-time model of consumption and labor supply, however, they assumed perfect certainty and perfect capital markets.

2. The authors reported, however, that "the correspondence among outcomes based on these alternative definitions (i.e. objective measures based on reductions in hours or wages) is relatively close, and the main conclusions of the paper remain unchanged using the alternative measure" (fn. 7, p. 405).

3. A statistical model is *degenerate* if a subset of its variables satisfy a relation with probability 1.

4. There have been recent advances in estimation methods for static discrete/continuous choice models by Dubin and McFadden (1984) and Haneman (1984). However, it is unclear whether these methods will extend to dynamic programming models. An alternative possibility is to attempt to merge the "orthogonality condition" method of Hansen and Singleton (1982) with the discrete choice framework of Rust (1986). A difficulty with this approach has been to specify a tractable stochastic process for the continuum of unobservables corresponding to each possible value of the continuous choice variable. Without such unobservables, one obtains a statistically degenerate model where the continuous choice variable is an exact function of other observed variables in the model.

5. The RHS has incomplete data on consumption expenditures. Rather than use this data directly, one can compute consumption from the budget equation $w_{t+1} = w_t + y_t - c_t$ since both income and wealth are measured much more completely and accurately in the RHS. An unfortunate complication is that the RHS records total income only for even-numbered years. Therefore, one must impute income in odd-numbered years based on retrospective information on labor force status in those years and a matched data file on Social Security earnings available for both even- and odd-numbered years.

6. These functional forms presented should be viewed as first guesses as to which specifications will "work." The final specification will be chosen from the results of a specification search over alternative functional forms using the NFXP algorithm.

7. Recent advances in simulation estimators by McFadden (1988) and Pakes and Pollard (1986) offer the hope of significantly extending the range of estimable distributions $q$ for the unobservables. However, it is not clear whether their methods, which depend heavily on having the simulation errors enter linearly and additively separately, directly extends to allow simulation instead of integration in the fixed point condition (8). In that case the simulation error is no longer additively separable, so the simulations must increase with the sample size to avoid inconsistency due to nonlinear "errors in variables".

8. Rust (1989) provides estimation results for workers' expectations using specifications outlined in this section.

9. A simple check of the numerical accuracy of the method is to compute the fixed point with $b$ and $u$ identically equal to 1. It is easy to see that in this case $v_\theta = 1/(1 - \beta)$, so the numerical results of the algorithm can be checked against this exact solution. Running the algorithm in 64-bit single precision with $\beta = .999999$, I found that the computed solution agreed with the theoretical solution to twelve significant digits.

10. A simulation analysis of the Cray-2 processor (on a MacIntosh) by Lawrence Liddiard (1986) suggests that a single processor can achieve a maximum rate of 433 megaflops for dense matrix multiplication. The highest rates that have been recorded for the University of Minnesota Cray-2 (as of March 1987) have been on the order of 360 megaflops. The single processor average of 220 megaflops reported in table 12.6 has been achieved using standard library kernels without special assembly language coding to optimize the flow of data from common memory to local memory and to the vector registers, and back

to common memory. The easiest way to get significant speed increases is to utilize all four processors of the Cray-2 simultaneously. The fixed point computation can be fairly easily decomposed into sets of four independent subtasks (e.g., a separate processor is dedicated to computing the fixed point $v_\theta$ and the remaining processors assigned to computing each of the derivatives $\partial v_\theta/\partial\theta$), allowing a sustainable processing rate approaching 880 megaflops.

11. For estimates of workers' expectations, $\hat{\pi}$, see Rust (1989).

# References

Aaron, Henry J., and Gary Burtless. 1984. *Retirement and economic behavior.* Washington, D.C.: Brookings Institution.

Anderson, K. H., R. V. Burkhauser, and J. S. Butler. 1988. Work and health after retirement: A semi-parametric bivariate interval hazard model. Manuscript, Vanderbilt University.

Anderson, K. H., R. V. Burkhauser, and J. F. Quinn. 1984. Do retirement dreams come true? The effect of unexpected events on retirement age. Working Paper no. 750-84, Institute for Research on Poverty, University of Wisconsin-Madison.

Barro, R. J. 1974. Are government bonds net worth? *Journal of Political Economy* 82(6):1095–1117.

———. 1978. *The impact of Social Security on private saving.* Washington, D.C.: The American Enterprise Institute.

Bernheim, D. 1984. Dissaving after retirement: Testing the pure life cycle hypothesis. NBER Working Paper no. 1409. Cambridge, Mass.: National Bureau of Economic Research.

Blackwell, D. 1965. Discounted dynamic programming. *Annals of Statistics* 36:226–35.

Blinder, A., R. H. Gordon, and D. E. Wise. 1983. Social Security, bequests, and the life-cycle theory of savings. In *The determinants of national saving and wealth,* ed. F. Modigliani and R. Hemming, 89–122. New York: St. Martin's Press.

Bodie, Z., and J. B. Shoven, eds. 1983. *Financial aspects of the United States pension system.* Chicago: University of Chicago Press.

Boskin, M., and L. J. Kotlikoff. 1985. Public debt and United States savings: A new test of the neutrality hypothesis. In *The "new monetary economics," fiscal issues and unemployment,* ed. K. Brunner and A. H. Meltzer, vol. 23. Amsterdam: North-Holland.

Boskin, M., L. J. Kotlikoff, D. J. Puffert, and J. B. Shoven. 1986. Social Security: A financial appraisal across and within generations. NBER Working Paper no. 1891. Cambridge, Mass.: National Bureau of Economic Research.

Boskin, M., and M. Hurd. 1974. The effect of Social Security on early retirement. *Journal of Public Economics* 10:361–77.

Boskin, M., and J. B. Shoven. 1986. Poverty among the elderly: Where are the holes in the safety net? NBER Working Paper no. 1923. Cambridge, Mass.: National Bureau of Economic Research.

Bound, J. 1986. The disincentive effects of the Social Security disability program. University of Michigan. Typescript.

Burkhauser, R. V. 1980. The early acceptance of Social Security: An asset maximization approach. *Industrial and Labor Relations Review* 33:484–92.

_____. 1979. The pension acceptance decision of older workers. *Journal of Human Resources* 14(1):63–75.

Burkhauser, R. V., and J. A. Turner. 1978. A time-series analysis of Social Security and its effect on the market work of men at younger ages. *Journal of Political Economy* 86:701–15.

Burtless, Gary, and R. Moffitt. 1984. The effect of Social Security benefits on the labor supply of the aged. In *Retirement and economic behavior,* ed. Henry J. Aaron and Gary Burtless. Washington, D.C.: Brookings Institution.

Cartwright, W. S., and R. B. Friedland. 1985. The President's Commission on Pension Policy Household Survey 1979. *Review of Income and Wealth* 31:285–308.

Chirikos, T. N., and G. Nestel. 1981. Impairment and labor market outcomes: A cross-sectional and longitudinal analysis. In *Work and retirement,* ed. H. Parnes. Cambridge, Mass.: MIT Press.

Congressional Quarterly, Inc. 1983. *Social Security and retirement.* Washington, D.C.: GPO.

Crawford, V. P., and D. M. Lilien. 1982. Social Security and the retirement decision. *Quarterly Journal of Economics* (August):505–29.

Danziger, S., R. Haveman, and R. Plotnick. 1981. How income transfers affect work, saving, and the income distribution. *Journal of Economic Literature* 19(3):975–1028.

Danziger, S., J. van der Gaag, E. Smolensky, and M. Taussig. 1982. The life-cycle hypothesis and the consumption behavior of the elderly. *Journal of Post-Keynesian Economics* 5:208–27.

Darby, M. R. 1979. *The effects of Social Security on income and the capital stock.* Washington, D.C.: American Enterprise Institute.

Davies, J. B. 1981. Uncertain lifetime, consumption, and dissaving in retirement. *Journal of Political Economy* 89(3):561–77.

Deaton, A. 1986. Life-cycle models of consumption: Is the evidence consistent with the theory? NBER Working Paper no. 1910. Cambridge, Mass.: National Bureau of Economic Research.

Diamond, P. 1977. A framework for Social Security analysis. *Journal of Public Economics* 8(3):275–98.

Diamond, P., and J. Hausman. 1984a. Individual retirement and savings behavior. *Journal of Public Economics* 23:81–114.

_____. 1984b. The retirement and unemployment behavior of older men. In *Retirement and economic behavior,* ed. H. Aaron and G. Burtless. Washington, D.C.: Brookings Institution.

Diamond, P., and J. A. Mirrlees. 1978. A model of social insurance with variable retirement. *Journal of Public Economics* 10:295–336.

Dubin, J., and D. McFadden. 1984. An econometric analysis of residential electric appliance holdings and consumption. *Econometrica* 52(2):345–62.

Duff, I. S. 1984. The solution of sparse linear equations on the Cray-1. In *High speed computation,* ed. J. S. Kowalik. Berlin: Springer-Verlag.

Feldstein, M. 1974. Social Security, induced retirement and aggregate capital accumulation. *Journal of Political Economy* 82:905–26.

_____. 1983. Social Security benefits and the accumulation of pre-retirement wealth. In *The determinants of national wealth and saving,* ed. F. Modigliani and R. Hemming, 3–23. New York: St. Martin's Press.

Feldstein, M., and A. J. Pellechio. 1979. Social Security and household wealth accumulation: New microeconometric evidence. *Review of Economics and Statistics* 61(3):361–68.

Fields, G. S., and O. S. Mitchell. 1985. *Retirement, pensions, and Social Security.* Cambridge, Mass.: MIT Press.

Fuchs, V. R. 1982. Time preference and health: An exploratory study. In *Economic aspects of health,* ed. V. Fuchs. Chicago: Univ. of Chicago Press.

Gordon, R. H., and A. S. Blinder. 1980. Market wages, reservation wages, and retirement decisions. *Journal of Public Economics* 14:277–308.

Gotz, G. A., and J. J. McCall. 1984. A dynamic retention model for Air Force officers. Research report R-3028-AF. Santa Monica, Calif.: The Rand Corporation.

Gustman, A. L., and T. L. Steinmeier. 1983. Minimum hours constraints and retirement behavior. *Economic Inquiry* 3:77–91.

––––––. 1984. Partial retirement and the analysis of retirement behavior. *Industrial and Labor Relations Review* 37:403–15.

––––––. 1986. A structural retirement model. *Econometrica* 54(3):555–84.

Hall, A., and T. Johnson. 1980. The determinants of planned retirement age. *Industrial and Labor Relations Review* 33(2):241–55.

Hamermesh, D. 1984. Consumption during retirement: The missing link in the life cycle. *Review of Economics and Statistics* 66:1–7.

Haneman, W. M. 1984. Discrete/continuous models of consumer demand. *Econometrica* 52(3):541–62.

Hansen, L. P., and K. Singleton. 1982. Generalized instrumental variables estimation of nonlinear rational expectations models. *Econometrica* 50(5):1269–86.

Harris, L. 1984. *Retirement and income.* New York: Garland Publishing.

Hurd, M. D. 1986. Savings and bequests. NBER Working Paper no. 1826. Cambridge, Mass.: National Bureau of Economic Research.

Irelan, L., D. Motley, K. Schwab, S. Sherman, and J. Murray. 1976. *Almost 65: Baseline data for the retirement history study.* HEW Research Report 49. Washington, D.C.

King, M. 1985. The economics of saving: A survey of recent contributions. In *Frontiers of economics,* ed. K. Arrow and S. Harkapohja. Oxford: Basil Blackwell.

King, M., and L. D. Dicks-Mireaux. 1982. Asset holdings and the life-cycle. *The Economic Journal* 92:247–67.

Kotlikoff, L. J. 1979. Testing the theory of Social Security and life cycle accumulation. *American Economic Review* 69:396–410.

––––––. 1986. Health expenditures and precautionary savings. NBER Working Paper no. 2008. Cambridge, Mass.: National Bureau of Economic Research.

Kotlikoff, L. J., and D. E. Smith. 1983. *Pensions in the American economy.* Chicago: University of Chicago Press.

Kotlikoff, L. J., and L. H. Summers. 1981. The role of intergenerational transfers in aggregate capital accumulation. *Journal of Political Economy* 89:706–32.

Kotlikoff, L. J., A. Spivak, and L. H. Summers. 1982. The adequacy of savings. *American Economic Review* 72(5):1056–69.

Kurz, M. 1981. The life-cycle hypothesis and the effects of Social Security and private pensions on family savings. IMSSS Technical Report 335, Stanford University.

––––––. 1984. Capital accumulation and the characteristics of private intergenerational transfers. *Economica* 51: 1–22.

––––––. 1985. Heterogeneity and savings behavior: A comment. In *Frontiers of economics,* ed. K. Arrow and S. Harkapohja. Oxford: Basil Blackwell.

Levhari, D., and L. J. Mirman. 1977. Savings and consumption with an uncertain horizon. *Journal of Political Economy* 85(2):265–81.

Liddiard, L. D. 1986. How to get the most out of a Cray-2. University of Minnesota. Typescript.

Lucas, R. E. 1976. Econometric policy evaluation: A critique. In *The Philips Curve and labor markets,* ed. K. Brunner and A. K. Meltzer. Carnegie-Rochester Conference on Public Policy 1. Amsterdam: North-Holland.

MaCurdy, T. E. 1983. A simple scheme for estimating an intertemporal model of labor supply and consumption in the presence of taxes and uncertainty. *International Economic Review* 24(2):265–89.

Marschak, J. 1953. Economic measurements for policy and prediction. In *Studies in econometric method,* ed. W. C. Hood and T. C. Koopmans. New York: Wiley and Sons.

McFadden, D. 1981. Econometric models of probabilistic choice. In *Structural analysis of discrete data with econometric applications,* ed. C. F. Manski and D. McFadden. Cambridge: MIT Press.

————. 1988. A method of simulated moments for estimation of multinomial probits without numerical integration. *Econometrica.* Forthcoming.

Menchik, P. L., and M. David. 1983. Income distribution, lifetime savings, and bequests. *American Economic Review* 73(4):672–90.

————. 1985. The effect of Social Security on lifetime wealth accumulation and bequests. *Economica* 52(208):421–34.

Miller, R. 1984. Job matching and occupational choice. *Journal of Political Economy* 92(6):1086–1120.

Mirer, T. W. 1979. The wealth-age relation among the aged. *American Economic Review* 69(3):435–43.

————. 1980. The dissaving behavior of the aged. *Southern Economic Journal* 46:1197–1205.

Mitchell, O. S., and G. S. Fields. 1984. The economics of retirement behavior. *Journal of Labor Economics* 2(1):84–105.

Modigliani, F. 1975. The life cycle hypothesis of saving twenty years later. In *Contemporary issues in economics,* ed. M. Pakin. Manchester: Manchester University Press.

Modigliani, F., and F. Brumberg. 1954. Utility analysis and the consumption function: An interpretation of cross-section data. In *Post-Keynesian economics,* ed. K. Kurihara. New Brunswick: Rutgers University Press.

Morrison, M. H. 1982. *Economics of aging: The future of retirement.* New York: Van Nostrand Reinhold.

Mott, F. L., and R. J. Haurin. 1981. The impact of health problems and mortality on family well-being. In *Work and retirement,* ed. H. Parnes. Cambridge: MIT Press.

Munnell, A. H. 1977. *The future of Social Security.* Washington, D.C.: Brookings Institution.

Pakes, A. 1986. Patents as options: Some estimates of the value of holding European patent stocks. *Econometrica* 54(4):755–84.

Pakes, A., and D. Pollard. 1988. The asymptotics of simulation estimators. *Econometrica,* forthcoming.

Parnes, H. S., ed. 1981. *Work and retirement.* Cambridge: MIT Press.

————, ed. 1983. *Policy issues in work and retirement.* Kalamazoo, Michigan: W. E. Upjohn Institute for Employment Research.

Parsons, D. O. 1982. The male labour force participation decision: Health, reported health, and economic incentives. *Economica* 49: 81–91.

Pellechio, A. J. 1979. Social Security financing and retirement behavior. *American Economic Review* 69(2):284–87.

Quinn, J. F. 1977. Microeconomic determinants of early retirement: A cross-sectional view of white married men. *Journal of Human Resources* 12: 329–46.

Quinn, J. F., and R. V. Burkhauser. 1983. Is mandatory retirement overrated?: Evidence from the 1970's. *Journal of Human Resources* 18(3):377–58.

Rust, J. 1987. Optimal replacement of GMC bus engines: An empirical model of Harold Zurcher. *Econometrica* 55(5):999–1033.

———. 1988. Maximum likelihood estimation of discrete control processes. *SIAM Journal on Control and Optimization* 26(5): 1–19.

———. 1989. Behavior of male workers at the end of the life-cycle: An empirical analysis of states and controls. In *Issues in the economics of aging,* ed. D. Wise. Forthcoming.

Sargent, T. J. 1981. Interpreting economic time series. *Journal of Political Economy* 89(2):213–48.

Schulz, J. H. 1976. *The economics of aging.* Belmont, Calif.: Wadsworth Publishing.

Sickles, R. C., and P. Taubman. 1986. An analysis of the health and retirement status of the elderly. *Econometrica* 54(6):1339–56.

Sheshinski, E. 1978. A model of Social Security and retirement decisions. *Journal of Public Economics* 10: 337–60.

Stein, B. 1980. *Social Security and pensions in transition.* New York: Free Press.

Sueyoshi, G. 1986. Social Security and the determinants of full and partial retirement: A competing risks analysis. M.I.T. Typescript.

Thompson, L. H. 1981. The Social Security reform debate. *Journal of Economic Literature* 21(4):1425–67.

Tobin, J. 1967. Life-cycle saving and balanced growth. In *Ten economic studies in the tradition of Irving Fisher,* ed. W. Fellner, 231–56. New York: Wiley and Sons.

White, B. 1978. Empirical tests of the life-cycle hypothesis. *American Economic Review* 68: 547–60.

———. 1984. Empirical tests of the life-cycle hypothesis: Reply. *American Economic Review* 74: 258–59.

Williams, C. A., Jr., J. G. Turnbull, and E. F. Cheit. 1982. *Economic and social security: Social insurance and other approaches.* New York: Wiley and Sons.

Wise, D., ed. 1985. *Pensions, labor, and individual choice.* Chicago: University of Chicago Press.

Wolpin, K. 1984. An estimable dynamic stochastic model of fertility and child mortality. *Journal of Political Economy* 92(5):852–74.

Yaari, M. E. 1965. Uncertain lifetime, life insurance, and the theory of the consumer. *Review of Economic Studies* 32: 137–50.

Zabalza, A., C. Pissarides, and M. Barton. 1980. Social Security and the choice between full-time work, part-time work, and retirement. *Journal of Public Economics* 14: 245–76.

## Comment    Gary Burtless

The author of this paper sets out to do a couple of notable things. First, he wants to set up a tractable "optimizing" model that workers follow

Gary Burtless is a senior fellow of the Brookings Institution.

in determining their period-by-period consumption and labor supply toward the end of life. Second, he attempts to embed this model within a defensible econometric framework so that the important unknown parameters in the model can be estimated with a longitudinal data base containing information on several thousand men. Third, he hopes to obtain empirical estimates of the unknown parameters within our lifetime and within a very, very large—although finite—computer budget. And finally, I guess, he would eventually like to describe his model and results in a paper that is accessible to an audience that includes, but is not *restricted* to, operations research specialists who are conversant with the internal architecture of the Cray-2 supercomputer.

Judging by the evidence in this paper, the last objective might turn out to be the hardest to attain.

You might ask: How does this set of objectives distinguish this paper from other papers on the subject? To my knowledge, no previous analyst has ever been quite so ambitious. Some analysts, including myself, have examined a *subset* of the issues treated in this paper: What determines the age at retirement? What determines an older worker's weekly hours? How can we explain the dynamic pattern of partial and full retirement? What are the determinants of the saving/consumption path, particularly the trends in saving before and after retirement? How do unexpected events, such as layoffs, poor health, and death, affect labor supply and consumption?

Many previous analysts—also including myself—make a ritual bow toward the idea that each of these issues can and should be treated within a unified life-cycle, labor supply/consumption model. But then in the empirical implementation we plead lack of data or an insufficient computer budget. We treat only one or occasionally two of the issues in the list I just mentioned. This author is after the whole nine yards: A unified framework that simultaneously treats *all* of the issues.

Devising such a framework is very, very hard. Before talking about the author's proposed solution, I would like to describe just how hard it is. In the canonical model of labor supply and consumption, economic agents are assumed to make decisions about current and future hours of work and saving based on current and future wage rates, current and anticipated wealth—including wealth accumulated through Social Security and pensions—current and anticipated health and family responsibilities, and individual tastes—specifically, the taste for work versus leisure, leisure versus goods consumption, and present versus future consumption and leisure.

To add to the analyst's problem, he or she is confronted with a very limited, and in some cases defective, data set. Frequently, the current wage rate is poorly measured. Even where it is well measured, we have no way of knowing the worker's potential future wages. Wealth is notoriously badly measured. Even where it is well measured, it is very tricky to provide simple conceptual definitions of future wealth, because such critical items as pension assets and Social Security accumulations are highly dependent on the exact sequence of potential wage rates and actual labor force participation decisions. (For example, wealth accumulation in Social Security occurs in a highly nonlinear way as the retirement age is delayed from 59 to 62, from 62 to 65, and from 65 to 68.)

Even if we can solve these measurement and conceptual problems in obtaining observations on a worker's wealth, there is still the problem that the wealth concept measured in the data usually does not represent the worker's initial endowment, which is, of course, the correct starting point for measuring his or her lifetime budget constraint. Instead, we observe wealth at some initial age (in this case, ages 58 to 63, which are the earliest ages observed in the Retirement History Survey). Practically speaking, wealth at those ages probably reflects most of the assets the worker is going to have available to finance his retirement. Moreover, those observed wealth levels embody all the worker's past consumption and labor supply decisions, given his initial endowment and potential market wage. In terms of the full life-cycle model, the observed wealth holdings at the start of the survey represent endogenous—not exogenous—variables.

If these measurement problems are not enough to deter even a stout-hearted graduate student seeking econometric glory, let me add one final point. In the canonical life-cycle model we are not really talking about a straightforward two-good problem—goods consumption and leisure. At a minimum we are talking about four goods—more probably $2 \times T$, where $T$ is the expected number of periods in the lifetime. That is, we are talking about consumption in the current period and in a future period, and leisure in the current period and in a future period. The large number of goods in the utility function gives rise to an integrability problem in deriving individual demand functions, except in forms of the function that are carefully specified a priori, and which might be unrealistic.

Armed with a guarantee of ten hours on a Cray-2, John Rust bravely confronts these problems and outlines a research program. His courage and high intelligence are everywhere evident in this paper. But, I would need a better weapon than mere CPU time before hazarding into this particular battle.

How does Rust overcome the problems I just mentioned? It is not clear that some of them are even treated. For example, I am not sure that Rust considers that the potential wage of workers might vary over time. He proposes to enter the wage or potential earnings of a worker at each conceivable level of work effort (here taken to be zero hours, part-time hours, and full-time hours) as explanatory variables. But does

he account for the fact that the potential market wage might decline
with advancing age? Or for the fact that the tax on wages must change
at different ages, depending on acceptance or rejection of a Social
Security pension? I do not know. But this is a central problem traditionally faced in the retirement literature, and it does not appear to be
mentioned here.

How does the author treat the issue of nonlinear accumulation of
pension and Social Security wealth? (These accumulations are nonlinear with respect to the age of retirement because of minimum pension
ages, early retirement penalties, and actuarially unfair compensation
for workers delaying retirement beyond the normal retirement age.)
The author handles the problem posed by private pensions by tossing
out every member of his sample who is covered by one. He handles
Social Security accumulations by assuming that the remaining members
of his sample perfectly anticipated in 1969 and 1971 that Social Security
wealth would be raised by the 1972 amendments. That is, he assumes
that all workers plan on receiving benefits as Social Security pensions
would be computed under the 1973 law. These people are indeed
farsighted.

Let me interject here that this measure of Social Security wealth is
extremely troubling. In this paper we have a general model that must
account for all anticipated and unanticipated events that might affect
retirement and consumption. Yet the author fails to use our best available information about when the workers learned of Social Security
benefit increases; namely, the date that real benefits were raised by
8–10 percent in late 1969 and a further 9–11 percent in late 1972.

Although I intuitively understand how the author will handle the
growth in Social Security wealth that can be anticipated, I am not really
sure how he will do it, because that issue is not explicitly treated in
the paper.

How does the author handle the endogeneity of his initial observation
on wealth? Here he cuts the Gordian knot and simply claims he does
not *need* to address the problem. All he needs to do is estimate parameters that generate transition probabilities between the many specified statuses, given an initial set of state variables, including initial
wealth. I find this claim difficult to reconcile with another objective of
the paper. Rust wants to use the estimated model to forecast the effect
of policy changes, such as reductions in Social Security retirement or
disability benefits. This implies that the parameter estimates recovered
from the analysis can be used to forecast the effect of policy changes
on any future cohort of men near retirement age.

Suppose we think of a sample of men whose wealth accumulations
occurred under a radically different sequence of state variables: different Social Security and income tax rates or different real interest

rates and patterns of capital gain. Then as I understand the paper, we are being told that the transition probabilities (i.e., the underlying parameters) estimated in this study can be applied to this new sample. Personally, I find this hard to believe, but I am willing to be persuaded.

I will not pretend that I understand how the author expects to estimate this model. It would be too easy for the alert reader to detect my ignorance of dynamic programming techniques. But I will open myself up to ridicule by admitting that I do not quite understand how he intends to organize his data and define an observation, e.g., a dependent variable. The paper lays great stress on a worker's decision about making an optimal plan at a given point in time. Does this mean that the author will rely on the worker's stated intentions to measure projected labor supply and consumption paths? That is, in defining the "state" variables presumed to exist at a given point in time, he will rely on the worker's observed employment status and some direct estimate of his recent consumption level. But how will the author measure the worker's "choice" in that period? By using the observed labor market and consumption path over the next two years? Or by using the worker's stated intention at that time to retire at a specified date in the future? Both of these options seem to me to have advantages and problems, but it is not entirely clear which option has been selected.

The reader should not interpret my comments as being especially critical. Many of the questions I raise will undoubtedly be cleared up in a subsequent paper, in which the estimation results are actually displayed. Other points I appear to criticize are probably necessary simplifications in order to make estimation possible. Anyone working in this area has had to make the same kinds of more or less defensible simplifications.

Some readers might feel that using the word "simplification" anywhere within ten miles of this paper is a little like using the word "integrity" in discussing the ethical standards of the advertising industry. But it is nonetheless the case that Rust has had to make a certain number of drastically simplifying assumptions to make estimation feasible. He will probably have to make even more before obtaining estimates.

Even with these simplifications, however, we might wonder whether the final result is simple enough to reflect the prosaic reality that surrounds us. In thinking about consumer decision models, I like to apply the "Paul Pepperbridge" test. Paul Pepperbridge was the average graduate of the average high school in the United States. If a decision model seems to call for more intellectual capacity than Paul can bring to bear, I am usually a little skeptical. If it calls for a couple of seconds of CPU time on a Cray-2 to assess all the consumption alternatives, I am a bit more skeptical. Let's face it, the Cray can probably make as many calculations in a second as Paul was willing and capable of making between the sixth and twelfth grades. I doubt he will spend much more time than that thinking about when he is going to retire.

So one thing the author might want to do is persuade the reader that the decision-making model provides a conceivable approximation to reality, as well as the best a consumer could do if he had a couple of hours on a Cray and the professional advice of a consulting economist. From the point of view of a fellow economist, however, the model described in this paper represents an extremely impressive achievement.

# Contributors

B. Douglas Bernheim
J. L. Kellogg Graduate School of
  Management
Northwestern University
2001 Sheridan Road
Evanston, IL 60201

David E. Bloom
Department of Economics
Columbia University
New York, NY 10027

Axel Börsch-Supan
Universität Dortmund
Gebäude Mathematik M-111
Postfach 50 05 00
D-4600 Dortmund 50
West Germany

John P. Bunker
Division of Health Services
  Research
HRP Building, Room 7-5093
Stanford University
Stanford, CA 94305

Gary Burtless
Brookings Institution
1775 Massachusetts Avenue, NW
Washington, DC 20030

Jonathan Feinstein
Graduate School of Business
Stanford University
Stanford, CA 94305

Alan M. Garber
National Bureau of Economic
  Research
204 Junipero Serra Boulevard
Stanford, CA 94305

Michael D. Hurd
Department of Economics
State University of New York at
  Stony Brook
Stony Brook, NY 11794

Yannis M. Ioannides
Department of Economics
Virginia Polytechnic Institute and
  State University
Blacksburg, VA 24061

Laurence J. Kotlikoff
National Bureau of Economic
  Research
1050 Massachusetts Avenue
Cambridge, MA 02138

Edward P. Lazear
Graduate School of Business
University of Chicago
1101 East 58th Street
Chicago, Il 60637

Daniel McFadden
Department of Economics
Massachusetts Institute of
  Technology
E52-271D
Cambridge, MA 02139

John N. Morris
The Hebrew Rehabilitation Center
   for the Aged
1200 Center Street
Roslindale, MA 02131

Ariel Pakes
Department of Economics
University of Wisconsin
Social Sciences Building
1180 Observatory Drive
Madison, WI 53706

Henry O. Pollakowski
Joint Center for Housing Studies
Massachusetts Institute of
   Technology and Harvard
   University
53 Church Street
Cambridge, MA 02138

James M. Poterba
National Bureau of Economic
   Research
1050 Massachusetts Avenue
Cambridge, MA 02138

John M. Quigley
School of Public Policy
University of California
2607 Hearst
Berkeley, CA 94720

John P. Rust
Department of Economics
University of Wisconsin
Social Sciences Building
1180 Observatory Drive
Madison, WI 53706

John B. Shoven
Department of Economics
Stanford University
Encina Hall, 4th Floor
Stanford, CA 94305

Konrad Stahl
Universität Mannheim
Department of Economics
P.O. Box 10 34 62
D-6800 Mannheim 1
West Germany

Jeffrey O. Sundberg
Department of Economics
Stanford University
Stanford, CA 94305

Paul Taubman
Department of Economics
521 McNeil Building/CR
3718 Locust Walk
University of Pennsylvania
Philadelphia, PA 19104

Steven F. Venti
Department of Economics
Dartmouth College
Hanover, NH 03755

David A. Wise
National Bureau of Economic
   Research
1050 Massachusetts Avenue
Cambridge, MA 02138

# Author Index

# Subject Index

Actuarial studies, S.S.A., 243
Age: ADL limitations and, 274; changing distribution of, in U.S., 119, 127; crude mobility vs., 57t; days hospitalized and, 270; expected retirement, 358; extreme, 50; housing consumption and, 101; income distribution and, 129; living arrangements and, 120, 125, 127, 132t, 133t, 141; mobility effects and, 2–3, 9, 17–31, 56–58, 73, 82t, 112; retirement, years of service, and, 323–28; role reversal and, 134t; vulnerability status and, 153, 154t, 156t; wealth holdings and, 197, 280, 284–87; West German population and, 94, 96
AHS. *See* Annual Housing Survey
Alternative living arrangements. *See* Extended families; Living arrangements
American Cancer Society, 234
American Housing Survey. *See* Annual Housing Survey
Annual Housing Survey (AHS), HUD (1973), 3, 13, 49, 84; limitations of, 121, 148; variables used in, 95–96
Annuities, defined, 220. *See also* Pensions; Social Security
Assets. *See* Financial status; Wealth; *specific type*

Baby boom, 228, 243
Bellman equation, 372

Bequeathable wealth, 11; defined, 220; housing sales and, 51; marginal utility of, 219, 221, 223, 228; marital status and, 179, 187, 190–92, 197, 212–13t, 215; Medicaid rules and, 261; moving choices and, 32–37; reserve mortgages and, 53; savings and, 362–63
Bernoulli model, moving choices and, 66–68, 88
Binary logit estimates, moving choices and, 108–12
Blackwell's theorem, 371, 373
British National Health Service, 232
Bureau of Labor Statistics (BLS), poverty definition of, 178, 204–8

Capital gains, 53, 56, 59
Careerism, women and, 228
Cash flow income. *See* Liquidity
Children, 119; contact with parents, 4, 151–75; differential mortality and, 187–88; as source of care, 7, 183; support from, 194. *See also* Bequeathable wealth; Extended families
Chronic disease, 257–59. *See also* Disabled elderly; Long-term health care
Cigarette smoking. *See* Smoking
Community Development Block Grants, 53
Construction Reports, U.S. Bureau of the Census, 59

411